A Companion to Late Medieval and Early Modern Augsburg

Brill's Companions to European History

VOLUME 20

The titles published in this series are listed at *brill.com/bceh*

A Companion to Late Medieval and Early Modern Augsburg

Edited by

B. Ann Tlusty and Mark Häberlein

BRILL

LEIDEN | BOSTON

Cover illustration: Stadtarchiv Augsburg, Schätze 203a, Plan XLIV (detail).

Library of Congress Cataloging-in-Publication Data

Names: Tlusty, B. Ann, editor. | Häberlein, Mark, editor.
Title: A companion to late medieval and early modern Augsburg / edited by B. Ann Tlusty, and Mark Häberlein.
Description: Leiden ; Boston : Brill, [2020] | Series: Brill's companions to European history, 2212-7410 ; volume 20 | Includes bibliographical references and index.
Identifiers: LCCN 2019055561 (print) | LCCN 2019055562 (ebook) | ISBN 9789004414952 (hardback) | ISBN 9789004416055 (ebook)
Subjects: LCSH: Augsburg (Germany)--History.
Classification: LCC DD901.A92 C66 2020 (print) | LCC DD901.A92 (ebook) | DDC 943/.375--dc23
LC record available at https://lccn.loc.gov/2019055561
LC ebook record available at https://lccn.loc.gov/2019055562

Typeface for the Latin, Greek, and Cyrillic scripts: "Brill". See and download: brill.com/brill-typeface.

ISSN 2212-7410
ISBN 978-90-04-41495-2 (hardback)
ISBN 978-90-04-41605-5 (e-book)

Copyright 2020 by Koninklijke Brill NV, Leiden, The Netherlands.
Koninklijke Brill NV incorporates the imprints Brill, Brill Hes & De Graaf, Brill Nijhoff, Brill Rodopi, Brill Sense, Hotei Publishing, mentis Verlag, Verlag Ferdinand Schöningh and Wilhelm Fink Verlag.
All rights reserved. No part of this publication may be reproduced, translated, stored in a retrieval system, or transmitted in any form or by any means, electronic, mechanical, photocopying, recording or otherwise, without prior written permission from the publisher.
Authorization to photocopy items for internal or personal use is granted by Koninklijke Brill NV provided that the appropriate fees are paid directly to The Copyright Clearance Center, 222 Rosewood Drive, Suite 910, Danvers, MA 01923, USA. Fees are subject to change.

This book is printed on acid-free paper and produced in a sustainable manner.

Contents

Acknowledgements IX
List of Figures X
Notes on Contributors XIII

PART 1
The City

1 Sources and Historiography 3
   Helmut Graser, Mark Häberlein and B. Ann Tlusty

2 Urban Topography, Population, Visual Representations 20
   Barbara Rajkay

3 Of Invisible Boundaries: Bodies, Plagues, and Healers 46
   Claudia Stein

4 Textual Representation: Chronicles 69
   Gregor Rohmann

PART 2
Economy, Politics, and the Law

5 Production, Trade, and Finance 101
   Mark Häberlein

6 Politics under the Guild Regime, 1368–1548 123
   Christopher W. Close

7 Politics under the Patrician Regime, 1548–1806 146
   Mark Häberlein and Barbara Rajkay

8 Crime and Punishment 171
   Allyson F. Creasman

9 Civil Law 196
   Peter Kreutz

PART 3
Religion and Society

10   The Urban Reformation   221
     Michele Zelinsky Hanson

11   Catholic-Protestant Coexistence   247
     Marjorie E. Plummer and B. Ann Tlusty

12   Urban Society: Inequality, Poverty, and Mobility   271
     Mark Häberlein and Reinhold Reith

13   Women, Family, and Sexuality   294
     Margaret Lewis

14   Sociability and Leisure   316
     B. Ann Tlusty

15   The Experience of War   342
     Andreas Flurschütz da Cruz

16   Jews as Ethnic and Religious Minorities   367
     Sabine Ullmann

PART 4
Communication, Cultural and Intellectual Life

17   The Dissemination of News   391
     Regina Dauser

18   Book Production and Trade   415
     Hans-Jörg Künast
     Translated by Christine R. Johnson

19   Dress and Material Culture   440
     Victoria Bartels and Katherine Bond

20   Learned Culture   470
     Wolfgang E.J. Weber
     Translated by Mark Häberlein and B. Ann Tlusty

21   The Arts   495
     Andrew Morrall

22   Architecture   526
     Dietrich Erben

23   Music   553
     Alexander J. Fisher

     Index   575

Acknowledgements

The editors would like to thank Andreas Flurschütz da Cruz (University of Bamberg) for collecting the images and reproduction rights for this volume as well as the institutions that kindly provided them. We also thank the anonymous reviewers for their helpful comments, Michael Williams for his expert copyediting, and André Arnold for preparing the index. Financial support for indexing was provided by the Provost's Office at Bucknell University. Finally, we are especially grateful to all the contributors who invested their time and expertise into this volume despite their busy schedules, and to the team of editors at Brill who guided it through the publication process.

Mark Häberlein
B. Ann Tlusty

Figures

2.1 View of Augsburg from the chronicle of Sigismund Meisterlin, 1457. Staats- und Stadtbibliothek Augsburg, 2° Cod. H. 1   22
2.2 Hans Rogel, city plan of Augsburg, woodcut, 1563. Staats- und Stadtbibliothek Augsburg, Graph 31/6   34
4.1a Paul Hektor Mair, Geschlechterbuch, 1538. P. xx. Staats- und Stadtbibliothek Augsburg, Rar 113   84
4.1b Paul Hektor Mair, Geschlechterbuch, 1538. P. xxi. Staats- und Stadtbibliothek Augsburg, Rar 113   85
5.1 Jakob Fugger the Rich and his bookkeeper Matthäus Schwarz, from the Schwarz costume book. Herzog Anton Ulrich-Museum, Hs 27 N. 67   106
6.1 Establishment of the guild regime in 1368 according to Clemens Jäger's *Consulatsbuch* (1545). Staats- und Stadtbibliothek Augsburg, Cim 21, fol. 37r   124
7.1 Troops parading in front of city hall during the Augsburg weavers' revolt of 1794, drawing by Franz Thomas Weber. Augsburg, Städtische Kunstsammlungen, Graphische Sammlung   160
9.1 Augsburg *Stadtbuch* of 1276. Stadtarchiv Augsburg, Stadtrechtsbuch 1276, fol. 7r   198
10.1 View of St. Moritz Church from the west, copperplate by Simon Grimm, 1687. Staats- und Stadtbibliothek Augsburg, Graph 17/3a   227
11.1 Failed attempt to expel the Protestant preacher Dr. Georg Müller from Augsburg, 1582, woodcut from illustrated broadsheet. Staats- und Stadtbibliothek Augsburg, Graph 22/12   259
12.1 Goldsmith's workshop in Augsburg, copperplate by Etienne Delaune (1518/19–1583). Augsburg, Städtische Kunstsammlungen, G20955   278
14.1 Sleigh ride in front of Augsburg's Gothic city hall, engraving by Wilhelm Peter Zimmermann, 1618. Augsburg, Städtische Kunstsammlungen, G 1387   321
14.2 Bathing scene, detail from the *Augsburger Monatsbild* April–June, workshop of Jörg Breu the Elder. Deutsches Historisches Museum Berlin, 1990/185.2   330
15.1 Siege and bombardment of Augsburg in December 1703. Staats- und Stadtbibliothek Augsburg, Graph 56/109/9   356
16.1 Drawing from the letterbook (*Missivbuch*) of the Augsburg city council depicting the proposed designation of Jews, 1434. Stadtarchiv Augsburg, Missivbuch III (1429–1435), no. 1387, f. 334r   370
17.1 *Copia der Newen [Z]eitung aus Presilg Landt*, c. 1515, title page. Munich, Bayerische Staatsbibliothek, Rar. 614, fol. 1r   396

FIGURES   XI

18.1   Map of trade routes from Jörg Gail's "Reisebüchlein der vornehmsten Lande
       und Städte", printed in Augsburg in 1563   429
19.1   "From summer until September this was my usual dress to walk the streets …",
       Book of Clothes, 1560, Veit Konrad Schwarz. Herzog Anton Ulrich-Museum,
       Hs 27 N. 67b, Ill. 36r   441
19.2   *Einspänniger* soldiers' livery, 3 July 1547, *Einspännigerbuch* (*Memorybuch über
       die ausgabe der Kleidung*), Paul Hektor Mair, c. 1569. Staats- und Stadtbibliothek
       Augsburg, 2° Cod S 228, fol. 13r   448
19.3   "This is a Castilian peasant as he goes into a city to market or rides upon an ass",
       Christoph Weiditz, Trachtenbuch, ca. 1529. Germanisches Nationalmuseum,
       Hs. 22474, Ill. 19r   449
19.4   Portrait of Christoph Fugger: oil on wood, Christoph Amberger, 1541, 97,5 ×
       80,4 cm Bayerische Staatsgemäldesammlungen, Munich, Alte Pinakothek. Bild-
       nachweis: bpk | Bayerische Staatsgemäldesammlungen   453
19.5   Dagger with sheath, cased in gold, silver, ivory, and steel, Christoph Weiditz,
       c. 1560, Staatliche Kunstsammlungen Dresden, Rüstkammer, inv. no. p203.
       Photo: Richard Andrich, SLUB / Deutsche Fotothek   455
19.6   An Augsburg bride going to church on her wedding day, *Kostüme der Männer
       und Frauen in Augsburg und Nürnberg, Deutschland, Europa, Orient und Afrika*,
       late 16th century. Munich, Bayerische Staatsbibliothek, BSB-HSS Cod.Icon. 341,
       fol. 2v   457
19.7   "In March 1523. The doublet of fustian, which has 4,800 slashes with velvet
       rolls all in white," Matthäus Schwarz, Book of Clothes. Herzog Anton Ulrich-
       Museum, Hs 27 N. 67a, Ill. 61v   460
19.8   "Langenmantel vom R.", *Bericht und Anzeigen aller Herren Geschlecht der lobli-
       chen Stadt Augspurg*, Strasbourg: Christoph Weiditz and David Kannel, Paul
       Hektor Mair, 1538. Munich, Bayerische Staatsbibliothek, Rar. 641, fol. 8   462
19.9   Costume harness of Wilhelm of Rogendorf (1481–1541): steel and leather,
       Kolman Helmschmid (German, Augsburg 1471–1532) and Daniel Hopfer
       (German, Kaufbeuren-Augsburg 1471–1536), 1523. Kunsthistorisches Museum
       Vienna, Court hunting and armory, No. A 374   464
19.10 Working sketch of the harness included in the letter from Andreas Brenker to
       Ferdinand II, Augsburg, 11 July 1557. Innsbruck, Tiroler Landesarchiv   465
21.1   Hans Holbein the Elder, The Basilica of San Paolo fuori le mura, oil on panel.
       Augsburg, Städtische Kunstsammlungen   498
21.2   Hans Burgkmair the Elder, The Emperor Maximilian I on Horseback,
       chiaroscuro woodcut, 1509   501
21.3   Fugger Funerary Chapel, St. Anna, Augsburg   502
21.4   Hans Daucher, The Holy Family and Angels, honestone limestone, c. 1520.
       Augsburg, Städtische Kunstsammlungen, Maximilianmuseum, no. 5703   504

21.5   Hans Burgkmair the Elder, Esther before Ahasuerus, oil on panel, 1528. Munich, Alte Pinakothek, no. 689   506
21.6   Adriaen de Vries, Hercules Fountain, 1602, bronze. Augsburg   510
21.7   Philipp Hainhofer, Ulrich Baumgartner, The Kunstschrank of Gustavus Adolphus, 1625–31 (240 cm high × 120 cm wide). Gustavianum, University of Uppsala   514
21.8   Christoph Schißler, *Horologium Achaz Hydrographicum*, 1578, gilded brass, 12 cm diam. Philadelphia, American Philosophical Society, inv. no. 58.66   516
21.9   Joachim Friess (ca. 1579–1620) Automaton in the form of Diana and the stag, ca. 1620. Partially gilded silver, enamel, jewels (case); iron, wood (movement), 14 3/4 × 9 1/2 in. (37.5 × 24.1 cm) Metropolitan Museum of Art, Gift of J. Pierpont Morgan, 1917, acc. no. 17.190.746   519
21.10 Gregorio Guglielmo, Ballroom, Schaezler Palace, Augsburg, 1765   521
22.1   City map of Augsburg from Braun und Hogenberg, *Civitates orbis terrarium* ..., colored woodcut, 1572. Augsburg, Städtische Kunstsammlungen, G30   527
22.2   View from the south of the east chancel of Augsburg Cathedral, constructed 1340–1431. Photo from 1990, Eberhard Lantz, Bayerisches Landesamt für Denkmalpfllege München   529
22.3   Late Gothic city hall, built 1385, expanded 1449 and 1515–1516. Wooden model, *c.* 1515–16. Augsburg, Städtische Kunstsammlungen, Graphische Sammlung, no. 3453   531
22.4   View from the north of the former abbey church of Sts. Ulrich and Afra, built from 1467 onwards, with the Protestant church of St. Ulrich in the foreground. Photo: Isabel Mühlhaus, Lehrstuhl für Theorie und Geschichte von Architektur, Kunst und Design, TU München   532
22.5   Marcus Welser's former garden house in the *Frauenvorstadt*, built after 1583, restored in 2013. Photo: Dietrich Erben   538
22.6   City library in the *Annahof*, built in 1562. Etching by Wolfgang Kilian, 1623. Augsburg, Städtische Kunstsammlungen, G274   542
22.7   City hall square with Augustus fountain and city hall. Etching by Wolfgang Kilian, 1623. Augsburg, Städtische Kunstsammlungen, G12069   544
22.8   Johann Heinrich von Schüle's cotton-printing manufacture, 1770–1772, demolition of the wings and modern rebuilding in 1996. Photo: Dietrich Erben   547
23.1   Portrait of Johann Andreas Stein (1728–1792), maker of keyboard instruments, by an anonymous artist, 1755/57 Augsburg, Städtische Museen, Mozarthaus   568

Notes on Contributors

Victoria Bartels
is a Ph.D. candidate in history at the University of Cambridge who specializes in the cultural history of early modern arms, armor, costume, and masculinity in sixteenth-century Italy and Germany.

Katherine Bond
is a Ph.D. candidate in history at the University of Cambridge. Her work focuses on the visual and material culture of early modern Europe, in particular costume books of the German-speaking lands, with an emphasis on the development of national sartorial styles.

Christopher W. Close
is Assistant Professor of History at Saint Joseph's University, where he specializes in the religious and political history of early modern Germany. He is the author of *The Negotiated Reformation: Imperial Cities and the Politics of Urban Reform, 1525–1550* (2009).

Allyson F. Creasman
is Associate Professor of History at Carnegie Mellon University. Her research focuses on religious reform and confessional relations, as well as issues of social discipline and criminality, in early modern German cities. She is the author of *Censorship and Civic Order in Reformation Germany, 1517–1648: "Printed Poison and Evil Talk"* (2012).

Regina Dauser
is Senior Lecturer in Early Modern History at the University of Augsburg. She specializes in communications history, the history of the international system, the circulation of knowledge, and the economic Enlightenment. She is the author of *Informationskultur und Beziehungswissen. Das Korrespondenznetz Hans Fuggers (1531–1598)* and has recently published *Ehren-Namen. Herrschertitulaturen im völkerrechtlichen Vertrag, 1648–1748* (2017).

Dietrich Erben
is Professor of Theory and History of Architecture, Art and Design at the Technical University of Munich, where he has been teaching since 2009. He works on art and architectural history of the early modern and modern periods. His publications include *Paris und Rom: Die staatlich gelenkten Kunstbeziehungen unter Ludwig XIV.* (2004) and *Die Kunst des Barock* (2008).

Alexander J. Fisher
is Professor of Music at the University of British Columbia, where he teaches courses on music history from the Middle Ages to the Baroque, and coordinates the School's Early Music Ensemble. A specialist in music, sound, and religious culture in early modern Germany, he is the author of two books, *Music and Religious Identity in Counter-Reformation Augsburg, 1580–1630* (2004), and *Music, Piety, and Propaganda: The Soundscapes of Counter-Reformation Bavaria* (2014).

Andreas Flurschütz da Cruz
teaches Early Modern History at the University of Bamberg. He specializes in the social, political, and cultural history of southern Germany and in military history. His publications include *Zwischen Füchsen und Wölfen* (2014), a study of noble conflict in early modern Franconia, and *Hexenbrenner – Seelenretter. Fürstbischof Julius Echter von Mespelbrunn und die Hexenverfolgungen im Hochstift Würzburg* (2017).

Helmut Graser
taught Germanic languages, literature, and linguistics at the University of Augsburg. His research interests include early modern grammar and morphology as well as the history of urban languages and dialects. He has recently co-edited *Jonas Losch, Teutscher Dichter und Componist. Die Lieder- und Reimspruchsammlung eines Augsburger Webers aus den Jahren 1579–1583* (with B. Ann Tlusty, 2015).

Mark Häberlein
is Professor of Early Modern History at the University of Bamberg, where he has been teaching since 2004. He has published widely on early modern trade and merchant networks, urban history, and eighteenth-century transatlantic migration. His recent publications include *The Fuggers of Augsburg: Pursuing Wealth and Honor in Renaissance Germany* (2012) and *Aufbruch ins globale Zeitalter. Die Handelswelt der Fugger und Welser* (2016).

Hans-Jörg Künast
is a specialist in Augsburg's printing and book trade in the early modern period. He is the author of *Getruckt zu Augspurg. Buchdruck und Buchhandel in Augsburg zwischen 1468 und 1555* (1997) as well as numerous articles on the subject; in addition, he co-edited *Die Bibliothek Konrad Peutingers* (2 vols., 2003–05).

Peter Kreutz

teaches Public Law, Roman Law, and European Legal History at the University of Augsburg. His publications include *Romidee und Rechtsbild in der Spätantike. Untersuchungen zur Ideen- und Mentalitätsgeschichte* (2008).

Margaret Lewis

is Assistant Professor of History at the University of Tennessee at Martin. She specializes in women's and gender history; her recent publications include *Infanticide and Abortion in Early Modern Germany* (2016).

Andrew Morrall

is Professor of Art History at the Bard Graduate Center in New York City. His research focuses on the art and material culture of early modern northern Europe, including Renaissance aesthetics, the history of collecting, and intersections of art and science. In addition to numerous articles, he is the author of *Jörg Breu the Elder. Art, Culture and Belief in Reformation Augsburg* (2001).

Marjorie E. Plummer

holds the Susan C. Karant-Nunn Chair in Reformation and Early Modern European History at the University of Arizona. She specializes in early modern European cultural, social, and gender history as well as the history of the Reformation and early modern religion. She is the author of *From Priest's Whore to Pastor's Wife: Clerical Marriage and the Process of Reform in the Early German Reformation* (2012) and co-editor of *Archeologies of Confession: Writing the German Reformation, 1517–2017* (2017).

Barbara Rajkay

is an independent historian in Augsburg who has worked on various aspects of the social and cultural history of Swabian cities in the early modern period. She is the co-editor of a three-volume edition of the autobiographical writings of Paul von Stetten the Younger (1731–1808), the last Protestant mayor of the imperial city of Augsburg.

Reinhold Reith

is Professor of Economic and Social History at the University of Salzburg. He has written several monographs and numerous articles on the history of journeymen, labor migration, technological change, and environmental history. He has recently published *Umweltgeschichte der Frühen Neuzeit* (2011) and co-edited *An Environmental History of the Early Modern Period: Experiments and Perspectives* (2014).

Gregor Rohmann

teaches Medieval History at the University of Frankfurt am Main and is a research fellow of the Gerda Henkel Foundation. He specializes in the history of medicine, religious concepts and practice, and kinship, as well as urban historiography and memory in the late Middle Ages. He is the editor of *Das Ehrenbuch der Fugger* (2 vols., 2004) and author of *Tanzwut. Kosmos, Kirche und Mensch in der Bedeutungsgeschichte eines spätmittelalterlichen Krankheitskonzepts* (2013).

Claudia Stein

is Associate Professor of History at the University of Warwick. Her current research focuses on the formation of the modern and postmodern subject since the seventeenth century at the intersection of science and medicine, politics and economy. She is the author of *Negotiating the French Pox in Early Modern Germany* (2009) and co-author of *Writing History in the Age of Biomedicine* (2013).

B. Ann Tlusty

is Professor of History at Bucknell University. She specializes in the social and cultural history of early modern cities, particularly in southern Germany. She is the author of *Bacchus and Civic Order: The Culture of Drink in Early Modern Germany* (2001) and *The Martial Ethic in Early Modern Germany: Civic Duty and the Right to Bear Arms* (2011), and editor of *Augsburg in the Reformation Era: An Anthology of Sources* (2012).

Sabine Ullmann

is Professor of Early Modern History and Regional History at the Catholic University of Eichstätt-Ingolstadt. She specializes in the history of early modern Jewry as well as in the political and judicial culture of the Holy Roman Empire. She is the author of *Nachbarschaft und Konkurrenz. Juden und Christen in den Dörfern der Markgrafschaft Burgau 1650 bis 1750* (1999) and *Geschichte auf der langen Bank. Die Kommissionen des Reichshofrats unter Kaiser Maximilian II. (1564–1576)* (2006).

Wolfgang E.J. Weber

is retired Professor of History at the University of Augsburg. He has published widely on early modern political thought, cultural and intellectual history, and historiography. His recent publications include *Luthers bleiche Erben. Kulturgeschichte der evangelischen Geistlichkeit des 17. Jahrhunderts* (2017) and (as co-editor) *Augsburg und Amerika. Aneignungen und globale Verflechtungen in einer Stadt* (2013).

Michele Zelinsky Hanson is an independent historian. She formerly taught at La Salle University and is the author of *Religious Identity in an Early Modern Community: Augsburg, 1517 to 1555* (2008).

PART 1

The City

∴

CHAPTER 1

Sources and Historiography

Helmut Graser, Mark Häberlein and B. Ann Tlusty

In many ways, Paul von Stetten the Younger (1731–1808) was a man between two worlds. As the imperial city of Augsburg's last Protestant mayor (*Stadtpfleger*), Stetten sought to implement administrative and financial reforms, but ultimately could not prevent the city's incorporation into the Kingdom of Bavaria in 1806. As an adherent of the Enlightenment, Stetten was familiar with contemporary ideas of toleration and individual rights; nonetheless, he remained a conservative patrician who clung to the imperial city's established constitutional order, which enshrined the political privileges of his social class and preserved a rigid system of confessional parity between Catholics and Protestants.[1] As a historian, Stetten was the heir to a family tradition of chronicle writing – his father Paul von Stetten the Elder had produced a voluminous history of the imperial city[2] – but he also wrote a number of works that pioneered a new approach to the city's past. His books on the history of the patriciate (*Geschichte der adelichen Geschlechter in der freyen Reichs-Stadt Augsburg*, 1762) and on the development of arts and crafts in Augsburg (*Kunst-, Gewerb- und Handwerks-Geschichte der Reichs-Stadt Augsburg*, 2 vols., 1779–88) bear witness to the author's pride in his native city's glorious history, but also demonstrate a thorough knowledge of the written and archival sources.[3]

The home-town history that served as a point of pride for the Stetten family was rooted in an illustrious past that still permeated the collective memory of its educated citizens, even if the city had lost some of its global reach by Paul Stetten the Younger's time. Established as a Roman settlement during the reign of Caesar Augustus, for whom it is named, Augsburg by the dawn of the early modern era was one of the largest and most prosperous cities in central Europe. A major center of textile production and the home of merchant companies who carried out long-distance trade and financial operations on a European (and in some cases a global) scale, the city's economic centrality gave it a significance well beyond the southern German lands. This economic prominence was matched by its political and cultural importance. Augsburg was a favorite

---

1 Bátori, "Paul von Stetten der Jüngere"; Pahnke, "Patriotismus ohne Nation".
2 Stetten, *Geschichte*.
3 See Chapter 4 of this volume.

destination for emperors from Maximilian I to Rudolph II, hosting no less than eight imperial diets over the course of the sixteenth century, at which some of the most crucial negotiations of the Reformation were hammered out. The Swabian city was also the largest producer of German-language books in the Empire and played a major role as a center of humanism and Renaissance art north of the Alps. While the Thirty Years' War resulted in heavy demographic and economic losses during the first half of the seventeenth century, Augsburg managed to recover at least some of its economic and cultural potential and was particularly notable in the eighteenth century for the output of its cotton-printing factories, printers, and goldsmiths.

Chronicles began to celebrate Augsburg's history from the early fifteenth century, and it has attracted the attention of historians ever since. A particular focus of this historiography is the city's zenith of prominence between the late fifteenth and the seventeenth centuries. Much of this historical tradition, however, is inaccessible to English-language readers, and a survey of Augsburg's history in English is lacking entirely. Our goal here, then, is to provide readers with a useful overview of the history of this important early modern center that is informed by recent scholarship. In combination, the contributions collected here provide a survey of the most significant scholarly approaches to Augsburg's colorful past from a variety of perspectives, disciplines, and methodological approaches, while at the same time introducing new research.

As a historian, the above-mentioned Paul von Stetten the Younger set the standard for a number of additional works by native sons or residents of Augsburg that appeared in the nineteenth and early twentieth centuries. These local histories were likewise based on familiarity with the local sources and provided in-depth accounts of major aspects of the city's past. The producers of this brand of local history included public officials like Franz Eugen von Seida und Landensberg (1772–1826), who wrote an account of the city's religious, educational, and welfare institutions in 1813 and a general history of the city in 1826;[4] librarians like Benedikt Greiff, who published the autobiography of the Renaissance merchant Lucas Rem in the 1860s;[5] or archivists like Pius Dirr (1875–1943), who authored several studies on the city's constitutional, economic, and cultural history.[6] A regional historical society, the *Historischer Verein für Schwaben und Neuburg*, provided these scholars with a forum of exchange and an outlet for their publications. While many of their books and articles still serve as essential starting points for research on late medieval and

---

4 Seida, *Historisch-statistische Beschreibung*; idem, *Augsburger Geschichte*.
5 E.g. Greiff, "Tagebuch".
6 These include Dirr, "Clemens Jäger"; idem, *Augsburgs Textilindustrie*; idem, "Zunftregiment".

early modern Augsburg, their impact was largely confined to the local and regional scene.

The work of the Munich professor Friedrich Roth was of a more ambitious nature: In the late nineteenth and early twentieth centuries, Roth edited several Augsburg chronicles in a series of urban historiographical works from the late medieval and Reformation periods (*Die Chroniken der deutschen Städte vom 14. bis ins 16. Jahrhundert*) under the auspices of the Bavarian Academy of Sciences.[7] Besides numerous articles, he also wrote a four-volume account of the Protestant Reformation in Augsburg. Drawing on a broad range of sources – council minutes, correspondence, chronicles, sermons, and pamphlets, among others – Roth published what remains the most comprehensive account of the city's religious and political history from 1517 to 1555.[8]

Apart from Augsburg's role as a center of the urban Reformation, late nineteenth- and early twentieth-century historiography concentrated on the place of the city's prominent families in the history of capitalism. The economist Richard Ehrenberg (1857–1921) set the stage for this historiographical focus with his two-volume work *Das Zeitalter der Fugger* ("The Age of the Fuggers") in 1896.[9] Ehrenberg made extensive use of the account books, balance sheets (*Generalrechnungen*), and correspondence of Augsburg's major mercantile firms to outline their history and their involvement in sixteenth-century capital markets. Several reprints and translations into French and English (as *Capital and Finance in the Age of the Renaissance: A Study on the Fuggers and Their Connections*) underscore the work's lasting significance as a pioneering exploration of Augsburg's role as a center of long-distance trade and government finance. A few years later, the economic historian Jakob Strieder (1877–1936) published a dissertation in which he presented Augsburg as a case study of the "genesis of modern capitalism" and demonstrated on the basis of tax records that, contrary to the economist Werner Sombart's claim, commerce instead of landed wealth provided the basis for the large fortunes of the city's leading families in the fifteenth and early sixteenth centuries.[10] Strieder went on to become a professor of economic and social history at the University of Munich, where he supervised numerous dissertations on individual merchant companies and wrote several studies on south German commerce in the sixteenth century as well as a bestselling biography of Jakob Fugger the Rich

---

7   For more on this series and on the individual chronicles, see Chapter 4 of this volume.
8   Roth, *Augsburgs Reformationsgeschichte*.
9   Ehrenberg, *Zeitalter der Fugger*.
10 Strieder, *Genesis des modernen Kapitalismus*.

(1459–1525), whom Strieder presented as the archetype of the modern capitalistic entrepreneur.[11]

The work of Roth, Ehrenberg, and Strieder established a historiographical focus on the sixteenth century, which was perceived as a "golden age" (*Blütezeit*) when Augsburg ranged among Europe's premier commercial, political, religious, and cultural centers. Throughout the twentieth century, this focus has been sustained in research on the city's most prominent family, the Fuggers. Much of this work has been supported by the Fugger family foundations.[12] Baron Götz von Pölnitz (1906–67), who succeeded Strieder as head archivist of the Fugger archives in 1936, wrote exhaustive biographies of Jakob Fugger the Rich and his nephew and successor as general manager of the Fugger firm, Anton Fugger (1493–1560). Although Pölnitz pursued a "great men make history" approach and his flowery style makes for difficult reading, his biographies remain indispensable for the sheer amount of information they contain.[13] Pölnitz's work was carried on by Hermann Kellenbenz (1913–90), a renowned and highly productive economic historian, whose many publications on the Fugger Company culminated in a three-volume study of its activities in Spain and Portugal.[14]

Pölnitz and Kellenbenz tended to regard Anton Fugger's successors as mere epigones who exploited the company's wealth for their individual pursuits and luxurious lifestyles; several researchers, however, have revised this view. Beginning with the French historian Robert Mandrou and the German historian Reinhard Hildebrandt in the late 1960s, they have shown that members of the Fugger family integrated themselves into the ranks of the imperial nobility and built up substantial territorial complexes in Swabia while successfully continuing their involvement in long-distance trade and government finance at the same time.[15] Among other topics, recent research has explored the fate of Jakob Fugger's foundations in the Reformation era,[16] the correspondence networks of individual family members,[17] and conflicts within the Fugger family,[18] thus showing that the Fuggers' manifold activities and the vast amount of

---

11 Strieder, *Jakob Fugger der Reiche*; see also Deininger (ed.), *Das reiche Augsburg*.
12 See Karg, "Betreff".
13 Pölnitz, *Jakob Fugger*; idem, *Anton Fugger*; idem, *Die Fugger*.
14 Kellenbenz, *Die Fugger in Spanien und Portugal*. On his life and work, see Granda, *Kellenbenz*.
15 Mandrou, *Les Fugger*; Hildebrandt, *Die "Georg Fuggerischen Erben"*; see also Mörke, "Die Fugger"; Egermann-Krebs, *Jacob Fugger-Babenhausen*.
16 Scheller, *Memoria an der Zeitenwende*.
17 Dauser, *Informationskultur*.
18 Schneider, *Fugger contra Fugger*.

documentation which these have generated still constitute a promising area of research.[19]

Whereas economic historians have concentrated on the sixteenth century because of the Fuggers' and other merchant families' importance to European – and in some instances even global – trade and finance, art historians focused on the same period due to Augsburg's central position as a producer of Renaissance art and architecture. In the 1950s, Norbert Lieb compiled two volumes on the Fuggers' role as patrons of the arts,[20] and a major exhibition staged in Augsburg in 1980 highlighted the city's artistic and cultural achievements during the Renaissance and early Baroque periods.[21] Since then, art historians and curators have continued to explore important monuments such as the Fugger chapel in the church of St. Anna and the cycle of representations of the months of the year (*Monatsbilder*) from the workshop of Jörg Breu the Elder,[22] as well as the careers and works of individual Renaissance artists within their respective aesthetic, political, and social contexts.[23]

Until the 1970s, sixteenth-century merchants and artists remained the two best-studied groups in pre-modern Augsburg, while research on the city's political and intellectual history was confined to important individuals like the city secretary and humanist Conrad Peutinger.[24] Other social groups were neglected, and neither the late medieval period nor the seventeenth and eighteenth centuries received much attention. Leonhard Lenk's 1968 dissertation on Augsburg's *Bürgertum* between 1580 and 1700, for example, largely confirmed the view that this period was marked by cultural and intellectual decline. Wolfgang Zorn's 1961 study, by contrast, presented strong evidence that the economy of Augsburg (and other Swabian cities) substantially recovered after the devastating period of the Thirty Years' War and attracted numerous enterprising merchants and bankers.[25] In 1971, Rolf Kießling's dissertation on the relationship between Augsburg's citizens and the local church offered a major reassessment of the city's religious and social history in the late Middle Ages.[26]

---

19 For a recent synthesis, see Häberlein, *The Fuggers of Augsburg*.
20 Lieb, *Die Fugger und die Kunst*. For a recent work on this topic, see Wölfle, *Kunstpatronage*.
21 *Welt im Umbruch*.
22 Bushart, *Fuggerkapelle*; Bellot, "Fuggerkapelle"; Grüber (ed.), *"Kurzweil viel ..."*
23 See Cuneo, *Art and Politics*; Morrall, *Jörg Breu*; Kranz, *Christoph Amberger*; Metzger, *Daniel Hopfer*; and on musicology, see Fisher, *Music*.
24 König, *Peutingerstudien*; Bauer, "Peutingers Gutachten"; Lutz, *Conrad Peutinger*.
25 Lenk, *Augsburger Bürgertum*; Zorn, *Handels- und Industriegeschichte*.
26 Kießling, *Bürgerliche Gesellschaft*.

For a number of reasons, the 1980s and 1990s mark a watershed in the historiography of Augsburg. First, the city's history now attracted the attention of international scholars who applied the new approaches of social and cultural history to Augsburg's rich store of late medieval and early modern sources. Influenced by the cultural turn of the 1970s, which emphasized the socially constitutive nature of humanist research, historians of Germany began in the 1980s to apply methodologies associated with social anthropology, feminist theory, and postmodernism to the mountains of archival documents held in many urban archives of the former Holy Roman Empire. Their self-conscious goal was to shift the emphasis from elite groups and dominant narratives and explore a more inclusive social and cultural history "from below". This new generation of historians focused on human lives less as elements in a movement or social organization, and more as individual agents, giving recognition to the diversity of experience and identity among historical actors who themselves were not able to pen their own histories.[27]

A second factor was the founding of a university in Augsburg in 1970 and the subsequent establishment of a history department there, which strengthened the academic basis for scholarly work on the imperial city. In the early 1990s, an Institute of European Cultural History was also established at the university, which at least in its early years was explicitly tasked with encouraging exploration of the rich collections of historical records held in Augsburg's repositories.[28] In pursuit of this mission, the Institute was able to support the work of foreign scholars in the city's archives and libraries, thus enhancing the internationalization of research on the pre-modern city. Finally, Augsburg celebrated the 2000th anniversary of its Roman founding in 1985, and a new general history of the city as well as a historical encyclopedia published on the occasion have provided students of Augsburg's history with a solid basis.[29]

In 1981 Claus-Peter Clasen, a German-born historian who was then teaching at UCLA, published the first modern study on the largest group of craftsmen in sixteenth-century Augsburg, the weavers. Mainly relying on tax lists, muster rolls, and administrative records, Clasen did much to deflate the myth of Augsburg's "golden age" by pointing out the widespread poverty and susceptibility to crisis in the craft sector that formed the backbone of Augsburg's

---

27 The term "history from below" was popularized by E.P. Thomson in the 1960s: Thompson, "History from Below".
28 See Brüning and Janota (eds.), *Augsburg in der Frühen Neuzeit*.
29 Gottlieb et al. (eds.), *Geschichte der Stadt Augsburg*. The historical encyclopedia was republished in a revised and extended edition in 1998: Grünsteudel et al. (eds.), *Augsburger Stadtlexikon*. This revised version is also accessible online: http://www.stadtlexikon-augsburg.de/.

economy.[30] Since then, Clasen has continued to explore the social and economic history of Augsburg's crafts in a series of monographs which are closely based on the local sources.[31] Bernd Roeck's work on the bakers during the Thirty Years' War, Reinhold Reith's dissertation on the working and living conditions of eighteenth-century journeymen, and Christine Werkstetter's study of women's work have likewise made substantial contributions to the social history of Augsburg's crafts.[32] At the University of Augsburg, several students of Wolfgang Reinhard, who held the chair of early modern history there during the 1980s, applied Reinhard's network approach to study kinship ties, social interactions, and factions within Augsburg's political elite.[33] This approach has subsequently been extended to the city's sixteenth-century merchant communities[34] and to the local printers.[35]

Two particularly influential monographs appeared in 1989. The first of these was Australian-born historian Lyndal Roper's *The Holy Household*, a pioneering exploration of gender roles and women's experiences in Augsburg during the Protestant Reformation. Drawing on an extensive range of sources, Roper provocatively argued that the Reformation actually reinforced notions of male honor and dominance, which were at the heart of the urban craftsmen's value system, by disciplining wayward women, abolishing the convents as spaces of female sociability, and curtailing the role of women in the public sphere. While stimulating debate on the social and gender dimensions of the urban Reformation, Roper also pointed historians to the wealth of court and guild records available in Augsburg's city archives.[36] In the same year, Bernd Roeck provided a magisterial account of Augsburg's history prior to and during the Thirty Years' War. Combining the methods of political, demographic, social, and cultural history, Roeck offered a comprehensive portrait of urban society in the years around 1600 as well as a detailed study of the war's effects on Augsburg's population, economy, and government.[37]

Roper's and Roeck's works provided stimulation for a new generation of Anglo-American and German scholars working on social-historical themes

---

30   Clasen, *Augsburger Weber*.
31   Clasen, *Streiks und Aufstände*; idem, *Textilherstellung*; idem, *Streiks der Augsburger Schuhknechte*.
32   Roeck, *Bäcker, Brot und Getreide*; Reith, *Arbeits- und Lebensweise*; Werkstetter, *Frauen im Augsburger Zunfthandwerk*.
33   Sieh-Burens, *Oligarchie*; Steuer, *Außenverflechtung*; Reinhard, "Oligarchische Verflechtung".
34   Reinhard (ed.), *Augsburger Eliten*; Häberlein, *Brüder, Freunde und Betrüger*.
35   Künast, *"Getruckt zu Augspurg"*.
36   Roper, *The Holy Household*.
37   Roeck, *Eine Stadt in Krieg und Frieden*.

including marginal(ized) groups,[38] forms of sociability,[39] and religious identities.[40] While most German-speaking historians publishing in the 1990s continued to take a more traditional approach to Augsburg's Reformation history, studying political developments or the roles of individual clergymen,[41] the collaboration of German and American historians a decade later resulted in a new look at the local Reformation at the parish level.[42]

Augsburg's status as a bi-confessional city in which Catholics and Protestants lived next to one another and shared political power has likewise attracted considerable scholarly attention. Paul Warmbrunn, Katarina Sieh-Burens, Peter Steuer, and Bernd Roeck had explored important political and social facets of confessional coexistence during the 1980s,[43] but the French historian Etienne François offered a particularly rich account of the topic in 1991. Focusing on the period between the Peace of Westphalia and the end of Augsburg's existence as an imperial city, François looked at confessional coexistence from various angles – demographic behavior, professional profiles, economic cooperation, marriage patterns, social relations in households and neighborhoods, religious ritual, and even naming patterns – to highlight that Augsburg's confessional groups were neither antagonistic nor tolerant in a modern sense. Instead, they cooperated in selected areas while remaining largely among themselves in others.[44] Thomas M. Safley has looked at the bi-confessional city through the lens of Augsburg's orphanages, tracing their institutional and economic history as well as the experiences of individual orphans.[45]

Taken together, the activities of Augsburg-based and international scholars have resulted in an extraordinary thematic and methodological breadth. In addition to the topics mentioned above, works that came out during the past quarter of a century have explored political norms and groups during the late Middle Ages;[46] the library of Augsburg's pre-eminent humanist, Conrad

---

38 Stuart, *Defiled Trades*; Kießling (ed.), *Judengemeinden*; Ullmann, *Nachbarschaft und Konkurrenz*.
39 Tlusty, *Bacchus and Civic Order*.
40 Zelinsky Hanson, *Religious Identity*.
41 Gößner, *Weltliche Kirchenhoheit*; Dellsperger et al. (eds.), *Wolfgang Musculus*.
42 Kießling et al. (eds.), *Im Ringen um die Reformation*.
43 Warmbrunn, *Zwei Konfessionen*; Sieh-Burens, *Oligarchie*; Steuer, *Außenverflechtung*; Roeck, *Eine Stadt in Krieg und Frieden*.
44 François, *Die unsichtbare Grenze*. See also the more recent study by Corpis, *Crossing the Boundaries*, which deals with religious conversion.
45 Safley, *Charity and Economy*; idem, *Children of the Laboring Poor*.
46 Rogge, *Für den Gemeinen Nutzen*.

Peutinger;[47] the city's role in sixteenth-century communication networks;[48] the production of chronicles and family books;[49] the learning of foreign languages;[50] medical practice;[51] and the making of scientific instruments.[52] The topic of merchant capitalism, one of the traditional areas of scholarship on early modern Augsburg, has also attracted new interest in studies on the early stages of globalization,[53] merchants as cultural agents,[54] and the causes and consequences of business failure.[55] Collections of essays present the current state of research on Augsburg's cultural history in the era of Renaissance Humanism,[56] the development of printing and publishing in the city,[57] and the history of important parish churches.[58]

Finally, a number of useful sources for studying the history of early modern Augsburg have become available in print during the past two decades. Apart from business records of important merchant companies like the Welsers[59] and the Paler-Weiß,[60] these include an anthology of sixteenth- and seventeenth-century sources concentrating on common people;[61] the extensive urban chronicle of Georg Kölderer, bookkeeper of the Weiß family's merchant company, covering the years 1576–1607;[62] the letterbooks of Hans Fugger, a member of the famous merchant family whose 4,700 letters offer fascinating glimpses of the material culture and consumption habits of a wealthy patrician in the late sixteenth century;[63] the personal memoir of Matheus (Matthäus) Miller, a seventeenth-century merchant;[64] and the letters written by the young

---

47   Künast and Zäh (eds.), *Bibliothek Konrad Peutingers*; Laube and Zäh (eds.), *Gesammeltes Gedächtnis*.
48   Dauser, *Informationskultur*; Bauer, *Zeitungen vor der Zeitung*; Ferber, "Scio multos te amicos habere".
49   Rohmann, *Clemens Jäger*; idem, *Ehrenbuch der Fugger*; Mauer, "Gemain Geschrey"; Emmendörffer and Zäh (eds.), *Bürgermacht und Bücherpracht*.
50   Glück et al., *Mehrsprachigkeit*.
51   Stein, *French Pox*.
52   Keil, *Augustanus Opticus*.
53   Johnson, *The German Discovery of the World*; Kalus, *Pfeffer – Kupfer – Nachrichten*; Häberlein, *The Fuggers of Augsburg*; idem, *Aufbruch ins globale Zeitalter*.
54   Häberlein and Bayreuther, *Agent und Ambassador*.
55   Häberlein, *Brüder, Freunde und Betrüger*; Safley, "Bankruptcy".
56   Müller (ed.), *Humanismus und Renaissance*.
57   Gier and Janota (eds.), *Augsburger Buchdruck und Verlagswesen*.
58   Müller (ed.), *St. Moritz*; Kießling (ed.), *St. Anna*.
59   Geffcken and Häberlein (eds.), *Rechnungsfragmente*; Schmidt (ed.), *Gewerbebuch*.
60   Hildebrandt (ed.), *Quellen und Regesten*.
61   Tlusty (ed.), *Augsburg During the Reformation Era*.
62   Weber and Strodel (eds.), *Georg Kölderer*.
63   Karnehm (ed.), *Korrespondenz Hans Fuggers*.
64   Safley (ed.), *Aufzeichnungen*; see also idem, *Matheus Miller's Memoir*.

patricians Friedrich and Hans Endorfer to their father during their commercial apprenticeship in Italy and France in the 1620s.[65] The "costume books" of the Fugger Company's chief bookkeeper Matthäus Schwarz (1497–1574) and his son Veit Konrad, which represent a unique blend of illustrated autobiography and Renaissance fashion book, have finally been published in full color.[66] The diaries of the above-mentioned mayor Paul von Stetten the Younger, a major source for Augsburg's history during the final decades of its existence as a free imperial city, are also now available in a three-volume edition.[67]

Apart from enriching the source base for studies on early modern Augsburg, the appearance of these editions reflects historians' growing interest in "ego-documents" (personal memoirs, autobiographies, letters, and diaries), which promise insights into the identities, experiences, reflections, and worldviews of individuals in the past.[68] While most ego-documents – in Augsburg as elsewhere in the early modern world – mirror the experiences and mentalities of the elites, growing attention has also been paid in this context to documents that reveal the experiences of ordinary citizens. With a close reading of the text, common voices and emotions can be gleaned not only from house books and letters, but also from petitions, supplications, and other legal and official documents prepared by professional scribes. Such efforts naturally require reading past the formulaic expressions of scribes in order to identify individual expressions, a process that can benefit from methods borrowed from socio-linguistics.[69]

The extraordinarily rich holdings of Augsburg's city archives also contain considerable amounts of material written by non-professional writers in their own hands, including documents displaying levels of writing ability that range from near-professional to semi-literate.[70] Adding new layers of socio-linguistic research based on texts from the borderline between oral and written culture reveals stages of development in dialect forms as well as highlighting the everyday use of written texts among semi- and sub-literate townspeople. This approach to "language from below" both complements socio-historical research and adds nuance to studies of the development of a unified written standard

---

65   Häberlein et al. (eds.), *Korrespondenz*.
66   Rublack and Hayward (eds.), *First Book of Fashion*.
67   Stetten, *Selbstbiographie*.
68   See Ulbrich et al. (eds.), *Mapping the 'I'*.
69   See for example the articles by Blickle, Fuhrmann et al., and Holenstein in Blickle (ed.), *Gemeinde und Staat*, pp. 241–357; Voss (ed.), *Petitions*; Ulbricht, "Supplikationen".
70   Graser, "Quellen vom unteren Rand".

in German, the process of which itself was influenced in considerable measure by the style of Augsburg's printers.[71]

Despite the presence of unusually rich and still largely unexploited collections, research on late medieval and early modern Augsburg has for the past decade not been easy. The city archives' old building in the city center was affected by structural and humidity problems, and an infestation of bread beetles (presumably from the adjacent city market) with a taste for early modern documents finally caused its temporary closure in 2010. Following closely on the collapse of the city archive of Cologne in the same year, this incident reminds us of the fragility of the historical record, particularly in the case of the many as-yet unexploited documents that exist in only one manuscript copy.

The Augsburg city archives have since moved to new premises in a former textile factory, and its holdings finally became fully accessible again only in 2015.[72] Meanwhile, Augsburg's other major repository of historic manuscripts, the state and city library (*Staats- und Stadtbibliothek*), went through a turbulent period of its own when the city of Augsburg faced massive budget cuts in 2010 and considered splitting up the library's holdings. In this critical situation, scholars and other patrons formed an initiative to support the institution and raise public awareness of its cultural significance. Prolonged negotiations have eventually resulted in the State of Bavaria's assumption of full financial responsibility for the library. The historic library building (opened in 1893) is currently undergoing a major restoration and expansion, and the Bavarian State Library's digitalization program will make the historic manuscripts more easily accessible for future generations of users.[73]

Bibliography

Published Primary Sources

Geffcken, P. and Häberlein, M. (eds.), *Rechnungsfragmente der Augsburger Welser-Gesellschaft 1496–1551. Oberdeutscher Fernhandel am Beginn der neuzeitlichen Weltwirtschaft*, Stuttgart, 2014.

Graser, H. and Tlusty, B.A. (eds.), *Jonas Losch, Teutscher Dichter und Componist. Die Lieder- und Reimspruchsammlung eines Augsburger Webers aus den Jahren 1579–1583*, Regensburg, 2015.

---

71 Graser, "Augsburg und die deutsche Sprachgeschichte"; Graser and Tlusty (eds.), *Jonas Losch*.
72 See the archive's official website: http://www.stadtarchiv.augsburg.de.
73 See the library's official website: https://www.sustb-augsburg.de.

Greiff, B., "Tagebuch des Lucas Rem aus den Jahren 1494–1541. Ein Beitrag zur Handelsgeschichte der Stadt Augsburg", *26. Jahresbericht des historischen Kreisvereins im Regierungsbezirk von Schwaben und Neuburg*, Augsburg, 1861, pp. 1–110.

Häberlein, M., Künast, H.-J. and Schwanke, I. (eds.), *Korrespondenz der Augsburger Patrizierfamilie Endorfer 1620–1627. Briefe aus Italien und Frankreich im Zeitalter des Dreißigjährigen Krieges*, Augsburg, 2010.

Hildebrandt, R. (ed.), *Quellen und Regesten zu den Augsburger Handelshäusern Paler und Rehlinger 1539–1642. Wirtschaft und Politik im 16./17. Jahrhundert*, 2 vols., Stuttgart, 1996–2004.

Künast, H.-J. and Zäh, H. (eds.), *Die Bibliothek Konrad Peutingers. Edition der historischen Kataloge und Rekonstruktion der Bestände*, 2 vols., Tübingen, 2003–05.

Safley, T.M. (ed.), *Die Aufzeichnungen des Matheus Miller. Das Leben eines Augsburger Kaufmanns im 17. Jahrhundert*, Augsburg, 2003.

Schmidt, S. (ed.), *Das Gewerbebuch der Augsburger Christoph-Welser-Gesellschaft (1554–1560). Edition und Kommentar*, Augsburg, 2015.

Stetten, P. von (the Elder), *Geschichte der Heil. Röm. Reichs Freyen Stadt Augspurg* […], Frankfurt and Leipzig, 1743.

Stetten, P. von (the Younger), *Paul von Stetten d.J. Selbstbiographie. Die Lebensbeschreibung des Patriziers und Stadtpflegers der Reichsstadt Augsburg (1731–1808)*, ed. H. Gier et al., 3 vols., Augsburg, 2009–16.

Tlusty, B.A. (ed.), *Augsburg During the Reformation Era: An Anthology of Sources*, Indianapolis, 2012.

Weber, W.E.J. and Strodel, S. (eds.), *Georg Kölderer, Beschreibunng vnnd Kurtze Vertzaichnus Fürnemer Lob vnnd gedenckhwürdiger Historien. Eine Chronik der Stadt Augsburg der Jahre 1576–1607*, Augsburg, 2013.

Secondary Literature

Bátori, I., "Paul von Stetten der Jüngere. Augsburger Staatsmann in schwieriger Zeit", *Zeitschrift des Historischen Vereins für Schwaben* 77 (1983), pp. 103–24.

Bauer, C., "Conrad Peutingers Gutachten zur Monopolfrage. Eine Untersuchung zur Wandlung der Wirtschaftsanschauungen im Zeitalter der Reformation", *Archiv für Reformationsgeschichte* 45 (1954), pp. 1–43, 145–96.

Bauer, O., *Zeitungen vor der Zeitung. Die Fuggerzeitungen (1568–1605) und das frühneuzeitliche Nachrichtensystem*, Berlin, 2011.

Bellot, C., "'Auf welsche art, der zeit gar new erfunden.' Zur Augsburger Fuggerkapelle", in Müller (ed.), *Humanismus und Renaissance*, pp. 445–90.

Blickle, P. (ed.), *Gemeinde und Staat im Alten Europa*, Munich, 1998.

Brüning, J. and Janota, J. (eds.), *Augsburg in der Frühen Neuzeit. Beiträge zu einem Forschungsprogramm*, Berlin, 1995.

Bushart, B., *Die Fuggerkapelle bei St. Anna in Augsburg*, Munich, 1994.

Clasen, C.-P., *Die Augsburger Weber. Leistungen und Krisen des Textilgewerbes um 1600*, Augsburg, 1981.

Clasen, C.-P., *Streiks und Aufstände der Augsburger Weber im 17. und 18. Jahrhundert*, Augsburg, 1993.

Clasen, C.-P., *Textilherstellung in Augsburg in der Frühen Neuzeit*, 2 vols., Augsburg, 1995.

Clasen, C.-P., *Streiks der Augsburger Schuhknechte. Freiheit und Gerechtigkeit*, Augsburg, 2002.

Corpis, D., *Crossing the Boundaries of Belief: Geographies of Religious Conversion in Southern Germany, 1648–1800*, Charlottesville and London, 2014.

Cuneo, P.F., *Art and Politics in Early Modern Germany: Jörg Breu the Elder and the Fashioning of Political Identity, c.1475–1536*, Leiden and Boston, 1998.

Dauser, R., *Informationskultur und Beziehungswissen – Das Korrespondenznetz Hans Fuggers (1531–1598)*, Tübingen, 2008.

Deininger, H.F. (ed.), *Das Reiche Augsburg. Ausgewählte Aufsätze Jakob Strieders zur Augsburger und süddeutschen Wirtschaftsgeschichte des 15. und 16. Jahrhunderts*, Munich, 1938.

Dellsperger, R., Freudenberger, R. and Weber, W. (eds.), *Wolfgang Musculus (1497–1563) und die oberdeutsche Reformation*, Berlin, 1997.

Dirr, P., "Clemens Jäger und seine Augsburger Ehrenbücher und Zunftbücher", *Zeitschrift des Historischen Vereins für Schwaben und Neuburg* 36 (1910), pp. 1–32.

Dirr, P., *Die Augsburger Textilindustrie im 18. Jahrhundert*, Augsburg, 1911.

Dirr, P., "Studien zur Geschichte der Augsburger Zunftverfassung 1368–1548", *Zeitschrift des Historischen Vereins für Schwaben und Neuburg* 39 (1913), pp. 144–243.

Egermann-Krebs, D., *Jacob Fugger-Babenhausen (1542–1598). Güterpolitik und Herrschaftspraxis*, Augsburg, 2015.

Ehrenberg, R., *Das Zeitalter der Fugger. Geldkapital und Creditverkehr im 16. Jahrhundert*, 2 vols., Jena, 1896. English translation: *Capital and Finance in the Age of the Renaissance: A Study on the Fuggers and Their Connections*, transl. H.M. Lucas, New York, 1928 (repr. New York, 1963).

Emmendörffer, C. and Zäh, H. (eds.), *Bürgermacht und Bücherpracht. Augsburger Ehren- und Familienbücher der Renaissance* (exhibition catalogue), 2 vols., Lucerne, 2011.

Ferber, M.U., *"Scio multos te amicos habere". Wissensvermittlung und Wissenssicherung im Späthumanismus am Beispiel des Epistolariums Marx Welsers d.J. (1558–1614)*, Augsburg, 2008.

Fisher, A.J., *Music and Religious Identity in Counter-Reformation Augsburg, 1580–1630*, Aldershot, 2004.

François, E., *Die unsichtbare Grenze. Protestanten und Katholiken in Augsburg 1648–1806*, Sigmaringen, 1991.

Gier, H. and Janota, J. (eds.), *Augsburger Buchdruck und Verlagswesen. Von den Anfängen bis zur Gegenwart*, Wiesbaden, 1997.

Glück, H., Häberlein, M. and Schröder, K., *Mehrsprachigkeit in der Frühen Neuzeit. Die Reichsstädte Augsburg und Nürnberg vom 15. bis ins frühe 19. Jahrhundert*, Wiesbaden, 2013.

Gößner A., *Weltliche Kirchenhoheit und reichsstädtische Reformation. Die Augsburger Ratspolitik des "milten und mitleren Wegs" 1520–1534*, Berlin, 1999.

Gottlieb, G., Baer, W., Becker, J., Bellot, J., Filser, K., Fried, P., Reinhard W. and Schimmelpfennig, B. (eds.), *Geschichte der Stadt Augsburg von der Römerzeit bis zur Gegenwart*, Stuttgart, 1984 (2nd ed. 1985).

Granda, J., *Hermann Kellenbenz (1913–1990). Ein internationaler (Wirtschafts-)Historiker im 20. Jahrhundert*, Berlin, 2017.

Graser, H., "Augsburg und die deutsche Sprachgeschichte", in E. Funk, W. König and M. Renn (eds.), *Bausteine zur Sprachgeschichte. Referate der 13. Arbeitstagung zur Alemannischen Dialektologie*, Heidelberg, 2000, pp. 47–58.

Graser, H., "Quellen vom unteren Rand der Schriftlichkeit – die Stimme der einfachen Leute in der Stadt der Frühen Neuzeit?", in S. Elspaß and M. Negele (eds.), *Sprachvariation und Sprachwandel in der Stadt der Frühen Neuzeit*, Heidelberg, 2011, pp. 15–48.

Grüber, P.M. (ed.), *"Kurzweil viel ohn' Maß und Ziel". Augsburger Patrizier und ihre Feste zwischen Mittelalter und Neuzeit* (exhibition catalogue), Munich, 1994.

Grünsteudel, G., Hägele, G. and Frankenberger, R. (eds.), *Augsburger Stadtlexikon*, 2nd ed., Augsburg, 1998.

Häberlein, M., *Brüder, Freunde und Betrüger. Soziale Beziehungen, Normen und Konflikte in der Augsburger Kaufmannschaft um die Mitte des 16. Jahrhunderts*, Berlin, 1998.

Häberlein, M., *The Fuggers of Augsburg: Pursuing Wealth and Honor in Renaissance Germany*, Charlottesville and London, 2012.

Häberlein, M., *Aufbruch ins globale Zeitalter. Die Handelswelt der Fugger und Welser*, Darmstadt, 2016.

Häberlein, M. and Bayreuther, M., *Agent und Ambassador. Der Kaufmann Anton Meuting als Vermittler zwischen Bayern und Spanien im Zeitalter Philipps II.*, Augsburg, 2013.

Hildebrandt, R., *Die "Georg Fuggerischen Erben". Kaufmännische Tätigkeit und sozialer Status, 1555–1620*, Berlin, 1966.

Johnson, C.R., *The German Discovery of the World: Renaissance Encounters with the Strange and Marvelous*, Charlottesville, 2008.

Kalus, M., *Pfeffer – Kupfer – Nachrichten. Kaufmannsnetzwerke und Handelsstrukturen im europäisch-asiatischen Handel am Ende des 16. Jahrhunderts*, Augsburg, 2010.

Karg, F., "'Betreff: Herstellung einer Geschichte des Hauses Fugger.' Die Fugger als Forschungsthema im 20. Jahrhundert", in J. Burkhardt (ed.), *Augsburger Handelshäuser im Wandel des historischen Urteils*, Berlin, 1996, pp. 308–321.

Keil, I., *Augustanus Opticus. Johann Wiesel (1583–1662) und 200 Jahre optisches Handwerk in Augsburg*, Berlin, 2000.

Kießling, R., *Bürgerliche Gesellschaft und Kirche in Augsburg im Spätmittelalter. Ein Beitrag zur Strukturanalyse der oberdeutschen Reichsstadt*, Augsburg, 1971.
Kießling, R. (ed.), *Judengemeinden in Schwaben im Kontext des Alten Reiches*, Berlin, 1995.
Kießling, R. (ed.), *St. Anna in Augsburg. Eine Kirche und ihre Gemeinde*, Augsburg, 2013.
Kießling, R., Safley, T.M. and Wandel, L.P. (eds.), *Im Ringen um die Reformation. Kirchen und Prädikanten, Rat und Gemeinden in Augsburg*, Epfendorf, 2011.
König, E., *Peutingerstudien*, Freiburg, 1914.
Kranz, A., *Christoph Amberger – Bildnismaler zu Augsburg. Städtische Eliten im Spiegel ihrer Porträts*, Regensburg, 2004.
Künast, H.-J., *"Getruckt zu Augspurg". Buchdruck und Buchhandel in Augsburg zwischen 1468 und 1555*, Tübingen, 1997.
Laube, R. and Zäh, H. (eds.), *Gesammeltes Gedächtnis. Konrad Peutinger und die kulturelle Überlieferung im 16. Jahrhundert* (exhibition catalogue), Lucerne, 2016.
Lenk, L., *Augsburger Bürgertum in Späthumanismus und Frühbarock (1580–1700)*, Augsburg, 1968.
Lieb, N., *Die Fugger und die Kunst*, 2 vols., Munich, 1952–58.
Lutz, H., *Conrad Peutinger. Beiträge zu einer politischen Biographie*, Augsburg, 1958.
Mandrou, R., *Les Fugger, propriétaires fonciers an Souabe 1560–1618. Étude de comportements socio-économiques à la fin du XVIe siècle*, Paris, 1969.
Mauer, B., *"Gemain Geschrey" und "teglich Reden". Georg Kölderer – ein Augsburger Chronist des konfessionellen Zeitalters*, Augsburg, 2001.
Metzger, C., *Daniel Hopfer. Ein Augsburger Meister der Renaissance* (exhibition catalogue), Berlin and Munich, 2009.
Mörke, O., "Die Fugger im 16. Jahrhundert: Städtische Elite oder Sonderstruktur? Ein Diskussionsbeitrag", *Archiv für Reformationsgeschichte* 74 (1983), pp. 141–61.
Morrall, A., *Jörg Breu the Elder. Art, Culture, and Belief in Reformation Augsburg*, Aldershot, 2002.
Müller, G.M. (ed.), *Das ehemalige Kollegiatstift St. Moritz in Augsburg*, Lindenberg, 2006.
Müller, G.M. (ed.), *Humanismus und Renaissance in Augsburg. Kulturgeschichte einer Stadt zwischen Spätmittelalter und Dreissigjährigem Krieg*, Berlin and New York, 2010.
Pahnke, G., "Patriotismus ohne Nation: Die patriotische Ideenwelt des Augsburger Patriziers Paul von Stetten d. J. (1731–1808)", in R. Kießling (ed.), *Neue Forschungen zur Geschichte der Stadt Augsburg*, Augsburg, 2011, pp. 165–230.
Pölnitz, G. von, *Jakob Fugger. Kaiser, Kirche und Kapital in der oberdeutschen Renaissance*, 2 vols., Tübingen, 1949–51.
Pölnitz, G. von, *Anton Fugger*, 5 vols., Tübingen, 1958–86.
Pölnitz, G. von, *Die Fugger*, Tübingen, 1960.

Reinhard, W., "Oligarchische Verflechtung und Klientel in oberdeutschen Städten", in A. Mączak (ed.), *Klientelsysteme im Europa der Frühen Neuzeit,* Munich, 1988, pp. 47–62.

Reinhard, W. (ed.), *Augsburger Eliten des 16. Jahrhunderts. Prosopographie wirtschaftlicher und politischer Führungsgruppen 1500–1620,* Berlin, 1996.

Reith, R., *Arbeits- und Lebensweise im städtischen Handwerk. Zur Sozialgeschichte der Augsburger Handwerksgesellen im 18. Jahrhundert, 1700–1806,* Göttingen, 1988.

Roeck, B., *Bäcker, Brot und Getreide in Augsburg. Zur Geschichte des Bäckerhandwerks und zur Versorgungspolitik der Reichsstadt im Zeitalter des Dreißigjährigen Krieges,* Sigmaringen, 1987.

Roeck, B., *Eine Stadt in Krieg und Frieden. Studien zur Geschichte der Reichsstadt Augsburg zwischen Kalenderstreit und Parität,* 2 vols., Göttingen, 1989.

Rogge, J., *Für den Gemeinen Nutzen. Politisches Handeln und Politikverständnis von Rat und Bürgerschaft in Augsburg im Spätmittelalter,* Tübingen, 1996.

Rohmann, G., *"Eines Erbaren Raths gehorsamer amptman". Clemens Jäger und die Geschichtsschreibung des 16. Jahrhunderts,* Augsburg, 2001.

Rohmann, G., *Das Ehrenbuch der Fugger. Darstellung – Kommentar – Transkription,* 2 vols., Augsburg, 2004.

Roth, F., *Augsburgs Reformationsgeschichte,* 4 vols., Munich, 1901–11.

Safley, T.M., *Charity and Economy in the Orphanages of Early Modern Augsburg,* Boston, 1997.

Safley, T.M., *Matheus Miller's Memoir: A Merchant's Life in the Seventeenth Century,* New York, 2000.

Safley, T.M., *Children of the Laboring Poor: Expectation and Experience among the Orphans of Early Modern Augsburg,* Leiden and Boston, 2005.

Safley, T.M., "Bankruptcy: Family and Finance in Early Modern Augsburg", *Journal of European Economic History* 29 (2000), pp. 53–72.

Scheller, B., *Memoria an der Zeitenwende. Die Stiftungen Jakob Fuggers des Reichen vor und während der Reformation (ca. 1505–1555),* Berlin, 2004.

Schneider, B., *Fugger contra Fugger. Die Augsburger Handelsgesellschaft zwischen Kontinuität und Konflikt,* Augsburg, 2016.

Seida und Landensberg, F.E. von, *Historisch-statistische Beschreibung aller Kirchen- Schul- Erziehungs- und Wohlthätigkeits-Anstalten in Augsburg,* Augsburg and Leipzig, 1813.

Seida und Landensberg, F.E. von, *Augsburger Geschichte von der Erbauung der Stadt bis zum Tode Maximilian Josephs,* Augsburg, 1826.

Sieh-Burens, K., *Oligarchie, Konfession und Politik im 16. Jahrhundert. Zur sozialen Verflechtung der Augsburger Bürgermeister und Stadtpfleger 1518–1618,* Munich, 1986.

Stein, C., *Negotiating the French Pox in Early Modern Germany,* Farnham, 2009.

SOURCES AND HISTORIOGRAPHY

Steuer, P., *Die Außenverflechtung der Augsburger Oligarchie von 1500–1620. Studien zur sozialen Verflechtung der politischen Führungsschicht der Reichsstadt Augsburg*, Augsburg, 1988.

Strieder, J., *Zur Genesis des modernen Kapitalismus. Forschungen zur Entstehung der großen bürgerlichen Kapitalvermögen am Ausgang des Mittelalters und zu Beginn der Neuzeit, zunächst in Augsburg*, Leipzig, 1904 (2nd ed. Munich, 1935).

Strieder, J., *Jakob Fugger der Reiche*, Leipzig, 1926.

Stuart, K., *Defiled Trades and Social Outcasts: Honor and Ritual Pollution in Early Modern Germany*, Cambridge, 1999.

Thompson E.P., "History from Below", *The Times Literary Supplement 3345* (Thursday, 7 April 1966), p. 279.

Tlusty, B.A., *Bacchus and Civic Order: The Culture of Drink in Early Modern Germany*, Charlottesville, 2001.

Ulbrich, C., Greyerz, K. von and Heiligensetzer, L. (eds.), *Mapping the 'I': Research on Self-Narratives in Germany and Switzerland*, Leiden, 2015.

Ulbricht, O., "Supplikationen als Ego-Dokumente. Bittschriften von Leibeigenen aus der ersten Hälfte des 17. Jahrhunderts als Beispiel", in W. Schulze (ed.), *Ego-Dokumente. Annäherung an den Menschen in der Geschichte*, Berlin, 1996, pp. 149–74.

Ullmann, S., *Nachbarschaft und Konkurrenz. Juden und Christen in Dörfern der Markgrafschaft Burgau 1650 bis 1750*, Göttingen, 1999.

Voss, L.H. van (ed.), *Petitions in Social History* (International Review of Social History, Supplement 9), Cambridge, 2001.

Warmbrunn, P., *Zwei Konfessionen in einer Stadt. Das Zusammenleben von Katholiken und Protestanten in den paritätischen Reichsstädten Augsburg, Biberach, Ravensburg und Dinkelsbühl von 1548 bis 1648*, Wiesbaden, 1983.

Welt im Umbruch. Augsburg zwischen Renaissance und Barock (exhibition catalogue), 3 vols., Augsburg, 1980.

Werkstetter, C., *Frauen im Augsburger Zunfthandwerk. Arbeit, Arbeitsbeziehungen und Geschlechterverhältnisse im 18. Jahrhundert*, Berlin, 2001.

Wölfle, S., *Die Kunstpatronage der Fugger 1560–1618*, Augsburg, 2009.

Zelinsky Hanson, M., *Religious Identity in an Early Reformation Community: Augsburg, 1517 to 1555*, Leiden and Boston, 2009.

Zorn, W., *Handels- und Industriegeschichte Bayerisch-Schwabens, 1648–1870*, Augsburg, 1961.

CHAPTER 2

Urban Topography, Population, Visual Representations

Barbara Rajkay

1   Geographical and Topographical Features

Augsburg is located in the northern Alpine foothills, close to the estuary area of the Alpine rivers Lech and Wertach.[1] It is characterized by a lengthy ridge with an altitude of approximately 490 m above sea level, extending through the entire city from south to north. This almost perfectly flat spur steeply drops by about twenty meters towards the north and the east into the Lech valley, while on the west side to the valley of the Wertach the altitude drops by only twelve meters, and by only six meters towards the low terrace in the southeast.[2]

The strategic advantages of this high terrace were already perceived by the Romans, who founded the provincial capital *Augusta Vindelicum*[3] at its northern end. The gentle ascent of the ridge in the south allowed easy access to the city by the major Roman road *Via Claudia Augusta*. In medieval times, the city clustered around the cathedral, located in what used to be the southern part of the Roman city area. Right in front of the gates of the episcopal city, a pre-urban market settlement started forming around the *Perlach* area and the church of St. Peter. The artisan quarter extended east of the lower terrace, while street markets developed along the old *Via Claudia* towards the south, all the way to the sepulchral pilgrimage church of St. Afra.[4] There, on the grounds of a Roman cemetery, a Benedectine monastery (founded around 1006) had developed out of a canon abbey. In addition, development continued north to the cathedral area.

Until the mid-twelfth century, the civilian settlement evinced the characteristics of a suburb. The first evidence of a wall surrounding the areas of the episcopal city, the civilian settlement, and the monastery district can be found in a

---

1   Frei, "Topographie – Geologie – Gewässer – Geographische Lage – Klima – Raumnutzung", pp. 23–26.
2   Fehn, "Probleme der frühen Augsburger Stadtentwicklung", p. 361.
3   Bakker, "Zur Topographie", pp. 41–50; Tremmel, *Kastellvicus*, pp. 13–14.
4   Kießling, *Bürgerliche Gesellschaft und Kirche*, p. 24.

document dated 1172.⁵ During the course of the thirteenth century, the artisan quarter spread out towards the River Lech. Although sparsely populated for a long time, this newly developed area was also eventually enclosed by fortifications and named *Jakobervorstadt* after the local church of St. Jacob. With this, the spatial development of Augsburg was essentially completed by the end of the fourteenth century.⁶

Historically the settlement can be divided into four areas: the episcopal city together with the so-called lower town, also called *Frauenvorstadt* (Our Lady's Suburb); to the south of it, the Upper Town, centered around the *Perlach* area; east of the high terrace the *Lechviertel* (Lech Quarter); and finally the *Jakobervorstadt* (St. Jacob's Suburb). In addition, a narrow strip of land between the town walls and the city limits was used for agricultural and commercial purposes.

Including its fortifications, Augsburg extended over an area of about 536 acres, with its length (north – south, 2270 m) almost twice its width (1140 m).⁷ Up until its integration into the Kingdom of Bavaria, the city's north-south orientation remained the decisive factor in its urban planning.⁸

Unlike Nuremberg or Ulm, Augsburg never managed to develop a larger territory. The eastern border with the Duchy of Bavaria was marked by the Lech River, which, due to frequent and intensive floods, kept altering its bed – in most cases to Augsburg's disadvantage.⁹ Today, the Lech River is artificially controlled by extensive river engineering measures. In the years 1554, 1570, 1589, 1744 and 1768 the river bed moved towards Bavaria; only once, in 1755, did it move back towards Swabia. During an on-site inspection on 10 October 1768, the fountain master Caspar Walter noted that the Lech had shifted entirely into Bavaria, without even leaving a backwater in Swabia, but rather retracting from the area and leaving only gravel.¹⁰ This literally fluid border necessitated recurring negotiations with Augsburg's powerful Bavarian neighbor.¹¹

Still, the Lech always was a symbolic border as well. Many ceremonial entries of emperors to the imperial diets of the sixteenth century started at the

---

5   Schröder, *Stadt Augsburg*, pp. 160–61.
6   Piper, *Stadtplan*, pp. 4–5.
7   Kießling and Lohrmann, "Türme – Tore – Bastionen", p. 15.
8   Roeck, "Urbanistische Entwicklung", p. 113.
9   Böhm, *Hochwassergeschichte*; Pfeuffer, *Der Lech*.
10 Stetten, *Geschichte*, pp. 506, 723, 724; Stadtarchiv Augsburg (StadtAA), Bauamt, 7, no. 213, Ordentliche Beschreibung aller Brunnenbäche; Bauamt 7, no. 201, Bericht Caspar Walters, Nov. 7, 1768.
11 Groos, "Beiträge zur Topographie", pp. 27–30; Cramer-Fürtig, "Der Lech als Grenze", pp. 6–12.

FIGURE 2.1 View of Augsburg from the chronicle of Sigismund Meisterlin, 1457
STAATS- UND STADTBIBLIOTHEK AUGSBURG, 2O COD. H. 1

bridge over the Lech River.[12] The Lech was also a clear dividing line for the development of dialects.[13] By comparison, the Wertach River in the west played only a secondary strategic and economic role, albeit a notable one: it marked the border to the margravate of Burgau. Adjacent towards the south were episcopal territories and the village of Haunstetten, belonging to the Benedictine monastery of Sts. Ulrich and Afra.[14] The area towards the north belonged to the Empire's bailiwick (*Vogtei*).[15]

The city and its inhabitants were closely interwoven with the surrounding territories in several ways. By the fifteenth century, citizens of Augsburg increasingly appeared as fief-holders of ecclesiastical estates, particularly of properties within a range of 15–20 km along the north- and southbound trade routes. The patriciate was primarily aiming to acquire property which entailed seigneurial rights.[16] The city council, on the other hand, continuously extended its influence over the charitable endowments, sinecures, and hospitals within the town and related properties in the surrounding area. Financial control over these institutions was the responsibility of the two mayors.[17] In this way the city council could exert partial or even full control over neighboring villages such as Pfersee and Oberhausen. The bailiwick north of Augsburg was directly attached to the council: based on a privilege conferred by King Sigismund in 1426, the city had the right to elect the bailiffs (*Vögte*) for the town and its region. This imperial fiefdom was combined with the rights of high jurisdiction. In the eighteenth century, the office was usually granted to the elder mayor, who in turn delegated the task to the municipal bailiff. Each time a new tenure of the city bailiff began, the borderline of the municipality and the adjacent regional bailiwick were inspected by the new office-holder, accompanied by a delegation of citizens and administrative officers. The extensive documentation of all boundary stones and landmarks highlighted the city's claim to power over the entire territory, including the regional bailiwick.[18]

---

12 Löser, "Flüsse im Mittelalter", pp. 15–30; Aulinger, "Augsburg und die Reichstage", p. 13.
13 König and Renn, *Kleiner Sprachatlas*, pp. 28–30.
14 Regarding the borders, see Schröder, *Stadt Augsburg*, pp. 168–70; Kießling, *Bürgerliche Gesellschaft*, pp. 203–14.
15 Jahn, "Aspekte der Zentralität Augsburgs", pp. 153–61.
16 Kießling, *Bürgerliche Gesellschaft*, pp. 197–214.
17 Bátori, *Reichsstadt Augsburg*, pp. 14, 50–51.
18 Staats- und Stadtbibliothek Augsburg (SuStBA), 2° Cod. Aug. 138, Augsburgische Gränzbeschreibung, 22 October 1755; Schröder, *Stadt Augsburg*, pp. 68–70. The villages of Gersthofen and Langweid as well as the hamlet of Stettenhofen were part of the regional bailiwick. Regarding the disputes over jurisdiction in the regional bailiwick, see Jahn, *Augsburg Land*, pp. 55–63.

Two locational factors played a very significant role in Augsburg's development. First, the abundant supply of water enabled the development of a wide range of trades and crafts. In the sixteenth century, fourteen grain mills, one powder mill, and three paper mills existed in the city along with spice mills, grinding mills, fulling mills, sawmills, and copper and iron hammer mills. In the following century, two stamp mills for the processing of scrap gold and silver were added. In the eighteenth century, some of the paper, grinding, and sawmills were converted into tobacco mills.[19] According to a precise inventory prepared by Caspar Walter in 1761, a total of 78 mills equipped with 163 water wheels were in use throughout the municipal territory inside and outside the fortifications.[20]

The second locational factor concerns the road system. In the late Middle Ages, a location close to important long-distance roads was a decisive factor for a prospering and expanding trade. A major traffic route was emerging between Italy in the south and Flanders and Brabant in the north. As a consequence, the ancient Roman *Via Claudia*, which ran through Augsburg and offered two alternative routes to traverse the Alps (Füssen – Fernpass and Mittenwald – Scharnitz), was intensively frequented once again. This route provided access to the entire Upper German region. Additional roads to the Lake Constance region and Switzerland as well as the ancient salt-traders' road to Munich, which continued towards Salzburg and Austria, turned the city into an important traffic hub.[21] Also of importance for the transport of goods was rafting on the rivers Lech and, to a lesser extent, Wertach, which ensured a cost-effective supply of wood and other construction materials such as stones and lime. Textile and leather goods as well as silverwork were also frequently rafted.[22] Sometimes even travelers chose this means of transportation.[23]

Despite the gradual emancipation of the citizenry from the bishop during the thirteenth and fourteenth centuries, Augsburg remained the bishop's residential city until 1806, when the city was incorporated into Bavaria.[24] In economic terms, the ecclesiastical institutions retained some assets. The heavily

---

19 StadtAA, KPS 03198 (map with all hydraulic structures from the sixteenth century); Bestand Mühlenwesen, no. 26 (reports of the master builders from 1802 with numerous examples of the transformation of mills).
20 Clasen, *Die Augsburger Getreidemühlen*, p. 2; Walter, *Beschreibung Aller ... Gumber-Werck*, pp. 27–30.
21 Kießling, "Augsburgs Wirtschaft", p. 172; Koch, *Trassen des Fernhandelsweges*.
22 Filser, "Lechflößerei", pp. 226–29; Schilling, "Wälder, Holzeinschlag und Flößer", pp. 31–46; Wangerow, "Handel und Wandel", pp. 126–33.
23 During his voyage in 1580, Michel de Montaigne travelled by raft from Füssen; Montaigne, *Tagebuch einer Reise*, pp. 71–72.
24 Wüst, "Augsburger Bürgerschaft, Domkapitel und Fürstbischöfe", pp. 65–95.

frequented bridges (across the Wertach towards Oberhausen and via two bridges across the Lech towards Friedberg and Lechhausen) remained the property of the clergy and yielded lucrative toll charges.[25] An attempt to incorporate the clergy, along with its servants, into the citizenry had failed in 1398, leading to the development of independent jurisdictions. From a legal perspective, a homogeneous population in which all residents shared citizenship existed only during the ten years between the introduction of the Protestant Reformation in 1537 and the restitution of Catholic property by Emperor Charles V in 1547–48.[26] Catholic ecclesiastical institutions spread across the entire city, with the highest concentration in the area around the cathedral with the bishop's residency and the 22 chapter houses.[27] For the later fifteenth century, Kießling estimates a minimum of 320 clergymen and -women (priests, friars, nuns); by 1774 their number had grown to 350.[28] From a legal perspective, this group also includes all secular members of clerical institutions, such as relatives living in the same household and servants. In a list of taxable households compiled in 1734 by the municipal envoy Abraham Streber, 399 individuals fell within this group, including 60 servants of the prince-bishop and 13 courtiers.[29] According to a 1781 estimate, a total of 1,800 members of ecclesiastical households lived within the city but were not subject to its jurisdiction. They enjoyed all the advantages of the infrastructure without contributing to its financing.[30]

Although the clerical institutions seemed like islands of special jurisdiction within the imperial city, they still were closely intertwined with it at many levels through the parishes, and remained so until the end of the imperial period. One of Augsburg's peculiarities was that all parishes were incorporated into the clerical institutions.[31] At the same time, the parishes also structured urban space. In medieval times, the parishes determined – among other things – the boundaries of the pastures. The imperial tax (*Gemeiner Pfennig*) was also levied on the basis of the same organizational structure in 1497.[32] The complex spatial and social interweaving between the imperial city's inhabitants and

---

25 Kießling, *Bürgerliche Gesellschaft und Kirche*, pp. 63–64.
26 See Chapter 10 in this volume.
27 François, *Die unsichtbare Grenze*, p. 24; Rummel, "Katholisches Leben".
28 Kießling, *Bürgerliche Gesellschaft*, p. 40; Rummel, "Katholisches Leben", p. 15.
29 StadtAA, Evangelisches Wesensarchiv, Tom. 448 2, Verzeichnis was in A.° 1734 allhier zu Augsburg an Bürgern, Beisitzern, Wittiben, wie ledige, sowohl Manns- als auch Weibspersonen, was steuerbar ist, und was sich sowohl in eigenen als in Zinshäusern dises Jahr hat befunden.
30 Fassl, *Konfession, Wirtschaft und Politik*, p. 85.
31 Kießling, "Eckpunkte der Augsburger Reformationsgeschichte", p. 31.
32 Geffcken, "Soziale Schichtung in Augsburg", p. 19.

the members of ecclesiastical institutions remained a characteristic feature of Augsburg from medieval times until the early nineteenth century.[33]

2   Population

Augsburg's static spatial structure, which remained unchanged for centuries, stands in stark contrast to its dynamic demographic development. All population figures for the fifteenth century cited in the literature rely on estimates based on the tax books and thus on the number of households.[34] According to these sources, the population grew between 1396 and 1492 from about 12,000 to about 19,000.[35]

For the following centuries, a so-called *Bevölkerungstafel* (population chart) in the literature lists annual rates of births, marriages, and deaths.[36] This table provides precise information about the fluctuation of the population, but not about its absolute size. Older research assumed that Augsburg's political and economic role must be reflected in the number of inhabitants,[37] a correlation challenged by Joachim Jahn. Based on an estimate by the city archivist Adolf Buff (18,000 inhabitants in the final third of the fifteenth century) and a critical evaluation of the *Bevölkerungstafel*, Jahn concluded that a figure of 35,000 inhabitants seems realistic for the 1530s.[38] Despite the lack of exact data for population size, the city council decided as early as 1539 to stop accepting new inhabitants, as housing was becoming scarce and rents were increasing.[39]

Further development up to 1648 has been documented in detail by Bernd Roeck. Taking an entirely new approach, Roeck based his conclusions about the number of inhabitants on an analysis of the consumption of grain. According to this method, the city's population was about 45,000 at the outbreak of the Thirty Years' War in 1618. Roeck attributes the rapid increase by 10,000 inhabitants in the course of a century mainly to immigration.[40] Following the

---

33   Kießling, *Bürgerliche Gesellschaft und Kirche*, p. 25.
34   For an overview of older estimates, see Paas, *Population Change*, p. 42.
35   Jahn, "Augsburger Sozialstruktur", p. 188.
36   The chronologically most complete table, covering the period from 1501 to 1830, is found in SuStBA, 11 PB 2, Geburts-, Hochzeits-, und Sterb-Calender von 1831.
37   For a comprehensive summary of the literature, cf. Roeck, *Bäcker, Brot und Getreide*, pp. 71–73.
38   Jahn, "Augsburgs Einwohnerzahl", pp. 379–96.
39   Roeck, *Bäcker, Brot und Getreide*, p. 71. The council, however, reserved the right to grant exceptions "under special circumstances"; StadtAA, Ratsprotokolle 1529–1542, entry for June 21, 1539.
40   Roeck, *Eine Stadt in Krieg und Frieden*, vol. 1, pp. 301–8.

demographic catastrophe of the years 1627 to 1635, caused by epidemics and famines, a census conducted by the city council counted only 16,432 inhabitants (12,017 Protestants and 4,415 Catholics), meaning that the entire population growth of the last 130 years had been wiped out within less than a decade. A subsequent census undertaken in 1645 registered moderate improvement, yielding a total of 21,018 inhabitants (13,790 Protestants, 6,170 Catholics, and 1,058 soldiers).[41] The final years of the war, however, were again dominated by mortality crises, mainly caused by food shortages. In particular, the siege by French and Swedish troops in 1646 was detrimental to the city.[42]

After 1650, the population began to grow again, but the massive loss of 62% would not be recovered until the nineteenth century. The major mortality crises of the eighteenth century – the War of the Spanish Succession, which claimed more than 3,000 lives in 1704 alone; the central European famine of 1771–72; and the Napoleonic Wars around 1800 – severely restricted population development. Around 1700, Augsburg's estimated population lay between 26,000 and 27,000. The largest number of inhabitants in the eighteenth century was probably reached around 1770, with an estimated population of 30,000 to 33,000. A statistical survey undertaken in 1807 after the transition to Bavaria counted 28,543 inhabitants.

In response to the significant population growth during the sixteenth century, existing houses were enlarged and elevated,[43] but the growth was hardly reflected in the number of buildings. 2,488 houses existed in 1498; their number grew to 2,521 by 1604 and reached about 3,000 around 1800.[44] The availability of property tax records, which have been preserved intermittently from 1346 and completely from 1396 until 1717, allows for precise conclusions about the social topography, at least from the fifteenth through the seventeenth century.[45] As is typical for historic cities, residential comfort in Augsburg declined from the center towards the outskirts. The ranking order started with the uptown area, followed by the Lech Quarter, Our Lady's Suburb, and at the bottom end, St. Jacob's Suburb.[46] The perimeter of the city was marked by the *Zwingerhäuser* ("barbican houses"), built between 1585 and 1597 on the city's

---

41 Roeck, *Eine Stadt in Krieg und Frieden*, vol. 2, pp. 775, 879–81.
42 See Chapter 15 of this volume.
43 Zimmer, "Veränderungen im Augsburger Stadtbild", p. 43.
44 Buff, *Augsburg in der Renaissancezeit*, p. 54; Schröder, *Stadt Augsburg*, p. 181. See also Chapter 22 of this volume.
45 Clasen, *Augsburger Steuerbücher*; Kraus, "Entwicklung und Topographie".
46 Roeck, *Eine Stadt in Krieg und Frieden*, vol. 1, p. 496.

southern and western ramparts to house the soldiers of the city guard. A total of 316 dwellings accommodated soldiers and their families.[47]

As in many European cities, social segregation was accelerated in sixteenth-century Augsburg by two trends. First, a concentration of upper-class buildings occurred in the city center. Whoever could afford it purchased neighboring buildings and converted two narrow houses, with their gables facing the street, into one larger and more imposing house, now with its eaves towards the street.[48] In Augsburg, this phenomenon can only be observed in the uptown area, where the number of houses fell from 216 in 1550 to 193 in 1618.[49]

Second, the rapid population increase mainly took place in the lower social stratum. Poor individuals were flooding the scarce housing market, mainly affecting St. Jacob's Suburb. Back in medieval times, this district had contained large gardens and several agricultural markets and had the lowest population density of all city districts. The large distance from the center as well as its close proximity to the Lech, posing a constant risk of flooding, adversely influenced the quarter's livability. The city council widened the social gap, as some immigrants without sufficient financial means were only granted citizenship on the condition that they reside in St. Jacob's Suburb.[50] Numerous new buildings were erected, including the Fuggerei in 1514–22, new buildings in the garden of the Meitting family (*Neues Sachsengäßlein*) in 1556, and construction at the *Bachenanger* (*Neue Gasse*) the following year.[51] The number of houses grew accordingly, from 561 in 1550 to 703 in 1618. Nevertheless, most inhabitants of this district were crowded into small premises housing four (or more) households. A similar, albeit less pronounced development can be observed in the northeastern part of Our Lady's Suburb. The Lech Quarter, a district dominated by craftspeople, proved very stable throughout the dynamic sixteenth century.[52] In general, by the beginning of the Thirty Years' War more than half of Augsburg's population possessed few or no taxable assets and was living in the most difficult housing conditions.[53]

The demographic catastrophe of the Thirty Years' War was most visible in the quarters rendering the lowest tax contributions. Roeck's meticulous analysis of the tax books allows the exact geographical mapping of social inequality caused by hunger and disease. The closer to the city outskirts, the higher the

---

47 Kraus, *Militärwesen der Reichsstadt Augsburg*, pp. 198–201.
48 Fuhrmann, *Geschichte des Wohnens*, pp. 71–72.
49 Roeck, *Eine Stadt in Krieg und Frieden*, vol. 1, pp. 493–94.
50 Piper, *Stadtplan*, p. 76; Kießling, "Jakober Vorstadt", pp. 38–49.
51 Stetten, *Geschichte*, pp. 520, 522.
52 Roeck, *Eine Stadt in Krieg und Frieden*, vol. 1, pp. 493–96.
53 Roeck, "'Arme' in Augsburg", pp. 515–58. See also Chapter 12 of this volume.

demographic losses were, as can be seen in St. Jacob's Suburb with its high rate of decline. The *Fischersiedlung* (settlement of fishermen), located just outside the fortifications near the *Wertachbrucker Tor* and the creek *Senkelbach*, was entirely abandoned and never repopulated.[54]

One of the traditionally poorest trades was that of the weavers. As they significantly contributed to the economic rise of Augsburg,[55] the city council promoted their settlement up to the 1530s by requiring lower property qualifications than for members of other crafts as a condition of citizenship.[56] Additionally, in 1529, the council ordered the construction of two rows of eave-oriented, two-storied houses with elevated basements to be used as workshops, each row comprising nine units, which were situated close by the northern city walls in Our Lady's suburb next to the Fishermen's Gate (*Fischertor*). However, this measure was just a drop in the ocean. Most weavers still lived in painfully cramped tenements in St. Jacob's Suburb.[57] The total number of weavers far exceeded that of the other crafts.[58] In 1601, 2,165 households of weavers, comprising 8,438 individuals, were counted in Augsburg. By 1653, however, only 500 master weavers were left – less than a quarter of the workshops in the pre-war period.[59] This dramatic decrease was the most significant change in the local population structure during the early modern period.

Of particular interest to further demographic development after 1648 is the relationship of the city's two confessions, the long-term trend of which was already indicated by the two censuses of 1635 and 1645. In the first census of 1635, about 73% of all residents were Protestants, while the count of non-residents enumerated 694 Catholics and only 37 Protestants. Two periods of Catholic ascendancy during the war – from 1629 to 1632 and from 1635 to 1648 – resulted in a rising proportion of Catholic inhabitants. Thus no Protestant citizens were admitted from August 30, 1629, onwards, and in May 1645 the tax officers were ordered not to tolerate any "non-Catholic outsiders" in the city without prior consultation of the council.[60]

While confessional parity, enshrined in Augsburg's constitution since the 1648 Peace of Westphalia, granted legal equality to both confessional parties, it had no influence on the stability of the numerical proportions. Before the war

---

54   Schröder, *Stadt Augsburg*, p. 164.
55   Kießling, "Techniktransfer und Wirtschaftsboom", pp. 36–51.
56   Clasen, *Die Augsburger Weber*, p. 17.
57   Pfaud, *Bürgerhaus*, pp. 98–100. The street is called *Herrenhäuser* even today: see Clasen, *Augsburger Weber*, p. 41.
58   Roeck, *Eine Stadt in Krieg und Frieden*, vol. 2, pp. 910–16.
59   Clasen, *Augsburger Weber*, pp. 18–19.
60   Stetten, *Geschichte*, vol. 2, pp. 53, 636.

broke out in 1618, the share of the Catholics was about 20 per cent; by the time of the 1645 census it had already increased to 30 per cent.[61] This development was not caused by mass conversions or higher fertility rates among Catholic families, but resulted from a combination of two factors: a constantly negative ratio of births versus deaths in the Protestant community, and the city's isolation within a region dominated by Catholic territories. Over the long run, the latter factor caused a constant increase of the Catholic share of the population in all confessionally mixed imperial cities in southern Germany.[62] Historical studies of migration identify a constant stream of migrants from rural areas into the cities, i.e. the population surplus of rural areas balanced the lack of births in the cities and contributed to their growth.[63] A similar development can be observed in the imperial city of Kaufbeuren, despite the Protestants enjoying a dominant political position there.[64] Small, temporary waves of immigration of Protestant religious refugees, such as the *Deferegger* in 1684 and exiles from the archbishopric of Salzburg in 1731–32, could not reverse the general trend.[65]

Even without further censuses, contemporaries were aware of the gradual "re-Catholization" caused by the imbalanced demographic development. The count of baptisms, weddings, and burials for population tables left no room for doubt. As early as 1696, the number of Catholic baptisms exceeded those of Protestants, and by 1710 the same held true for marriages. The author Christian Friedrich Daniel Schubart, who lived in Augsburg for several months in 1774–75, expressed his observations in a rather polemical way: "If things continue like this, the Papal pike will soon have devoured all Lutheran gobies."[66] The full dimensions of "Catholic expansion", as this process was termed by Etienne François, became evident at the occasion of a census conducted by the Bavarian authorities in 1811–12. According to it, 11,646 Lutherans and 17,721 Catholics lived in the city in the early nineteenth century.[67] While Protestant marriages and baptisms remained on an almost constant level from 1650 to 1800, several phases can be identified for the Catholics. The sustained expansion after 1650 stagnated in the 1730s. During this decade, the demographic ratios reached a balance. In the second half of the eighteenth century, the

---

61   François, *Die unsichtbare Grenze*, p. 45.
62   Fassl, *Konfession, Wirtschaft und Politik*, pp. 17–26.
63   Lengger, *Leben und Sterben*, vol. 1, pp. 153–214.
64   Dieter, *Reichsstadt Kaufbeuren*, pp. 110–29.
65   Link, "Deferegger in Augsburg"; idem, "Lendler, Deferegger, Salzburger", pp. 35–83.
66   Schubart, *Schubart's Leben und Gesinnungen*, Part 2, pp. 17–18.
67   François, *Die unsichtbare Grenze*, p. 47.

development is characterized by strong fluctuations among the Catholic population, albeit years of growth prevailed.[68]

The patrician Wolfgang Jakob Sulzer the Younger (1685–1751), who later became a Protestant mayor, had recognized the problem as early as 1715, when he compared the number of master craftsmen by confession and developed ideas for countermeasures. He made the regional preponderance of Catholics a subject of discussion and argued for the targeted recruitment of Protestants from other cities, combined with offers of financial support for their settlement.[69] Most Protestant immigrants – men as well as women – actually came from other cities, predominantly from free imperial cities, whereas Catholic immigrants mainly came from rural areas around the rivers Danube, Lech and Iller – territories with traditionally strong social and economic ties with Augsburg. While the share of Protestant immigrants with a rural background did increase during the eighteenth century, the fundamental differences between the migration patterns of both confessions remained unchanged. Not only had the Lutheran community become a minority in Augsburg by 1800, the Protestants born there had also become a minority within their own confessional camp.[70]

The origins of migrants also had a large impact on their economic standing. Those moving to Augsburg from rural areas often became journeymen or day laborers, mainly in the building trades, or worked in the textile industry.[71] To avoid further exacerbation of the poverty problem, the city council changed its population policy in the second half of the eighteenth century. Especially after the famine of 1770–71, couples wanting to marry were intensively audited to ensure that they possessed sufficient financial means.[72] But this kind of emergency brake could not change the fact that due to contrasting migration patterns, Catholics and Protestants were also divided by their economic circumstances. Nevertheless, no ghettoization took place and the city districts essentially retained their social structure between 1650 and 1806.[73]

The geographic setting of Augsburg – at the confluence of two mountain rivers, with substantial differences in altitude between its quarters – can figuratively be regarded as a mirror image of its historic development: Augsburg remained an episcopal city while also evolving into a bi-confessional free

---

68 François, *Die unsichtbare Grenze*, pp. 47–52.
69 StadtAA, EWA 1600, Zufällige Gedanken von der Anzahl der alhiesigen beyderseits Religions Verwandten Bürgerschaft und Inwohner, 8 June 1715.
70 François, *Die unsichtbare Grenze*, pp. 52–64.
71 François, *Die unsichtbare Grenze*, p. 91.
72 Fassl, *Konfession, Wirtschaft und Politik*, pp. 20–21. Regarding the criteria for approval of marriage requests among craftspeople, see Werkstetter, "Gesellenehen".
73 François, *Die unsichtbare Grenze*, pp. 89–110.

imperial city. The long-term development between 1400 and 1800 was characterized by social and demographic extremes. Altogether, one might speak of a structured coexistence of geographic, economic, social, and confessional opposites.

3   Visual Representations

Augsburg's visual representation can be described on three levels: the coat of arms and signet respectively as the most important symbol and emblem; visual messages in public spaces and on public buildings; and a range of movable items such as maps, views, coins, and medals. While the development of Augsburg's spatial form had been completed by the end of the fourteenth century, a canon of motifs and thematic images only emerged under the influence of Humanism between the later fifteenth and the early seventeenth century.

The emancipation of the civic community from the bishop's claim to power is illustrated by the use of a discrete municipal signet. The oldest preserved imprint dates back to 1237 and shows open city gates with two crenellated towers under a six-armed star. In the center of the open gate, a stylized tree with an oval shape grows out of a trimount – the tree could be interpreted as a tree of life. The signet used by the city since 1260 shows two changes: the trimount has been replaced by a curved base, and it now holds a stylized fruit, which according to contemporary observers was interpreted variously as a bunch of grapes, a berry, or a pine cone. Over time, the coat of arms was reduced to a depiction of a cembra nut (or cedar nut), also referred to as the *Pyr*. In the present day, a green *Pyr* is centered on a shield party per pale in red and silver. The first reference to these colors used in the city flag can be found in the master builders' book of 1372.

There is still no final consensus on the interpretation of this fruit and its changes over time. It is undisputed that Augsburg's Roman past only came to play a meaningful role in the historical constructs of chroniclers after 1500. The frequently used term *Statpir* ("city pyr" or "city berry") underwent etymological reinterpretations as well. The Benedictine monk Sigismund Meisterlin, who authored a history of Augsburg in 1456,[74] derived it from the Latin word *pyra* (fire, flame). This was picked up by the councilor and chronicler Hector Mülich (*c*. 1420–89/90), who amended Meisterlin's chronicle in the 1480s. Mülich claimed to have identified the Augsburg coat of arms in Mainz on the tomb of Drusus, stepson of Emperor Augustus. Drusus was supposed to have

---

74   See Chapter 3 of this volume.

converted Augsburg into a city by surrounding it with a wall.[75] In 1467, close to Sts. Ulrich and Afra, a Roman pine cone, standing on a column decorated with a small head of the goddess Kybele, was found and related to the Augsburg coat of arms. This interpretation became established under the influence of Renaissance Humanism and eclipsed all other explanations until well into the nineteenth century.[76]

The individuals most influential in establishing Augsburg's Roman history – Sigismund Gossembrot, Hektor Mülich, Conrad Peutinger, Marcus Welser – were all humanists, who were part of or had close relationships with the political elite.[77] Referencing ancient Roman history became a useful tool for dealing with contemporary political challenges on several occasions. The legal claims of Bishop Peter von Schaumberg (1424–69), for example, could thus be contained within historically justified limits.[78] Conrad Peutinger elaborated on emperorship from ancient times up to the Habsburg dynasty, establishing close and advantageous relations with Emperor Maximilian I, both personally and on behalf of the city.[79] Marcus Welser also dealt with Bavaria's latent claims to power by pointing out the special status of Augsburg as the capital of the Roman province of Raetia.[80]

As republics in their own right, the free imperial cities strongly relied on particular visions of their historical identity. Visual images helped to merge ancient stories with present realities to form a meaningful whole. In his 1457 version of the Meisterlin chronicle, Hektor Mülich correlated historic events with colored pen drawings of the townscape. The depiction of the sermon of the saint King Lucius (see page 22) supposedly represents the oldest image of Augsburg's cityscape. On this view from the East, the characteristic outlines of the Red Gate, the church of Sts. Ulrich and Afra, the triple-gabled city hall, the Perlach tower and the cathedral can be identified.[81] While Mülich's illustrations were only accessible to a small circle of viewers, a larger public could be reached by means of façade paintings: in cooperation with Emperor Maximilian I, Conrad Peutinger developed a genealogy of Roman and Habsburg emperors that was executed as a painting on the three gables of Augsburg's city hall in 1516.[82]

---

75   Johanek, "Geschichtsschreibung und Geschichtsüberlieferung", pp. 162–66.
76   Roper, "The Gorgon of Augsburg", pp. 113–36.
77   Müller, ed., *Humanismus und Renaissance*. See Chapter 3 of the present volume.
78   Kah, "Die Sichtbarkeit des Reichs", p. 65; Saurma-Jeltsch, "Die Wahrheit der Fiktion", p. 11.
79   West, "Conrad Peutinger and the Visual Arts"; Johanek, "Geschichtsschreibung und Geschichtsüberlieferung", p. 180.
80   Mauer, "Der Patrizier als Archäologe", p. 97; Roeck, "Der Brunnen der Macht", p. 28.
81   Pataki, "Ein Bürger blickt auf seine Stadt", p. 128.
82   Hascher, *Fassadenmalerei in Augsburg*, pp. 50–51.

FIGURE 2.2 Hans Rogel, city plan of Augsburg, woodcut, 1563
STAATS- UND STADTBIBLIOTHEK AUGSBURG, GRAPH 31/6

Commemoration of the city's supposed foundation 1600 years before provided the occasion for the erection in 1594 of the *Augustusbrunnen*, a fountain with a sculpture of the Roman Emperor Augustus, according to an inscription on the statue's base. The emperor's bronze statue portrays Augustus with the attitude of a peacemaker (*pacificator*). This subject as a monumental fountain provided plenty of clues for identification to local as well as foreign onlookers: The personification of the emperor was a reference to Augsburg's place within the Holy Roman Empire, while the perimeter of the basin anchored the statue in the local topography. The four most important rivers and creeks, personified as antique river deities, reside at the emperor's feet. The same combination of Roman history with the present imperial city was subsequently applied to the design of additional fountains with Mercury and Hercules as crowning figures.[83] The erection of these fountains inaugurated a period of massive

---

83   Emmendörffer, "Fortitudo Augustaea", pp. 197–209.

urban and architectural renewal under the architect Elias Holl.[84] Public buildings which were not replaced by new constructions, including several innercity towers in 1610–11 and the weavers' guildhouse in 1605–07, were redecorated with elaborate façade paintings.[85] Apart from subjects related to salvation history, the extensive picture cycles mainly referred to local historic events such as the battle on the Lech plain in 955, which celebrated the pre-Reformation order by depicting how a bishop and an emperor jointly saved the city and the Empire from their enemies.[86]

The visual decorations of town halls in imperial cities often referred to the Empire, personified by the emperor (or entire series of emperors), thus referencing Roman history.[87] Moreover, from about 1600, a highly sophisticated implementation of this imagery came to dominate other important public spaces in Augsburg in unique ways.[88] An example is provided by the monumental fountains noted above, which by the choice of their material, size, and location in proximity to the city hall or major markets represented a self-confident expression of the council's sense of art and history as well as its financial capabilities. This message was to be conveyed in particular to princely neighbors beyond the city walls.[89] The painter Franz Aspruck was therefore commissioned by the council to make a drawing of the Augustus Fountain as a template for a copperplate.[90] The template was converted into print by Lucas Kilian as early as 1598; his brother Wolfgang produced etchings of the Hercules Fountain in 1612 and the Mercury Fountain in 1614. The bronze fountains, along with Holl's representative new buildings, became a persistent element of Augsburg's thematic canon for etchings.[91]

Until well into the eighteenth century, images of the entire city usually took the form of cityscapes or maps from a bird's-eye view. After several years of surveying work, the goldsmith Jörg Seld (about 1454–1527) created in 1521 the first map from a bird's-eye perspective ever produced in Germany. Seld chose a view of Augsburg from the west and took great care to reproduce all the details of the streets and alleys as well as the houses and gardens. He also considered

---

84 See Chapter 22 of this volume.
85 Netzer, *Johann Matthias Kager*, pp. 64–86.
86 Zimmer, *Cives propagantur*; Netzer, *Johann Matthias Kager*, pp. 85–86.
87 Hafner, *Republik im Konflikt*, pp. 199–220; Larsson, "Die großen Brunnen", pp. 135–47.
88 Roeck, "Die ästhetische Inszenierung", pp. 220–22.
89 Jachmann, *Die Kunst des Augsburger Rates*, pp. 68–69.
90 Friedel, *Bronzebildmonumente in Augsburg*, p. 123.
91 Schmidt, *Augsburger Ansichten*, pp. 61–63, 221.

the intensively utilized zone outside the city walls, including the bleaching fields and pastures.[92]

Despite Seld's great achievement, the view from the east prevailed in the long run, combined with the exaltation of the most important buildings to the detriment of all other structures. The fortifications, which had been fundamentally renovated in 1538–53, hermetically framed the city. This graphic presentation followed common sixteenth- and seventeenth-century paradigms.[93] Augsburg is first pictured in this way in 1550, in the second edition of Sebastian Münster's *Cosmographia universalis*. The artist remains unknown; apparently the council had sent the plan to Münster. The selection of the 59 depicted objects represents a clear authoritarian perspective: communal and ecclesiastical buildings, complemented by the *Herrenstube* (patrician drinking hall) and the *Kaufleutestube* (Merchants' drinking hall). The presence of a fulling mill indicates the city's economic base. With this image, the council – dominated by the Catholic patricians since the constitutional change of 1548 – presents its new official self-perception.[94] In 1563, the mould carver Hans Rogel essentially completed Münster's plan based on measurements he had taken over several years. Like Seld, Rogel included all local buildings, and he also produced a three-dimensional model that he donated to the council.[95] Rogel's 1563 bird's-eye-view map and its reduced version from 1565 became the templates for many mapmakers for decades to follow.

By order of the city, the surveyor Christoph Schissler and the illustrator and copper engraver Alexander Mair jointly produced another bird's-eye-view plan in 1598–1600, this time also including the peripheral zones beyond the fortifications. As Augsburg's urban renewal had just begun, however, this map rapidly became outdated.

In the long run, the plans that remained in use as references into the eighteenth century were those created in 1626, 1637, and 1660 by Wolfgang Kilian (1581–1661), based on Schißler's measurements. Kilian's templates can be found in the *Topographia suevia*, published by Matthäus Merian the Elder in 1656, or, heavily simplified, in Johann Baptist Homann's contemporary illustrations of the siege and fall of Augsburg in 1703.[96] The surveyor and military engineer Johann Thomas Krauss (1697–1775) based his plan on his own measurements but retained Kilian's ground plan and viewing angle. Engraved into copper by

---

92   Schmidt, *Augsburger Ansichten*, pp. 29–33.
93   Michalsky, "Vom himmlischen Jerusalem", p. 49.
94   Kießling and Plaßmeyer, "Augsburg", p. 134; Knoll, *Die Natur der menschlichen Welt*, p. 222.
95   Schmidt, *Augsburger Ansichten*, pp. 38–39.
96   Kießling and Plaßmeyer, "Augsburg", p. 136; Schmidt, *Augsburger Ansichten*, pp. 43–48.

Matthäus Seutter, the plan was first published in 1730–31 by his own publishing house and from 1762 onward by Tobias Conrad Lotter.[97]

Unlike bird's-eye-view maps with their precise rendering of streets and buildings, skyline views maintain only the outlines of the dominant buildings and thus allow for a high level of recognizability. In 1563, Hans Rogel produced a skyline view of Augsburg from the east, which in 1600 was used as a template by the famous punchcutter Valentin Mader for a gold medal commissioned by the city council. Like the pool edge of the Augustus Fountain, the major waters, personified by fluvial gods, appear on this medal. With a price of ten ducats, however, it was only the privileged few who could afford it. More widely distributed was the Augsburg *Taler* issued in 1624. This was the first time that a German municipal government had chosen to mint a city view along with the outlines of the newly built city hall on a coin used for payment.[98]

In the German-speaking lands, series of engravings depicting important urban buildings only started to appear in the seventeenth century. The first such series for Augsburg, comprising 50 plates and titled *Augsburg Sambt dero vornembste Kirchen, Statt-Thor, Gebäude und Spring-Brunnen* ("Augsburg including its most prominent churches, city gates, buildings, and fountains"), was produced by the painter and engraver Simon Grimm in 1682.[99] A generation later, around 1724, Karl Remshart (1678–1755) chose a different approach by depicting entire streets and squares instead of singular buildings. The publisher Matthäus Seutter and his draughtsman Jacob Christian Weyermann created a series of 48 views of important buildings in 1742. His innovative selection of buildings, which was not confined to prominent edifices but also included functional institutions like the hospital, graveyards, bleaching fields, and the building yard, proved very successful. Consequently, several other publishers continued to complete and update the popular series and issued new editions.[100]

After the Thirty Years' War, the council withdrew from its active role in designing public space and disseminating the city's image in various media. New public constructions now became rare exceptions and were no longer related to the city center. During the early eighteenth century, the focus of urban government lay on repairing the damage caused by the War of the Spanish Succession, during which the fortifications had suffered significantly.[101] Maintenance and renovation of the complex water supply system and the

---

97 Ritter, *Die Welt aus Augsburg*, p. 52.
98 Jachmann, *Die Kunst des Augsburger Rates*, p. 71; Zink, "Die frühesten Stadtansichten", p. 201; Pfeuffer, "Flussgötter auf Medaillen und Münzen", pp. 149–50.
99 Schmidt *Augsburger Ansichten*, pp. 76–83, 135.
100 Schmidt, "Moderne und Romantik", pp. 208–10.
101 For a detailed list of the damage, see Crophius. *Das mit Krieges-Last gedrückte ... Augspurg*.

representative fountains remained the construction office's main tasks throughout the century. The only time the city council influenced the cityscape was with its update of the building code in 1740. Instead, wealthy bankers and businessmen set new standards with their sumptuously decorated houses.[102] Outstanding artists such as Matthäus Günther, Johann Georg Bergmüller, and Johann Josef Anton Huber took façade painting to new heights and made the city center resemble an open-air art gallery.[103]

In the mid-1790s the painter and etcher Johann Michael Frey created a series of views combining the architecture outside the city walls with the landscape. Garden sheds, inns, mills, and Johann Heinrich Schüle's gorgeous textile factory are the focal points of his 36 colored etchings. From Frey's wide-angle view, even the fortifications no longer isolate the city from the country. Frey's choice of motifs and perspective are clearly indicative of nineteenth-century trends.[104]

It was also during the 1790s that Mayor Paul von Stetten the Younger instructed the illustrator and engraver Franz Thomas Weber (1761–1828) to depict important local events – not as a public official, however, but as an art lover. The series comprised 18 pages, ranging from Marie Antoinette's visit in 1770 to the weavers' uprising in 1794 and the occupation of the city by French troops. Stetten himself wrote a comprehensive autobiography, which he also intended as a documentation of Augsburg's history during his tenure. With Stetten's contribution, the pioneer work of the Mülich brothers comes full circle in the twilight years of the free imperial cities.[105]

Bibliography

Unpublished Primary Sources
Stadtarchiv Augsburg (StadtAA)

Evangelisches Wesensarchiv, no. 448 2, Verzeichnis was in A.° 1734 allhier zu Augsburg an Burgern, Beisizern, Wittiben, wie ledige, sowohl Manns- als auch Weibspersonen, was steuerbar ist, und was sich sowohl in eigenen als in Zinshäusern dises Jahr hat befunden.

Evangelisches Wesensarchiv, no. 1600, Zufällige Gedanken von der Anzahl der alhiesigen beyderseits Religions Verwandten Bürgerschaft und Inwohner, 8 June 1715.

---

102   Nagler, "Augsburger Bürgerhäuser", pp. 30–46.
103   Hascher, *Fassadenmalerei*, pp. 82–120.
104   Schmidt, "Moderne und Romantik", pp. 216–18.
105   Weber, "Biografische Mittheilungen", p. 184; Stetten, *Selbstbiographie*.

Bauamt 8, no. 213, Ordentliche Beschreibung aller Brunnenbäche, derer Wasser Strassen durch die Churbayrische Möhringer Au wie auch Haunstötter und Stadt Au herunter gehen [...] von Caspar Walter.

Bauamt 8, Nr. 201, Bericht Caspar Walters vom 7 November 1768.

Mühlenwesen, no. 26, Gutachten der Baumeister von 1802 mit zahlreichen Beispielen zu Umwandlungen einzelner Mühlen.

Karten- und Plansammlung 03198, Karte mit allen Wasserbauten aus dem 16. Jahrhundert.

Ratsprotokoll 1539.

Staats- und Stadtbibliothek Augsburg (SuStBA)

11 PB 2, Geburts-, Hochzeits-, und Sterb-Calender von 1831.

2° Cod. Aug. 138, Augsburgische Gränzbeschreibung, 22 October 1755.

Published Primary Sources

Crophius, P.J., *Das mit Krieges-Last gedrückte und durch Wunder-Hülff erquickte Augspurg, oder wahrhaffte und unpartheyische Erzehlung, was sich vor, in und nach der Belagerung und Bombardirung ... in diser deß H.R. Reichs Freyen Stadt Augspurg zugetragen*, Augsburg, 1710.

Montaigne, M. de, *Tagebuch einer Reise nach Italien über die Schweiz und Deutschland von 1580–1581*, transl. and ed. H. Stilett, Frankfurt am Main, 2002.

Schubart, C.F.D., *Schubart's Leben und Gesinnungen: von ihm selbst, im Kerker aufgesetzt. Zweiter Theil*, ed. L. Schubart, Stuttgart, 1793.

Stetten, P. von (the Elder), *Geschichte Der Heil. Röm. Reichs Freyen Stadt Augspurg. Aus bewährten Jahr-Büchern und Tüchtigen Urkunden gezogen, Und an das Licht gegeben*, 2 vols., Frankfurt am Main, Leipzig, 1743–58.

Stetten, P. von (the Younger), *Paul von Stetten d.J. Selbstbiographie. Die Lebensbeschreibung des Patriziers und Stadtpflegers der Reichsstadt Augsburg (1731–1808)*, 3 vols., ed. H. Gier et al., Augsburg, 2009–16.

Walter, C., *Beschreibung Aller hölzternen, und derer mit 2. messenen Stüfelen versehen, oder gemachten sogenannten Gumber-Werck, Wie viel derer in Löbl. Reichs-Stadt Augspurg vorhanden*, Augsburg, 1761.

Secondary Literature

Aulinger, R., "Augsburg und die Reichstage im 16. Jahrhundert", in *Welt im Umbruch. Augsburg zwischen Renaissance und Barock* (exhibition catalogue), Augsburg, 1980, vol. 3, pp. 9–24.

Bakker, L., "Zur Topographie der Provinzhauptstadt Augusta Vindelicum", in G. Gottlieb, W. Baer, J. Becker, J. Bellot, K. Filser, P. Fried, W. Reinhard and B. Schimmelpfennig (eds.), *Geschichte der Stadt Augsburg von der Römerzeit bis zur Gegenwart*, Stuttgart, 1984, pp. 41–50.

Bátori, I., *Die Reichsstadt Augsburg im 18. Jahrhundert. Verfassung, Finanzen, Reformversuche*, Göttingen, 1969.

Böhm, O., *Hochwassergeschichte des bayerischen Alpenvorlandes. Die Hochwasser der Sommermonate im Kontext der Klimageschichte Mitteleuropas*, Augsburg, 2011.

Buff, A., *Augsburg in der Renaissancezeit*, Bamberg, 1893.

Clasen, C.-P., *Die Augsburger Steuerbücher um 1600*, Augsburg, 1976.

Clasen, C.-P., *Die Augsburger Weber. Leistungen und Krisen des Textilgewerbes um 1600*, Augsburg, 1981.

Clasen, C.-P., *Die Augsburger Getreidemühlen 1500–1800*, Augsburg, 2000.

Cramer-Fürtig, M., "Der Lech als Grenze der Reichsstadt Augsburg mit dem Herzogtum Bayern", *Schriften des Heimatvereins Friedberg* 5 (2011), pp. 6–12.

Dieter, S., *Die Reichsstadt Kaufbeuren in der frühen Neuzeit. Studien zur Wirtschafts-, Sozial-, Kirchen- und Bevölkerungsgeschichte*, Thalhofen, 2000.

Emmendörffer, C., "Fortitudo Augustaea – Zur Neugestaltung Augsburgs um 1600", in C.A. Hoffmann, M. Johanns, A. Kranz, C. Trepesch and O. Ziedler (eds.), *Als Frieden möglich war. 450 Jahre Augsburger Religionsfrieden* (exhibition catalogue), Regensburg, 2005, pp. 197–209.

Fassl, P., *Konfession, Wirtschaft und Politik. Von der Reichsstadt zur Industriestadt. Augsburg 1750–1850*, Sigmaringen, 1988.

Fehn, K., "Probleme der frühen Augsburger Stadtentwicklung", *Mitteilungen der Geographischen Gesellschaft in München* 53 (1968), pp. 361–75.

Filser, K., "Lechflößerei: Konjunktur und Niedergang eines Gewerbes während der Industrialisierung", in R.A. Müller (ed.), *Aufbruch ins Industriezeitalter. Vol. 2: Aufsätze zur Wirtschafts- und Sozialgeschichte Bayerns von 1750–1850*, Munich, 1985, pp. 226–37.

François, E., *Die unsichtbare Grenze. Protestanten und Katholiken in Augsburg 1648–1806*, Sigmaringen, 1991.

Frei, H., "Topographie – Geologie – Gewässer – Geographische Lage – Klima – Raumnutzung", in G. Grünsteudel, G. Hägele and R. Frankenberger (eds.), *Augsburger Stadtlexikon*, 2nd ed., Augsburg, 1998, pp. 22–28.

Friedel, H., *Bronzebildmonumente in Augsburg 1589–1606. Bild und Urbanität*, Augsburg, 1974.

Fuhrmann, B., Meteling, W., Rajkay, B. and Weipert, M., *Geschichte des Wohnens vom Mittelalter bis heute*, Darmstadt, 2008.

Geffcken, F.P., "Soziale Schichtung in Augsburg 1396–1521", Ph.D. diss., Munich, 1995.

Groos, W., "Beiträge zur Topographie von Alt-Augsburg", *Bericht der Naturforschenden Gesellschaft Augsburg* 21 (1967), pp. 1–127.

Haberstock, E., *Der Augsburger Stadtwerkmeister Elias Holl (1573–1646). Werkverzeichnis*, Petersberg, 2016.

Hafner, U., *Republik im Konflikt. Schwäbische Reichsstädte und bürgerliche Politik in der frühen Neuzeit*, Tübingen, 2001.

Hascher, D., *Fassadenmalerei in Augsburg vom 16. bis zum 18. Jahrhundert*, Augsburg, 1996.

Jachmann, J., *Die Kunst des Augsburger Rates 1588–1631*, Munich and Berlin, 2008.

Jahn, J., "Augsburgs Einwohnerzahl im 16. Jahrhundert – Ein statistischer Versuch", *Zeitschrift für bayerische Landesgeschichte* 39 (1976), pp. 379–96.

Jahn, J., *Augsburg Land* (Historischer Atlas von Bayern, Teil Schwaben, 11), Munich, 1984.

Jahn, J., "Die Augsburger Sozialstruktur im 15. Jahrhundert", in G. Gottlieb, W. Baer, J. Becker, J. Bellot, K. Filser, P. Fried, W. Reinhard and B. Schimmelpfennig (eds.), *Geschichte der Stadt Augsburg von der Römerzeit bis zur Gegenwart*, Stuttgart, 1984, pp. 187–93.

Jahn, J., "Aspekte der Zentralität Augsburgs", in R.A. Müller (ed.), *Aufbruch ins Industriezeitalter, Vol. 2: Aufsätze zur Wirtschafts- und Sozialgeschichte Bayerns 1750–1850*, Munich, 1985, pp. 153–61.

Johanek, P., "Geschichtsschreibung und Geschichtsüberlieferung in Augsburg am Ausgang des Mittelalters", in J. Janota and W. Williams-Krapp (eds.), *Literarisches Leben in Augsburg während des 15. Jahrhunderts*, Tübingen, 1995, pp. 160–82.

Kah, D., "Die Sichtbarkeit des Reichs in der 'wahrhaft königlichen Stadt'. Augsburg im späten Mittelalter", in H. Wittmann (ed.), *Reichszeichen. Darstellungen und Symbole des Reichs in Reichsstädten*, Petersberg, 2015, pp. 55–72.

Kapfhammer, G., *Augsburger Stadtsagen*, Regensburg, 1985.

Kießling, R., *Bürgerliche Gesellschaft und Kirche in Augsburg im Spätmittelalter*, Augsburg, 1971.

Kießling, R., "Augsburgs Wirtschaft im 14. und 15. Jahrhundert", in G. Gottlieb, W. Baer, J. Becker, J. Bellot, K. Filser, P. Fried, W. Reinhard and B. Schimmelpfennig (eds.), *Geschichte der Stadt Augsburg von der Römerzeit bis zur Gegenwart*, Stuttgart, 1984, pp. 171–81.

Kießling, R., "Techniktransfer und Wirtschaftsboom in Augsburg/Schwaben im 14. Jahrhundert", in M. Kaufhold (ed.), *Augsburg im Mittelalter*, Augsburg, 2009, pp. 36–51.

Kießling, R., "Eckpunkte der Augsburger Reformationsgeschichte", in idem, T.M. Safley and L.P. Wandel (eds.), *Im Ringen um die Reformation. Kirchen und Prädikanten, Rat und Gemeinden in Augsburg*, Epfendorf, 2011, pp. 29–42.

Kießling, R., "Die Jakober Vorstadt und ihre Kirchen. Ein Augsburger Stadtteil in Mittelalter und Früher Neuzeit", in M. Thierbach (ed.), *Barfuß vor St. Max. Von der Klosterkirche der Franziskaner zur Pfarrkirche St. Maximilian*, Augsburg, 2013, pp. 38–49.

Kießling, R. and Lohrmann U., *Türme – Tore – Bastionen. Die reichsstädtischen Befestigungsanlagen Augsburgs*, Augsburg, 1987.

Kießling, R. and Plaßmeyer, P., "Augsburg", in W. Behringer and B. Roeck (eds.), *Das Bild der Stadt in der Neuzeit 1400–1800*, Munich, 1999, pp. 131–37.

Knoll, M., *Die Natur der menschlichen Welt. Siedlung, Territorium und Umwelt in der historisch-topographischen Literatur der Frühen Neuzeit*, Bielefeld, 2013.

Koch, A., *Die Trassen des Fernhandelsweges Augsburg im 15. und 16. Jahrhundert*, Landsberg am Lech, 2007.

König, W. and Renn, M., *Kleiner Sprachatlas von Bayerisch-Schwaben*, 2nd ed., Augsburg, 2007.

Kraus, J., *Das Militärwesen der Reichsstadt Augsburg 1548–1806. Vergleichende Untersuchungen über städtische Militäreinrichtungen in Deutschland vom 16.–18. Jahrhundert*, Augsburg, 1980.

Kraus, J., "Entwicklung und Topographie der Augsburger Steuerbezirke", *Zeitschrift des Historischen Vereins für Schwaben* 86 (1993), pp. 115–83.

Krüger, T.M., "Die Anfänge des Augsburger Stadtsiegels und die Emanzipation der Bürgerschaft", in M. Kaufhold (ed.), *Augsburg im Mittelalter*, Augsburg, 2009, pp. 19–35.

Larsson, L.O., "Die großen Brunnen und die Stadterneuerung um 1600", in W. Baer, H.-W. Kruft and B. Roeck (eds.), *Elias Holl und das Augsburger Rathaus* (exhibition catalogue), Regensburg, 1985, pp. 135–47.

Lengger, W., *Leben und Sterben in Schwaben. Studien zur Bevölkerungsentwicklung und Migration zwischen Lech und Iller, Ries und Alpen im 17. Jahrhundert*, 2 vols., Augsburg, 2002.

Link, A., "Lendler, Deferegger, Salzburger: Arme Exulanten in Augsburg", in D. Schiersner, A. Link, B. Rajkay and W. Scheffknecht (eds.), *Augsburg, Schwaben und der Rest der Welt. Neue Beiträge zur Landes- und Regionalgeschichte. Festschrift für Rolf Kießling zum 70. Geburtstag*, Augsburg, 2011, pp. 35–83.

Link, A., "Deferegger in Augsburg. Kirchenbücher als Quelle der Migrationsforschung", in R. Baumann and R. Kießling (eds.), *Mobilität und Migration in der Region*, Constance and Munich, 2014, pp. 127–61.

Löser, F., "Flüsse im Mittelalter: der Lech", in M. Krauss, S. Lindl and J. Soentgen (eds.), *Der gezähmte Lech. Ein Fluss der Extreme*, Munich, 2014, pp. 15–30.

Mauer, B., "Der Patrizier als Archäologe", in B. Kirchgässner and H.-P. Becht (eds.), *Stadt und Archäologie*, Stuttgart, 2000, pp. 81–100.

Michalsky, S., "Vom himmlischen Jerusalem bis zu den Veduten des 18. Jahrhunderts – Symbolik und Darstellungsparadigmen der Stadtprofilansichten", in W. Behringer and B. Roeck (eds.), *Das Bild der Stadt in der Neuzeit 1400–1800*, Munich, 1999, pp. 46–55.

Müller, G.M. (ed.), *Humanismus und Renaissance in Augsburg. Kulturgeschichte einer Stadt zwischen Spätmittelalter und Dreißigjährigem Krieg*, Berlin and New York, 2010.

Nagler, G., "'Es sind welche darunter, welche sich in Rom und Genua auszeichnen würden'. Augsburger Bürgerhäuser im 18. Jahrhundert", in G. Haindl (ed.), *Die Kunst zu wohnen. Ein Augsburger Klebealbum des 18. Jahrhunderts*, Berlin and Munich, 2010, pp. 30–45.

Netzer, S., *Johann Matthias Kager. Stadtmaler von Augsburg*, Munich, 1980.

Paas, M.W., *Population Change, Labor Supply, and Agriculture in Augsburg 1480–1618: A Study of Early Demographic-Economic Interactions*, New York, 1981.

Pataki, Z.A., "Antike Form und humanistischer Sinn – Die Illustrationen der Göttin Cisa in den Augsburger Abschriften der Stadtchronik Sigismund Meisterlins", in L.E. Saurma-Jeltsch and T. Frese (eds.) *Zwischen Mimesis und Vision. Zur städtischen Ikonographie am Beispiel Augsburgs*, Berlin, 2010, pp. 59–100.

Pataki, Z.A., "Ein Bürger blickt auf seine Stadt. Zur Rezeption und Funktion des Stadtbildes bei Hektor Mülich 1455/57", in S. Albrecht (ed.), *Stadtgestalt und Öffentlichkeit. Die Entstehung politischer Räume in der Stadt der Vormoderne*, Cologne, Weimar and Vienna, 2010, pp. 121–46.

Pfaud, R., *Das Bürgerhaus in Augsburg*, Tübingen, 1976.

Pfeuffer, E., *Der Lech*, Augsburg, 2010.

Pfeuffer, E., "Flussgötter auf Medaillen und Münzen der Freien Reichsstadt Augsburg", *Zeitschrift des Historischen Vereins für Schwaben* 108 (2016), pp. 145–62.

Piper, E., *Der Stadtplan als Grundriss der Gesellschaft. Topographie und Sozialstruktur in Augsburg und Florenz um 1500*, Frankfurt and New York, 1982.

Ritter, M., *Die Welt aus Augsburg. Landkarten von Tobias Conrad Lotter (1717–1777) und seinen Nachfolgern* (exhibition catalogue), ed. A. Lotter and C. Trepesch, Munich and Berlin, 2014.

Roeck, B., "'Arme' in Augsburg zu Beginn des 30jährigen Krieges", *Zeitschrift für bayerische Landesgeschichte* 46 (1983), pp. 515–58.

Roeck, B., "Urbanistische Entwicklung im 19. Jahrhundert", in R.A. Müller (ed.), *Aufbruch ins Industriezeitalter. Vol. 2: Aufsätze zur Wirtschafts- und Sozialgeschichte Bayerns 1750–1850*, Munich, 1985, pp. 112–23.

Roeck, B., *Bäcker, Brot und Getreide in Augsburg. Zur Geschichte des Bäckerhandwerks und zur Versorgungspolitik der Reichsstadt im Zeitalter des Dreißigjährigen Krieges*, Sigmaringen, 1987.

Roeck, B., *Eine Stadt in Krieg und Frieden. Studien zur Geschichte der Reichsstadt Augsburg zwischen Kalenderstreit und Parität*, 2 vols., Göttingen, 1989.

Roeck, B., "Der Brunnen der Macht. Kunst und Mythos im späthumanistischen Augsburg", in M. Kühlenthal (ed.), *Der Augustusbrunnen in Augsburg*, Munich, 2003, pp. 13–46.

Roeck, B., "Die ästhetische Inszenierung des Reichs – Aspekte seiner frühneuzeitlichen Ikonographie", in H. Schilling, W. Heun and J. Götzmann (eds.), *Heiliges Römisches Reich Deutscher Nation 962–1806. Altes Reich und neue Staaten 1495–1806*, Dresden, 2006, pp. 215–28.

Roper, L., "The Gorgon of Augsburg", in S. Broomhall and S. Trabin (eds.), *Women, Identities and Communities in Early Modern Europe*, Aldershot, 2008, pp. 113–36.

Rummel, P., "Katholisches Leben in der Reichsstadt Augsburg", *Jahrbuch des Vereins für Augsburger Bistumsgeschichte* 18 (1984), pp. 9–161.

Saurma-Jeltsch, L.E., "Die Wahrheit der Fiktion", in idem and T. Frese (eds.), *Zwischen Mimesis und Vision. Zur städtischen Ikonographie am Beispiel Augsburgs*, Berlin, 2010, pp. 1–33.

Schilling, L., "Wälder, Holzeinschlag und Flößer am Lech", in M. Krauss, S. Lindl and J. Soentgen (eds.), *Der gezähmte Lech. Ein Fluss der Extreme*, Munich, 2014, pp. 31–46.

Schmidt, A., *Augsburger Ansichten. Die Darstellung der Stadt in der Druckgraphik des 15. bis 18. Jahrhunderts*, Augsburg, 2000.

Schmidt, A., "Zwischen Moderne und Romantik. Ansichten von Augsburg um 1800", in J.R. Paas, J.H. Biller and M.-L. Hopp-Gantner (eds.), *Gestochen in Augsburg. Forschungen und Beiträge zur Augsburger Druckgrafik*, Augsburg, 2013, pp. 207–20.

Schröder, D., *Stadt Augsburg* (Historischer Atlas von Bayern, Teil Schwaben, 10), Munich, 1975.

Stoll, U., "Pinienzapfen und Zirbelnuß. Ein Beitrag zur Deutung der römischen Pinienzapfen und zur Geschichte des Augsburger Stadtwappens", *Zeitschrift des Historischen Vereins für Schwaben* 79 (1985), pp. 55–110.

Tremmel, B., *Der Kastellvicus des 1. Jahrhunderts nach Chr. von Augusta Vindelicum / Augsburg*, Augsburg, 2012.

Wangerow, H.-H., "Handel und Wandel auf der Donau von Ulm bis Wien", *Zeitschrift des Historischen Vereins für Schwaben* 105 (2013), pp. 101–161.

Weber, F.T., "Biographische Mittheilungen über das Leben der Künstler Franz Thomas und Josef Karl Weber von Augsburg. Ein Beitrag zur Künstlergeschichte der Stadt Augsburg", *Zeitschrift des Historischen Vereins für Schwaben* 19 (1892), pp. 181–97.

Werkstetter, C., "… daß seine Ehewürthin ebenfalls wie Er ihren täglichen und erklecklichen Verdienst hat – 'Gesellenehen' in der diversifizierten Arbeitswelt Augsburgs im 18. Jahrhundert", in D. Schiersner, A. Link, B. Rajkay and W. Scheffknecht (eds.) *Augsburg, Schwaben und der Rest der Welt. Neue Beiträge zur Landes- und Regionalgeschichte. Festschrift für Rolf Kießling zum 70. Geburtstag*, Augsburg, 2011, pp. 111–40.

West, A.D., "Conrad Peutinger and the Visual Arts: Collaborating with Hans Burgkmair the Elder", in R. Laube and H. Zäh (eds.), *Gesammeltes Gedächtnis. Konrad Peutinger und die kulturelle Überlieferung im 16. Jahrhundert*, Lucerne, 2016, pp. 62–73.

Wüst, W., "Augsburger Bürgerschaft, Domkapitel und Fürstbischöfe im 17. und 18. Jahrhundert: geistlich-weltliche Allianz oder politisch-ständischer Gegensatz?", in B. Kirchgässner and W. Baer (eds.), *Stadt und Bischof*, Sigmaringen, 1988, pp. 65–95.

Zimmer, J., "Die Veränderungen im Augsburger Stadtbild zwischen 1530 und 1630", in *Welt im Umbruch. Augsburg zwischen Renaissance und Barock* (exhibition catalogue), Augsburg, 1980, vol. 3, pp. 25–65.

Zimmer, J., *Cives propagantur: Also werden die Burger gepflantzet und gezüglet. Bemerkungen zu öffentlichen Kunstwerken in Augsburg um 1600*, Munich, 1988.

Zink, F., "Die frühesten Stadtansichten auf deutschen Medaillen und Münzen", *Anzeiger des Germanischen Nationalmuseums* 1954–1959, pp. 192–221.

CHAPTER 3

Of Invisible Boundaries: Bodies, Plagues, and Healers

Claudia Stein

During 1728 and 1729 the French aristocrat, jurist, and *homme de lettres* Charles-Louis de Secondat, Baron de Montesquieu (1689–1755) traveled Europe. Nothing escaped the traveler's enlightened critical eye, and his observations filled several notebooks. These detailed notes would later serve Montesquieu in the composition of his most famous work, *The Spirit of the Laws* (1748), a legal-philosophical treatise that would inspire all modern constitutional theories.[1] His visit to the imperial city of Augsburg, where he arrived on 16 August 1729 with a crippling cold, was important for Montesquieu's political and legal reflections.[2] The city's bi-confessional status within the political system of the Holy Roman Empire fascinated him. An early advocate of a separation of political powers and an admirer of the federal organization of the Empire, which had offered imperial cities like Augsburg a considerable degree of independence, Montesquieu declared Augsburg's citizens the happiest subjects in the German-speaking lands. The strict religious parity in the city's administration, which was established after the Peace of Westphalia in 1648 and structured everything from the highest magistrates to the city's street cleaners, offered citizens a certain protection from political arbitrariness, he believed.[3]

Although Montesquieu did not think that parity was a magic formula against all political injustice, he still considered it a superior system of political organization to that of his absolutist, centralized fatherland France. What such a strict bi-confessional organization meant for daily life in the city, though, he also learned towards the end of his stay. His cold had steadily worsened, and eventually Montesquieu felt the need to ask his Augsburg banker for a good physician.[4] The banker recommended a "Catholic doctor". Despite feeling rotten, Montesquieu could not deny himself a joke and asked for a good Turkish

---

1 Montesquieu, *Reisen*, pp. 11–35. For Montesquieu in Augsburg, see also François, "Augsburger Freiheit".
2 For his visit to the city's tourist attractions, see Montesquieu, *Reisen*, pp. 92–93.
3 Ibid., p. 95.
4 Ibid., p. 94.

doctor instead. The banker, somewhat consternated by this request and oblivious to its irony, responded apologetically that unfortunately there was none available in town.

For visitors like Montesquieu, the banker's response highlighted some of the absurdities of bi-confessional life. For Augsburg's citizens, however, one's denomination was a dead serious matter; indeed it was *the* central ordering force in most of their life decisions. It is therefore not surprising that the city's health care system was also structured around what Etienne François has called an "invisible boundary" between Catholics and Protestants.[5] This bi-confessional organization of Augsburg's medical marketplace, officially controlled by a board of local academic physicians, the *Collegium Medicum*, remained remarkably stable until the dissolution of the *Collegium* by the Bavarian government in 1806.

The city's wealth of civic health care institutions, in particular, remained a source of pride. The Augsburg engineer and architect Lucas Voch (1728–85) proudly claimed in his bestselling *The Civic Art of Building* of 1781 that no other German city had as many hospitals and other "civic works of charity" (*bürgerliche Liebeswerke*).[6] However, other enlightened visitors to Augsburg's hospitals did not share Voch's pride. The Marburg physician and medical reformer Ernst Gottfried Baldinger (1738–1804) was shocked by what he encountered in 1796.[7] All health institutions, he reported, were overcrowded and unbelievably dirty. None of the staff and medical personnel met Baldinger's enlightened standards. Their ignorance, he claimed, had even killed some inmates. Baldinger's damning judgment was not exceptional; another visiting doctor found the hospitals' conditions simply "disgusting" (*abscheulich*).[8]

Whether these depictions of messy wards and hordes of ignorant healers matched the reality of Augsburg's eighteenth-century health care institutions remains uncertain. Historians of medicine have cautioned us not to take everything reform-minded physicians like Baldinger had to say about their competitors as a given.[9] In the eyes of enlightened physicians, everyone and everything besides their own medical ideas and practice was found wanting. Whether such considerations also colored Baldinger's views on Augsburg we do not know, because, so far, no research has been conducted on the city's

---

5 François argued that, while pragmatism reigned in most business and political relations, a strong but "invisible boundary" was drawn in family and social life. See François, *Unsichtbare Grenze*, pp. 70–72, 84–142, 190–243.
6 Voch, *Bürgerliche Baukunst*, p. 37.
7 Baldinger, "Nachrichten von Wien, München und Augsburg".
8 Bisle, *Die öffentliche Armenpflege*, p. 116.
9 Lindemann, *Health and Healing*, pp. 3–21.

eighteenth-century medical marketplace.[10] This chapter does not aspire to close this gap. Instead, it traces the emergence and organization of the city's larger medical institutions and the range of official and illicit medical services that enlightened contemporaries either praised or condemned.

In order to understand the structure and dynamics of Augsburg's early modern medical marketplace, we need to take into account two invisible boundaries. Apart from the city's bi-confessional administrative and institutional structure, civic health care institutions were equally shaped by the ancient division of the human body in terms of an "inner" (invisible) and an "outer" (visible) sphere. As we shall see, it is this distinction, and the professional struggles that unfolded over who was responsible for the "inner" body, that structured professional relationships and explains the specific hierarchy of the city's healer community from the sixteenth until the end of the eighteenth century.

1   Institutional Care for the Sick and Poor

In 1812, the Augsburg patrician, lawyer, and Bavarian civil servant Franz Eugen von Seida und Landensberg (1772–1826) published a history of the city's charitable and medical foundations. His *Historical and Statistical Description of All Ecclesiastical, Educational, and Charity Institutions in Augsburg* reflected recent radical changes in the city's political status and the identity of its citizens.[11] In 1806, Augsburg had lost its status as an imperial city and become part of the Bavarian kingdom. This entailed a complete overhaul of communal affairs, including civic charity and health care institutions.[12] The *Collegium Medicum*, which had officially overseen the city's medical provisions since 1582, was dissolved in 1807, and some of its responsibilities were transferred to the newly defined local *Polizeydirection*. Seida's historical overview was to serve the new Bavarian administrators as a guide in their attempt to integrate the local health system into a centralized Bavarian *Medizinalwesen*.[13] It traced the decline and marked the end of a long tradition of charity and health care that had its roots in the late Middle Ages.

Seida's account showed that Augsburg's main health care institutions, like those in other cities of the Holy Roman Empire, originated in an alliance of the

---

10   For information on Augsburg's eighteenth-century itinerant healers, see Probst, *Fahrende Heiler*.
11   Seida, *Beschreibung*.
12   Dietrich, *Integration*.
13   Probst, "Reform des Medizinalwesens".

Catholic Church with lay initiatives.[14] The primary objective of these foundations was the organization of Christian charity for those in need due to illness or other infirmities.[15] Augsburg's largest institution was the Hospital of the Holy Ghost, which since the thirteenth century had been located within the inner city walls, near the Red Gate.[16] Given a new home in the early seventeenth century by Augsburg's famous architect Elias Holl (1573–1646), it housed about 250 elderly and frail citizens, including the mentally disturbed and those afflicted with falling sickness (a form of what is known today as epilepsy).[17] Leprosy is first mentioned in civic sources in the thirteenth century, when its sufferers were separated from the healthy population in special leper houses.[18] The first of these, St. Servatius, was established in the mid-thirteenth century with donations from various pious burghers. When it proved too small, two further leprosaria were opened in the early fifteenth century, St. Sebastian and St. Wolfgang. The Pilgrim House, founded in the fourteenth century by the bequest of a wealthy local merchant, created additional space for the curable poor and infirm.[19] By the mid-sixteenth century it was re-located to the Mendicant Gate (*Barfüsser Tor*), thanks to another pious bequest, and housed about 70 poor and sick residents.

Like the Pilgrim House, all local facilities owed their existence to private initiatives and the generosity of pious citizens or to the Catholic Church. But by the end of the sixteenth century this was no longer the case. The number of private or church-run institutions had plummeted, while the city council became the most important benefactor. An exception were the two private French pox hospitals of the Fugger family, established in their social housing project, the Fuggerei, in St. Jacob's Suburb (*Jakobervorstadt*) in 1523–24 and 1572, and the family's private surgery on the Horse Market.[20] New health care institutions, such as the civic French pox hospital (*Blatterhaus*), established in 1495 and likewise situated in St. Jacob's Suburb, were founded at the council's behest, while the council also attempted to seize the administration of

---

14   Kießling, *Bürgerliche Gesellschaft*.
15   Despite several new studies, a fundamental work on German hospital history remains Reike, *Das deutsche Spitalwesen*.
16   Lengle, "Heilig-Geist-Spital".
17   Voch, *Baukunst*, pp. 89–99; Seida, *Beschreibung*, pp. 772–76.
18   On leprosy, see Kießling, *Bürgerliche Gesellschaft*, pp. 169–73; Hammond, "Origins of Civic Health Care", pp. 81–83.
19   Trompeter, "Pilgerhaus", p. 10.
20   The French pox are often identified with the modern disease entity of venereal syphilis. For the problems of such "retrospective diagnosis", i.e. the identification of past diseases with modern disease entities, see Stein, "'Getting the Pox". For a detailed history of the pox hospitals, see Stein, *French Pox*, pp. 91–110.

the existing charitable institutions. Augsburg is not the only city in which this process can be observed. Social historians have explained it as the culmination of an extended process of communalization that had begun roughly two centuries earlier. It aimed at weakening the power of the local Church by bringing the most important care institutions into the hands of citizens and their representative body, the council.[21]

The magistrates' efforts to re-organize poor relief under their own auspices gained momentum during the sixteenth century. New civic institutions were founded, such as the city's two plague hospitals in 1521 and in the early 1570s (to quarantine the victims of the plague that had regularly been visiting the city since 1349), and the "house for the needy" (*Nothaus*), which by the 1560s came to be used as a shelter for sick foreigners.[22] In accordance with the critique of traditional forms of Catholic charity during the Reformation, access to these civic institutions was restricted: poor citizens were to be provided with relief only after careful examination and evaluation of their individual circumstances.[23] This process of centralization peaked with the official establishment of the Reformation in the 1530s. Responsibility for all local charitable institutions passed into the hands of the council, now dominated by evangelical-minded guild members. The council's control over health care institutions remained in force even after Charles v enforced the re-establishment of Catholicism and the adoption of a patrician regime in 1548. The council was subsequently dominated by a small group of Catholic patricians who ruled over a largely Protestant population, yet both denominations managed to coexist more or less peacefully until the Thirty Years' War.[24] This coexistence was reflected in the administration of civic health care institutions.

The fortune of these institutions during the seventeenth century has received limited attention from historians, but the records indicate that the general deterioration of the city's finances and administration during and after the Thirty Years' War resulted in dwindling financial support for civic institutions.[25] Epidemics due to hunger and disease accompanied the periods of warfare and economic crisis. These were especially difficult times for the city's poor and sick, whose numbers rose correspondingly and increased dramatically when poor people from the devastated countryside poured into Augsburg, seeking

---

21 For an overview, see Jütte, *Obrigkeitliche Armenfürsorge*.
22 The *Nothaus* was administratively joined with the Pilgrim House. During the eighteenth century it served as a shelter for poor single and pregnant women: see Bisle, *Armenpflege*, pp. 119–22.
23 Such tendencies can also be observed in Catholic cities. For socio-economic background, see Ludyga, *Obrigkeitliche Armenfürsorge*, pp. 178–82.
24 See Chapters 7 and 11 in this volume.
25 Bátori, *Reichsstadt Augsburg*.

additional support from already strapped civic institutions. Moreover, during successive occupations by foreign armies, the larger health care institutions were temporarily converted into barracks or stables to accommodate the soldiers, or were destroyed.[26] However, despite wartime losses, destruction, and serious financial constraints, the majority of the city's larger health institutions managed to survive and remained under civic authority until 1806. Despite the difficulties they faced, they retained their bi-confessional character from the mid-sixteenth century to 1806. Members of both denominations were equally entitled to admission, and both Catholic and Protestant inmates had access to religious services. While female and male patients were admitted to separate wards in the sixteenth and seventeenth century, a separation by denomination does not seem to have been established; although by the late eighteenth century, Voch's architectural overview reveals that the patients in the Holy Ghost hospital and the Pilgrim House were separated by their denomination as well as their sex. Whether the occasional disputes among inmates and staff over religious issues recorded in the archival sources led to a spatial demarcation of this invisible confessional boundary remains to be ascertained. However, as both Catholic and Protestant administrators and patients feared the wrath of God in response to sinful behavior, confessional separation may have been the logical outcome.

2   Admission Practices

While a Christian applicant's denomination did not subject him or her to discrimination in Augsburg's health-care institutions, the council devised other strategies to restrict access in order to cope with rising numbers of applicants and increasing financial difficulties. As in other cities, the distinction between "deserving" and "undeserving" poor was imposed in terms of residency and civic status.[27] By far the most important criterion for admission in all civic institutions, however, was the applicant's physical condition. From the 1520s onward, no one was to be admitted without a previous *Geschau*, a physical examination conducted by a learned physician and/or barber-surgeon.[28] Admission was granted only if the applicant's physical condition matched the institution's specific criteria. The general entrance ticket to the Hospital of the Holy Ghost was the applicant's age, since the institution served as a retirement home for old and needy citizens (who often brought their own endowment to pay for

---

26   See Chapter 15 in this volume.
27   Clasen, "Armenfürsorge".
28   For this and the following, see Stein, *French Pox*, pp. 76–79.

their stay until they died). Eligible patients were only accepted if their bodies did not manifest open lesions or (even worse) "infected matter". Supplicants diagnosed by the medical team as openly infectious were immediately transferred to another institution that specialized in the treatment of such conditions: the Pilgrim House, the leper houses, or the civic French pox house.

The Pilgrim House, which from the later sixteenth century onwards treated about five hundred sufferers per year, catered for all those "afflicted with open wounds and other vile diseases" but specified that the wounds must be "curable".[29] Concerns for the health of other inmates along with financial considerations played a crucial role in this restriction. The chronically cash-strapped administrators sought to avoid the admission of those who were incurably ill, fearing extra costs for their institution. Definitely barred from entry were sufferers from leprosy, who had to apply at one of the three leper houses. Interestingly, by the sixteenth century leprosy was no longer perceived as necessarily "incurable", making the leper houses attractive for idlers who, without any signs of leprosy, were simply hanging about there because of "bad weather", at least according to the council and the attending physicians.[30] Visitations by civic physicians to "winkle out" those inmates who were already cured or were otherwise there under false pretenses became common. The chronic shortage of beds in the three leper houses also led the chief administrators to refuse admission of cases in which the medical staff failed to reach an unambiguous and unanimous diagnostic verdict.[31]

This was the fate of Anna Nidermair, who was diagnosed as "afflicted with loathsome scabs" in October 1609, but, because the medical practitioners were unable to agree on whether these were related to leprosy or the French pox, was refused admission by the guardians of the leper homes.[32] She was then referred to the pox house, whose guardians also refused to accept her. Only after the council's intervention was her case resolved: she was to be exceptionally accepted to the civic French pox house for observation until a place in one of the leper houses became available.[33] This, in turn, upset the pox house guardians, who had been instructed since 1495 (when the hitherto unknown disease made its first appearance in the city) only to accept those showing unambiguous symptoms of the French pox. The guardians had been instructed

---

29 Clasen, "Armenfürsorge", p. 104.
30 For this and other cases, see Stein, *French Pox*, pp. 79–80.
31 For the *examen leprosorum*, see Sudhoff, "Was geschah", pp. 150–52.
32 For her case, see Stein, *French Pox*, pp. 81–82.
33 Stadtarchiv Augsburg (StadtAA), St. Martin, Fasz. 6, Prod. 88: Bericht der Pfleger des St. Servatius Siechenhauses; ibid., Bericht der Oberpfleger über das Blatterhaus, 16 January 1610.

not to accept and always discharge ambiguous cases in order to protect their own inmates from being "contaminated" with other ailments. The substantial number of cured inmates demonstrates that the civic French pox house was indeed a therapeutic success story (as were the two private "woodhouses" of the Fugger family). This success was largely attributed to the use, beginning in the 1520s, of a new therapeutic drug from the New World, guaiacum wood.[34]

Victims of the most dreaded of all diseases, the plague or Black Death, which first appeared in the city in 1349, were treated in the two civic plague houses, which only opened their gates during plague epidemics.[35] Transfer to the two plague house or *Lazarethe* was decreed by the council as soon as medical practitioners identified a case. The barber-surgeon Joseph Schmidt (1601?–67), who had worked for years as *Chyrurgus lazarethanus* (plague surgeon), recalled that such a verdict was never proclaimed lightly and its public announcement was delayed as long as possible.[36] The council thus hoped to prevent a sudden panic among the population, possibly followed by a serious interruption or even a breakdown of all civic and economic life. Moreover, time was needed to prepare the necessary quarantine measures and staff the plague houses. Although recent studies on early modern Augsburg have pointed out that the official and public response to the plague was rather less dramatic than the older historiography suggested, spreading the news of a possible outbreak was considered a grave offense for any physician or barber-surgeon and was officially prosecuted.[37] By the mid-eighteenth century, the plague had ceased to terrorize the city, but the memory of its devastations continued to haunt even enlightened contemporaries.[38] In his discussion of the city's plague houses, the architect Voch thanked the Lord that he and his family had never had to experience an outbreak. He reported in 1781 that the plague houses were instead treating cases of dysentery, smallpox, scabies, venereal disease, cancer, scurvy, and many other diseases deemed infectious.[39]

---

34   This was why the Fugger hospital in the Fuggerei was called the woodhouse. Contrary to widespread historical opinion, the Fuggers never held a monopoly on the sale of the wood. For the history of this myth, see Stein, *French Pox*, pp. 101–5.

35   To what extent mid-fourteenth-century Swabia and Augsburg were affected by the plague is a matter of debate; see Krug, "Pest in Augsburg?"; Horanin, "Die Pest". For an impressive reconstruction of the city's response to the plague of 1627–28, see Roeck, *Eine Stadt in Krieg und Frieden*, vol. 2, pp. 630–54; for the reactions of the council, see his pp. 639–42.

36   See Ecker-Offenhäußer, "'Pest, Frantzosen, Scharbock'".

37   See Mauer, "*Gemein Geschrey*", p. 204.

38   The last outbreak of the plague in Western Europe occurred in Marseilles in the early 1720s.

39   Voch, *Baukunst*, pp. 43–45.

3 Invisible Bodily Worlds: God, Stars, Humors, and Disease

The diagnostic verdict of medical practitioners, which was at the core of the admission process in all civic institutions, was based on an understanding of the human body that was fundamentally different from ours. The decision reached in the case of Anna Nidermair – which, from a modern perspective, might appear a sign of colossal medical incompetence – has to be understood in the context of the division of the human body into an "outer" visible and "inner" invisible sphere – a major symbolic opposition in Western medicine from its first formulation in ancient Greek Hippocratic medical treatises.[40] In order to comprehend what was happening within the invisible depths of the body, the outer signs of disease needed to be interpreted by taking into account the multiple links between the human body (the microcosm) and the surrounding God-created world (the macrocosm). The tenets of this understanding of the body's functioning remained powerful well into the eighteenth century.[41] Archival records in Augsburg demonstrate that these explanations were shared by medical practitioners and patients alike, and this continued to be the case despite the rise of new materialistic, mechanical, and chemical theories of the body and new medical practices such as pathological anatomy or cowpox inoculation during the late-seventeenth and eighteenth centuries.[42]

The surgeon Joseph Schmid's explanation for why he had never caught the plague (or the French pox) while he worked in the *Blatterhaus* offers a point of entry into the complete otherness of this world. The Almighty, he explained, specially protected medical practitioners so that they were able to fulfill their God-given duty.[43] Anyway, he believed, plague or pox victims could only infect healthy persons if their complexion, their individual mixture of humors and qualities, were similar. Schmid's firm belief in God as the *prima causa* for all illness was shared by Protestants and Catholics alike.[44] No one doubted that illness and pain were God's reminder of humanity's original sin, which had tainted mankind forever. Physical suffering was a divine punishment with which the Almighty chastised the sins of mankind. Illness therefore always had a higher purpose, and to cope with it necessarily involved a coming-to-

---

40 For these ideas, see Lindemann, *Medicine and Society*, pp. 19–20; Jütte, *Ärzte, Heiler und Patienten*.
41 See Duden, *Women Beneath the Skin*.
42 On eighteenth-century medicine, see Broman, *Transformation*. On the theory of vitalism, which rejected materialistic theories of nature and the human body, see Reill, *Vitalizing Nature*.
43 See Schmid, *Kurtzer iedoch Gewisser bericht*, pp. 29–31.
44 Stein, *French Pox*, pp. 23–30.

terms with one's Maker. In the case of plague, for example, Augsburg's terrified citizens hoped to appease God's anger and attract his mercy with 24-hour processions, mass public prayers, and – if Catholic – pilgrimages to nearby shrines of saints.[45] It was only with the Reformation, which stressed individual redemption through faith and grace, that Protestants increasingly considered certain Catholic practices, like miracle healings or the veneration of holy relics, suspect. How this affected spiritual responses to illness in bi-confessional Augsburg requires further investigation.[46]

It was widely believed that via his "helpers", the stars and planets, God was able to express His disapproval of sinful human actions by altering the four elements (air, earth, water and fire) that made up the earthly sphere and everything in it, including the human body.[47] This idea of a God-created and controlled cosmos accounts for the great importance that contemporaries attached to the readings and interpretation of the skies to explain all kinds of medical issues. Augsburg's physicians had studied astronomy and astrology during their university years. That some of them possessed extensive knowledge in this area is demonstrated by the work of Achilles Pirmin Gasser (1505–77).[48] His writings on the plague and other diseases, in Latin for his academic peers and in German to instruct Augsburg's common people, indicate how important astrology was (and would remain) not only for the explanation of disease causation but also for the prognostication of its possible outcome.[49] Every year the council asked the academic physicians to produce the city's official astrological calendar, which informed all local practitioners about the most appropriate astrological times for bloodletting, bathing, cupping, and even the cutting of one's hair. Serious surgical operations outside the appropriate times were deemed dangerous, possibly even lethal.[50]

The close interconnection between the body and the cosmos was mediated through the ancient ideas of elements, complexion, and humors. Each person was believed to be endowed with an innate mixture of the four elements and their related qualities (dry, moist, hot, and cold) which defined his or her

---

45   Horanin, "Die Pest", p. 5.
46   For the Protestant critique of such practices, see, e.g., Daston, "Wunder".
47   Recent scholarship has argued that there were few differences between Protestants and Catholics regarding the belief in medical astrology. See Kusukawa, "'Aspectio divinorum operum'".
48   Burmeister, *Gasser*.
49   Gasser published several astronomical and astrological treatises between 1531 and 1546 and was open to Copernicus' then controversial idea of a heliocentric universe: see Burmeister, *Gasser*, vol. 1, pp. 62–80.
50   Hoffmann, "Augsburger Bäder", p. 29.

"complexion" or "temperament", acquired at the moment of conception and kept more or less intact throughout life.[51] A person's complexion depended on the internal balance of the four humors and their individual qualities: blood (hot/wet), phlegm (cold/wet), yellow bile (hot/dry), and black bile (cold/dry). Depending on which humor dominated a person's innate complexion, he or she was either sanguine, phlegmatic, choleric, or melancholic. Produced from the foodstuffs in the stomach and distributed through the body via the liver, humors fulfilled two central functions in the body's economy: they nourished the individual organs and body parts, and collectively served to maintain an individual's overall complexional balance and health. Any alteration of one's innate humoral balance carried the risk of disease.

Information about how to keep one's humoral balance and hence remain healthy was easy to obtain in Augsburg, one of the major European printing centers.[52] Medical advice literature in the German vernacular was published here as early as the fifteenth century. The *Ordnung der Gesundheit* (Regiment of Health, 1475) was in fact the first published medical regiment in German and contained a section on how to behave in times of plague.[53] The advice provided did not differ much from that which Achilles Pirmin Gasser offered the public roughly a century later.[54] The key to survival, according to Gasser's *Unterricht wider die Pestilenz* (Instruction against Pestilence, 1565), was a strictly regular lifestyle that observed the "six non-naturals", influences to which the human body was incessantly exposed, namely air, evacuation and retention, food and drink, motion and rest, sleeping and waking, and the passions.

All medical treatment aimed at "correcting" the imbalance of humors. The "poisonous" disease matter would first be expelled through bloodletting, cupping, purging, and sweating. If already too deeply "rooted" in the body, specific medication and drugs whose qualities were opposed to those of the diagnosed imbalance were administered. The appearance of the French pox at the end of the fifteenth century triggered a virtual explosion of printed treatment advice by Augsburg's physicians, surgeons, and apothecaries, praising the benefits of the new drug guaiacum and offering recipes for the preparation of the wood drink and treatment at home. Augsburg was also the origin of a narrative in which an early patient shared his experience with the French pox with fellow sufferers in print. The imperial knight, poet, and reformer Ulrich von Hutten (1481–1523) undertook a guaiacum cure in one of Augsburg's private

---

51   For an excellent general overview, see Siraisi, *Medieval and Early Renaissance Medicine*.
52   See Chapter 18 in this volume.
53   Horanin, "Die Pest", p. 34.
54   Gasser, *Unterricht*. See the facsimile of this tract in Burmeister, *Gasser*, pp. 142–43.

pox houses and published his gruesome experiences after his alleged miraculous recovery.[55]

Sufferers like Hutten held their bodies to be a seething mass of humors and fluids rather than an assembly of discrete organs or cells. A constant exchange took place between the body's inside and outside through its invisible boundary and through openings such as the nose, ears, eyes, and pores. No early modern person perceived a disease as etiologically, morphologically, or symptomatically separate from other diseases, as we tend to do today. Patients' hospital records and surviving diagnosis certificates show that a disease like the pox could manifest itself in different ways in different individuals.[56] Moreover, diseases were able to metamorphose into each other. There were hundreds of species of leprosy, plague, or the pox, which were believed to originate from innumerable subtle differences in the mixture of the four vital humors, hidden in the invisible depths of the individual inner body. Diagnosing disease was therefore an intricate business that relied as much on the sufferer's opinions and interpretation as on the medical practitioner's professional expertise. The verdict of the medical team reached in the case of Anna Nidermair was therefore not a sign of the incompetence of medical theory and practice, but a reflection of its core tenets and strengths. In what follows, we shall see how this conception of the human body not only explains the logic of many diagnostic verdicts and choices of medical treatment, but was also the basis for the hierarchical organization of Augsburg's medical healers until the end of the eighteenth century.

4   Professional Hierarchies and the Body's Invisible Boundary

In 1806, the Catholic physician and dean of Augsburg's *Collegium Medicum*, Joseph Ahorner von Ahornrain (1764–1839),[57] and his colleagues lost control over the city's medical marketplace. Following a Bavarian royal decree, the city's board of health, consisting of Catholic and Protestant academic physicians,

---

55   The tract was first published in Latin and translated by Thomas Murner into German: Hutten, *Von der wunderbarlichen artzney*. For Hutten's suffering and dramatic therapy, see Stein, *French Pox*, pp. 27–29, 32–34, 39–40.

56   On medical semiotics, see Siraisi, "Disease and Symptoms". For the slow development of modern monocausal concepts of disease during the nineteenth century, see Carter, *Rise of Causal Concepts*.

57   Seidl, "Joseph von Ahorner".

was officially dissolved, and a long history came to an abrupt end.[58] Since 1582, the *Collegium* had presided over the organization of the civic hospitals and had undertaken the examination and licensing of local surgeons, barbers, and midwives as well as the visitations of the local pharmacies. Its members had also acted as arbiters in cases of professional dispute and malpractice. Besides monitoring the official healer community, the *Collegium* kept track of the many illicit healers from inside and outside the city, testing their potions and alleged wonder cures and issuing prohibitions when they found them potential health threats to patients. In times of epidemics, the members of the *Collegium* became official city diplomats, negotiating quarantines and rights of passage for foodstuffs and goods with the representatives of neighboring communities and territories. Altogether, the *Collegium* enjoyed considerable social prestige and political power. Moreover, Ahorner's biographies of the *Collegium's* physicians show that membership also entailed significant economic opportunities. Due to Augsburg's political and economic importance as an imperial city (particularly during the sixteenth century), some academic physicians established a European clientele of wealthy merchants, noblemen, diplomats, and visitors who paid generously for their services. Some even treated kings and queens, and many were well-known intellectuals who made significant contributions to Augsburg's cultural and scientific development and international fame. Ahorner himself was a widely-known naturalist and collector of natural specimens, whose collection of butterflies attracted many foreign visitors.[59] But these prosperous times were now definitely over, as Ahorner and his colleagues realized only too painfully. Not everyone, and Ahorner is an example, was able to continue his career in the newly established Bavarian medical system, controlled by the central medical office in Munich.[60]

Reading Ahorner's celebratory biographies of *Collegium* members, written at a time when academic physicians' social, political, and economic standing had been undermined, conveys the impression that their leading position in Augsburg had always rested on their academic medical and scientific expertise. The archival sources, however, particularly those of the earlier sixteenth century, present a rather different story. The power of academic physicians and

---

58 Deininger, "Collegium Medicum Augustanum"; Salzbrunn, "Ende"; Gensthaler, *Medizinalwesen*.

59 For his collection and his publications, see Pfeuffer (ed.), *Von der Natur fasziniert*, pp. 85–86. Ahorner was also an accomplished draftsman and published two beautifully illustrated volumes on shells and butterflies, which are held at the Staats- und Stadtbibliothek Augsburg. For a comprehensive overview of eighteenth-century scientific collecting in Germany, see Siemer, *Geselligkeit und Methode*.

60 Probst, "Medizinalwesen".

their representative body, the *Collegium Medicum*, was never uncontested. Due to the particular understanding of the human body discussed above, academic physicians constantly had to negotiate their position in the marketplace with other healers and consumers. Only after a long struggle did they establish the superiority of their knowledge of the "inner" body and successfully claim control over Augsburg's medical marketplace. The foundation of the *Collegium Medicum* in 1582 was the official and highly visible outcome of their strategic maneuvering, which began in the early sixteenth century.

The earliest example of the physicians' ambitions is the struggle over cures in the civic *Blatterhaus*. In the early years of the institution, much to the physicians' chagrin, treatment lay entirely in the hands of non-academic "empirics". Only in the 1520s, after intense lobbying and the proposition of a new miraculous treatment – the wood guaiacum, whose workings, the physicians claimed, was known only to them – were they able to gain control of the institution. By 1522, the *Blatterhaus* ordinance installed a physician firmly at the top of the staff hierarchy.[61] For the first time, academic medical expertise on the inner invisible body was officially acknowledged by the council as superior to the work of barber-surgeons. The latter were now officially restricted to the "outer" sphere of the patient's body (and remunerated significantly lower) and had to work in the presence of an academic physician.

The unity that the physicians displayed as a professional group in this case was to become one of their strategic tools in dealing with the council and competing medical practitioners. Occasional disputes among the group of physicians over the correct medical theory and practice, one of which erupted over the local publications of the maverick physician Paracelsus (1493–1541), eventually strengthened their professional unity, which they eagerly demonstrated to the city council in all matters of public health.[62] This appearance of unity, however, was not only based on (and strengthened by) shared academic expertise and its vocal public defense against medical outsiders such as Paracelsus. The key to the physicians' success was their social and political relations. During the sixteenth century, marriages between physicians, often immigrants and/or from prosperous backgrounds, and the daughters of wealthy local patricians became increasingly common. They were indicative of the rising reputation and social status accorded to widely travelled, university-trained humanist physicians in one of Europe's leading economic and cultural centers.[63] A telling example is the aforementioned Lutheran physician and

---

61 For house organization, see Stein, *French Pox*, pp. 107–14.
62 Weeks, *Paracelsus*. On Paracelsus in Augsburg, cf. Hammond, "Paracelsus".
63 For their university studies, see Martz, "Gesundheitswesen".

humanist scholar Achilles Pirmin Gasser, who married a rich widow from one of the most influential patrician families soon after his arrival in Augsburg.[64] Financially secure, Gasser gained immediate access to the city's highest political decision-making bodies, which offered him the opportunity to advise the council in questions of public health. His social and personal ties with the elite were further strengthened when, during times of plague, he acted as Augsburg's official plague physician. Instructing the public through his own publications, Gasser also ran a lucrative private practice and corresponded with many humanist intellectuals, so that his medical advice came to be sought by the rich and powerful all over Europe.[65] Some of his children and grandchildren followed him in his successful career, a phenomenon that can also be observed in other physician families.[66] Medical dynasties such as the Gassers, Occos or Jungs became increasingly frequent. That physicians used their social ties to their professional advantage is also evident in the organization of the city's midwifery system, which came under the control of the doctors – and their patrician wives – from the 1520s onwards.[67] By the eighteenth century, as elsewhere in Europe, midwifery was entirely under the control of a specially appointed academic physician, the *accoucheur*.[68]

The physicians not only exploited their family relations and prominent political status; they also elevated themselves by exploiting ongoing disputes among their most serious competitors on the medical marketplace, the bath masters, barbers, and barber-surgeons such as Joseph Schmid. These practitioners of "trades of the body" ran the city's bathhouses, cut hair, shaved, performed bloodletting, treated external injuries, and performed more serious surgical operations, such as fixing broken bones, extracting bladder stones (lithotomy), and performing hernia operations or amputations.[69] Some local barber-surgeons were as famous as their academic colleagues; their skills were in high demand and well-paid all over Europe. Without professional representation on the council, however, they had difficulties exerting any sustained influence on the council's decision-making in questions of public health. This

---

64 For his family relations, see Burmeister, *Gasser*, p. 109.
65 On his European networks see Burmeister, *Gasser*, pp. 135–42.
66 Most famous was his grandson Johann Ulrich Rumler (1565–1626), who allegedly treated Queen Anne of England: Burmeister, *Gasser*, p. 119.
67 Hammond, *Health Care*, pp. 98–101. On the development of male midwifery in Germany, see Labouvie, *In anderen Umständen*.
68 For details on these 'accoucheurs' in Augsburg's *Nothaus*, which served as the local *Achouchir-Anstalt* in the eighteenth century, see Baldinger, "Nachrichten von Wien, München und Augsburg", pp. 19–20.
69 Hoffmann, "Augsburger Bäder"; Ecker-Offenhäußer, "'Pest, Franzosen, Scharbock'", pp. 28–33; Hammond, "Origins of Civic Health Care", pp. 74–75, 166–80.

situation was exploited by the physicians,[70] who particularly targeted the barber-surgeons who had traditionally performed "inner medicine" (administering medications that affected the composition of the humors) under their own auspices. By the mid-sixteenth century, this was now forbidden by the council. Further decrees confirmed that barber-surgeons could only treat external and surgical wounds. As the barber-surgeons apparently lacked knowledge of the hidden secrets of the body, the physicians explained to the council, they should only be allowed to perform their trade under the supervision of academic colleagues. That the physicians exaggerated their case and the barber-surgeons were well aware of this is revealed in many official complaints about the impossibility of keeping up this invisible professional boundary. Thus Joseph Schmid's publications, directed at instructing local barber-surgeon apprentices, clearly show how sophisticated surgical knowledge actually was. It included the theory of complexion and humors, and extensive knowledge of herbs, minerals and plants, as well as astrology.[71]

Less acrimonious were the relationships between physicians and local apothecaries, who also came under the physicians' control during the sixteenth century. Traditionally, apothecaries had often been local grocers and spice traders, dealing, among other things, with medicinal drugs. Increasingly, however, sixteenth-century apothecaries were recruited via the international patronage networks of local physicians.[72] Of course, such patronage relations came at a cost for these apothecaries. The initiative of four physicians (including Gasser) and one apothecary resulted in the *Pharmacopaea Augustana* of 1564 (one of the earliest works of its kind and much copied thereafter), which listed all medications officially permitted in the city, fixed their prices, established rules for their preparation, and granted the physicians the right to control observance of these new rules in all apothecary shops several times a year on the basis of their academic knowledge.[73] Once again, the physicians managed to turn their expertise on the inner body into a professional boundary. The founding of the *Collegium Medicum* in 1582, which acknowledged the physicians at the top of the city's hierarchy of healers, sanctioned these professional distinctions. Officially, control over the Augsburg medical marketplace was finally theirs.

The sources suggest, however, that this control was far from complete or comprehensive. How could it be otherwise? The ancient invisible distinction

---

70 See StadtAA, Collegium Medicum, Ordnungen und Decreta, 1625–1804, 4 June 1532.
71 On education, see Ecker-Offenhäußer, "'Pest, Franzosen, Scharbock'", pp. 17–28, 44–48.
72 Gensthaler, *Medizinalwesen*, pp. 60–69.
73 See Gensthaler, *Medizinalwesen*, pp. 95–100.

between the inner and the outer body, which had emerged as the demarcation line among Augsburg's official healers during the sixteenth century, was too weak to serve as a barbed-wire boundary between them. As already mentioned, the barber-surgeons found it impossible to respect this imaginary boundary in their daily business, particularly in the case of accidents.[74] Equally important, the great majority of the surgeons' patients did not possess the financial means to pay the academic physicians' higher fees. The barber-surgeons' suggestion that the physicians were motivated by financial considerations was immediately denied by the latter, who in turn depicted their competitors as ignorant "empirics" who themselves robbed the innocent sick whenever possible.[75] These aggressive exchanges between physicians and barber-surgeons (which increased after 1582) tend to hide the fact that both groups generally shared professional responsibilities in dealing with the dualistic body. Indeed, many of the civic surgeons' and physicians' activities required teamwork, such as the daily rounds through the wards of the civic health care institutions or autopsies to establish the causes of deaths involving cases of physical violence or possible malpractice.[76] Both professions also shared certain political aims. Central was their joint battle against a heterogeneous group of healers, both local and itinerant, who had not undergone an officially acknowledged medical training and/or lacked the residency or citizenship status necessary to officially practice it. From the 1530s onwards the physicians increasingly acted as advocates for all official healer groups in their fight against these unlicensed "quacks" and "ignorant empirics".[77] They repeatedly reminded the council of its God-given obligation to protect all local medical trades against outside encroachments. But although the founding of the *Collegium Medicum* made the physicians the council's official advisers in questions of public health, the council continued to act independently of its recommendations and often allowed itinerant healers to practice. The local executioner, for example, who derived his medical expertise from the performance of physical punishments and whose knowledge of human anatomy often surpassed that of authorized healers, was allowed to offer his skills as a bone-setter. Kathy Stuart has observed that Augsburg's executioners regarded medical practice as a legitimate right of their profession well into the eighteenth century, even advertising that they were executioners to draw more patients (to the annoyance of the authorized healer community).[78] One of their bestselling products was human fat (or "poor

---

74   Joseph Schmid's work shows this clearly: Stein, *French Pox*, pp. 117–20.
75   StadtAA, Collegium Medicum, Fasz. 1, Gegenbericht der Doktoren auf die Supplikation der sechs geschworenen Meister der Wundärzte, 8 and 22 April 1568.
76   Hammond, "Origins of Civic Health Care", pp. 168–80.
77   Stein, *French Pox*, pp. 119–22.
78   Stuart, *Defiled Trades*, pp. 149–88.

sinner's fat") derived from executed bodies, a popular ingredient for all sorts of medical ointments that was sold in local pharmacies and frequently used by surgeons to treat wounds.

Besides unorthodox local healers like the executioner, the council also granted many itinerant healers permission to sell their medication in the city, usually for a limited period of time and only for specific therapies or illnesses. The council also officially entrusted the members of the *Collegium Medicum* with testing applicants' knowledge and skills and sometimes their products in order to avoid potential health damage to the public. Once in possession of a permit from the *Collegium*, these healers were free to roam the streets and sell their wares. To enhance their public visibility during their limited stay, they often performed on stage or printed and distributed advertisement pamphlets.[79] Some of them, like Doctor Johann Georg Kiesow (1718–86), a former military surgeon from Paris who arrived in Augsburg in 1762, played their cards so cleverly that they not only gained riches, but were also invited by the council to become citizens (to the horror of the local physicians).[80] Kiesow's famous and bestselling *Lebenselexir* (elixir of life), a distilled potion containing, amongst other things, aloe and rhubarb, is still sold today.[81] Whether healers like Kiesow actually increased in number during the seventeenth and eighteenth centuries, as increasingly vociferous complaints by the local community of authorized healers suggest, requires further investigation. It is likely, however, that the increasing pressure on itinerant healers in the surrounding Bavarian territories, particularly under the rule of the enlightened Bavarian medical reformer Anton von Wolter (1711–97), caused more of them to take refuge within the safe walls of the imperial city.[82]

The consumers of medical services in Augsburg cared little about the endless disputes among the local practitioners or their disputes with unauthorized competitors. And they cared even less for the strategic power games the council played with academic physicians and the *Collegium Medicum*. To cope with illness without ever consulting a healer was not uncommon among Augsburg's sick, poor and rich alike. It is indeed striking to what extent the sick were accustomed to diagnose and treat themselves, usually turning to family and friends before seeking professional help. Even sufferers from the lower echelons of society often considered themselves competent judges of their

---

79   See Stein, "Quack", pp. 193–95.
80   For the following, see Probst, *Fahrende Heiler*, pp. 116–18.
81   The *Elisabeth-Apotheke* in Lechhausen continues to sell the elixir.
82   Stein, "Johann Anton von Wolter". For the rise of medical police, see Möller, *Medizinalpolizei*.

physical conditions. Cases like that of the single mother Walburga Reuchard are common: in 1564, Reuchard openly defied the civic medical practitioners' diagnosis of her three-year-old daughter and appealed to the authorities to accept the correctness of her own interpretation of her daughter's symptoms.[83] Applications received by the civic institutions reveal that Augsburg's patients mixed medical advice and services, disregarding the carefully drawn professional boundaries between the local authorized healers. Nor did they care whether the healer they finally chose was a member of the official community or an itinerant "quack". On the other hand, poor patients were willing to seek the advice of academic physicians if they deemed it necessary, while a closer look at the clientele of itinerant healers reveals that those with more education or money, such as members of the Fugger or Welser families, also valued their skills.[84] The rich sources in the Augsburg archives show that, while divided by wealth inequalities, the sick and their medical practitioners lived in a unitarian medical world. They shared the same language about the functioning of the human body and drew on shared knowledge about its relationship to the wider God-created natural world.[85]

5   Conclusion

Early modern Augsburg offered a wide range of medical services to its ailing public. To understand the specific structure and dynamics of this medical landscape, the invisible religious boundaries of the body politic and, even more importantly, of the human body have to be taken into account. The latter, respected by practitioners and patients alike, was a powerful force in organizing the structure and daily life of the city's health care institutions and the hierarchy of its healers. Although the academic physicians, the guardians of the invisible boundary, began to control other healer groups from the 1520s on, their *Collegium Medicum* never became an entirely secure stronghold of academic power over the city's medical marketplace. The understanding of the human body did not allow any healer group to force its competitors out of business, even if they strongly disagreed on many issues and tried their best to depict each other's skills and knowledge as inferior or even dangerous to the public. Close cooperation between specialists of the inner body (the physicians) and

---

83   See Stein, *French Pox*, pp. 143–44.
84   See Stein, "Quack", pp. 192–96.
85   For the concept of the "unitarian medical world", see Jones and Brockliss, *The Medical World*, p. 237; for my own use of it, see Stein, *French Pox*, pp. 15–16.

those of the outer (barber-surgeons in particular) remained the norm. In each medical encounter the voice of the sick – rich or poor, educated or not – was central. Indeed, Augsburg's patients, used to competently judging their own physical state as well as that of others and skilled in medicating themselves, were their healers' most feared critics.

When Augsburg lost its status as an imperial city and became part of the new Bavarian kingdom, the organization of its medical marketplace changed. New institutional power structures were created and older ones, such as the *Collegium Medicum*, disappeared. Further research will have to investigate whether or not these new structures were able to cut across the two persistent but largely invisible boundaries that had stood at the core of the city's medical marketplace since the sixteenth century.

Bibliography

Unpublished Primary Sources
Stadtarchiv Augsburg (StadtAA)
    Collegium Medicum, Ordnungen und Decreta, 1625–1804.
    Collegium Medicum, Fasz. 1.
    St. Martin, Fasz. 6, Prod. 88.

Published Primary Sources
Baldinger, E.G., "Nachrichten von Wien, München und Augsburg über dortige Hospital-Anstalten", *Neues Magazin für Aerzte* 18 (1796), pp. 14–20.
Gasser, A.P., *Unterricht Wieder die Pestilenz*, Augsburg, 1565.
Hutten, U. von, *Von der wunderbarlichen artzney des holtz Guaiacum genant, und wie man die Frantzosen oder blattern heilen sol*, Augsburg, 1519.
Montesquieu, C.-L. de Secondat, Baron de la Brède et de, *Meine Reisen in Deutschland 1728–1729*, transl. H.W. Schumacher, ed. J. Overhoff, Stuttgart, 2014.
Schmid, J., *Kurtzer iedoch Gewisser bericht, dreyer Erblicher kranckheiten, alß da sein Pest, Frantzosen, und Scharbock, wie sie mögen curiert werden ...*, Augsburg, 1667.
Voch, L., *Bürgerliche Baukunst. Zweyter Theil, worinnen von Hospitälern, Lazarethen, Waysen-, Armen- und Findlingshäusern, wie auch von einer besonderen Anlage eines Tollhauses gehandelt wird ...*, Augsburg, 1781.

Secondary Literature
Bátori, I., *Die Reichsstadt Augsburg im 18. Jahrhundert. Verfassung, Finanzen, Reformversuche*, Göttingen, 1969.

Bisle, M., *Die öffentliche Armenpflege der Reichsstadt Augsburg mit Berücksichtigung der einschlägigen Verhältnisse in anderen Reichsstädten Süddeutschlands*, Paderborn, 1904.

Broman, T.H., *The Transformation of German Academic Medicine 1750–1820*, Cambridge, 1996.

Burmeister, K.-H., *Achilles Primin Gasser (1505–1577). Arzt und Naturforscher, Historiker und Humanist. Vol. 1: Biographie*, Wiesbaden, 1970.

Carter, C.K., *The Rise of Causal Concepts of Disease*, Aldershot, 2003.

Clasen, C.-P., "Armenfürsorge in Augsburg vor dem Dreißigjährigen Krieg", *Zeitschrift des Historischen Vereins für Schwaben* 78 (1984), pp. 65–115.

Daston, L., "Wunder, Naturgesetze und die wissenschaftliche Revolution des 17. Jahrhunderts", *Jahrbuch der Akademie der Wissenschaften zu Göttingen* (1991), pp. 99–112.

Deininger, H.-F., "Das Collegium Medicum Augustanum", *Deutsches Ärzteblatt* 61 (1964), pp. 1239–43.

Dietrich, R., *Die Integration Augsburgs in den bayerischen Staat (1806–1821)*, Sigmaringen, 1993.

Duden, B., *The Women Beneath the Skin: A Doctor's Patients in Eighteenth-Century Germany*, Cambridge, MA, 1991.

Ecker-Offenhäußer, U., "'Pest, Frantzosen, Scharbock'. Krankheitserfahrung und medizinischer Alltag des 17. Jahrhunderts im Spiegel der Werke des Augsburger Wundarztes Joseph Schmid", M.A. thesis, University of Augsburg, 1994.

François, E., *Die unsichtbare Grenze. Protestanten und Katholiken in Augsburg 1648–1806*, Sigmaringen, 1991.

François, E., "Augsburger Freiheit und preußische Tyrannei. Montesquies Reisetagebuch durch Deutschland 1729", in J. Burkhardt, T.M. Safley and S. Ullmann (eds.), *Geschichte in Räumen: Festschrift für Rolf Kießling*, Constance, 2006, pp. 73–81.

Gensthaler, G., *Das Medizinalwesen der Freien Reichsstadt Augsburg bis zum 16. Jahrhundert mit Berücksichtigung der ersten Pharmakopöe von 1564 und ihren weiteren Ausgaben*, Augsburg, 1973.

Hammond, M.L., "The Origins of Civic Health Care in Early Modern Germany", Ph.D. diss., University of Virginia, 2000.

Hammond, M.L., "Paracelsus and the Boundaries of Medicine in Early Modern Augsburg", in G.S. Williams and C.D. Gunnoe, Jr. (eds.), *Paracelsian Moments: Science, Medicine, and Astrology in Early Modern Europe*, Sixteenth Century Essays and Studies Series, vol. 64, Kirksville, 2002, pp. 19–33.

Hoffmann, R., "Die Augsburger Bäder und das Handwerk der Bader", *Zeitschrift des Historischen Vereins für Schwaben und Neuburg* 6 (1875), pp. 1–33.

Horanin, M., "Die Pest im frühneuzeitlichen Augsburg. Soziale Konstruktion einer Krankheit", Ph.D. diss., University of Göttingen, 2003.

Jones, C. and Brockliss, L., *The Medical World of Early Modern France*, Cambridge, 1997.

Jütte, R., *Obrigkeitliche Armenfürsorge in deutschen Reichsstädten der frühen Neuzeit. Städtisches Armenwesen in Frankfurt a. M. und Köln*, Cologne, 1984.

Jütte, R., *Ärzte, Heiler und Patienten. Medizinischer Alltag in der frühen Neuzeit*, Munich, 1991.

Kießling, R., *Bürgerliche Gesellschaft und Kirche in Augsburg im Spätmittelalter. Ein Beitrag zur Strukturanalyse der oberdeutschen Reichsstadt*, Augsburg, 1971.

Krug, R.M., "Pest in Augsburg 1348–1351? Eine Studie zur Frage des Pestvorkommens zu Zeiten des Schwarzen Todes in Europa", in R. Kießling (ed.), *Stadt und Land in der Geschichte Ostschwabens*, Augsburg, 2005, pp. 285–321.

Kusukawa, S., "'Aspectio divinorum operum': Melanchton and Astrology for Lutheran Medics", in O.P. Grell and A. Cunningham (eds.), *Medicine and the Reformation*, London, 1993, pp. 33–56.

Labouvie, E., *In anderen Umständen. Eine Kulturgeschichte der Geburt*, Cologne, 2000.

Lengle, P., "Das Augsburger Heilig-Geist-Spital", in W. Pötzl and P. Fassl (eds.), *Herrschaft und Politik. Vom Frühen Mittelalter bis zur Gebietsreform*, Augsburg, 2003, pp. 206–15.

Lindemann, M., *Health and Healing in Eighteenth-Century Germany*, Baltimore, 1996.

Lindemann, M., *Medicine and Society in Early Modern Europe*, Cambridge, 1999.

Ludyga, H., *Obrigkeitliche Armenfürsorge im deutschen Reich vom Beginn der Frühen Neuzeit bis zum Ende des Dreißigjährigen Krieges (1495–1648)*, Berlin, 2010.

Martz, E., "Gesundheitswesen und Ärzte in Augsburg im 16. Jahrhundert", Med. diss., University of Munich, 1950.

Mauer, B., *"Gemein Geschrey" und "teglich Reden". Georg Kölderer – ein Augsburger Chronist des konfessionellen Zeitalters*, Augsburg, 2001.

Möller, C., *Medizinalpolizei. Die Theorie des staatlichen Gesundheitswesens im 18. und 19. Jahrhundert*, Frankfurt, 2005.

Pfeuffer, E. (ed.), *Von der Natur fasziniert ... Frühe Augsburger Naturforscher und ihre Bilder*, Augsburg, 2003.

Probst, C., "Die Reform des Medizinalwesens in Bayern zwischen 1799 und 1808", in E. Weis (ed.), *Reformen im rheinbündischen Deutschland*, Munich, 1984, pp. 195–212.

Probst, C., "Das Medizinalwesen in Bayern im frühen 19. Jahrhundert", in R.A. Müller (ed.), *Aufbruch ins Industriezeitalter. Vol. 2: Aufsätze zur Wirtschafts- und Sozialgeschichte Bayerns von 1750–1850*, Munich, 1985, pp. 479–491.

Probst, C., *Fahrende Heiler und Heilmittelhändler. Medizin von Marktplatz und Landstraße*, Rosenheim, 1992.

Reike, S., *Das deutsche Spitalwesen und sein Recht im Mittelalter*, 2 vols., Stuttgart, 1932 (repr. Amsterdam, 1970).

Reill, P.H., *Vitalizing Nature in the Enlightenment*, Berkeley, 2005.

Roeck, B., *Eine Stadt in Krieg und Frieden. Studien zur Geschichte der Reichsstadt Augsburg zwischen Kalenderstreit und Parität*, 2 vols., Göttingen, 1989.

Salzbrunn, I., "Das Ende des Augsburger Collegium Medicum", *Bayerisches Ärzteblatt* 28 (1973), pp. 156–62.
Seida und Landensberg, F.E. von, *Historisch-statistische Beschreibung aller Kirchen-, Schul-, Erziehungs-, und Wohltätigkeitsanstalten in Augsburg. Von ihren Ursprüngen an bis auf die neuesten Zeiten*, 2 vols., Augsburg, 1812.
Seidl, E., "Der katholische Arzt Joseph von Ahorner (1765–1839)", in C.A. Hoffmann and R. Kießling (eds.), *Die Integration in den modernen Staat*, Constance, 2007, pp. 181–200.
Siemer, S., *Geselligkeit und Methode. Naturgeschichtliches Sammeln im 18. Jahrhundert*, Mainz, 2004.
Siraisi, N.C., *Medieval and Early Renaissance Medicine: Introduction to Knowledge and Practice*, Chicago, 1990.
Siraisi, N.C., "Disease and Symptoms as Problematics Concepts in Renaissance Medicine", in E. Kessler and I. Maclean (eds.), *Res et Verba in the Renaissance*, Wiesbaden, 2002, pp. 217–40.
Stein, C., "Johann Anton von Wolter (1711–1778): A Bavarian Court Physician between *Aufklärung* and *Reform*", in O.P. Grell and A. Cunningham (eds.), *Medicine and Religion in Enlightenment Europe*, Farnham, 2007, pp. 173–93.
Stein, C. *Negotiating the French Pox in Early Modern Germany*, Farnham, 2009.
Stein, C., "'Getting' the Pox: Reflections by an Historian on How to Write the History of Early Modern Disease", *Nordic Journal of Science and Technology Studies* 2, 1 (2014), 53–60.
Stuart, K., *Defiled Trades and Social Outcasts: Honor and Ritual Pollution in Early Modern Germany*, Cambridge, 1999.
Sudhoff, K., "Was geschah mit den (nach erneuter Schau) als leprafrei erklärten und aus den Leprosorien wieder Freigelassenen von behördlicher Seite", *Archiv für Geschichte der Medizin* 6 (1912), pp. 149–54.
Trompeter, J., "Das Augsburger Pilgerhaus", M.A. thesis, University of Augsburg, 1997.
Weeks, A., *Paracelsus: Speculative Theory and the Crisis of Early Modern Reformation*, Albany, 1997.

CHAPTER 4

Textual Representation: Chronicles

Gregor Rohmann

Within the essential series *Die Chroniken der deutschen Städte* ("Chronicles of German Cities"), the Augsburg chronicles comprise no less than nine volumes.[1] Among all German-speaking cities, only the 11 volumes of the Basel chronicles (*Basler Chroniken*) score better[2] – and some important Augsburg texts did not even make it into these edited volumes. This sheer quantity of material calls for further scrutiny, even if we take into account that the *Chroniken der deutschen Städte* series was edited under the auspices of the Bavarian Academy of Sciences in nearby Munich, which has resulted in a regional imbalance.[3] But how do we situate urban chronicles as a literary genre between contemporary conception and scholarly construction? And what other forms of writing about the past were in use in late medieval and early modern Augsburg? This chapter first considers chronicles as a genre; then family books as a specific form of domestic writing; and finally the professionalization of historiography, which seems to be a characteristic feature of Augsburg.

1 Why People Wrote, Exhibited (and Possibly Read) Historiography

Unlike most media of memory, historical writing is marked by the verbal fixing of information. Ritual, ceremony, and other forms of symbolic communication as well as ephemeral, non-written communication forms like the spoken word or songs typically produce a memory that is unstable in content and interpretation. Architecture, monuments, and inscriptions are at the least marked by interpretive ambiguity. Hence, the writing of history as a form of communication about the past has a special quality. But at the same time, its origins are shaped by its interaction with non-verbal media of memory.[4] Within this interplay of communicative forms, the production, possession, and exhibition of history books in the broadest sense may have served a function apart from the

---

1 *Städtechroniken Augsburg*, 9 vols.
2 *Basler Chroniken*, 11 vols.
3 Meyer, *Die Stadt als Thema*, pp. 58–70; idem, "Zur Edition".
4 Graus, "Funktionen", pp. 37–39.

written content.[5] Apparently the book in many cases existed not specifically for reading, but to serve as a token of authority.

As a means of transmitting historical knowledge and political legitimacy, written history was relatively weak compared to other media.[6] Since only a minority of the populace could read and write, the written word must have been a subordinate form of communication.[7] We must therefore consider its functions and usage within the interior communication processes of political and economic elites on the one hand and among urban populations on the other.

Well into early modern times, communication primarily took place in nonliterate forms. Even written texts were usually received not by reading, but by collective listening.[8] Thus they served not only as media of information, but also as focal points of group integration via reproduction of tradition.[9] While earlier research assumed regular readings in ceremonial or ritual contexts,[10] recent studies have called this into question. Possibly most chronicles would be better situated in the context of domestic writing. Few of these works acquired an "official" character or reached a broader urban public.[11] Official transmission of historical memory more often used ephemeral media like performances, plays, and processions, or artefacts, monuments, fountains, inscriptions, and murals inside and outside public buildings.[12] Additionally, by the sixteenth century, broadsheets and other types of printed works began to play a major role in designing and disseminating tradition.

Without doubt, considering the past was often simply a pastime.[13] But this does not mean that memory had no political or socio-cultural functions, even if it was good entertainment. Just as the public tended to enjoy history for its entertaining qualities, the author may have presented it as a didactic means of making a point. Historical writing is thus always marked by an intersection of educational, ceremonial, and entertainment functions.

On the other hand, historical writing could serve the entirely material function of proving legal tenures.[14] During the fifteenth and sixteenth centuries, this authoritative role may have become less important than archival evidence

---

5   Johnston and Dussen (eds.), *The Medieval Manuscript Book*.
6   Graus, "Funktionen", pp. 28–30.
7   Bauer, "Die 'gemein sag'", pp. 40–52.
8   Johanek, "Gedächtnis der Stadt", pp. 356–60.
9   Menke, "Geschichtsschreibung", pt. 1, p. 28.
10 Menke, "Geschichtsschreibung", pt. 2, p. 166.
11 Droste, "Gebrauch und Wirkung".
12 Johanek, "Gedächtnis der Stadt", pp. 353–56 (ritual and performance), 343–47 (monuments), 361–66 (inscriptions).
13 Sprandel, "Kurzweil durch Geschichte".
14 Studt, *Fürstenhof und Geschichte*, pp. 348–49, 381–82, 409–20.

and juridical expertise.[15] But urban chronicles in particular emerged in close proximity to the administrative records of city councils and may thus have preserved their status as a means of supporting political and legal claims, at least temporarily. Equally important for the emergence of town chronicles was the preservation of exemplary knowledge.[16] Thus chronicles had a tangible relation to political practice.

Furthermore, the historical record provided authority for social positions in a twofold sense: The author rendered an account of his own and his peers' actions,[17] and the ruling elite, or part of it, accumulated and monopolised knowledge on how and why to act in a given situation.[18] According to Jan Assmann, this represents the normative function of memory, answering the question: "What shall we do?" The other main function of history, according to Assmann, is formative, responding to the question: "Who are we?"[19] For the most universal function of history may be 'tradition', i.e. the endowment of persons, groups, and institutions with a common understanding of themselves, their origins, position, destiny, status, and goals.[20] As people experienced their world in terms of genealogy and tradition, they defined their status within that world by referencing their origins.[21] An accepted common history served as an integrating core of group-building and established the political and social order. Thus, tradition shaped the production and reception of knowledge about the past. The provenance of a person, group, or institution, however, was less likely to be distinguished by its singularity than by its embeddedness in contemporary imaginations, affiliation with heroic figures and important historical or mythical events, and mobilisation of symbolic power for the construction of tradition. The shaping of history as 'tradition' was thus not fiction, but the truth-status of an account about the past depended on the social status of the speaker and his audience. The more writing was established as a method of recording and communicating history, the more the (re-)construction of tradition became the major concern of historical writing. This goal came to determine the etymological and genealogical efforts of humanist scholars to enhance the seniority and venerability of their and their patrons' country, hometown, or pedigree.[22]

---

15   Graus, "Funktionen", p. 23.
16   Johanek, "Geschichtsbild", pp. 559–61.
17   Johanek, "Geschichtsbild", p. 569.
18   Studt, *Fürstenhof und Geschichte*, pp. 381–82.
19   Assmann, *Das kulturelle Gedächtnis*, pp. 139–42.
20   Graf, *Gmünder Chroniken*, pp. 69–74.
21   Schmidt, *Städtechroniken*, pp. 111–26.
22   Graus, "Funktionen", pp. 43–50.

While *herkommen* ("ancestry", "provenance") attempts to base social status retrospectively on tradition, *gedechtnus* ("memory" in Middle High German) strives to ensure continuation of status into the future. Only the commemoration of forefathers secures the social standing of their progeny.[23] Hence "memory" always implies concern for both salvation and secular remembrance as a generator of social capital. Memory and ancestry are thus just two sides of the same coin, only differing in perspective.[24]

All these functions were usually closely interrelated: example, authority, and provenance are all complementary functions of memory.[25] Conversely, knowledge about the past was and is defined by these functions: Only those memories that are meaningful for the present will be sustained. Every power tells its own history, and every history is determined by power (even if it is told by dissidents).[26] This also determines the norms of production and reproduction of knowledge about the past.

2   Burghers as Historians: Town Chronicles between Genre and Construction

From the thirteenth century onwards, forms of historical writing emerged in cities north of the Alps.[27] The writing of history originated in four specific urban settings: bishops' courts,[28] (mendicant) monasteries,[29] merchants' offices,[30] and councils' chancelleries.[31] Research on urban chronicles as a genre has tended to focus on texts produced in municipal offices and monasteries, neglecting the reciprocity of urban, dynastic, and episcopal historiography.[32]

The origins of urban historiography in a narrower sense were closely linked to the political and economic elites.[33] Historical writing in this context first emerged in the form of singular, isolated records produced within government

---

23   Graus, "Funktionen", pp. 22–23.
24   Müller, *Gedechtnus*, pp. 80–100.
25   Graf, *Exemplarische Geschichten*, pp. 117–18, 228–30.
26   Assmann, *Das kulturelle Gedächtnis*, pp. 32, 66–68.
27   Schmid Keeling, "Town Chronicles"; Johanek, "Gedächtnis der Stadt"; idem (ed.), *Städtische Geschichtsschreibung*.
28   Plessow, *Die umgeschriebene Geschichte*, pp. 173–84; Eckhart, *Ursprung und Gegenwart*.
29   Menke, "Geschichtsschreibung", pt. 2, pp. 169–70.
30   Schmidt, *Städtechroniken*, pp. 23–24.
31   Menke, "Geschichtsschreibung", pt. 1, pp. 2–3.
32   Stein, "Selbstverständnis oder Identität?"
33   Weber, *Geschichtsschreibung*, pp. 25, 171–80.

circles and often concerning crises or conflicts between different elite groups.[34] Such reports ("relations") were intended for internal use within the administration, with a goal of establishing and communicating an official understanding of political events as well as of gathering administrative and political experience.[35] Due to their affinity with administrative routine and their legitimising character, the "relations" typically strove for factual precision and documented legal claims, especially charters and other testimonials.[36] From the fourteenth century onwards, these relations turned into single entries or series of reports in urban administrative accounts.[37] In some cases chancelleries collected such historical notes in special codices, initiating their transformation from isolated reports to regular chronicles.[38]

During the fifteenth century, chronicle writing instigated by the town council became in some places institutionalised as a regular task of the town clerks,[39] the members of a local collegiate church,[40] or the monks of a monastery close to the city's elites. In the archives of early modern cities, chronicles and similar accounts served as reference works for the historical expertise required by city councils.[41] Other roots of urban chronicle writing were independent of the administration, emerging from the everyday writing practices of councilors, merchants, or town officials.[42] But just as official chronicles were kept confidentially for a long time, those written by private persons were usually stored, added to, and read only within the household.[43] Perhaps the most intriguing feature of urban chronicles is the vast number of copies, continuations, edited versions, and excerpts passed down in collections that are very diverse in content, form, and coverage from the fifteenth to the seventeenth century. These collections indicate the broad exchange of historical writing among literate members of the urban population.[44] As this potential public grew with advances in literacy and the popularity of vernacular reading after the late fifteenth century, urban historiography expanded in quantity and quality. Now people from the middling strata of society, albeit excluded from political and

---

34   Menke, "Geschichtsschreibung", pt. 1, p. 3.
35   Ibid., pt. 1, pp. 4, 73–76; pt. 2, pp. 164–66.
36   Ibid., pt. 2, p. 180.
37   Weber, *Geschichtsschreibung*, pp. 11–24.
38   Menke, "Geschichtsschreibung", pt. 1, pp. 57–59; Schmidt, *Städtechroniken*, pp. 24–26.
39   Schmidt, "Über Geschichtsschreibung", pp. 631–32.
40   Schmidt, *Städtechroniken*, pp. 27–28.
41   Schmid, *Geschichte im Dienst der Stadt*.
42   Schmidt, *Städtechroniken*, pp. 23–25.
43   Rohmann, *Clemens Jäger*, pp. 63–67.
44   Rau, *Geschichte und Konfession*, pp. 435–44.

economic decision-making, wrote and read chronicles, some on behalf of elite patrons, but most simply out of individual interest.[45]

But prior to the advent of printing, historical writing had remained limited in dissemination, reception and efficacy. Authors, patrons, and potential readers had lived in relatively exclusive social circles, be they princely courts, urban oligarchies, or monastic communities.[46] This may also be the reason why histories were so seldom published in print before the late sixteenth century. As printing was only profitable if 300 to 500 copies were expected to be sold,[47] works lacking general interest continued to be produced in manuscript form. Only world chronicles, national histories, antique subjects, and the like, which generated a more general interest, were printed regularly.[48] The history of a particular town was transmitted only in comparatively small numbers, and it was cheaper to copy such books than to print them.[49] There were, however, exceptions to the rule: The Strasbourg chronicle of Jakob Twinger von Königshofen was printed in Augsburg in 1474 (apparently successfully, as a second edition was released in 1476).[50] In 1483, Anton Sorg published Ulrich Richenthal's chronicle of the Council of Constance.[51] Augsburg printers like Johannes Bämler seem to have experimented with chronicles at a comparatively early date.[52] And apparently printed urban history could be successful: An anonymous mixture of world and town chronicle named *Chronica von vil vnd mancherlay historien* was printed in Augsburg three times between 1518 and 1521, with a precursor in 1515.[53]

At the same time, print increasingly influenced the contents of urban historiography: Printed books began to be used as sources and models and were copied and integrated into collected volumes along with manuscript material.[54] Broadsides and pamphlets especially, the new media of the Reformation era, found their way into chronicles.[55]

Nearly all publications and interpretations of chronicles have omitted the images that were often integrated into the codex. They have also ignored

---

45   Schneider, *Heinrich Deichsler*, pp. 29–31, 38–40.
46   Johanek, "Historiographie und Buchdruck", pp. 91–93.
47   Brandis, "Handschriften- und Buchproduktion", p. 187.
48   Johanek, "Historiographie und Buchdruck", pp. 116–18.
49   Warken, *Mittelalterliche Geschichtsschreibung*, pp. 354–62.
50   Wolf, "Konrad Bollstatter", p. 63.
51   Happes, "Transformation und Nutzung", p. 77.
52   Wolf, "Konrad Bollstatter", pp. 53–54.
53   Eckhart, *Ursprung und Gegenwart*, pp. 109–17.
54   Johanek, "Historiographie und Buchdruck", pp. 100–2.
55   Tschopp, "Nachrichten", pp. 37–39; on dissemination of news via broadsheet see Chapter 17 in this volume.

specific features such as layout and diagrams. Only recently has research started to consider chronicles as hybrid media.[56] Additionally, we should scrutinise them not as ready-made products of an individual author, but as open texts, marked by intertextuality, mutilation, transfer, and bricolage.[57]

Until very recently, German scholarship considered town chronicles a peculiarity of the Holy Roman Empire, and especially of the autonomous imperial cities.[58] The alleged decline of their autonomy and the integration of many cities into the emerging early modern territorial states was held responsible for a disintegration of the urban chronicle as a genre. Today we know about analogous forms of writing in Italian, French, English, and Netherlandish towns.[59] In addition, not only imperial cities, but also smaller towns that were dependent on a princely ruler knew forms of historical writing.

In general, the concept of a specific genre of 'urban chronicle' seems in need of reappraisal.[60] As Robert Stein has shown, this supposed genre is to a considerable extent the product of existing editions: Until recently, editions of urban chronicles have appeared mainly in Germany with a primary focus on the fourteenth and fifteenth centuries. For later periods, the editors tended to abridge the manuscript texts in typical ways, omitting everything not considered useful for an understanding of that particular town's history. Moreover, they excluded all Latin chronicles. Thus scholars using the resulting editions were led to conclude that town chronicles had been a German phenomenon, especially of the later Middle Ages; predominantly focussed on the town's past; and written in the vernacular.[61] If we scrutinise all urban historical writing, however, we find that people recorded not only the history of their town, but also that of the surrounding territory, the ruling dynasty, the church, and even events on a European scale. Unfortunately, we lack research on urban chronicles after the mid-sixteenth century.[62] Thus the reception, usage, and continuation of urban historiography as reflected in chronicles during early modern times largely remains to be studied.

---

56 Pataki, "Bilder schaffen Identität"; idem, "Antike Form"; idem, "Ein Bürger"; Ott, "Ausstattungsanspruch"; idem, "Von der Handschrift zum Druck".
57 Serif, "Städtische Geschichtsschreibung".
58 Lottes, "Stadtchronistik".
59 Stein, "Selbstverständnis oder Identität".
60 Plessow, *Umgeschriebene Geschichte*, pp. 167–73.
61 Less critical: Johanek, "Gedächtnis der Stadt", pp. 372–79, 397–98.
62 Johanek, "Hofhistoriograph und Stadtchronist", pp. 58, 67–68.

3 "An extraordinarily vivid historical culture"[63]

In Augsburg, the earliest surviving chronicle is an anonymous account of the period from 1368 to 1406.[64] It is followed by Erhard Wahraus' chronicle of events from 1126 to 1445.[65] Both render coherent accounts of their reference periods. Thus the writing of urban history started comparably late here;[66] there was no earlier stage of isolated "relations".[67] This may be due to the fact that medieval Augsburg housed two prolific clerical centers of learning: the cathedral and the Benedictine monastery of Sts. Ulrich and Afra.

Moreover, a rich tradition of historical knowledge was already represented in the city streets in the form of inscriptions and murals on the façades of some wealthy houses.[68] At least one early chronicle was explicitly written as a pattern for such paintings, namely the *Reimchronik* (historical poem) composed by a cleric called Küchlin from 1437 to 1442 for the murals of the mayor Peter von Argon's estate.[69] These were designed to sway the city's founding history in favor of Argon's individual representation of it. Accordingly, Küchlin traced the origins of Augsburg back to the Roman Aeneas tradition and consequently to Troy.[70] In opposition to this vision, the influential councilor Sigismund Gossembrot the elder commissioned Sigismund Meisterlin, a learned monk of Sts. Ulrich and Afra, to write his *Chronographia Augustensium*, covering the period down to 1456. Meisterlin carefully refuted Küchlin's construction of tradition and proposed an autochthonous explanation for the city's origins, which was allegedly founded by the *Vindeliker* people long before Troy or Rome. As the *Chronographia* was first written in Latin, the council commissioned a German translation which became a kind of paradigm of Augsburg's history.[71] Thirty years later, Meisterlin also wrote a seminal chronicle of Nuremberg.[72] Thus the employment of the past in political debates determined Augsburg's historical writing from the beginning. Competing factions within the city council struggled for interpretive hegemony concerning the town's history. This dispute also

---

63 Johanek, "Geschichtsschreibung in Augsburg", p. 179.
64 *Städtechroniken Augsburg* 1, pp. 1–200; Weber, *Geschichtsschreibung*, pp. 32–35.
65 *Städtechroniken Augsburg* 1, pp. 201–62; Weber, *Geschichtsschreibung*, p. 34.
66 Kießling, "Augsburg-Bild", pp. 185–86; Schnith, "Zur Erforschung".
67 Kießling, "Augsburg-Bild", pp. 185–86.
68 Johanek, "Geschichtsschreibung in Augsburg", p. 178.
69 Johanek, "Geschichtsschreibung in Augsburg", p. 167–69.
70 Giersch, "Augsburger Gründungslegende"; Schnith, "Gründungslegenden".
71 *Städtechroniken Augsburg* 1, p. 335–56; Müller, "Humanistische Aspekte"; Müller, "Beitrag der Mönche".
72 Meyer, *Stadt als Thema*, pp. 130–78.

engaged the new tools of the emerging humanist historiography. Due to its political value, the Meisterlin chronicle was printed as early as 1522.[73]

While mendicant monasteries elsewhere played a crucial role in the development of historical writing, the highly respected Benedictines of Sts. Ulrich und Afra provided Augsburg with historical accounts for generations,[74] even establishing their own printing press as early as 1470. Apart from Meisterlin, several other monks from the abbey wrote chronicles: Johannes Frank (1430–62),[75] Clemens Sender (1475–1537),[76] and Veit Bild (1481–1529).[77] Around 1500, Augsburg became one of the centres of the reign of Emperor Maximilian I, whose highly idiosyncratic political ideology exerted strong influence on knowledge about the past.[78] Geographical and cultural affinity to Italian humanism gave Augsburg's historiography its distinctive character well into early modern times, especially when Conrad Peutinger, Achilles Pirmin Gasser, and Marcus Welser turned their attention to the city's Roman origins in the sixteenth century.[79]

From the late fifteenth century onwards, we also know chronicles written by members of the city's elite.[80] Among these, the apologetic reports of the burgomaster Ulrich Schwarz (1422–78), who was eventually executed on charges of tyranny, merit special consideration,[81] as they seem to have initiated the genre of "relations" in Augsburg. A few years later the councilor Hektor Mülich (c. 1420–89/90) wrote his chronicle.[82] Together with his brother Jörg, he was also commissioned to produce a richly illustrated edition of Meisterlin's chronicle, which served as a model for his own writing.[83] But in contrast to the Benedictine Meisterlin, the merchant and politician Mülich was no humanist scholar.[84] At the beginning of the sixteenth century, Mülich's chronicle

---

73   Ott, "Von der Handschrift zum Druck", pp. 21–29.
74   Wolf, "Bollstatter", p. 53.
75   *Städtechroniken Augsburg* 5, pp. 285–42; Weber, *Geschichtsschreibung*, pp. 39–40.
76   *Städtechroniken Augsburg* 4, pp. 1–404; *Städtechroniken Augsburg* 5, pp. 343–409; see also Kramer-Schlette, *Augsburger Chronisten*.
77   Müller and Ziesak, "Veit Bild".
78   Böhm, *Reichsstadt Augsburg*.
79   Goerlitz, "Zur Genese"; Burmeister, *Achilles Pirmin Gasser*, vol. 1, pp. 162–272; vol. 2, pp. 16–25, 49–61; Mauer, "Patrizier als Archäologe"; see also Chapter 22 in this volume.
80   Weber, *Geschichtsschreibung*, pp. 39–41; Kießling, "Augsburg-Bild", pp. 201–15.
81   Weber, *Geschichtsschreibung*, pp. 41–42.
82   *Städtechroniken Augsburg* 3; Pataki, "Bürger"; Weber, *Geschichtsschreibung*, pp. 47–68; Rogge, "Schweigen der Chronisten".
83   Pataki, "Bilder schaffen Identität"; idem, "Antike Form".
84   Johanek, "Geschichtsschreibung in Augsburg", p. 176.

was copied and continued by Jörg Demer, Marx Walther, and Wilhelm Rem.[85] Another influential chronicle by a member of a patrician family was Matthäus Langenmantel's, which survives in several copies and continuations.[86]

But the production of chronicles also spread to the offices of middle-class people, for example the merchant Burkhard Zink, a social climber whose history ranges from 1368 to 1468.[87] More than half a century later, impressed by the events of the Reformation, the painter Jörg Breu the Elder began to document contemporary history.[88] In the later sixteenth century, this sort of domestic recording of events by middle-class people became more frequent; examples include the municipal *Baumeister* (architect and chief engineer) Elias Holl and the brewer Georg Siedeler.[89] A comparatively traditional chronicle was produced by the merchant and councilor Jakob Wagner (1570–1649) during the Thirty Years' War.[90] A similar account, but more detailed and comprehensive, was provided by the teacher Ludwig Hainzelmann.[91]

At the turn of the seventeenth century, the clerk Georg Kölderer (c. 1550–1607) produced a work which in fact is much more than a "chronicle" in the late medieval sense.[92] Kölderer gathered broadsheets, *Zeitungen* (handwritten news circulated within merchants' networks[93]), hearsay, and other information from all over town and processed it into a comprehensive survey of contemporary history. His work thus testifies to the shift from individual writing to the collection of ephemeral information.

Moreover, everyday political business resulted in the production of administrative, propagandistic, and historical texts. The political and confessional conflicts of the Reformation era were expressed in pamphlets, memoranda, surveys, and a range of other texts,[94] which were repeatedly copied, re-written, rearranged, and mingled together with edited versions of older chronicles. These collections of historical records, compiled according to the composer's or his patron's specific requirements, fill the stacks of Augsburg's archive and library today. At least until the end of the seventeenth century, historical writing

---

85   *Städtechroniken Augsburg* 4, pp. 405–71; *Städtechroniken Augsburg* 5, pp. iii–246.
86   *Städtechroniken Augsburg* 5, pp. 361–401; Mauer, "Patrizisches Bewusstsein", pp. 172–74.
87   Johanek, "Geschichtsschreibung in Augsburg", pp. 174–76.
88   *Städtechroniken Augsburg* 6; Cuneo, *Art and Politics*.
89   Meyer (ed.), *Hauschronik*; Kormann, *Ich, Welt und Gott*, pp. 289–94; Stadtarchiv Augsburg, Chroniken 20.
90   Baer et al. (eds.), *Elias Holl*, no. 171; Roeck, *Eine Stadt in Krieg und Frieden*, vol. 1, p. 45.
91   Roeck, *Eine Stadt in Krieg und Frieden*, vol. 1, pp. 45–46.
92   Weber and Strodel (eds.), *Georg Kölderer*; Mauer, "*Gemain Geschrey*"; Tschopp, "Nachrichten".
93   See Chapter 17 of this volume.
94   See Chapter 10 of this volume.

was not only a concern of municipal authorities, but also of domestic interest in wider urban circles.[95] The exploration of this material largely remains a desideratum.

Eighteenth-century historiography in Augsburg is characterized by an intriguing interplay of old and new: Along with the declining influence of the Holy Roman Empire, the status of the free imperial cities was increasingly questioned. Against this background, authors from old patrician families tried to reinvigorate the traditional basis of the city's political order. In 1713, David Langenmantel (1643–1716) published his *Historie des Regiments in des Heiligen Römischen Reichs Stadt Augspurg*. Printed in Frankfurt with later editions in 1725 and 1734, this book exemplifies the general interest which the history of Augsburg received outside its immediate surroundings.[96]

Two generations later, Paul von Stetten the Younger (1731–1808), the last *Stadtpfleger* (mayor) of Augsburg, produced an entire series of books on the history and present state of his hometown. In 1762 he published the *Geschichte der adelichen Geschlechter in der freyen Reichs-Stadt Augsburg*, a comprehensive survey of the town's patrician dynasties.[97] This was followed by the *Neues Ehrenbuch oder Geschichte des adeligen Geschlechtes der von Stetten* (1766),[98] a history of his own family that explicitly referred to their sixteenth-century books of honor (see below). Finally, between 1779 and 1788 he published an economic history of Augsburg in two volumes.[99]

As Augsburg had to defend its independence against neighboring Bavaria,[100] the "golden age" of its history gained new relevance for the identity of urban elites. While authors of the Enlightenment era developed a ground-breaking systematisation of history, they also referred to the tradition of late medieval chronicles in significant ways. They not only copied entire passages from older historical works, but also adapted images from fifteenth- and sixteenth-century codices. But this was no mere imitation: Apparently these models had attained canonical status, so that authors had to refer to them in order to legitimize their own constructions of tradition. Simultaneously, Georg Wilhelm Zapf and Franz Anton Veith, two typical representatives of the antiquarian character of late seventeenth- and eighteenth-century German historiography, published bibliographical collections of scholarly knowledge on the history of

---

95 Rohmann, *Clemens Jäger*, pp. 217–19.
96 Langenmantel, *Historie des Regiments*.
97 Stetten, *Geschichte der adelichen Geschlechter*.
98 Stetten, *Neues Ehrenbuch*.
99 Stetten, *Kunst-, Gewerb- und Handwerks-Geschichte*.
100 Bátori, *Reichsstadt Augsburg*, pp. 174–95; see also Mährle, *Wissenschaftliche Stadtchronistik*.

Augsburg.[101] The urban historiography of eighteenth-century Augsburg thus seems to have adapted to new scholarly developments while at the same time remaining deeply grounded in late medieval learned practice.

4   Augsburg Fathers and Their Books

Within the oligarchic elites, the history of the kin group was linked to that of the town, as the latter was always shaped by the leading families.[102] In some southern German cities, as in Italy or France, it was common practice to record the history of one's own family in a particular book, written usually by the father and stored within the house – a *Familienbuch*.[103]

While noblemen regularly delegated historical writing to local clerics or officials, urban householders almost invariably defined their own historical tradition. Endowed with a position of authority in family and society, they were able to tell their descendants who was part of the kin group and what its history was like. Although most authors were male, there are some instances of female chroniclers, for example the Augsburg brewer's wife Apollonia Hefelin (1582–1619).[104] Women may have produced chronicles as keepers of domestic authority, because their husbands or fathers had died or were tied up with business, or simply because they were more of the bookish type than their husbands.

Typically these records were inherited by the son with the family estate. The younger generation often continued the writing of the elder, using blank pages or creating a new book – not without explicitly invoking the authority of the originator. Thus the family as a diachronic formation was documented in writing: memory created the group, as the name, the house, the coat of arms, the pedigree, and the city's past were interwoven.[105] By securing and defining memory, the father became the founder of his house. Simultaneously, the family book could serve as an inventory for the family's legal evidence. The proper fixation of burials and pious endowments, sometimes including pictorial

---

101   Veith, *Bibliotheca Augustana*; Zapf, *Augsburgische Bibliothek*.
102   Monnet, "La mémoire".
103   Studt, "Haus- und Familienbücher"; idem (ed.), *Haus- und Familienbücher*; Tomaszewski, *Familienbücher*.
104   Staats- und Stadtbibliothek Augsburg, 4° Cod. S. 10; Lenk, *Augsburger Bürgertum*, pp. 169–70; Roeck, *Eine Stadt in Krieg und Frieden*, vol. 1, p. 44.
105   Monnet, *Rohrbach*.

copies of epitaphs, altars, and tombstones, was also a means of securing the ancestors' salvation.[106]

The author could embed his family history into that of his town and its territory, thus sometimes writing a chronicle rather than a family book proper. He could also incorporate the details of his own life at considerable length in order to preserve his experiences for his descendants and ensure his own remembrance. In this case the text assumed characteristics of an autobiography – accordingly, many family books are perceived by modern researchers more as ego-documents than as expressions of collective memory.[107] But the author might also hide his own personality, merely recording it as a link within a long genealogical chain. Hence, chronicle, autobiography, and genealogy intersected within the genre "family book".

The urban elites primarily defined ancestry in terms of the alliances constituted via marriage and through personal and economic communication. It is not accidental, then, that family books tended to record these alliances meticulously, because knowledge of them provided immediate grounds for social dominance. If a family considered itself very old, this knowledge could reach deep into history (often employing apparently fictitious elements). But in many cases it included only three or four generations: grandparents, parents, siblings, and children.

The shape of these family books could take the form of everyday writing. But some were fashioned as richly decorated "coffee-table books",[108] with portraits of family members, coats of arms, calligraphic lettering, and other images. The outward appearance did not always correlate with the family's social position: some noble houses had simple daybooks, while middle-class fathers occasionally commissioned gorgeously illuminated codices.[109] These valuable works of art were not commonly displayed for status representation. Like ancestors' portraits, they were often stored behind closed doors and only exhibited to trustworthy friends and relatives, subject to the same confidentiality as other chronicles.[110] However, access may have been variable, and it was this flexibility that gave the family book the power to define social affiliation. Everybody who participated in knowledge of the kin's past was included in the group. Family books thus circulated within kinship and friendship circles. Knowledge about past alliances made people conscious of their social

---

106 Staub, "Zwischen Denkmal und Monument"; Rohmann, *Clemens Jäger*, pp. 123–205.
107 Ulbrich, "Family and House Books".
108 Paravicini, "Gruppe und Person", pp. 344–45.
109 Bock, "Bebilderte Geschlechterbücher".
110 Rohmann, *Clemens Jäger*, pp. 179–87.

networks and stabilised them as well. Finally, in the process of circulation, knowledge about the past itself became a means of constituting social networks.[111]

As mentioned above, the genres of urban chronicle and family book, construed by later scholars, are so closely intertwined that it is often impossible to keep them apart. For example, the chronicles of Burkhard Zink,[112] Jakob Wagner,[113] Lukas Rem,[114] or Jörg Siedeler[115] merge urban and family history inseparably. Likewise, many middle-class chroniclers cannot be distinguished from fathers writing family books. In both cases, people writing household chronicles tried to retain knowledge about the past primarily for their descendants. Only in retrospect was one particular text perceived as a city chronicle and perhaps stored in the city archive while another was categorized as a private record. In the last twenty years, scholars have finally begun to scrutinise all these codices, as shifting paradigms within historical research led to new questions, such as the anthropology of European kinship, the construction of individual and collective identities, and the cultural reproduction of habitus and social order.[116] Exhibitions in Munich (2010) and Augsburg (2011) paved the way for a more thorough investigation of these books, most of which remain unpublished.[117]

The rich stock of family books in Augsburg has led scholars to presume that the genre may have originated there.[118] In fact, Nuremberg may have been the first German city to produce family books, although from a quantitative perspective Augsburg might sustain the lead. As early as 1469, the patrician Hans Gossembrot collected a combined armorial and family chronicle.[119] Richly decorated books survive for the Welser[120] and Sulzer families.[121] A more pragmatic form was used by the Hainhofers.[122] Some family books produced in Augsburg have not survived, but are identifiable as models for others that were preserved, for example by the Mülich and Meuting families.[123] Matthäus

---

111 Rohmann, "Wissensproduktion", pp. 104–9.
112 Zahnd, *Aufzeichnungen*, pp. 345–56.
113 Baer et al. (eds.), *Elias Holl*, no. 171; Roeck, *Eine Stadt in Krieg und Frieden*, vol. 1, p. 44.
114 Zahnd, *Aufzeichnungen*, pp. 290–92.
115 Tlusty (ed.), *Augsburg during the Reformation Era*, p. 29.
116 Rohmann, *Clemens Jäger*, pp. 170–74; Mauer, "Patrizisches Bewusstsein", pp. 163–76.
117 *Die Fugger im Bild*; Emmendörffer and Zäh (eds.), *Bürgermacht und Bücherpracht*.
118 Rieber, "Patriziat", p. 319.
119 Emmendörffer and Zäh (eds.), *Bürgermacht und Bücherpracht*, no. 19.
120 Mauer, "Patrizisches Bewusstsein", pp. 165–166.
121 Emmendörffer and Zäh (eds.), *Bürgermacht und Bücherpracht*, no. 21.
122 Baer et al. (eds.), *Elias Holl*, no. 184.
123 Rohmann, "Wissensproduktion", p. 107.

Schwarz, grandson of the notorious Ulrich Schwarz and head bookkeeper of the Fugger Company, gave his account a more autobiographical shape by combining it with a series of costume images,[124] while Marx Walther commissioned an illustrated account of his victories in tournaments, and used some free pages to add a short family chronicle and a record of foundations which his father had written.[125]

Around 1550, the town clerk Clemens Jäger began providing urban dignitaries with accounts of their pedigrees (see below). These *Ehrenbücher* (books of honor) soon became a model for other Augsburg families, including the von Stetten, Thenn, Sulzer, Bimmel, and Seitz families.[126] Jäger's most influential book may have been the *Fuggerchronik*, a history of the famous merchant family, which was continuously maintained, re-transcribed, and frequently rewritten until the eighteenth century.[127] Fifty-six copies can still be verified.[128] While this conglomerate of texts is almost unexplored, a coeval and complementary medium of familial memory has recently found proper scrutiny: the *Fuggerorum et Fuggerarum Imagines*, a collection of engraved portraits of all members of the house, published in 1618.[129] The written narrative of the *Fuggerorum Imagines* was reproduced time and again, while the portrait gallery was even printed. Both works far exceeded the boundaries of their original genre. But even the printed collection of engravings presumably was not produced to be sold on the open market. Rather, it appeared as a form of private publishing for distribution among noble circles of kinship and friendship.

The same might be true for the printed *Augsburgische Geschlechterbücher* (Augsburg books of lineage) which began to be published after the number of patrician families was expanded in 1538. First the town clerk Paul Hektor Mair, in collaboration with the artist Christoph Weiditz, produced a collection of engravings, each showing a fantastic knight in shining armour holding the coat of arms of one of the families belonging to the newly constituted urban elite (figures 4.1a–b). In 1545, Hans Burgkmair the Younger and Heinrich Vogtherr the Younger produced a similar work. This concept was repeated after the imperial revision of the city's constitution in 1548, which clearly shows that the volumes met with some success.[130] As other historical information was lacking in these books, they only depicted visually who was part of the urban nobility.

---

124 Groebner, "Kleider des Korpers"; see also Chapter 19 in this volume.
125 Huber (ed.), *Marx Walthers Turnierbuch*.
126 Rohmann, *Clemens Jäger*, pp. 238–88.
127 Meyer (ed.), *Chronik der Familie Fugger*.
128 Rohmann, *Clemens Jäger*, pp. 271–73, 311–15.
129 *Fugger im Bild*, pp. 115–99; Rohmann, *Ehrenbuch*, vol. 1, pp. 41–42.
130 Kaulbach and Zäh (eds.), *Augsburger Geschlechterbuch*.

FIGURE 4.1a Paul Hektor Mair, Geschlechterbuch, 1538. P. xx
STAATS- UND STADTBIBLIOTHEK AUGSBURG, RAR 113

TEXTUAL REPRESENTATION: CHRONICLES 85

FIGURE 4.1b Paul Hektor Mair, Geschlechterbuch, 1538. P. XXI
STAATS- UND STADTBIBLIOTHEK AUGSBURG, RAR 113

While "ordinary" family books, as texts circulating within a social network, constituted the historical knowledge of the municipal elite, these comprehensive *Geschlechterbücher* represent a sort of meta-discourse about collective familial history.

Hence, the Augsburg family book as a specific genre was not limited to textual representation, but often relied on an interplay of text and image. The books were visual representations as much as textual ones, which became even more the case as the production of historical knowledge was commercialized.

5   Professionalizing Historical Knowledge

From its beginnings, powerful patrons who commissioned the writing of history determined its form. But because history as arcane or private knowledge relies especially on the writer's personal authority, in some genres the author's position depended on his own participation in the events or groups described. At the very least, explicit mention of a commission legitimized the text through reference to the patron. Thus Küchlin wrote under commission for Peter von Argon; Sigismund Meisterlin for Sigismund Gossembrot; and Hektor Mülich re-worked Meisterlin's chronicle on behalf of the city council. Some years later, Konrad Bollstatter began to provide several patrons with texts compiled from a standard repertoire of chronicles, including the Saxon world chronicle, the Strasbourg chronicle of Jakob Twinger von Königshofen, and others.[131] Bollstatter also compiled a version of Meisterlin's chronicle, and presumably in 1483 he published a small account of Augsburg's history and holy shrines with the printer Johannes Bämler.[132] In 1536 the Benedictine monk Clemens Sender dedicated his city chronicle to the notorious bonvivant and patron Hieronymus Fugger.

Hence, the political elite of Renaissance Augsburg became used to delegating the production of historical tradition early on. Spending their days at their manors in rural Swabia and Bavaria or visiting other courts, they met noblemen who might have shown them their own splendid historiographical manuscripts. Additionally, they all knew about the magnificent products of imperial propaganda, especially during the reign of Maximilian I. Most of these works had been written by clerics and scholars commissioned by their aristocratic patrons. But the emperor loved to pose as an autobiographic narrator in "his"

---

131   Wolf, "Stadt-Weltchronik", pp. 17–20.
132   Wolf, "Stadt-Weltchronik", pp. 23–28; idem, "Bollstatter", pp. 75–77, 84; Johanek, "Geschichtsschreibung in Augsburg", pp. 178–80.

works. Augsburg fathers were thus familiar with the idea of a "ghost-writer" producing their history.[133]

The most prominent case was the cobbler, town clerk, and toll keeper Clemens Jäger (c. 1500–61). In 1541 the council commissioned him with the organisation of the archival records stored within the city hall. This gave him the opportunity to systematically survey old manuscripts for evidence concerning the city's past. As early as 1532, he had written a report on the 1524 riots concerning the preacher Johann Schilling. As treasurer of the cobblers' guild, he also compiled a chronicle of this corporation. Around 1541 Jäger composed a long poem on the *Herkomen der uralten des heiligen reichs stat Augspurg* ("Origins of the Ancient Holy Imperial City of Augsburg"), which was displayed in the parlor of the cobblers' guildhall. In 1543 a copy of this poem was dedicated to the council. From then on, Jäger became a public historian *avant la lettre*, producing a series of historical accounts for paying wealthy patrons.

Between 1544 and 1548, Jäger wrote a chronicle of the important weavers' guild and two so-called "books of honor" (*Ehrenbücher*) containing the history of the town's constitution and bailiwick (*Vogtei*). The guild mayor Jakob Herbrot received an illustrated history of the commune's government, and his patrician colleague Georg Herwart an *Ehrenbuch* of his family. For Hans Jakob Fugger (1516–75), Jäger wrote the *Fuggersches Ehrenbuch*. In addition, he produced legal surveys and historical memoranda and the marriage register of the patrician *Herrentrinkstube* ("Lords' drinking hall"). Similar to the *Ehrenbücher* of the Herwart and Fugger families, Jäger crafted splendid manuscripts for the Pfister and Linck; a genealogical table for the Welsers; a survey of the pedigree and presumably also a proper family book for the Rehlingers; and a genealogical survey for a branch of the Langenmantels. Hans Jakob Fugger also commissioned him with the prototype of the *Fuggerchronik* and the so-called *Habsburgisches Ehrenwerk*, a two-volume history of the imperial dynasty and its intersections with Augsburg and the Fugger family.[134]

Yet Clemens Jäger was not the only supplier on Augsburg's history market. His colleague as *Ratsdiener* ("apparitor", a town clerk), Paul Hektor Mair, published not only the printed *Geschlechterbuch*, but also a city chronicle which he distributed to interested recipients.[135] Jäger's predecessor as city clerk, Hans Tirol, likewise produced richly illuminated historical manuscripts. He was married to a daughter of the painter and chronicler Jörg Breu the Elder and was thus a brother-in-law of Jörg Breu the Younger, whose workshop

---

133   Rohmann, "Public History"; Mauer, "Patrizisches Bewusstsein", pp. 168–73.
134   Buzási and Pálffy, *Augsburg – Wien – München – Innsbruck*; Kagerer, *Macht und Medien*.
135   *Städtechroniken Augsburg* 7 and 8; Mauer, "Sammeln und Lesen".

carried out the artistic decoration of Jäger's works.[136] Together, Tirol and Breu produced what Heidrun Lange has called the "climax of Renaissance illumination in Augsburg".[137] Tirol wrote an imperial chronicle from Julius Caesar to Charles V; a history of the Habsburg dynasty, the other European monarchies, and their realms; and finally, a comprehensive armorial of the nobility of the Holy Roman Empire. In 1541 the mayor Jakob Herbrot dedicated a gorgeously decorated three-volume copy of these works to King Henry VIII of England; and in 1547, Augsburg's bishop Otto Truchsess of Waldburg presented another set to Charles' son Philip, later Philip II of Spain.

Here we can detect a network of writers and artists connected by marriage, friendship, neighborhood, and collaboration. They acted as creative producers who were more or less dependent on their patrons, none of them gaining an autonomous intellectual position. Rather, Jäger and his peers remained dependent on the market which they had opened up, providing political actors with public relations material on demand.[138] But the fact that they were working simultaneously in the same place might be the most important reason for the unrivalled proliferation of historical writing in Augsburg during the sixteenth century. Their supply met the demands of an urban elite, which after the creation of new patrician families in 1538 and the regime change of 1548 had developed a special demand for familial and historical tradition. Against this background, they constructed textual and visual representations of the city's and its families' origins and ancestry. Additionally, their work stimulated imitators. Together they shaped the identity of Augsburg and its inhabitants down to today.

6   Perspectives

As one of the largest urban centers in the Holy Roman Empire, Augsburg provided the critical mass necessary for the production and reception of historiography. Even compared with the few other cities of similar population size and cultural importance, the output remains remarkable. What distinguishes Augsburg is the emergence of a professionalized body of work as early as the late fifteenth century and especially during the crucial era of the Reformation.

But we should remember that the writing of history was not the only or even the most important medium available for gaining knowledge of the past.

---

136   Rohmann, *Clemens Jäger*, pp. 33–34.
137   Lange, "Einführung", p. 7.
138   Adrian, *Augsbourg*, pp. 319–20; see also Rohmann, *Clemens Jäger*.

Compared with non-written forms of creating memory, it was in fact a peripheral and derivative phenomenon. Its social and cultural functions can only be understood in its specific interrelatedness with these other media. Domestic chronicles in particular may sometimes have been no more than the peculiar hobby of bookish householders, possibly succumbing primarily to local or temporal fashion.

The importance of history for Augsburg's self-conception as a free imperial city, however, is obvious. From its beginnings, Augsburg's historiography was shaped by references to its ancient Roman origins. From the early sixteenth century onwards, interest in the city's past intersected with the emergence of humanist antiquarianism. While academics like Conrad Peutinger, Marcus Welser, or Hieronymus Wolf "invented" modern disciplines like archaeology or Byzantine studies,[139] urban historiography remained the more down-to-earth pursuit of monks, artisans, merchants, urban officials, and councilors.

However, these forms of historical writing mutually influenced one another, as Augsburg was one of the few places in Germany where they could refer to the same points in the past. From the time of the argument between Küchlin and Meisterlin, the autochthonous origins of pagan *Vindelica* constituted a kind of consensual model for the urban society as a whole. Similarly, reference to the battle on the Lechfeld in 955 could serve the needs of different groups and thus form a bridge within the urban cultural environment. Roman republicanism acted as an original myth for the city's administration, and the Roman Empire as a reference point for its relationship to *Kaiser und Reich*.

But simultaneously, historical imagination gained its dynamics from the fact that the past was always used as an arsenal for current political debates.[140] The constitutional change of 1368 legitimized the political status of both guilds (*Gemeinde*) and patricians (*Geschlechter*). The scandalous history of Ulrich Schwarz served as a prototype for the political conflicts of the sixteenth century. Additionally, knowledge about the past as a reservoir of competing traditions became intertwined with Reformation disputes, the remembrance of which later determined historical thinking in a society permanently divided in denominational terms.

Generally speaking, research on late medieval and early modern historiography in Augsburg seems to have peaked about twenty years ago, and unfortunately so, because some desiderata are clearly obvious. Apart from the classical canon of the *Chroniken der deutschen Städte*, we lack philologically sound editions of most works that focus equally on text, image, and transmission.

---

139   Ott, "Konrad Peutinger".
140   Kießling, "Augsburg-Bild", pp. 200–1, 213–15.

In particular, the vast number of later copies and miscellaneous collections, mostly by anonymous writers, is nearly unexplored. Moreover, we need to understand chronicles as open texts, shaped by intertextuality, variation, and bricolage. The interactions of hand-written and printed texts in various contexts also remain to be examined. The enhanced techniques of digital editions may give us new options for the appropriate display of these texts. This would finally enable us to take into account the interrelation of different media: composite forms of text and image, diagrams, and layout could possibly be scrutinised in comparison. The growing engagement with song, pamphlet, pasquil, and other ephemeral forms of textual communication could be made visible. Even the practical context of historical texts in relation to ritual and ceremony may become more comprehensible through a thorough examination of the vast number of unpublished manuscripts in the Augsburg *Stadtarchiv* and the *Staats- und Stadtbibliothek*.

All this would possibly free the exploration of urban chronicles from its traditional context, which at least in Germany has mostly been confined to research on medieval urban society. Simultaneously, one should consider urban chronicle-writing in its widest sense as a subject of its own, not as merely a deficient form of humanist or pre-Enlightenment historiography. If we grasp urban historiography as a genuine phenomenon, we gain new insights into the cultures of memory during a secular media shift.

Bibliography

Unpublished Primary Sources

Staats- und Stadtbibliothek Augsburg, 4° Cod. S. 10.
Stadtarchiv Augsburg, Chroniken 20.

Published Primary Sources

Die Basler Chroniken, ed. Historische und Antiquarische Gesellschaft in Basel (vols. 1–11), Leipzig, 1915–87.
Die Chroniken der schwäbischen Städte, Augsburg
Vol. 1, ed. F. Frensdorff (*Die Chroniken der deutschen Städte vom 14. bis ins 16. Jahrhundert* [CDS] 4), Leipzig, 1865 (repr. Stuttgart, 1966):
  I. Chronik von 1368–1406 mit Fortsetzung bis 1447.
  II. Chronik des Erhard Wahraus 1126–1445 mit Nachträgen zum Jahr 1462.
  III. Chronik von der Gründung der Stadt Augsburg bis zum Jahr 1469.
  Beilage: Die Reimchronik des Küchlin.

Vol. 2, ed. F. Frensdorff (CDS 5), Leipzig, 1866 (repr. Stuttgart, 1966):
   IV. *Chronik des Burkard Zink. 1368–1468.*
Vol. 3, ed. F. Frensdorff (CDS 22), Leipzig, 1892 (repr. Stuttgart, 1966):
   V. *Chronik des Hector Mülich 1348–1487. Mit Zusätzen von Demer, Walther und Rem.*
   VI. *Anonyme Chronik 991–1483.*
Vol. 4, ed. F. Roth (CDS 23), Leipzig, 1894 (repr. Stuttgart, 1966):
   VII. *Die Chronik von Clemens Sender von den ältesten Zeiten der Stadt bis zum Jahre 1536.*
   Anhang: Fortsetzungen der Chronik des Hector Mülich von Demer, Walther und Rem.
Vol. 5, ed. F. Roth (CDS 25), Leipzig, 1896 (repr. Stuttgart, 1966):
   VIII. *"Cronica newer geschichten" von Wilhelm Rem 1512–1527.*
   IX. *Fr. Johannes Franks Augsburger Annalen vom Jahre 1430 bis zum Jahre 1462.*
   Beilagen zur Chronik des Clemens Sender.
Vol. 6, ed. F. Roth (CDS 29), Leipzig, 1906 (repr. Stuttgart, 1966):
   X. *Die Chronik des Augsburger Malers Georg Preu des Älteren. 1512–1537.*
Vol. 7, ed. F. Roth (CDS 32), Leipzig, 1917 (repr. Stuttgart, 1966):
   [XI.] *Paul Hektor Mairs 1. Chronik von 1547–1565.*
Vol. 8, ed. F. Roth (CDS 33), Stuttgart, 1928 (repr. Stuttgart, 1966):
   Das Diarium Paul Hektor Mairs von 1560–63.
   Paul Hektor Mairs 2. Chronik von 1547–65.
Vol. 9, ed. F. Roth (CDS 34), Stuttgart, 1929 (repr. Stuttgart, 1966):
   Die Weberchronik von Clemens Jäger (Der erbern Zunft von Webern Herkommen, Cronika und Jarbuch 955–1545).
Huber, D.J.M. (ed.), *Marx Walthers Turnierbuch. Mit Familienchronik und Stiftungsverzeichnis*, Königsbrunn, 2014.
Langenmantel, D., *Historie des Regiments in des Heiligen Römischen Reichs Stadt Augspurg*, Frankfurt am Main 1713, 2nd ed. 1725, 3rd ed. 1734.
Meyer, C. (ed.), *Chronik der Familie Fugger vom Jahr 1599*, Munich, 1902.
Meyer, C. (ed.), *Die Hauschronik der Familie Holl, insbesondere die Lebensaufzeichnungen des Elias Holl, Baumeisters der Stadt Augsburg*, Munich, 1910.
Rohmann, G., *Das Ehrenbuch der Fugger. Darstellung – Kommentar – Transkription*, 2 vols., Augsburg, 2004.
Stetten, P. von (the Younger), *Geschichte der adelichen Geschlechter in der freyen Reichs-Stadt Augsburg*, Augsburg, 1762.
Stetten, P. von (the Younger), *Neues Ehrenbuch oder Geschichte des adeligen Geschlechtes der von Stetten*, Augsburg, 1766.
Stetten, P. von (the Younger), *Kunst-, Gewerb- und Handwerks-Geschichte der Reichs-Stadt Augsburg*, 2 vols., Augsburg, 1779–88.
Tlusty, B.A. (ed.), *Augsburg during the Reformation Era: An Anthology of Sources*, Indianapolis, 2012.

Veith, F.A, *Bibliotheca Augustana, complectens notitias varias de vita et scriptis eruditorum quos Augusta Vindelica orbi litterato vel dedit vel aluit*, 12 vols., Augsburg, 1785–96.

Weber, W.E.J. and Strodel, S. (eds.), *Georg Kölderer, Beschreibunng vnnd Kurtze Vertzaichnus Fürnemer Lob vnnd gedenckhwürdiger Historien. Eine Chronik der Stadt Augsburg der Jahre 1576–1607*, Augsburg, 2013.

Zapf, G.W., *Augsburgische Bibliothek, oder historisch-kritisch-literarisches Verzeichnis aller Schriften, welche die Stadt Augsburg angehen und deren Geschichte erläutern*, 2 vols., Augsburg, 1795.

Secondary Literature

Assmann, J., *Das kulturelle Gedächtnis. Schrift, Erinnerung und politische Identität in frühen Hochkulturen*, Munich, 1992.

Baer, W., Kruft, H.W. and Roeck, B. (eds.), *Elias Holl und das Augsburger Rathaus*, Regensburg, 1985.

Bátori, I., *Die Reichsstadt Augsburg im 18. Jahrhundert. Verfassung, Finanzen, Reformversuche*, Göttingen, 1969.

Bauer, M., "Die 'gemein sag' im späteren Mittelalter. Studien zu einem Faktor mittelalterlicher Öffentlichkeit und seinem historischen Auskunftswert", Ph.D. diss., Univ. Erlangen-Nuremberg, 1981.

Bayerische Staatsbibliothek (ed.), *Die Fugger im Bild. Selbstdarstellung einer Familiendynastie der Renaissance* (exhibition catalogue), Lucerne, 2010.

Bock, H., "Bebilderte Geschlechterbücher", in Emmendörffer and Zäh (eds.), *Bürgermacht und Bücherpracht*, vol. 1, pp. 57–66.

Böhm, C., *Die Reichsstadt Augsburg und Kaiser Maximilian I. Untersuchungen zum Beziehungsgeflecht zwischen Reichsstadt und Herrscher an der Wende zur Neuzeit*, Sigmaringen, 1998.

Brandis, T., "Handschriften- und Buchproduktion im 15. und frühen 16. Jahrhundert", in L. Grenzmann and K. Stackmann (eds.), *Literatur und Laienbildung im Spätmittelalter und in der Reformationszeit*, Stuttgart, 1984, pp. 176–96.

Burmeister, K.H., *Achilles Pirmin Gasser 1505–1577. Arzt und Naturforscher, Historiker und Humanist*, 3 vols., Wiesbaden, 1970–75.

Buzási, E. and Pálffy, G., *Augsburg – Wien – München – Innsbruck. Die frühesten Darstellungen der heiligen Krone Ungarns und die Entstehung der Exemplare des Ehrenspiegels des Hauses Österreich. Gelehrten- und Künstlerbeziehungen im Mitteleuropa in der zweiten Hälfte des 16. Jahrhunderts*, Budapest, 2015.

Cuneo, P.F., *Art and Politics in Early Modern Germany: Jörg Breu the Elder and the Fashioning of Political Identity, ca. 1475–1536*, Leiden, 1998.

Droste, H., "Zu zeitgenössischem Gebrauch und Wirkung von Stadtchroniken – das Beispiel Lüneburg", *Niedersächsisches Jahrbuch für Landesgeschichte* 73 (2001), pp. 271–93.

Dunphy, R.G. (ed.), *The Encyclopedia of the Medieval Chronicle*, 2 vols., Leiden, 2010.

Eckhart, P., *Ursprung und Gegenwart. Geschichtsschreibung in der Bischofsstadt und das Werk des Konstanzer Notars Beatus Widmer (1475–ca. 1533)*, Stuttgart, 2016.

Emmendörffer, C. and Zäh, H. (eds.), *Bürgermacht und Bücherpracht. Augsburger Ehren- und Familienbücher der Renaissance* (exhibition catalogue), 2 vols., Lucerne, 2011.

Giersch, P., "Die Augsburger Gründungslegende – Motiventwicklung und Motivverknüpfung im Mittelalter", *Zeitschrift des Historischen Vereins für Schwaben* 97 (2004), pp. 7–46.

Goerlitz, U., "'… sine aliquo verborum splendore …'. Zur Genese frühneuzeitlicher Mittelalter-Rezeption im Kontext humanistischer Antike-Transformation: Konrad Peutinger und Kaiser Maximilian I.", in J. Helmrath, A. Schirrmeister and S. Schlelein (eds.), *Historiographie des Humanismus. Literarische Verfahren, soziale Praxis, geschichtliche Räume*, Berlin, 2013, pp. 85–110.

Graf, K., *Gmünder Chroniken im 16. Jahrhundert. Texte und Untersuchungen zur Geschichtsschreibung der Reichsstadt Schwäbisch Gmünd*, Schwäbisch Gmünd, 1984.

Graf, K., *Exemplarische Geschichten. Thomas Lirers 'Schwäbsche Chronik' und die 'Gmünder Kaiserchronik'*, Munich, 1987.

Graus, F., *Funktionen der spätmittelalterlichen Geschichtsschreibung*, in H. Patze (ed.), *Geschichtsschreibung und Geschichtsbewußtsein im späten Mittelalter*, Sigmaringen, 1987, pp. 11–55.

Groebner, V., "Die Kleider des Körpers des Kaufmanns: Zum 'Trachtenbuch' eines Augsburger Kaufmanns im 16. Jahrhundert", *Zeitschrift für Historische Forschung* 25 (1998), pp. 329–58.

Happes, J., "Transformation und Nutzung der Konstanzer Konzilschronik im späten 15. Jahrhundert", *Mitteilungen der Residenzen-Kommission der Akademie der Wissenschaften zu Göttingen* n.s. 4 (2015), pp. 69–81.

Janota, J. and Williams-Krapp, W. (eds.), *Literarisches Leben in Augsburg während des 15. Jahrhunderts*, Tübingen, 1995.

Johanek, P. (ed.), *Städtische Geschichtsschreibung im späten Mittelalter*, Cologne, 2000.

Johanek, P., "Historiographie und Buchdruck im ausgehenden 15. Jahrhundert", in K. Andermann (ed.), *Historiographie am Oberrhein im späten Mittelalter und in der frühen Neuzeit*, Sigmaringen, 1988, pp. 89–120.

Johanek, P., "Hofhistoriograph und Stadtchronist", in W. Haug and B. Wachinger (eds.), *Autorentypen*, Tübingen, 1991, pp. 50–68.

Johanek, P., "Geschichtsschreibung und Geschichtsüberlieferung in Augsburg am Ausgang des Mittelalters", in Janota and Williams-Krapp (eds.), *Literarisches Leben*, pp. 160–82.

Johanek, P., "Geschichtsbild und Geschichtsschreibung in den sächsischen Städten im 15. und 16. Jahrhundert", in M. Puhle (ed.), *Hanse – Städte – Bünde. Die sächsischen Städte zwischen Elbe und Weser um 1500*, vol. 1, Magdeburg, 1996, pp. 557–74.

Johanek, P., "Das Gedächtnis der Stadt. Stadtchronistik im Mittelalter", in G. Wolf and N.H. Ott (eds.), *Handbuch Chroniken des Mittelalters*, Berlin, 2016, pp. 337–98.

Johnston, M. and Dussen, M. van (eds.), *The Medieval Manuscript Book: Cultural Approaches*, Cambridge, 2015.

Kagerer, A., *Macht und Medien um 1500. Selbstinszenierungen und Legitimationsstrategien von Habsburgern und Fuggern*, Berlin, New York, 2017.

Kaulbach, H.M. and Zäh, H. (eds.), *Das Augsburger Geschlechterbuch – Wappenpracht und Figurenkunst*, Lucerne, 2012.

Kießling, R., "Zum Augsburg-Bild in der Chronistik des 15. Jahrhunderts", in Janota and Williams-Krapp (eds.), *Literarisches Leben*, pp. 183–215.

Kormann, E., *Ich, Welt und Gott. Autobiographik im 17. Jahrhundert*, Cologne, 2004.

Kramer-Schlette, K., *Vier Augsburger Chronisten der Reformationszeit. Die Behandlung und Deutung der Zeitgeschichte bei Clemens Sender, Wilhelm Rem, Georg Preu und Paul Hektor Mair*, Lübeck, 1970.

Lange, H., "Einführung", in Emmendörffer and Zäh (eds.), *Bürgermacht und Bücherpracht*, vol. 2, p. 7.

Lenk, L., *Augsburger Bürgertum im Späthumanismus und Frühbarock (1580–1700)*, Augsburg, 1968.

Lottes, G., "Stadtchronistik und städtische Identität. Zur Erinnerungskultur der frühneuzeitlichen Stadt", *Mitteilungen des Vereins für Geschichte der Stadt Nürnberg* 87 (2000), pp. 47–58.

Mährle, W., "Wissenschaftliche Stadtchronistik im Zeitalter der Aufklärung. Die Geschichte der Heiligen Römischen Reichs Freyen Stadt Augsburg (1743/58) von Paul IV. von Stetten", in O. Fejtová et al. (eds.), *Historiography Connected with Cities: Historiography of Cities and in Cities*, Prague, 2018, pp. 543–73.

Mauer, B., "Der Patrizier als Archäologe: Markus Welser und Augsburgs römische Vergangenheit", in B. Kirchgässner and H.P. Becht (eds.), *Stadt und Archäologie*, Stuttgart, 2000, pp. 81–100.

Mauer, B., "Patrizisches Bewusstsein in Augsburger Chroniken, Wappen- und Ehrenbüchern", in W. Rösener (ed.), *Adelige und bürgerliche Erinnerungskulturen*, Göttingen, 2000, pp. 163–76.

Mauer, B., "Sammeln und Lesen – Drucken und Schreiben. Die vier Welten des Augsburger Ratsdieners Paul Hector Mair", in F. Mauelshagen and B. Mauer (eds.), *Medien und Weltbilder im Wandel der Frühen Neuzeit*, Augsburg, 2000, pp. 107–32.

Mauer, B., *"Gemain Geschrey" und "teglich Reden". Georg Kölderer – ein Augsburger Chronist des konfessionellen Zeitalters*, Augsburg, 2001.

Menke, J.B., "Geschichtsschreibung und Politik in den deutschen Städten des Spätmittelalters. Die Entstehung deutscher Geschichtsprosa in Köln, Braunschweig, Lübeck, Mainz und Magdeburg [Pt. I]", *Jahrbuch des Kölnischen Geschichtsvereins* 33 (1958), pp. 1–84.

Menke, J.B., "Geschichtsschreibung und Politik in den deutschen Städten des Spätmittelalters. Die Entstehung deutscher Geschichtsprosa in Köln, Braunschweig, Lübeck, Mainz und Magdeburg [Pt. II]", *Jahrbuch des Kölnischen Geschichtsvereins* 34–35 (1960), pp. 85–194.

Meyer, C., *Die Stadt als Thema. Nürnbergs Entdeckung in Texten um 1500*, Ostfildern, 2009.

Meyer, C., "Zur Edition der Nürnberger Chroniken in den 'Chroniken der deutschen Städte'", *Mitteilungen des Vereins für Geschichte der Stadt Nürnberg* 97 (2010), pp. 1–29.

Monnet, P., *Les Rohrbach de Francfort. Pouvoirs, affaires et parenté à l'aube de la Renaissance allemande*, Genève, 1997.

Monnet, P., "La mémoire des élites urbaines dans l'Empire à la fin du Moyen Âge entre écriture de soi et histoire de la cité", in H. Brand, P. Monnet and M. Staub (eds.), *Memoria, Communitas, Civitas. Mémoire et conscience urbaines en occident à la fin du Moyen Âge*, Ostfildern, 2003, pp. 49–70.

Müller, G.M., "'Quod non sit honor Augustensibus si dicantur a Teucris ducere originem'. Humanistische Aspekte in der Chronographia Augustensium des Sigismund Meisterlin", in idem (ed.), *Humanismus und Renaissance*, pp. 237–74.

Müller, G.M. (ed.), *Humanismus und Renaissance in Augsburg. Kulturgeschichte einer Stadt zwischen Spätmittelalter und Dreißigjährigem Krieg*, Berlin, 2010.

Müller, H., "Der Beitrag der Mönche zum Humanismus im spätmittelalterlichen Augsburg. Sigismund Meisterlin und Veit Bild im Vergleich", in Müller (ed.), *Humanismus und Renaissance*, pp. 389–407.

Müller, H. and Ziesak, A.K., "Der Augsburger Benediktiner Veit Bild und der Humanismus", *Zeitschrift des Historischen Vereins für Schwaben* 95 (2002), pp. 27–52.

Müller, J.D., *Gedechtnus. Literatur und Hofgesellschaft um Maximilian I.*, Munich, 1982.

Pataki, Z.A., "Bilder schaffen Identität. Zur Konstruktion eines städtischen Selbstbildes in den Illustrationen der Augsburger Chronik Sigismund Meisterlins 1457–1480", in C. Dartmann and C. Meyer (eds.), *Identität und Krise? Zur Deutung vormoderner Selbst-, Welt- und Fremderfahrungen*, Münster, 2007, pp. 99–118.

Ott, M., "Konrad Peutinger und die Inschriften des römischen Augsburg. Die 'Romanae vetustatis fragmenta' von 1505 im Kontext des gelehrten Wissens nördlich und südlich der Alpen", in Müller (ed.), *Humanismus und Renaissance*, pp. 275–91.

Ott, N.H., "Zum Ausstattungsanspruch illustrierter Stadtchroniken", in S. Füssel and J. Knape (eds.), *Poesis et pictura. Studien zum Verhältnis von Text und Bild in Handschriften und alten Drucken, Festschrift für Dieter Wuttke zum 60. Geburtstag*, Baden-Baden, 1989, pp. 77–109.

Ott, N.H., "Von der Handschrift zum Druck und retour: Sigismund Meisterlins Chronik der Stadt Augsburg in der Handschriften- und Druck-Illustration", in J.R. Paas (ed.), *Augsburg, die Bilderfabrik Europas*, Augsburg, 2001, pp. 21–29.

Paravicini, W., "Gruppe und Person. Repräsentation durch Wappen im späteren Mittelalter", in O.G. Oexle and A. von Hülsen-Esch (eds.), *Die Repräsentation der Gruppen: Texte – Bilder – Objekte*, Göttingen, 1998, pp. 327–89.

Pataki, Z.A., "Antike Form und humanistischer Sinn – Die Illustrationen der Göttin Cisa in den Augsburger Abschriften der Stadtchronik Sigismund Meisterlins 1457–1530", in L.E. Saurma-Jeltsch and T. Frese (eds.), *Zwischen Mimesis und Vision: Zur städtischen Ikonographie am Beispiel Augsburgs*, Münster, 2010, pp. 59–100.

Pataki, Z.A., "Ein Bürger blickt auf seine Stadt. Zur Rezeption und Funktion des Stadtbildes bei Hektor Mülich 1455/57", in: S. Albrecht (ed.), *Stadtgestalt und Öffentlichkeit: Die Entstehung politischer Räume in der Stadt der Vormoderne*, Cologne, 2010, pp. 121–46.

Plessow, O., *Die umgeschriebene Geschichte: Spätmittelalterliche Historiographie in Münster zwischen Bistum und Stadt*, Cologne, 2006.

Rau, S., *Geschichte und Konfession: Städtische Geschichtsschreibung und Erinnerungskultur im Zeitalter von Reformation und Konfessionalisierung in Bremen, Breslau, Hamburg und Köln*, Hamburg, 2002.

Rieber, A., "Das Patriziat von Ulm, Augsburg, Ravensburg, Memmingen, Biberach", in H. Rößler (ed.), *Deutsches Patriziat 1430–1740*, Limburg a.d. Lahn, 1968, pp. 299–351.

Roeck, B., *Eine Stadt in Krieg und Frieden. Studien zur Geschichte der Reichsstadt Augsburg zwischen Kalenderstreit und Parität*, 2 vols., Göttingen, 1989.

Rogge, J., "Vom Schweigen der Chronisten. Überlegungen zu Darstellung und Interpretation von Ratspolitik sowie Verfassungswandel in den Chroniken von Hektor Mülich, Ulrich Schwarz und Burkhard Zink", in Janota and Williams-Krapp (eds.), *Literarisches Leben*, pp. 216–39.

Rohmann, G., *"Eines Erbaren Raths gehorsamer amptman": Clemens Jäger und die Geschichtsschreibung des 16. Jahrhunderts*, Augsburg, 2001.

Rohmann, G., "'mit ser grosser muhe vnd schreiben an ferre Ort'. Wissensproduktion und Wissensvernetzung in der deutschsprachigen Familienbuchschreibung des 16. Jahrhunderts", in Studt (ed.), *Haus- und Familienbücher*, pp. 87–120.

Rohmann, G., "Public History im 16. Jahrhundert. Clemens Jäger (1500–1561) und die Augsburger Ehrenbücher", in Emmendörffer and Zäh (eds.), *Bürgermacht und Bücherpracht*, vol. 1, pp. 37–42.

Schmid, R., *Geschichte im Dienst der Stadt: Amtliche Historie und Politik im Spätmittelalter*, Zurich, 2009.

Schmid Keeling, R., "Town Chronicles", in Dunphy (ed.), *Encyclopedia of the Medieval Chronicle*, vol. II, pp. 1432–38.

Schmidt, H., *Die deutschen Städtechroniken als Spiegel des bürgerlichen Selbstverständnisses im Spätmittelalter*, Göttingen, 1958.

Schmidt, H., "Über Geschichtsschreibung in norddeutschen Städten des späten Mittelalters und der Reformationszeit", in C. Meckseper (ed.), *Stadt im Wandel*.

Kunst und Kultur des Bürgertums in Norddeutschland 1150–1650, Stuttgart, 1985, pp. 627–42.

Schneider, J., *Heinrich Deichsler und die Nürnberger Chronistik des 15. Jahrhunderts*, Wiesbaden, 1991.

Schnith, K., "Mittelalterliche Augsburger Gründungslegenden", in *Fälschungen im Mittelalter. Internationaler Kongreß der Monumenta Germaniae Historica, München, 16.–19. September 1986*, Hanover, 1988, vol. 1, pp. 497–517.

Schnith, K., "Zur Erforschung der spätmittelalterlichen Augsburger Historiographie in den letzten fünfzig Jahren", *Zeitschrift für Bayerische Landesgeschichte* 60 (1997), pp. 479–89.

Serif, I., "Städtische Geschichtsschreibung in neuen Kontexten. Vernetzung, Aneignung, (Re-)Funktionalisierung", *Mitteilungen der Residenzen-Kommission der Akademie der Wissenschaften zu Göttingen* n.s. 4 (2015), pp. 83–90.

Sprandel, R., "Kurzweil durch Geschichte. Studien zur spätmittelalterlichen Geschichtsschreibung in Deutschland", in E. Ruhe and R. Behrens (eds.), *Mittelalterbilder aus neuer Perspektive: Diskussionsansätze zur amour courtois, Subjektivität in der Dichtung und Strategien des Erzählens*, Munich, 1985, pp. 344–63.

Staub, M., "Zwischen Denkmal und Monument. Nürnberger Geschlechterbücher und das Wissen von der Vergangenheit", in idem and K. Vogel (eds.), *Wissen und Gesellschaft in Nürnberg um 1500*, Nuremberg, 1999, pp. 83–104.

Stein, R., "Selbstverständnis oder Identität? Städtische Geschichtsschreibung als Quelle für die Identitätsforschung", in H. Brand, P. Monnet and M. Staub (eds.), *Memoria, Communitas, Civitas. Mémoire et conscience urbaines en occident à la fin du Moyen Âge*, Ostfildern, 2003, pp. 181–202.

Studt, B., *Fürstenhof und Geschichte: Legitimation durch Überlieferung*, Cologne, 1992.

Studt, B., "Haus- und Familienbücher", in J. Pauser, M. Scheutz and T. Winkelbauer (eds.), *Quellenkunde zur Habsburgermonarchie in der frühen Neuzeit (16.–18. Jahrhundert)*, Vienna, 2004.

Studt, B. (ed.), *Haus- und Familienbücher in der städtischen Gesellschaft des Spätmittelalters und der frühen Neuzeit*, Cologne, 2007, pp. 753–66.

Tomaszewski, M., *Familienbücher als Medien städtischer Kommunikation: Untersuchungen zur Basler Geschichtsschreibung im 16. Jahrhundert*, Tübingen, 2017.

Tschopp, S.S., "Wie aus Nachrichten Geschichte wird: Die Bedeutung publizistischer Quellen für die Augsburger Chronik des Georg Kölderer", *Daphnis* 37 (2008), pp. 33–78.

Ulbrich, C., "Family and House Books in Late Medieval German Speaking Areas. A Research Overview", in idem, K. von Greyerz and L. Heiligensetzer (eds.), *Mapping the 'I'. Research on Self-Narratives in Germany and Switzerland*, Leiden, 2015, pp. 209–26.

Warken, N., "Mittelalterliche Geschichtsschreibung in Straßburg: Studien zu ihrer Funktion und Rezeption bis zur frühen Neuzeit", Ph.D. diss., Saarbrücken, 1995.

Weber, D., *Geschichtsschreibung in Augsburg. Hektor Mülich und die reichsstädtische Chronistik des Spätmittelalters*, Würzburg, 1984.

Wolf, J., "Die 'Augsburger Stadt-Weltchronik' Konrad Bollstatters: Untersuchung und Edition", *Zeitschrift des Historischen Vereins für Schwaben* 87 (1994), pp. 13–38.

Wolf, J., "Konrad Bollstatter und die Augsburger Geschichtsschreibung. Die letzte Schaffensperiode", *Zeitschrift für deutsches Altertum und Literatur* 125 (1996), pp. 51–86.

Zahnd, U.M., *Die autobiographischen Aufzeichnungen Ludwig von Diesbachs. Studien zur spätmittelalterlichen Selbstdarstellung im oberdeutschen und schweizerischen Raume*, Berne, 1986.

PART 2

Economy, Politics, and the Law

∵

CHAPTER 5

Production, Trade, and Finance

Mark Häberlein

Along with Nuremberg, Augsburg emerged as the major center of production, trade, and finance in south Germany in the later Middle Ages and was among the pre-eminent commercial cities of Europe in the sixteenth century. The city's merchant companies – among whom the Fuggers and Welsers were only the most prominent – extended loans to European monarchs, controlled a significant share of the continent's silver and copper production, and engaged in sophisticated financial operations. Sporadically, they even ventured into the spice, gemstone, and sugar trades with Asia and the New World, thus playing a pioneering role in the forging of intercontinental connections and the emergence of global markets. But while some historians working on the great merchant corporations have tended to see their activities as manifestations of a "golden age" of Augsburg's commerce, others have maintained that these achievements were tarnished by economic woes (especially an unbalanced craft sector dominated by a veritable army of poor weavers) and by an unstable business environment that led to numerous bankruptcies.

Building on the extensive literature, the following chapter examines fustian weaving and long-distance trade as the twin foundations of the economy of early modern Augsburg and identifies their strengths and weaknesses. It also considers several other aspects that affected the city's economic well-being: the specialized production of luxury goods, credit markets, and the role of the public sector. Moreover, it provides a diachronic perspective by surveying the expansion of Augsburg's economy during the fifteenth and sixteenth centuries, the disastrous impact of the Thirty Years' War, and the city's postwar recovery as a center of textile production, banking, and metal-working, which highlights its remarkable resilience in the face of economic and political disruption.

1 Fustian Weaving and Commercial Expansion: The Late Medieval Economy

In the latter half of the fourteenth century, Swabian weavers began to combine cotton, imported from the eastern Mediterranean by merchants trading in Venice, with homegrown flax yarn. The resulting fabric, fustian (*Barchent* in German), had been developed in Italy, but now it triggered an economic boom in Swabia. As production processes were standardized and urban authorities monitored quality standards, the new product acquired a sound reputation on European markets. Weavers in the imperial cities of Augsburg, Ulm, Ravensburg, Memmingen, Biberach, and Kaufbeuren concentrated on fustian production, while urban merchants used their commercial relations with Venice and Genoa to import cotton and distribute the finished cloth in important market centers. In the course of the fifteenth century, merchants also came to play a growing role in the organization of regional textile production by advancing credit to weavers. These activities led to the emergence of one of the great late medieval European regions of craft production, which extended from Lake Constance to the rivers Danube and Lech.[1]

As the fifteenth century wore on, Augsburg and Ulm left other Swabian cities behind and established themselves as the leading centers of fustian production and long-distance commerce. Excise (*Ungeld*) lists, which record the indirect taxes collected by the city of Augsburg, reveal an annual production of 12,000 pieces of cloth in 1385; only 25 years later the figure had risen to over 85,000 pieces per year. The weavers' guild was able to purchase its own guild house in 1389, and shortly afterwards Augsburg fustians were traded at the important fairs in Frankfurt am Main. By around 1400, they were also marketed in Cologne, Prague, Wrocław, Krakow, and Vienna. But the fustian boom was accompanied by rising social tensions: local riots broke out 1397 in which poor weavers protested against the imposition of new excise taxes.[2]

The boom's main beneficiaries were long-distance merchants. Some hailed from established patrician families, while others, like the Artzt and Hämmerlin families, emerged from the ranks of the weavers' guild, and still others were immigrants from smaller Swabian textile towns like Lauingen, Nördlingen, and Donauwörth.[3] Between 1293 and 1440, at least 36 Augsburg merchants visited the Nördlingen Pentecost fair, a major rendezvous for south German trade in the late Middle Ages; nearly all of them were marketing textiles.[4]

Augsburg experienced substantial economic growth in the fifteenth century, as the number of taxpayers increased from slightly less than 3,000 in 1408 to almost 4,800 in 1461 and to 5,351 in 1498.[5] But the urban economy was subject to recurrent crises as well. Some of these slumps were caused by political

---

1 Kießling, *Kleine Geschichte Schwabens*, p. 53.
2 Kießling, "Augsburgs Wirtschaft", p. 175; idem, *Die Stadt und ihr Land*, pp. 721, 723–25.
3 Kießling, "Augsburgs Wirtschaft", p. 177; Jahn, "Augsburger Sozialstruktur", p. 188.
4 Steinmeyer, *Nördlinger Pfingstmesse*, pp. 84–89.
5 Jahn, "Augsburger Sozialstruktur", p. 188; Kießling, *Die Stadt und ihr Land*, pp. 715–17.

and military conflict: Emperor Sigismund repeatedly imposed trade bans on Venice, the major supplier of cotton to German merchants, between 1412 and 1433. At mid-century, the Second City War interrupted trade routes once again, and the war of the Holy Roman Empire against Duke Ludwig of Bavaria-Landshut in the 1460s likewise had adverse effects on the economy of Swabian cities. Augsburg's indirect tax revenues indicate a severe crisis of urban production from about 1450 to 1480. Amidst this difficult period, new excise riots broke out in 1466 when poorer artisans vented their frustration over high taxes. Nonetheless, fustian production continued on a large scale: In 1475, when the crisis was not yet over, 550 weavers brought 43,400 pieces to the urban bleachery. When inferior types of cloth, which were not bleached but dyed, are included, the production volume may have come to 65,000 pieces. By the end of the century, 900 to 1,000 weavers were producing 70,000 to 80,000 pieces of cloth per annum. Augsburg's craft sector was decidedly unbalanced, as about one-quarter of the city's guild members were involved in the making and finishing of fustian.[6]

City authorities responded to the vulnerability of the local textile sector by imposing restrictions on the putting-out system, in which merchants advanced cotton to rural weavers and collected the finished cloth from them. When urban weavers protested against competition from the countryside in 1411, Augsburg prohibited the putting-out system in the textile sector within a radius of three German miles (c. 20 km) around the city. This prohibition was subsequently renewed on several occasions. Yet the production of flax yarn and *Wepfen* (a semi-finished product) in the countryside remained of great importance to urban fustian production. In 1443, Augsburg established a *Wepfenschau*, an institution for monitoring the quality of this flax fabric. While this institution survived only a short time, yarn and *Wepfen* imports from the countryside were a well-established feature of the urban textile economy in the later fifteenth century. The region supplying flax yarn to Augsburg extended as far as the Allgäu (the southernmost part of Swabia) and Bavaria.[7]

As the century drew to a close, flax yarn imports from central Germany and Silesia caused massive conflicts once again. Whereas poorer weavers maintained that these imports increased their dependence on the merchants and voiced concern over declining cloth prices and increasing competition, the merchants supporting the yarn imports pointed to a shortage of raw materials, the high quality of central German flax yarn, and the prospects for increasing

---

6 Kießling, "Augsburgs Wirtschaft", pp. 174, 176; idem, *Die Stadt und ihr Land*, p. 725; Jahn, "Augsburger Sozialstruktur", pp. 188–89; Rogge, *Für den Gemeinen Nutzen*, pp. 30–41.

7 Kießling, *Die Stadt und ihr Land*, pp. 725–29; idem, "Augsburgs Wirtschaft", pp. 175–77.

production. The city council initially sided with the merchants' arguments, but ultimately restricted yarn imports in 1501 and published a detailed ordinance on quality control.[8]

Whereas textile production formed the backbone of the urban economy, other sectors contributed to its overall performance. In 1475, 280 to 300 guild members were engaged in the fur- and leather-working crafts. The furriers regularly visited the Nördlingen fairs, and the shoemakers began to produce for export markets at the end of the century. Other important craft guilds worked primarily for domestic consumption: In the late fifteenth century the butchers', bakers' and brewers' guilds counted more than 100 members each. At the same time, the metal-working sector became increasingly diversified and sophisticated as well.[9]

The financial sector in south Germany was dominated by merchant companies from Nuremberg around 1400, but Augsburg firms were already carrying out transactions with the courts of Bavaria and France and handling monetary transfers from central European dioceses to the Roman curia. The most dynamic local trading firm of the mid-fifteenth century, the Meuting Company, had close commercial ties with Venice, Genoa, and Bruges. In 1456 it granted Duke Sigismund of Tyrol a loan of 35,000 gulden, in return for which it was assigned silver from the Tyrolean mines.[10] Other companies were looking towards Saxony, where another important mining area was developing at the time: In 1479, Lukas Welser and his brothers, whose business activities extended from Bruges to Naples, invested in silver mining near Zwickau.[11] These were the first forays of Augsburg companies into a field that would become extremely important for the city's merchants in the following century.

2 The Fugger Company: Augsburg's First "Global Players"

In 1896, Richard Ehrenberg titled his pioneering work on the emergence of merchant capitalism and international capital markets in the Renaissance period "The Age of the Fuggers", and while this shorthand formula has subsequently been questioned,[12] there is no doubt that the Fugger Company accounted for the most spectacular success story in the business world of the sixteenth

---

8   Rogge, *Für den Gemeinen Nutzen*, pp. 107–18.
9   Kießling, *Die Stadt und ihr Land*, pp. 731–32; idem, "Augsburgs Wirtschaft", p. 176.
10 Ehrenberg, *Zeitalter der Fugger*, vol. 1, pp. 187–88; Kießling, "Augsburgs Wirtschaft", p. 177.
11 Geffcken, "Die Welser und ihr Handel", pp. 125–45.
12 See Landsteiner, "Kein Zeitalter der Fugger".

century. Their participation in various overseas ventures, but even more so their role in the management of global bullion flows, turned the Fuggers into the first "global players" among south German merchant corporations.[13]

While the company of Ulrich Fugger and his brothers had already established itself in the long-distance trade in textiles and luxury goods by the 1480s, Ulrich's younger brother Jakob opened up an entirely new field when he began extending loans to Archduke Sigismund of Tyrol in return for silver from the mines of the Inn Valley in 1485. Taking advantage of a favorable economic and political climate, the Fuggers advanced the enormous sum of 624,000 gulden to Sigismund and his successor, King (later Emperor) Maximilian I, until 1494, in return for 200,000 marks ($c.$ 56 tons) of silver. In the 1490s, the Fuggers also began to obtain Alpine copper in return for their loans to the Habsburg rulers. Moreover, Jakob Fugger and the Krakow mining expert Johann Thurzo leased the mines of Neusohl in upper Hungary (present-day Slovakia) in 1494. They subsequently built smelting works in Neusohl, Hohenkirchen (Thuringia) and Fuggerau near Villach (Carinthia) and organized a far-flung distribution network for Hungarian copper. Initially, Venice was their major market. In 1498, the Fuggers joined three other companies who were active in the Alpine copper trade – the Gossembrot and Herwart firms of Augsburg and the Baumgartners of Kufstein – forming a syndicate to stabilize prices. By 1500, however, the Fuggers had found an alternative outlet for Hungarian copper, shipping it to the Baltic ports of Gdańsk and Szczecin and across the Baltic and North Seas to Antwerp. This route turned out to be extremely profitable, as the Portuguese crown, which needed large amounts of copper and silver for its developing African and Asian trades, selected Antwerp as its major outlet for Asian spices in the first years of the sixteenth century. Within a few years, the Fuggers redirected a large share of their Hungarian copper towards Antwerp, reaping huge profits from the soaring demand for metals, which were about to become the backbone of a budding world economy.[14]

Although of secondary importance to the marketing of silver and copper, the Fuggers's office in Rome, established in 1495, came to play an important role in financial transfers to the papal curia, including revenues from the sale of letters of indulgence. As these kinds of financial services had long been the domain of Tuscan merchant-bankers, the Fuggers' rise to the position of papal bankers signaled the shifting balance of power among the European financial

---

13   See Häberlein, *Aufbruch ins globale Zeitalter*.
14   Häberlein, *Fuggers of Augsburg*, pp. 31–45, 49–54; idem, *Aufbruch ins globale Zeitalter*, pp. 56–69; Rössner, *Deflation – Devaluation – Rebellion*, pp. 251–301. On Jakob Fugger, see Steinmetz, *The Richest Man*.

FIGURE 5.1   Jakob Fugger the Rich and his bookkeeper Matthäus Schwarz, from the Schwarz costume book
HERZOG ANTON ULRICH-MUSEUM, HS 27 N. 67

elite in the years around 1500. The Augsburg company also helped to recruit Swiss soldiers for the pope (the origins of the Vatican's still-existing Swiss guard) and leased the papal mint (*zecca*) for a number of years. The company curtailed its operations in Rome in the 1520s, when the popes came to prefer the services of Tuscan bankers once again and the Protestant Reformation led to a collapse of the market for letters of indulgence. The Fuggers closed their Roman office for good after the sack of Rome by imperial troops in 1527.[15]

After Emperor Maximilian's death, Jakob Fugger supported the election of Maximilian's grandson Charles, Duke of Burgundy and King of Spain, as Emperor Charles V in 1519, providing more than half of the 850,000 gulden spent in Charles' campaign for the imperial throne. Subsequently the Fugger Company, headed by Jakob Fugger's nephew Anton after his uncle's death in 1525, remained a major financier of the emperor and his brother, Archduke (later King) Ferdinand. From 1521 to 1555, the dozens of loans extended to Charles V by the Fuggers in return for revenues of the Castilian crown totaled about five and a half million ducats. These royal taxes and rents, along with revenues from the lands of the Spanish knightly orders (*Maestrazgos*), were farmed by the Fuggers, usually at handsome returns. Charles V also rewarded his bankers by elevating them into the ranks of the hereditary nobility of the Holy Roman Empire and shielding them from political attacks on the large merchant companies during the so-called monopoly dispute of the 1520s. This mutually beneficial relationship ran into difficulties, however, when Charles' son and successor Philip II failed to honor his financial obligations to the Augsburg company, ordering the confiscation of bullion shipments which had been assigned to it in 1557.[16]

By that time, Anton Fugger had already embarked on a restructuring of his firm. In 1546, when the Fugger Company's net assets peaked at more than five million gulden, he decided to discontinue the lease of the Hungarian mines due to declining returns and military conflict between the house of Habsburg and the Ottoman Turks in the Balkans. Two years later, he also reorganized Fugger holdings in the Tyrolean mining areas, which were consolidated in response to declining output. Anton Fugger's son and successor Marx, who headed the company from 1563 to 1595, continued this strategy of consolidation, reducing the number of branch offices in European cities and concentrating on the core areas of mining, banking, and government finance. Of crucial importance was the lease of the Spanish *Maestrazgo* lands, which the Fuggers

---

15 Häberlein, *Fuggers of Augsburg*, pp. 45–49, 71–72.
16 Häberlein, *Fuggers of Augsburg*, pp. 64–67, 75–87, 92–94; Tracy, *Emperor Charles V*, pp. 63–65, 89–106 and passim.

held continuously from 1562 to 1647, and which included the mercury mines of Almadén. The demand for mercury soared when the amalgamation process, a method of extracting silver from ore by adding a mercury compound, was introduced in Mexico and Peru. The Fuggers garnered huge returns from the sale of Almadén mercury to the Spanish authorities for shipment to America in the final third of the sixteenth century.[17]

These profits enabled family members to acquire extensive rural properties in eastern Swabia in a practice that had begun under Jakob Fugger and was continued by succeeding generations. By 1618, members of the Fugger family owned lands and feudal rights in more than 100 Swabian villages. Apart from being a secure investment that yielded modest but safe returns, these properties, along with the emperors' favor, became the foundation for the family's establishment within the ranks of the imperial nobility.[18]

3 Beyond the Fuggers: Commerce, Mining, and Banking in the Long Sixteenth Century

While the scope of their business activities and their success were extraordinary, the Fuggers also exemplify the general expansion of Augsburg's long-distance commerce and involvement in mining and banking from the late fifteenth century onwards. Like the Fugger firm, other Swabian mercantile companies typically were family enterprises whose members were more or less closely related to one another, and they increased their working capital by accepting deposits at fixed interest rates from family members, relatives, aristocrats, and wealthy townspeople. They established permanent branch offices in important commercial cities like Antwerp, Lyons, Milan, Venice, or Lisbon, which were headed by junior members of the firm or salaried employees. Company contracts were limited to a certain number of years, but were frequently renewed as long as the parties involved agreed to continue the partnership.[19]

Mining and the marketing of metals played a major role in the commercial rise of Augsburg. There were three major mining areas producing silver and copper for export in the sixteenth century: Tyrol, upper Hungary, and the Mansfeld region in central Germany. Between 1500 and 1620, Augsburg

---

17 Häberlein, *Fuggers of Augsburg*, pp. 87–90, 99–115; idem, *Aufbruch ins globale Zeitalter*, pp. 141–51.
18 Mandrou, *Les Fugger*; Häberlein, *The Fuggers of Augsburg*, pp. 201–13.
19 Lutz, *Die rechtliche Struktur*; Kellenbenz, "Wirtschaftsleben", pp. 270–84.

companies effectively controlled more than 70 per cent of the Tyrolean copper output and more than 90 per cent of Hungarian copper, while Nuremberg companies managed to ward off their Swabian competitors in the Mansfeld region.[20]

Of crucial importance was the provision of credit to the lords of the mines. King Maximilian, his grandson Ferdinand, and Ferdinand's successors borrowed enormous sums from their Augsburg bankers, assigning silver and copper from the Tyrolean mines to them in return. In the Alps, the Baumgartner, Manlich, Herwart, Bimmel, and Hoechstetter firms joined the Fuggers as major investors in the early sixteenth century. The Hoechstetters aggressively competed with the Fuggers on the copper market and leased the mercury mines in Idria in present-day Slovenia. Ambrosius Hoechstetter even attempted to establish a European-wide monopoly on the mercury trade in the 1520s, but overextended his credit and spectacularly failed in 1529.[21]

Around mid-century, Augsburg's mining entrepreneurs began to sell unproductive mines and smelting works and to consolidate their operations in the Alps due to declining output, falling copper prices, and the influx of American silver. In 1565, the three remaining firms in the Tyrolean mining business – the Fugger, Haug-Langnauer, and Manlich-Katzbeck companies – fused their holdings in the newly-formed Jenbach Company. When the Fuggers withdrew from upper Hungary, the Augsburg merchant Matthias Manlich took over operations in Neusohl in 1548. Manlich was in turn succeeded by other Augsburg firms. Wolfgang Paler took over the marketing of Hungarian copper in 1569, which his partners and heirs controlled until the early 1620s. The Idria mercury mines remained in the hands of successive Augsburg companies – the Baumgartner, Herwart, and Haug-Langnauer – until the late 1570s, while other mining entrepreneurs were active in the Salzburg mountains, Saxony, and Thuringia.[22] In the 1560s, the Haug-Langnauer also invested in the "Company of Mines Royal", which sought to exploit copper deposits in Cornwall and was backed by the English government. After the Haug-Langnauer's bankruptcy in 1574, their manager Daniel Hoechstetter and his heirs continued to operate the English copper mines until the 1630s.[23]

On a more general level, Augsburg mercantile companies' involvement in English mining illustrates the propensity for risk-taking and the exploration

---

20   Hildebrandt, "Kupferhandel".
21   Kellenbenz, "Kapitalverflechtung", pp. 20–39; Safley, "Konkurs der Höchstetter".
22   Kellenbenz, "Kapitalverflechtung", pp. 39–45; idem, "Wirtschaftsleben", pp. 264–65; Hildebrandt, "Kupferhandel", pp. 210–15.
23   Hammersley (ed.), *Daniel Hoechstetter the Younger*.

of new investment opportunities. Participation in maritime trade likewise testifies to their quest to expand into new business areas. After the Portuguese had opened the sea route to India in 1497–99, the Fugger, Welser-Vöhlin, and Hoechstetter companies hastened to establish branch offices in Lisbon and to obtain commercial privileges from the Portuguese crown. In 1505, they were part of a German-Italian consortium that invested in a Portuguese fleet to India. After King Manoel of Portugal had excluded private merchants from direct involvement in the Asian spice trade in 1506, the Welser Company continued to purchase large amounts of pepper and other exotic spices from Portuguese officials in Lisbon and Antwerp. The Welsers' interest in overseas trade is evinced by their opening of an office on the island of Madeira, an early center of sugar production in the Atlantic world, in 1509, and their purchase of a sugar estate on La Palma, one of the Canary Islands, around the same time.[24]

Like the Fuggers, the Welsers consolidated their role as early "global players" when they became involved in trade with America – including the notorious transatlantic slave trade – in the 1520s. Soon after Emperor Charles V had opened trade with Spanish America to foreigners in 1525, the Welsers sent employees to the New World, who established a branch office on the island of Hispaniola. Capitalizing on the company's role as bankers of Charles V, the Welser representatives Ulrich Ehinger and Hieronymus Sailer contracted with the Spanish crown for the colonization of a province on the northern coast of South America (eventually named Venezuela) and the shipment of 4,000 African slaves to the Caribbean in 1528. While the slave-trading venture turned out to be profitable for the company, the attempt to colonize Venezuela resulted in financial as well as human losses. Instead of focusing on settlement and commercial opportunities, the men on the spot merely sought to garner quick returns by conquering a Native American empire and looting its treasures. A series of brutal, but ultimately unsuccessful forays were undertaken into the interior of Venezuela and Colombia, in the course of which thousands of Indians were killed, maimed, tortured, and enslaved. Responding to settlers' and officials' complaints about the Welser Company's negligence and mismanagement, the Spanish crown suspended the company's colonization privileges in 1546 and rescinded them a decade later.[25]

Although direct forays of Swabian merchants into overseas trade were sporadic,[26] they continued in the later sixteenth century. In the 1570s, Konrad

---

24 Pohle, *Deutschland und die überseeische Expansion*, pp. 97–134; Häberlein, *Aufbruch ins globale Zeitalter*, pp. 82–93, 107–16.
25 Denzer, *Konquista*; Häberlein, *Aufbruch ins globale Zeitalter*, pp. 116–30.
26 See Johnson, *German Discovery*, pp. 88–122; Häberlein, "Augsburger Handelshäuser".

Rott unsuccessfully sought to monopolize Portuguese pepper purchases in India and their marketing in Europe. The firms of Marx & Matthäus Welser and Georg Fugger's Heirs invested in the Portuguese spice trade in 1585 and sent their own representatives to Goa, the capital of the Portuguese colonial empire in India.[27] When warfare between the Ottoman Empire and an alliance of European powers threatened to cut off the flow of goods between Venice and the Eastern Mediterranean in the early 1570s, Melchior Manlich and his associates in Augsburg sought to profit from the situation by entering the Levant trade from the French port of Marseilles. But the Manlich Company overextended its credit and went bankrupt in 1574.[28]

As indicated above, the provision of credit to European monarchs constituted another potentially profitable, albeit risky, field of investment. The Fugger and Welser companies were among the major backers of Charles V, putting up more than 36 per cent of the 28 million ducats which the Spanish crown loaned from merchant-bankers between 1521 and 1555.[29] Other firms were lured by the promise of high interest rates on loans to the French crown, the emperor's major competitor in European politics, in the 1540s and 1550s. Bartholomäus Welser and his associates had begun to lend money to King Francis I of France in the 1520s, and the Meuting, Herwart, Zangmeister, and Weyer Companies joined them at mid-century. Several of these firms were bankrupted when Henry II of France failed to honor his debts in the late 1550s.[30] Still others became bankers to the kings of Portugal and Denmark, the electors of Saxony, and the dukes of Bavaria. Thus Jakob Herbrot, an ambitious social climber from the furrier's guild who was elected mayor of Augsburg in the mid-1540s, provided substantial loans to Protestant princes who opposed Charles V in imperial politics – but this did not distract him from lending money to the emperor's brother Ferdinand as well.[31]

The expansion and growing complexity of long-distance trade and banking led to the emergence of a specialized market for bills of exchange and mercantile credit. In the 1550s, the city's licensed brokers recorded thousands of credit and exchange transactions involving several dozen firms. Bills of exchange drawn on Antwerp between 1551 and 1558 totaled one million gulden, while bills drawn on Venice amounted to 240,000 ducats. The most active participants on the Augsburg capital market included the Fugger, Welser, Krafter, Manlich,

---

27 Hildebrandt, *Die "Georg Fuggerischen Erben"*, pp. 145–72; Kalus, *Pfeffer – Kupfer – Nachrichten;* Häberlein, *Fuggers of Augsburg*, pp. 117–20.
28 Seibold, *Manlich*; Kellenbenz, "Melchior Manlich".
29 Tracy, *Emperor Charles V*, pp. 100–1; Häberlein, *The Fuggers of Augsburg*, pp. 75–76.
30 Häberlein, *Brüder, Freunde und Betrüger*, pp. 120–47.
31 Häberlein, "Jakob Herbrot".

Imhof, and Herwart companies. Multiple financial transactions among these firms created networks of trust that reinforced the kinship networks underlying urban long-distance trade.[32]

As the above-mentioned bankruptcies indicate, however, business failure was a significant hazard for risk-taking merchant companies. Economic downturns, princely debtors who neglected to repay loans, military conflict, imprudent investment decisions, and sheer misfortune caused the failure of dozens of firms – particularly those who relied too heavily on outside capital. These failures multiplied in the later sixteenth century, when the Spanish and French monarchies defaulted on their debts, the output of major mining areas declined, warfare in France and the Netherlands cut off south German merchants from important markets, and Flemish and Italian firms expanded their activities in central Europe. Bankruptcy strained the networks of credit and trust within the urban elite; charges of negligence and fraud resulted in intense litigation and prompted the city council to pass three ordinances between 1564 and 1580 that regulated the settling of bankruptcy cases and penalized fraudulent behavior.[33]

But the failure of dozens of prominent firms and the withdrawal of others from active commerce did not signify a general decline of Augsburg's mercantile community, as newcomers quickly filled their spots. Many leading mercantile companies around 1600 abstained from risky ventures and concentrated on established business fields like the importation of cotton, silk, and velvet from northern Italy, the marketing of linen and fustian at central European fairs, and the supply of raw materials like wool, dyestuffs, and furs. The volume of freight transported between Venice and south Germany doubled in the course of the sixteenth century, confirming the viability of this central axis of Augsburg's trade. Some firms also reacted to shifts in the European economy by establishing offices in the burgeoning port cities of Hamburg and Amsterdam, and several merchants permanently moved to these rising commercial centers or migrated to Venice or Lyons.[34] Finally, there were individuals like Philipp Hainhofer, who embarked on a distinguished career as an art dealer and supplied a variety of finely wrought precious objects to princely clients.[35] In sum, Augsburg's merchants in the late sixteenth and early seventeenth century

---

32   Blendinger (eds.), *Zwei Augsburger Unterkaufbücher*; Häberlein, *Brüder, Freunde und Betrüger*, pp. 97–119; Jeannin, *Change, crédit et circulation monétaire*.

33   Häberlein, *Brüder, Freunde und Betrüger*, pp. 224–337; idem, "Merchants' bankruptcies"; Safley, "Bankruptcy".

34   Hildebrandt, "Effects of Empire"; idem, "Die wirtschaftlichen Beziehungen"; idem, "Commercium – Confessio – Conubium".

35   Roeck, "Philipp Hainhofer".

demonstrated considerable resilience and the capacity to adjust to a changing business environment.

4 The Urban Economy on the Eve of the Thirty Years' War

Whereas long-distance trade continued to thrive on the eve of the Thirty Years' War, the general economic situation was more complex. About three per cent of Augsburg's taxpayers were traders, but the majority was engaged in household-based craft production, which retained its focus on the textile sector. Weavers continued to account for more than 20 per cent of Augsburg's taxpayers, as their number rose from 1,451 in 1536 to more than 2,000 in the early seventeenth century, when 400,000 pieces of fustian were annually presented for inspection at the weavers' guildhall. Although impressive by itself, this figure indicates considerable overproduction, as Swabian fustian faced increasing competition from central German linen as well as Dutch and English cloth. After cloth sales plummeted during the economic crisis of the 1570s, the city council sought to stabilize the situation and support the city's independent master weavers by limiting the amount of debt which a weaver could contract, prohibiting the exchange of cotton for finished cloth, and establishing a public pawn vault where weavers could bring their unsold fustian to raise money. These measures may have prevented the spread of the putting-out system on a large scale, but they failed to resolve the basic problem of overproduction. A disproportionate number of weavers were poor: 56 per cent were not taxed for any property, and another 25 per cent paid only minimal taxes. Thus more than four-fifths belonged to the lowest economic ranks, compared for example to 20 per cent of the bakers and 34 per cent of the dyers. More than half of the weavers had only a single loom in their workshop, and many received public alms either sporadically or permanently.[36] A variety of other trades – dyeing, bleaching, finishing – complemented weaving and underscore the pivotal importance of the textile sector.[37]

The weavers' craft was more than ten times larger than any other craft in Augsburg in 1610. Eight other crafts counted more than 100 members; the tailors, goldsmiths, butchers, day laborers, carpenters, bakers, joiners, and shoemakers. While most of these large crafts produced basic goods for mass consumption, the goldsmiths and other specialized artisans, including watchmakers,

---

36 Clasen, *Augsburger Weber*, pp. 17–69, 211, 261–85, 330–32.
37 Clasen, *Textilherstellung*, vol. 2, pp. 97–351.

harness-makers, and printers, stand out for the quality of their products.[38] The goldsmiths in particular managed to combine high aesthetic standards with marketing success. The number of master goldsmiths tripled from 63 in 1555 to 200 in 1594, and individual masters created works that adorned the palaces of the emperor and other European princes. In 1615, 185 master goldsmiths worked alongside 108 journeymen. By that time a specialized group of silver traders and jewelers had emerged who mediated between individual workshops and well-to-do clients.[39]

But even the provision of certain basic needs could be capital-intensive: thus several thousand oxen from Hungary were annually imported to meet the demand for meat. To finance these imports, some butchers formed associations that pooled their capital and mobilized credit for purchases in Vienna. Those butchers who handled these complex operations most effectively, particularly members of the Burkhart family, rose into the ranks of the city's economic elite, while their economic strength caused considerable tension within the craft.[40] The shoemakers were involved in export production as well, exporting footwear to the Tyrolean mining region in addition to supplying the local market.[41]

Augsburg's position as a commercial center was only possible on account of an efficient transportation and information sector. Horse-drawn wagons transported goods over long distances, and on the north side of the Alps, rafts on the Lech River offered a convenient alternative to tedious road transportation. Regular messenger service also connected Augsburg with cities like Venice, and the imperial city was a major hub in the emerging European-wide network of postal routes organized by the Taxis family.[42]

As the examples of merchants' bankruptcies and the crisis-prone weavers' craft indicate, the city council intervened in urban economic life in numerous ways. Apart from monitoring quality standards and regulating crafts and markets, the city was a major employer, with hundreds of citizens working in the public sector and taxes financing the construction or improvement of fortifications, public buildings, roads, and waterways. Between 1590 and 1620, revenues from consumption and property taxes enabled Augsburg to realize an ambitious construction program that featured a new city hall, arsenal, slaughterhouse, and several city gates and towers. Best known as a phase of architectural

---

38 Clasen, *Augsburger Weber*, p. 22; Roeck, *Eine Stadt in Krieg und Frieden*, vol. 1, pp. 406–26.
39 Schürer, "ein erbar handwerckh", pp. 58–60.
40 Dalhede, *Ochsenhandel*; Roeck, *Eine Stadt in Krieg und Frieden*, vol. 1, pp. 419–20.
41 Kießling, "Aspekte der Lederbeschaffung".
42 Kellenbenz, "Wirtschaftsleben der Blütezeit", pp. 265–69.

renewal on the eve of the Thirty Years' War,[43] this effort has to be seen as an economic investment and employment program, too. From 1608 to 1620, Elias Holl, the architect and chief engineer in charge of the project, had 10,000 to 15,000 gulden annually at his disposal and oversaw a workforce of several hundred artisans and day laborers. Thus urban renewal not only demonstrated the city's wealth and prestige but also helped to alleviate poverty and preserve social peace.[44] Finally, hospitals, orphanages, and other charitable foundations contributed to urban economic life by managing properties, extending credit, employing laborers, and purchasing supplies at urban markets.[45]

5 Collapse and Revival: The Thirty Years' War and Its Aftermath

For a city so heavily dependent on long-distance trade and export production, the Thirty Years' War (1618–48) had disastrous economic consequences. Although merchant companies managed to keep the vital connection with northern Italy alive during the war,[46] a string of economic, demographic, and military crises – runaway inflation in the early 1620s, a plague epidemic in 1627–28, the Swedish occupation in 1632–35, a lengthy siege in 1634–35, and the costs of forced quartering of imperial troops – caused dramatic losses. Many firms went out of business or drastically reduced their activities. In 1646, the total assessed wealth of Augsburg's merchants stood at merely one-sixth of the pre-war level. The population had been reduced by more than 50 per cent (from roughly 45,000 in 1618 to 21,000 in 1646), and the number of weavers had dropped by a staggering 80 per cent.[47]

But despite these dramatic losses, the foundations of Augsburg's former economic strength had not been completely destroyed. Within years after the Peace of Westphalia, merchants re-established commercial ties with Vienna, Linz, Bolzano, Venice, and Lyons and were once again doing business at the Frankfurt and Leipzig fairs.[48] To be sure, urban merchants failed to revive some of the links that had contributed to the city's pre-eminence in the sixteenth century, such as the commercial relations with Spain and Portugal that had been a hallmark of the "age of the Fuggers". Yet Augsburg's comeback was remarkable nonetheless. Historians have identified three major fields of

---

43 See Chapter 22 of this volume.
44 Roeck, "Voraussetzungen".
45 Safley, *Charity and Economy*.
46 Blendinger, "Augsburger Handel".
47 Roeck, *Eine Stadt in Krieg und Frieden*, vol. 2, pp. 914–49.
48 Zorn, *Handels- und Industriegeschichte*, pp. 11–14.

economic revival: banking and metal trade; fine crafts; and textile production. All three branches were export-oriented, and they combined technical know-how and substantial capital investment.[49]

While most prominent merchant families of the sixteenth century had died out or withdrawn from active trade, new individuals and families – often immigrants from other south German cities and northern Italy – filled the depleted ranks of the commercial community. In the final quarter of the seventeenth century, the Gullmann, Greiff & Köpf, Rad & Hößlin, and Rauner companies profitably combined gold and silver trading with banking services. Founded by Protestant immigrants from cities like Nuremberg, Frankfurt, and Lindau, these firms delivered precious metal objects to the princely courts in Vienna, Potsdam, Munich, and Dresden, as well as to noble households and clerical institutions. By 1690, they also began to extend loans to governments and to accept commissions for army supplies, which became a major field of business in an era of almost constant warfare with the France of Louis XIV and the Ottoman Empire. Samuel Bertermann, who hailed from Wrocław, supplied imperial troops and speculated in mercury during the 1690s but overextended his credit. Johann Thomas Rauner invested in the Bavarian salt trade, while his son Johann Thomas the Younger and his son-in-law Christian (von) Münch granted large loans to the elector of Bavaria during the 1720s and 1730s. Rad & Hößlin, a prosperous silver trading company with branches in Vienna and Warsaw, was a major contractor of the Vienna court and the imperial army. In addition to providing government loans, Augsburg merchant-bankers engaged in large-scale production. Thus Markus von Schnurbein took over a manufactory for gold and silver objects in Köthen in the principality of Anhalt in 1724 and became involved in the distribution of copper from the Mansfeld and Eisleben regions in Thuringia to central European markets a few years later. Christian von Münch was active in the copper trade of the Banat (in present-day Romania) in the mid-1730s. The importance of these merchant-bankers to the imperial court is illustrated by the fact that several were granted titles of nobility.[50]

Protestants dominated Augsburg's mercantile sector in the early decades of the eighteenth century, and their ranks were reinforced by the arrival of the silver traders and bankers Philipp Adam Benz, Joseph Halder (both from Lindau), and Johann Adam Liebert (from Biberach). At the same time, Catholic

---

49 See François, *Die unsichtbare Grenze*, pp. 73–84.
50 Zorn, *Handels- und Industriegeschichte*, pp. 14–38; Fassl, *Konfession, Wirtschaft und Politik*, pp. 123–24, 126–27, 133; Seibold, *Wirtschaftlicher Erfolg*, vol. 1, pp. 89–96, 237–57, 269–74, 301–22.

immigrants from Tyrol and northern Italy – Tomaso Carli, who hailed from Tremezzo on the banks of Lake Como, members of the Brentano-Mezzegra clan from the same region, and Johann Obwexer from Klausen in South Tyrol – also joined Augsburg's merchant community. Protestant and Catholic merchant-bankers cooperated after mid-century to supply the imperial mints in Hall (Tyrol) and Günzburg (Swabia) with silver for the minting of large coins. These so-called Maria Theresia Talers were a major article of export to the eastern Mediterranean. In 1769, the Liebert, Köpf, and Carli firms formed a syndicate that leased the entire production of the Hall and Günzburg mints for a period of eight years in return for yearly payments of four million Talers. In the 1780s, the Obwexer, Schwarz, Carli, Cobres, und Pedroni companies joined forces to supply the city of Venice with oxen and tallow.[51]

The success of the silver traders and their rise into the ranks of government bankers eventually rested on the reputation of Augsburg's gold- and silversmiths and other metal-working crafts. In a sophisticated division of labor, silver traders commissioned orders from princely clients and organized production in a kind of putting-out system that combined efficiency with high quality standards. The number of master goldsmiths rose from 160 in 1661 to 190 35 years later, and peaked at 275 around 1740.[52] Another prospering field of specialized production was the making of copper prints and illustrated books. Whereas most printers had been Protestants before the Thirty Years' War, printing and publishing now became a Catholic domain. Augsburg's publishing houses played a crucial role in the distribution of books in Catholic areas of south Germany and the Habsburg Empire, selling large numbers of printed works to monastic libraries. There were 23 publishers in 1788, some of them existing for several generations.[53]

The recovery in the late seventeenth century of the textile sector, which had been hit especially hard by the Thirty Year's War, was due to major innovations. Weavers began to shift from fustian to cotton fabrics, and Georg Neuhofer, who had learned about new cotton printing techniques during a tour of England and the Netherlands in 1688–89, brought the new technique to Augsburg. Cotton printing expanded slowly in the first half of the eighteenth century and dramatically after 1750, when several entrepreneurs opened large factories. The most ambitious of these was Johann Heinrich Schüle, whose

---

51   Zorn, *Handels- und Industriegeschichte*, pp. 47–51, 60; François, *Die unsichtbare Grenze*, pp. 77–78; Seibold, *Wirtschaftlicher Erfolg*, vol. 1, pp. 50–51, 96–111, 190–202, 207–17, 227–37.
52   Schürer, "ein erbar handwerckh", p. 61; Fassl, *Konfession, Wirtschaft und Politik*, pp. 127–29.
53   Fassl, *Konfession, Wirtschaft und Politik*, pp. 137–42; François, *Die unsichtbare Grenze*, pp. 78–81.

cotton-printing factory became the largest in south Germany within a few years of its inception in 1759. In 1785, the cotton-printing industry was producing about 170,000 pieces per year. Printing was centralized in large-scale factories, but the preliminary processes of weaving and bleaching continued to be carried out in small workshops. The entrepreneurs purchased large amounts of cloth from local weavers but also imported increasing quantities of East Indian cotton via Amsterdam. The weavers blamed their bleak situation on these imports and on the low prices offered by the entrepreneurs, and they demanded a ban on cotton imports. The resulting conflicts occupied the city authorities for decades and eventually erupted into open rebellion in 1794.[54]

As they had two centuries earlier, prosperity and crisis existed side by side in late eighteenth-century Augsburg. Even as many craftsmen faced declining fortunes and recurrent economic crises – the number of goldsmiths declined from 275 in 1740 to 126 in 1800, for example – a small group of entrepreneurs amassed large fortunes. Apart from the aforementioned Johann Heinrich Schüle, big players in the cotton-printing industry included Schüle's nephew Matthäus, Schoeppler & Hartmann, and the widow Anna Barbara Gignoux.[55] Their operations were financed by the local merchant-bankers, for example the Obwexer banking house, who extended large loans to Johann Heinrich Schüle and his nephew Matthäus. During the American War of Independence, the brothers Joseph Anton and Peter Paul Obwexer once again involved Augsburg in overseas trade by exporting locally printed cottons along with linen from Silesia and Saxony to the Dutch Caribbean island of Curaçao, which served as a distribution point to the French West Indies and Spanish South America.[56]

In sum, Augsburg's economy demonstrated remarkable resilience, as merchants, entrepreneurs, and craftsmen adapted to changing demand and pursued innovative production and marketing strategies. Nonetheless, signs of crisis were clearly evident in the final decades of the eighteenth century, and they multiplied as the French Revolutionary Wars threw the urban economy into disarray. The number of printed cottons fell by half in the 1790s, several large banking houses went bankrupt, and up to 1,400 of Augsburg's 30,000 inhabitants were dependent on poor relief.[57] The city's commercialized, export-oriented and decidedly unbalanced economy thus remained susceptible to

---

54 Fassl, *Konfession, Wirtschaft und Politik*, pp. 144–70; Clasen, *Textilherstellung*, vol. 2, pp. 353–500.
55 See Seibold, *Wirtschaftlicher Erfolg*, vol. 1, pp. 67–73, 129–34, 330–45.
56 Häberlein and Schmölz-Häberlein, *Die Erben der Welser*; Seibold, *Wirtschaftlicher Erfolg*, vol. 1, pp. 227–37.
57 Fassl, *Konfession, Wirtschaft und Politik*, pp. 131–36, 141–42, 155–57.

external shocks, and it continued to be marked by sharp contrasts between prosperity and poverty.

Bibliography

Published Primary Sources

Blendinger, F. and E. (eds.), *Zwei Augsburger Unterkaufbücher aus den Jahren 1551 bis 1558. Älteste Aufzeichnungen zur Vor- und Frühgeschichte der Augsburger Börse*, Stuttgart, 1994.

Hammersley, G. (ed.), *Daniel Hoechstetter the Younger. Memorabilia and Letters 1600–1639*, Stuttgart, 1988.

Secondary Literature

Blendinger, F., "Augsburger Handel im Dreißigjährigen Krieg nach Konzepten von Fedi di Sanità, Politen, Attesten u.ä.", in J. Schneider (ed.), *Wirtschaftskräfte und Wirtschaftswege. Festschrift für Hermann Kellenbenz*, Stuttgart, 1978, vol. 2, pp. 287–323.

Clasen, C.-P., *Die Augsburger Weber. Leistungen und Krisen des Textilgewerbes um 1600*, Augsburg, 1981.

Clasen, C.-P., *Textilherstellung in Augsburg in der Frühen Neuzeit*, 2 vols., Augsburg, 1995.

Dalhede, C., *Zum europäischen Ochsenhandel. Das Beispiel Augsburg 1560 und 1578*, St. Katharinen, 1992.

Denzer, J., *Die Konquista der Augsburger Welser-Gesellschaft in Südamerika 1528–1556. Historische Rekonstruktion, Historiografie und lokale Erinnerungskultur in Kolumbien und Venezuela*, Munich, 2005.

Ehrenberg, R., *Das Zeitalter der Fugger. Geldkapital und Creditverkehr im 16. Jahrhundert*, 2 vols., Jena, 1896. English translation: *Capital and Finance in the Age of the Renaissance: A Study of the Fuggers and their Connections*, transl. H.M. Lucas, New York, 1928 (repr. New York, 1963).

Fassl, P., *Konfession, Wirtschaft und Politik. Von der Reichsstadt zur Industriestadt: Augsburg 1750–1850*, Sigmaringen, 1988.

François, E., *Die unsichtbare Grenze. Protestanten und Katholiken in Augsburg 1648–1806*, Sigmaringen, 1991.

Geffcken, P., "Die Welser und ihr Handel 1246–1496", in M. Häberlein and J. Burkhardt (eds.), *Die Welser. Neue Forschungen zur Geschichte und Kultur des oberdeutschen Handelshauses*, Berlin, 1996, pp. 17–167.

Häberlein, M., "Jakob Herbrot (1490/95), Großkaufmann und Stadtpolitiker", in W. Haberl (ed.), *Lebensbilder aus dem Bayerischen Schwaben*, vol. 15, Weißenhorn, 1997, pp. 69–111.

Häberlein, M., *Brüder, Freunde und Betrüger. Soziale Beziehungen, Normen und Konflikte in der Augsburger Kaufmannschaft um die Mitte des 16. Jahrhunderts*, Berlin, 1998.

Häberlein, M., *The Fuggers of Augsburg: Pursuing Wealth and Honor in Renaissance Germany*, Charlottesville and London, 2012.

Häberlein, M., "Merchants' bankruptcies, economic development, and social relations in German towns during the long sixteenth century", in T.M. Safley (ed.), *The History of Bankruptcy: Economic, Social and Cultural Implications in Early Modern Europe*, London, 2013, pp. 19-33.

Häberlein, M., "Augsburger Handelshäuser und die Neue Welt: Interessen und Initiativen im atlantischen Raum (16. bis 18. Jahrhundert)", in P. Gassert, G. Kronenbitter, S. Paulus and W.E.J. Weber (eds.), *Augsburg und Amerika. Aneignungen und globale Verflechtungen in einer Stadt*, Augsburg, 2013, pp. 19-37.

Häberlein, M., *Aufbruch ins globale Zeitalter. Die Handelswelt der Fugger und Welser*, Darmstadt, 2016.

Häberlein, M. and Schmölz-Häberlein, M., *Die Erben der Welser. Der Karibikhandel der Augsburger Firma Obwexer im Zeitalter der Revolutionen*, Augsburg, 1995.

Hildebrandt, R., *Die "Georg Fuggerischen Erben". Kaufmännische Tätigkeit und sozialer Status 1555-1618*, Berlin, 1966.

Hildebrandt, R., "Augsburger und Nürnberger Kupferhandel, 1500-1619: Produktion, Marktanteile und Finanzierung im Vergleich zweier Städte und ihrer wirtschaftlichen Führungsschicht", in H. Kellenbenz (ed.), *Schwerpunkte der Kupferproduktion und des Kupferhandels in Europa 1500-1650*, Cologne, 1977, pp. 190-224.

Hildebrandt, R., "The Effects of Empire: Changes in the European Economy after Charles V", in I. Blanchard, A. Goodman and J. Newman (eds.), *Industry and Finance in Early Modern History: Essays Presented to George Hammersley to the Occasion of his 74th Birthday*, Stuttgart, 1992, pp. 58-76.

Hildebrandt, R., "Die wirtschaftlichen Beziehungen zwischen Oberdeutschland und Venedig um 1600: Konturen eines Gesamtbildes", in B. Roeck, K. Bergdolt and A.J. Martin (eds.), *Venedig und Oberdeutschland. Beziehungen zwischen Kunst und Wirtschaft*, Sigmaringen, 1993, pp. 277-88.

Hildebrandt, R., "Commercium – Confessio – Conubium. Augsburger Kaufleute in europäischen Städten 1560-1650", in R. Kießling (ed.), *Stadt und Land in der Geschichte Ostschwabens*, Augsburg, 2005, pp. 9-28.

Jahn, J., "Die Augsburger Sozialstruktur im 15. Jahrhundert", in G. Gottlieb, W. Baer, J. Becker, J. Bellot, K. Filser, P. Fried, W. Reinhard and B. Schimmelpfennig (eds.), *Geschichte der Stadt Augsburg von der Römerzeit bis zur Gegenwart*, 2nd ed., Stuttgart, 1985, pp. 187-93.

Jeannin, P., *Change, crédit et circulation monétaire à Augsbourg au milieu du XVIe siècle*, Paris, 2001.

Johnson, C.R., *The German Discovery of the World: Renaissance Encounters with the Strange and Marvelous*, Charlottesville, 2008.

Kalus, M., *Pfeffer – Kupfer – Nachrichten. Kaufmannsnetzwerke und Handelsstrukturen im europäisch-asiatischen Handel am Ende des 16. Jahrhunderts*, Augsburg, 2010.

Kellenbenz, H., "Wirtschaftsleben der Blütezeit", in G. Gottlieb, W. Baer, J. Becker, J. Bellot, K. Filser, P. Fried, W. Reinhard and B. Schimmelpfennig (eds.), *Geschichte der Stadt Augsburg von der Römerzeit bis zur Gegenwart*, 2nd ed., Stuttgart, 1985, pp. 258–301.

Kellenbenz, H., "Kapitalverflechtung im mittleren Alpenraum: Das Beispiel des Bunt- und Edelmetallbergbaus vom fünfzehnten bis zur Mitte des siebzehnten Jahrhunderts", *Zeitschrift für bayerische Landesgeschichte* 51 (1988), pp. 13–50.

Kellenbenz, H., "From Melchior Manlich to Ferdinand Cron: German Levantine and Oriental Trade Relations", *Journal of European Economic History* 19 (1990), pp. 611–22.

Kießling, R., "Augsburgs Wirtschaft im 14. und 15. Jahrhundert", in G. Gottlieb, W. Baer, J. Becker, J. Bellot, K. Filser, P. Fried, W. Reinhard and B. Schimmelpfennig (eds.), *Geschichte der Stadt Augsburg von der Römerzeit bis zur Gegenwart*, 2nd ed., Stuttgart, 1985, pp. 171–81.

Kießling, R., *Die Stadt und ihr Land. Umlandpolitik, Bürgerbesitz und Wirtschaftsgefüge in Ostschwaben vom 14. bis ins 16. Jahrhundert*, Cologne, 1989.

Kießling, R., *Kleine Geschichte Schwabens*, Regensburg, 2009.

Kießling, R., "Aspekte der Lederbeschaffung und des Lederabsatzes in Oberdeutschland im 15./16. Jahrhundert", in A. Westermann and S. von Welser (eds.), *Beschaffungs- und Absatzmärkte oberdeutscher Firmen im Zeitalter der Welser und Fugger*, Husum, 2011, pp. 205–33.

Landsteiner, E., "Kein Zeitalter der Fugger: Zentraleuropa 1450–1620", in F. Edelmayer, P. Feldbauer and M. Wakounig (eds.), *Globalgeschichte 1450–1620: Anfänge und Perspektiven*, Vienna, 2002, pp. 95–123.

Lutz, E., *Die rechtliche Struktur süddeutscher Handelsgesellschaften in der Zeit der Fugger*, 2 vols., Tübingen, 1976.

Mandrou, R., *Les Fugger, propriétaires fonciers an Souabe 1560–1618. Étude de comportements socio-économiques à la fin du XVIe siècle*, Paris, 1969.

Pohle, J., *Deutschland und die überseeische Expansion Portugals im 15. und 16. Jahrhundert*, Münster, 2000.

Roeck, B., "Wirtschaftliche und soziale Voraussetzungen der Augsburger Baukunst zur Zeit des Elias Holl", *Architectura* 14 (1984), pp. 119–38.

Roeck, B., *Eine Stadt in Krieg und Frieden. Studien zur Geschichte der Reichsstadt Augsburg zwischen Kalenderstreit und Parität*, 2 vols., Göttingen, 1989.

Roeck, B., "Philipp Hainhofer: Unternehmer in Sachen Kunst", in L. Carlen and G. Imboden (eds.), *Kräfte der Wirtschaft. Unternehmergestalten des Alpenraums im 17. Jahrhundert*, Brig, 1992, pp. 9–53.

Rössner, P.R., *Deflation – Devaluation – Rebellion. Geld im Zeitalter der Reformation*, Stuttgart, 2012.

Rogge, J., *Für den Gemeinen Nutzen. Politisches Handeln und Politikverständnis von Rat und Bürgerschaft in Augsburg im Spätmittelalter*, Tübingen, 1996.

Safley, T.M., *Charity and Economy in the Orphanages of Early Modern Augsburg*, Boston, 1997.

Safley, T.M., "Bankruptcy: Family and Finance in Early Modern Augsburg", *Journal of European Economic History* 29 (2000), pp. 53–72.

Safley, T.M., "Der Konkurs der Höchstetter in Abhängigkeit von Beschaffungs- und Absatzmärkten für Quecksilber", in A. Westermann and S. von Welser (eds.), *Beschaffungs- und Absatzmarkte oberdeutscher Firmen im Zeitalter der Welser und Fugger*, Husum, 2011, pp. 273–86.

Schürer, R. "ein erbar handwerckh von goldschmiden", in R. Baumstark and H. Seling (eds.), *Gold und Silber. Augsburger Goldschmiedekunst für die Höfe Europas*, 2 vols., Munich, 1994, vol. 1, pp. 57–65.

Seibold, G., *Die Manlich. Geschichte einer Augsburger Kaufmannsfamilie*, Sigmaringen, 1995.

Seibold, G., *Wirtschaftlicher Erfolg in Zeiten des politischen Niedergangs. Augsburger und Nürnberger Unternehmer in den Jahren zwischen 1648 und 1806*, 2 vols., Augsburg, 2014.

Steinmetz, G., *The Richest Man Who Ever Lived: The Lives and Times of Jacob Fugger*, New York, 2014.

Steinmeyer, H., *Die Entstehung und Entwicklung der Nördlinger Pfingstmesse im Spätmittelalter*, Nördlingen, 1960.

Tracy, J.D., *Emperor Charles V, Impresario of War: Campaign Strategy, International Finance, and Domestic Politics*, Cambridge, 2002.

Zorn, W., *Handels- und Industriegeschichte Bayerisch Schwabens 1648–1870. Wirtschafts-, Sozial- und Kulturgeschichte des schwäbischen Unternehmertums*, Augsburg, 1961.

CHAPTER 6

Politics under the Guild Regime, 1368–1548

Christopher W. Close

On the evening of 22 October 1368, hundreds of artisans in the city of Augsburg took up arms against their government. Frustrated at a lack of representation in the city's political institutions, the craftsmen occupied Augsburg's city hall and demanded a greater voice in civic governance. They also called for the creation of new guilds to regulate the city's economy. Within 24 hours, the artisans had completed a bloodless revolution that gave them control of the city. The new government structure they introduced, the guild regime, transformed Augsburg's economic and political organization in ways that persisted for almost 200 years.[1] Their actions belonged to a wave of guild revolutions that swept across urban communities in the late fourteenth century.[2] As in most places, an interplay of factors within and outside the city shaped how Augsburg's guild-based political system operated. Scholars have examined Augsburg's internal political dynamics in great detail, and many studies emphasize how interactions among different actors inside the city walls guided politics under the guild regime. This approach has produced remarkable insights, but it risks obscuring the numerous external impulses that shaped guild regime policies as well. Augsburg's magistrates participated in multiple networks that linked them to other authorities in Swabia and elsewhere. By integrating Augsburg's guild regime more completely into these wider constellations, historians can achieve a more holistic understanding of its policies, especially as they related to social movements such as the Reformation.

Three patterns of political activity reveal the interdependence between internal and external factors in shaping civic politics under Augsburg's guild regime. First, as the government became increasingly oligarchical during the fifteenth and sixteenth centuries, Augsburg's magistrates developed an identity as the arbiters of "peace and unity" within their community.[3] This principle served as justification for almost every domestic policy the guild regime pursued, even as government control shifted among different factions. Second, Augsburg's governing council sought to extend its authority over neighboring

---

1   Blendinger, "Zunfterhebung", pp. 150–51.
2   Eitel, *Zunftherrschaft*.
3   On the importance of these ideals beyond Augsburg, see Rublack, "Grundwerte".

FIGURE 6.1 Establishment of the guild regime in 1368 according to Clemens Jäger's *Consulatsbuch* (1545)
STAATS- UND STADTBIBLIOTHEK AUGSBURG, CIM 21, FOL. 37R

communities. The push for an expanded sphere of influence outside the city fed off related attempts to subjugate internal aspects of civic life, such as the appointment of clerics, to the council's regulation. Third, city leaders employed alliances with other political authorities to promote Augsburg's external interests and to protect its internal freedoms. These three policy strands coalesced together most clearly in the gradual introduction of the Reformation in the 1520s and 1530s, which represented one of the guild regime's most important legacies but ultimately led to its demise. Examining these trends throughout the entire period of its existence displays the remarkable continuities and important political transitions that marked the two centuries of guild regime government in Augsburg.

1   The Guild Regime's Structure

Augsburg's guild constitution, which lasted from 1368 to 1548, underwent minor modifications during its lifetime. Nevertheless, its basic parameters remained intact, which gave Augsburg an institutional stability that promoted its economic and political ascendancy in the fifteenth century. The guild regime's structure reflected the division of Augsburg's ruling classes into two groups: patricians and guildsmen. The patricians belonged to an exclusive, hereditary class that possessed landed wealth and was barred from performing manual labor. They could undertake mercantile activity, however, and the leaders of some of the city's biggest banking firms came from Augsburg's patriciate. Guildsmen embodied a wide variety of socioeconomic statuses, ranging from some of the city's richest traders down to some of its poorest weavers.[4] Seventeen guilds operated in Augsburg. A hierarchy existed among them, with some corporations such as the merchant guild sending more representatives to the city government than other, less prestigious guilds such as the bakers. The office of mayor, whose occupants frequently came from the merchant guild, epitomized this imbalance. Since the leaders of individual guilds also occupied civic offices, significant overlap existed between guild leadership and membership in Augsburg's government.[5]

The largest body within Augsburg's political leadership was the Large Council (*Großer Rat*), with 233 members. Each guild sent its 13 highest ranking officials to this assembly, along with 12 patricians that the guilds

---

4   Sieh-Burens, *Oligarchie*, pp. 24–28. On Augsburg's patriciate, see Gloor, *Politisches Handeln*, pp. 66–96.
5   Gloor, *Politisches Handeln*, pp. 164–89; Sieh-Burens, "Stadtverfassung", pp. 127–30.

elected. Because of its size, the Large Council only met when Augsburg's mayors convened it.[6] It could exact taxes but served mainly as a venue for garnering popular support for decisions made in the other two organs of government, the Small Council and the Council of Thirteen. The Large Council therefore stabilized Augsburg's political system by ensuring that the institutions managing the city's day-to-day affairs remained accountable to the guilds. While it rarely formulated policy on its own, its backing legitimized the actions of the smaller, more exclusive councils.[7]

The Small Council (*Kleiner Rat*), which handled much of the city's daily business, included 42 members, all of whom came from the Large Council. When scholars refer to "Augsburg's council", they usually mean this institution. Two guildmasters from each guild sat on the Small Council, along with eight patricians. From the fifteenth century onwards, the records of this group's meetings, which occurred roughly every three days, have survived in the *Ratsbücher* (council books) and *Ratsprotokolle* (council protocols).[8] Within the Small Council, an elite group managed the de facto government of the city. This subcommittee – known as the *Dreizehner*, or Council of Thirteen – met almost daily. Its detailed records, which became especially thorough in the sixteenth century, display the Thirteen's importance, especially in matters of external policy.[9] Membership in the Thirteen was limited to a small group of men. Between the years 1486 and 1518, for example, only 30 individuals served on the Thirteen. Of that number, nine members served once or twice, meaning this 32-year period saw 21 individuals serve three or more annual terms.[10] Once on the Thirteen, one tended to remain in this select committee, a fact that created continuity and cultivated political experience among Augsburg's top magistrates. The Thirteen's exclusive nature meant that shifts in its membership could alter the city's politics in significant ways.

At the top of Augsburg's political hierarchy sat the two mayors (*Bürgermeister*), one patrician and one guildsman, whom the Small Council elected for one-year terms. Both mayors belonged to the Thirteen. Augsburg's constitution barred individuals from serving as mayor for two consecutive years, but mayors were routinely re-elected every other year. From 1518 to 1534, for example, Hieronymus Imhoff served as guild mayor nine times, while Georg Vetter occupied the office of patrician mayor eight times, both in the even years.[11] Such

---

6   Rogge, *Für den Gemeinen Nutzen*, p. 14.
7   Rogge, *Für den Gemeinen Nutzen*, pp. 231–46.
8   On these sources, see Kluge, *Macht des Gedächtnisses*, pp. 293–306.
9   Sieh-Burens, "Stadtverfassung", pp. 134–37.
10 Böhm, *Reichsstadt Augsburg*, pp. 375–76.
11 Sieh-Burens, "Bürgermeisteramt", p. 62, n. 8.

continuity provided consistency in Augsburg's external and internal policies. It allowed officeholders to accrue practical expertise, an important characteristic for mayors, since they served as Augsburg's main representatives in dealings with other authorities. Most correspondence received by the city was addressed to the "mayor and council", and the mayors often held responsibility for communicating with council representatives away on diplomatic missions. As members of the Thirteen and the only individuals with authority to convene the Large Council, the mayors influenced all aspects of guild regime politics.

Council elections occurred every January. After each guild selected its leaders by majority vote, another round of voting took place to certify their membership in the Large Council. This primarily symbolic act made visible to the community the council's legitimacy. As with the mayors, council members were often re-elected to their posts year after year.[12] Once the composition of the Small Council and the Thirteen had been determined, Augsburg's new mayors appeared on the balcony of the city hall to swear their oath of office in public before the populace. Augsburg's citizens responded by reiterating their oath of obedience to the council.[13] This yearly ritual bound the community together and certified the government's authority by making explicit the reciprocal duties of council and citizen. With minor variations, similar political systems developed in many south German imperial cities. The excellent preservation of sources in Augsburg, coupled with its political and economic prominence, make it a useful case study for understanding the guild-based system of governance that dominated late medieval German cities.

2   Politics in the Fifteenth Century

During the 1400s, Augsburg developed into one of the richest, most populous, and most powerful cities in southern Germany. Its population swelled from approximately 10,000 inhabitants in 1400 to around 30,000 inhabitants by the 1510s, a sign of the economic growth the city experienced during this period.[14] Augsburg's magistrates sought to promote "peace and unity" within this burgeoning community by establishing council supervision over numerous aspects of civic life. Their attempts to gain control of clerical appointments to the city's churches epitomized this trend. As in all late medieval cities, a variety

---

12   On the process of voting, see Rogge, *Für den Gemeinen Nutzen*, pp. 16–27.
13   Sieh-Burens, "Stadtverfassung", pp. 141–42.
14   Gloor, *Politisches Handeln*, pp. 388–89.

of Catholic clergy lived in Augsburg: parish priests, monks and nuns, cathedral canons, endowed preachers, and others. Many positions came with a right of patronage, which gave the owner the authority to appoint a new cleric when a post became vacant. Numerous entities possessed appointment rights in the city, with Augsburg's bishop, corporate institutions such as monasteries, and even some private citizens naming clerics to specific positions. Throughout the fifteenth century, Augsburg's council worked hard to acquire for itself as many patronage rights as possible in order to provide better spiritual care for its community.[15] These efforts provoked conflict with the bishop, who desired to centralize clerical appointments in his own hands. Such competition fed into an on-going rivalry between civic leaders and the bishop stretching back to 1276, when Augsburg gained independence from the bishop's political authority.[16] The council's ownership of appointment rights remained far from complete, but its actions reveal that long before the Reformation, Augsburg's authorities felt a duty to safeguard their community's spiritual well-being. Their sense of responsibility for their subjects' religious welfare motivated attempts to limit the bishop's jurisdiction within the city, and it caused magistrates to lump social and religious deviants together as "bad citizens" who disrupted public order.[17]

At the same time that Augsburg's council sought to centralize authority in its hands, it underwent a process of oligarchization that restricted access to its most important offices. By the second half of the fifteenth century, a limited group of individuals from the most prestigious guilds and the patriciate had come to dominate the Small Council. Many guildsmen found themselves shut out of positions of power. They reacted by agitating for increased participation from all the guilds in civic governance. This movement culminated in Ulrich Schwarz's reign as guild mayor.[18] A member of the carpenter guild, Schwarz first became mayor in 1469. From 1475 to 1478, he occupied the office for four straight years, a novelty that breached the tradition prohibiting consecutive mayoral terms. Schwarz shepherded through several constitutional reforms that gave the less prestigious guilds more representation in the Small Council and replaced the Thirteen with an expanded Council of Eighteen. Schwarz and his supporters argued that these innovations "made for better peace" by

---

15 Kießling, *Bürgerliche Gesellschaft*, p. 179.
16 On this rivalry, see Tyler, *Sacred City*.
17 Smelyansky, "Urban Order", p. 20.
18 On the following, see Gloor, *Politisches Handeln*, pp. 300–304; Rogge, *Für den Gemeinen Nutzen*, pp. 48–82.

integrating every guild into the city's innermost decision-making process.[19] For Schwarz's opponents, his actions threatened Augsburg's political stability and worked "to the detriment of the common good".[20] A struggle ensued that in 1477 resulted in the execution of Schwarz's two main political enemies. Rather than subdue his detractors, the executions galvanized resistance to Schwarz. With the help of imperial agents, in April 1478 Schwarz's opponents had the mayor arrested, placed on trial for treason, and eventually executed. The city's new leaders re-established the Thirteen and rolled back many of Schwarz's other reforms, although they allowed each guild to retain equal membership in the Small Council.

The turmoil caused by Schwarz's call for wider inclusion in political decision-making encouraged the Small Council and the Thirteen to accelerate the concentration of authority in their own hands. In the aftermath of Schwarz's execution, Augsburg's magistrates worked especially to curtail the independence of the guilds, a process Jörg Rogge has dubbed the "intensification" of rule from the top.[21] Similar to the struggle over clerical appointments, the Schwarz Affair dramatized an on-going debate over how Augsburg's government could best promote internal peace and the common good of all its citizens. Both sides in the conflict appealed to these cardinal values, which operated as living, breathing concepts that formed the basis of civic politics, even as their exact meaning remained open to interpretation.

In concert with the intensification of council rule within the city, Augsburg's external politics during the fifteenth century aimed to secure the city's independence against the aggression of neighboring princes. The council also sought to increase its economic and political jurisdiction over nearby communities through a policy that Rolf Kießling has labelled "indirect lordship".[22] The fifteenth century marked a period of expansion for many German cities, as urban governments subjugated surrounding rural territories to their rule.[23] In Augsburg, the council's attempts to gain jurisdiction in the countryside proved challenging, as the city bordered two large territorial states: the duchy of Bavaria and the prince-bishopric of Augsburg. Competition with these authorities limited opportunities for direct control of rural communities.[24] Many citizens controlled sizeable possessions in the countryside, however, as did

---

19 Quoted at Rogge, *Für den Gemeinen Nutzen*, p. 66. Unless otherwise noted, translations are my own.
20 Quoted at Gloor, *Politisches Handeln*, p. 302, n. 1389.
21 Rogge, *Gemeinen Nutzen*, pp. 284–85.
22 Kießling, "Augsburg", p. 247.
23 Scott, *City-State*, pp. 137–64.
24 Lutz, "Umwelt", pp. 413–14.

the city's ecclesiastical institutions. Augsburg's council exploited this situation by exercising authority indirectly in rural communities through these intermediaries. Since those individuals with rural possessions tended to cluster in the city's governing elite, the use of indirect lordship complemented the council's oligarchization. It also strengthened the desire to expand the council's control of clerical appointments, since the more influence magistrates could exert on the staffing of ecclesiastical institutions, the more effectively they could pursue policies beneficial to the council in those institutions' rural holdings.[25] This symbiosis between internal and external policies highlights the importance of Augsburg's wider geopolitical context for understanding guild regime initiatives.

Part of Augsburg's strategy to protect itself against neighboring princes involved cultivating ties to the imperial house of Habsburg. Here the city's prosperity proved vital. During the 1400s, Augsburg developed into one of the richest merchant-banking centers in central Europe. This wealth drew the interest of several Habsburg rulers, who constantly needed money and saw a ready source of capital in Augsburg's banking firms. In exchange for granting the Habsburgs substantial loans, Augsburg's firms gained numerous rights to mining operations in the Alps, along with other privileges. This activity augmented the city's visibility on the level of imperial politics and increased the funds at the disposal of its political leaders. In a similar way to the policy of indirect lordship, the possessions of individual citizens and the expansion of the city's political influence went hand in hand.[26]

This dynamic became especially prominent at the end of the fifteenth century during the reign of Emperor Maximilian I, who visited Augsburg 55 times while emperor and granted the council new privileges on 19 separate occasions. In return, from 1489 to 1517, Augsburg's council loaned Maximilian over 70,000 gulden.[27] In addition, Maximilian took out loans from the Fugger banking house that by 1518 totaled over 1,300,000 gulden.[28] These financial ties to the emperor bolstered Augsburg's program of indirect lordship, as many of the new imperial privileges expanded the council's rights in nearby rural areas on terms that the city's magistrates themselves suggested.[29] This interplay between imperial and urban prerogatives speaks to the unique position of imperial cities. Augsburg needed the emperor's support and protection to

---

25 Kießling, *Bürgerliche Gesellschaft*; Sieh-Burens, "Stadtverfassung", pp. 142–44.
26 Gloor, *Politisches Handeln*, pp. 386–87; Lutz, "Umwelt", pp. 416–17.
27 Böhm, *Reichsstadt Augsburg*, pp. 378–92.
28 Brady, *Turning Swiss*, p. 82. See Chapter 5 in this volume.
29 Böhm, *Reichsstadt Augsburg*, pp. 355–68.

strengthen its external policies, while Maximilian saw Augsburg as a financial and political resource he could exploit. This interdependence created opportunities for Augsburg's council even as it threatened to subjugate the city's political agenda to imperial interests.

A final hallmark of guild regime politics during the fifteenth century involved the use of alliances to promote Augsburg's regional policies. Alliances united multiple political authorities for a collective benefit, often the preservation of public peace or the resolution of neighborly conflicts. Their collaborative decision-making process and ability to pool resources made leagues attractive to urban magistrates. Beginning in 1379 and continuing throughout the fifteenth century, Augsburg's council participated in several alliances as bulwarks against the expansion of neighboring territories, particularly Bavaria. Some alliances proved more successful than others, and membership carried risks, as Augsburg's magistrates discovered in 1449 when an urban league they had joined suffered military defeat and collapsed.[30] On the whole, however, leagues offered an effective tool for protecting the city's external interests, especially when alliances brought princes and cities together around a common cause.

This feature marked the most powerful alliance that Augsburg joined in the fifteenth century, the Swabian League.[31] Founded in 1488 under Habsburg leadership, the League sought to maintain public peace in its member territories, which included princely estates and many imperial cities. It provided a forum for the coordination of common policies that lasted until 1534. Imperial cities held an influential position within the League's structure, and some urban magistrates characterized the Swabian League as the "proper form of the German nation", an indication of the importance they ascribed to its operation.[32] For Augsburg's council, the League offered protection against Bavarian expansion and a way to institutionalize influence over other Swabian cities. Augsburg therefore assumed a leadership position among the League's cities, a role it shared with its main urban rival, Ulm. Similar to many of its other fifteenth-century policies, Augsburg's participation in alliances, especially large ones like the Swabian League, established a pattern of political behavior that persisted into the sixteenth century and framed how the city's authorities confronted the challenges of the Reformation era.

---

30 Schnith, "Reichsstadt Augsburg", p. 161.
31 On the Swabian League, see Carl, *Der Schwäbische Bund*.
32 Quoted in Carl, *Der Schwäbische Bund*, p. 501.

3 Politics in the Early Sixteenth Century

The sixteenth century opened with Augsburg's involvement in two wars conducted by Emperor Maximilian and the Swabian League. The 1499 Swabian War ended with the League's defeat by the Swiss Confederation, which effectively removed the Swiss from the Empire's jurisdiction. A few years later, in 1504, war again erupted in southern Germany, this time on Augsburg's doorstep, over a contested succession in the duchy of Bavaria. This conflict proved more successful for Augsburg, resulting in a League triumph that neutered the Bavarian threat to the city for the next decade.[33] Money from Augsburg and other imperial cities played a critical role in funding both campaigns. This dynamic, with alliance leaders relying on urban finances to conduct military operations, characterized many leagues. It augmented the political importance of the city's merchant-banking houses, which continued to grow during the first two decades of the sixteenth century.[34]

The large firms' wealth and the influence it bought stoked resentment among the Empire's princes and common folk, which boiled over in the early 1520s in legal attempts to dismantle the merchant houses on the basis that they operated as "monopolies". This term implied that the firms manipulated economic markets in an illicit fashion to serve their own interests at the expense of the common good.[35] Augsburg's magistrates saw this anti-monopoly movement as a threat to the city's financial and political stability. Much of the city's wealth derived from its banking houses, and many magistrates had a family connection to one or more firms. The council therefore fought to preserve the houses at all costs. The famous humanist and city secretary Conrad Peutinger, who had married into the Welser house, took the lead. As Augsburg's city secretary, Peutinger oversaw the council's correspondence with external authorities and wrote several tracts defending the merchant firms during the monopoly debate. His treatises argued that unregulated profit-seeking served the common good rather than hurt it.[36] Such a claim embodied the mercantile ethos of many Augsburg councilors in a way that tapped into their goal of maintaining peace and unity. Ultimately, Augsburg's officials persuaded Maximilian's grandson and successor Emperor Charles V to issue decrees protecting the large houses from prosecution. This move owed much to Charles's financial dependence on Augsburg's firms, which had funded his 1519 election as emperor.

---

33 Brady, *Turning Swiss*, pp. 57–79.
34 See Chapter 5 in this volume.
35 Brady, *Turning Swiss*, pp. 120–29; Johnson, *German Discovery*, pp. 132–44.
36 Bauer, "Gutachten"; Johnson, *German Discovery*, pp. 168–77; Lutz, *Peutinger*.

Augsburg's victory came at a cost, however, as the council's unwillingness to compromise upset magistrates in cities such as Ulm and Nuremberg, where councilors had been willing to make concessions on monopolies to quiet other attacks on urban liberties.[37] While Augsburg's council repaired its relations with these cities in the ensuing years, its actions in the monopoly debate left lingering doubts in other council chambers about the loyalties of Augsburg's magistrates.

At the same time that Augsburg's council dealt with the external challenge against merchant monopolies, it undertook several measures to increase the effectiveness of its internal governance. In 1519, for example, the council reorganized the city's court system, while in March 1522 it issued a new alms ordinance that complemented the council's desire to strengthen its jurisdiction vis-a-vis the city's ecclesiastical institutions. Traditionally, the Catholic Church controlled the administration of alms, but the 1522 ordinance transferred this responsibility to the city government. It centralized almsgiving into a new civic institution headed by six "alms lords", whom the council appointed. Each alms lord received sole authority to collect donations for the poor in one of six districts and to determine the most appropriate way to distribute these funds to the needy.[38] A similar shift in jurisdiction occurred in many imperial cities in the early sixteenth century, as city governments claimed authority over public charity. In Augsburg, the 1522 ordinance offered another way for the council to regulate the city's internal peace that continued the policies of centralization it had pursued since the Schwarz affair.

These initiatives provide part of the context for how Augsburg's political authorities reacted to the Reformation, which tested the council's ability to maintain peace and unity among its populace. Reform ideas found early entry into Augsburg and circulated freely among the general citizenry and elites. In early 1518, for example, Peutinger received a copy of Martin Luther's *95 Theses* through his ties to humanist circles. When Luther visited the city later that year and came under threat, the son of Augsburg's patrician mayor helped smuggle him out of the city. The connections councilors possessed to other cities enabled many officials to develop personal relationships with reformers, as Ulrich Langenmantel's correspondence with the Zurich reformer Ulrich Zwingli shows.[39] The diversity of ideas that characterized the early Reformation gripped Augsburg's populace, and throughout the 1520s, supporters of Lutheran reform, Zwinglian or Upper German reform, and Catholicism

---

37 Brady, *Turning Swiss*, pp. 120–50; Mertens, *Monopole*.
38 Gößner, *Weltliche Kirchenhoheit*, pp. 39–40; Sieh-Burens, *Oligarchie*, pp. 147–51.
39 Sieh-Burens, "Bürgermeisteramt", pp. 65–66; Sieh-Burens, *Oligarchie*, p. 134.

co-existed within the council and jockeyed for position. This internal split undermined the council's ability to formulate a religious policy palatable to all its members.[40] It therefore adopted a neutral approach that upheld Catholic primacy but did not suppress evangelical ideas. For example, the council published the papal bull excommunicating Luther and refused to sanction the marriage of a priest in 1523.[41] It also officially barred printers from producing polemical religious texts, but it did little to enforce the prohibition.[42] In a similar vein, it gave lip service to the 1521 Edict of Worms but did not implement it in any stringent manner, and it turned a blind eye to reformed preaching in the city's churches.[43] This laissez-faire attitude reflected the religious divisions among Augsburg's magistrates, but it also proved consistent with the council's long-standing commitment to fostering "good unity, as well as proper Christian order, government, and peace".[44] The only way magistrates saw to preserve these values was to avoid taking an official stance for or against religious reform. In the Reformation's early stages, Augsburg's political leaders tried to overcome its challenges by incorporating them into the pre-existing framework of council policies.

This approach came under fire in 1524. While the council tried to remain aloof from theological debates, it felt compelled to intervene when a cleric's message fomented social and political unrest. In August 1524, the council moved against Johann Schilling, a preacher in the city's Franciscan Church. Schilling's sermons harshly criticized Catholic practices, called for greater economic equality between Augsburg's rich and poor, and condemned the council's refusal to introduce religious reform. These arguments made him very popular, but they also led members of the Small Council to fear that his sermons could trigger social disturbances or even an uprising. They therefore arranged Schilling's removal in secret and sent him away from Augsburg in order to preserve "peace and tranquility among the poor and rich in this city".[45] Word of Schilling's dismissal spread quickly, however, and on 6 August, a large crowd numbering well over 1,000 people assembled outside city hall during a meeting of the Small Council and demanded Schilling's reinstatement. After several failed attempts to appease the crowd, the council agreed to recall Schilling, and

---

40   Sieh-Burens, "Bürgermeisteramt", pp. 69–70. On diversity of belief among the general populace, see Zelinsky Hanson, *Religious Identity*. See also Chapter 10 in this volume.
41   Sieh-Burens, *Oligarchie*, pp. 150–51.
42   Creasman, *Censorship*, pp. 68–71.
43   Immenkötter, "Kirche", p. 396.
44   Quoted in Gößner, *Weltliche Kirchenhoheit*, p. 40.
45   Rogge, *Für den Gemeinen Nutzen*, pp. 250–54, quote at p. 253; Amberg, *Real Presence*, pp. 49–62.

the protesters dispersed. Tensions remained high, and armed conflict almost broke out on 12 August, but Schilling's reappearance that evening calmed the situation. The Schilling affair dramatized the Reformation's explosive political power and marked the collapse of the council's policy of non-involvement in reform matters. It taught Augsburg's magistrates the importance of getting ahead of popular reform movements in order to curtail their potential for socio-political upheaval. In the weeks following the August 1524 disturbances, therefore, Augsburg's magistrates reasserted their authority by rounding up some of the principal actors in the demonstrations and charging them with plans to overthrow the council. On 15 September, it executed the ringleaders. In November, Schilling left the city again for good.[46]

Augsburg's experience in the Schilling affair derived from the city's specific context, but it was not entirely unique. Other urban communities witnessed similar clashes between the general populace and council during the late fifteenth and early sixteenth centuries.[47] These uprisings rarely toppled the government. Instead, they often strengthened the reciprocal relationship between the council and its citizenry. In Augsburg, the Schilling affair encouraged the council to crack down on dissidents, but it also forced magistrates to become more open to religious reform as an official policy and to respond in clearer terms to the demands of its citizens. The ability of regular people to influence the council's actions, however restricted that capacity might have been, goes a long way toward explaining why moments of violent internal upheaval like the Schilling affair proved exceptions rather than the rule under the guild regime.

4 The Political Move toward Reform (1525–37)

In 1524–26, a massive revolt gripped the Holy Roman Empire. Known as the Peasants' War, the disruptions it caused to Augsburg's commerce, and the danger of revolution linked to religious reform that it displayed, made lasting impressions on the city's leadership. Together with the Schilling affair, the Peasants' War pushed Augsburg's council to adopt a new approach toward the Reformation that Conrad Peutinger termed "the middle way". This policy advocated a gradual move toward church reform that could avoid alienating those Augsburgers who remained loyal to the Catholic Church. Taking "the middle way" meant maintaining close ties to the emperor and preserving Catholicism

---

46 Rogge, *Für den Gemeinen Nutzen*, pp. 254–83; Amberg, *Real Presence*, pp. 70–81.
47 Brady, *Turning Swiss*, pp. 13–15; Isenmann, *Deutsche Stadt*, pp. 412–14; Panzer, *Sozialer Protest*.

in the city while simultaneously allowing the establishment of evangelical ideas and practices. Similar to most council policies, "the middle way" sought to protect the city's freedoms in its dealings with external authorities while also maintaining social harmony among its inhabitants.[48]

The notion of religious coexistence inherent to "the middle way" became a lasting feature of Augsburg's landscape throughout the early modern period. In the 1520s, it meant that Augsburg's council prohibited religious polemics but for the most part permitted the city's inhabitants to believe as they pleased. With their eyes on the Schilling affair and the Peasants' War, magistrates drew the line at ideas that threatened the city's peace and political order.[49] Those individuals who linked socio-political change to religious reform, such as some Anabaptists, fell under suspicion. In April 1528, civic authorities arrested over 100 people on charges of practicing Anabaptism, many of whom they expelled from Augsburg.[50] The crackdown on radicals supported the council's desire to maintain internal harmony, as it denounced Anabaptist ideas as causing "quarrels, division, fighting, rebellion, and repudiation of the government ordained by God".[51] It also helped rebuff allegations from other authorities that the city harbored dangerous revolutionaries, an accusation leveled at Augsburg and other cities in the wake of the Peasants' War.[52]

Externally, Augsburg's "middle way" pushed the council into a no-man's-land between those estates that opposed the Reformation and those authorities that embraced it. In trying to please everyone, Augsburg's magistrates pleased no one. In 1529, the council accepted the controversial recess of the Imperial Diet of Speyer, and it initially refused to take sides at the 1530 imperial diet held in Augsburg. These positions separated Augsburg from the religious policies of many other imperial cities, a development whose roots stretched back to urban divisions during the monopoly debate. The 1530 diet did mark a turning point for Augsburg's religious politics, however. The council refused to certify the diet's decision condemning evangelical reform, even as it promised Emperor Charles V that it would continue to allow Catholic worship in the city. While it did not openly join the reform camp, therefore, Augsburg's council broke its neutrality.[53] In the wake of the 1530 diet, attitudes among the city's leaders shifted in favor of the Reformation, and the political movement toward formal religious reform received a boost in January 1531 from a

---

48   Sieh-Burens, "Bürgermeisteramt", p. 72.
49   Zelinsky Hanson, *Religious Identity*, pp. 48–50.
50   On Augsburg's Anabaptists, see Zelinsky Hanson, *Religious Identity*, pp. 79–105.
51   Quoted in Creasman, *Censorship*, p. 95. Translation is Creasman's.
52   Carl, *Der Schwäbische Bund*, pp. 174–75.
53   Gößner, *Weltliche Kirchenhoheit*, pp. 56–61; Sieh-Burens, *Oligarchie*, pp. 152–53.

change in council membership. The annual elections saw eight Catholic loyalists replaced by reform supporters, giving those favorable to the Reformation the upper hand within the Small Council. This election formed part of a larger rotation of new individuals into the Small Council and the office of mayor, as stalwarts who had served for years either passed away or became too old to hold office. The reform party's majority position allowed it to employ several reform-minded jurists as council advisors, some of whom, like Georg Frölich, played prominent roles in civic politics until the guild regime's end.[54]

The council also used its influence over some of the city's ecclesiastical institutions to appoint new evangelical clerics. Ironically, the conditions that Emperor Charles V imposed on Augsburg for hosting the 1530 imperial diet facilitated this move. In advance of the diet, the emperor ordered a halt to reform preaching in the city, which caused many preachers to leave. Once the diet recessed, Augsburg's council had a blank slate to summon whichever clerics it desired to fill the empty positions.[55] Councilors looked principally to Strasbourg, which sent Augsburg five preachers in 1531–32, and Augsburg's emerging official reformation developed close ties to the Alsatian city. These preachers pressured the council to introduce full-scale religious reform in the city's churches, something Augsburg's magistrates continued to avoid, in part for fear of external repercussions. In January 1533, the local preachers even formally petitioned the council "to perform its assigned, divinely ordained office and immediately eliminate everything that according to God's commandments and His Word should be eliminated".[56] In a parallel to the Schilling affair, segments of urban society outside the council sought to push the city's political leadership toward greater open support for the Reformation.

Augsburg's council responded by asking its jurists to study the legality of religious reform. Only two of the five recommendations came back positive.[57] Despite the shift in council membership, deep rifts remained within Augsburg's leadership circles, a fact that helps explain why the council waited until mid-1534 to adopt any kind of official reform. External factors also played a role. The Swabian League, which opposed the Reformation in its member territories, threatened action against the city if it adopted reform. In order to strengthen its position, Augsburg formed a Three Cities' League in 1533 with Nuremberg and Ulm. This new alliance pooled the financial resources of the three communes in a way that provided for their common defense and supported Augsburg's

---

54 Gößner, *Weltliche Kirchenhoheit*, pp. 63–85; Sieh-Burens, "Bürgermeisteramt", pp. 73–76.
55 Gößner, *Weltliche Kirchenhoheit*, pp. 85–87; Sieh-Burens, *Oligarchie*, pp. 143–45.
56 Quoted in Roth, *Augsburgs Reformationsgeschichte*, vol. 2, p. 135.
57 Gößner, *Weltliche Kirchenhoheit*, pp. 96–147.

ambition to expand its sphere of influence over surrounding territories.[58] With this regional support structure in place, Augsburg's reform-minded magistrates seized the opportunity when the Swabian League dissolved in early 1534. On 29 July, the council mandated that only clerics that it appointed could preach within the city. It claimed this move would "preserve sound teaching, beloved peace, and praiseworthy unity among its subjects, whom God has entrusted [to the council's care]". The council also ordered all but eight of the city's churches to stop celebrating the Latin Mass. Those churches where the bishop retained rights of clerical appointment could continue Catholic services. In the city's other churches, the council permitted the introduction of evangelical worship.[59]

While Augsburg's 1534 reform decree prohibited Catholic clergy from preaching in public, therefore, it did not eliminate Catholicism entirely from the city. It continued the practice of religious co-existence, albeit recast in favor of evangelical reform. In order to take the final step toward a full-scale reformation that banned Catholicism, Augsburg's council needed stronger external backing than the Three Cities' League could offer. It set its sights on a new Protestant alliance that included urban and princely members from across the Empire: the Schmalkaldic League. Founded in 1531, the League provided for the collective defense of the Reformation in its members' territories. After years of negotiation, Augsburg finally entered the alliance in January 1536.[60] One year later, shortly after the annual elections again strengthened the council's reform party, Augsburg's magistrates took the final step toward official reform. On 17 January 1537, they expelled the city's remaining Catholic clergy, outlawed the Latin Mass, and ordered the implementation of a new church ordinance. In explaining its actions, Augsburg's council cited the experiences of "Nuremberg and Ulm, which years ago decided they would permit no Catholic foundation to take root in their cities. For this reason, they above all others enjoy peace and tranquility."[61] As they had in so many other instances, Augsburg's magistrates fell back on the cardinal values of guild regime politics to justify their new religious direction.

Augsburg's incremental move toward official reform highlights the gradual process by which the urban Reformation often occurred. In most cities, the introduction of reform resulted from a lengthy give and take between the

---

58   Stadtarchiv Augsburg (StadtAA), Literaliensammlung, 26 May 1533.
59   Gößner, *Weltliche Kirchenhoheit*, pp. 190–97, quote at p. 195, n. 28.
60   Close, *Negotiated Reformation*, pp. 69–76. On the League's wider history, see Brady, *Protestant Politics*.
61   StadtAA, Literaliensammlung, 17 January 1537.

council, its preachers, and the common people. Each city's reform path also depended on the constellation of external pressures on the city. This process of negotiation, both internally within the city and externally among different authorities, shaped the Reformation in almost every urban community.[62] In Augsburg's case, the council hoped "the middle way" would placate supporters of reform while maintaining good relations with Catholic powers like Bavaria and the emperor. Once it shifted policy in the early 1530s, the council drew on connections to cities that had already adopted the Reformation, such as Strasbourg and Ulm, to guide and protect its actions. The Three Cities' League offered additional structural support, but Augsburg's council sought the security that only the Schmalkaldic League could provide. Once Schmalkaldic membership became a reality, Augsburg's council felt empowered to embark on a new religio-political path that dominated the guild regime's final 11 years.

5   The Reformation Council (1537–48)

The 1537 introduction of the Reformation occurred under the leadership of Wolfgang Rehlinger, who became patrician mayor in 1534 at the young age of 29. A committed advocate of reform, Rehlinger dominated Augsburg's politics until his resignation from the council in 1543. To consolidate his influence, Rehlinger shifted the Council of Thirteen's responsibilities to a new Secret Council comprised of only six individuals. Initially a sub-committee of the Thirteen, the Secret Council under Rehlinger took over the city's daily governance, supplanting the Thirteen and guiding Augsburg's introduction of religious reform.[63] This concentration of power in the Secret Council marked the pinnacle of the guild regime's oligarchization and magnified the intertwining of religion and politics in its operation.

Implementing the Reformation was one of the Secret Council's biggest challenges. The January 1537 decree placed all of Augsburg's churches under the council's sole authority. The council finally controlled all clerical appointments in the city, and it sought to ensure conformity to its official version of Protestant reform. For assistance, it again turned to Strasbourg and petitioned its Schmalkaldic ally to send the reformer Martin Bucer to "help complete the ongoing construction of our Christian church".[64] Bucer's activity codified Augsburg's Protestant church ordinance and catechism. The council also issued

---

62   Close, *Negotiated Reformation*.
63   Roth, *Augsburgs Reformationsgeschichte*, vol. 2, pp. 286–87; Sieh-Burens, *Oligarchie*, p. 150.
64   StadtAA, Literaliensammlung, 17 April 1537.

a new discipline ordinance and created a marriage and morals courts to enforce the Reformation's principles.[65] Nevertheless, attempts to create religious unity encountered some resistance from the population. Some Augsburgers, such as the wealthy Fuggers, retained Catholic sympathies.[66] As city secretary Georg Frölich noted with dismay in 1538, other inhabitants refused to attend the regular sermons. Instead, many "common folk are meeting once again in private houses, reading and reciting to each other. Your honors can well understand how false belief, religious sects, and schism may result".[67] Frölich described clandestine groups gathering within the boundaries of Johann Schilling's old stomping grounds, the Franciscan Church. This association raised the specter of renewed political unrest rooted in deviant religiosity. Social order and proper religious belief went hand in hand for the Reformation council, but the legacy of the policy of coexistence ensured that not all of Augsburg's inhabitants followed the council's demands once an official version of reform existed.

The council's efforts to reshape religious practice in the city coincided with an increase in the number of Augsburg's patricians, whose ranks had shrunk through death and emigration to a mere eight families. Many officials feared this downward trend meant that patrician posts in the city's government would soon go unfilled. With the guild regime's viability in question, Augsburg's magistrates elevated 39 new families to the patriciate in October 1538. A majority of these families supported religious reform, which has led Katarina Sieh-Burens to characterize the expansion as an attempt to institutionalize government backing for the Reformation. Georg Herwart, one of the move's leading proponents, gave the moment explicit religious meaning by explaining that since Augsburg "through God's grace has achieved true and right belief in its church services and ceremonies, this city needs many intelligent, god-fearing, and pious men". Including such people in the patriciate promoted "more unity ... and protected against many evil intrigues".[68] As a result, after the January 1539 elections, almost no open Catholics remained on the Small Council.

Despite the clear upper hand that supporters of reform enjoyed, not all councilors agreed on which direction the city should take. Many magistrates chafed under the exclusivity of the Secret Council, accusing Rehlinger of abusing the office of mayor to serve his own interests.[69] In 1543, this disgruntlement shifted power within the Small Council to a faction led by Georg Frölich

---

65   On these courts, see Roper, *Holy Household*, pp. 56–88.
66   Häberlein, *Fuggers*, pp. 181–88.
67   StadtAA, Literaliensammlung, Personalselekt Cellarius, 23 November 1538.
68   Sieh-Burens, "Bürgermeisteramt", pp. 81–86, quotes at p. 82.
69   See, for example, Lenz (ed.), *Briefwechsel*, pp. 339–40.

and the mayors Jakob Herbrot and Georg Herwart. This group eliminated the Secret Council and returned authority to the Thirteen.[70] Many of its other actions proved more radical. To ensure the proper staffing of the city's churches, the Herbrot council recruited preachers from Switzerland, specifically from the Zwinglian city of Zurich. This move provoked controversy with Augsburg's Schmalkaldic allies, many of whom condemned Zwinglian reform as heretical. Undeterred, Augsburg's leaders used the Swiss preachers to underwrite an aggressive external policy meant to enshrine Augsburg's regional religious influence.[71] From 1544 to 1546, Augsburg's magistrates shipped multiple preachers to neighboring communities with the goal of bringing them into line with Augsburg's Reformation. In rural villages, the council hoped to bolster its policy of indirect lordship by creating new ties of religious authority to Augsburg. It took a similar approach with the imperial cities Donauwörth and Kaufbeuren.[72] By sending preachers to convert these cities to Augsburg's version of reform, the council hoped to create, in the words of the preacher Michael Keller, "right-believing flank town[s] ... that, God willing, will stand beside Augsburg in religious matters and other Christian and neighborly affairs as well".[73] In the mid-1540s, religion and politics became one and the same for Augsburg's leaders as they acted to realize long-held regional objectives.[74]

These expansionist policies culminated in the 1546–47 Schmalkaldic War, which pitted Emperor Charles V against the Schmalkaldic League. Augsburg's leaders viewed the war as a righteous religious struggle that presented the opportunity "to bring [rural territories] into possession in such a way that, if the main affair succeeds, no one will be able to drive us out again".[75] By opposing the emperor and "undertaking the Christian work of improving the corrupted churches of these poor subjects now, God will grant us victory more quickly and allow the newly won Christians to remain with us".[76] The war's religious and political dimensions fed off each other for Augsburg's magistrates, and their program of evangelizing surrounding communities escalated in the conflict's opening phases. Unfortunately for Augsburg's council, Charles V proved victorious. In the closing months of 1546, the emperor subdued the Schmalkaldic cities one by one. On 29 January 1547, Augsburg's council surrendered. A few

---

70   Roth, *Augsburgs Reformationsgeschichte*, vol. 3, pp. 218–26.
71   Close, "Zurich".
72   Close, *Negotiated Reformation*, pp. 110–208.
73   StadtAA, Reichsstadtakten 541, 27 August 1545.
74   See Close, *Negotiated Reformation*; Kießling, "Eine italienische Option?".
75   Quoted in Roth, *Augsburgs Reformationsgeschichte*, vol. 3, p. 398.
76   Herberger (ed.), *Sebastian Schertlin*, p. 146. See also Häberlein, "Interessen", p. 35.

days later, imperial troops occupied the city, bringing with them the return of Catholicism.

Augsburg's military defeat meant the collapse of its expansionist policies and the end of the guild regime. In the war's aftermath, Augsburg's Protestant leaders endured the imposition of the *Interim*, which restored Catholic worship in the city and returned many of the buildings confiscated from the Catholic Church in the 1530s. On 3 August 1548, Charles V also dissolved Augsburg's guild government along with the city's seventeen guilds on the grounds that their "disorderly regime" had produced not peace and unity among the citizenry, but rather "division and misunderstanding, and even revolt and rebellion".[77] In their stead, the emperor introduced a new political order that placed government control in the hands of patricians, a group Charles believed would prove more sympathetic to the Catholic Church and imperial interests. Augsburg's experience formed part of a wider destruction of urban guild regimes that followed the emperor's victory in the Schmalkaldic War.[78] The city's new patrician-led council remained in place for two and a half centuries, but the legacy of guild regime policies lived on in the city's Protestant community and bi-confessional society, which persisted long after the guild regime itself disappeared.

6   Conclusion

Throughout its nearly 200-year existence, Augsburg's guild regime enacted policies that it believed would maintain peace and unity within its community. This goal remained remarkably consistent across the decades, even as its pursuit produced shifts in policy between eras. The focus on preserving internal civic unity complemented the guild regime's persistent desire to increase its sphere of influence, which provided a way to shore up the city's autonomy. The council made frequent use of indirect lordship and alliances with other authorities in patterns that recurred throughout the guild regime's history. All these policies found their most radical expression under the Reformation council.

While scholars have studied these various policy strands individually, the interdependencies between the council's internal and external politics require more investigation and represent a promising area for new scholarship. Future research on the guild regime should work to integrate Augsburg's politics into

---

77   Naujoks (ed.), *Kaiser Karl V.*, p. 57. See also Chapter 7 in this volume.
78   See Naujoks (ed.), *Kaiser Karl V.*

wider regional frameworks that reveal how those structures influenced guild regime policies and vice versa. In particular, scholars can illuminate how the guild regime's politics of alliance fit into its larger domestic and external political agendas, a crucial issue given the council's membership in multiple alliances during the fifteenth and sixteenth centuries. New studies of Augsburg's guild regime, and indeed of all guild regimes, should move beyond the city walls to chart how reciprocal influences between the city and surrounding territories shaped council actions. Augsburg's rich survival of sources makes it a valuable laboratory for exploring issues that can alter how scholars conceptualize urban politics across central Europe.

Bibliography

Unpublished Primary Sources
Stadtarchiv Augsburg (StadtAA)
    Literaliensammlung, 26 May 1533, 17 January 1537, 17 April 1537.
    Literaliensammlung, Personalselekt Cellarius, 23 November 1538.
    Reichsstadtakten 541, 27 August 1545.

Published Primary Sources
Herberger, T. (ed.), *Sebastian Schertlin und seine an die Stadt Augsburg geschriebenen Briefe*, Augsburg, 1852.
Lenz, M. (ed.), *Briefwechsel Landgraf Philipp's des Grossmüthigen von Hessen mit Bucer*, vol. 3, Leipzig, 1891.
Naujoks, E. (ed.), *Kaiser Karl V. und die Zunftverfassung. Ausgewählte Aktenstücke zu den Verfassungsänderungen in den oberdeutschen Reichsstädten (1547–1556)*, Stuttgart, 1985.

Secondary Literature
Amberg, J. van, *A Real Presence: Religious and Social Dynamics of the Eucharistic Conflicts in Early Modern Augsburg 1520–1530*, Leiden, 2012.
Bauer, C., "Conrad Peutingers Gutachten zur Monopolfrage", *Archiv für Reformationsgeschichte* 45 (1954), pp. 1–43, 145–96.
Blendinger, F., "Die Zunfterhebung von 1368", in Gottlieb et al. (eds.), *Geschichte der Stadt Augsburg*, pp. 150–53.
Böhm, C., *Die Reichsstadt Augsburg und Kaiser Maximilian I.*, Sigmaringen, 1998.
Brady, T., *Turning Swiss: Cities and Empire, 1450–1550*, Cambridge, 1985.
Brady, T., *Protestant Politics: Jacob Sturm (1489–1553) and the German Reformation*, Boston, 1995.

Carl, H., *Der Schwäbische Bund 1488–1534*, Leinfelden-Echterdingen, 2000.
Close, C., *The Negotiated Reformation: Imperial Cities and the Politics of Urban Reform, 1525–1550*, Cambridge, 2009.
Close, C., "Zurich, Augsburg, and the Transfer of Preachers during the Schmalkaldic War", *Central European History* 42 (2009), pp. 595–619.
Creasman, A., *Censorship and Civic Order in Reformation Germany, 1517–1648: "Printed Poison and Evil Talk"*, Farnham, 2012.
Eitel, P. *Die oberschwäbischen Reichsstädte im Zeitalter der Zunftherrschaft*, Stuttgart, 1970.
Gloor, M., *Politisches Handeln im spätmittelalterlichen Augsburg, Basel und Strassburg*, Heidelberg, 2010.
Gößner, A., *Weltliche Kirchenhoheit und reichsstädtische Reformation. Die Augsburger Ratspolitik des "milten und mitleren weges" 1520–1534*, Berlin, 1999.
Gottlieb, G., Baer, W., Becker, J., Bellot, J., Filser, K., Fried, P., Reinhard, W. and Schimmelpfennig, B. (eds.), *Geschichte der Stadt Augsburg von der Römerzeit bis zur Gegenwart*, Stuttgart, 1984.
Häberlein, M., "Interessen, Parteien und Allianzen. Gereon Sailer als 'Makler' in der oberdeutschen Reformation", in P. Burschel, M. Häberlein, V. Reinhardt, W.E.J. Weber and R. Wendt (eds.), *Historische Anstöße. Festschrift für Wolfgang Reinhard zum 65. Geburtstag am 10. April 2002*, Berlin, 2002, pp. 14–39.
Häberlein, M., *The Fuggers of Augsburg: Pursuing Wealth and Honor in Renaissance Germany*, Charlottesville and London, 2012.
Immenkötter, H., "Kirche zwischen Reformation und Parität", in Gottlieb et al. (eds.), *Geschichte der Stadt Augsburg*, pp. 391–412.
Isenmann, E., *Die deutsche Stadt im Mittelalter 1150–1550. Stadtgestalt, Recht, Verfassung, Stadtregiment, Kirche, Gesellschaft, Wirtschaft*, Vienna, 2012.
Johnson, C.R., *The German Discovery of the World: Renaissance Encounters with the Strange and Marvelous*, Charlottesville, 2008.
Kießling, R., "Augsburg zwischen Mittelalter und Neuzeit", in Gottlieb et al. (eds.), *Geschichte der Stadt Augsburg*, pp. 241–51.
Kießling, R., *Bürgerliche Gesellschaft und Kirche in Augsburg im Spätmittelalter: Ein Beitrag zur Strukturanalyse der oberdeutschen Reichsstadt*, Augsburg, 1971.
Kießling, R., "Eine italienische Option? Zur Politik der schwäbischen Reichsstädte in der Mitte des 16. Jahrhunderts", in W.E.J. Weber and R. Dauser (eds.), *Faszinierende Frühneuzeit. Reich, Frieden, Kultur und Kommunikation 1500–1800. Festschrift für Johannes Burkhardt zum 65. Geburtstag*, Berlin, 2008, pp. 95–112.
Kluge, M., *Die Macht des Gedächtnisses. Entstehung und Wandel kommunaler Schriftkultur im spätmittelalterlichen Augsburg*, Leiden, 2014.
Lutz, H., "Augsburg und seine politische Umwelt", in Gottlieb et al. (eds.), *Geschichte der Stadt Augsburg*, pp. 413–33.

Lutz, H., *Conrad Peutinger: Beiträge zu einer politischen Biographie*, Augsburg, 1958.

Mertens, B., *Im Kampf gegen die Monopole. Reichstagsverhandlungen und Monopolprozesse im frühen 16. Jahrhundert*, Tübingen, 1996.

Panzer, M., *Sozialer Protest in süddeutschen Reichsstädten 1485 bis 1525*, Munich, 1982.

Rogge, J., *Für den Gemeinen Nutzen. Politisches Handeln und Politikverständnis von Rat und Bürgerschaft in Augsburg im Spätmittelalter*, Tübingen, 1996.

Roper, L., *The Holy Household: Women and Morals in Reformation Augsburg*, Oxford, 1989.

Roth, F., *Augsburgs Reformationsgeschichte*, 4 vols., Munich, 1901–11.

Rublack, H-C., "Grundwerte in der Reichsstadt im Spätmittelalter und in der Frühen Neuzeit", in H. Brunner (ed.), *Literatur in der Stadt*, Göppingen, 1982, pp. 9–36.

Schnith, K., "Die Reichsstadt Augsburg im Spätmittelalter (1368–1493)", in Gottlieb et al. (eds.), *Geschichte der Stadt Augsburg*, pp. 153–65.

Scott, T., *The City-State in Europe, 1000–1600*, Oxford, 2012.

Sieh-Burens, K., "Die Augsburger Stadtverfassung um 1500", *Zeitschrift des Historischen Vereins für Schwaben* 77 (1983), pp. 125–49.

Sieh-Burens, K. "Bürgermeisteramt, soziale Verflechtung und Reformation in der freien Reichsstadt Augsburg 1518 bis 1539", in P. Fried (ed.), *Miscellanea Suevica Augustana*, Sigmaringen, 1985, pp. 61–88.

Sieh-Burens, K., *Oligarchie, Konfession und Politik im 16. Jahrhundert. Studien zur sozialen Verflechtung der Augsburger Bürgermeister und Stadtpfleger von 1518 bis 1618*, Munich, 1986.

Smelyansky, E., "Urban Order and Urban Other: Anti-Waldensian Inquisition in Augsburg, 1393", *German History* 34, 1 (2016), pp. 1–20.

Tyler, J.J., *Lord of the Sacred City: The Episcopus Exclusus in Late Medieval and Early Modern Germany*, Leiden, 1999.

Zelinsky Hanson, M., *Religious Identity in an Early Reformation Community: Augsburg, 1517 to 1555*, Leiden and Boston, 2009.

CHAPTER 7

Politics under the Patrician Regime, 1548–1806

Mark Häberlein and Barbara Rajkay

1   Regime Change

Charles V (1500–58) conceived of himself as the supreme monarch in Christian Europe, and as Holy Roman Emperor, King of Spain and Duke of Burgundy he in fact wielded unprecedented power. Yet throughout his reign, Charles was confronted by rebellions in his extensive domains. Cities in particular, which resented heavy taxation and/or the emperor's religious policies, repeatedly rose in revolt. As early as 1521, the young emperor had to hurry back to Spain from Germany in order to help suppress a civic uprising in Castile known as the Comunero Revolt. Almost two decades later, Charles V entered his native city of Ghent in the southern Netherlands (now Belgium) at the head of an army to quell a local uprising. During the Schmalkaldic War in 1546–47, the majority of south German cities sided with the Protestant princes against Charles. As he had done in Castile and Ghent before, the victorious emperor vented his anger on the unruly cities, punishing them for their disobedience and implementing lasting constitutional changes that were of enormous significance for their future history.[1]

Following his victory over the Schmalkaldic League, Charles V summoned an imperial diet in Augsburg in 1547 which lasted 43 weeks, making it the longest of his entire reign. Due to the presence of Spanish troops, this conference of the imperial estates became known as the "Armored Diet". Toward the end of his stay in Augsburg, the emperor pressured the city to conclude a treaty with the bishop of Augsburg, Otto Truchsess von Waldburg, on 2 August 1548, which restored the bishop and the cathedral chapter to their former rights and privileges and provided for the return of Catholic clergy to the city, from which it had been ousted a decade before, along with the restitution of the dissolved monasteries and collegiate chapters.[2] Moreover, Charles V decreed the so-called Interim, a religious settlement which the Catholic-dominated diet imposed unilaterally on Protestant imperial cities and territories.

---

1   For an overview, see Reinhard, "Governi Stretti e Tirannici".
2   Warmbrunn, *Zwei Konfessionen*, pp. 98–103; Kießling, "Augsburg in der Reformationszeit", pp. 37–38.

While the Interim was framed as a preliminary compromise between Catholic and Protestant doctrinal positions until the Council of Trent, which had opened in 1545, would decide them for good, it actually favored Catholic positions and had to be enforced against tenacious local resistance.[3] These measures had far-reaching consequences for the religious situation in Augsburg, as the Catholic faith could now be practiced there for the first time since 1537 and local Protestantism, which had been inclined towards Martin Bucer's and Ulrich Zwingli's teachings during the 1530s and 1540s, subsequently took on a decidedly Lutheran character.[4] The latter development was reinforced by the expulsion during the next imperial diet in 1551 of those Protestant preachers who would not accept the Interim. Several hundred veiled women, who asked the emperor to have mercy on the preachers, were dispersed by the city guard.[5]

Finally, Charles V ordered the abolition of the craft guilds and the introduction of a patrician regime in Augsburg on 5 August 1548. This measure had earlier been suggested by Catholic patricians like Hans Baumgartner, Hans Jakob Fugger, and the city advocate Dr. Claudius Pius Peutinger, who denounced the guildsmen in Augsburg's city government as poor, unfit plebeians who merely fostered strife and sedition. Referring to the example of Nuremberg – a patrician-controlled city that had remained loyal to the emperor during the Schmalkaldic War – they argued that the patricians should rule the city due to their superior experience, wealth, and "wisdom". While many guildsmen on the city council were in fact wealthy and experienced men, the implied negative image obviously suited the emperor's predilection for authoritarian rule. When the imperial vice-chancellor Dr. Georg Sigmund Seld, himself a native of Augsburg, announced the emperor's decision in a speech before the city council on 3 August 1548, he largely followed the patricians' line of reasoning. He blamed the guild regime for Augsburg's internal divisions and disobedience to Charles V and emphasized the emperor's wish to restore harmony and order as well as promote the common good.[6]

Seld then presented the council with a list of 41 persons whom the emperor had appointed to the Small Council (*Kleiner Rat*). Among these men, 31 hailed from patrician families, giving the urban nobility a three-quarters majority in the new governing body. Three individuals were *Mehrer* (merchants related to

---

3 Warmbrunn, *Zwei Konfessionen*, pp. 71–80.
4 Kießling, "Konfession als alltägliche Grenze", pp. 50–51.
5 Warmbrunn, *Zwei Konfessionen*, pp. 80–88; Sieh-Burens, *Oligarchie*, p. 177.
6 Naujoks (ed.), *Karl V. und die Zunftverfassung*, pp. 50–53; Warmbrunn, *Zwei Konfessionen*, pp. 106–07; Sieh-Burens, *Oligarchie*, p. 170; Roeck, *Stadt in Krieg und Frieden*, vol. 1, pp. 232–37; Reinhard, "Governi Stretti e Tirannici", pp. 409, 414–15; Finkl, *Administrative Verdichtung*, p. 404.

patrician families), one was a merchant, and six were commoners. At the top of the government hierarchy, the two mayors (*Bürgermeister*), one of whom had been a guildsman, were replaced by two patrician mayors (*Stadtpfleger*). The mayors together with five patrician secret councilors (*Geheime Räte*) subsequently formed the inner circle of power. The Secret Council set the course in foreign and financial policy, and only its members were entitled to full information on the city's revenues and expenditures. Significantly, Charles v appointed his major bankers, Anton Fugger and Bartholomäus Welser, to this important body. The office of *Bürgermeister* was nominally retained, but its responsibilites were sharply reduced: in the future, the six *Bürgermeister* acted as arbitrators of conflicts and as police officers. Although the Small Council was roughly evenly balanced between Catholics and Protestants, the emperor's appointments clearly favored Catholics, who made up only a small minority of the city's population in the mid-sixteenth century but were heavily overrepresented at the highest echelons of political power. A 300-member Large Council (*Großer Rat*), composed of 44 patricians, 36 *Mehrer*, 80 merchants, and 140 commoners, met only once a year and had largely symbolic functions. In sum, the regime change of 1548 set the stage for an oligarchic city government dominated by wealthy families with close ties to the emperor. Moreover, Charles v agreed in 1551 that the councilors and other officials should be adequately remunerated, thus offering patricians a financial incentive to serve in the city government. The guilds, by contrast, were dissolved, most guildhalls were sold, and the council appointed its own principals (*Vorgeher*) to monitor the crafts.[7] Apart from a brief episode in 1552, when the guild regime was temporarily revived during the Princes' Revolt against Charles v, the patrician regime survived until Augsburg's incorporation into the Kingdom of Bavaria in 1806. The number of seats on the Small Council was raised from 41 to 45 in 1555, slightly improving the representation of *Mehrer*, merchants, and commoners.[8]

The new regime also bolstered the local power of individual families, particularly Augsburg's most important Catholic clan, the Fuggers. When Anton Fugger, the head of the family company, resigned his post on the Secret Council in 1551, his nephew Hans Jakob took his seat, and Anton Fugger's brother-in-law Heinrich Rehlinger served as mayor from 1549 until his death in 1574. During the 1550s, Rehlinger and Hans Jakob Fugger were the major protagonists of a moderate political course that sought to maintain confessional peace

---

7 Naujoks (ed.), *Karl V. und die Zunftverfassung*, pp. 54–55; Warmbrunn, *Zwei Konfessionen*, pp. 108–13; Roeck, *Eine Stadt in Krieg und Frieden*, vol. 1, pp. 239–62.
8 Naujoks (ed.), *Karl V. und die Zunftverfassung*, pp. 56–59, 105–7, 109–11; Warmbrunn, *Zwei Konfessionen*, pp. 113–14, 122–23; Reinhard, "Governi Stretti e Tirannici", 408–13; Finkl, *Administrative Verdichtung*, pp. 398–403.

within the city as well as good relations with the emperor and neighboring Catholic territories.[9] According to Katarina Sieh-Burens, the Fuggers and their allied families "became the decisive factor supporting the new political system because of their economic power and influence, which extended far beyond the boundaries of the city".[10] Along with the "Fugger network", the Welsers and allied families, whose members included Protestants as well as Catholics, shaped the course of urban politics during the following decades.[11]

On the other hand, some Protestant leaders of the old guild regime were not only removed from power but even driven from the city. After briefly reassuming a leading position during the Princes' Revolt of 1552, the former guild mayor Jakob Herbrot, a wealthy merchant, became the target of libelous poems and songs denouncing him as a social upstart, treacherous deceiver, and political troublemaker. Worn down by this barrage of anonymous attacks and haunted by his creditors, Herbrot moved to nearby Lauingen in 1553, where he became a district official of the Duke of Pfalz-Neuburg. A few years later he gave up his Augsburg citizenship and handed his business over to his sons.[12] Another Protestant merchant and former mayor, Georg Österreicher, was banished from the city for supporting the abortive attempt to restore the guild regime in 1552. Österreicher went to Electoral Saxony, where he became a district official, and unsuccessfully petitioned the imperial diets of 1555 and 1558 for permission to return to Augsburg. When Emperor Ferdinand I and the city council turned down his requests, he eventually became a citizen of Regensburg.[13]

Finally, the new regime that Charles V imposed on Augsburg in 1548 served as a model for the constitutional change imposed by imperial officials on 26 other imperial cities in south Germany in 1551–52. In a pun on the last name of the imperial councilor Dr. Heinrich Haas (or Hase), who announced the emperor's decision to the city councils, the new patrician councils became known as *Hasenräte* (rabbit councils).[14] While this designation indicated lingering

---

9   See Warmbrunn, *Zwei Konfessionen*, pp. 146–48; Sieh-Burens, *Oligarchie*, pp. 178–79, 184–87.
10 Sieh-Burens, *Oligarchie*, pp. 171; see also Mörke and Sieh, "Führungsgruppen", p. 303; Kießling, "Augsburg in der Reformationszeit", p. 38; Häberlein, *The Fuggers of Augsburg*, p. 191.
11 Sieh-Burens, *Oligarchie*, pp. 171–73.
12 Häberlein, *Brüder, Freunde und Betrüger*, pp. 235–41. On the libels against Herbrot, see Kuhn, *Politik des Pasquino*.
13 Roth, *Augsburgs Reformationsgeschichte*, vol. 4, pp. 512–14; Sieh-Burens, *Oligarchie*, pp. 174, 180.
14 For a documentary history of these regime changes, see Naujoks (ed.), *Karl V. und die Zunftverfassung*. See also Warmbrunn, *Zwei Konfessionen*, pp. 104–30; Reinhard, "Governi Stretti e Tirannici", p. 412.

resentment at the abolition of old corporate privileges, the new, aristocratic city constitutions survived until the Napoleonic era.

2 Political Norms and Administrative Consolidation

Although the regime change of 1548 marked a break in the city's political history, there were elements of continuity as well. To begin with, the old guild regime had already perceived itself as Augsburg's divinely elected authority (*Obrigkeit*),[15] and this self-perception was reinforced when the patriciate assumed political power. Accordingly, the patrician-dominated council saw itself as the guardian of peace, order, honor, and social harmony in the city. From a Christian perspective, discipline and public morality had to be maintained not merely for worldly reasons, but also because they contributed to the preservation of a divinely sanctioned order and helped avert God's wrath from the community. The city council thus took a patriarchal stance in its decrees and proclamations, often assuming the posture of "fatherly authority" (*vätterliche Obrigkeit*) toward its subjects.[16]

Second, the council had created a large number of offices and courts since the fifteenth century, and the process of administrative consolidation continued unabated after 1548. Apart from the Small Council, there were numerous salaried posts in the city's financial offices (*Baumeister-, Einnehmeramt*), tax administration (*Steuer-, Ungeldamt*), office of poor relief (*Almosenamt*), and various other bureaucracies, including the administration of parishes, schools, and charitable foundations. When it came to selecting officers for these positions, the council tended to favor patricians, and some patrician councilors garnered a sizable income from the accumulation of various civic offices.[17]

Third, the patrician-dominated city council continued to pass numerous regulations on social and economic life, including wedding, sumptuary, alms, market, and bankruptcy ordinances. Without referring to specific confessional positions, these ordinances typically invoked the principles of order, discipline, and the common good, reflecting trends prevalent throughout Germany and much of Europe.[18] Both urban and princely governments viewed themselves as guardians of public order, security, and welfare and took numerous measures

---

15   See Chapter 6 of this volume.
16   Roeck, *Eine Stadt in Krieg und Frieden*, vol. 1, pp. 215–32.
17   Roeck, *Eine Stadt in Krieg und Frieden*, vol. 1, pp. 262–69; Finkl, *Administrative Verdichtung*, pp. 408–57.
18   See Hildebrandt, "Zum Verhältnis" (on bankruptcy ordinances); Roeck, *Eine Stadt in Krieg und Frieden*, vol. 1, pp. 235–36. For English translations of several council decrees and

to promote these social and political goals while simultaneously reaffirming their own authority.[19]

3   Confessional Polarization and Local Opposition

For about a quarter century, Augsburg's political leaders gave their highest priority to maintaining confessional peace within the city walls. This policy of compromise had its basis in the Religious Peace of Augsburg, which legally sanctioned Catholicism and Lutheranism in 1555 and stipulated that both faiths should continue unmolested where they were already practiced.[20] The number of Catholics and Protestants on the Small Council was roughly equal, and Protestants even gained a slight majority in the early 1570s. From 1574 onward, however, the balance shifted in favor of the Catholic side, which controlled 26 of the 45 seats by 1583.[21] Moreover, in the years around 1580, the founding of a Jesuit college (with strong financial support from the Fugger family) and the Protestant college of St. Anna signaled a hardening of confessional fronts,[22] and two dedicated Catholics, Marx Fugger and Anton Christoph Rehlinger, now held the top position of mayor. Fugger had only accepted this office in 1576 after urgent appeals to his civic duty, however, and repeatedly asked to be relieved of the post.[23]

In early 1583, the growing confessional tensions escalated into open rebellion when the city council decided to adopt the new calendar introduced by Pope Gregory XIII the year before. This decision was justified by potential economic disadvantages for the city if Augsburg's religious holidays should diverge from those of its powerful Catholic neighbors, the duchy of Bavaria and the prince-bishopric of Augsburg, which had already introduced the new calendar. Although some Protestants consented to the adoption of the Gregorian calendar, dissenting Protestant councilors and church wardens perceived this reform as a violation of the principles of the Religious Peace of

---

ordinances, see Tlusty (ed.), *Augsburg During the Reformation Era*. See also Chapter 9 of this volume.
19   Scribner, "Police and the Territorial State"; Iseli, *Gute Policey*; Härter, "Security".
20   See Naujoks, "Vorstufen der Parität"; Kießling, "Vom Ausnahmefall zur Alternative", pp. 120–21.
21   Warmbrunn, *Zwei Konfessionen*, pp. 132–37; Sieh-Burens, *Oligarchie*, pp. 183–85.
22   Warmbrunn, *Zwei Konfessionen*, pp. 248–49, 285; Sieh-Burens, *Oligarchie*, pp. 195, 200–1, 203; Wallenta, *Konfessionalisierung*, pp. 194–96, 199–203; Häberlein, *The Fuggers of Augsburg*, pp. 192–93.
23   Sieh-Burens, *Oligarchie*, pp. 187–88; Häberlein, *The Fuggers of Augsburg*, p. 193.

Augsburg and appealed the decision at the Imperial Chamber Court in Speyer. When the council went ahead and implemented the new calendar anyway, the Protestant majority of Augsburg's inhabitants reacted by ignoring the new dates for Sundays and religious holidays. The council retaliated by punishing numerous artisans, especially butchers, for illegally working on holidays. Anonymous libels accused the council of attempting to convert Augsburg into a *Pfaffenstadt* – a city controlled by the Catholic clergy – and threatened that the common people would take matters into their own hands if the papal calendar were not repealed. The Protestant preachers acted as spokesmen of the opposition; their superintendent Dr. Georg Müller (Mylius) was particularly outspoken, denouncing the city councilors as hypocrites and tyrants.[24]

The council for its part did nothing to relieve the tensions, but recruited soldiers for its own safety and then proclaimed that it would fill two vacant preaching positions itself. Protestant preachers had traditionally been nominated by the clergy's corporation, the *Ministerium*, but this body's recommendations were now rejected by the council. When a verdict by the Imperial Chamber Court upheld the introduction of the Gregorian calendar, the council took vigorous action and dismissed the leaders of the Protestant opposition from their posts. The preachers reacted by encouraging their parishioners to civil disobedience. Their stance was supported by a legal opinion of the Protestant University of Tübingen, which argued that Catholics and Protestants enjoyed equality in Augsburg.

In early June 1584, the lingering conflict erupted into open riot when the preachers summoned their parishioners from the pulpits to celebrate the upcoming festival of Ascension according to the old Julian calendar. The council reacted by forbidding the closing of shops on that day and expelling the superintendent Dr. Müller. This attempt to remove the leading Protestant preacher backfired: an angry crowd stopped Müller's carriage and freed the preacher. Several thousand Augsburgers then assembled in St. Jacob's Suburb (*Jakober Vorstadt*), an area mostly inhabited by poor craftsmen and day laborers. Although the council ordered the closing of the inner city gates, the crowd forced its way into the city center. Gunshots were fired in the vicinity of the city hall, where the soldiers recruited by the council awaited the crowd. The Protestant preachers managed to calm the angry multitude, however, probably averting major bloodshed.

---

24   For this and the following paragraph, see Sieh-Burens, *Oligarchie*, pp. 191, 197–206; Roeck, *Eine Stadt in Krieg und Frieden*, I, pp. 125–33; Warmbrunn, *Zwei Konfessionen*, pp. 360–75; Wallenta, *Konfessionalisierung*, pp. 102–16; and Chapter 11 in this volume.

While the city council subsequently entered into negotiations with the citizenry to resolve the calendar conflict, disagreements about the right to select new preachers continued. In the summer of 1584, an imperial commission questioned more than 100 citizens of Augsburg, whose answers revealed widespread dissatisfaction with the council's policies. Craftsmen and laborers also complained about rising food prices and worsening economic conditions. The list of grievances included the Catholic majority in the city council; the kinship ties between councilors; an unfair electoral system; the council's interference in the affairs of the Protestant church; the activities of the Jesuits; and the tax privileges of rich patrician families, above all the Fuggers.[25] These statements reveal that opposition to the "papal" calendar was closely intertwined with social and political grievances, which not only fomented unrest in Augsburg but also caused uprisings in numerous other German cities during this period.[26]

In the end, the city government, which enjoyed the support of imperial officials and Catholic princes,[27] remained adamant. After the imperial commission had failed to reach a compromise between the confessional camps, the council relieved 18 Protestant hardliners of their posts in 1585, including members of prominent patrician and merchant families, and expelled ten of them from the city. Eleven preachers and several Protestant officials, among them the city physician and Oriental traveler Leonhard Rauwolf, also lost their jobs. Whereas most Protestant citizens refrained from open opposition, a dramatic decline in church donations between 1583 and 1591 demonstrated their rejection of the council-appointed preachers. It was only in 1591 that a compromise was reached on the vocation of Protestant preachers: the three patrician church wardens were supplemented by three adjuncts from the community at large. These six persons had the right to nominate suitable candidates, whereas the right of confirmation remained with the council. Although this compromise calmed open tensions, the writings of Protestant authors like the chronicler Georg Kölderer (c. 1550–1607) show that disaffection with the council and the "papal" calendar lingered below the surface.[28]

---

25   Roeck, *Stadt in Krieg und Frieden*, vol. 1, pp. 133–37; Sieh-Burens, *Oligarchie*, p. 205.
26   See Friedrichs, "German Town Revolts"; Schilling, "European Crisis"; Roeck, *Eine Stadt in Krieg und Frieden*, vol. 1, pp. 137–40.
27   On the conflict's external ramifications, see Sieh-Burens, *Oligarchie*, pp. 198–200; Steuer, *Außenverflechtung*, pp. 147–85.
28   Roeck, *Eine Stadt in Krieg und Frieden*, vol. 1, pp. 169–88; see also Sieh-Burens, *Oligarchie*, pp. 191–92, 198, 202, 206; Mauer, *"Gemain Geschrey"*, pp. 163–98.

4   Urban Politics during the Thirty Years' War

The Thirty Years' War marked not only the worst demographic and economic crisis faced by Augsburg during the early modern era;[29] it also highlighted the limitations of the city's biconfessional patrician regime, which was repeatedly overwhelmed by external pressures. To begin with, the economic crisis caused by runaway inflation in the early 1620s forced the council to sharply increase its expenditures on poor relief, thus emptying the city treasury.[30] After his armies had dealt crushing defeats to his opponents, Emperor Ferdinand II then proclaimed the Edict of Restitution in 1629, which sought to restore secularized ecclesiastical properties to the Catholic Church. Overruling the council's objections, Ferdinand and the bishop of Augsburg, Heinrich von Knöringen, used military pressure to enforce the edict in Augsburg, ordering the closure of Protestant churches and the removal of Lutheran councilors. Although several Catholic families were newly designated as patricians to fill their seats, it proved difficult to find enough suitable Catholic candidates for posts in the city government.[31]

When the victorious Swedish King Gustavus Adolphus entered the city with his army in 1632,[32] he replaced this Catholic council with an exclusively Protestant governing body, in turn elevating several Lutheran families to the patriciate.[33] The handover of the city to an imperial army after a devastating siege in early 1635 brought yet another regime change, as the "Swedish Council" gave way to a Catholic city government, and the army colonel Ott Heinrich Fugger, a scion of Augsburg's pre-eminent Catholic family, temporarily exerted the powers of an imperial military governor.[34] The Peace of Westphalia, which terminated the Thirty Years' War in 1648, eventually enshrined the principle of confessional parity for Augsburg (and three other imperial cities: Dinkelsbühl, Biberach, and Ravensburg). Protestants and Catholics were granted complete equality and were assigned the same number of seats on the city council as well as in numerous administrative positions, large and small. In addition, both confessions were to handle their internal affairs autonomously. Confessional

---

29   See Chapter 15 of this volume.
30   Roeck, *Eine Stadt in Krieg und Frieden*, vol. 2, pp. 615–30; see also Chapter 12 of this volume.
31   Warmbrunn, *Zwei Konfessionen*, pp. 163–64; Roeck, *Eine Stadt in Krieg und Frieden*, vol. 2, pp. 655–68.
32   For more on this, see Chapter 15 of this volume.
33   Warmbrunn, *Zwei Konfessionen*, pp. 166–68; Roeck, *Eine Stadt in Krieg und Frieden*, vol. 2, pp. 715–20.
34   Roeck, *Eine Stadt in Krieg und Frieden*, vol. 2, pp. 871–74; Haberer, *Ott Heinrich Fugger*, pp. 308–27; Häberlein, *The Fuggers of Augsburg*, pp. 216–17.

parity signaled a notable victory for Augsburg's Protestants, who had long resented the city's pro-Catholic politics and whose delegate Hans David Herwart had worked tirelessly throughout the peace negotiations for just such a solution. In the long run, however, both confessional camps accepted parity as the basis for peaceful local coexistence.[35]

5   The Urban Constitution and the Patriciate, 1650–1806

Augsburg's constitution, established with the Peace of Westphalia, survived until the end of the Holy Roman Empire with only slight modifications. After receiving complaints about the concentration of power among a handful of patrician families, the Imperial Aulic Council in Vienna imposed a revised government ordinance (*Regimentsordnung*) and new rules for public office-holding (*Ämterrecess*) in 1719. The major changes limited the number of seats on the Small Council that any one family could hold to a maximum of four, while prohibiting first- or second-degree relatives from sitting together in the Secret Council. Other amendments imposed limitations on the accumulation of offices, rules governing behavior during council meetings, and the balance of power among mayors, Secret Council, and Small Council.[36] While the Catholic party held a numerical majority of one vote in the council, the Peace of Westphalia had established the principle of *itio in partes*, both on the imperial level and in Augsburg. According to this principle, only an *amicabilis compositio* (i.e. an amicable compromise between both confessional parties) could acquire legal force. Numerous council protocols and legal memorandums show that politics in Augsburg were not merely shaped by two separate confessional blocs. In many cases, representatives of both camps formed a third party, a *minora mixta*. This phenomenon had already come to the attention of the imperial commission in 1719, but its constitutional status remained unclear.[37]

A constitutional amendment (*Additionalrezess*) in 1740 grouped the public offices into four classes according to their significance. The salaries awarded to office-holders mirrored this hierarchy. To prevent abuse arising from holding multiple offices, certain combinations were ruled out; councilors, for example, were entitled to a maximum of two first-class offices.[38] Due to massive conflicts

---

35   Warmbrunn, *Zwei Konfessionen*, pp. 173–74, 181–83; Roeck, *Eine Stadt in Krieg und Frieden*, II, pp. 949–74.
36   Bátori, *Reichsstadt Augsburg*, pp. 36–39.
37   Stetten, *Selbstbiographie*, vol. 1, p. 253.
38   Stetten, *Selbstbiographie*, vol. 3, p. 240.

between the city government, merchants, and weavers in the 1790s, the council made two attempts to restore direct citizen participation in political decision-making. The first occurred in the immediate aftermath of the weavers' revolt in March 1794, when the council conceded that each of the eight city districts could directly elect two deputies from among the citizenry. The second took place in April 1795, when the Large Council formed a committee of 12 men that included members of all estates. Both reform attempts were quickly ended by the Imperial Aulic Council, which feared the spread of revolutionary turmoil.[39]

In much more profound ways than these piecemeal modifications of the 1548 constitution, a long-term process of juridification (*Verrechtlichung*) changed political life in Augsburg. Along with the establishment of confessional parity in 1649, six positions were created for legal counselors, three for each confessional camp.[40] These jurists enjoyed high social reputations, as numerous nominations to the patriciate or marriages with women from patrician families demonstrate.[41] The council's legal advisers were selected by the Secret Council, before whom they swore an oath of office, and were usually jurists with university doctorates. They prepared all legislation and wrote memorandums that served as the basis of council decisions. Their other obligations included the interrogation of prisoners and the writing of protocols. At least one legal adviser was present at all official receptions and delegations.[42] The degree to which the law provided room for political maneuvering became evident when the *Kunst-, Gewerb- und Handwerksgericht* (court of arts, trades, and crafts) was set up in 1722. This commercial court held jurisdiction of first instance over all local artisans except the salt-traders and the weavers. While two patrician council members formally presided over the court, two jurists (*Referendare*) and two assistants (*Aktuare*) formed the body's core.[43]

The constant expansion of communal responsibilities made urban governance increasingly time-consuming. In the eighteenth century, the Small Council convened every Tuesday, Thursday, and Saturday at 10:00 AM. In addition, there were sessions of the various council offices, which took place weekly or even daily according to their respective fields of duty. Therefore the incumbents of the major offices were released from regular council sessions. These exempt positions included the directors of the receivers' office (*Einnehmeramt*), building office (*Bauamt*), tax office (*Steueramt*), guardians'

---

39   Möller, *Bürgerliche Herrschaft*, p. 84; Bátori, *Reichsstadt Augsburg*, pp. 139–51.
40   Stetten, *Geschichte der Reichsstadt*, vol. 2, pp. 1164–65.
41   Gößner, *Rechtsgelehrte in Reichsstädten*.
42   Stetten, *Selbstbiographie*, vol. 2, pp. 69–70.
43   Stetten, *Selbstbiographie*, vol. 3, p. 247.

office (*Pflegamt*), and the chief judges (*Oberrichter*). Only when particularly important business was transacted were all councilors required to be present in a session called the "required council" (*gebotener Rat*). In order to discuss the execution of decrees and resolutions, the so-called directorate met in the city hall at 7:30 AM on council days. This body included the two mayors and the acting *Bürgermeister* as well as the city secretary and the council clerk.

Due to this heavy workload, the regular visits to markets and fairs or business trips necessary for long-distance merchants were no longer compatible with the requirements of political office-holding. At the same time, a political career had the benefit of lifetime financial security, as the higher council offices in particular were amply rewarded.[44] One consequence of this was the progressive withdrawal of the old patrician families from active involvement in commerce. Their sons no longer received a commercial education, but were instead sent to universities, primarily to study the law.[45] The Fugger family, on the other hand, which ostensibly harbored no more political ambitions in eighteenth-century Augsburg, left the patriciate, but nonetheless remained important in the city's social life.[46]

6 The Lords' Drinking Hall

While Charles V had granted the patriciate a decisive role in urban politics, the radical constitutional change he imposed in 1548 left regulation of the Lords' or Patricians' drinking hall (*Herrenstube* or *Geschlechterstube*), the symbol of their corporate status, untouched.[47] This ostentatious building directly across from the city hall housed gatherings of a peculiar mixture of feudal nobility, holders of high office, and wealthy men, with some of the latter still active in banking and commerce. From 1650 to 1800, the number of patrician families oscillated between 27 and 28.[48] Confessional differences regarding the reception of new members were already evident in the seventeenth century and continued into the eighteenth. Whereas new Protestant members often came from other imperial cities and owed their standing to their economic ascent, most Catholic newcomers were ennobled public officials from neighboring

---

44 Bátori, *Reichsstadt Augsburg*, pp. 73–75.
45 Rajkay, "Totentanz", pp. 106–7; see also Häberlein, "Sozialer Wandel".
46 Hetzer, "Augsburger Theaterwesen", p. 531; Huber, "Konzerte".
47 On the establishment of the Lords' and Merchants' drinking halls and their symbolic role in defining elite status, see Tlusty, *Bacchus*, 29–31.
48 Bátori, "Reichsstädtisches Regiment", p. 461; Fassl, *Konfession, Wirtschaft und Politik*, pp. 30–42.

territories.[49] A largely endogamous choice of spouses reinforced the discrepancies between the two groups with each succeeding generation. In the long run, the complete withdrawal from commercial business was only sustainable for those patrician families who managed to acquire new fortunes through favorable marriages.

The decline of economic resources was mostly caused by the "random fate of genealogy",[50] as the number of heirs heavily influenced the wealth of noble and patrician families. Expenses for dowries, status-appropriate wedding feasts, or an extended education usually followed up by an expensive grand tour severely strained family finances. Friedrich Endorfer the Elder (c. 1567–1628), a patrician director of the tax office, tried to solve this problem in the 1620s by embezzling large sums from the city treasury.[51] In 1764, the Langenmantel family asked the bishop of Augsburg if the family foundation, which had been established in 1731 to finance apprenticeships for the sons of poor citizens, might be used for the education of scions of the three family branches. Considering that the family's fortunes had gravely declined, the bishop gave his assent.[52] Yet the Langenmantels' financial straits continued: in the context of the weavers' unrest in 1784, Joseph Anton Leopold Wolfgang von Langenmantel (1736–99), a council deputy at the weavers' hall, was found guilty of corruption.[53] Two unmarried Langenmantel daughters were financially supported by charitable foundations in the 1790s, as were two sisters of the building office director Joseph Johann Adam von Seida and several children of the ancient Ilsung family.[54]

Excepting Endorfer, all these examples refer to Catholic patricians. The sources offer very few hints that Protestant patricians were in similar straits. The reasons for this are structural and can be explained by a combination of demographic, economic, and confessional factors. On the one hand, numerous Protestant patrician families had established foundations for the support of needy members by 1751.[55] On the other hand, patricians also benefited from the superior financial resources of the Protestant citizenry,[56] for the old urban nobility and the new aristocracy of wealth were closely entwined by marriage. The Protestant von Stetten family in particular employed a strategy of forging

---

49   Kießling, "Patriziat", p. 26.
50   Zürn, "Stillstand im Wandel", p. 246.
51   Häberlein et al. (eds.), *Endorfer*, pp. 30–42.
52   Werner, *Stiftungen*, p. 59.
53   Clasen, *Streiks und Aufstände*, p. 205.
54   Stetten, *Selbstbiographie*, vol. 3, pp. XVIII–XIX.
55   Stetten, *Selbstbiographie*, vol. 1, pp. 360, 368–70.
56   Bátori, "Reichsstädtisches Regiment", p. 460.

remunerative marriage alliances both purposefully and successfully over several generations, thus reducing its dependence on incomes derived from political office-holding.[57]

Catholic patrician families, however, suffered from a lack of choices when it came to selecting marriage partners, for a significant part of Augsburg's Catholic economic elite in the eighteenth century was made up of immigrants from south of the Alps.[58] While this group was liberal in its choice of business partners, it selected marriage partners – with few exceptions – from its native regions or from the local migrant community. A prime example is the Obwexer family of merchant-bankers, which originally hailed from South Tyrol. Despite their enormous business success and ennoblement in 1778, the Obwexers did not form marriage alliances with the patriciate, instead remaining members of the Merchants' drinking hall.[59]

On the whole, three career options befitted members of Augsburg's patriciate: office-holding, commerce, and the military. Catholic families had the additional option of providing for members by placing them in ecclesiastical chapters, but this path often proved to be a dead end. First, it required a stainless ancestral pedigree; in this regard, alliances with wealthy merchant families would have spoiled the family tree for generations. And second, the fight for equality with the ecclesiastical nobility (*Stiftsadel*) in Vienna and Rome was very costly. Access to Augsburg's cathedral chapter remained barred to the city's patricians in the eighteenth century, all their appeals to Rome notwithstanding. They also failed in their attempt to reserve for local citizens the exclusive right to be provosts of Augsburg's three collegiate chapters.[60]

These developments resulted in a growing gap between the patricians' political ascendancy and their economic means. Therefore they found it increasingly difficult in the eighteenth century to fulfill their self-image as selfless and wise rulers seeking fair compromises among diverging interests among the citizenry. This became particularly evident during the large-scale weavers' revolts of 1784 and 1794.[61] These uprisings focused on economic demands for an import quota – or even an import ban – for foreign cotton cloth, and did not aim at constitutional change.[62] Under pressure from the street, the council initially made far-reaching concessions to the weavers in February 1794. Alarmed

---

57 Stetten, *Selbstbiographie*, vol. 3, pp. 236–38.
58 Fassl, *Konfession, Wirtschaft und Politik*, pp. 48–49.
59 Häberlein and Schmölz-Häberlein, *Erben der Welser*, pp. 21–34; Staats- und Stadtbibliothek Augsburg, 2° Cod. S 87-2, Stubenzettel 1696.
60 Seiler, *Augsburger Domkapitel*, pp. 16–71.
61 Bayer, *Streiks*, pp. 55–85.
62 Kießling, "Augsburg im Aufstand", p. 171.

by developments in France since 1789, however, the Imperial Aulic Council in Vienna and the Swabian Imperial Circle interpreted these decisions as a "total capitulation" and forced their annulment.[63] When new riots threatened to break out in November 1794, military intervention by the Swabian Circle was considered the only remaining option.

FIGURE 7.1   Troops parading in front of city hall during the Augsburg weavers' revolt of 1794, drawing by Franz Thomas Weber
AUGSBURG, STÄDTISCHE KUNSTSAMMLUNGEN, GRAPHISCHE SAMMLUNG

63   Fimpel, *Reichsjustiz*, p. 283.

7 Economic and Financial Policies

The withdrawal of most old patrician families from active economic life went hand in hand with the council's abstention from economic investment. From the Middle Ages to the Thirty Years' War, the city had pursued a highly ambitious policy of improving its infrastructure. Costly treaties with the duchy of Bavaria had succeeded in securing important rights to channel water from the Lech River into the city.[64] Along these canals, the council oversaw the construction of various kinds of mills; the Lech master Jörg Renner recorded more than 30 building projects during his tenure (1517–c. 1540) alone. These included powder mills, grist mills, sawmills, and fulling mills.[65] A century later, the famous master builder Elias Holl likewise participated in the construction or renovation of numerous urban mills.[66] Especially when it came to the important textile industry, the city asserted its control, running all three bleaching facilities and the assorted fulling mills along with two cloth presses.[67]

The enormous debts caused by the Thirty Years' War, however, necessitated a complete turnaround. From the 1650s onward, the city began to sell urban properties, retaining the right of first refusal in each case.[68] Due to the war, one of the bleaching facilities – the *mittlere Bleiche* outside the Jakober Gate – had been abandoned as early as 1633, while the other two were purchased by the widow of the merchant Gerhard Greiff in 1693.[69] Eventually, however, the community had to shoulder considerable running expenses for most of these alienated objects. In a letter dated 1 March 1721, the directors of the building office complained that the city had traded away benefits (*commoda*) while retaining burdens (*onera*). More particularly, they listed numerous mills whose water supply had to be maintained at the city's expense.[70]

According to a 1711 survey, the War of the Spanish Succession burdened the city treasury with 3.8 million gulden, although the expenses for renovating the heavily damaged fortifications were settled only in the 1740s.[71] The above-mentioned burdens notwithstanding, the city remained able to stabilize its budget until 1770. It was only the additional expense of 400,000 gulden caused

---

64 Stetten, *Geschichte der Reichsstadt*, vol. 1, pp. 524–26, 738–41, 786; Bátori, *Reichsstadt Augsburg*, pp. 86–88.
65 Stadtarchiv Augsburg (StadtAA), Reichsstadt, Akten 1, no. 1061, Lechmeister und Brunnenmeister. See also Chapter 2 in this volume.
66 Haberstock, *Werkverzeichnis*, pp. 60–64, 84, 109, 139.
67 Clasen, "Augsburger Bleichen"; StadtAA, Bauamt 4, no. 103, Einstandsrechte der Stadt.
68 Bátori, "Reichsstädtisches Regiment", pp. 457–59.
69 Clasen, "Augsburger Bleichen", pp. 184–85.
70 StadtAA, Bauamt 7, Karton 29.
71 Bátori, *Reichsstadt Augsburg*, p. 93; Kraus, *Militärwesen*, pp. 361–66.

by the famine of the early 1770s that put the local economy into a downward spiral that could not be stopped before the end of the Holy Roman Empire. While debt service spun out of control, the costs of social projects skyrocketed.[72] In 1789, the damages caused by flooding of the Lech River eventually exposed the disastrous state of Augsburg's finances.[73] Numerous reform attempts to stabilize the system were undertaken up until 1804, but none of them yielded substantial results.[74] The enormous additional expenses triggered by the French Revolutionary Wars made the city's default more and more likely.

In 1803, the council entered into negotiations about further loans with the city's merchants as well as with three Jewish exchange banks. The latter offered favorable conditions, asking for the right to take up residence in the city in return. The merchants for their part had demanded far-reaching securities and control of the city budget before they would advance the sum of 500,000 gulden. They also made every effort to prevent the admission of Jews, who had been driven from Augsburg en masse in the fifteenth century. Ultimately the city reached an agreement with the Jewish bankers on 12 November 1803,[75] which from the merchants' point of view marked their final rupture with the city council. Together with the retailers, they lodged a complaint with the Imperial Aulic Council in Vienna in the spring of 1804, demanding not only information about the state of the budget but also the rectification of constitutional grievances. The case was still pending when the Holy Roman Empire was dissolved in 1806.[76]

The progressive deterioration of the city budget described by Ingrid Bátori was also a matter of mentalities. The council protocols contain numerous hints at another reason for the holes in the treasury, which has hardly been studied to this day. Various entries refer to large-scale tax evasion, but a lenient council did little to prevent fraud – even during the direst periods of financial strain. These cases pertain to merchants and artisans rather than patricians, which is all the more astonishing insofar as the tax burden in Augsburg was actually very moderate.[77] Yet the council showed its largesse even in cases where the tax evaders' heirs were living abroad. It seems that the amount of outstanding taxes was often less a legal matter than a game for time, which

---

72   Bátori, *Reichsstadt Augsburg*, pp. 98–105.
73   Bátori, "Reichsstädtisches Regiment", p. 463.
74   Stetten, *Selbstbiographie*, vol. 2, pp. 2–4, 9–14, 18–20, 30–37.
75   Bátori, *Reichsstadt Augsburg*, pp. 123–28; Dotterweich and Reissner, "Finanznot und Domizilrecht". See also Chapter 16 of this volume.
76   Bátori, *Reichsstadt Augsburg*, pp. 165–69; Stetten, *Selbstbiographie*, vol. 3, pp. 2–4, 9–14, 18–20, 26–27, 30–37.
77   Fassl, *Konfession, Wirtschaft und Politik*, p. 47.

many people played very astutely. Persons who owed water fees were shown similar lenience.[78] Perhaps the council thought it was simply good policy to put mercy before justice.[79]

8 Social and Cultural Policies

The substantial increase in expenses after 1771 was partly caused by far-reaching social reforms. As early as 1755, a correctional institution and workhouse had been established upon the initiative, and under the direction of, Paul von Stetten the Elder. This measure aimed at solving the problem of poverty by confining beggars. The famine of 1770–71, however, led to a dramatic increase in the number of alms recipients, while the revenues from alms collections plummeted due to massive price increases. The deficit in the alms chest was balanced by direct transfers from the city treasury.[80] In reaction to reform projects suggested by merchants and some dedicated councilors, the "new alms office" (*Neue Armenanstalt*) was created in 1781. This institution was based on a completely new form of financing poor relief, which aimed at permanently relieving the city budget through an institutionalized system of donations organized by the council. At the same time, a new measure was taken to integrate the able-bodied poor into the economy; they were to supply the weavers with spun yarn. Maximum transparency in the registration of donations and the support of the poor was meant to ensure the inhabitants' willingness to donate in the long run.

Implementation of the new system required substantial preparations, however. Numbering all local buildings with a combination of alphabetic letters and numbers provided all donors and recipients with clear addresses.[81] Well-respected citizens were chosen as collectors in each of the eight city districts, where they collected the promised amounts from the donors on a monthly basis.[82] Annual reports were printed to familiarize the public with the new institution's financial operations. After a few years, the recipients' names and the sums paid to them were likewise published.[83] Although donations plummeted

---

78 Rajkay, "Augsburger Wasserwirtschaft", pp. 76–77.
79 Stetten, *Selbstbiographie*, vol. 3, pp. XXXIII–XXXIV.
80 Stetten, *Selbstbiographie*, vol. 1, pp. 57–59; Bátori, "Reichsstädtisches Regiment", p. 460.
81 For a detailed description of the new institution, see anon., "Augspurgische Verfügungen".
82 Stetten, *Selbstbiographie*, vol. 1, pp. 110–18.
83 Staats- und Stadtbibliothek Augsburg, 4° Cod. Aug. 973, Nachricht an das Reichsstadt-Augsburgische Publikum über den gegenwärtigen Zustand der neuen Armenanstalt (1782–1813).

in the 1790s due to warfare, the quartering of troops, and additional taxes, the institution was maintained.[84]

The construction of a new theater in 1776 was also connected to the financing of poor relief. As in other cities, the rental of the theater facilities was conceived as a means to increase alms revenues. The construction project made Augsburg one of a number of communities that deliberately distanced themselves from court theater and established a public theater with an educational mission.[85] Although the theater's site on the *Lauterlech*, in the poor St. Jacob's Suburb, attracted criticism, the facilities offered by this new symbol of civic pride were anything but miserable.[86] Masked balls in the fashionable inn *Drei Mohren* were another means to raise funds for the alms office. For the concession to stage balls during carnival season, the innkeeper had to pay 75 to 100 gulden to the alms office.[87]

The Augsburg Academy of Arts, founded as a private institution in 1670–74 by Joachim Sandrart (1606–88), was taken over by the city council in 1710 and had its premises in the upper floor of the butchers' hall (*Stadtmetzg*) from 1712 onward. On the initiative of Paul von Stetten the Younger, the council created a committee in 1779 to reform the academy. The premises were renovated and enlarged, and some of the most advanced writings on art theory were read to the students during nude figure drawing lessons. As in other academies and drawing schools, Augsburg's institution staged annual public exhibitions, where prizes were awarded each Tuesday after Easter; special medals were created for the occasion.[88] The council also set up another drawing school, where artisans who lacked the time and money to attend the academy's regular classes could go on Sundays. In the eighteenth century, drawing schools were considered as an ideal means to enhance the local crafts' competitiveness in trans-regional markets. The reform was also successful because it was accompanied by the establishment of a supporting association named *Privat-Gesellschaft zur Ermunterung der Künste und des Kunstfleißes* (private society for encouraging the arts and creativity), comprising councilors and merchants as well as specialized artisans.[89]

The council also became active in other areas of public interest during the Age of Enlightenment. Thus the doctors forming the *Collegium Medicum* compiled instructions on the handling of suicides and drowning people, which

---

84 Stetten, *Selbstbiographie*, vol. 3, pp. 51, 106.
85 Möller, "Zwischen Kunst und Kommerz", p. 21.
86 Dussler (ed.), *Reiseberichte*, vol. 2, p. 260.
87 Rajkay, "Totentanz", p. 108; see also Chapter 14 in this volume.
88 Mančal, *Augsburger Kunstakademie*, pp. 20–34; Grieger, "Kunst und Öffentlichkeit", p. 132.
89 Mančal, *Augsburger Kunstakademie*, pp. 59–64.

were published as council decrees in 1756 and once more in 1777.[90] Based on the model of Hamburg, financial awards and honorary medals sought to encourage the inhabitants' propensity to help.[91] In 1804, a circle of citizens formed an association to promote life-saving and rescue activities.[92]

9 Conclusion

In the final analysis, the institutions of the Holy Roman Empire circumscribed the imperial city's internal and external spheres of political action. Juridification and the expansion of communal responsibilities were long-term processes that decisively shaped urban politics. Following the radical constitutional reform of 1548, the patriciate accommodated to its new position of power, educated its sons to become professional politicians, and sought to minimize confessional and social antagonisms by pursuing a policy of consensus. It was only the economic and social dislocations of the French Revolutionary Wars that decisively undermined the social consensus and the council's authority. Attempts by the city's governing body to reform the political system and promote more citizen participation were not thwarted by the patricians' quest for continual dominance, but by the veto coming from the imperial capital of Vienna.

Bibliography

Unpublished Primary Sources

Stadtarchiv Augsburg (StadtAA)
    Bauamt 4, no. 103, Einstandsrechte der StadtBauamt 7, Karton 29.
    Reichsstadt, Akten 1, no. 1061, Lechmeister und Brunnenmeister.
Staats- und Stadtbibliothek Augsburg (SuStBA)
    2° Cod. S 87–2, Stubenzettel 1696.
    4° Cod. Aug. 973, Nachricht an das Reichsstadt-Augsburgische Publikum über den gegenwärtigen Zustand der neuen Armenanstalt (1782–1813).

---

90 Beyschlag, *Rettungsanstalten*, pp. 10–19; Stetten, *Selbstbiographie*, vol. 3, p. 52.
91 Schambach, *Patriotische Gesellschaft*, pp. 26–28. The authorities were struggling to overcome popular fears of helping potential suicide victims because of the risk of defamation resulting from handling the body: Stuart, *Defiled Trades*, pp. 197–200, 243–44.
92 Stetten, *Selbstbiographie*, vol. 3, p. 52.

Published Primary Sources

[anon.], "Augspurgische Verfügungen wider den Bettel. 1781", *Ephemeriden der Menschheit* 1 (1782), pp. 223–44.

Beyschlag, E., *Etwas zur Beantwortung der Frage: Was können und sollen öffentliche Schulen zum glücklichen Erfolg der Rettungsanstalten für Scheintodte beytragen?* [...], Augsburg, 1804.

Dussler, P.H. (ed.), *Reisen und Reisende in Bayerisch-Schwaben und seinen Randgebieten in Oberbayern, Franken, Württemberg, Vorarlberg und Tirol. Reiseberichte aus sechs Jahrhunderten*, Reiseberichte und Selbstzeugnisse aus Bayerisch-Schwaben vol. 2, Weissenhorn, 1974.

Häberlein, M., Künast, H.-J. and Schwanke, I. (eds.), *Die Korrespondenz der Augsburger Patrizierfamilie Endorfer 1620–1627. Briefe aus Italien und Frankreich im Zeitalter des Dreißigjährigen Krieges*, Augsburg, 2010.

Naujoks, E. (ed.), *Kaiser Karl V. und die Zunftverfassung. Ausgewählte Aktenstücke zu den Verfassungsänderungen in den oberdeutschen Reichsstädten (1547–1556)*, Stuttgart, 1985.

Stetten, Paul von [the Younger], *Selbstbiographie. Die Lebensbeschreibung des Patriziers und Stadtpflegers der Reichsstadt Augsburg (1731–1808)*

Vol 1: Die Aufzeichnungen zu den Jahren 1731–1792, ed. H. Gier, comp. B. Rajkay and R. von Stetten, Augsburg, 2009.

Vol. 2: Die kalendarischen Aufzeichnungen 1791 bis 1804, ed. H. Gier, comp. B. Rajkay and A. Schlenkrich, Augsburg, 2015.

Vol. 3: Die Aufzeichnungen zu den Jahren 1804 bis 1807, ed. H. Gier, comp. B. Rajkay and R. von Stetten, Augsburg, 2016.

Tlusty, B.A. (ed.), *Augsburg During the Reformation Era: An Anthology of Sources*, Indianapolis, 2012.

Ulrich, T.L., "Regimentsordnung der Reichsstadt Augsburg aus dem Jahre 1719", *Juristisches Magazin für die deutschen Reichsstädte* 3 (1793), pp. 1–749.

Ulrich, T.L., "Ämterreceß der Reichsstadt Augsburg von 1719", *Juristisches Magazin für die deutschen Reichsstädte* 4 (1795), pp. 292–372.

Ulrich, T.L., "Augspurgischer Additionalreceß von 1740", *Juristisches Magazin für die deutschen Reichsstädte* 5 (1795), pp. 154–94.

Secondary Literature

Bátori, I., *Die Reichsstadt Augsburg im 18. Jahrhundert. Verfassung, Finanzen und Reformversuche*, Göttingen, 1969.

Bátori, I., "Reichsstädtisches Regiment, Finanzen und bürgerliche Opposition", in: G. Gottlieb, W. Baer, J. Becker, J. Bellot, K. Filser, P. Fried, W. Reinhard and B. Schimmelpfennig (eds.), *Geschichte der Stadt Augsburg von der Römerzeit bis zur Gegenwart*, Stuttgart, 1984, pp. 457–68.

Bayer, H.-W., "Streiks in Augsburg im Wandel vom 18. zum 19. Jahrhundert", Ph.D. diss., University of Constance, 1992.

Clasen, C.-P., "Die Augsburger Bleichen im 18. Jahrhundert", in R.A. Müller (ed.), *Aufbruch ins Industriezeitalter. Vol. 2: Aufsätze zur Wirtschafts- und Sozialgeschichte Bayerns 1750–1850*, Munich, 1985, pp. 184–222.

Clasen, C.-P., *Streiks und Aufstände der Augsburger Weber im 17. und 18. Jahrhundert*, Augsburg, 1993.

Fassl, P., *Konfession, Wirtschaft und Politik: Von der Reichsstadt zur Industriestadt. Augsburg 1750–1850*, Sigmaringen, 1988.

Fimpel, M., *Reichsjustiz und Territorialstaat. Württemberg als Kommissar von Kaiser und Reich im Schwäbischen Kreis (1648–1806)*, Tübingen, 1999.

Finkl, N., *Administrative Verdichtung und Konfessionalisierung. Die Verwaltung der Reichsstadt Augsburg im 16. Jahrhundert*, Neustadt an der Aisch, 2011.

Dotterweich, V. and Reissner, B., "Finanznot und Domizilrecht. Zur Aufnahme jüdischer Wechselhäuser in Augsburg 1803", in R. Kießling (ed.), *Judengemeinden in Schwaben im Kontext des Alten Reiches*, Berlin, 1995, pp. 282–305.

Friedrichs, C.R., "German Town Revolts and the Seventeenth-Century Crisis", *Renaissance and Modern Studies* 26, 1 (1982), pp. 27–51.

Gößner, A., "Rechtsgelehrte in Reichsstädten. Identitätsmerkmale eines Berufsstandes in Süddeutschland", in: *Zeitschrift des Historischen Vereins für Schwaben* 92 (1999), pp. 75–89.

Grieger, A., "Kunst und Öffentlichkeit in der zweiten Hälfte des 18. Jahrhunderts", in H.-W. Jäger (ed.), *Öffentlichkeit im 18. Jahrhundert*, Göttingen, 1997, pp. 117–35.

Haberer, S., *Ott Heinrich Fugger (1592–1644). Biographische Analyse typologischer Handlungsfelder in der Epoche des Dreißigjährigen Krieges*, Augsburg, 2004.

Häberlein, M., *Brüder, Freunde und Betrüger. Soziale Beziehungen, Normen und Konflikte in der Augsburger Kaufmannschaft um die Mitte des 16. Jahrhunderts*, Berlin, 1998.

Häberlein, M., "Sozialer Wandel in den Augsburger Führungsschichten des 16. und frühen 17. Jahrhunderts", in G. Schulz (ed.), *Sozialer Aufstieg. Funktionseliten im Spätmittelalter und in der frühen Neuzeit*, Munich, 2002, pp. 73–96.

Häberlein, M., *The Fuggers of Augsburg: Pursuing Wealth and Honor in Reformation Germany*, Charlottesville and London, 2012.

Häberlein, M. and Schmölz-Häberlein, M., *Die Erben der Welser. Der Karibikhandel der Augsburger Firma Obwexer im Zeitalter der Revolutionen*, Augsburg, 1995.

Haberstock, E., *Der Augsburger Stadtwerkmeister Elias Holl (1573–1646). Werkverzeichnis*, Petersberg, 2016.

Härter, Karl, "Security and 'gute Policey' in Early Modern Europe: Concepts, Laws and Instruments", *The Production of Human Security in Premodern and Contemporary History*, special issue of *Historical Social Research* 35 (2010), pp. 41–65.

Hetzer, G., "Augsburger Theaterwesen zwischen 1770 und 1850", in R.A. Müller (ed.), *Aufbruch ins Industriezeitalter. Vol. 2: Aufsätze zur Wirtschafts- und Sozialgeschichte Bayerns 1750–1850*, Munich, 1985, pp. 527–43.

Hildebrandt, R., "Zum Verhältnis von Wirtschaftsrecht und Wirtschaftspraxis im 16. Jahrhundert. Die Fallitenordnungen des Augsburger Rates 1564–1580", in A. Mächler, E. Grünert and H. Kraemer (eds.), *Historische Studien zu Politik, Verfassung und Gesellschaft. Festschrift für Richard Dietrich zum 65. Geburtstag*. Berne and Frankfurt, 1976, pp. 154–63.

Huber, H., "Die Konzerte im Fugger'schen Saal in Augsburg", *Zeitschrift des Historischen Vereins für Schwaben*, 103 (2011), pp. 225–302.

Iseli, A., *Gute Policey. Öffentliche Ordnung in der frühen Neuzeit*, Stuttgart, 2009.

Kießling, R., "Augsburg in der Reformationszeit", in E. Brockhoff, W. Jahn and J. Kirmeier (eds.), *"… wider Laster und Sünde". Augsburgs Weg in die Reformation*, Cologne, 1997, pp. 17–43.

Kießling, R., "Konfession als alltägliche Grenze – oder: Wie evangelisch waren die Reichsstädte?" in: W. Jahn, T. Berger, J. Kirmeier and E. Brockhoff (eds.), *"Geld und Glaube". Leben in evangelischen Reichsstädten* (exhibition catalogue), Augsburg, 1998, pp. 48–66.

Kießling, R., "Vom Ausnahmefall zur Alternative. Bikonfessionalität in Oberdeutschland", in C.A. Hoffmann, M. Johanns, A. Kranz, C. Trepesch and O. Zeidler (eds.), *Als Frieden möglich war. 450 Jahre Augsburger Religionsfrieden* (exhibition catalogue), Regensburg, 2005, pp. 119–30.

Kießling, R., "Augsburg im Aufstand. Ein systematischer Vergleich von Unruhen des 14./16. mit denen des 17./18. Jahrhunderts", in A. and E. Westermann (eds.), *Streik im Revier. Unruhe, Protest und Ausstand vom 8. bis 20. Jahrhundert*, St. Katharinen, 2007, pp. 153–75.

Kießling, R., "Das Patriziat in Augsburg vom 15. bis ins 17. Jahrhundert", in C. Emmendörfer and H. Zäh (eds.), *Bürgermacht & Bücherpracht. Augsburger Ehren- und Familienbücher der Renaissance* (exhibition catalogue), Lucerne, 2011, vol. 1, pp. 19–36.

Kraus, J., *Das Militärwesen der Reichsstadt Augsburg 1548 bis 1806*, Augsburg, 1980.

Kuhn, C., *Die Politik des Pasquino. Schmähschriften, Protestgelächter und Öffentlichkeiten in politischen Konflikten Alteuropas (ca. 1540–1750)*, Berlin, 2020 (in press).

Mančal, J., *Augsburger Kunstakademie in reichsstädtischer Zeit* (exhibition catalogue), Augsburg, 2010.

Mauer, B., *"Gemain Geschrey" und "teglich Reden". Georg Kölderer – ein Augsburger Chronist des konfessionellen Zeitalters*, Augsburg, 2001.

Möller, F., "Zwischen Kunst und Kommerz. Bürgertheater im 19. Jahrhundert", in D. Hein and A. Schulz (eds.), *Bürgerkultur im 19. Jahrhundert*, Munich, 1996, pp. 19–33.

Möller, F., *Bürgerliche Herrschaft in Augsburg 1790–1880*, Munich, 1998.

Mörke, O. and Sieh, K., "Gesellschaftliche Führungsgruppen", in G. Gottlieb, W. Baer, J. Becker, J. Bellot, K. Filser, P. Fried, W. Reinhard and B. Schimmelpfennig (eds.), *Geschichte der Stadt Augsburg. 2000 Jahre von der Römerzeit bis zur Gegenwart*, 2nd ed., Stuttgart, 1985, pp. 301–11.

Naujoks, E., "Vorstufen der Parität in der Verfassungsgeschichte der schwäbischen Reichsstädte (1555–1648). Das Beispiel Augsburgs", in J. Sydow (ed.), *Bürgerschaft und Kirche*, Sigmaringen, 1980, pp. 38–66.

Rajkay, B., "Totentanz oder Maskenbälle? Anmerkungen zur Geschichte Augsburgs im 18. Jahrhundert", in B. Rajkay, D. Schiersner, A. Link and W. Scheffknecht (eds.), *Augsburg, Schwaben und der Rest der Welt. Neue Beiträge zur Landes- und Regionalgeschichte. Festschrift für Rolf Kießling zum 70. Geburtstag*, Augsburg, 2011, pp. 85–109.

Rajkay, B., "Die trockene Seite der Augsburger Wasserwirtschaft. Organisationsstrukturen und Aufgaben der reichsstädtischen Bauverwaltung bei der Trinkwasserversorgung und beim Wasserbau", in Stadt Augsburg (ed.), *Augsburg und die Wasserwirtschaft. Studien zur Nominierung für das UNESCO-Welterbe im internationalen Vergleich*, Augsburg, 2017, pp. 68–85.

Reinhard, W., "Governi Stretti e Tirannici. Die Städtepolitik Karl V.", in A. Kohler and H. Lutz (eds.), *Karl V. 1500–1558. Neue Perspektiven seiner Herrschaft in Europa und Übersee*, Vienna, 2002, pp. 407–34.

Roeck, B., *Eine Stadt in Krieg und Frieden. Studien zur Geschichte der Reichsstadt Augsburg zwischen Kalenderstreit und Parität*, 2 vols., Göttingen, 1989.

Roth, F., *Augsburgs Reformationsgeschichte*, 4 vols., Munich, 1901–11.

Schambach, S., *Aus der Gegenwart die Zukunft gewinnen. Die Geschichte der Patriotischen Gesellschaft von 1765*, Hamburg, 2004.

Schilling, H., "The European Crisis of the 1590s: The Situation in German Towns", in P. Clark (ed.), *The European Crisis of the 1590s*, London 1985, pp. 135–56.

Scribner, R.W., "Police and the Territorial State in Sixteenth-Century Württemberg", in E.I. Kouri and T. Scott (eds.), *Politics and Society in Reformation Europe: Essays for Sir Geoffrey Elton on his Sixty-Fifth Birthday*, London, 1987, pp. 103–20.

Seiler, J., *Das Augsburger Domkapitel vom Dreißigjährigen Krieg bis zur Säkularisation (1648–1802). Studien zur Geschichte seiner Verfassung und seiner Mitglieder*, St. Ottilien, 1989.

Sieh-Burens, K., *Oligarchie, Konfession und Politik im 16. Jahrhundert. Studien zur sozialen Verflechtung der Augsburger Bürgermeister und Stadtpfleger von 1518 bis 1618*, Munich, 1986.

Stuart, K., *Defiled Trades and Social Outcasts: Honor and Ritual Pollution in Early Modern Germany*, Cambridge, 1999.

Steuer, P., *Die Außenverflechtung der Augsburger Oligarchie von 1500–1620: Studien zur sozialen Verflechtung der politischen Führungsschicht der Reichsstadt Augsburg*, Augsburg, 1988.

Tlusty, B.A., *Bacchus and Civic Order: The Culture of Drink in Early Modern Germany*, Charlottesville, 2001.

Wallenta, W., *Katholische Konfessionalisierung in Augsburg, 1548–1648*, Hamburg, 2003.

Warmbrunn, P., *Zwei Konfessionen in einer Stadt. Das Zusammenleben von Katholiken und Protestanten in den paritätischen Reichsstädten Augsburg, Biberach, Ravensburg und Dinkelsbühl von 1548 bis 1648*, Wiesbaden, 1983.

Werner, A., *Die örtlichen Stiftungen für die Zwecke des Unterrichts und der Wohltätigkeit in der Stadt Augsburg*, Augsburg, 1899.

Zürn, M., "Stillstand im Wandel oder Wandel im Stillstand. Waldburg und Habsburg im 18. Jahrhundert", in C. Bumiller, M. Hengerer and E.L. Kuhn (eds.), *Adel im Wandel. 200 Jahre Mediatisierung in Oberschwaben*, Ostfildern, 2006, vol. 1, pp. 241–54.

CHAPTER 8

Crime and Punishment

Allyson F. Creasman

The history of crime has proven to be a particularly valuable lens through which to study the major developments transforming European society and culture in the early modern period. The years between 1400 and 1800 were marked by increasing political centralization across much of Europe, accompanied by expanding state bureaucracies and greater legal oversight of both public and private affairs. In the German context, this trend toward "social disciplining" is evident in the growth of legal institutions and statutory law at the imperial, territorial, and local levels.[1] Over the course of the early modern period, these developments helped to create an increasingly standardized legal culture that strongly bolstered the interests of the state and enhanced its investigatory powers.[2]

The imperial city of Augsburg left behind an unusually rich collection of sources illustrating these transformations of early modern law and society. Between the thirteenth and sixteenth centuries, jurisdictional conflicts, changes in criminal procedure, and an expanding corpus of substantive criminal law consolidated judicial authority in the hands of Augsburg's ruling city council. By the early sixteenth century, it exercised exclusive authority to define, try, and punish crime, and over the course of the early modern period it erected an extensive legal bureaucracy to enforce a vision of communal order regulating both public and private conduct. But in Augsburg, as elsewhere in Europe, the practical limitations of early modern policing and enforcement often frustrated official controls. However much the social disciplining impulse might undergird the regulatory power of the state, the practical realities of controlling crime in Augsburg and other early modern communities meant that authorities always had to rely on the citizenry's active participation in the process. As a result, magistrates had to be ever alert to public expectations of justice in their administration of the criminal law.

---

1 On social disciplining, see Oestreich, *Strukturprobleme*; Schulze, "Gerhard Oestreichs Begriff Sozialdisziplinierung", pp. 265–302; Po-chia Hsia, *Social Discipline in the Reformation*. On the limitations of the concept, see Schmidt, "Sozialdisziplinierung?", pp. 639–82.
2 Schulze, "Gerhard Oestreichs Begriff Sozialdisziplinierung", p. 278; Wieacker, *A History of Private Law in Europe*, pp. 101, 111; Coing, *Römisches Recht in Deutschland*, pp. 31–33.

1 Building on Medieval Foundations

Augsburg's governing city council entered the sixteenth century as the city's supreme judicial authority. From then until the dissolution of the Empire in 1806, the council defined the city's substantive criminal law and oversaw the policing, adjudication, and punishment of crime.[3] High justice in Augsburg, however, rested on early medieval foundations. Of particular importance to the evolution of this system were the jurisdictional battles between the medieval city and its bishops, and the gradual reformulation of its customary laws and procedures in Roman terms.

Medieval Augsburg had risen to prominence under the protection of a storied line of bishops. The 1156 *Stadtrecht* (civic law) issued by Emperor Frederick I recognized the bishop's lordship over the city and placed the administration of criminal justice exclusively in the hands of his representative, the *Vogt* (bailiff).[4] But tensions repeatedly arose in the ensuing years between the episcopal administration and the local population, and with imperial support, Augsburg's city council gradually assumed control over the city's political and legal affairs.[5]

Key to this process was the 1276 codification of the civic law code, the *Stadtbuch*, at the command of King Rudolf I. In authorizing the code, the king recognized the local authority of the city council and confirmed its right to define the city's laws independently of the bishop.[6] One of the earliest urban law codes in Germany, the Augsburg *Stadtbuch* was continuously expanded until 1512.[7] It addressed criminal offenses such as murder, manslaughter, rape, robbery and theft, arson, adultery, heresy, and sorcery and authorized the use of punishments such as beheading, hanging, breaking on the wheel, burning, and live burial.[8]

In this period, continental European law was also undergoing a profound transformation brought about by the renewed study of Roman law and procedure. In early medieval Germanic law, criminal trials had largely followed "accusatorial" procedure, where the onus was on the victim or his kin to initiate a case via formal complaint and to muster evidence against the accused in

---

3 Schorer, *Strafgerichtsbarkeit*, p. 166; Bátori, *Reichsstadt Augsburg*, p. 41.
4 Baer, "Das Stadtrecht von Jahre 1156", pp. 132–33.
5 Schorer, *Strafgerichtsbarkeit*, pp. 50–62; Tyler, *Lord of the Sacred City*, pp. 77–102; Kießling, *Bürgerliche Gesellschaft und Kirche*, pp. 23–30.
6 Schmidt, "Das Stadtbuch von 1276", pp. 140–44.
7 Schmidt, "Das Stadtbuch von 1276", p. 140; Pötzl, "Gesetze und Ordnungen", p. 18; Hoffmann, "Strukturen und Quellen", p. 62. See also Chapter 9 in this volume.
8 Meyer (ed.), *Stadtbuch*; Pötzl, "Gesetze und Ordnungen", pp. 18–24.

public, oral proceedings.[9] Jurors pronounced guilt or innocence based either on the results of the ordeal or trial by combat or on compurgation – the accused's sworn oath of innocence backed by "oath-helpers" who attested to his honesty and good reputation.[10]

Beginning in eleventh-century Italy, continental European jurists began to systematize customary law and practice in accordance with the sixth-century Roman *Corpus Juris Civilis*.[11] This process – called the "Reception" of Roman law – also introduced Roman inquisitorial procedure into medieval European criminal law. In contrast to customary accusatorial procedure, the inquisitorial model tasked public magistrates with the primary responsibility for conducting investigations, evaluating evidence, and deciding verdicts. Rather than having to wait for victims to initiate prosecutions, they could investigate suspected crimes upon their own authority, thus substantially augmenting the magistrate's prosecutorial power.[12] Inquisitorial procedure also shifted virtually all stages of the trial process from public, oral proceedings to private hearings before the magistrates, documented in official, written records.[13]

The introduction of inquisitorial procedure roughly coincided with a transformation in the continental European law of proof. After the Fourth Lateran Council's 1215 prohibition of clerical involvement in the ordeal, reliance on this and other "non-rational" forms of proof gradually declined.[14] In empowering judges to rationally weigh the evidence before them, inquisitorial procedure could offer an alternative, but European jurists worried about substituting the potentially faulty judgment of human judges for the divinely-ordained certainty of the ordeal. To minimize the risk of human error, they required convincing evidence of guilt, typically the testimony of two eyewitnesses or, ideally, the confession of the accused.[15] While satisfying the moral demand for certainty of guilt, this heavy emphasis on confession also fostered the gradual reintroduction of the Roman practice of judicial torture in order to secure it. Between the thirteenth and eighteenth century, this reliance on judicial torture empowered continental prosecutors to secure convictions in otherwise questionable cases, often to deadly effect.[16]

---

9   Langbein, *Prosecuting Crime*, pp. 130–32.
10 Langbein, *Prosecuting Crime*, p. 142–44.
11 Wieacker, *A History of Private Law*, pp. 360–73.
12 Langbein, *Prosecuting Crime*, pp. 130–32.
13 Trusen, "Strafprozeß und Rezeption", p. 79.
14 Trusen, "Strafprozeß und Rezeption", p. 54.
15 Langbein, *Prosecuting Crime*, pp. 134–37; idem, *Torture and the Law of Proof*, pp. 4–8.
16 Langbein, *Torture and the Law of Proof*, pp. 3–17; Peters, *Torture*, pp. 40–73.

In Germany, inquisitorial procedure had been in use in canon law courts since the thirteenth century, but the Reception did not begin to make substantial inroads into secular law until the fifteenth century.[17] Although the Reception did not proceed uniformly across the German territories, administrations at both the imperial and local levels were increasingly staffed by jurists trained in Roman law and procedure, and by the early seventeenth century its influence was widespread.[18]

The Augsburg sources indicate that inquisitorial procedure was in use there at least by the beginning of the fifteenth century.[19] Although criminal proceedings could still be initiated by private complaint, public magistrates were authorized to commence investigations on their own authority, and compurgation gave way to the magistrates' objective evaluation of the evidence.[20] King Frederick IV (later Emperor Frederick III) ratified the city's Roman procedures in a 1446 decree, authorizing the Augsburg council to conduct criminal proceedings and pronounce judgments "in secret", that is, the private hearings and official adjudications characteristic of inquisitorial procedure.[21]

2   Augsburg's Early Modern Courts

At the dawn of the sixteenth century, these medieval developments had securely established Augsburg's city council as the city's highest criminal court. Its judicial functions were carried out by the Small Council (*Kleiner Rat*), a body of 42 men selected from the guilds and patricians.[22] Although restructured in Emperor Charles V's 1548 reform of Augsburg's constitution, the Small Council retained its criminal jurisdiction.[23] Only the Small Council could impose the death penalty, and its decisions could not be appealed to any higher authority.[24] It also adjudicated a variety of non-capital crimes deemed important to

---

17   Wieacker, *A History of Private Law*, pp. 109, 113–58.
18   Wieacker, *A History of Private Law*, pp. 104–5, 109, 113–58; Coing, *Römisches Recht*, p. 30. On German opposition to Roman law in the sixteenth century, see Strauss, *Law, Resistance, and the State*.
19   Schorer, *Strafgerichtbarkeit*, pp. 163–64.
20   Ibid., pp. 162, 165–66.
21   Ibid., pp. 165–66.
22   Liedl, *Gerichtsverfassung und Zivilprozess*, p. 111; Rogge, *Für den Gemeinen Nutzen*, p. 301; see also Chapter 6 in this volume.
23   Roeck, *Eine Stadt in Krieg und Frieden*, vol. 1, p. 239; Bátori, *Reichsstadt Augsburg*, p. 41. On these governmental changes, see Chapters 6 and 7 in this volume.
24   Liedl, *Gerichtsverfassung*, p. 111.

communal order and security, such as seditious gossip, disorderly assembly, or violation of censorship laws.

In this period, Augsburg's city council also created a variety of lower magistracies to handle minor criminal offenses. These tribunals were typically staffed by councilmen, and their judgments were appealable to the Small Council.[25] An extensive corpus of decrees and ordinances spelled out their respective jurisdictions and procedures.

Chief among these tribunals in the fifteenth century were the *Einunger*, a panel of five magistrates appointed by the Small Council. Charged with resolving minor disputes and breaches of the peace, their jurisdiction was quite broad.[26] Between 1472 and 1537, however, the *Einunger*'s criminal authority was gradually shifted to a new magistracy, the *Strafherren* ("punishment lords").[27] From the early sixteenth century onwards, this body functioned as Augsburg's major lower criminal tribunal. Originally a panel of six (later four) men, the *Strafherren* were appointed from the members of the Small and Large Councils. Their jurisdiction was most fully spelled out in the 1537 Discipline and Police Ordinance (*Zucht und Policey Ordnung*).[28] Issued after Augsburg's adoption of the Protestant Reformation, the Discipline and Police Ordinance has sometimes been seen as an expression of the council's religious concern to reform public and private morality.[29] It outlawed offenses such as blasphemy, swearing, gambling, drunkenness, adultery, and slander. In addition to these offenses, the *Strafherren* were also responsible for punishing brawling and other minor breaches of the peace. Given their focus on moral discipline and public order, the *Strafherren* are also sometimes described in the Augsburg sources as the *Zuchtherren*, or "discipline lords".[30]

Prior to 1548, the city council also allowed the guilds to punish minor offences committed in their guildhalls. If guild officials failed to act within eight days, or if the matter involved non-guild members, the *Strafherren* were to decide

---

25 Sieh-Burens, "Augsburger Stadtverfassung", p. 147.
26 Sieh-Burens, "Augsburger Stadtverfassung", pp. 152–54; Hoffmann, "Strukturen und Quellen", p. 79.
27 Schorer, *Strafgerichtsbarkeit*, p. 159; Finkl, *Administrative Verdichtung*, pp. 157–68.
28 Stadtarchiv Augsburg (StadtAA), Ordnungen, Zucht-und-Policey Ordnung 1537; Schorer, *Strafgerichtsbarkeit*, pp. 187–88; Hoffmann, "Strukturen und Quellen", p. 77. The Police Ordinances were periodically revised, with few substantive changes, throughout the early modern period.
29 Köhler, *Zürcher Ehegericht*, vol. 2, pp. 28–322; Roper, *The Holy Household*, p. 54.
30 Schorer, "Die Strafherren", p. 183.

the case.[31] The city council gradually withdrew such authority from the guilds, however, and the *Strafherren* assumed full jurisdiction over such cases.[32]

These various officials applied a loosely defined collection of laws governing crime. Although the 1276 *Stadtbuch* was never formally rescinded, its authority dwindled over time. New legislation supplemented and eventually superseded it, but occasionally still cited its authority, as for example, in the 1529 *Stadtgerichtsordnung* (civic judicial ordinance), which grounded its penalties for manslaughter on the punishments established in the *Stadtbuch*. After the early sixteenth century, the *Stadtbuch* seems to have been seldom consulted, but no new codification of Augsburg's laws took place in the early modern period.[33] While many other German imperial cities, such as Nuremberg and Frankfurt am Main, undertook comprehensive revisions and restatements of their laws in the fifteenth and sixteenth centuries, such a legal "reformation" never occurred in Augsburg. City officials periodically compiled the various council decrees and ordinances in use, but none of these volumes had official status.[34] As a result, early modern Augsburg lacked a clearly identifiable and coordinated body of laws regulating crime and punishment.[35]

3 Policing the City

In the mid-sixteenth century, Augsburg was one of the largest and most prosperous cities of the Holy Roman Empire, but was deeply divided economically. This stratification of wealth continued into the seventeenth century, with the top 10% of the city's taxpayers controlling 92% of its taxable property by 1618.[36] In light of the city's sizable but often impoverished and disenfranchised underclass, Augsburg's ruling elites were wary of any hint of civic disorder and looked upon the lower orders with nervous suspicion.

The city's crowded living conditions, combined with its religious and socioeconomic divisions, created ample opportunities for conflict but, like most

---

31 Hoffmann, "Strukturen und Quellen", pp. 80–81.
32 Schorer, *Strafgerichtsbarkeit*, pp. 204–07.
33 Hoffmann, "Strukturen und Quellen", pp. 62, 65–66.
34 In the 1590s, the city advocates Georg Tradel and Matthaeus Laimann proposed such a revision, but the council did not follow through. See Becker (ed.), *Consvetudines almae Reipublicae Augustanae* and Chapter 9 in this volume.
35 Binswanger, "Zur äusseren Rechtsgeschichte", pp. 16–19; Liedl, *Gerichtsverfassung und Zivilprozess*, pp. 53–54.
36 For more on Augsburg's population and socio-economic structure, see Chapters 2 and 5 in this volume.

early modern communities, Augsburg lacked a professional police force. Its legal system was thus, by necessity, dependent upon citizen reporting and voluntary compliance. All citizens were required to swear an oath pledging obedience to the council and its mandates and were obligated to report law-breakers and suspicious persons.[37] Denunciations in Augsburg's criminal files suggest that residents generally accepted these duties, actively policing each other's conduct on the council's behalf. Although the social and religious conflicts of the period sometimes shook public confidence in the city council, Augsburgers generally accepted its oversight as essential to the maintenance of public order and actively participated in enforcing its rule. This could never be entirely taken for granted, however, and the practical realities of urban policing meant that the council's rule had to reflect communal expectations of justice.[38]

In addition to citizen reporting, local authorities also relied on a network of informants who were paid according to the severity of the penalties levied against the people they accused.[39] They also retained a small paid constabulary force, the *Scharwächter* (watch regiment), and a four-person guard, the *Stadtknechte* (civic guard).[40] Under the command of the city bailiff (*Stadtvogt*),[41] the *Stadtknechte* carried out the orders of the *Bürgermeister*[42] and *Strafherren*,[43] summoning witnesses or taking suspects into custody. Together with the *Stadtvogt*, they were charged with escorting banished criminals out of the city, quelling public disturbances, and patrolling taverns, streets, and markets in search of suspicious activity.[44]

Like many early modern German cities, Augsburg also relied on a citizen militia to help maintain order. Every adult male citizen was expected to serve in the militia and arm himself for this purpose. In times of public emergency,

---

37 Schorer, *Strafgerichtsbarkeit*, pp. 173–75.
38 See Hoffmann, "Bürgersicherheit".
39 StadtAA, Bürgermeisteramt, Instruction die Herren Bürgermeister betreffend, fol. 132.
40 Schorer, *Strafgerichtsbarkeit*, p. 175.
41 Originally the highest judicial officer in medieval Augsburg, the *Stadtvogt* primarily had a policing function by the sixteenth century, serving essentially as Captain of the Guard. Schorer, *Strafgerichtsbarkeit*, pp. 185–87.
42 Once a mayoral office under the guild government, the city's *Bürgermeister* assumed mainly policing duties after the 1548 Caroline constitutional reform. On the changes in Augsburg's governmental structure during this period, see Chapters 6 and 7 in this volume.
43 See StadtAA, Schätze, no. ad 36/3, Zucht unnd Execution Ordnung, 1553, Ordnung und Pflicht der Straffherren, auch wie Sÿ auff aines Erbarn Raths, furgenomne Zucht Ordnung, hanndeln, Procediern, und Straffen sollen; StadtAA, Bürgermeisteramt, Instruction die Herren Bürgermeister betreffend.
44 Schorer, *Strafgerichtsbarkeit*, pp. 175–76, 182.

they were to muster under a designated "quarter captain" for the city's defense. They were also called upon to help patrol the city as a nightly watch.[45] While on their rounds, they were instructed to look out for "all that may be troublesome or dangerous", especially "dangerous, suspicious persons".[46]

This entire system, with its heavy reliance on citizen reporting and policing, depended on neighbors to know one another's affairs and assess one another's characters. This points to a central feature of early modern European life – the importance attached to honor and reputation. Honor, in Richard Evans' words, was the "glue" that held early modern society together.[47] But reputation, or *fama*, also had a long history in criminal law.[48] Honor and reputation were critical to determining both who had access to the courts and who was targeted by them. Judges could open a case based on bad reputation alone, as manifested through hearsay about an individual's habits and associates.[49] Magistrates also weighed the reputations of accusers when deciding whether to launch an investigation, and anyone who testified had to be of honorable repute.[50] People with dishonorable reputations were more likely to fall under suspicion and were less able to be heard in court.

For early modern Germans, both those caught up in the penal system and those who administered it were tainted with dishonor. Although the community relied on them to keep order, constables, bailiffs, jailors, and other low-level officials in close contact with prisoners and instruments of punishment were often decried as dishonorable. They and their children could be barred from guilds and higher public offices, and honorable people were expected to avoid social contact with them. Executioners were the most highly dishonorable of all, and their mere touch was thought to be defiling.[51] Although the law extolled the importance of these judicial officers to the civic order, they occupied highly ambivalent positions in early modern German communities.

---

45   Tlusty, *The Martial Ethic*, pp. 11–45; Kraus, *Militärwesen*, pp. 74–94. Obligatory militia service made wearing a weapon – and being prepared to use it – an identifying mark of honorable male citizenship; indeed, Augsburg magistrates sometimes shamed male offenders by forbidding them to carry weapons. The centrality of weapons among urban men made delimiting their proper use a major concern for magistrates attempting to police urban violence.
46   StadtAA, Schätze, no. 16, Anschläge, fol. 56r.
47   Evans, *Rituals of Retribution*, p. 54.
48   On *fama*, see Fenster and Smail, *Fama*.
49   See sections 6 and 25 of the 1522 *Constitutio Criminalis Carolina* (§§ 6, 25 *Carolina*).
50   § 66 *Carolina*.
51   Stuart, *Defiled Trades*, pp. 3–4, 97–102; Dülmen, *Der ehrlose Mensch*, pp. 43–54. On the status and functions of executioners in early modern Germany, see Harrington, *The Faithful Executioner*.

4 Trial Procedure and Punishment

Once suspects were taken into custody, the next stage of the proceedings depended upon the nature of the accusations against them. The *Bürgermeister* would determine whether there were sufficient grounds to warrant jailing the defendant pending a formal investigation. In cases involving petty offenses or minor disputes, the *Bürgermeister* was authorized to settle matters in summary hearings, typically imposing small fines (*Busen*) or requiring a formal apology (*Abbitte*) to the victim.[52]

In more serious cases, the prisoner would be "laid in irons" to await investigation by the appropriate officials, usually in the dungeon under the city hall.[53] Offenses falling under the discipline and police ordinances – blasphemy, swearing, drunkenness, adultery, insults, and the like – were referred to the *Strafherren* for adjudication. Persons awaiting a hearing before the *Strafherren* might be held in the "fool's house" (*Narrenhaus*) – a cage-like cell located next to the city hall where passers-by might jeer at them.[54]

The *Strafherren* met on Mondays, Wednesdays, and Saturdays to adjudicate cases. For all but the most serious offenses, they were authorized to decide punishments; the police ordinances set forth fines for most minor offenses, but depending on the nature and severity of the crime, the *Strafherren* could also order banishment or corporal punishment.[55] Where a case fell outside their jurisdiction or presented difficult legal questions or threats to public order, the *Strafherren* could refer it to the Small Council, often with a report and recommended sentence.[56]

More serious crimes, and all crimes potentially subject to the death penalty, were reserved for adjudication by the Small Council. In Augsburg, as in early modern Europe generally, a wide variety of offenses were punishable by death. In addition to violent crimes such as murder, manslaughter, and rape, offenses such as major theft, witchcraft, sodomy, incest, and bestiality were also potential capital crimes in Augsburg.[57]

---

52   StadtAA, Bürgermeisteramt, Instruction die Herren Bürgermeister betreffend; Liedl, *Gerichtsverfassung*, p. 111.
53   Schorer, *Strafgerichtsbarkeit*, p. 177.
54   Tlusty, *Bacchus and Civic Order*, p. 85.
55   Punishments levied by the *Strafherren/Zuchtherren* are recorded in the *Zuchtprotokolle* held in the Augsburg Stadtarchiv. Usually titled *Zuchtbücher* or *Protokolle der Zucht- und Strafherren*, they extend – almost without interruption – from 1537 to the mid-eighteenth century.
56   Hoffmann, "Strukturen und Quellen", pp. 78–79.
57   Pötzl, "Listen von Hingerichteten", pp. 360–73.

Cases to be decided by the Small Council were investigated by two interrogators, or *Auditores* (literally, "hearers"), appointed from its ranks on a rotating basis.[58] In addition to summoning and interviewing witnesses, they could apply torture in capital cases with the council's prior approval. As there was no requirement that members of the Small Council have any formal legal education, trained jurists, or city attorneys (*Stadtadvocaten*), acted as advisors, opining on legal questions and recommending verdicts. Their opinions were compiled for the council's reference in future cases.[59]

Consistent with inquisitorial procedure, criminal interrogations were recorded by a city clerk, who was expected to record the defendant's words, actions, and demeanor as nearly as possible. As in most continental European jurisdictions in this period, all hearings were conducted in closed-door sessions, and the accused was not entitled to legal counsel.[60] Witnesses were typically interrogated according to a list of questions (*Fragstücke*) prepared in advance by the Small Council for each case.[61] The prisoner's answers, along with the question list, formed the official trial record, known locally as the *Urgicht*.[62]

Criminal trial procedure in early modern Augsburg largely coincided with the standards outlined in the 1532 imperial criminal code, the *Constitutio Criminalis Carolina*. The *Carolina* spelled out the various stages of the inquisitorial process from arrest to final judgment, establishing the circumstances warranting an arrest and the opening of a formal inquiry as well as the procedures for interrogating witnesses.[63] The process included an initial inquiry to establish whether a crime had indeed occurred, followed by a more formal investigation in which the presiding magistrates interrogated the accused and the witnesses under oath.[64] If the suspect's guilt was established by his confession or the sworn testimony of two credible eyewitnesses, the *Carolina* authorized a conviction.[65] Where the requisite proof was lacking, but strong circumstantial evidence of guilt existed, the *Carolina* authorized the magistrates to question the accused under torture in capital cases.[66] They were to

---

58 Schorer, *Strafgerichtsbarkeit*, p. 168.
59 Schorer, *Strafgerichtsbarkeit*, pp. 170–71.
60 Dülmen, *Theatre of Horrors*, p. 28.
61 Schorer, *Strafgerichtsbarkeit*, p. 168.
62 The Augsburg Stadtarchiv holds an extensive collection of *Urgichten* from 1479 through the eighteenth century, although coverage is uneven before the 1550s.
63 On the *Carolina* generally, see Schmidt, "Sinn und Bedeutung"; Langbein, *Prosecuting Crime*, pp. 140–209.
64 § 6 *Carolina*.
65 §§ 60, 67 *Carolina*.
66 §§ 18–44 *Carolina*.

use torture only as a last resort, after having repeatedly warned the defendant, and were required to personally supervise its application.[67] To be valid, confessions extracted under torture had to be later ratified by the defendant "freely" – that is, not under torture.[68] Although this requirement was intended to guard against false confessions, judges could re-apply torture if the defendant retracted his confession.[69] There was, in fact, no limit in the *Carolina* on the number of times torture could be applied.[70]

Although intended to provide a model for criminal procedure, evidentiary rules, and criminal punishment, the *Carolina* did not mandate its use across the Empire. In the "savings clause" of its preamble, the *Carolina* made clear that the customary laws and procedures of the Empire's constituent territories remained in effect.[71] This resulted in significant regional variation in its implementation.[72]

In Augsburg, the influence of the *Carolina* is clear by the late sixteenth century. In 1587, for example, the city modified its customary procedures in applying torture to conform to the *Carolina*'s standards. Officials noted that "it had previously been customary to allow the executioner to torture suspects alone, in the absence of the [*Auditores*], but he often exceeded the appropriate measure of torture". To put an end to this "bad practice", the *Auditores* were henceforth required to be personally present during torture sessions, as the *Carolina* advised.[73]

As the *Carolina* envisioned, Augsburg officials used torture only in capital cases and only as a last resort. Interrogators employed three stages of questioning, and any escalation of the interrogation had to be approved in advance by the Small Council.[74] Each prisoner's *Urgicht* recorded which form of interrogation was applied at each stage of the proceedings: "friendly" (*gütlich*) questioning meant that the prisoner answered the interrogators' questions voluntarily, without any express or implicit threat of torture. Prisoners subjected to "grave" (*ernstlich*) questioning were warned that they were strongly suspect and might be tortured if they remained uncooperative. To increase the psychological pressure on the prisoner, he or she might be questioned in the presence of the torture instruments, with the executioner standing by. "Painful" (*peinlich*)

---

67 §§ 46–47 *Carolina*.
68 § 56 *Carolina*.
69 § 57 *Carolina*.
70 § 58 *Carolina*.
71 Preamble, *Carolina*.
72 Langbein, *Prosecuting Crime*, pp. 196–98.
73 Stetten, *Geschichte*, vol. 1, p. 701.
74 Schorer, *Strafgerichtsbarkeit*, p. 169.

questioning denoted interrogation under torture, sometimes preceded by a demonstration by the executioner of the workings of the torture device. Where interrogations proceeded to "painful" questioning, the Augsburg *Urgichten* note the methods and intensity of the torture applied, as well as the prisoner's responses under torture.[75]

In Augsburg, men were typically tortured with the *strappado*, a device which hoisted the prisoner by the arms, often dislocating his shoulders; women were generally tortured with thumb-screws, and sometimes the *strappado* in witchcraft cases.[76] Torture was always administered by the city executioner, whose very touch was thought to be defiling. Even if acquitted, prisoners who had been tortured "under the executioner's hand" might be shunned as dishonorable upon their release.[77]

After concluding an investigation, the two presiding *Auditores* had to confirm the accuracy of the interrogation record with the defendant. The defendant's *Urgicht*, as well as related comments from the city attorneys, were read out before the Small Council, which would decide whether to punish or pardon. If the case involved a capital crime, a date was fixed for the *Peinlicher Rechtstag* (high court day) when the council's final sentence would be decided. At this point (if not before) the defendant was offered the opportunity to consult with a clergyman. Two officials were also deputized to receive petitions of clemency on the defendant's behalf.[78]

At the *Peinlicher Rechtstag*, at least 24 of the 45 members of the Small Council had to be in attendance to make the sentence legally valid; the defendant was neither present nor represented.[79] The defendant's interrogation record was again read aloud, along with the relevant passages of the city's criminal laws and any opinions of the city attorneys thereon. The city bailiff, carrying his staff of office, asked each of the mayors (*Stadtpfleger*) and the assembled councilmen under oath whether the defendant's crime merited death, and if so, by what means. He was also to inquire whether there were any extenuating or aggravating factors warranting a milder or harsher punishment.[80]

Although early modern European law prescribed death for a wide range of violent and non-violent crimes, the penal system also allowed magistrates wide discretion to mitigate punishments as they deemed just in any given case.

---

75   Hoffmann, "Strukturen und Quellen", p. 91–96.
76   Hoffmann, "Strukturen und Quellen", p. 92; Roper, *Oedipus and the Devil*, pp. 226–48.
77   Stuart, *Defiled Trades*, pp. 140–42.
78   Rau, *Augsburger Kinderhexenprozesse*, pp. 64–65.
79   Rau, *Augsburger Kinderhexenprozesse*, pp. 61, 65–66.
80   The proceedings of the *Peinlicher Rechtstag* are described in StadtAA, Strafamt, no. 161, Modus procedendi, wann Malefiz-Recht gehalten wird in Malefiz Sachen, fols. 3–11.

Indeed, the public show of mercy to deserving individuals was understood as central to the legitimate administration of justice.[81] Whether the death penalty was imposed depended substantially on the circumstances of the crime, the criminal record of the accused, as well as the age, gender, and social standing of both the offender and his or her victim.[82] In lieu of the death penalty, Augsburg officials could impose punishments ranging from the imposition of fines to public shaming, corporal punishment, imprisonment, or banishment.[83]

Most minor offenses were punished with monetary fines and/or brief terms of imprisonment in one of the local jails. Lengthy incarceration was not generally used as a punishment before the eighteenth century, as most local jails were unequipped to house prisoners long-term. Rather, the jails were reserved for the holding of prisoners pending interrogation and sentencing, and when the council ordered imprisonment as a punishment, it typically limited the term to a brief confinement in a tower, sometimes ordering in addition that the prisoner subsist on limited rations of bread and water.

In 1715, Augsburg established Catholic and Lutheran prison workhouses or "discipline houses" (*Zuchthäuser*) to punish a variety of minor offenses. The establishment of local workhouses reflects a European-wide trend toward greater reliance on incarceration. First established in London and Amsterdam in the late sixteenth century to deal with a perceived upsurge in begging and vagrancy, prison workhouses aimed to reform the idle poor through hard work and moral discipline. The model was widely imitated across the continent in the seventeenth century and gradually evolved from a reformatory into a penal sanction for a variety of petty crimes, forming the basis for the advent of the modern prison.[84]

The Augsburg institutions reflect the inherent tensions between the workhouse's rehabilitative and punitive goals. Beggars, lazy or insolent journeymen and apprentices, disobedient youths, or anyone "who misbehaves and leads a sinful and idle life"[85] might be sentenced to a term of labor in the *Zuchthaus* in hopes that they might mend their ways. But in the popular imagination, all things associated with criminal punishment were tainted with dishonor. Although local officials stressed that the inmates of the *Zuchthaus* had never

---

81 Harrington, *The Faithful Executioner*, pp. 67, 169, 236–37.
82 Harrington, *The Faithful Executioner*, pp. 170–74; Dülmen, *Theatre of Horror*, pp. 28–32.
83 The fate of prisoners was recorded in the city's *Strafbücher* (punishment books), listing the individual's name and usually his or her occupation, the charged offense, the ultimate resolution of the case, and sometimes the rationale behind it. A nearly continuous series of *Strafbücher* from 1509 through 1699 is extant in the Augsburg Stadtarchiv.
84 Spierenburg, *Prison Experience*, pp. 12–86, 135–70.
85 Stuart, *Defiled Trades*, p. 144.

been "under the executioner's hand", they nonetheless found it difficult to return to honorable society upon their release, thus frustrating the institution's rehabilitative goal.[86]

Other common criminal penalties included corporal punishment, public shaming, and banishment. In the years immediately following Augsburg's adoption of Protestant reform, the council sometimes ordered that blasphemers and slanderers have their tongues ripped out.[87] Other maiming punishments, such as blinding, or the amputation of the offender's hands or ears, are also recorded for the early sixteenth century, but became increasingly rare by mid-century.[88] More often, prisoners were sentenced to a public whipping, sometimes as a prelude to exposure on the pillory. The public nature of corporal punishments made them all deeply dishonoring. Although not always intended to be permanently defiling, they could so disrupt the offender's communal standing and social relationships as to be a kind of "social death".[89]

Augsburg's magistrates also used banishment to punish a wide range of offences. For serious crimes, banishment might be coupled with some form of corporal punishment, and prisoners were often whipped out of the city gates. Although some individuals were banished for life or might even be shipped to Venice as galley slaves,[90] the council allowed most offenders to re-enter the city after a suitable period, particularly where the prisoner left behind dependents requiring support.[91] For many individuals, even temporary banishment could sever the economic and social ties upon which they and their families depended, and thus expulsion could mean serious hardship for them. But the Augsburg records also indicate that many exiled offenders maintained their local contacts, and the more dauntless among them returned without the council's permission – some of them multiple times.[92] These various sanctions allowed Augsburg officials considerable flexibility in tempering justice with mercy, but they offered limited protection against truly violent criminals or serial offenders. The trials of these most dangerous and determined criminals, therefore, often led to the gallows.

---

86   Stuart, *Defiled Trades*, pp. 143–44; Spierenburg, *Prison Experience*, pp. 161–66.
87   See, for example, StadtAA, Strafamt, Urgichten, Gregory Frey (17 June 1539); Endris Steirer (16 May 1544).
88   Kohlberger, "Ehren-, Verstümmelungs- und Todesstrafen", pp. 91–94.
89   Dülmen, *Theatre of Horror*, pp. 43–55; idem, *Der ehrlose Mensch*, pp. 67–82.
90   Schlosser, "Der Mensch als Ware".
91   Hoffmann, "Stadtverweis", pp. 204–5, 227–36.
92   Hoffmann, "Stadtverweis", pp. 215–23. On banishment in early modern Germany generally, see Coy, *Strangers and Misfits*.

Death sentences were publicly announced and carried out at the *Endlicher Rechtstag* (final court day) – the only public stage of the entire trial process.[93] The *Carolina* required that the condemned prisoner be given at least three days to prepare for death, during which time clergymen counseled the "poor sinner" to repent and seek God's grace.[94] On the eve of the last day, the prisoner shared a ceremonial final meal with the judges and executioner, signifying that he or she accepted the sentence as just.[95] When the day of the *Endlicher Rechtstag* dawned, the council secretary read out the judgment to the assembled Small Council. With their assent, the sentence was recorded and announced by the court bailiff to the crowd assembled in the Perlach Square. As the great storm bell in the Perlach Tower sounded, the crowd accompanied the "poor sinner" in procession from the city hall to the gallows, where they watched the condemned person die.[96]

In pre-modern Europe, executions were public events, often drawing substantial crowds. Although some later reformers decried the public executions of this era as carnivalistic celebrations of human suffering,[97] executions were in fact highly formalized rituals, with strict expectations governing each participant's role. Each stage of the proceedings was calculated to reassert the council's sovereign power to defend the rule of law, restore communal solidarity, and reaffirm the promise of redemption.[98] The assembled community stood as witnesses and guarantors of the council's justice, but if the ceremony went awry and the crowd judged that the prisoner had been treated improperly, they might rise up – as happened in Augsburg in 1464, when the crowd stoned an executioner following a botched execution.[99]

The various methods of execution employed were also understood to communicate something of the prisoner's crime and degree of moral guilt. Individuals condemned to die by "the bloody hand" were to be beheaded with the sword; those to die by "the dry hand" were sentenced to hang – these were the most common forms of execution in early modern Augsburg. Hanging was considered the more disreputable death, as it required more polluting contact

---

93 On the *Endlicher Rechtstag* in Germany, see Dülmen, *Theatre of Horror*, pp. 34–42; Langbein, *Prosecuting Crime*, pp. 188–92.
94 § 79 *Carolina*.
95 Stuart, *Defiled Trades*, pp. 173–77.
96 Rau, *Augsburger Kinderhexenprozesse*, pp. 66–67.
97 Evans, *Rituals of Retribution*, pp. 191–321. Some later scholarship also reflects this assessment; see, e.g., Foucault, *Discipline and Punish*, pp. 3–69.
98 On rituals of execution, see Dülmen, *Theatre of Horror*, pp. 58–129; Evans, *Rituals of Retribution*, pp. 65–86; Harrington, *The Faithful Executioner*, pp. 76–88.
99 Dülmen, *Theatre of Horror*, p. 113; Harrington, *The Faithful Executioner*, pp. 85–88.

with the executioner and the public exposure of the prisoner's corpse on the gallows. Beheading, as the quicker, more honorable death, was commonly used against high-status offenders, or when the council wished to show mercy to prisoners condemned to die by other means.[100]

Less common forms of execution also appear in the local records. Of these, breaking on the wheel was perhaps the most common. Last used in Augsburg in 1768, it was typically reserved for aggravated murder, as in the 1568 execution of Michael Schwartzkopf for highway robbery, arson, and more than twenty homicides.[101] Burning at the stake – the prescribed penalty for witchcraft under the *Carolina* – also appears in the local sources.[102] Although Augsburg did not experience the intense witch panics that gripped many other early modern German communities, it executed at least 18 people for this crime between 1625 and 1699,[103] typically first beheading them and then burning their corpses.[104]

The *Stadtbuch* had also prescribed live burial as an appropriate punishment in certain instances, but this seems to have been exceedingly rare. A merchant was buried alive for raping a young girl in 1428, and a 1504 source records a similar execution of a woman who had murdered a nobleman, but the practice seems to have ended in the early sixteenth century. More common in this period was death by drowning, but this was likewise largely phased out in Augsburg by the late sixteenth century.[105] In both Augsburg and the Empire as a whole, beheading and hanging became the preferred forms of execution, and other traditional forms of capital punishment gradually fell into disuse.[106]

Between 1545 and 1806, Augsburg executed a total of 327 persons, comparatively fewer than in some other German imperial cities. Frankfurt am Main, for example, executed roughly the same number of people just between 1592 and 1696, although the city's population was only about half Augsburg's size.[107] Augsburg's population more closely matched that of Nuremberg, but the latter city far outstripped the former in numbers of executions, putting to death

---

100 Dülmen, *Theatre of Horror*, pp. 97–102.
101 Kohlberger, "Ehren-, Verstümmelungs- und Todestrafen", p. 98; Pötzl, "Listen von Hingerichteten", p. 369.
102 § 109 *Carolina*.
103 Rau, *Augsburger Kinderhexenprozesse*, pp. 104–10; Roper, *Witch Craze*, p. 220.
104 As in the case of Augsburg's first executed witch, Dorothea Braun in 1625: StadtAA, Strafbuch, no. 105 (1615–32), fol. 492. See also Rau, *Augsburger Kinderhexenprozesse*, pp. 216–17, 274–75, 295.
105 Kohlberger, "Ehren-, Verstümmelungs- und Todestrafen", p. 100.
106 Dülmen, *Theatre of Horror*, pp. 82–87.
107 Dülmen, *Theatre of Horror*, p. 83 (339 persons between 1592 and 1696). On Frankfurt's population, see Boes, *Crime and Punishment*, pp. 13–23.

665 people between 1550 and 1700 (compared to 281 in Augsburg for the same time span).[108] Chronologically, the Augsburg executions break down as follows:

```
1545–1562 = 29
1563–1580 = 72
1581–1596 = 66
1596–1615 = 41
1615–1632 = 30
1632–1653 = 8
1653–1699 = 35
1700–1806 = 46[109]
```

The use of the death penalty in Augsburg corresponds to trends discernible across the Empire, reaching a high point of executions in the later sixteenth century, followed by a significant decline over the next two centuries. Some scholars have attributed the high rates of execution in late sixteenth-century Germany to a general economic downturn in this period, fueling perceptions of a rising tide of criminality and a corresponding intensification of criminal punishments.[110] The growing influence of the *Carolina* in this period may have also been a factor, as it provided a model of criminal procedure and punishment that expanded magistrates' prosecutorial powers and sharpened many prescribed criminal penalties.[111]

The overall decline in executions after 1600 may be due to a number of factors. For Augsburg, whose population declined from 45,000 to 21,000 in the Thirty Years' War, the low number of executions in 1632–53 could simply reflect wartime demographic losses. Record-keeping was spotty during the crisis years of the 1630s, and it is also likely that some otherwise punishable behavior was to some degree normalized during this period.[112] But in Augsburg and other communities hit hard by the war, the rate of executions remained lower even after local populations began to expand in the postwar years.

Executions similarly declined across Europe over the seventeenth and eighteenth centuries, and a number of theories have been advanced to account for

---

108 Dülmen, *Theatre of Horror*, p. 83. On Nuremberg, see Harrington, *The Faithful Executioner*, pp. 94–97.
109 Dülmen, *Theatre of Horror*, p. 83.
110 Dülmen, *Theatre of Horror*, pp. 100–2; Harrington, *The Faithful Executioner*, p. 30; Rau, *Augsburger Kinderhexenprozesse*, p. 67.
111 See Harrington, *The Faithful Executioner*, pp. 28–32; Heydenreuter, "Strafverfahren", pp. 70–83; Lewis, *Infanticide and Abortion*, pp. 16–81.
112 Roeck, *Eine Stadt in Krieg und Frieden*, vol. 2, pp. 739–41.

this development. Some scholars have argued that the death penalty gradually fell into disuse due to the increased availability of alternative punishments, particularly long-term incarceration.[113] This turn from the death penalty to the prison has been credited, at least in part, to the humanitarian efforts of Enlightenment reformers. Prompted by Enlightenment epistemology's focus on the perfectibility of human nature, reformers sought to redirect punishment from retribution to rehabilitation.[114] Other scholars see not merely changing perceptions of punishment in this period, but of violence in general. For Pieter Spierenburg, such trends reflect Norbert Elias' concept of a "civilizing process", whereby European social and cultural norms increasingly demanded emotional self-restraint and the suppression of violent, impulsive behavior.[115] This process, Spierenburg contends, also fostered greater empathy for the suffering of others and a corresponding distaste for the violent spectacle of executions.[116] Michel Foucault takes a darker view, arguing that Enlightenment discourse merely shifted the focus of the state's coercion from the criminal's body to the criminal's mind through the institution of a "carceral state".[117]

While each of these theories captures important features of European law and culture, they all have limitations.[118] It is unclear how much practical influence Enlightenment reformers had on penal policy, for example, and while prisons expanded in the eighteenth century, long-term incarceration did not become widespread in Europe until the nineteenth century. There is likewise little concrete historical evidence for a pervasive shift in popular mentalities regarding suffering and violence. While some studies have posited a long-term decline in interpersonal violence between the seventeenth and twentieth centuries,[119] evaluating these claims is problematic given the fragmentary evidence and the practical limits of early modern policing. Even in a community as well-documented as early modern Augsburg, there are significant gaps in the records. And even if complete, such records cannot reveal the extent of criminal activity that went unreported or undetected. Rather than measuring actual rates of violent crime, these records are probably best approached as

---

113 Langbein, *Torture and the Law of Proof*, pp. 27–44.
114 Evans, *Rituals of Retribution*, pp. 121–40.
115 Elias, *The Civilizing Process*.
116 Spierenburg, *Spectacle of Suffering*, pp. 183–99.
117 Foucault, *Discipline and Punish*, pp. 73–308.
118 For a critique of these various theories, and an alternative analysis of the death penalty in Germany between the sixteenth and twentieth centuries, see Evans, *Rituals of Retribution*, pp. 880–905.
119 Evans, *Rituals of Retribution*, pp. 118–23.

indicators of what early modern magistrates understood to be criminal, and therefore worthy of prosecution.

These shifting patterns of persecution and punishment, while driven by broader social and cultural factors, also reflect important changes in early modern European legal culture. A growing standardization and professionalization in legal education and practice in this era fostered stricter observance of evidentiary standards and procedural rules[120] as well as wider recognition of legal principles safeguarding the rights of the accused.[121] These developments made it more difficult to secure convictions in questionable cases, and some crimes traditionally punishable by death, such as sodomy or witchcraft, were either prosecuted less frequently in the later seventeenth and eighteenth centuries, or punished less severely.[122]

Changes in Augsburg's approach to infanticide illustrate many of these themes. Influenced in part by the *Carolina*'s harsh stance on infanticide, local officials stepped up prosecutions in the mid-sixteenth century, reaching a high point between 1590 and 1610, when half of the city's infanticide trials ended in execution. Thereafter, trials dropped dramatically and punishments abated.[123] Advances in forensic medicine highlighted the difficulty of conclusively establishing the causes of infant death, and jurists' rigorous application of the rules of evidence made the crime increasingly difficult to prove.[124] Enlightenment discourse also recast the crime and the moral guilt of the perpetrators. The typically young, unwed mothers who killed their infants were no longer seen as unnatural monsters deserving the harshest punishments, but as the hapless victims of male degeneracy and inflexible social mores. As throughout the Empire, Augsburg officials shifted focus, sentencing convicted mothers not to death on the gallows but to moral correction in the *Zuchthaus*.[125]

These trends toward declining prosecutions and milder punishments in the seventeenth century, however, are complicated – at least in the short-term – by Augsburg's approach to witchcraft. Sixteenth-century Augsburg had prosecuted witchcraft at about the same rate as its neighbors, but none of these cases ended in execution. In the following century, however, the city prosecuted far fewer people for witchcraft, but executed more of them.[126] At least

---

120   Lessafer, *European Legal History*, pp. 358–64, 449–55.
121   On these developments in Germany, see Köster, *Rechtsvermutung der Unschuld*, pp. 39–94.
122   On the impact of these developments on witchcraft prosecutions, see Levack, *Witch-Hunt*, pp. 231–40; Robisheaux, *Last Witch of Langenburg*, pp. 91–132, 228–321.
123   Lewis, *Infanticide and Abortion*, pp. 51–52.
124   Ibid., pp. 133–42.
125   Ibid., pp. 176–78.
126   Behringer, *Witchcraft Persecutions*, pp. 44, 102.

18 people were executed for witchcraft after 1625, all but two of these after 1650.[127] Although Augsburg executed its last witch in 1699, fear of witches did not entirely abate. Local prosecutions – mostly of alleged child-witches – continued through the early eighteenth century, but these cases ended either in acquittal or banishment (for adults) or "moral correction" (for children).[128] The legal pursuit of witches ended in Augsburg after 1730, brought about by shifting cultural perceptions of witchcraft and changes in legal practice.[129]

5 Conclusion

The evidence from Augsburg highlights both the expansion of regulatory power and the practical limitations of that authority in early modern Europe. Between the fifteenth and the eighteenth centuries, criminal law emerged as a powerful vehicle for the consolidation and expansion of governmental power at multiple levels. Across much of Europe, officials asserted their exclusive and sovereign authority to wield high justice in defense of the collective order. Augsburg's city government likewise secured its political independence by assuming the sole authority to define, try, and punish crime. As in Europe generally, the coming of the Reformation, with its renewed emphasis on the regulation of private conduct and belief, brought more activities under the council's oversight and sanction. In the ensuing years, councilors used that power to enforce a civic and moral order rooted in communally-agreed understandings of the "common good". But while these developments fostered legal controls and expanded official bureaucracies, the regulation of crime was never a simple matter of governmental control imposed "from above". Given the practical limitations of early modern policing and enforcement, the cooperation of the community was essential to these systems. As in Augsburg, policing crime required the citizenry's active participation, and the law necessarily had to reflect their understandings of the appropriate targets of enforcement and means of punishment.

The patterns of prosecution and punishment in Augsburg between 1400 and 1800 illustrate these changing understandings of what constitutes crime and its legitimate punishment. While corresponding in large measure to broader trends across Germany and Europe, they also highlight unique local

---

127   Rau, *Augsburger Kinderhexenprozesse*, p. 106.
128   Rau, *Augsburger Kinderhexenprozesse*, pp. 190, 296–323, 346.
129   Roper, *Witch Craze*, pp. 204–21.

conditions, whether demographic pressures in wartime or vagaries in record-keeping. These local variations are an important reminder that, however much the expansion of the criminal law facilitated centralized state-building, governmental regulation remained fragmentary in this era. Although becoming increasingly standardized, the administration of criminal justice remained a predominantly local affair both in Augsburg and across the Empire, and had to be responsive to communal concerns.

Bibliography

Unpublished Primary Sources
Stadtarchiv Augsburg (StadtAA)
  Bürgermeisteramt, Instruction die Herren Bürgermeister betreffend, fol. 132.
  Ordnungen, Zucht-und-Policey Ordnung 1537.
  Schätze, no. 16, Anschläge, fol. 56r.
  Schätze, no. ad 36/3, Zucht unnd Execution Ordnung, 1553.
  Strafamt, no. 161, Modus procedendi ... in Malefiz Sachen.
  Strafamt, Urgichten, Gregory Frey (17 June 1539), Endris Steirer (16 May 1544).
  Strafbuch, no. 105 (1615–32).

Published Primary Sources
Becker, C. (ed.), *"Consvetudines almae Reipublicae Augustanae" von Matthaeus Laimann und Georg Tradel mit "Notwendigs Bedenckhen" von Georg Tradel. Eine Zusammenstellung Augsburger Stadtrechts mit einer Denkschrift zu seiner Reform vom Ende des sechzehnten Jahrhunderts (Handschrift der Staats- und Stadtbibliothek Augsburg 2° Cod. Aug. 168)*, Berlin, 2008.

Meyer, C. (ed.), *Das Stadtbuch von Augsburg, insbesondere das Stadtrecht vom Jahre 1276, nach der Originalhandschrift zum ersten Male herausgegeben und erläutert*, Augsburg, 1872.

Radbruch, G. (ed.), *Die Peinliche Gerichtsordnung Kaiser Karl V. von 1532. Constitutio Criminalis Carolina*, Stuttgart, 1996.

Stetten, P. von (the Elder), *Geschichte der Heil. Röm. Reichs Freyen Stadt Augspurg [...]*, Frankfurt and Leipzig, 1743.

Secondary Literature
Baer, W., "Das Stadtrecht von Jahre 1156", in G. Gottlieb, W. Baer, J. Becker, J. Bellot, K. Filser, P. Fried, W. Reinhard and B. Schimmelpfennig (eds.), *Geschichte der Stadt Augsburg von der Römerzeit bis zur Gegenwart*, Stuttgart, 1984, pp. 132–34.

Bátori, I., *Die Reichsstadt Augsburg im 18. Jahrhundert. Verfassung, Finanzen, Reformversuche*, Göttingen, 1969.

Behringer, W., *Witchcraft Persecutions in Bavaria: Popular Magic, Religious Zealotry and Reason of State in Early Modern Europe*, Cambridge, 1997.

Binswanger, J., "Zur äusseren Rechtsgeschichte der Stadt Augsburg", *Festschrift zum 22. Deutschen Juristentag*, Augsburg, 1893, pp. 15–20.

Boes, M.R., *Crime and Punishment in Early Modern Germany: Courts and Adjudicatory Practices in Frankfurt am Main, 1562–1696*, Farnham, 2013.

Coing, H., *Römisches Recht in Deutschland*, Milan, 1964.

Coy, J.P., *Strangers and Misfits: Banishment, Social Control, and Authority in Early Modern Germany*, Leiden, 2008.

Dülmen, R. van, *Theatre of Horrors: Crime and Punishment in Early Modern Germany*, Cambridge, 1990.

Dülmen, R. van, *Der ehrlose Mensch. Unehrlichkeit und soziale Ausgrenzung in der Frühen Neuzeit*, Cologne, 1999.

Elias, N., *The Civilizing Process: The History of Manners and State Formation and Civilization*, Oxford, 1994.

Evans, R.J., *Rituals of Retribution: Capital Punishment in Germany, 1600–1987*, Oxford, 1996.

Fenster, T. and Smail, D.L., *Fama: The Politics of Talk and Reputation in Medieval Europe*, Ithaca, NY, 2003.

Finkl, N., *Administrative Verdichtung und Konfessionalisierung. Die Verwaltung der Reichsstadt Augsburg im 16. Jahrhundert*, Neustadt an der Aisch, 2011.

Foucault, M., *Discipline and Punish: The Birth of the Prison*, 2nd ed., New York, 1977.

Harrington, J.F., *The Faithful Executioner: Life and Death, Honor and Shame in the Turbulent Sixteenth Century*, New York, 2013.

Heydenreuter, R., "Das Strafverfahren im Hochstift Augsburg vom Mittelalter bis ins 18. Jahrhundert", in W. Pötzl (ed.), *Mörder, Räuber, Hexen. Kriminalgeschichte des Mittelalters und der Frühen Neuzeit*, Gersthofen, 2005, pp. 64–85.

Hoffmann, C.A., "Strukturen und Quellen des Augsburger reichsstädtischen Strafgerichtswesens in der ersten Hälfte des 16. Jahrhunderts", *Zeitschrift des Historischen Vereins für Schwaben* 88 (1995), pp. 57–108.

Hoffmann, C.A., "Der Stadtverweis als Sanktionsmittel in der Reichsstadt Augsburg in der Frühen Neuzeit", in H. Schlosser and D. Willoweit (eds.), *Neue Wege strafrechtsgeschichtlicher Forschung*, Cologne, 1999, pp. 193–237.

Hoffmann, C.A., "Außergerichtliche Einigungen bei Straftaten als vertikale und horizontale soziale Kontrolle im 16. Jahrhundert", in A. Blauert and G. Schwerhoff (eds.), *Kriminalitätsgeschichte: Beiträge zur Sozial-und Kulturgeschichte der Vormoderne*, Constance, 2000, pp. 563–79.

Hoffmann, C.A., "Bürgersicherheit und Herrschaftssicherung im 16. Jahrhundert – Das Wechselverhältnis zweier frühmoderner Sicherheitskonzepte", in M. Dinges and F. Sack (eds.), *Unsichere Großstädte? Vom Mittelalter bis zur Postmoderne*, Constance, 2000, pp. 101–23.

Kießling, R., *Bürgerliche Gesellschaft und Kirche in Augsburg im Spätmittelalter*, Augsburg, 1971.

Köhler, W., *Zürcher Ehegericht und Genfer Konsistorium, vol. 2: Das Ehe-und Sittengericht in den süddeutschen Reichsstädten, dem Herzogtum Württemberg und in Genf*, Leipzig, 1942.

Kohlberger, A., "Ehren-Verstümmelungs-und Todesstrafen", in W. Pötzl (ed.), *Mörder, Räuber, Hexen. Kriminalgeschichte des Mittelalters und der Frühen Neuzeit*, Gersthofen, 2005, pp. 86–103.

Köster, R.-J., *Die Rechtsvermutung der Unschuld. Historische und dogmatische Grundlagen*, Bonn, 1979.

Kraus, J., *Das Militärwesen der Reichsstadt Augsburg, 1548–1806*, Augsburg, 1980.

Langbein, J.H., *Prosecuting Crime in the Renaissance: England, Germany, France*, Cambridge, MA, 1974.

Langbein, J.H., *Torture and the Law of Proof: Europe and England in the Ancient Regime*, Chicago, 2006.

Lesaffer, R., *European Legal History: A Cultural and Political Perspective*, Cambridge, 2009.

Levack, B.P., *The Witch-Hunt in Early Modern Europe*, 4th ed., London, 2016.

Lewis, M., *Infanticide and Abortion in Early Modern Germany*, New York, 2016.

Liedl, E., *Gerichtsverfassung und Zivilprozess der Freien Reichsstadt Augsburg*, Augsburg, 1958.

Oestreich, G., *Strukturprobleme der frühen Neuzeit. Ausgewählte Aufsätze*, Berlin, 1980.

Peters, E., *Torture*, Philadelphia, 1996.

Po-chia Hsia, R., *Social Discipline in the Reformation: Central Europe, 1550–1750*, London, 1989.

Pötzl, W., "Gesetze und Ordnungen", in idem (ed.), *Mörder, Räuber, Hexen. Kriminalgeschichte des Mittelalters und der Frühen Neuzeit*, Gersthofen, 2005, pp. 10–63.

Pötzl, W., "Listen von Hingerichteten", in idem (ed.), *Mörder, Räuber, Hexen: Kriminalgeschichte des Mittelalters und der Frühen Neuzeit*, Gersthofen, 2005, pp. 360–73.

Rau, K., *Augsburger Kinderhexenprozesse, 1625–1730*, Vienna, 2006.

Robisheaux, T., *The Last Witch of Langenburg: Murder in a German Village*, New York, 2009.

Roeck, B., *Eine Stadt in Krieg und Frieden. Studien zur Geschichte der Reichsstadt Augsburg zwischen Kalenderstreit und Parität*, 2 vols., Göttingen, 1989.

Rogge, J., *Für den Gemeinen Nutzen. Politisches Handeln und Politikverständnis von Rat und Bürgerschaft in Augsburg im Spätmittelalter*, Tübingen, 1996.

Roper, L., *The Holy Household: Women and Morals in Reformation Augsburg*, Oxford, 1989.

Roper, L., *Oedipus and the Devil: Witchcraft, Sexuality and Religion in Early Modern Europe*, London, 1994.

Roper, L., *Witch Craze: Terror and Fantasy in Baroque Germany*, New Haven, 2004.

Schlosser, H., "Der Mensch als Ware. Die Galeerenstrafe in Süddeutschland als Reaktion of Preisrevolution und Großmachtpolitik (16.–18. Jahrhundert)", in R. Blum and M. Steiner (eds.), *Aktuelle Probleme der Marktwirtschaft in gesamt- und einzelwirtschaftlicher Sicht. Festgabe zum 65. Geburtstag von Louis Perridon*, Berlin, 1986, pp. 87–114.

Schmidt, G., "Sinn und Bedeutung der *Constitutio Criminalis Carolina* als Ordnung des materiellen und prozessualen Rechts", *Zeitschrift der Savigny-Stiftung für Rechtsgeschichte. Germanistische Abteilung* 83 (1966), pp. 239–57.

Schmidt, H.R., "Sozialdisziplinierung? Ein Plädoyer für das Ende des Etatismus in der Konfessionalisierungsforschung", *Historische Zeitschrift* 265 (1997), pp. 639–82.

Schmidt, R., "Das Stadtbuch von 1276", in G. Gottlieb, W. Baer, J. Becker, J. Bellot, K. Filser, P. Fried, W. Reinhard and B. Schimmelpfennig (eds.), *Geschichte der Stadt Augsburg von der Römerzeit bis zur Gegenwart*, Stuttgart, 1984, pp. 140–44.

Schorer, R., *Die Strafgerichtsbarkeit der Reichsstadt Augsburg, 1156–1548*, Cologne, 2001.

Schorer, R., "Die Strafherren – ein selbständiges Organ der Rechtspflege in der Reichsstadt Augsburg in der Frühen Neuzeit", in H. Schlosser and D. Willoweit (eds.), *Neue Wege strafrechtsgeschichtlicher Forschung*, Cologne, 1999, pp. 175–91.

Schulze, W., "Gerhard Oestreichs Begriff Sozialdisziplinierung in der frühen Neuzeit", *Zeitschrift für historische Forschung* 14 (1987), pp. 265–302.

Sieh-Burens, K., "Die Augsburger Stadtverfassung um 1500", *Zeitschrift Historischen Vereins Schwaben* 77 (1983), pp. 125–49.

Spierenburg, P., *The Spectacle of Suffering: Executions and the Evolution of Repression*, Cambridge, 1984.

Spierenburg, P., *The Prison Experience: Disciplinary Institutions and Their Inmates in Early Modern Europe*, New Brunswick, NJ, 1991.

Stuart, K., *Defiled Trades and Social Outcasts: Honor and Ritual Pollution in Early Modern Germany*, Cambridge, 1999.

Tlusty, B.A., *Bacchus and Civic Order: The Culture of Drink in Early Modern Germany*, Charlottesville, 2001.

Tlusty, B.A., *The Martial Ethic in Early Modern Germany: Civic Duty and the Right of Arms*, New York, 2011.

Trusen, W., "Strafprozeß und Rezeption. Zu den Entwicklungen im Spätmittelalter und den Grundlagen der *Carolina*", in P. Landau and F. Schroeder (eds.), *Strafrecht, Strafprozeß und Rezeption. Grundlagen, Entwicklung und Wirkung der Constitutio Criminalis Carolina*, Frankfurt am Main, 1984, pp. 29–118.

Tyler, J.J., *Lord of the Sacred City: The Episcopus Exclusus in Late Medieval and Early Modern Germany*, Leiden, 1999.

Wieacker, F., *A History of Private Law in Europe, with Particular Reference to Germany*, Oxford, 1995.

CHAPTER 9

Civil Law

Peter Kreutz

The roots of civil law, as it evolved in Augsburg during the early modern period, lie in the high Middle Ages. In order to understand the specifics of the imperial city's legal history, it is therefore necessary to move beyond the temporal framework of this volume and briefly consider these medieval origins before developments during the period from 1400 to 1800 can be properly addressed. Central to this discussion is the municipal law code of 1276, which remained the basis of legal practice well into the sixteenth century. Although it was gradually amended and superseded by statute law, no comprehensive revision took place until the end of Augsburg's history as a free imperial city.

1   Medieval Municipal Law

The oldest existing document on the legal history of Augsburg dates from 21 June 1156. On that day Emperor Frederick I (1120–90), called Barbarossa, decided a conflict of authority between the local bishop, his burgrave (*Burggraf*), and the local bailiff (*Vogt*). The incident was recorded in a legal instrument which has survived down to the present day.[1] Apart from the bishop and the emperor, this document names *urbani* (townsmen),[2] who had asked the emperor to resolve the dispute.[3] The townsmen successfully claimed the right to participate in the investigation of the episcopal burgrave, and they prompted the delimitation of the burgrave's and the reeve's respective authority.[4] The competences of the three parties involved – the bishop, the emperor, and the

---

1   Stored now in the Staatsarchiv Augsburg, Hochstift Augsburg, Urkunden 27. On the incident, see Baer, "Stadtrecht", pp. 132–33.
2   Baer, "Stadtrecht", p. 134.
3   See Liedl, *Gerichtsverfassung und Zivilprozeß*, p. 15.
4   While Berner, *Verfassungsgeschichte*, pp. 87–89, and Beyerle, *Grundherrschaft und Hoheitsrechte*, p. 96, count the reeve among the bishop's officials, Wolff, "Gerichtsverfassung und Prozess", p. 142 (with note 1), claims that he was in the imperial service. See also Liedl, *Gerichtsverfassung und Zivilprozeß*, pp. 16–18.

evolving municipality – were not fixed precisely at the time, however, but continued to evolve over the following century.[5]

On March 9, 1276, the confirmation of the municipal law code (*Stadtbuch*) by King Rudolf of Habsburg (1218–91) strengthened the position of the municipality vis-à-vis the bishop, constituting a milestone in the evolution of civic law.[6] Its special place in the legal history of south Germany[7] results from the facts that the *Stadtbuch* was the first written municipal law code and that it was closely related to the so-called *Spiegelrecht* (code law), especially the *Schwabenspiegel*.[8] Detailed comparisons of the textual versions of the *Schwabenspiegel* and the *Stadtbuch* of Augsburg have demonstrated the influence of the former law code on municipal law.[9]

The *Stadtbuch* consists of three parts.[10] The first describes the jurisdictional rights of the king, the bishop, the reeve, and the burgrave and comprises regulations concerning numerous local trades. The second part, which concerns the reeve's court, focuses on matters of criminal and procedural law but also includes rules governing various other areas, such as markets and crafts. The third part is concerned with the burgrave's jurisdiction, which is limited to matters of policing the city and administrative offences. As a whole, the *Stadtbuch* of 1276 deals with an abundance of topics, which it tries to define normatively.[11] Apart from the subjects mentioned above, it covers aspects of civil status law, family and inheritance law, and customs and tax law as well as trade law. These diverse legal areas are not arranged in a way that modern readers would consider systematic, however.[12] Rather, the municipal law code reflects

---

5   This process is reviewed in Becker, "Einleitung", pp. XI–XV.
6   The law code is inventoried as Staatsarchiv Augsburg, Reichsstadt Augsburg, Literalien 32, but is on permanent loan in the Stadtarchiv Augsburg (StadtAA). Edition: Meyer (ed.), *Das Stadtbuch von Augsburg*. Older editions can be found in Walch (ed.), *Vermischte Beyträge*, chapter 'Alte Augsburgische Statuten vom Jahr 1276' (pp. 1–418), and Freyberg (ed.), *Sammlung teutscher Rechts-Alterthümer*, vol. 1. An edition that had been planned before 1739 was not finalized; the drafts are archived in the Staats- und Stadtbibliothek Augsburg (SuStBA), 2° Cod. Aug. 151. On the history of these editions, see Schmidt, "Augsburger Stadtbuch", pp. 113–71.
7   On the character of the Stadtbuch, see Ciriacy-Wantrup, *Familien- und erbrechtliche Gestaltungen*, pp. 156–57; Pettinger, *Vermögenserhaltung*, pp. 67–69.
8   Edition: Lassberg, *Der Schwabenspiegel*. For further information, see Eckhardt, *Rechtsbücherstudien*, pp. 108–24; Liedl, *Gerichtsverfassung und Zivilprozeß*, pp. 20–22; Schmidt, "Stadtbuch von 1276", pp. 140–43.
9   A detailed comparison of the three legal codes can be found in Eckhardt, *Rechtsbücherstudien*, pp. 108–24.
10 For further details, see Ciriacy-Wantrup, *Familien- und erbrechtliche Gestaltungen*, p. 156.
11 Schmidt, "Stadtbuch von 1276", pp. 141–42.
12 Kroppenberg, "Kodifikation", cols. 1918–30.

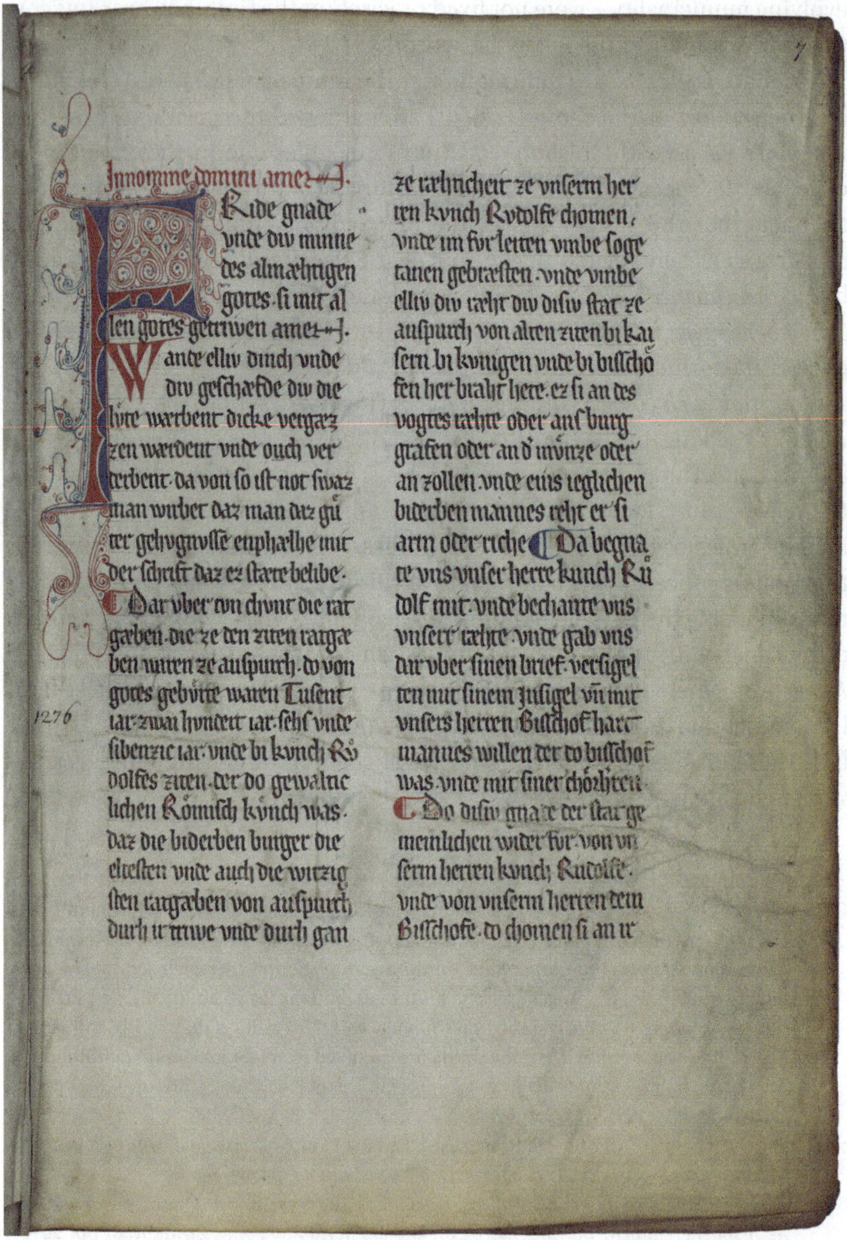

FIGURE 9.1 Augsburg *Stadtbuch* of 1276
STADTARCHIV AUGSBURG, STADTRECHTSBUCH 1276, FOL. 7R

contemporary legal training and takes specific local conditions and daily experience into account.[13] Roman law, as it was taught at northern Italian universities at the time, did not exert a significant influence on the municipal law code, at least in its original form. The learned tradition of Roman law began significantly to impact Augsburg's legal culture only in the early modern period, as handwritten addenda to the *Stadtbuch* show.

The municipal law code of 1276 remained in force for centuries and was not replaced by a comprehensive codification of civil law throughout the period considered here. In order to highlight how it shaped what we nowadays term civil law, three subjects will briefly be examined here: contract law, matrimonial law, and inheritance law. These areas affected the daily lives of medieval and early modern townspeople in crucial ways and have recently been researched in detail.[14]

Sales of goods, which undoubtedly constituted essential legal transactions in everyday life, were mainly treated as aspects of trade, customs, and tax law.[15] Article 125 spells out that a sale was valid when either a so-called God's penny (*Gottespfennig*) had passed hands or wine had been purchased in advance of the actual sale. For the sale to become effective, the buyer and seller had to drink the wine together in a symbolic act, thereby affirming their mutual intentions.[16] Warranties concerning possible material defects or defects of title were laid down only selectively.[17] Other regulations deal with the sale of bread not properly baked[18] or spoiled pork.[19] At some later point a rule governing the purchase of horses[20] was added. The settlement of disputes arising from sales of other goods seems to have been unproblematic – at least it did not require codification. It is possible that the experiences of local merchants who had travelled to Italy on business and had become familiar with local adaptations of Roman law there may also have played a role.

---

13 Binswanger, *Rechtsgeschichte der Stadt Augsburg*, p. 11.
14 Ciriacy-Wantrup, *Familien- und erbrechtliche Gestaltungen*; Pettinger, *Vermögenserhaltung*; Becker (ed.), *"Consvetudines almae Reipublicae Augustanae"*; Mayer, *Kauf nach dem Augsburger Stadtrecht*; Birnbaum, *Konkursrecht*. See also Becker, "Akten des Augsburger Notars Johann Spreng"; idem, "Einfluss der Rechtsschule"; idem, "Tierschaden"; Pettinger, "Entwicklung der gewillkürten Erbfolge".
15 For details, see Mayer, *Kauf nach dem Augsburger Stadtrecht*, pp. 45–54.
16 Mayer, *Kauf nach dem Augsburger Stadtrecht*, pp. 45–50; on the ritual tradition of the contract drink, see Tlusty, *Bacchus*, pp. 103–14.
17 Mayer, *Kauf nach dem Augsburger Stadtrecht*, pp. 129–41, 154–66.
18 Stadtbuch, art. 118 § 7.
19 Stadtbuch, art. 103. On other kinds of meat, see art. 121 § 4.
20 Stadtbuch, art. 125 amendment 10.

Matrimonial law is treated in the *Stadtbuch* along similar lines. Marriage and family are not dealt with in any systematic way. Rather, the municipal law code proceeds from specific everyday situations and focuses on matrimonial property law, including the dower (*Morgengabe*)[21] and the consequences of divorce.[22] In the latter case, the wife's entire estate had to be delivered to her, no matter whether she had obtained it through inheritance, gifts, or marriage. Later this rule was amended by specifying that assets which had been given to children could be excluded from the compensation of a divorced spouse.[23] A sixteenth-century draft for a municipal law reform adopts these regulations in abbreviated form,[24] thus highlighting the fundamental importance and timeless authority of this medieval law code. While the *Stadtbuch* originally did not include rules governing marriage itself, wedding ordinances were added from the end of the thirteenth century onwards.[25]

The rules governing inheritance law in the *Stadtbuch* are inspired by the *Erbenwartrecht* (waiting heir's claim), which stipulated that substantial parts of the inheritance had to remain within the family of the deceased person.[26] The legal code distinguishes between real estate, fiefs, and movable goods.[27] While fiefs and movable goods could be directly transferred to children, surviving husbands retained the right of priority regarding real estate ownership. An enumeration of valuable goods in article 76 includes such items as bowls, porringers, belts, clothing, harnesses, and arms. Moreover, the law code addresses various specific constellations, such as childless marriages, the prior death of husbands and wives, the status of orphaned children, or valuables handed down within the family. In general, the *Stadtbuch* established the principle of generational succession, which marked a significant departure from medieval Germanic law.[28]

The municipal law code also addresses the line of succession designed by the testator,[29] for example the possibility to donate *Seelgerät*[30] (salvation gifts). In its original form, the *Stadtbuch* does not recognize an unrestricted right to make last wills and testaments. It was only the later *ius commune*

---

21 Stadtbuch, art. 84 §§ 3 and 4.
22 Stadtbuch, art. 85 § 2.
23 Stadtbuch, art. 85 amendment 2.
24 See the edition in Becker (ed.), *"Consvetudines almae Reipublicae Augustanae"*, pp. 8–9.
25 Edited in Meyer (ed.), *Stadtbuch von Augsburg*, pp. 240–44.
26 Pettinger, "Entwicklung der gewillkürten Erbfolge".
27 Stadtbuch, art. 72.
28 Stadtbuch, art. 73 § 1 amendment 1.
29 Pettinger, *Vermögenserhaltung*, pp. 65–69.
30 Regulated in Stadtbuch, art. 73 § 8 and in an amendment to art. 112.

which initiated progress in this area, putting a strong emphasis on inheritance law.[31] The background for this is easy to identify, as the legal basis of most local trading companies rested on testamentary dispositions.[32] After a merchant's death, his heirs continued to run the company according to the testator's will. Remarkably, some testamentary dispositions can already be observed in Augsburg in the later Middle Ages.[33] This suggests that there was a generally accepted way of identifying the status of heirs, although the *Stadtbuch* did not state so. This fact can in turn be attributed to the influence of territories which were thoroughly shaped by Roman law, for example the Italian city states. The evolution of inheritance law also reveals a significant change in the concept of asset ownership. According to the medieval legal tradition north of the Alps, the allocation of goods remained within the family, even upon the death of the previous owner. Changes in the line of succession were only permissible within very narrow limits. Probably due to Italian influences, this legal concept changed in Augsburg at the beginning of the early modern era in ways which may be termed radical. The line of succession after the owner's death not only became a matter of free disposition; business interests could now actually supersede family obligations. In this respect, Augsburg's inheritance law adopted innovative early modern developments.

2   Augsburg and the Reception of Central European Common Law

Based on the general evolution of civil law in central Europe, one might expect that the legal history of Augsburg would culminate in a comprehensive reformation of urban law in the late fifteenth or early sixteenth century. Important milestones in the process of reformulating medieval urban law according to the spirit of Roman law include Nuremberg (1479), Worms (1498), and Freiburg im Breisgau (1520). Augsburg, by contrast, never realized a reformation of its municipal law. An attempt to do so at the end of the sixteenth century did not advance beyond the draft stage.[34] The materials compiled in this process were eventually handed over to the municipal library.[35] The *Stadtbuch* in its 1276 form thus remained the basis for municipal law of Augsburg, but it was repeatedly adjusted in the course of the later Middle Ages. The original manuscript

---

31   Pettinger, *Vermögenserhaltung*, pp. 87–91.
32   Ciriacy-Wantrup, *Familien- und erbrechtliche Gestaltungen*, pp. 215–55.
33   For a detailed analysis, see Pettinger, *Vermögenserhaltung*, pp. 92–100.
34   Liedl, *Gerichtsverfassung und Zivilprozeß*, pp. 53–54.
35   Located in SuStBA, 2° Cod. Aug. 253.

was designed in a way that left considerable free space on its parchment leaves to register amendments, which were added in accordance with decisions of the city council.[36] The bulk of these undated amendments go back to the period before 1324, which is evident from a copy produced in that year.[37] The frequency of additions subsequently declined. The last such amendment was added by the influential humanist, lawyer, and city secretary Conrad Peutinger[38] to article 62 in 1512.[39] It can be assumed that the paradigm shift regarding the form in which legal norms were issued in early modern Augsburg was partly set in motion by Peutinger, who had received his legal training in Italy.[40]

The municipal legal courts of the early modern period generally relied on handwritten compilations of excerpts and paraphrases from the *Stadtbuch*. The first private handbook of this type dates from 1529; it was revised in 1540 and has survived in numerous copies.[41] For use in the municipal court, the sources refer to a *Schwarzes Büchlein* ("little black book"), which was probably an extract from the municipal law code as well. Unfortunately, its character cannot be clarified because it seems to have been lost,[42] despite having been in use as late as the eighteenth century.[43] This "little black book" inspired two municipal lawyers of the late sixteenth century, Georg Tradel and Matthaeus Laimann,[44] to compile an agenda for the reform of municipal law.[45] As mentioned above, however, this reform never materialized.

3 Statutory Law

When the tradition of adding amendments to the *Stadtbuch* ended in the sixteenth century, law-making by the municipal authorities did not come to an

---

36 On Augsburg's political regime, see Sieh-Burens, "Augsburger Stadtverfassung", and Chapter 6 in this volume.
37 Meyer (ed.), *Stadtbuch von Augsburg*, pp. XXIV–XXVII.
38 For a biographical sketch, see Künast and Müller, "Peutinger". See also Becker, "Konrad Peutinger".
39 Meyer (ed.), *Stadtbuch von Augsburg*, p. XXII.
40 For further information, see Becker, "Konrad Peutinger".
41 SuStBA, 4° Cod. Aug. 122; 4° Cod. Aug. 123; 2° Cod. Aug. 254; 2° Cod. Aug. 255; 2° Cod. Aug. 257; and 2° Cod. Aug. 290.
42 Becker, "Einleitung", p. XVII; Liedl, *Gerichtsverfassung und Zivilprozeß*, p. 53.
43 Morell, *De iure statutario illustris Reipublicae Augustanae*, § 13, 30, (note bb).
44 For their biographies, see Kreutz, "Matthaeus Laimann und Georg Tradel", pp. XXI–XXIX.
45 The original is preserved in SuStBA, 2° Cod. Aug. 168. Edited in Becker (ed.), *"Consvetudines almae Reipublicae Augustanae"*.

end, of course, but rather took different forms.[46] Instead of formally revising and updating the municipal law code, civic authorities issued individual legislative acts, such as council decrees or judgements, which regulated a large variety of topics in response to specific local problems and developments. The medieval municipal law code was thus supplemented by separate *statuta*,[47] the body of which constitutes the statutory law of Augsburg (*Augsburger Statutarrecht*).[48]

The sheer number of civil law statutes issued in the early modern period is remarkable; a solid census enumerates no fewer than 81 positions.[49] These include procedural law, legal rules governing public offices, commercial and trade law, matrimonial and family law, inheritance law, and bankruptcy law.[50] This piecemeal legislation did not follow a long-term program or overall concept, but contemporaries obviously did not consider this a problem. In this regard, there is no difference between Augsburg and other early modern communities. Endeavors to systematize the local municipal law and readjust it were undertaken several times, but were carried on in a lackluster way and were eventually abandoned. At the time of the city's incorporation into the Bavarian state, Augsburg had accumulated a time-honored and multi-faceted body of civil law. To convey an overall impression of early modern urban law, the following section focuses on three selected areas presented in some detail.

3.1 *Commercial and Corporate Law*

In a city that functioned as a central node in European trade networks, mercantile companies in particular and corporations in general were of crucial importance. We therefore might expect to find a solid indigenous body of commercial and especially of corporate law. This was indeed the case in both Nuremberg and Frankfurt,[51] although surprisingly not in Augsburg. In this area

---

46 On this transformation, see Kießling, "Wirtschaft und Recht".
47 See the sophisticated classification in Chittolini, "Statuten und städtische Autonomien", as well as Schlosser, "Statutarrecht und Landesherrschaft", pp. 7–37, 177–93; Schmieder, "Stadtstatuten deutscher Städte?"; Hermann, "Vielerlei Zungen"; Sbriccoli, *L'interpretazione dello statuto*, pp. 49–83.
48 Hecker, "Augsburger Statutarrecht"; idem, "Recht der Reichsstadt Augsburg". An older work is Huber, *Abhandlung über die Abweichung*. Contemporary descriptions can be found in Herwart, *Disputatio iuridica inauguralis de successione*; Cadensky, *Dissertatio iuridica*; Morell, *De iure statutario illustris Reipublicae Augustanae*; Brucker, *Dissertatio inauguralis iuridica*; Lipp, *Commentatio de curatoribus minorum*; and Neunhoefer, *Analecta iuris statutarii Augustani*.
49 Huber, *Abhandlung über die Abweichung*, pp. 2–6.
50 Birnbaum, *Konkursrecht*, pp. 5–10; Becker, "Bancarottierer"; Fischer, "Bankruptcy".
51 Lutz, *Die rechtliche Struktur*, vol. 1, pp. 61–71, 134–37.

the regulations of the 1276 *Stadtbuch* formally remained in force throughout the early modern era.[52] The attempted legal reformation of 1596 did include norms governing the formation of companies, which would have copied the respective Nuremberg regulations more or less verbatim,[53] but as mentioned above, this reform was never implemented. Besides the medieval municipal law code, the legal basis for Augsburg's commercial companies was provided by supra-local legislation, i.e. imperial law,[54] which regulated issues of monopoly, for example, and by the *ius commune*, which was adopted with growing intensity in the sixteenth century and included Roman law concepts like the *societas*.[55] Apart from such isolated points of reference, however, neither the *ius commune* nor canon law offered suitable models for the formulation of a contemporary corporate law. This may have been one of the main reasons for the failure to codify commercial law in Augsburg in a systematic way.[56] There was no apparent need to harmonize local law and common law; instead, legal requirements were mainly of a practical nature, and according to contemporary opinion, these requirements could be met by individual decisions and their consolidation in the practice of common law. Another factor has to be taken into account for Augsburg as well: It was customary practice to establish mercantile companies with the tools of family and inheritance law, especially testamentary and family contract law, and merchants could not only pass their property on to their relatives and heirs but might also use wills or contracts to either sustain an existing company or form a new one with their property. In addition, they could use these legal instruments to stipulate the manner of the company's organization.[57]

3.2 Exchange Law

It is well known that Augsburg was a center of the evolving banking sector and therefore the site of a major capital market. Of crucial importance, then, was the ability to transfer capital through bills of exchange, an early manner of cashless payment that became widespread throughout Europe. Among other factors, Augsburg's strategic location within this European system of

---

52   Lutz, *Die rechtliche Struktur*, vol. 1, p. 63.
53   Ciriacy-Wantrup, *Familien- und erbrechtliche Gestaltungen*, p. 211.
54   Lutz, *Die rechtliche Struktur*, vol. 1, pp. 71–133; Ciriacy-Wantrup, *Familien- und erbrechtliche Gestaltungen*, pp. 149–50.
55   Ciriacy-Wantrup, *Familien- und erbrechtliche Gestaltungen*, pp. 152–54.
56   For details, see Lutz, *Die rechtliche Struktur*, vol. 1, pp. 138–41.
57   For details, see Ciriacy-Wantrup, *Familien- und erbrechtliche Gestaltungen*, pp. 256–314, and Pettinger, *Vermögenserhaltung und Sicherung der Unternehmensfortführung*, pp. 137–61.

exchange[58] resulted from its favorable position in relation to the north Italian commercial centers. Augsburg's law governing bills of exchange largely arose from practical necessity and was legally circumscribed by several council decrees in the course of the seventeenth and eighteenth centuries.[59] A first exchange ordinance, which was clearly modeled on the respective Nuremberg regulations, was passed in 1665, relatively late compared to other central European commercial cities. Further ordinances followed in 1707 and 1716.[60] The 1778 exchange ordinance is particularly important, as it resonated in large parts of Europe – a fact that once again underscores Augsburg's centrality in cashless payment transfers.[61]

The exchange system articulated in the 1778 exchange ordinance is remarkably coherent, reflecting more than a century of experience and combining structural consistency with practical usefulness. Thus the right to draw or accept bills of exchange was dependent upon membership in the merchants' association (*Kaufleutestube*). It was also possible to attain this right through listing in a special register, the *Raggionbuch*, but it is likely that this option was only available to individuals with a certain affinity to the merchant class. Other persons needed to have their bills of exchange certified with the burgomaster's office, where they were alerted to possible risks. Regarding the formal criteria which a bill of exchange had to meet, mature Augsburg law took common commercial practice as its starting point. Matters were different when it came to accepting bills of exchange: Here a specific type, the so-called *Augsburger Akzept*, had come into use, which was declared obligatory for long-term bills in the 1778 ordinance. In practice, this was a restricted kind of acceptance, on the basis of which payment could be demanded no sooner than two weeks before the bill's expiration date. This gave the drawee a chance to secure adequate cover, which the issuer of the bill had to provide.[62]

3.3 Marriage and Family Law

The legal character of marriage and family draws attention to an area of law that specifically reflects gendered social roles.[63] Like most areas of practical civil law, marriage and family law at the beginning of the sixteenth century

---

58 Zorn, *Handels- und Industriegeschichte*, pp. 12–70, as well as Chapter 5 in this volume.
59 Ludyga, "Augsburg als europäischer Wechselplatz".
60 Walder, *Wechselrecht der Reichsstadt Augsburg*, p. 7.
61 Fassl, "Von der freien Reichsstadt zur bayerischen Industriestadt"; see also Chapter 5 in this volume.
62 For details on the *Augsburger Akzept*, see Walder, *Wechselrecht der Reichsstadt Augsburg*, pp. 47–57; Ludyga, "Augsburg als europäischer Wechselplatz", pp. 65–68.
63 Roper, *The Holy Household*, pp. 7–55.

was strongly shaped by overlapping local and trans-local legal influences. Traditional local law coexisted with Roman and canon law, although the former superseded the latter in cases of dispute.[64] During the early modern period, the character of marriage and family underwent substantial change in Augsburg under the influence of learned jurisprudence.[65] Thus separation of property in marriage emerged as an alternative to the traditional practice of joint property, which remained in use only in certain segments of the urban population. In cases of bankruptcy, wives retained certain privileges with respect to the property they brought into the marriage, which could therefore be considered at least partially their own. Principles of the Roman system of civil law, such as the *senatus consultum Velleianum*, were modified for widows who administered their husbands' estates, and especially for those who continued their mercantile companies. In this case widows could actually exert the rights of commercial partners. As these selected examples demonstrate, the changes in Augsburg's marriage law at the beginning of the early modern era were of a piecemeal nature. A comprehensive and systematic reform never took place. This also applies to the structure of regulation: Numerous new rules can be found in almost all aspects of the increasingly differentiated local statutory law, including bankruptcy ordinances, police ordinances, and individual council decrees.[66]

4 Judicial Procedure

The structural changes observable in Augsburg's civil law at the outset of the early modern period are particularly evident in the case of judicial procedure, which only now emerges as a distinct field of legal regulation. The legal foundations of civil justice within the city remained unchanged, to be sure. The privileges that since the Middle Ages had guaranteed Augsburg's independence from foreign jurisdiction (excepting the emperor himself) remained in force.[67] The medieval municipal law code likewise retained its formal validity, although it was supplemented and eventually superseded by specific legislation. The recalibration of court procedure, especially in the area of civil jurisdiction – a process that started in the Holy Roman Empire with the adoption of an ordinance

---

64 Koch, "Die Frau im Recht der Frühen Neuzeit".
65 Weber (ed.), *Darstellung*, pp. 360–82, provides extensive coverage.
66 For individual examples, see Weber (ed.), *Darstellung*, pp. 360–82. Additional references may be found in Scholz-Löhnig, *Bayerisches Eherecht*, pp. 91–93.
67 Liedl, *Gerichtsverfassung und Zivilprozeß*, pp. 15–17.

for the Imperial Chamber Court, and which was strongly influenced by legal scholarship – had its counterpart in Augsburg shortly afterwards. Here a separate ordinance governing court procedure was drawn up in 1529[68] and subsequently revised several times.[69] In structural terms this ordinance, which was the work of the Augsburg court scribe Franz Kötzler, is no more than a compilation of recorded common law supplemented by references to relevant council resolutions and court rulings. Nevertheless, the fact that this document was obviously compiled as a handbook for practical use testifies to a certain professionalization of civic jurisdiction, which corresponded with the formalization of court procedure derived from precedence. This, in turn, hints at the author's familiarity with scholarly methods of dealing with normative texts like council decrees or important court rulings. In retrospect, the fact that this compilation focused on judicial procedure reflects general tendencies of the early modern period – an age in which not only material civil law in central Europe, but civil trial law as well was increasingly shaped by the impulses of learned jurisprudence.[70] In this respect, Augsburg's civil trial law appears modern by contemporary standards and otherwise in line with the developments of its time.

After the Thirty Years' War, the strict enforcement of confessional parity, which had been established in Augsburg on the basis of Article 5, Section 3 of the Treaty of Osnabrück in 1648,[71] initially impeded the further development of civil trial law.[72] Under the pressure of various measures which the Imperial Aulic Court in Vienna had taken in response to massive complaints about the local situation, Augsburg's city officials succeeded in passing an up-to-date trial ordinance in 1771.[73] This legal document marks the first instance in which the imperial city acquired an autonomous, innovative civil trial law that adapted to local circumstances the more recent principles of common civil procedure

---

68   Preserved in SuStBA, 4° Cod. Aug. 104.
69   Liedl, *Gerichtsverfassung und Zivilprozeß*, pp. 51–52; Pettinger, *Vermögenserhaltung*, pp. 88–89.
70   For further information, see Schlinker, *Litis Contestaio*.
71   Edited in Repgen (ed.), *Acta pacis Westphalicae* pp. 95–170, esp. p. 111.
72   Kreutz, "Prozessordnung der Reichsstädte", pp. 229–33.
73   Printed versions are stored in StadtAA, A 105-0-1-3-1; SuStBA, 2° Cod. Aug. 243–38; 2° Cod. Aug. 243–38a; 4° Cod. Aug. 1020–122; 4° Cod. Aug. 1020–122a; 4° Cod. Aug. 1021–2,11; 2° Cod. S 270; 2° Cod. S 271; 2° Cod. S 271a; 2° Cod. S 271b; Bayerische Staatsbibliothek München, 4° J. pract. 163; Bibliothek der Ludwig-Maximilians-Universität München, 0001/2° Jus 1467; 0312/Bav 106; and Staatliche Bibliothek Regensburg, 999/Bav. 1684.

law, which had come into increasingly wide usage in the Holy Roman Empire[74] after the imperial diet's final resolution (*Jüngster Reichsabschied*) of 1654.[75]

4.1 Court Structure and Civil Proceedings

By the time the trial ordinance of 1771 was passed, some fundamental changes in legal structures had taken place compared to the late Middle Ages, when most cases were brought before the civic court (*Stadt-Gericht*).[76] While the civic court was retained in the 1771 trial ordinance, it was supplemented by a number of special courts whose common designation as "offices" (*Ämter*) indicates that they originated from administrative practice but over time acquired the power to pass sentence in individual cases. According to the 1771 trial ordinance,[77] these offices included the main guardianship office (*Ober-Pflegamt*), which was responsible for what we nowadays consider to be matters of family law, especially cases of guardianship. According to the 1771 ordinance, the burgomaster's office (*Burgermeister-Amt*) constituted the imperial city's regular court of the first instance, but also held jurisdiction in matters of arrest, bills of exchange, criminal law with summary procedure, inheritance, and debt. The jurors' office (*Geschworne-Amt*) was in charge of cases involving real estate, especially easements, and construction law. The court of arts, trades, and crafts (*Kunst- Gewerb- und Handwerks-Gericht*) decided legal cases concerning the local economy. While the name of the imperial city's bailiff office (*Reichs-Stadt-Vogt-Amt*) refers to the medieval tradition of Augsburg's judicial personnel, in 1771 it actually took care of registers and inventories in cases of real estate sales and was in charge of securing debts and regulating city markets. The *Stadt-Gericht* now decided cases that nominally pertained to the *Burgermeister-Amt* but were conducted in writing, in addition to handling cases of bankruptcy and instances involving the privileged rank of patricians.

This elaborate system of courts, which evolved in Augsburg – as in comparable cities – between 1500 and 1800,[78] is of interest in several respects. It provides evidence of an increasingly sophisticated and comprehensive judicial system that mirrors the growing complexity of regulating everyday matters. In a process termed juridification (*Verrechtlichung*), civil law, which was now

---

74 Kreutz, "Prozessordnung der Reichsstädte", pp. 243–55; for further details, see Schumann, "Die geschichtlichen Grundlagen", pp. 101–02.
75 Edited in Laufs (ed.), *Der jüngste Reichsabschied*, pp. 7–99.
76 Liedl, *Gerichtsverfassung und Zivilprozeß*, pp. 55–56, and Finkl, *Administrative Verdichtung*, pp. 175–79.
77 Kreutz, "Prozessordnung der Reichsstädte", pp. 247–48.
78 Finkl, *Administrative Verdichtung*, pp. 294–309.

largely based on learned jurisprudence, came to permeate all areas of social life and render them subject to judicial procedure.

4.2 Notaries

Originating in Italy, where an *ars notaria* was taught at institutions of higher learning, the office of notary spread north of the Alps from the end of the Middle Ages.[79] Emperor Maximilian's imperial notary ordinance (*Reichsnotariatsordnung*) of 1512[80] provided a solid legal foundation for this office.[81]

In the imperial city of Augsburg, the activities of notaries are documented from the beginning of the early modern era, revealing that a number of notaries were working there during the sixteenth century on the basis of the imperial notary ordinance. The survival of the nearly completely intact archive of notary Johann Spreng (1524–1601), initially a schoolteacher at St. Anna, from the final third of the sixteenth century provides us with particularly comprehensive information about the functions and activities of local notaries.[82] The archive contains both Latin and German drafts of notarial documents; the Latin documents were presumably conceived for usage outside the German-speaking area.[83] Among Spreng's files we find legal mandates, powers of attorney, certified translations of important documents, wills and household inventories (including those of prominent members of the Fugger family[84]), and protested bills of exchange. Remarkably, real estate transactions were evidently not registered by contemporary notaries. It is likely that these had to be transacted before the civic court or the imperial city's bailiff office.

4.3 Bankruptcy Law

During the early modern period, instances of what we nowadays term insolvency – a loss of economic capability, which entailed the failure to honor one's financial obligations – came to the attention of lawmakers as well. On the imperial level, various police ordinances dealt with insolvency (*Falliment*) during the sixteenth century.[85] Local law in Augsburg also addressed the matter,

---

79 Surveys can be found in Ciriacy-Wantrup, *Familien- und erbrechtliche Gestaltungen*, pp. 15–36, and Schmoeckel (ed.), *Bild des Notariats*, pp. 8–35. See also Konow, *Johannes Halder*, and Becker, "Akten des Augsburger Notars".
80 Edited in Grziwotz (ed.), *Kaiserliche Notariatsordnung*.
81 For further details see Ciriacy-Wantrup, *Familien- und erbrechtliche Gestaltungen*, pp. 56–82.
82 The archive is preserved in the Stadtarchiv Augsburg.
83 Becker, "Akten des Augsburger Notars", pp. 480–81.
84 For further details, see Simnacher, *Fuggertestamente*, pp. 101–59.
85 For detailed references, see Becker, "Bancarottierer", pp. 10–13.

beginning in 1564 to standardize bankruptcy proceedings in publicized decrees for the use of the civic court. Additional bankruptcy decrees were passed in 1574 and 1580.[86] Together with the priority ordinances the city council had passed since 1540,[87] these decrees established specific judicial proceedings for the legal handling of bankruptcy cases,[88] which were increasing significantly among Augsburg's family companies at this time.[89]

In terms of the issues these decrees and ordinances addressed, we find that the norms and regulations had become much tighter and more specific within less than two decades. If the 1564 decree appears rather fragmentary, dealing only with inventorying the bankrupt's estate and with individual cases of criminal behavior, it did at least stipulate a general public obligation to assist in preventing the insolvent debtor's flight and securing his or her arrest. The first of two decrees passed in 1574 amended the norms regulating the initial securing and administration of the bankrupt's estate, while the second addressed the process of decision-making among the creditors. Additional criminal norms were introduced as well, applicable for instance when it turned out that the debtor's estate, including relevant documents, had been manipulated. Finally, in 1580 the existing standards were given more differentiated treatment and the privileges of spouses in insolvency cases were specified.[90] This body of norms provided the basis for the handling of bankruptcy cases in Augsburg for the remainder of the early modern period. In close correspondence with imperial law, bankruptcy cases were resolved on a legal basis with a clearly discernible focus on the creditors' interests in realizing their claims.[91] As a rule, these claims were satisfied by auctioning off the debtor's estate (*Vergantung*).[92] As a logical consequence of the strong position attributed to creditors by Augsburg's law, creditors occasionally put forward demands against their debtors which appear rather extreme.[93]

---

86 Hildebrandt, "Verhältnis von Wirtschaftsrecht und Wirtschaftspraxis"; Häberlein, *Brüder, Freunde und Betrüger*, pp. 323–24, 331–36; Birnbaum, *Konkursrecht*, pp. 7–9; Fischer, "Bankruptcy".
87 Birnbaum, *Konkursrecht*, pp. 9–10.
88 The bankruptcy ordinance of 3 July 1574 is edited in Haßler, *Ausgang der Augsburger Handelsgesellschaft*, pp. 52–53.
89 Hildebrandt, "Verhältnis von Wirtschaftsrecht und Wirtschaftspraxis", p. 154; Häberlein, *Brüder, Freunde und Betrüger*, pp. 397–99 and passim; Safley, "Bankruptcy".
90 For details on the decrees, see Birnbaum, *Konkursrecht*, p. 8.
91 Becker, "Bancarottierer", pp. 12–13; see also Häberlein, "Merchants' Bankruptcies", pp. 26–27.
92 For more on this, see Liedl, *Gerichtsverfassung und Zivilprozeß*, pp. 102–03.
93 Safley, "Standardisierung".

CIVIL LAW

The observation that the imperial city's insolvency law was primarily governed by practical considerations is borne out by the fact that the normative basis for the law remained unchanged (in 1749 it had only been restructured[94]) until Augsburg was incorporated into the Kingdom of Bavaria in 1806, and even beyond. This provides us with a clear indication that the further development of legal practice rested on routine case law. Even the fundamental revision of Augsburg's civil trial law stipulated by the 1771 ordinance left bankruptcy law, as it had evolved since the sixteenth century, essentially untouched.[95] In this respect, Augsburg differed from its neighbor Bavaria, where insolvency law had been incorporated into the 1753 *Codex Judiciarii*.[96]

5 Conclusion

An examination of medieval and early modern civil law in the imperial city of Augsburg reveals a multi-layered system of sources for legal practice, the basis for which was neither purely Germanic nor exclusively Roman. Instead, local legal thinking combined with external legal influences in various ways. Learned Roman and canon law exerted a stronger influence than has long been presumed. Within the different fields of legal regulation, a complex and multi-faceted system developed that blended indigenous legal concepts with received ideas, in particular those of common law. In addition, the way in which legal matters were regulated changed during the early modern period. Unlike during the medieval period, a single legal code no longer formed the basis of urban civil law. While the municipal law code of 1276 formally remained in force, it was almost completely superseded by a multiplicity of individual statutes. Another notable feature is the progressive differentiation of local judiciary offices. In conjunction with the regulation of numerous aspects of daily life, various courts with circumscribed jurisdictions were set up, thus marking the first steps toward a system of specialized courts.

---

94   *Eines HochEdlen, und Hochweisen Raths Verordnung Die Falliten Betreffend*, Augsburg 1749; Fischer, "Bankruptcy", pp. 173–74.
95   On the character of early modern Augsburg bankruptcy law, see Safley, "Standardisierung".
96   For more on this, see Bornhorst, *Das bayerische Insolvenzrecht*, pp. 4–21. For eighteenth-century insolvency law, see Vollmershausen, *Vom Konkursprozess zum Marktbereinigungsverfahren*, pp. 53–288.

Bibliography

Unpublished Primary Sources
Bayerische Staatsbibliothek München, 4° J. pract. 163.
Bibliothek der Ludwig-Maximilians-Universität München
  0001/2° Jus 1467.
  0312/Bav 106.
Staatsarchiv Augsburg
  Hochstift Augsburg, Urkunden 27.
  Reichsstadt Augsburg, Literalien 32.
Staats- und Stadtbibliothek Augsburg (SuStBA)
  2° Cod. Aug. 151; 2° Cod. Aug. 168; 2° Cod. Aug. 243–38; 2° Cod. Aug. 243–38a; 2° Cod. Aug. 253; 2° Cod. Aug. 254; 2° Cod. Aug. 255; 2° Cod. Aug. 257; 2° Cod. Aug. 290; 4° Cod. Aug. 104; 4° Cod. Aug. 122; 4° Cod. Aug. 123; 4° Cod. Aug. 1020–122; 4° Cod. Aug. 1020–122a; 4° Cod. Aug. 1021–2,11; 2° Cod. S 270; 2° Cod. S 271; 2° Cod. S 271a; 2° Cod. S 271b.
Staatliche Bibliothek Regensburg, 999/Bav. 1684.
Stadtarchiv Augsburg (StadtAA), A 105-0-1-3-1.

Published Primary Sources
Becker, C. (ed.), *"Consvetudines almae Reipublicae Augustanae" von Matthaeus Laimann und Georg Tradel mit "Notwendigs Bedenckhen" von Georg Tradel. Eine Zusammenstellung Augsburger Stadtrechts mit einer Denkschrift zu seiner Reform vom Ende des sechzehnten Jahrhunderts (Handschrift der Staats- und Stadtbibliothek Augsburg, 2° Cod. Aug. 168)*, Berlin, 2008.
Brucker, C.H., *Dissertatio inauguralis iuridica de tutoribus et curatoribus ex more Augustano*, Erlangen, 1765.
Cadensky, S.T., *Dissertatio iuridica conferens potißimam partem Tit. XI. Aug. Ord. polit. ref. ac. anno MDCXXX*, Strasbourg, 1713.
Freyberg, M.P. von (ed.), *Sammlung teutscher Rechts-Alterthümer*, vol. 1/1, Mainz, 1828.
Grziwotz, H. (ed.), *Kaiserliche Notariatsordnung von 1512. Spiegel des Europäischen Notariats*, Munich, 1995.
Herwart, D.U., *Disputatio iuridica inauguralis de successione coniugum ab intestato, secundum mores Augustanos*, Jena, 1703.
Lassberg, F.L.A. von (ed.), *Der Schwabenspiegel oder Schwäbisches Land- und Lehen-Rechtbuch, nach einer Handschrift vom Jahr 1287 herausgegeben*, 3rd ed. of the reprint of the 1840 edition, Aalen, 1972.
Laufs, A. (ed.), *Der jüngste Reichsabschied von 1654. Abschied der Römisch Kaiserlichen Majestät und gemeiner Stände, welcher auf dem Reichstag zu Regensburg im Jahr Christi 1654 aufgerichtet ist*, Berne, 1975.

Lipp, G.A., *Commentatio de curatoribus minorum, speciatim ex moribus Augustanis*, Jena, 1765.

Meyer, C. (ed.), *Das Stadtbuch von Augsburg, insbesondere das Stadtrecht vom Jahre 1276, nach der Originalhandschrift zum ersten Male herausgegeben und erläutert*, Augsburg, 1872.

Morell, J.G., *De iure statutario illustris Reipublicae Augustanae*, Altdorf, 1743.

Neunhoefer, C., *Analecta iuris statutarii Augustani ad singularia quaedam doctrinae de hypothecis et pignoribus*, Tübingen, 1784.

Repgen, K. (ed.), *Acta pacis Westphalicae*, series 3 B, vol. 1/1, Münster 1998.

Walch, C.F. (ed.), *Vermischte Beyträge zu dem deutschen Recht*, vol. 4, Jena, 1774.

Weber, G.M. von (ed.), *Darstellung der sämmtlichen Provinzial- und Statutar-Rechte des Königreichs Bayern, mit Ausschluß des gemeinen, preußischen und französischen Rechts, nebst den allgemeinen, dieselben abändernden, neueren Gesetzen*, vol. 4/1, Augsburg, 1841.

Secondary Literature

Baer, W., "Das Stadtrecht vom Jahre 1156", in G. Gottlieb, W. Baer, J. Becker, J. Bellot, K. Filser, P. Fried, W. Reinhard and B. Schimmelpfennig (eds.), *Geschichte der Stadt Augsburg von der Römerzeit bis zur Gegenwart*, 2nd ed., Stuttgart, 1985, pp. 132–34.

Becker, C., "Bancarottierer", *KTS. Zeitschrift für Insolvenzrecht* 69 (2008), pp. 3–19.

Becker, C., "Die Akten des Augsburger Notars Johann Spreng (1524–1601) – Ein Einblick in das Rechtsleben eines frühneuzeitlichen europäischen Wirtschaftszentrums", in H.-G. Hermann, T. Gutmann, J. Rückert, M. Schmoeckel and H. Siems (eds.), *Von den Leges Barbarorum bis zum ius barbarum des Nationalsozialismus. Festschrift für Hermann Nehlsen zum 70. Geburtstag*, Cologne, 2008, pp. 477–91.

Becker, C., "Einleitung", in idem (ed.), *"Consvetudines almae Reipublicae Augustanae"*, pp. IX–XX.

Becker, C., "Der Einfluss der Rechtsschule von Bologna auf das Wirtschaftsrecht in Augsburg", *Zeitschrift des Historischen Vereins für Schwaben* 102 (2010), pp. 369–86.

Becker, C., "Tierschaden – Über den Zusammenhang augsburgischen und gemeinen Rechts am Beispiel menschlicher Haftung für vom oder am Tier verursachte Schäden", in D. Schiersner, A. Link, B. Rajkay and W. Scheffknecht (eds.), *Augsburg, Schwaben und der Rest der Welt. Neue Beiträge zur Landes- und Regionalgeschichte. Festschrift für Rolf Kießling zum 70. Geburtstag*, Augsburg, 2011, pp. 1–20.

Berner, E., *Zur Verfassungsgeschichte der Stadt Augsburg vom Ende der römischen Herrschaft bis zur Kodifikation des zweiten Stadtrechts im Jahre 1276*, Breslau, 1879.

Beyerle, K., *Grundherrschaft und Hoheitsrechte des Bischofs von Konstanz in Arbon. Zugleich ein Beitrag zur Geschichte der deutschen Staatsverfassung*, Frauenfeld, 1904.

Binswanger, J., "Zur äusseren Rechtsgeschichte der Stadt Augsburg", in *Festschrift zum XXII. Deutschen Juristentag vom 7. bis 9. September 1893 in Augsburg*, Augsburg, 1893.

Birnbaum, S., *Konkursrecht der frühen Augsburger Neuzeit mit seinen gemeinrechtlichen Einflüssen*, Berlin, 2014.

Bornhorst, R., "Das bayerische Insolvenzrecht im 19. Jahrhundert und der Einfluß Bayerns auf das Entstehen der Reichskonkursordnung von 1877", Diss. jur., Univ. Würzburg, 2002.

Chittolini, G., "Statuten und städtische Autonomien. Einleitung", in idem and D. Willoweit (eds.), *Statuten, Städte und Territorien zwischen Mittelalter und Neuzeit in Italien und Deutschland*, Berlin, 1992, pp. 7–37.

Ciriacy-Wantrup, K. von, *Familien- und erbrechtliche Gestaltungen von Unternehmen der Renaissance: Eine Untersuchung der Augsburger Handelsgesellschaften der frühen Neuzeit*, Berlin, 2007.

Eckhardt, K.A., *Rechtsbücherstudien. Vol. 1: Vorarbeiten zu einer Parallelausgabe des Deutschenspiegels und Urschwabenspiegels*, Berlin, 1927.

Fassl, P., "Von der freien Reichsstadt zur bayerischen Industriestadt: Augsburg 1750/1850 – ein Überblick", in R.A. Müller (ed.), *Aufbruch ins Industriezeitalter*, Munich, 1985, vol. 2, pp. 81–102.

Finkl, N., *Administrative Verdichtung und Konfessionalisierung. Die Verwaltung der Reichsstadt Augsburg im 16. Jahrhundert*, Neustadt an der Aisch, 2011.

Fischer, P. "Bankruptcy in Early Modern German Territories", in T.M. Safley (ed.), *The History of Bankruptcy: Economic, Social and Cultural Implications in Early Modern Europe*, London, 2013, pp. 173–83.

Häberlein, M., *Brüder, Freunde und Betrüger. Soziale Beziehungen, Normen und Konflikte in der Augsburger Kaufmannschaft um die Mitte des 16. Jahrhunderts*, Berlin, 1998.

Häberlein, M., "Merchants' bankruptcies, economic development, and social relations in German towns during the long sixteenth century", in T.M. Safley (ed.), *The History of Bankruptcy: Economic, Social and Cultural Implications in Early Modern Europe*, London, 2013, pp. 19–33.

Haßler, F., *Der Ausgang der Augsburger Handelsgesellschaft David Haug, Hans Langnauer und Mitverwandte (1574–1606)*, Augsburg, 1928.

Hecker, H.-J., "Das Augsburger Statutarrecht", in R.A. Müller (ed.), *Aufbruch ins Industriezeitalter*, Munich, 1985, vol. 2, pp. 162–74.

Hecker, H.-J., "Das Recht der Reichsstadt Augsburg und die Versuche zu seiner Kodifizierung im 18. Jahrhundert", *Zeitschrift der Savigny-Stiftung für Rechtsgeschichte. Germanistische Abteilung* 113 (1996), pp. 391–96.

Hermann, H.-G., "Vielerlei Zungen: Intervention zum Beitrag von Felicitas Schmieder", in G. Drossbach (ed.), *Von der Ordnung zur Norm. Statuten in Mittelalter und Früher Neuzeit*, Paderborn, 2009, pp. 225–28.

Hildebrandt, R., "Zum Verhältnis von Wirtschaftsrecht und Wirtschaftspraxis im 16. Jahrhundert. Die Fallitenordnungen des Augsburger Rates 1564–1580", in A. Mächler, E. Grünert and H. Kraemer (eds.), *Historische Studien zu Politik, Verfassung und*

Gesellschaft. Festschrift für Richard Dietrich zum 65. Geburtstag, Berne, 1976, pp. 154–63.

Huber, J. von, *Abhandlung über die Abweichung der Augsburgischen Statuten vom gemeinen Recht, oder: kurzer Abriß des Augsburgischen Statutar-Rechts*, 2nd ed., Augsburg, 1858.

Kießling, R., "Wirtschaft und Recht auf dem Weg zur Moderne. Überlegungen zu den Entwicklungsfaktoren und Rahmenbedingungen in den oberdeutschen Städten, vor allem Augsburg, im Spätmittelalter und in der beginnenden Neuzeit", in T.M.J. Möllers (ed.), *Standardisierung durch Markt und Recht*, Baden-Baden, 2008, pp. 231–45.

Koch, E., "Die Frau im Recht der Frühen Neuzeit. Juristische Lehren und Begründungen", in U. Gerhard (ed.), *Frauen in der Geschichte des Rechts. Von der Frühen Neuzeit bis zur Gegenwart*, Munich, 1997, pp. 73–93.

Konow, K.-O., *Johannes Halder. Apostolischer und kaiserlicher Notar in Frankfurt am Main: Ein Beitrag zur Geschichte des deutschen Notariats im Spätmittelalter*, Frankfurt, 1959.

Kreutz, P., "Die Prozessordnung der Reichsstädte Dinkelsbühl und Augsburg: Konfessionelle Parität und gemeinrechtliche Prozesslehre", *Zeitschrift des Historischen Vereins für Schwaben* 107 (2015), pp. 223–56.

Kreutz, P., "Matthaeus Laimann und Georg Tradel. Ein Lebensbild zweier Augsburger Juristenpersönlichkeiten zu Beginn der Frühen Neuzeit", in C. Becker (ed.), *"Consvetudines almae Reipublicae Augustanae"*, pp. XXI–XXX.

Kroppenberg, I., "Kodifikation", in A. Cordes, H.-P. Haferkamp, H. Lück, D. Werkmüller and R. Schmidt-Wiegand (eds.), *Handwörterbuch zur deutschen Rechtsgeschichte*, 2nd ed., Berlin, 2012, vol. 2, col. 1918–30.

Künast, H.-J. and Müller, J.D., "Peutinger, Conrad", in *Neue Deutsche Biographie*, vol. 20, Berlin, 2001, pp. 282–84.

Liedl, E., *Gerichtsverfassung und Zivilprozeß der Freien Reichsstadt Augsburg*, Augsburg, 1958.

Ludyga, H., "Augsburg als europäischer Wechselplatz. Die städtische Wechselordnung von 1778", in C. Becker and H.-G. Hermann (eds.), *Ökonomie und Recht. Historische Entwicklungen in Bayern*, Berlin, 2009, pp. 55–72.

Lutz, E., *Die rechtliche Struktur süddeutscher Handelsgesellschaften in der Zeit der Fugger*, 2 vols., Tübingen, 1976.

Mayer, M.A., *Der Kauf nach dem Augsburger Stadtrecht von 1276 im Vergleich zum gemeinen römischen Recht*, Berlin, 2009.

Pettinger, S., *Vermögenserhaltung und Sicherung der Unternehmensfortführung durch Verfügungen von Todes wegen. Eine Studie der Frühen Augsburger Neuzeit*, Berlin, 2007.

Pettinger, S., "Die Entwicklung der gewillkürten Erbfolge in der freien Reichsstadt Augsburg", in C. Becker and H.-G. Hermann (eds.), *Ökonomie und Recht. Historische Entwicklungen in Bayern*, Berlin, 2009, pp. 99–118.

Roper, L., *The Holy Household: Woman and Morals in Reformation Augsburg*, Oxford, 1989.

Safley, T.M., "Bankruptcy: family and finance in early modern Augsburg", *Journal of European Economic History* 29 (2000), pp. 53–72.

Safley, T.M., "Die Frage einer frühneuzeitlichen Standardisierung des Rechtsprozesses in Bankrottfällen am Beispiel des Höchstetter-Konkurses 1529", in T.M.J. Möllers (ed.), *Vielfalt und Einheit – Wirtschaftliche und rechtliche Rahmenbedingungen von Standardbildungen*, Baden-Baden, 2008, pp. 107–25.

Sbriccoli, M., *L'interpretazione dello statuto: Contributo allo studio della funzione dei giuristi nell' età comunale*, Milan, 1969.

Schlinker, S., *Litis contestatio. Eine Untersuchung über die Grundlagen des gelehrten Zivilprozesses in der Zeit vom 12. bis zum 19. Jahrhundert*, Frankfurt, 2008.

Schlosser, H., "Statutarrecht und Landesherrschaft in Bayern", in G. Chittolini and D. Willoweit (eds.), *Statuten, Städte und Territorien zwischen Mittelalter und Neuzeit in Italien und Deutschland*, Berlin, 1992, pp. 177–93.

Schmidt, R., "Zum Augsburger Stadtbuch von 1276. Beschreibung der Originalhandschrift und der in Augsburg liegenden Abschriften des Augsburger Stadtbuches", *Zeitschrift des Historischen Vereins für Schwaben* 70 (1976), pp. 80–171.

Schmidt, R., "Das Stadtbuch von 1276"", in G. Gottlieb, W. Baer, J. Becker, J. Bellot, K. Filser, P. Fried, W. Reinhard and B. Schimmelpfennig (eds.), *Geschichte der Stadt Augsburg von der Römerzeit bis zur Gegenwart*, 2nd ed., Stuttgart, 1985, pp. 140–45.

Schmieder, F., "Stadtstatuten deutscher Städte? Einige Überlegungen im europäischen Vergleich", in G. Drossbach (ed.), *Von der Ordnung zur Norm: Statuten in Mittelalter und Früher Neuzeit*, Paderborn, 2009, pp. 217–24.

Schmoeckel, M. (ed.), *Das Bild des Notariats seit der Frühen Neuzeit*, Würzburg, 2012.

Scholz Löhning, C., *Bayerisches Eherecht von 1756 bis 1875 auf dem Weg zur Verweltlichung*, Berlin, 2004.

Schumann, E., "Die geschichtlichen Grundlagen des heutigen Zivilprozesses", in F. Stein (ed.), *Kommentar zur Zivilprozeßordnung/Stein-Jonas. Erster Band. §§ 1–252*, 20th ed., Tübingen, 1984, pp. 79–121.

Sieh-Burens, K., "Die Augsburger Stadtverfassung um 1500", *Zeitschrift des Historischen Vereins für Schwaben* 77 (1983), pp. 125–49.

Simnacher, G., *Die Fuggertestamente des 16. Jahrhunderts*, 2nd ed., Weißenhorn, 1994.

Tlusty, B.A. *Bacchus and Civic Order: The Culture of Drink in Early Modern Germany*, Charlottesville, 2001.

Vollmershausen, C.E., *Vom Konkursprozess zum Marktbereinigungsverfahren. Das deutsche Konkursverfahren vom Jahr 1700 bis heute. Eine exemplarische Untersuchung*, Berlin, 2007.

Walder, F., *Das Wechselrecht der Reichsstadt Augsburg*, Erlangen, 1922.

Wolff, A., "Gerichtsverfassung und Prozess im Hochstift Augsburg in der Rezeptionszeit", *Archiv für die Geschichte des Hochstifts Augsburg* 4 (1912–15), pp. 129–369.

Zorn, W., *Handels- und Industriegeschichte Bayerisch-Schwabens. 1648–1870: Wirtschafts-, Sozial- und Kulturgeschichte des schwäbischen Unternehmertums*, Augsburg, 1961.

PART 3

Religion and Society

CHAPTER 10

The Urban Reformation

Michele Zelinsky Hanson

Augsburg played a key role in historic events that shaped the course of the Reformation. As one of the largest and wealthiest cities in the Holy Roman Empire, a center of trade and banking, and closely tied to the emperor, Augsburg witnessed some of the most critical diplomatic negotiations that determined the religious and political future of the Empire during the first half of the sixteenth century. Augsburg hosted the emperor, papal legates, princes and territorial representatives, and their entourages at momentous imperial diets in 1518, 1530, 1547–48, 1550–51 and 1555. At the same time, the Reformation transformed the city in every possible aspect, from its government to its architecture. Forms of worship changed, of course, but social and political structures also underwent dramatic upheavals that shook the city and affected its destiny for centuries to come.

Augsburg did not take a straightforward path to church reform. The city experienced internal divisions among various religious adherents, including Catholics, Lutherans, Zwinglians, and Anabaptists, which made official alliance with one particular group difficult. Augsburg also had a complicated array of connections to foreign powers, including its overlord the Holy Roman Emperor and the dukes of Bavaria, as well as economic interests ranging from its upper German neighbors to cities all over Europe and, beginning in the 1520s, the Americas. Affiliation with a religious confession could jeopardize valuable financial or political alliances. The city council initially attempted to remain neutral on religious matters but eventually yielded to popular demand for reform, which influenced policy mostly through peaceful elections of magistrates sympathetic to Reformation ideas. When Augsburg finally declared itself for Protestant reform, which occurred much later than in most upper German cities that turned Protestant, this affront to the Catholic emperor provoked retaliations that resulted in radical alterations to the city's political and religious constitution. By the conclusion of the Religious Peace of Augsburg at the diet of 1555, the city emerged as one of only a few imperial cities with bi-confessional communities that openly tolerated and protected both Protestants and Catholics within their walls. This chapter focuses on the events that took place in Augsburg during the Reformation era and the agency of the community that steered the city through this period of upheaval.

1 On the Eve of the Reformation

Religious life in medieval Augsburg came in many forms. Its numerous religious foundations included the collegiate canons at the Cathedral of Our Lady and St. Moritz church, as well as the Augustinian canons at Holy Cross and St. Georg. The canons sang liturgies in their churches and provided pastoral care for nearby residents. Several mendicant orders, including the Franciscans, Dominicans, and Carmelites, served the lay population with dynamic sermons in the vernacular, held in preaching houses attached to the convents' churches. In addition to these foundations for men, women from both burgher and noble families pursued monastic life with the canonesses of St. Stephan, the Benedictines of St. Nicholas, the Franciscans of St. Clara, St. Martin, and Maria Stern, and the Dominicans of St. Katharina, St. Margaret, and St. Ursula.[1]

The bishop had his seat in the northern quarter of the city at the Cathedral of Our Lady, and he also ruled over his diocese in the surrounding territory of Swabia from his residence in Dillingen. He and the cathedral canons, however, did not have sole authority over religious life in the city. The imperial abbey of St. Ulrich governed independently the Benedictines' possessions at the southern end of the city and the villages that it owned outside the city walls. Moreover, religious personnel belonging to the mendicant orders fell under the jurisdiction of their respective orders. Lastly, the city council also exercised some influence over local religious life by acting as trustees for the preaching houses attached to many of the monastic churches to serve the lay community.[2] Augsburg's city council had no legal jurisdiction over any of the resident clergy, however, because clerics were not citizens and paid no taxes – a source of irritation for many residents. Lay Christians participated as worshippers and contributed to religious life as custodians, members of confraternities, and generous donors who endowed masses, artwork, altars, and chapels.[3] One of the most impressive surviving examples from the early sixteenth century is the Fugger chapel at the Carmelite church of St. Anna, which the brothers Jakob and Ulrich Fugger commissioned in the architectural style of the Italian Renaissance as a burial place for members of their family.[4]

As a pillar of medieval urban life, the Church could hardly hide its flaws. Everyone from the university-educated humanist, who scoffed at superstition

---

[1] Wandel, "Geschichte des Christentums"; Kießling, *Bürgerliche Gesellschaft*, pp. 38–41, 323–52.
[2] In the course of the Reformation, the *Zechpfleger* (financial custodians) could exert considerable influence by implementing or resisting religious policy.
[3] Kießling, *Bürgerliche Gesellschaft*, pp. 70–130, 235–40, 254–94.
[4] Scheller, *Memoria*, pp. 47–90; Bellot, "Fuggerkapelle"; see also Chapters 21 and 22 in this volume.

and groaned at the price of offices, to the disenfranchised poor, who could not afford to buy a mass or indulgence[5] for a departed loved one, felt the need for change. On 20 October 1517, the newly elected bishop of Augsburg, Christoph von Stadion, a humanist, cathedral canon, and Swabian noble, opened his tenure by convening a synod in Dillingen with reform in mind. A week and a half before Martin Luther posted his controversial attack on the sale of indulgences, Stadion had already introduced his plans to reform the diocese. An ardent admirer of Desiderius Erasmus of Rotterdam, Stadion admonished his clergy to remove the excesses and abuses of their privileged positions, to live more modestly, follow their vows more closely, and serve the laity more conscientiously.[6] He sought to root out the errors and scandals that plagued the Christian Church in the Middle Ages by reminding his clerics of the apostolic example of the simple Christian life. The new bishop anticipated a renewal of spiritual life in his diocese from the top down by a purification of the clergy based on a closer study of Scripture.

2   Martin Luther in Augsburg

News of Martin Luther's protest against the sale of plenary indulgences spread quickly. After Luther circulated his Ninety-Five Theses in Wittenberg in November 1517, printing presses soon made copies available everywhere and the theses became the subject of correspondence throughout the Empire. In Augsburg, Conrad Peutinger, city secretary and leader of a humanist circle, received a copy of Luther's theses from his friend Christoph Scheuerl of Nuremberg. Luther's arguments found fertile ground among both clerical and lay humanists. The prior of the Carmelite cloister of St. Anna, Johann Frosch, had studied with Luther at Wittenberg and would soon earn his doctorate there. Frosch, like Peutinger and other humanists including Veit Bild, the cathedral canons Christoph Langenmantel and brothers Bernard and Konrad Adelmann, not to mention Bishop von Stadion, shared Luther's desire to reform the Church and were among his earliest supporters in Augsburg.[7]

The first Reformation event in Augsburg with empire-wide implications took place in October 1518, when Martin Luther arrived and met with the papal legate, Cardinal Thomas de Vio da Gaeta, called Cajetan. Luther was hosted by

---

5   A remission of punishment due for sin granted by the pope.
6   Jesse, *Geschichte*, pp. 62–64; Kießling, "Augsburg in der Reformationszeit", p. 22.
7   Kießling, "Augsburg in der Reformationszeit", pp. 22–23; Immenkötter, "Kirche", pp. 392–93. See also Chapter 20 in this volume.

Prior Frosch and the Carmelites at their monastery from 7 to 20 October. The papal legate had been present since July for the imperial diet, at which the old emperor, Maximilian I, pressed the princes to elect his grandson Charles as his heir. The wealthy Augsburg merchant-banker Jakob Fugger provided the financial means to persuade the electors, and also hosted Cardinal Cajetan at the palatial Fugger residence while Cajetan awaited Luther's arrival.[8] As Pope Leo X's representative, Cajetan maintained belief in the efficacy of indulgences and the pope's right to grant them, and he apparently expected Luther to recant and throw himself on the pope's mercy once confronted. Over the course of three nerve-wracking meetings at the Fugger palace, however, it became clear that neither Cajetan nor Luther would waver. The result was only that the battle lines were more distinctly drawn.[9] Cajetan began to put the Church's legal machinery into motion, and Luther drafted a letter of appeal to the pope with Prior Frosch's support. Fearing arrest, Luther secretly fled the city, with the aid of the cathedral canon Christoph Langenmantel, on the night of 20 October 1518 by exiting through a small gate in the city walls.[10] Two days after his escape, Frosch publicized Luther's ongoing rebellion by nailing his letter to the doors of the Augsburg cathedral. In the letter Luther affected a tone of respectful regret and humility but unabashedly maintained that he had not been proved wrong, and therefore could not go against his conscience. Luther's refusal to cooperate with Cajetan caused a watershed in the history of the Roman Church.[11] After this confrontation, Christians would begin to choose sides.

3   Early Support for Reform

Luther's protest against the sale of indulgences to poor, unwitting Christians found friendly ears in Augsburg beyond the small circle of humanists. Progressive priests led the attack from within by criticizing the clergy's immorality and fiscal abuses. They found ready listeners among wealthy patricians and guild leaders as well as common artisans, laborers, and domestic servants.[12]

---

8   As administrators of the papal indulgence, the Fugger family's interests lay in defeating the monk's protest: Häberlein, *The Fuggers of Augsburg*, pp. 183–84.
9   Roper, *Martin Luther*, pp. 97–105.
10 Immenkötter, "Kirche", p. 393.
11 Rabe, *Deutsche Geschichte*, pp. 215–16.
12 Kießling, "Augsburg in der Reformationszeit", pp. 23–24. Friedrich Roth's four-volume *Augsburgs Reformationsgeschichte* remains the authoritative history of Reformation Augsburg; it also includes extensive transcriptions of contemporary sources.

Augsburg's economy had boomed since the late 1400s, but had benefited the populace unequally. By 1518, the wealthiest merchant-banking families were reaping great profits from their strong positions in European trade and finance, while ordinary artisans and laborers found their wages stagnating in the face of soaring food prices. The disparity between rich and poor thus increased dramatically as the number of people whose tax payments identified them as propertyless ("have-nots") rose significantly.[13] With anti-clericalism already rampant, listeners suffering hard times deeply resented wealthy and luxury-loving prelates and canons who were exempt from paying taxes. Priests like Johannes Eck and Ottmar Nachtigall, who defended bankers charging interest on loans, seemed like hypocrites.[14] Luther, meanwhile, sought to expose the selling of indulgences as exploitative of the gullible and the poor and argued that Christians did not need the Church to mediate for them with God at all; their faith was all they needed. Preaching the priesthood of all believers, Luther and his followers began to remove the barriers between clerics and laypeople by asserting that the laity could read the Bible for themselves and receive wine at communion just like priests. Moreover, priests should marry, become citizens, and pay taxes just like everyone else.

Augsburg's already vigorous printing industry boomed as interest in Luther's conflict with the papacy grew.[15] Printers produced a seemingly endless stream of anti-clerical pamphlets that excoriated the clergy for their worldliness and false piety and called for an end to abuses. The council's first reaction to Luther's growing popularity was thus to suppress texts that might spark public disturbances. In August 1520, council deputies Conrad Peutinger and Jakob Fugger admonished printers not to publish writings that discussed the religious debates or defamed personalities involved in the controversy.[16] Printers who violated the council's policy faced arrest and sometimes the closing of their workshops. Nonetheless, Augsburg's printers continued to provide numerous writings by Luther and his sympathizers.[17]

Although Bishop von Stadion sympathized with the reformers' point of view, he could neither disobey the pope nor protect priests who disobeyed him. In December 1520, he found himself forced to publish the papal ban on Luther and his written works. During Lent in 1521, Stadion ordered diocesan

---

13 Propertyless residents paid only a head tax called *habnit Steuer*: Broadhead, "Popular Pressure". For an explanation of Augsburg property taxes, see Chapter 12 of this volume.
14 On Eck, see Wurm, *Johannes Eck*.
15 Künast, *"Getruckt zu Augsburg"*, pp. 225–26, 231–34; idem., "Martin Luther".
16 Künast, *"Getruckt zu Augsburg"*, p. 201; Immenkötter, "Kirche", p. 393; Creasman, *Censorship*, pp. 68–69.
17 Künast, "Martin Luther".

priests not to grant absolution to people who refused to turn in their copies of Luther's works.[18] In the meantime, more local priests had joined Prior Frosch in his support of evangelical reform, including Urbanus Rhegius at the cathedral and Johann Speiser at St. Moritz. Johannes Eck, a theology professor at the University of Ingolstadt, delivered the pope's demand to Bishop von Stadion that he must force Rhegius either to recant his support of Luther or lose his position as preacher at the cathedral. Rhegius refused to recant and subsequently left the city.[19]

In these early years of the Reformation, the multiplicity of authorities who had jurisdiction over religious life created a confusing array of forces for and against Luther and his supporters. The bishop reluctantly enforced the decisions of the papacy, but popular pressure convinced the city council to protect priests who dissented. In August 1523, for example, 400 citizens at St. Moritz organized a deputation to the council to protect Speiser from charges of heresy. The deputation argued that the trustees should have some say in the appointment after sponsoring the preachership with their own funds.[20] Mayor Ulrich Rehlinger, a supporter of Luther, assured the preachers that the city council would protect them within its jurisdictional boundaries – essentially the city walls – as long as "they preached from the Holy Gospel and only what could be supported by Holy Scripture".[21] With support from parishioners and protection from the council, reformers continued to flourish. Frosch stepped down from his post as prior of the Carmelite convent in 1523, accepting instead a position as preacher at St. Anna; two years later he married, and St. Anna began to offer communion in both kinds. Ardent Lutherans Stephan Agricola and Urban Rhegius, who returned to the city in August 1524, soon joined Frosch in preaching reform.[22]

At the Franciscan church, the community exercised its corporate muscle to support reform even more dramatically. Historically, Franciscan preachers had served the population with effective preaching in the vernacular, drawing large audiences from among the city's craftspeople and laborers.[23] In 1522, the Franciscan lector Blasius Kern offended listeners by defending the papacy in his sermons, becoming so unpopular with the parishioners that the council sought to replace him before the hostilities turned violent. The trustees then hired a new preacher, the Franciscan Johann Schilling. An avid reformer,

---

18 Immenkötter, "Kirche", p. 394.
19 Kießling, "Augsburg in der Reformationszeit", pp. 23.
20 Kießling, "Doppelgemeinde", p. 116; Scheller, *Memoria*, pp. 207–08.
21 Stadtarchiv Augsburg (StadtAA), Geheime Ratsprotokolle, 13 October 1523.
22 Kießling, "Augsburg in der Reformationszeit", pp. 23–24.
23 Safley, "Zentrum und Peripherie", pp. 45–48.

THE URBAN REFORMATION 227

FIGURE 10.1   View of St. Moritz Church from the west, copperplate by Simon Grimm, 1687
STAATS- UND STADTBIBLIOTHEK AUGSBURG, GRAPH 17/3A

Schilling's passionate sermons on the evils of the Roman papacy filled the large church to capacity and encouraged listeners to take matters into their own hands. Inspired by Schilling, one shoemaker's young servant vandalized artwork in the cathedral in April 1524;[24] a few weeks later, parishioners harassed a group of Franciscan monks who were performing a traditional blessing of water and salt. Defending their actions before the magistrates, one participant explained, "[We] hear daily in the sermons that holy water does not take away sin and is useless, and that [we] should put [our] hope in God alone, and not in the water." When the monk tried to proceed anyway, the parishioner cried, "give me the book and get out of here, because you are turning us away from the truth of the Gospel that they preach to us every day".[25] The parishioner's

---

24   StadtAA, Urgichten, 8 May 1524, Georg Näßlin. Näßlin was later arrested on the suspicion of Anabaptist sympathies: Zelinsky Hanson, *Religious Identity*, pp. 37–40.
25   StadtAA, Urgichten, 8 May 1524, Bartholome Nussfelder; see also Tlusty (ed.), *Augsburg*, pp. 215–17.

testimony revealed to the council the power of persuasive preachers to inspire followers. The incident also demonstrated that permitting old practices to operate in the same space with new teachings confused and upset people. Narrowly avoiding violence again, the magistrates banished the ringleaders of the demonstration from the city for a year and reconsidered Schilling's employment.

Tensions exploded the following August when the council tried to dismiss Johann Schilling from his post. Schilling had stirred his listeners with tales of injustice, fiscal abuses, and the whole system of elite privileges and oppression by the city government and the wealthy merchants who ran it.[26] The council convinced Schilling to leave Augsburg secretly to avoid a riot, but their plan backfired. When Schilling disappeared, over a thousand protestors gathered in front of the city hall, demanding not only Schilling's return, but also the incorporation of the clergy into the citizenry (making them subject to city taxes and civic law) and the removal of certain taxes on wine and beer, which were particularly hard on the poor.[27] This uprising took place on the eve of the Peasants' War, and the magistrates worried about a full-scale revolt from the city's largest guild, the weavers, who had close ties to their rural neighbors and suffered from the domination of the cloth trade by Augsburg's wealthy merchants. The council called out the city guard to protect them in the city hall, and several wealthy citizens hastily fled for safety. The magistrates offered to discuss the protesters' demands and install Rhegius at the Franciscan church, but the leaders of the rebellion refused. The crowd dispersed only after the council agreed to recall Schilling. Once the magistrates had ensured their own safety and restored public order, they cracked down with a show of exemplary justice, executing the leaders of the riot, the weavers Hans Kag and Hans Speiser.[28] Schilling's triumphant return, meanwhile, did not last long; the council replaced him permanently in November 1524.[29]

The Schilling uprising is seen as something of a revelation point in Augsburg's Reformation history. It illustrated the power of charismatic preachers to motivate laypeople, especially those with economic grievances, to demand changes. It also demonstrated the potential for grassroots reform movements to be co-opted by magistrates.[30] During the Schilling negotiations, the council

---

26   Broadhead, "Popular Pressure", p. 82.
27   Rogge, *Für den Gemeinen Nutzen*, pp. 249–83, esp. p. 270 for a list of demands. On the council's reaction, see Chapter 6 of this volume.
28   StadtAA, Urgichten, 12–14 Sep. 1524, Hans Kag and Hans Speiser.
29   Kießling, "Augsburg in der Reformationszeit", pp. 24–25.
30   See Chapter 6 in this volume; see also Blickle, *The Revolution of 1525*, on the Peasants' War and the adoption of reforming policies by magistrates in order to control communal demands.

preserved its authority and managed to contain the popular reform movement by acknowledging the community's demand for sympathetic preachers. Although the magistrates did crack down on public disturbances – especially if they threatened violence – they also continued to support church reform by hiring reformers as preachers.[31] The Peasants' War terrorized much of southern Germany from 1524 to 1526 but largely bypassed Augsburg, in part because the city did not rule extensive territory outside its walls and in part because the guild-run government responded to its reform-minded citizens by appointing preachers that met their demands. In Schilling's place, the council appointed Michael Keller, a charismatic reformer influenced by Ulrich Zwingli of Zurich. Keller initially managed to ease the magistrates' concerns by preaching obedience to authority while railing against the abuses of the church, criticizing the greed of the wealthy, and attacking Luther for conservatism, ultimately establishing the Franciscan church as a center of reformed zeal in the city.[32] The hiring of Keller showed that engaged citizens could defend their interests while also marking a turning point in the council's policy towards directing reform. Augsburg's guild regime, in which citizens elected guild leaders who represented them in the council and the highest civil offices, provided a forum for carrying out reform in a relatively peaceful process that was neither strictly magisterial nor communal.[33]

4 The "Middle Way"

Augsburg's magistrates instituted reform later than most imperial cities, such as Nuremberg, Strasbourg, or Ulm.[34] Until the early 1530s, the council remained officially neutral. Various authorities had jurisdiction over church property and personnel, and in the past there had been little dispute over matters of doctrine. Now the church itself was divided on the most essential questions, and there was no mechanism or precedent for resolving conflicts of this scale. Bishop von Stadion's efforts failed to stifle reforming priests, some inspired by Luther and others – more and more – by the Swiss reformer Ulrich Zwingli. Many council members had long wished to see the Church reformed, but they disagreed amongst themselves on what form it should take or whether they had the authority to carry it out. Lutherans often sided with Catholics to avoid

---

31 Broadhead, "Guildsmen"; Kießling, "Augsburg in der Reformationszeit", p. 25.
32 Safley, "Zentrum und Peripherie", pp. 56, 67–71.
33 Kießling, "Augsburg in der Reformationszeit", pp. 26–28. See Chapter 6 in this volume for the structure of Augsburg's guild government.
34 See Cameron, *European Reformation*, pp. 217–21; Brady, *German Histories*, pp. 162–63.

yielding to the more extreme Zwinglians. Aside from their religious differences, leaders also considered the city's close relationship with its Habsburg overlord, Emperor Charles v, which even Protestants did not want to jeopardize. Moreover, with little territorial jurisdiction outside its walls, Augsburg depended on agricultural resources from the countryside, which was ruled by the Catholic dukes of Bavaria and the bishop of Augsburg.[35]

The city secretary Conrad Peutinger advocated a moderate "middle way" characterized by remaining loyal to the Habsburg emperor while acknowledging popular demands for reform. The council continued to promote peace and protect property while refusing to endorse a particular religious position as official policy.[36] In ordinances issued during the 1520s, it admonished residents not "to insult others concerning our holy Christian faith and godly evangelical teaching, nor dishonor them with offensive, heated, riotous, or shameful words".[37] During this time, residents still had the freedom to choose what type of Christian service to attend, and most of them identified their religious preferences – if at all – by the church they attended, not by a confessional name.[38] There were occasional disturbances over religious matters, but these were usually minor and directed specifically at the clergy rather than at fellow citizens. For the most part, Augsburgers seem to have been content to follow their own interests and let their neighbors do the same.

Though support for reform increased in the 1520s, there was no consensus on religious matters among city leaders either. This was not a matter of elites versus commoners; Augsburgers were divided at every economic and social level. Many members of the wealthiest and most powerful families (i.e., the Fuggers, Welsers, Langenmantels, Rehlingers, and Baumgartners) supported the papacy and upheld the pope's right to decide matters of church reform.[39] They were also among those most closely tied to the Catholic Habsburg dynasty through extensive loans and enterprises in Habsburg territories like Spain, Hungary, and the Netherlands. The Fuggers used their position as patrons, for example, to hire the outspoken Catholic priest Otmar Nachtigall at St. Moritz, but in 1528 complaints against him were so intense that the council felt compelled to ban him from walking the streets (a form of house arrest).[40] Being

---

35   Kießling, "Augsburg in der Reformationszeit", p. 28.
36   Gößner, *Weltliche Kirchenhoheit*, pp. 34–52.
37   StadtAA, Literaliensammlung, Zuchtordnung, 5 December 1529.
38   Zelinsky Hanson, *Religious Identity*, pp. 27–37.
39   Häberlein, *The Fuggers of Augsburg*, 176–81. On other members of the patriciate and merchant circles, see Sieh-Burens, *Oligarchie*, esp. pp. 134–55.
40   In his defense, Nachtigall was recorded as stating that, "Although he did as he admits call some of the preachers heretics, he does not remember preaching anything that could

on the right side of the law did not help, for Nachtigall's real crime was to be unpopular; he preached against reform in a city that was overwhelmingly in favor of it. Catholic citizens still attended mass at St. Moritz, the cathedral, and the Dominican church, but contemporary reports indicate that Catholics were in the minority by the late 1520s. By 1526, mass attendance had dwindled to the point at Holy Cross church that control of the preaching house fell into Protestant hands, requiring lay trustees to take up door-to-door collections in order to finance their choice of a preacher. By this means the congregation was able to maintain autonomy and fill the post by appointing the reform-minded Wolfgang Haug.[41]

Other magistrates, some from the same patrician families noted above, supported various types of Protestant reform. Konrad and Ulrich Rehlinger and Lukas Welser, for example, supported Lutheran reform, as did members of other patrician families including Hieronymous Imhof and Hans Honold. St. Anna's church became a center for Lutheran preaching, led by the so-called "three doctors" Johann Frosch, Urbanus Rhegius, and Stephan Agricola, all of whom enjoyed the moral and financial support of Luther's earliest supporters. Other civic leaders (including Wolfgang Rehlinger, Hans Welser, and the guild principal Mang Seitz) preferred the direction taken by Zwingli. Luther's initial popularity in the city eventually suffered in comparison to the growing influence of Zwingli, whose communal reform movement became far more popular among the self-governing cities of upper Germany. The new preacher at the Franciscan church, Michael Keller, drew large crowds with his Zwinglian-based sermons. These developments led Bishop von Stadion to report to Erasmus in August 1533 that "the Augsburgers still vacillate between Zwingli and Luther, but the scale appears to be tipping toward Zwingli".[42]

At the risk of over-simplifying the nuances of theological controversies, the most significant differences were fairly elementary and not easily reconciled. Catholics and Protestants disagreed on the fundamental premise of whether or not the institutional church was essential to the salvation of believers. Followers of the pope said yes; Protestants said no. For Protestants, the gulf between the two main leaders, Luther and Zwingli, divided the parties almost as thoroughly over the degree of reform required. Lutherans believed anything not forbidden by the Gospel could remain; Zwinglians believed everything not

---

have caused any uproar ... since their Imperial Majesty called the same preachers heretics in his edict." StadtAA, Ratsprotokolle 15, 12 Sep. 1528; Scheller, *Memoria*, pp. 211–17.

41 Gray, "Ottmarskapelle", 221–23. According to Gray, Wolfgang Haug may have been a supporter of Zwingli when he was first hired at Holy Cross, but he appears to have shifted his support to Luther in the 1530s.

42 Jesse, *Geschichte*, p. 114; Kießling, "Augsburg in der Reformationszeit", pp. 25–27.

expressly supported by the Gospel must go. Lutherans and Zwinglians also disagreed passionately on the doctrine of Christ's presence in the celebration of the Eucharist.[43] The debate over whether Christ's body was truly present in the consecrated bread and wine (as Catholics and Luther believed) or (as Zwingli believed) Christ was only spiritually present in the sacrament as a symbolic reenactment, aggravated tensions and delayed the implementation of reform on the local level. Augsburg's preachers argued the matter heatedly in pulpits and pamphlets, and their inability to resolve the controversy complicated their relationships with other Protestant communities.[44]

This religiously diverse environment meant that, during the 1520s, one could attend Catholic, Lutheran, or Zwinglian sermons within shouting distance of one another. For many people this was a perplexing rather than a liberating experience. As testified by the soldier's wife Agnes Vogel in 1528, "the preachers here moved her to [adult] baptism, for she attended their sermons for a good four years, while one preached this [and] the other that. One held the Sacrament for a symbol, the other would have it be flesh and blood. Thus they preached against one another and confused her so much that she didn't know what to believe, and so she wanted to listen to the others too."[45]

The "others" that Vogel found were the Anabaptists, who attracted followers in Augsburg as early as 1524, when small groups began meeting to read the Bible. People from all walks of life shared the Anabaptists' desire to live simply and mark their conversions to a truly Christian way of life with adult baptism. King Ferdinand banned Anabaptists in the Holy Roman Empire in February 1527, however, and since none of Augsburg's churches welcomed them, they began meeting in private homes and gardens in and around the city, thus acquiring the nickname of *Gartenbrüder* or *Gartenschwestern* ("garden brothers" or "garden sisters") from contemporaries.[46] Augsburg became a center for Anabaptist worship in the late 1520s, sending out preachers to lead ministries elsewhere and welcoming displaced Anabaptists in search of work or temporary shelter. In August 1527, Anabaptist leaders from southern Germany and Switzerland gathered in Augsburg for a historic meeting to discuss and unify their teachings. This fateful gathering became known as the "Martyrs' Synod" because so many attendees perished in persecutions afterwards. The meeting did not unify

---

43 Jesse, *Geschichte*, p. 76; Wandel, *Companion to the Eucharist*.
44 Amberg, *A Real Presence*.
45 StadtAA, Urgichten, 14 May 1528, Agnes Vogel. See also Zelinsky Hanson, *Religious Identity*, pp. 1–2, 15, 80, 86; Tlusty (ed.), *Augsburg*, p. 26.
46 Guderian, *Täufer in Augsburg*; Packull, *Mysticism*.

their doctrine, and most groups followed local leaders. Augsburg's Anabaptists noted, for example, that they differed from other Anabaptist groups because they preferred spiritual conversion to rebellion and did not subscribe to millenarian beliefs.[47]

Meanwhile, the dukes of Bavaria, who ruled much of the territory surrounding the city, cracked down hard on the movement in southern Germany with the aid of the Swabian League, which executed all arrested Anabaptists, even those who recanted.[48] Augsburg was milder by comparison, but the council could not tolerate large groups of Anabaptists meeting in secret inside its walls. Most clergy despised them, and the magistrates worried that they might be plotting rebellion at their illicit meetings. The council prohibited adult baptism in October 1527, and took more drastic action as the group continued to grow in spring 1528. The council arrested over one hundred people and exiled those who refused to recant, executing only one leader, Hans Leupold, while another, Hans Hut, died in a botched attempt to escape from jail.[49] The devastating breakup of numerous families, achieved by exiling zealots, successfully suppressed the local movement. Encouraged by the Zwinglians' ascendancy, the Anabaptist movement briefly revived in the early 1530s, but was again quickly suppressed.[50] Ultimately, most local crypto-Anabaptists appear to have assimilated to one of the mainstream Protestant faiths or pursued their faith privately, which was apparently tacitly tolerated in later years as long as their religious activities remained behind closed doors.[51]

5   The Imperial Diet of 1530

The imperial diet convened in Augsburg in 1530 influenced the future of reform in the Holy Roman Empire as a whole and in Augsburg particularly. Charles V sought his brother Archduke Ferdinand's election as King of the Romans, with the financial support of the Fuggers, which would secure a Catholic heir for

---

47   Zelinsky Hanson, *Religious Identity*, pp. 79–94.
48   The Swabian League was a military organization of princes, bishops, cities, and knights for mutual protection and enforcement of peace, primarily in southern Germany. It lasted from 1488 to 1534, when religious differences among leading members caused its dissolution; see also Chapter 6 of this volume.
49   Immenkötter, "Kirche", pp. 396–97.
50   This time there were no executions, although leaders who would not convert were held in prison for years until they recanted.
51   Zelinsky Hanson, *Religious Identity*, p. 82.

the imperial throne.[52] He also hoped to settle the religious controversies. In response to an official *Protestation* signed by princes and cities at Speyer the previous year,[53] the emperor now demanded a statement of their beliefs, and so they arrived in Augsburg with their theologians in tow. Charles suspected that the Protestants (as they came to be called after their support of the 1529 *Protestation*) disagreed too much among themselves to present a united front, and the exposure of their differences would weaken their position. The emperor's stated goal of resolving grievances and avoiding war, however, led some participants to arrive at the diet believing that reconciliation might be possible. The outcome proved them wrong.[54]

Philip Melanchthon, renowned Wittenberg professor, led the Lutheran party at the imperial diet with Luther's support. He carefully distilled the Lutheran position to its most essential and least offensive points, including communion in both forms (bread and wine), the marriage of priests, and a very modest statement on justification by faith alone. The *Confessio Augustana* or Augsburg Confession produced by Melanchthon and other Lutheran theologians attempted to find common ground with the Catholic Church without betraying essential Protestant beliefs. However, Charles v was proved correct; the Protestants failed to unify at Augsburg. Four imperial cities, Strasbourg, Lindau, Memmingen, and Kempten, found the Augsburg Confession too moderate and composed their own Tetrapolitan Confession, influenced by Zwingli but unique to the upper German cities.[55]

As the diet progressed, Augsburg's Bishop Christoph von Stadion urged his colleagues to seek compromise with the reformers, but the emperor did not ask the Catholic theologians to produce a statement of their faith. Instead, they drafted a scathing rebuttal to Melanchthon's *Confessio Augustana* that was so bitter that even Charles v insisted they moderate their tone. The resulting refutation (known as the *Confutatio Augustana*) entertained no thought of reconciliation, only capitulation. The emperor concluded that they had

---

52 When the election succeeded, Raymund, Anton, and Hieronymus Fugger and their heirs were elevated to the rank of imperial counts. Zorn, *Augsburg*, p. 178.

53 At Speyer in 1529, King Ferdinand led a majority of the imperial diet to ban further religious changes and uphold the concept of transubstantiation. The elector of Saxony and landgrave of Hesse, as well as the cities of Strasbourg, Ulm, and Nuremberg, objected to the diet's resolution by signing and later publishing a *Protestation*: Cameron, *European Reformation*, pp. 341–42.

54 On the imperial diets from 1530 to 1555, see Lutz, *Ringen*, pp. 253–310; Gößner, *Weltliche Kirchenhoheit*, pp. 54–61.

55 Ford, *Wolfgang Musculus*, p. 112.

disproved the reformers' position and declared the Protestant cause lost. He called for all Christians to return to the old church and wait for a papal council to institute reforms.[56]

Despite rejection by the emperor, the Catholic Church, and even some Protestant parties, the Augsburg Confession received the support of several pro-Lutheran princes and cities, including Elector Johann of Saxony, Landgrave Philip of Hesse, and the city of Nuremberg. For years to come, it remained the only form of Protestantism legally recognized in the Empire. While many leaders wished for a peaceful resolution, the mood of the times did not celebrate peace-makers or compromise. The diet of 1530 heightened tensions between the Catholic and Protestant parties in the Empire, and undermined the princes' confidence in the emperor to respect their religious choices. It also highlighted the divisions among Protestants, who nonetheless grasped the need to unify themselves rather urgently.

The diet altered conditions in Augsburg in several ways. First, it placed a huge burden on the city's resources to house, feed, and serve the numerous attendees and their retinues. Though some benefited from the added employment and commerce associated with the hospitality trade, the demands on food and fuel drove up prices on essential goods for those who could least afford it, adding fuel to existing discontent over economic polarization. Second, the emperor forbade all Protestant preaching from the pulpit for the duration of the diet and threatened violators with arrest, causing most of the preachers to flee the city. Though these changes temporarily stifled Protestant worship, they also incited public outrage. When the emperor turned the Franciscan church over to the Catholics at the end of the diet, the council feared an uprising. In its first really defiant act, the council refused to endorse the diet's resolution and spurned the emperor's offer of troops to assist in suppressing popular resistance.[57]

Finally, the delineation of even clearer boundaries by the various confessions and the failure to reconcile religious differences increased the pressure on the city council to choose sides. The emperor, bishop, the Bavarian dukes, and Augsburg's leading Catholic patricians all demanded that the city stay with the old church, while Protestant trade partners, including the cities of Nuremberg, Strasbourg, and Ulm, pressured Augsburg to take a stand with them against the emperor. Still, the council wavered; it rejected the Catholic *Confutatio* but did not declare itself for either of the dominant Protestant confessions; after

---

56 For this and the following paragraph, see Rabe, *Deutsche Geschichte*, pp. 323–26.
57 Jesse, *Geschichte*, pp. 97–98; Kießling, "Eckpunkte", pp. 33–34.

the emperor's departure, the city recalled both the Lutheran and Zwinglian preachers to their posts.[58]

6   Implementation of Reform

After 1530, local support for reform grew more passionate and the preference for Zwinglian preachers over Lutherans more obvious. Citizens encouraged these developments by choosing magistrates who supported reform. In January 1531, more Protestants were elected to positions of leadership in the guilds, and they formed a greater proportion of city councilors. They chose as mayors two leaders from the weavers' guild, Mang Seitz and Anton Bimmel, who favored Zwinglian reform.[59] The new mayors sought to settle the dispute over the Eucharist by muzzling the Lutheran preachers who were attacking the Zwinglian position in their sermons. In March 1531 the influential Lutheran preachers Frosch, Agricola, and Rhegius left the increasingly inhospitable city. The departure of Luther's earliest supporters marked another turning point in Augsburg's path to reformation. Following the model of other upper German cities, the council sought preachers from Strasbourg (Wolfgang Musculus, Bonifacius Wolfart, and Theobald Niger) to replace them.[60] Lutheran citizens who received the Eucharist in the "old form" from the remaining Carmelites at the convent of St. Anna now found themselves on the wrong side of law; they were reprimanded in June and again in October 1531.[61]

Keller, Musculus, and Wolfart now used their pulpits to push for a complete reformation of the city based on the upper German model exemplified in Strasbourg. In 1533, they petitioned the council to ban the Catholic Mass once and for all.[62] Their efforts highlight another difference between Lutherans and Zwinglians; Lutheran reformers promoted a purely spiritual renaissance and generally avoided the political sphere, instead endorsing the authority of rulers and obedience of their subjects. Zwingli, who influenced the upper German reform movement, demanded a thorough reformation of public and private life, guided by the preachers and executed by representatives of the people. The Zwinglian message resonated deeply with the people of Augsburg because the reformers' desire for religious reform coincided with popular views of what a

---

58   Immenkötter, "Kirche", p. 398; see also Gößner, *Weltliche Kirchenhoheit*, pp. 56–61.
59   Gößner, *Weltliche Kirchenhoheit*, pp. 6–69.
60   Ford, *Wolfgang Musculus*, pp. 111–29; Kießling, "Augsburg in der Reformationszeit", p. 29; see also Link, "Augsburg".
61   Jesse, *Geschichte*, p. 111; Kießling, "Doppelgemeinde", pp. 131–32.
62   Gößner, *Weltliche Kirchenhoheit*, pp. 92–94.

Christian community should be: the populace wanted to address economic and social inequities through the creation of a truly Christian society, while leaders embraced new opportunities to expand their guardianship.

In 1534, the guild-led government took a decisive step in favor of reform. It formed a committee on religious affairs and sought the endorsement of the city's legal advisors, a new group led by Doctors Konrad Hel, Claudius Pius Peutinger, and Lucas Ulstett. The council confidently declared its jurisdiction over preaching at the buildings they controlled: the Franciscan church, its dependent chapel of St. Jacob, and the preaching houses attached to three diocesan churches.[63] The Carmelite monks at St. Anna, who had once hosted Luther, turned over the convent in exchange for pensions, and the church remained closed until 1548. The council advanced the reformation of the city's churches by controlling the hiring of preachers, but the magistrates did not control all local churches. Catholic priests could still celebrate mass in the bishop's churches, as well as in the abbey of Sts. Ulrich and Afra, which was independent of both the city and the bishop. The council confined Catholic services to these churches and forbade them to hold their traditional public processions. Protestant preachers now reigned in the pulpits and enthusiastically urged their listeners to complete the Reformation.[64]

In 1537 they succeeded. Enthusiastic citizens elected an overwhelming number of Zwinglians to leadership positions in the guilds. The mayors, Hans Welser and Mang Seitz, and the new council immediately carried out a thorough reform of local church life. With a resounding seven-eighths majority, the council voted on 17 January to seize the bishop's churches for evangelical services, ban the Catholic Mass, and expel all clergy, monks, or nuns who would not become citizens and submit to taxation. Most Catholic clergymen and religious chose to leave the city peacefully; some turned over their property to the council for a pension or repurposing for charitable causes. Many monks and nuns resettled in affiliated convents in the region. Those nuns who refused to leave were consolidated in only two remaining houses, St. Ursula and St. Katharina, where they remained under the strict control of the authorities and were forbidden from hearing mass or receiving sacraments. Benedictines from the abbey of Sts. Ulrich and Afra departed peacefully but fought to retain ownership of their property. The schools at the cathedral, at St. Ulrich, and at St. Moritz were closed. Catholic residents were forbidden to leave the city to

---

63 Peutinger's father, the long-term city secretary Conrad Peutinger, opposed this move, but his influence on the council had waned: Gößner, *Weltliche Kirchenhoheit*, pp. 69, 77, 103–13; Kießling, "Augsburg in der Reformationszeit", pp. 29–30.

64 Immenkötter, "Kirche", pp. 398–99; Kießling, "Augsburg in der Reformationszeit", p. 30.

attend mass in the countryside, and the guards at the city gates were instructed to report those who did so. Wealthy Catholics retired to their country estates in protest.[65]

Although Augsburg had several popular and persuasive preachers, none influenced the design of Augsburg's Reformation as much as Martin Bucer of Strasbourg. The council called him to the city's service five times between 1531 and 1537. Bucer played an especially instrumental role in reconciling the differences between Lutheran and Zwinglian positions of the Eucharist, the interpretation of which had led to a bitter debate between Luther and Zwingli.[66] The controversy threatened to derail any chance of unity among Protestants and made it difficult for Zwinglian-leaning cities like Augsburg to cooperate with the Lutheran Saxons as members of the Schmalkaldic League,[67] which Augsburg had joined in January 1536. Ultimately, Bucer and Melanchthon orchestrated the Wittenberg Concord together with Luther in May 1536, which smoothed relations among League members by accepting a limited but real presence of body and blood in the Eucharist, a position that allowed room for interpretation.[68] Bucer also negotiated employment conditions for Augsburg's pastors in 1535 and was a major architect of the Augsburg church ordinance of 1537.[69]

This new church ordinance reflected the upper German reform movement based on the Strasbourg model. The upper German reformers were influenced by Zwingli, especially in terms of liturgy, but their reform differed in the degree of control placed in the hands of the city council. For example, Augsburg's ministers would not be allowed to use excommunication to discipline parishioners; rather, secular authorities would be firmly in charge of both public and private life, with clergy confined solely to preaching and spiritual guidance of their parishes.[70] The ordinance also made extensive changes in Christian worship, reducing the sacraments to two (baptism and the Eucharist) and the holy days to six, and abolishing private confession and clerical robes for the

---

65 Roth, *Augsburgs Reformationsgeschichte*, vol. 2, pp. 309–23; Immenkötter, "Kirche", pp. 400; Roper, *Holy Household*, pp. 212–14; Kießling, "Augsburg in der Reformationszeit", p. 31.
66 See Wandel (ed.), *Companion to the Eucharist*.
67 An alliance intended to provide collective defense for Protestant cities and territories from attempts to enforce the demands of the diet of 1530; see Chapter 6 of this volume.
68 Cameron, *European Reformation*, p. 165.
69 Roth, *Augsburgs Reformationsgeschichte*, vol. 2, pp. 309–71; Jesse, *Geschichte*, pp. 111–23.
70 Kießling, "Augsburg in der Reformationszeit", p. 31. The disastrous Anabaptist Kingdom of Münster in 1535 served as a warning to magistrates not to let spiritual leaders take over the government: see Arthur, *The Tailor-King*.

ministers, who took oaths of citizenship and loyalty to the council. Not surprisingly, the document remained vague on the matter of the Eucharist.

These changes meant that the Reformation in Augsburg ushered in changes in the governing of social life as well as changes in church doctrine and liturgy. The medieval church had held jurisdiction over the sacrament of marriage and the education of children, but the Augsburg council appropriated these powers for itself rather than turning them over to the new clergy.[71] The council established seven lay trustees (*Kirchenpröpste*) to oversee the churches, took control of the city's schools and poor-relief programs, and created a marriage court run by council members. In addition, it issued a police and discipline ordinance and appointed magistrates to police behavior and morals. The council thus managed to settle the religious controversies that had been plaguing Augsburg for the past twenty years while also expanding its own authority by assuming far greater control over religious and social life, with a goal of reforming not only the church, but also the moral lives of its citizens.[72]

7 Protestant Triumph and Eclipse

Despite its ambitious design, the church ordinance of 1537 resulted in barely a decade of official religious uniformity, let alone peace. Resistance remained passive but never disappeared.[73] Having defied the emperor, the council now sought protection through membership in the Schmalkaldic League, which eagerly welcomed the financial backing Augsburg could provide in case of war. Three civil servants, Dr. Gereon Sailer (civic physician), Georg Frölich (city secretary), and Sebastian Schertlin von Burtenbach (captain of the guard), cultivated close ties to Landgrave Philip of Hesse, one of the League's leaders. The city stockpiled weapons and ammunition, built up fortifications, and hired men-at-arms. Meanwhile, ministers like Keller and Musculus encouraged parishioners to embrace war and place themselves in God's hands.[74] Jakob Herbrot, a self-made businessman who rose through the ranks of the furrier's guild to become mayor, led the "war party" and welcomed the opportunity to defend the city's Reformation. On 1 July 1546 the city council voted in favor

---

71 Roper, *The Holy Household*, pp. 7–55.
72 Kießling, "Augsburg in der Reformationszeit", p. 31; Roper, *The Holy Household*, pp. 56–88, 165–205.
73 See Kießling et al. (eds.), *Im Ringen um die Reformation*, for case studies of the implementation of and resistance to reform in individual parishes.
74 Roth, *Augsburgs Reformationsgeschichte*, vol. 3, pp. 4–21; Kießling, "Augsburg in der Reformationszeit", pp. 32–33.

of war. Several of the wealthiest residents, including members of the Fugger, Welser, Baumgartner, Rehlinger, and Herwart families, declared their loyalty to the Habsburg emperor and departed. They paid fines to retain their citizenship rights, but loaned far greater sums to the emperor to support his war efforts.[75]

Under the command of Schertlin von Burtenbach, the League's troops conquered much of the territory south of Augsburg. The council envisioned creating a territory out of the bishop's diocese and spreading reform. Disorganized leadership within the League and a crucial alliance between Charles V and the Lutheran Duke Moritz of Saxony, however, led to the war's rather abrupt end. The emperor subdued one city after another, and Augsburg surrendered at the end of January 1547. On April 24, Charles V defeated the remaining Protestant princes at the Battle of Mühlberg and took the Elector Johann Frederick of Saxony and Landgrave Philip of Hesse (Duke Moritz's father-in-law) captive. The emperor then made his way to Augsburg for an extended stay.[76]

From August 1547 to August 1548, the city hosted the so-called "Armored Diet", during which the emperor, his brother King Ferdinand, and their allies occupied the city with their troops. This imperial diet produced the settlement known as the Augsburg Interim, which reinstated the old faith with very few concessions to Protestant sentiments in the hope that the Protestants would thus be guided back to Catholicism. The emperor viewed the Interim as a temporary measure that would eventually be superseded by the results of the church council underway at Trent. On 5 August 1547 Catholic Mass was celebrated in the cathedral for the first time in ten years.[77]

Augsburg's populace experienced the Schmalkaldic League's defeat up close by having to quarter hundreds of the emperor's troops in their homes, while financing the extravagant sums demanded as war reparations primarily via a steep hike in excise taxes on wine and beer.[78] Another casualty of war was the city's guild-led government; the emperor not only dismissed the standing council and mayors but removed the guilds from power entirely. In their stead, he gave patricians a disproportionate number of council seats and required that a majority of magistrates and one of the two mayors (now termed city wardens) always be Catholic to ensure the survival of the minority religion.[79]

---

75   Kießling, "Augsburg in der Reformationszeit", pp. 33–36; see also Häberlein, *The Fuggers of Augsburg*, pp. 188–89.
76   Kießling, "Augsburg in der Reformationszeit", p. 37.
77   Kießling, "Augsburg in der Reformationszeit", pp. 37–39; Immenkötter, "Kirche", pp. 401–02; Warmbrunn, *Zwei Konfessionen*, pp. 71–80.
78   Tlusty, "Public House"; see also Chapter 15 in this volume.
79   Naujoks (ed.), *Kaiser Karl V.*, pp. 56–59. See also Chapter 7 in this volume.

The cardinal-bishop of Augsburg, Otto Truchsess von Waldburg, also returned to take possession of the Catholic church's former buildings, rights, and privileges. He took his opportunity and obligation to renew the Catholic faith very seriously, employing effective preachers who appealed to secular audiences and inviting the Society of Jesus (Jesuits) to settle in the city. Nicholas Bobadilla, one of Ignatius of Loyola's original companions, came to Augsburg with 120 Spanish confessors who vividly demonstrated public displays of penitence during Lent of 1548. Monks and nuns from the various religious orders returned and reclaimed the convents that had belonged to them. Truchsess von Waldburg began the Counter-Reformation of Augsburg through spiritual leadership, but he also assiduously defended the church's rights and pursued compliance with the Interim.[80]

In addition to changes in government and the return of Catholicism, Protestants suffered attacks on their own worship and practices. The imposition of the Interim preserved only the Eucharist in both forms, clerical marriage, and a weak statement of justification by faith. All other revisions to doctrine and liturgy were revoked. When the new city council endorsed the Interim, a number of ministers, including Musculus and Johannes Karg, left the city because they would not comply with the new regulations after having preached against them.[81] Many ministers in the preaching houses under council jurisdiction, however, conformed outwardly in order to remain with their congregations. Worship services during the Interim often involved a minister giving the sermon, while a priest administered the sacraments. Meanwhile, a moderate form of Lutheranism based on the Augsburg Confession developed at St. Anna and the Franciscan church.

Considerable resentment was directed at the city government for bowing to the emperor and the Interim. Naturally, many citizens began to associate the return of Catholicism with the disempowerment of the guilds and occupation by foreign troops along with the loss of reformed worship. In the years after 1548, conflicts that arose between citizens identifying with different confessions reflect a level of animosity that was barely evident before the Schmalkaldic War and the Interim. Some altercations demonstrated open hostility to the city government for failing to protect the Protestants, with complainants advocating overturning the Interim and removing the Catholic clergy.[82] Tensions emerged from the association of confessional identities with

---

80   Immenkötter, "Kirche", p. 402. See also Groll (ed.), *Otto Truchseß von Waldburg*.
81   Jesse, *Geschichte*, pp. 136–40; Kießling, "Augsburg in der Reformationszeit", p. 39.
82   Zelinsky Hanson, *Religious Identity*, pp. 138–215.

political and social conditions. Unfortunately for Augsburg, this situation was only the beginning of the struggles to come.[83]

The next imperial diet took place in Augsburg in 1550–51, during which Charles V sought to enforce compliance with the Interim and unsuccessfully attempted to ensure the election of his Spanish son Philip as his heir in the Empire. In the process, he expelled nearly all local preachers and most of the teachers at the Protestant *Gymnasium*, as well as the lay custodians who had been overseeing the preaching houses. Protestant resentments continued to seethe in Augsburg as elsewhere in the Empire; when Elector Moritz of Saxony led a rebellion of princes against Charles V in 1552, a group of merchants rallied by the wealthy furrier Jakob Herbrot refused to defend the city, instead welcoming the Saxon army and seizing the opportunity to regain power and turn back the clock to 1537. Briefly, they resurrected the guild regime and renewed church reform. Backed by the Fuggers again, however, the emperor soon emerged victorious, retaking the city in August 1552. Once again, Augsburg was burdened with reparations and the quartering of imperial troops.[84]

By this time, however, the Interim was a moot point. On August 10, 1552, in negotiations with Moritz and other German princes, Charles had agreed to temporary religious freedom for Lutherans throughout the Empire and revoked the Interim. The Treaty of Passau signaled the recognition that coexistence of the two faiths was the only path to peace, laying the groundwork for the conclusion of a permanent agreement to be worked out at the next imperial diet. In the meantime, with Lutheranism the only legally recognized Protestant faith, the council sought Lutheran ministers rather than Zwinglians for the vacated posts in the preaching houses.

The most famous of the imperial diets that met in Augsburg during the Reformation era took place in 1555. At this historic conference, King Ferdinand (Charles's brother and now heir to the imperial throne) and the princes and cities of the Empire agreed to disagree on matters of religion.[85] Putting into effect a principle later termed *cuius regio, eius religio* ("whose realm, his religion"), the princes and magistrates secured the right to choose the religion of the subjects within their realms and enforce conformity or exile on dissenters. The peace again recognized only Lutheranism (i.e., adherents to the Augsburg Confession) and Roman Catholicism as viable choices. Despite the suppres-

---

83   See e.g. Warmbrunn, *Zwei Konfessionen*.
84   Kießling, "Augsburg in der Reformationszeit", p. 39. Herbrot was subsequently to face much of the blame for the disastrous result of the alliance: see Chapters 7 and 15 in this volume.
85   Charles V had by this time begun divesting himself of his imperial duties and did not attend: Kohler, *Karl V.*, pp. 341–84.

sion of Zwinglian or upper German reform, the Religious Peace of Augsburg prevented war in the Empire for over sixty years.[86]

The peace treaty excluded the free cities of mixed confession from the principle of "whose realm, his religion", creating a policy out their inclination to tolerate the minority religion inside their walls. In cities with a bi-confessional population like Augsburg, this resulted in an unusual circumstance for the day: Catholics and Protestants living openly in close proximity to each other and even sharing government, if somewhat unevenly. Any attempt to infringe upon each other's religious beliefs or practice, from any quarter, was considered a violation of the peace.[87] Though this move reflected political and economic expediency, it was an early step in encouraging the development of the principle of religious freedom for its own sake. The new status quo in Augsburg created a sometimes fragile atmosphere of cooperation and competition that shaped the city's development in the following centuries.[88]

Augsburg is often cited as a microcosm of the Empire in the sixteenth century. It experienced religious upheavals that permanently transformed the old society and overturned assumptions about the universal church and the sacred commune. Secular authorities expanded their jurisdiction into matters of conscience, and the Catholic Church lost control over all Christians who identified as Protestants. At various phases of its development, Augsburg nurtured varieties of reformers (from humanists to Anabaptists) and negotiated tough choices on a subject fraught with disagreements. Despite the sometimes overwhelming desire to eliminate controversy and create a unified religion for the sake of stability, coexistence and a policy of enforced tolerance emerged as the best option for establishing peace.

Bibliography

Unpublished Primary Sources
Stadtarchiv Augsburg (StadtAA)
  Geheime Ratsprotokolle.
  Literaliensammlung, Zuchtordnung, 5 December 1529.
  Urgichten.

---

86 On the imperial diet of Augsburg and the ensuing religious peace, see Hoffmann et al. (eds.), *Als Frieden möglich war*; Gotthard, *Augsburger Religionsfrieden*.
87 Warmbrunn, *Zwei Konfessionen*, p. 1; Kießling, "Vom Ausnahmefall zur Alternative", pp. 120–21.
88 Corpis, *Crossing the Boundaries;* Warmbrunn, *Zwei Konfessionen*, pp. 125–30; see also Chapter 11 in this volume.

Published Primary Sources

Naujoks, E. (ed.), *Kaiser Karl V. und die Zunftverfassung: Ausgewählte Aktenstücke zu den Verfassungsänderungen in den oberdeutschen Reichsstädten (1547–1556)*, Stuttgart, 1985.

Tlusty, B.A. (ed.), *Augsburg in the Reformation Era: An Anthology of Sources*, Indianapolis, 2012.

Secondary Literature

Amberg, J. van, *A Real Presence: Religious and Social Dynamics of the Eucharistic Conflicts in Early Modern Augsburg 1520–1530*, Leiden, 2012.

Arthur, A., *The Tailor-King: The Rise and Fall of the Anabaptist Kingdom of Münster*, New York, 1999.

Bellot, C., "'Auf welsche art, der zeit gar new erfunden.' Zur Augsburger Fuggerkapelle", in G.M. Müller (ed.), *Humanismus und Renaissance in Augsburg: Kulturgeschichte einer Stadt zwischen Spätmittelalter und Dreißigjährigem Krieg*, Berlin and New York, 2010, pp. 445–90.

Blickle, P., *The Revolution of 1525: The German Peasants' War from a New Perspective*, Baltimore, 1981.

Brady, T.A., *German Histories in the Age of Reformations, 1400–1650*, Cambridge, 2009.

Broadhead, P., "Popular Pressure for Reform in Augsburg, 1524–1534", in W.J. Mommsen, P. Alter and R.W. Scribner (eds.), *Stadtbürgertum und Adel in der Reformation*, Stuttgart, 1979, pp. 80–87.

Broadhead, P., "Guildsmen, Religious Reform, and the Search for the Common Good: The Role of Guilds in the early Reformation in Augsburg", *The Historical Journal* 39, 3 (1996), pp. 577–97.

Cameron, E., *The European Reformation*, 2nd ed., Oxford, 2012.

Corpis, D., *Crossing the Boundaries of Belief: Geographies of Religious Conversion in Southern Germany*, Charlottesville and London, 2014.

Creasman, A., *Censorship and Civic Order in Reformation Germany, 1517–1648: "Printed Poison and Evil Talk"*, Farnham, 2012.

Ford, J.T., "Wolfgang Musculus and the Struggle for Confessional Hegemony in Reformation Augsburg, 1531–1548", Ph.D. diss., University of Wisconsin, 2000.

Gößner, A., *Weltliche Kirchenhoheit und reichsstädtische Reformation: Die Augsburger Ratspolitik des "milten und mitleren weges" 1520–1534*, Berlin, 1999.

Gotthard, A., *Der Augsburger Religionsfrieden*, Münster, 2004.

Gray, E.F., "Von der Ottmarskapelle zur Gemeindekirche: Heilig Kreuz", in Kießling, Safley and Wandel (eds.), *Im Ringen um die Reformation*, pp. 215–40.

Groll, T. (ed.), *Kardinal Otto Truchseß von Walburg (1514–1573)*, Neustadt an der Aisch and Augsburg, 2015.

Guderian, H., *Die Täufer in Augsburg. Ihr Geschichte und ihr Erbe. Ein Beitrag zur 2000-Jahr-Feier der Stadt Augsburg*, Pfaffenhofen, 1984.

Häberlein, M., *The Fuggers of Augsburg: Pursuing Wealth and Honor in Renaissance Germany*, Charlottesville and London, 2012.

Hoffmann, C.A., Johanns, M., Kranz, A., Trepesch, C. and Ziedler, O. (eds.), *Als Frieden möglich war. 450 Jahre Augsburger Religionsfrieden* (exhibition catalogue), Regensburg, 2005.

Immenkötter, H., "Kirche zwischen Reformation und Parität", in G. Gottlieb, W. Baer, J. Becker, J. Bellot, K. Filser, P. Fried, W. Reinhard and B. Schimmelpfennig (eds.), *Geschichte der Stadt Augsburg von der Römerzeit bis zur Gegenwart*, Stuttgart, 1984, pp. 391–412.

Jesse, H., *Die Geschichte der Evangelischen Kirche in Augsburg*, Pfaffenhofen, 1983.

Kießling, R., "Eckpunkte der Augsburger Reformationsgeschichte", in idem, Safley and Wandel (eds.), *Im Ringen um die Reformation*, pp. 29–42.

Kießling, R., "Eine 'Doppelgemeinde': St. Moritz und St. Anna", in idem, Safley and Wandel (eds.), *Im Ringen um die Reformation*, pp. 105–71.

Kießling, R., "Vom Ausnahmefall zur Alternative: Bikonfessionalität in Oberdeutschland", in Hoffmann et al. (eds.), *Als Frieden möglich war*, pp. 119–30.

Kießling, R., *Bürgerliche Gesellschaft und Kirche in Augsburg im Spätmittelalter. Ein Beitrag zur Strukturanalyse der oberdeutschen Reichsstadt*, Augsburg, 1971.

Kießling, R., "Augsburg in der Reformationszeit", in J. Kirmeier, W. Jahn and E. Brockhoff (eds.), *"... wider Laster und Sünde". Augsburgs Weg in die Reformation* (exhibition catalogue), Cologne, 1997, pp. 17–43.

Kießling, R., T.M. Safley and L.P. Wandel (eds.), *Im Ringen um die Reformation. Kirchen und Prädikanten, Rat und Gemeinden in Augsburg*, Epfendorf, 2011.

Kohler, A., *Karl V, 1500–1558. Eine Biographie*, Munich, 2005.

Künast, H.-J., "Martin Luther und der Buchdruck in Augsburg, 1518–1530", in H. Gier and R. Schwarz (eds.), *Reformation und Reichsstadt – Luther in Augsburg*, Augsburg, 1996, pp. 65–77.

Künast, H.-J., *"Getruckt zu Augspurg". Buchdruck und Buchhandel in Augsburg zwischen 1468 und 1555*, Tübingen, 1997.

Link, A., "Augsburg – Wolfgang Musculus", in M. Welker, M. Beintker and A. de Lange (eds.), *Europa Reformata. Reformationsstädte Europas und ihre Reformatoren*, Leipzig, 2016, pp. 35–44.

Lutz, H., *Das Ringen um deutsche Einheit und kirchliche Erneuerung, 1490–1648*, Frankfurt and Berlin, 1983.

Packull, W.O., *Mysticism and the Early South German – Austrian Anabaptist Movement, 1527–1531*, Scottsdale, 1977.

Rabe, H., *Deutsche Geschichte 1500–1600. Das Jahrhundert der Glaubensspaltung*, Munich, 1991.

Rogge, J., *Für den Gemeinen Nutzen. Politisches Handeln und Politikverständnis von Rat und Bürgerschaft in Augsburg im Spätmittelalter*, Tübingen, 1996.

Roper, L., *The Holy Household: Women and Morals in Reformation Augsburg*, Oxford, 1989.

Roper, L., *Martin Luther: Renegade Prophet*, London, 2016.

Roth, F., *Augsburgs Reformationsgeschichte*, 4 vols., Munich, 1901–11.

Safley, T.M., "Zentrum und Peripherie: Die Gemeinden Zu den Barfüßern und St. Georg", in Kießling, Safley and Wandel (eds.), *Im Ringen um die Reformation*, pp. 45–104.

Scheller, B., *Memoria an der Zeitenwende. Die Stiftungen Jakob Fuggers des Reichen vor und während der Reformation (ca. 1505–1555)*, Berlin, 2004.

Sieh-Burens, K., *Oligarchie, Konfession und Politik im 16. Jahrhundert. Studien zur sozialen Verflechtung der Augsburger Bürgermeister und Stadtpfleger von 1518 bis 1618*, Munich, 1986.

Tlusty, B.A., "The Public House and Military Culture in Germany, 1500–1648", in B. Kümin and B.A. Tlusty (eds.), *The World of the Tavern: The Public House in Early Modern Europe*, Aldershot, 2002, pp. 136–56.

Wandel, L.P., "Die Geschichte des Christentums", in Kießling, Safley and Wandel (eds.), *Im Ringen um die Reformation*, pp. 15–24.

Wandel, L.P. (ed.), *A Companion to the Eucharist in the Reformation*, Leiden, 2014.

Wurm, J.P., *Johannes Eck und der oberdeutsche Zinsstreit 1513–1515*, Münster, 1997.

Zelinsky Hanson, M., *Religious Identity in an Early Reformation Community: Augsburg, 1517 to 1555*, Leiden and Boston, 2009.

Zorn, W., *Augsburg. Geschichte einer europäischen Stadt*, 3rd ed., Augsburg, 1995.

CHAPTER 11

Catholic-Protestant Coexistence

Marjorie E. Plummer and B. Ann Tlusty

During the early Reformation in Germany, various reformed ideologies were debated not only in churches, courts, and council houses, but also in the streets, shops, and public houses where ordinary residents lived their day-to-day lives. The confessional directions usually associated with reform movements (Lutheran, Zwinglian, Schwenckfelders, Anabaptists, and others) were not yet fully conceptualized at the outset of the Reformation. Boundaries of religious identifications emerged gradually over the course of the sixteenth and seventeenth centuries in a process that involved laypeople and politicians as well as theologians and clergy. According to standard historiography, this process of confession-building or "confessionalization" was characterized by a mostly top-down process of social disciplining and state-building designed to enforce doctrinal conformity and create alliances between rulers and institutionalized religion. Rulers imposed Christian morality and discipline on a populace that was often receptive, in part because of their own views of a moral community.[1] The result was both a stronger sense of religious and communal identity and a more powerful role for secular rulers in controlling the lives of their populace.[2] Critics of the confessionalization theory point to its failure to differentiate sufficiently among the many competing ideas and interest groups that characterized the Reformation, while recent scholarship recognizes the fluid nature of confessional boundaries and raises questions about the top-down emphasis, highlighting instead the negotiating power of popular demands for reform.[3]

In Augsburg, decisions by local rulers to remain neutral and follow a "middle way" in the early years of the Reformation allowed multiple religious viewpoints to flourish, at times openly. Even after the Religious Peace of 1555 established Catholicism and the Augsburg Confession as the only acceptable

---

1 Roper, *Holy Household*, esp. pp. 7–55.
2 Zeeden, *Entstehung der Konfessionen*; Schilling, "Konfessionalisierung"; Reinhard, "Gegenreformation"; Hsia, *Social Discipline*, pp. 1–3.
3 Lotz-Heumann, "The Concept of 'Confessionalization'"; Broadhead, "Guildsmen"; Corpis, *Crossing the Boundaries*, p. 8; Ziegler, "Kritisches zur Konfessionalisierungsthese"; see also Brady, "Confessionalization", and the other contributions in *Confessionalization in Europe*; and Chapters 6 and 10 in this volume.

religious practices, evidence suggests that some thoughtful residents continued to follow non-conformist religious paths. As long as they did so quietly and did not appear to pose a threat to the authorities or to civic peace, repercussions were limited. Of greater concern to civic leaders were those who violated the Religious Peace by openly insulting rival faiths or inciting violence in the name of religion. Local rulers had good reason to fear the effects of this kind of harsh rhetoric. By the end of the sixteenth century, increasingly volatile language from preachers and pamphleteers contributed to a greater sense of confessional solidarity among Lutherans and Catholics, hardening the lines between them and stoking a culture of mutual fear that threatened civic peace.

Relations between the confessions in Augsburg and throughout the Empire reached their breaking point during the destructive Thirty Years' War (1618–48), which left Augsburg's population traumatized by violence and reduced in number by more than half as a result of military action, disease, war-induced famine, and migration.[4] The institution of religious parity at the conclusion of the war is often cited as an early step towards a secular, tolerant society; at the same time, however, the agreement effectively institutionalized religious difference, in effect calcifying the confessional divide.[5]

1 The Struggle for Identity, 1548–82

At twilight on the evening of 5 October 1582, subprioress Anna Jacobäa Fuggerin (1547–87) unexpectedly fled St. Katherina's convent after 18 years as a nun, letting herself out of the garden with a key made by Hans Jacob Hermann, a neighboring goldsmith.[6] Two theories emerged in Augsburg about why she had done this. The first assumption was that Anna Jacobäa had been seduced by the goldsmith, so the city council arrested and questioned Hermann.[7] Only after his testimony revealed that the goldsmith had been an unwitting party to the escape did a second conjecture gain traction. The Fuggers argued that Anna Jacobäa had come into contact with evangelical ideas about female monastic life through letters sent by her Lutheran uncle Ulrich Fugger from Württemberg, including one containing her escape plan delivered by a Württemberg student in town for the 1582 Diet of Augsburg.

---

4   See Chapter 15 in this volume.
5   Corpis, *Crossing the Boundaries*, pp. 9–10.
6   Fugger Archives Dillingen 1.1.33, fol. 6v (6 October 1582). Letter from Philip Eduard Fugger to Octavian Secundus Fugger.
7   StadtAA, Strafamt Urgichten 1582, Hans Jacob Hermann.

The timing of Anna Jakobäa's flight could not have been more problematic for the Fugger family, whose members had been striving to expand their local influence and to boost Catholicism over the previous decades as part of their ongoing political and business interests.[8] While the church and political authorities assumed that evangelical books must have been smuggled in, they did not entertain another possibility: that there may well have been older nuns in the convent who were well-versed in evangelical rituals, ideas, and practices. St. Katherina's convent, like the rest of Augsburg, had undergone a series of significant confessional shifts over the previous decades that left the religious identity of its residents fluid and volatile. The spiritual and personal life of Anna Jakobäa was directly influenced by those changes. Like many others living in Augsburg during the mid-sixteenth century, Anna Jakobäa lived with elements of various different faiths and probably could not be fully categorized as either Catholic or Protestant, even as she fled her convent.

Between the 1547–48 Diet of Augsburg and that of 1582, the fluidity of confessional politics and personal beliefs within the city and beyond led to sometimes turbulent and sometimes surprisingly harmonious interactions among individuals professing various religious beliefs and embracing a spectrum of religious rituals and practices. These differences and exchanges fed the continued religious diversity within the city, which characterized the local spiritual landscape. At the same time, Augsburg emerged as a battleground for political and religious policies of the emperor and pope on one side and various political and religious leaders supporting the Augsburg Confession on the other, as each party sought to achieve religious uniformity. The six imperial diets that took place in the city during this period contributed to ongoing discussions of religion and sparked both intra- and inter-confessional conflicts. Continued daily interactions among merchants, neighbors, families, and individuals of differing religious beliefs, however, necessitated tentative accommodations and pragmatic toleration. Thus, any study of religious relations in Augsburg needs to consider how both conflict and coexistence shaped the diverse and dynamic religious situation during this period.

Confessional relations in Augsburg between the Religious Peace and the Thirty Years' War have received less attention from scholars than the more volatile periods before 1555 and after 1618, perhaps in part because it was a stage of relative peace. Those who have examined this period are often influenced by the legal system of bi-confessionalism and political parity established by the Peace of Westphalia after 1648, thus seeking to understand the process of confessionalization from the assumption that the city was characterized by a

---

8 Dauser, *Informationskultur*, pp. 113–15, 337–38.

clearly defined bi-confessional system prior to the seventeenth century. More recent historians of the Reformation have argued that such a clearly bifurcated system could not yet have existed because the confessions themselves had not fully formed. Concentrating instead on religious diversity and hybridity as more useful concepts for understanding religious practice and belief during the mid- to late sixteenth century, scholars are beginning to differentiate between labels that were leveled at non-conformists, often derogatorily, and the actual religious identity and practice of those so described.[9]

As scholars have paid more attention to labeling in the sixteenth century, patterns of belief start to look somewhat different. While it is not uncommon to see individuals and groups being accused of being *unchristian* or *uncatholic*, other terms describing distinct confessional groups in contemporary documents indicate that neither the terminology nor the associated belief systems were clearly defined before the seventeenth century. The use of sectarian terms such as Zwinglian (*zwinglische*), Anabaptist (*wiedertäuferisch*), heretical (*ketzerisch*), and devilish (*teufelisch*) by polemical authors and politicians often served only to distance the religious activities of targeted others from the faith these authors defined as true and Christian.[10] Such terms did not accurately depict the belief, self-understanding, or rituals of the other, but rather served as shorthand for describing something perceived as not truly Christian.

This approach raises questions about the assumptions of previous generations of historians, who often took such labels at face value. Recent scholars, for example, have begun to question the categorization of the so-called "Zwinglian" phase of Augsburg's Reformation because practices and beliefs associated with this movement did not necessarily follow Zwingli's theology. The label "Zwinglian" was more likely levied at anyone who deviated from a specific practice of the Augsburg Confession, or whose beliefs were hybrid, fluid, or merely different from the perceived right religion. This does not mean, however, that true religious diversity did not exist. As microstudies have shown, a significant number of followers of Zwingli, Bucer, Luther, Schwenckfeld, the various Anabaptist sects, and other religious groups continued to reside in Augsburg during the later sixteenth century and beyond.[11]

---

9   Strecker, *Augsburger Altäre*, pp. 20–22. Strecker makes this point by demonstrating the difficulty of identifying specific "confessional" art. For a model for future research, see Luebke, *Hometown Religion*, esp. pp. 1–19.

10 See Burnett, "Picards"; Mayes, "Triplets"; and Luebke, "*Confessionisten*".

11 Clasen, *Anabaptism*; Zelinsky Hanson, *Religious Identity*, pp. 19–105; Gritschke, "*Via Media*". More work needs to be done to understand how these groups interacted with the official religious groups and what role they played in local religious interactions.

It was into this diverse religious environment that Emperor Charles V arrived for the "Armored Diet" of 1547–48.[12] Fresh from his victory in the Schmalkaldic War, Charles had sent ahead a request to the Augsburg city council that he and his party be allowed to hold Catholic services in St. Katherina's for the duration of the imperial diet. The directive appeared to promise that the Catholic devotional services would end with the conclusion of the diet.[13] A few days later, however, the city council also ordered that chalices, monstrances, and other devotional objects be handed over to Cardinal Otto Truchsess von Waldburg, bishop of Augsburg.[14] Charles' intentions to recatholicize the city became clear in 1548 with the conclusion of the Interim decree requiring a return to the religious practices of the Roman church. To ensure that his religious policies remained in place, Charles replaced the predominantly evangelical, guild-dominated town council with a largely Catholic, patrician, oligarchical council.[15]

Estimates on the confessional makeup of the population prior to the Interim suggest that approximately 30,000 Augsburgers attended churches that had broken with Rome or participated in other religious communities, while only 3,000, or about ten per cent, continued to attend traditional services overseen by priests adhering to Rome, a proportion that remained static until the 1560s.[16] These numbers are of course generalized, given that confessional identities remained fluid and ambiguous. Thus it is hardly surprising that the Interim decree proved hard to implement in practice in spite of the Catholic-dominated government, the continued presence of imperial troops, and pressure from imperial officials. Augsburgers felt the intent of the Interim in many areas of daily life, especially when the new marriage court was suspended and the educational reforms overturned. On 12 August 1548, the new city council summoned all Augsburg clergy to swear an oath to obey the emperor, not to speak against the Interim decrees, and to return to previous religious practices, such as wearing their vestments and celebrating mass.[17] Most clergymen signed, but attempted to continue some form of modified religious service at least for a while.[18] Failure to follow the new regulations had consequences. Most of the schoolmasters at St. Anna's refused to comply on 31 August 1551

---

12   See Chapter 10 in this volume.
13   StadtAA, Ratsbücher, no. 21, fol. 41r (22 October 1547).
14   StadtAA, Ratsbücher, no. 21, fol. 42r (24 October 1547). For more on the bishop, see the articles in Groll (ed.), *Kardinal Otto Truchseß von Waldburg*.
15   See Chapter 7 in this volume.
16   Hoffmann, "Das kirchliche Augsburg", p. 272; Warmbrunn, *Zwei Konfessionen*, p. 136.
17   Roth, *Augsburg Reformationsgeschichte*, vol. 4, pp. 206–12.
18   See, for instance, the departure of Johannes Ehinger: Wallenta, "Ehinger".

and were banished.[19] The nuns of St. Katherina's, many of whom had complied with previous commands to wear secular clothing, were informed in July that they needed to return to their traditional habits. A month later, Charles' court counselor Heinrich Haas (or Hase) arrived at the convent and threatened the women: either they start wearing their habits or they "would be tossed from the convent with nary a Heller or penny".[20]

Catholic clergy, who have received less scholarly attention than Protestants, seem to have renewed public practice, but much of this shift back to traditional practice occurred under pressure from outside forces. Cardinal Otto, for instance, returned to his residence in the city after the banishment of the bishop of Augsburg to Dillingen; and in 1550–51, the emperor brought back his military forces for a new imperial diet, reassembling soldiers, imperial officials, and Catholic clergy in Augsburg and launching a renewed effort to ensure compliance from clergy and laity.[21] The result of this constant oversight was local upheaval. Riots broke out between evangelical laity and Spanish soldiers outside of St. Ulrich's in late summer 1551, and most of the evangelical clergy were banished from the city in late August. The emperor and his officials continued their attempts to root out the remnants of non-Catholic devotional practice until their departure in late October 1551.[22]

The decade following the Interim decree complicated the balance between religious beliefs and obedience to secular authority, but had a limited impact on the religious practices of the population.[23] Although individual devotional practice during this period remains under-researched, what we do know suggests that clergy and laity continued to practice according to their beliefs in church and at home between 1548 and 1552. After the signing of the Treaty of Passau in August 1552, which allowed toleration of the Augsburg Confession in the Empire, some of the local evangelical clergymen returned to their parishes and the city council filled vacant positions in previously Protestant churches with clergy from Wittenberg recommended by Lutheran theologian Philipp Melanchthon.[24] By 1553, the city accepted a new church order written by the

---

19 Hoffmann, "Das kirchliche Augsburg", p. 281.
20 StadtAA, Ratsbücher, no. 22, 2, fols. 22r (7 July 1548), 40r–v (7 Aug. 1548); on Haas see Chapter 7 in this volume.
21 Roth, *Augsburg Reformationsgeschichte*, vol. 4, pp. 293–389.
22 Roth, *Augsburg Reformationsgeschichte*, vol. 4, pp. 383–86; Warmbrunn, *Zwei Konfessionen*, pp. 132–37.
23 For recent discussions of the impact of the Interim on the confessional politics of the city council, see Dunwoody, *Conflict*, pp. 140–203; on the clergy during the Interim, see Hough, *The Peace of Augsburg*, ch. 2.
24 Warmbrunn, *Zwei Konfessionen*, p. 8; Hough, *The Peace of Augsburg*, ch. 2.

local clergy, restored the marriage court, and reintroduced the evangelical schoolmasters.[25]

The quick overturning of the imperial attempts to restore religion to its traditional form did not mean anything like a unified Protestantism within the city. Theological debates between Georg Melhorn, a clergyman from Wittenberg, and Johann Bächlin and Johannes Meckhart, local Augsburg clergy, showed that divisions still existed among those professing the Augsburg Confession.[26] Such debates were not unique to Augsburg: concern about dissent led the emperor to include a clause in his imperial police ordinance of 1548 censoring texts coming from outside of the city during the Interim, and the Augsburg city council enforced his decree.[27] Non-conformist groups such as the Schwenckfelders also continued to attract local laypeople.[28] Nor did relations between Catholics and non-Catholics improve; the Interim left Catholics in a better legal and political position, but the events had increased hostility among the populace. Evidence collected by Michele Zelinsky Hanson suggests a rising number of cases of anti-Catholic polemic and insults against Catholics coming before the city council, related to growing hostility against Catholics during the occupation of the city between 1548 and 1552.[29]

In the resolution of the diet of 1555, known commonly as the Religious Peace of Augsburg, the emperor granted the legal right of the "adherents of the Augsburg Confession" to worship, but also protected "adherents of the Catholic belief."[30] Provision 27 required imperial cities with significant numbers of both Catholics and Protestants within their walls to grant to both confessions freedom of "religion, belief, devotional customs, and rituals" and the right to remain without losing their property or rights.[31] Based on what had become a longstanding reality, Augsburg remained bi-confessional.[32] Like many earlier imperial agreements on religion, the 1555 Religious Peace of Augsburg was intended as a temporary measure in preparation for a church council to resolve theological differences.

The Religious Peace validated the return of the evangelical clergy but did not eliminate religious diversity within the city. The agreement did not address the

---

25 Weidemann, *Augsburger Pfarrerbuch*.
26 StadtAA, Literaliensammlung, Melhorn-Selekt; Gritschke, *"Via Media"*, pp. 269–74; Hough, *The Peace of Augsburg*, ch. 4.
27 Creasman, *Censorship*, pp. 51–56.
28 Zelinsky Hanson, *Religious Identity*, pp. 144, 149–51, 200–7; Gritschke, *"Via Media"*, pp. 27–37.
29 Zelinsky Hanson, *Religious Identity*, pp. 144–46, 174–200; see also Chapter 10 in this volume.
30 *Augsburger Reichsabschied, 1555*, pars. 15 and 16.
31 *Augsburger Reichsabschied, 1555*, par. 27; Creasman, *Censorship*, pp. 119–20.
32 Dixon, "Urban Order", pp. 8–9; see also Chapter 10 for more on this provision.

emergence of new variations within the faith groups, nor did it address the ongoing ambiguity of those considering themselves "adherents of the Augsburg Confession". Conflicts continued among the clergy as each sought to propagate their theological interpretations of how the Augsburg Confession and the "old Catholic belief" should be practiced. While both religious groups shared the government, Catholics retained a slim majority in the council disproportionate to their numbers at large, which did not help local confessional relations.[33]

As one of only a handful of towns in which both government and populace were confessionally mixed, Augsburg's city council issued repeated decrees over the next decades forbidding confessional slurs and demanding that clergy promote "peaceful and friendly cohabitation", thus introducing new definitions of what constituted a religious crime.[34] Instead of targeting one particular confession, the council now sought to maintain peace by focusing on those who insulted other religions or threatened violence. At the same time, experiments with various kinds of religious diversity emerged within each faith group as clergy, councilmen, and the laity struggled to figure out how religious groups would relate to one another and what the limits of these designations meant.

There were periodic attempts to discourage more radical forms of religious practice. In 1563, for instance, the city council renewed the questioning of individuals suspected of being Schwenckfelders, a process they continued sporadically against both Schwenckfelders and Anabaptists throughout the late sixteenth century, although with considerably less virulence than had been the case three decades earlier.[35] They were even less likely to question those suspected of mild dissent from the still broadly-defined acceptable religious practices. Meanwhile, Catholics and Protestants continued to share living and working spaces. In 1580, Montaigne commented upon a visit to Augsburg that harmonious mixed marriages were common there, the party more eager for the match often happily converting to please their marriage partner.[36] Some scholars have defined this moment as evidence of peaceful coexistence and a precursor to tolerance.[37]

---

33   Warmbrunn, *Zwei Konfessionen*, pp. 132–33.
34   Tlusty (ed.), *Augsburg*, pp. 24–25. For comparisons of the bi-confessional cities, see Warmbrunn, *Zwei Konfessionen*, and François, *Unsichtbare Grenze*, pp. 231–36. Other bi-confessional towns included Biberach, Dinkelsbühl, Kaufbeuren, and Ravensburg, all relatively small by comparison.
35   Gritschke, *"Via Media"*, pp. 34–35; see also Chapter 10 in this volume.
36   Hoffmann, "Das kirchliche Augsburg", p. 286. Montaigne was lodging at the time with a Catholic innkeeper whose wife was Protestant: Tlusty, *Bacchus*, pp. 155, 242, n. 39.
37   See, for instance, Schulze, "Augsburg und die Entstehung der Toleranz".

But the peace remained tenuous, and was repeatedly undermined by rumors circulating among the laity that the Catholic city council intended to banish the Protestant clergy and repress Lutheran practice. Whether inspired by the memory of the 1551 banishments, contemporary banishments in neighboring towns, or lurid reports of bloody massacres in far-away France, the claims violated the Religious Peace, leading perpetrators to be investigated. Their testimony reveals a high level of anxiety among Protestants.[38] Neighbors of different faiths also occasionally engaged in religious disputes, which sometimes started over unrelated issues and escalated to include confessional insults. In order to avoid provoking further confessional quarrels, the authorities tended to handle such incidents cautiously, allowing private rather than public retractions of insults and levying only standard fines for quarreling rather than the harsher punishments allowed by the law. Only in the case of dissemination of inflammatory literature were more serious penalties imposed.[39]

Confessional lines were drawn more sharply as the century progressed, particularly after the final session of the Catholic Council of Trent in 1563 and movement within the Augsburg Confession towards the 1577 Formula of Concord, both of which established clearer religious creeds. As the confessions clarified their doctrinal positions, a new cohort of clergy replaced the older generation of pastors and priests. Among the first of these was Petrus Canisius, a Jesuit, who took over as cathedral preacher in 1559 at the invitation of Cardinal Otto Truchsess von Waldburg. Canisius held the position until 1566.[40] Several Wittenberg-educated clergymen came to Augsburg as well, most notably Georg Müller (Mylius), who arrived in 1572 to serve as deacon at Holy Cross and eventually (from 1579) as pastor and superintendent at St. Anna.[41] Both men were informed by the new confessional orthodoxy and sought to establish greater conformity to these dictates within their jurisdictions.

The lay reaction to Canisius was particularly divisive in part because of his ties to the city council and the bishop. On one side, several individuals were brought before the council for spreading rumors and participating in verbal

---

38 Hoffmann, "Konfessionell motivierte und gewandelte Konflikte", pp. 99–100; Creasman, *Censorship*, pp. 124–25.
39 The volume of such incidents is difficult to assess, as local records of fines for insults rarely include the nature of slurs: Hoffmann, "Konfessionell motivierte und gewandelte Konflikte", pp. 110–13; on censorship see Creasman, *Censorship*, pp. 48–49.
40 Rummel, "Petrus Canisius", pp. 48–49.
41 Appold, "Der Fall Georg Mylius", pp. 157–58.

and written attacks both against Canisius and against the city council for supporting him.[42] On the other, a growing number of Augsburgers were swayed to attend Catholic churches. Most notably, Canisius was able to convert Ursula von Liechtenstein, wife of Georg Fugger, and Sibilla von Eberstein, wife of Marcus (Marx) Fugger, to Catholicism in 1561.[43] Besides demonstrating the success of Canisius' efforts, these two conversions are also evidence of the prevalence of mixed marriages even among the most ardent Catholic elite families. According to later reports, it was Canisius himself who convinced Ursula von Liechtenstein to have her teenage daughter Anna Jakobäa profess at St. Katherina's, only for her to flee the bonds of her vows eighteen years later. These conversions among the Fuggers were not the only successes for Canisius and the Jesuits in strengthening local Catholicism. Through a combination of conversion and immigration from the surrounding countryside, the share of Catholics grew from around ten per cent of the population in the 1560s to 20 per cent in 1583 and 27 per cent by 1618.[44]

During the 1570s and early 1580s, both religious groups pursued greater institutional legitimacy by founding schools, educating and appointing clergy, and establishing set texts and liturgies. In 1579, Hans Fugger donated 30,000 gulden to establish the Jesuit school of St. Salvator, which was opened in 1582. This move prompted the development of a foundation for the expansion and support of the Protestant high school (*Gymnasium*) at St. Anna's to ensure that it could continue to support educating students despite the competition of a free education at St. Salvator.[45]

The Fuggers' activist efforts to promote Jesuit teaching proved to be a thorn in the side of local Protestant theologians, Müller in particular. Theological differences between the Jesuits and Müller were reflected in bitter accusations from the pulpit and in print that hardened the lines of confessional identity among the populace and led to numerous episodes of recalcitrant behavior justified on the basis of religious conscience.[46] Müller openly accused the Catholics – under increasing Jesuit influence – of forcing Protestant servants and hospital patients to participate in Catholic worship, taking weapons into Protestant church services, and replacing the local guard with foreign spies. Müller's claim that Catholics married to Protestants were encouraged by the

---

42   Creasman, *Censorship*, pp. 124–28.
43   Fisher, *Music and Religious Identity*, p. 8, n. 9; Schad, *Die Frauen*, pp. 59–69; Conrad, "Stifterinnen und Lehrerinnen", pp. 215–16.
44   Hoffmann, "Das kirchliche Augsburg", pp. 272, 280; Warmbrunn, *Zwei Konfessionen*, pp. 135–36.
45   Hoffmann, "Das kirchliche Augsburg", pp. 280, 282.
46   Hoffmann, "Konfessionell motivierte und gewandelte Konflikte", pp. 110–12.

Jesuits to pressure their spouses into conversion and to refuse to honor promises to raise the children as Lutherans suggest that mixed marriages were still a reality; his constant attacks, however, hardly supported peaceful coexistence in the household.[47] The council, meanwhile, had continued its policy of holding both confessions to the Religious Peace and warning them to ignore "reckless and unfounded talk" by trouble-makers.[48] But the repeated admonitions did little to stem the tide of partisan polemic. The stage was set for violence.

2   The Calendar Conflict and the Road to Religious War, 1582–1618

Stoked in part by Müller's divisive rhetoric, rumors of an impending suppression of Lutheranism reached a fever pitch in the early 1580s, when the introduction of the new (Gregorian) calendar put relations between Catholics and Protestants in the city to the test. The revised and more accurate calendar was introduced by Pope Gregory XIII in 1582, and adopted by Augsburg's city council in early 1583. Named after the pope and endorsed by the Catholic emperor, the calendar appeared to many Protestants, including members of Augsburg's bi-confessional council, as an interference with the celebration of church holidays.[49] Less than two months after announcing the reform, the council began issuing decrees admonishing the Augsburgers to ignore inflammatory talk and "hostile rumors" about the calendar, which, they insisted, was simply a political expediency and not a religious decision. Rumors of an imminent forced recatholicization continued to spread, however, not only from the pulpit, but also through the streets in the form of gossip, protest songs, printed pamphlets, and anonymous pasquinade.[50]

Fears were exacerbated by the decision of the emperor and the Catholic-dominated council to recruit professional mercenaries in late 1583 for protection against "rebellious and disobedient" elements among the townsmen, and to increase the presence of foreign troops again in the spring of 1584. The citizenry regarded these outsiders not only as tools of the Catholic powers, but also as usurpers of the local militia's right to provide for defense of their own homes and neighborhoods. According to Müller, the Catholic soldiers, many of

---

47   StadtAA, Kalenderstreitakten 26, fol. 41r; SuStBA, 4° Cod. Aug. 152, G2v–G4v.
48   "leichtferttige, doch vngegründte reden". StadtAA, Chroniken 10, Jörg Siedeler, fols. 155r–158r.
49   See Chapter 7 in this volume.
50   Tlusty, *Martial Ethic*, pp. 247–58.

whom were Spanish, were just waiting for the go-ahead to begin their "Parisian Wedding" or "Antwerp Martin's Night", terms that recalled the bloody massacres of Protestants on St. Bartholomew's Day in Paris (1572) and in Antwerp during the "Spanish Fury" (1576).[51] Civic authorities were particularly concerned because some artisans arrested for anti-authoritarian talk who repeated these fears under interrogation cited multiple sources for their information, including neighbors, anonymous pasquinade, or visiting peasants from the Bavarian countryside.[52]

Things came to a head in June 1584, when the council decided to remove Müller from his post as pastor and superintendent at St. Anna's and escort him out of the city. News of Müller's arrest spread quickly through the streets, seeming to verify the worst fears of the Lutheran populace. A crowd interfered with the guards and freed Müller. In a state of collective fear, Protestant men, armed with the weapons and military equipment required of every householder as a condition of citizenship, swarmed into the streets and gathered at the city hall.[53] Having been fed rumors of impending plunder and massacres for weeks, householders living near the city hall panicked at the sight of the crowd, and shots were fired from windows, one of them injuring the captain of the guard. For a moment, the city teetered on the brink of armed insurrection.

Yet the incident ended peacefully. Augsburg's civic leaders moved quickly to defuse the situation, and the crowd soon dispersed. In order to avoid creating martyrs and increasing confessional animosity, most participants in the uprising were later pardoned, some with imperial intercession, and the city returned to a state of fragile peace. The council, whose members were also divided on the calendar issue, reached a compromise and took steps to consolidate their power.[54]

But the traumatic events of 1584 left their mark on the populace as well as on council politics. Interrogations both of citizens involved in the incident and of council members reveal that many of their concerns stemmed from political and economic grievances rather than from religious conviction.[55] What

---

51   Müller, *Augspurgische Händel*, F2r–v, G2v; Kingdon, *Myths*, pp. 1–6. Müller blamed the Jesuits for the bloodbath in Paris (*Augspurgische Händel*, C1r–v).
52   Tlusty (ed.), *Augsburg*, pp. 39–45.
53   Keeping and bearing arms for local defense was a right and duty of all male citizens: Tlusty, *Martial Ethic*. The oft-repeated but incorrect claim that Augsburg's citizens stormed the armory to obtain weapons in this incident apparently originated with an erroneous statement produced in the nineteenth century by Ferdinand Kaltenbrunner: Kaltenbrunner, "Der Augsburger Kalenderstreit", p. 521.
54   See Chapter 7 in this volume.
55   Ibid.

FIGURE 11.1 Failed attempt to expel the Protestant preacher Dr. Georg Müller from Augsburg, 1582, woodcut from illustrated broadsheet
STAATS- UND STADTBIBLIOTHEK AUGSBURG, GRAPH 22/12

followed, however, was not a segregation of religion from politics, but the opposite. The coalescing of confessional identity around concerns that included social and economic hierarchies and collective fear of political oppression widened the confessional divide. The resulting bonds of solidarity fostered within the rival denominations did not disappear any time soon. City authorities, having found common ground in their pursuit of stability, thus returned to a policy of enforcing tolerance while taking steps to reduce the threat of another armed insurrection by curbing the role of civilian men in civic defense and forbidding them to assemble publicly without permission from the authorities.[56]

The threat of violence between Catholics and Protestants ensured that the council would continue primarily to target incendiary talk and confessional insults rather than enforcing strict religious conformity, leaving room for some non-conformist religious experimentation to continue. An example is provided by a group of Schwenckfeld-leaning citizens arrested and interrogated in

---

56   StadtAA, Kalenderstreitakten 26, fol. 53.

1598 for failing to attend church. Although Schwenckfeld's teachings were officially forbidden, the men were released with merely a warning once it became clear that their unconventional religious practice was limited to quiet contemplation of alternative ideas at home. This was in spite of the fact that the goldsmith David Altenstetter had testified rather remarkably that "He has in the matter of religion thus far been free … [H]e doesn't really adhere to either one or the other of the confessions." Altenstetter's neighbor Martin Künle, a furrier, went even further, admitting that although he read both Schwenckfelder and Lutheran texts at home, "if he [were] to tell the truth, then he has to say that Schwenckfelder's books, writings, and faith appeal to him the most".[57] In contrast, the Lutheran loden weaver Anton Riedenburger, who also attracted attention in the same year for staying away from church, was banished after admitting to worshipping at home in accordance with the old calendar, criticizing local religious leaders, and accusing Lutheran pastors of spying for the council.[58]

These cases of religious non-conformity testify to the diversity of religious expression that continued to challenge Catholic and Lutheran dominance. Notable is that Riedenburger, a pious but disobedient Lutheran, was treated much more harshly than either Altenstetter, who professed no specific denomination at all, or Künle, who openly admitted preferring a forbidden faith.[59] Throughout the latter half of the sixteenth century, punishments for seditious talk and public slurs against established confessions were significantly more severe than those imposed on religious eccentrics whose religious experimentation took place in private. They would become even harsher as the Empire headed into the Thirty Years' War: by 1618, composers of texts deemed to be aimed "only at embittering and inflaming the common folk" faced public whipping, defaming on the pillory, and permanent banishment.[60]

---

57   Not until a decade later, in 1609, was Altenstetter finally recalled before the magistrates and released again after testifying that he had decided on the Lutheran faith; Künle had died in the meantime: Tlusty (ed.), *Augsburg*, pp. 54–62. See also Roeck, *Ketzer, Künstler und Dämonen*.
58   Hoffmann, "Konfessionell motivierte und gewandelte Konflikte", p. 115.
59   Social status may have played a role as well: goldsmiths and furriers were considerably higher on the socio-economic scale than loden weavers. According to Caroline Gritschke, Altenstetter, Künle, and others in their circle were in contact with other Schwenckfelders in Augsburg and elsewhere: *"Via Media"*, pp. 36–37; see also StadtAA, Literaliensammlung, Schwenckfelder-Selekt.
60   StadtAA, Anschläge und Dekrete 1490–1649, part 1, no. 61; Creasman, *Censorship*, pp. 205–12.

3 The Winds of War, 1618-48

As was the case throughout the Holy Roman Empire, Augsburg suffered greatly during the Thirty Years' War, often as a result of confessional politics. The city went through a series of confessional shifts between 1629 and 1648, each of which led to religious repression of one confession or the other depending on the fortunes of war. Details about these shifts and the experiences of Augsburg's citizenry are provided elsewhere in this volume.[61] Here the emphasis will be on specific confessional strategies employed by the populace and the authorities to assert their own faith and triumph over that of their rivals. Inevitably, wartime abuses created a culture of martyrdom on both sides that only strengthened internal identification with the respective faiths.

Against a background of social tension resulting from rising food prices and a widening gap between rich and poor, the early seventeenth-century city faced waves of extreme inflation, inclement weather, shortages of grain, and (in 1628) a virulent attack of bubonic plague. All these combined to convince many Christians that they were suffering punishment for having angered God. Naturally, what God was so angry about was a matter of opinion, so blaming and punishing those with different beliefs became one of many strategies for dealing with crisis. Others included hoarding and withholding grain stores, calling for increased shows of collective piety, refining military weaponry and tactics, casting spells and saying blessings, identifying witches for execution as enemies of God, and doing whatever was necessary to prepare oneself for the final Day of Judgment. All of these strategies helped to keep people from feeling powerless in the face of uncertainty.

During the worst phases of the war, many citizens found comfort in their faith. Confessional solidarity was supported in these troubled times by a network of printed, oral, and handwritten media that provided both news and religious affirmation. Confessional polemic, political propaganda, and sensational news stories, in many cases based on little more than rumor or speculation, flooded the Empire during the Thirty Years' War, leading to repeated efforts on the part of Augsburg's magistrates to impose censorship. The common man, they lamented in 1618, naively believing "lies to be the truth," was "moved to anger, hate, envy, unrest, and quarreling" by these wartime rumors, which were transmitted orally even to those who could not read.[62]

Religious messaging often took the form of song, especially among Protestants, who had made a tradition of singing as protest and fellowship.

---

61 See Chapters 7 and 15.
62 Creasman, *Censorship*, p. 187.

Several of those arrested in the wake of the calendar conflict of 1584 had been specifically accused of writing and singing political and confessional songs, which gave the authorities ample reason for concern. Songs about the calendar conflict in Augsburg were extremely popular and made the rounds throughout Germany, keeping the flames of dissent alive for years. The medium of song had a number of advantages over the written word as a means of communicating controversial ideas and confronting institutions of power, including its appeal to many audiences and its capacity to invoke emotion and invite sympathy from listeners.[63] This was particularly true in the case of familiar psalms and religious songs, as well as songs of protest that used the same melodies, which was a standard tactic for writers and singers of seditious songs. Reusing recognizable melodies also made the songs easier to remember and repeat, meaning they could be orally transmitted, which made them much more difficult for censors to control than written or printed texts. Singing in these contexts was an inherently social activity that fostered bonds of identity and belonging among singers and listeners.[64] For these reasons, popular songs appeared subversive to early modern authorities.

Singing became even more suspect in wartime, particularly during the imperial occupation that began in 1629 to enforce the Edict of Restitution. With Protestantism forbidden in the city, expressions of faith in song helped to raise Lutheran spirits and strengthen networks of confessional identity that now lacked institutional support. Arrests of several singers and songwriters during this phase of the war reveal that anti-Catholic songs were circulating widely in manuscript and oral form. Protestants also gathered by the hundreds to sing at the graveyard of St. Stephan's, and in 1630 the weaver Thomas Schueler, holding Lutheran prayer meetings in his home, led visitors in singing hymns so loudly that neighbors were able to join in from their own homes in a pious neighborhood sing-along. Arguments by these perpetrators that their songs were intended only for comfort, that they were moved to sing by the Holy Spirit, or (in Schueler's case) that they were only singing psalms "at home" did not placate the authorities. Producers and purveyors of protest songs and anti-authoritarian texts of any kind were treated harshly by wartime censors, typically leading to defamation and banishment.[65]

---

63   Guillorel, "Folksongs", pp. 304–05.
64   Grijp and Dieuwke "Introduction", p. 4.
65   Creasman, *Censorship*, pp. 194–211; Tlusty (ed.), *Augsburg*, pp. 63–64; Stuart, *Defiled Trades*, pp. 128–48. Schueler was banished without defamation for leading the neighborhood in singing psalms, but craftsmen who composed and circulated anti-Catholic songs received harsher punishments. As Stuart argues, public whipping, exposure on the pillory, and interrogation under torture all had a defaming effect.

Another confessional tool that was applied regularly by both Catholic and Protestant officials in Augsburg was a policy of forced quartering of foreign troops as a kind of punishment. The practice began when Gustavus Adolphus entered the city in 1632 and took over Catholic schools, the various buildings associated with the cathedral, and the Catholic welfare settlement known as the Fuggerei as quarters for his Swedish troops; eventually, soldiers were placed in Catholic homes as well. The ruinous costs of maintaining these troops also fell largely upon the unfortunate Catholic citizenry.[66] When the city again fell into the hands of the Catholics in 1635, the situation quickly reversed, with the physical and financial burdens of quartering now falling upon the Protestant members of the bi-confessional city. Wealthier citizens for the most part avoided having to put up with soldiers in their homes by paying ruinously large contributions, which were also extracted overwhelmingly from Protestants after 1635.[67]

The case of the well-known architect Elias Holl[68] is illustrative of how quartering intensified the confessional bitterness festering at this stage of the war. Because of his Protestant faith, the architect was dismissed as master builder in 1629, reinstated during the Swedish occupation, and then fired again in 1635. Soon after his second dismissal, Holl filed a request for relief from the "unbearable burden" of quartering four soldiers in his home. Now unemployed and an old man, he lamented, he had neither the funds nor the physical strength to deal with the burden of quartering. Holl tried to shore up his request by recalling his important service to the city in creating beautiful buildings, noting that he had made "no difference between the religions" in his artistic efforts. His arguments, however, fell on deaf ears. The Catholic chief quartermaster in his response accused the "non-Catholic city builder" of hypocrisy and affectation, pointing out that "during the time of the Swedish trouble" Holl had treated Catholics with "ill will, terror, defiance, derision, mockery, and prejudice", and had even supported the imposition of quartered troops on Catholics. The accuracy of the quartermaster's accusations is difficult to assess, but as the city was now in Catholic hands, the soldiers remained in Holl's home.[69]

Also contributing to confessional division was the Catholic council's decision to disarm the Protestant populace in the wake of the Swedish occupation. In 1635, Protestants were forced to relinquish individually-owned property consisting of 1,681 firearms, 2,443 swords, 2,374 pole arms, 1,531 sets of armor,

---

66 SuStBA, 2° Cod. Aug. 123 (Singularia Augustana), fol. 33.
67 Tlusty, "The Public House and Military Culture".
68 See Chapter 22 of this volume.
69 StadtAA, Militaria 55, 1518–1638, 21–28 July 1635.

and numerous pistols, crossbows, battle axes, and daggers. Disarmament was an act imbued with significant meaning for early modern German men, serving not just to limit their capacity to resort to arms, but also to shame them, for it stripped them of their right to resist and thus relegated them to unarmed roles normally held by women, children, and marginal groups who did not share the rights of citizens.[70] Protestants remained at a disadvantage in weapons ownership vis-à-vis Catholics until the end of the war: according to the military muster of 1645, Lutheran households held only about half as many guns and swords as Catholics. The numbers were especially low in the poorer neighborhoods of St. Jacob's Suburb (*Jakober Vorstadt*), where most of the artisans who participated in the armed riot of 1584 had resided.[71]

4   Parity

The Peace of Westphalia, concluded in 1648, reestablished the principle of *cuius regio, eius religio*, now also recognizing Calvinism, which had meanwhile gained considerable ground throughout Europe. Calvinism was not an option in Augsburg, however, which remained bi-confessional. The principle of religious parity within all government offices as it was instituted in Augsburg was absurdly detailed, but by remaining in force until the dissolution of the Empire in 1806, it achieved its aim of institutionalizing power-sharing for good.[72] The parity rules in Augsburg required equal representation not only on the Large and Small Councils, but at every level of the civic bureaucracy, from tax collectors to city guards.

Meanwhile, the local Catholic minority had grown to around a third of the populace and continued to grow (due more to migration from the countryside than to conversion) so that Catholics made up a majority of the populace by the later eighteenth century.[73] Over the course of this period both Catholics and Lutherans coalesced around separate identities that were cultural as well as religious. According to Etienne François, the confessions between 1650 and 1800 were divided by an "invisible boundary" that was made increasingly visible by behavioral choices such as the differentiation of given names, confessionally-defined gestures (kneeling, genuflecting, etc.), use of identifying architectural

---

70   Tlusty, *Martial Ethic*, pp. 72, 142–43, 262.
71   Economic hardship between 1635 and 1645 would have made replacing relinquished arms difficult; at the same time, some Protestants may have been hesitant to reveal weapons in their homes out of fear they would again be taken away: Tlusty, *Martial Ethic*, pp. 142–43.
72   *Die Westfälischen Friedensverträge vom 24. Oktober 1648*, Art. 5, pars. 3–10.
73   François, *Die unsichtbare Grenze*, pp. 252–60.

features on homes and churches, and external and internal domestic decor. The two confessions eventually came to occupy parallel worlds in which social life and family relationships rarely overlapped. Mixed marriages and conversions were viciously condemned from the pulpit and became increasingly rare. The hardening of boundaries between the confessions in some ways functioned as a stabilizing factor, since clear boundaries are less likely to be disputed. Thus despite hostile attitudes in matters of religion, Augsburgers during the hundred years following the Peace of Westphalia rarely engaged in the kind of open conflict that would endanger economic relationships or civic peace.[74]

Even if religious conversions were less common, they nonetheless continued, sometimes for reasons of economic or social expediency – suggesting that religious convictions were not always as firm as demanded by doctrine.[75] Ironically, the institution of parity itself could occasionally force conversions, for example among people belonging to the so-called "dishonorable" trades, whose options for marriage partners were limited. These social outcasts included the local executioner, skinner, and outhouse cleaner, all city positions held by only one person at a time.[76] According to the parity decree issued in 1664 to address these cases, the executioner would always be Catholic and the outhouse cleaner Protestant, leaving the skinner's post having to alternate by confession. This meant that when a skinner died, his heirs either had to convert or seek employment elsewhere. When the Catholic skinner Michael Leichnam died in 1664, therefore, he was replaced by Johann Scheppelin, a Protestant skinner from Memmingen, and the Leichnam family relocated to Burgau. A skinner, however, like any master craftsman, was expected to marry upon taking up an independent position, and the most obvious match for a member of this highly dishonorable trade was the daughter of the Catholic executioner, Susanna Hartmann. So Hartmann converted to Lutheranism in order to make the match. Twelve years later, Scheppelin died and was replaced by a Catholic skinner from Bavaria. In a tradition resembling that of artisans in other trades, the new skinner married his predecessor's widow, and Susanna Hartmann converted a second time. Suffering from complications in childbed a year later, however, Hartmann demonstrated the internalization of her twelve-year Lutheran identity by a deathbed conversion back to Lutheranism, a decision that was opposed by her husband but remained her legal right under the terms

---

74   François, *Die unsichtbare Grenze*, pp. 167–219, 227–30.
75   Corpis, *Crossing the Boundaries*, pp. 178–225.
76   Stuart, *Defiled Trades*, p. 1. Skinners were tasked with removing animal carcasses, disposing of the bodies of suicide victims, destroying wild and rabid dogs, and assisting the executioner.

of the Religious Peace.[77] Many soldiers' wives also decided to convert in order to adapt to local circumstances as a result of their mobile lifestyles.[78]

Conversions remind us that throughout the period from the Reformation to the eighteenth century, Lutherans and Catholics – and at times people of less clearly-defined denomination – continued to share the city's spaces, institutions, resources, and government, and usually did so peacefully. Even in the worst phases of the Thirty Years' War, there was nothing unusual about people of mixed confessions attending the same wedding or mixing at other social occasions. In fact, many confessional conflicts between neighbors that have left traces in the records resulted from arguments that broke out in public houses while Catholics and Protestants were sharing tables and drinks.[79] As neighbors and co-workers who continued to share space and government, the confessions learned to cooperate in a spirit of peaceful coexistence that privileged a common civic identity over confessional sectarianism, even if it was not always characterized by tolerance.[80] Confessional conflicts continued to arise, sometimes encouraged from the pulpit by exuberant preachers, but serious religious violence was kept in check.

Both confessional groups also staged public demonstrations of their faith to affirm their confessional identities and delineate religious boundaries. On the Catholic side, sermons by visiting mendicant preachers, who voiced polemical attacks on Protestant "heretics", often drew large crowds, and processions highlighted the presence of Catholics in the public sphere. Augsburg's Protestants, on the other hand, annually celebrated the *Friedensfest* (peace festival) to commemorate their liberation through the Peace of Westphalia from "papism" and religious despotism. Special artworks were commissioned from local artists for the occasion and distributed among Protestant schoolchildren as illustrated leaflets. The *Friedensfest* continues to be celebrated in Augsburg as a local holiday on 8 August down to the present day.[81]

Augsburg was unusual in 1648 as the only bi-confessional city with large populations of both Catholics and Protestants. These distinctive local conditions increased pressure for peaceful coexistence. The city's uniqueness lessened by the later eighteenth century, however, as confessional difference took a back seat to economic development and was increasingly depoliticized, so that a growing number of other cities accepted confessionally-mixed governments

---

77 Stuart, *Defiled Trades*, pp. 80–82.
78 Corpis, *Crossing the Boundaries*, pp. 10, 64.
79 Tlusty, *Bacchus*, pp. 155–56; Corpis, *Crossing the Boundaries*, pp. 1–4.
80 Gray, *Good Neighbors*, pp. 213–17.
81 François, *Die unsichtbare Grenze*, pp. 143–67, 177–90.

and eventually embraced enlightened notions of religious freedom.[82] The citizens of Augsburg, meanwhile, continued overwhelmingly to identify themselves either as Catholic or Lutheran well into the twentieth century.

Bibliography

Unpublished Primary Sources
Stadtarchiv Augsburg (StadtAA)
    Anschläge und Dekrete 1490–1649.
    Chroniken 10, Jörg Siedeler.
    Kalenderstreitakten 26.
    Literaliensammlung, Melhorn-Selekt and Schwenckfelder-Selekt.
    Militaria 55, 1518–1638.
    Ratsbücher 21, 22.
    Strafamt, Urgichten 1582.
Staats- und Stadtbibliothek Augsburg (SuStBA)
    2° Cod. Aug. 123 (Singularia Augustana).
    4° Cod. Aug. 152.
Fugger Archives Dillingen
    1.1.33.

Published Primary Sources
Müller, G., *Augspurgische Händel*, Wittenberg, 1586.
Tlusty, B.A. (ed.), *Augsburg During the Reformation Era: An Anthology of Sources*, Indianapolis, 2012.

Secondary Literature
Appold, K., "Der Fall Georg Mylius: Biographie als Mittel konfessioneller Identitätsbildung", in I. Dingel and G. Wartenberg (eds.), *Die Theologische Fakultät Wittenberg 1502 bis 1602*, Leipzig, 2007, pp. 155–72.
Brady, T.A., "Confessionalization: The Career of a Concept", in Headley, Hillerbrand and Papalas (eds.), *Confessionalization in Europe, 1555–1700*, pp. 1–17.
Broadhead, P.J., "Guildsmen, Religious Reform, and the Search for the Common Good: The Role of Guilds in the Early Reformation in Augsburg", *The Historical Journal* 39, 3 (1996), pp. 577–97.

---

82   François, *Die unsichtbare Grenze*, pp. 23–43.

Burnett, A.N., "Picards, Karlstadtians, and Oecolampadians: (Re-)Naming the Early Eucharistic Controversy", in J.F. Harrington and M.E. Plummer (eds.), *Names and Naming in Early Modern Germany*, Oxford, 2019.

Clasen, C.-P., *Anabaptism. A Social History, 1525–1618: Switzerland, Austria, Moravia, South and Central Germany*, Ithaca, 1972.

Conrad, A., "Stifterinnen und Lehrerinnen: Der Anteil von Frauen am jesuitischen Bildungswesen", in R. Berndt S.J. (ed.), *Petrus Canisius S.J. (1521–1597). Humanist und Europäer*, Berlin, 2000, pp. 205–24.

Corpis, D., *Crossing the Boundaries of Belief: Geographies of Religious Conversion in Southern Germany*, Charlottesville and London, 2014.

Creasman, A., *Censorship and Civic Order in Reformation Germany, 1517–1648: "Printed Poison and Evil Talk"*, Farnham, 2012.

Dauser, R., *Informationskultur und Beziehungswissen. Das Korrespondenznetz Hans Fuggers (1531–1598)*, Tübingen, 2008.

Dixon, C.S., "Urban Order and Religious Coexistence in the German Imperial City: Augsburg and Donauwörth, 1548–1608", *Central European History* 40 (2007), pp. 1–33.

Dunwoody, S., "Conflict, Confession, and Peaceful Coexistence in Augsburg, 1547–1600", Ph.D diss., University of Chicago, 2012.

Fisher, A.J., *Music and Religious Identity in Counter-Reformation Augsburg, 1580–1630*, Farnham, 2004.

François, E., *Die unsichtbare Grenze. Protestanten und Katholiken in Augsburg, 1648–1806*. Sigmaringen, 1991.

Gray, E.F., "Good Neighbors: Architecture and Confession in Augsburg's Lutheran Church of Holy Cross, 1525–1661", Ph.D. diss., University of Pennsylvania, 2004.

Grijp, L.P. and van der Poel, D., "Introduction", in idem and W. van Anrooij (eds.), *Identity, Intertextuality, and Performance in Early Modern Song Culture*, Leiden, 2016, pp. 1–38.

Gritschke, C., *"Via Media". Spiritualistische Lebenswelten und Konfessionalisierung. Das süddeutsche Schwenckfeldertum im 16. und 17. Jahrhundert*, Berlin, 2006.

Groll, T. (ed.), *Kardinal Otto Truchseß von Walburg (1514–1573)*, Neustadt an der Aisch and Augsburg, 2015.

Guillorel, É., "Folksongs, Conflicts and Social Protest", in D. van der Poel, L.P. Grijp, and W. van Anrooij (eds.), *Identity, Intertextuality, and Performance in Early Modern Song Culture*, Leiden, 2016, pp. 287–307.

Headley, J.M., Hillerbrand, H.J. and Papalas, A.J. (eds.), *Confessionalization in Europe, 1555–1700: Essays in Honor and Memory of Bodo Nischan*, Aldershot, 2004.

Hoffmann, C.A., "Konfessionell motivierte und gewandelte Konflikte in der zweiten Hälfte des 16. Jahrhunderts: Versuch eines mentalitätsgeschichtlichen Ansatzes am Beispiel der bikonfessionellen Reichsstadt Augsburg", in P. Frieß and R. Kießling (eds.), *Konfessionalisierung und Region*, Constance, 1999, pp. 99–120.

Hoffmann, C.A., "Das kirchliche Augsburg in der konfessionellen Konkurrenz", in H. Flachenecker and R. Kießling (eds.), *Urbanisierung und Urbanität. Der Beitrag der kirchlichen Institutionen zur Stadtenentwicklung in Bayern*, Munich, 2008, pp. 269–94.

Hough, A., *The Peace of Augsburg and the Meckhart Confession: Moderate Religion in an Age of Militancy*, Oxford, 2019.

Hsia, R.P., *Social Discipline in the Reformation: Central Europe 1550–1750*, London and New York, 1988.

Kaltenbrunner, F., "Der Augsburger Kalenderstreit", *Mittheilungen des Instituts für Oesterreichische Geschichtsforschung* 1 (1880), pp. 497–539.

Kingdon, R.M., *Myths about the St. Bartholomew's Day Massacres 1572–1576*, London, 1988.

Lotz-Heumann, U., "The Concept of 'Confessionalization': A Historiographical Paradigm in Dispute", *Memoria y Civilización* 4 (2001), pp. 93–114.

Luebke, D.M., *Hometown Religion: Regimes of Coexistence in Early Modern Westphalia*, Charlottesville and London, 2016.

Luebke, D.M., "*Confessionisten, Calvinisten, Tibben*: Nomenclatures of Legal Exclusion in Northwestern Germany, 1535–1650", in J. Harrington and M.E. Plummer (eds.), *Names and Naming in Early Modern Germany*, Oxford, 2019.

Mayes, D., "Triplets: The Holy Roman Empire's Birthing of Catholics, Lutherans, and Reformed in 1648", in J. Harrington and M.E. Plummer (eds.), *Names and Naming in Early Modern Germany*, Oxford, 2019.

Reinhard, W., "Gegenreformation als Modernisierung? Prolegomena zu einer Theorie des konfessionellen Zeitalters", *Archiv für Reformationsgeschichte* 68 (1977), pp. 226–52.

Roeck, B., *Eine Stadt in Krieg und Frieden. Studien zur Geschichte der Reichsstadt Augsburg zwischen Kalenderstreit und Parität*, 2 vols., Göttingen, 1989.

Roeck, B., *Ketzer, Künstler und Dämonen. Die Welten des Goldschmieds David Altenstetter*, Munich, 2009.

Roper, L., *The Holy Household: Women and Morals in Reformation Augsburg*, Oxford, 1989.

Roth, F., *Augsburgs Reformationsgeschichte*, 4 vols., Munich, 1901–11.

Rummel, P., "Petrus Canisius und Otto Kardinal Truchseß von Waldburg", in J. Oswald and P. Rummel (eds.), *Petrus Canisius: Reformer der Kirche. Festschrift zum 400. Todestag*, Augsburg, 1996, pp. 41–66.

Schad, M., *Die Frauen des Hauses Fugger von der Lilie (15.–17. Jahrhundert). Augsburg – Ortenburg – Trient*, Tübingen, 1989.

Schilling, H., "Die Konfessionalisierung im Reich: Religiöser und gesellschaftlicher Wandel in Deutschland zwischen 1555 und 1620", *Historische Zeitschrift* 246 (1988), pp. 1–45.

Schulze, W., "Augsburg und die Entstehung der Toleranz", in J. Burkhardt and S. Haberer (eds.), *Das Friedenfest. Augsburg und die Entwicklung iner neuzeitlichen Tolerenz-, Friedens-, und Festkultur*, Augsburg, 2000, pp. 43–60.

Strecker, F., *Augsburger Altäre zwischen Reformation (1537) und 1635. Bildkritik, Repräsentation und Konfessionalierung*, Münster, 1998.

Stuart, K., *Defiled Trades and Social Outcasts: Honor and Ritual Pollution in Early Modern Germany*, Cambridge, 1999.

Tlusty, B.A., *Bacchus and Civic Order: The Culture of Drink in Early Modern Augsburg*, Aldershot, 2001.

Tlusty, B.A., "The Public House and Military Culture in Early Modern Germany", in B. Kümin and B.A. Tlusty (eds.), *The World of the Tavern: The Public House in Early Modern Europe*, Aldershot, 2002, pp. 136–56.

Tlusty, B.A., *The Martial Ethic in Early Modern Germany: Civic Duty and the Right of Arms*, Basingstoke, 2011.

Wallenta, W., "Ehinger", in G. Grünsteudel, G. Hägele and R. Frankenberger (eds.), *Augsburger Stadtlexikon*, 2nd ed., Augsburg, 1998, p. 374.

Warmbrunn, P., *Zwei Konfessionen in einer Stadt. Das Zusammenleben von Katholiken und Protestanten in den paritätischen Reichsstädten Augsburg, Biberach, Ravensburg und Dinkelbühl von 1548 bis 1648*, Wiesbaden, 1983.

Weidemann, H., *Augsburger Pfarrerbuch. Die evangelischen Geistlichen der Reichsstadt Augsburg, 1524–1806*, Nuremberg, 1962.

Zeeden, E.-W., *Die Entstehung der Konfessionen. Grundlagen und Formen der Konfessionsbildung im Zeitalter der Glaubenskämpfe*, Munich, 1965.

Zelinsky Hanson, M., *Religious Identity in an Early Reformation Community: Augsburg, 1517 to 1555*, Leiden and Boston, 2009.

Ziegler, W., "Kritisches zur Konfessionalisierungsthese", in P. Frieß and R. Kießling (eds.), *Konfessionalisierung und Region*, Constance, 1999, pp. 41–53.

Electronic Resources

Augsburger Reichsabschied, 1555. URL: http://www.lwl.org/westfaelische-geschichte/portal/Internet/finde/langDatensatz.php?urlID=739&url_tabelle=tab_quelle [30.04.2018].

Die Westfälischen Friedensverträge vom 24. Oktober 1648: Texte und Übersetzungen (Acta Pacis Westphalicae, Supplementa electronica, 1). URL: http://www.pax-westphalica.de/ipmipo/ [14.01.2018].

CHAPTER 12

Urban Society: Inequality, Poverty, and Mobility

Mark Häberlein and Reinhold Reith

Like most pre-modern urban societies, Augsburg was highly stratified. While some inhabitants were wealthy and a few were fabulously rich, most were living in humble circumstances. The first part of this chapter surveys the evidence for the city's social stratification from Augsburg's outstanding set of tax records. The tax data suggest that social inequality grew in times of economic expansion and was reduced during the crisis of the Thirty Years' War; nonetheless it remained a persistent feature of urban life over the centuries. The following two sections focus on craftsmen and their families, who made up the majority of Augsburg's population, first concentrating on the household and guild organization of production and on patterns of labor recruitment, and then exploring labor markets. The migration patterns of journeymen underscore that Augsburg was perceived as a place of opportunity for some crafts, while others experienced little inter-regional mobility. Considering that a substantial portion of the population was living at or below the poverty line, the city's major public and private welfare initiatives and institutions will be surveyed next. The final section of this chapter shows that Augsburg's economic and social woes manifested themselves in numerous instances of labor unrest, with journeymen regularly expressing their grievances through strikes and other disturbances and weavers resorting to open revolt in the late eighteenth century.

1   Wealth and Inequality: The Evidence from Tax Registers

The imperial city's tax office kept annual registers, which were organized topographically and listed each household's property assessment. A series of these tax registers that begins in 1346 and continuously extends from 1389 to 1717 survives, providing historians with the opportunity to reconstruct the social structure of Augsburg over a period of more than three centuries. Tax payments were based on a proportional assessment of householders' taxable wealth, with real estate being assessed at half the rate of movable property (especially cash and financial investments). Items of daily use like furniture, clothes, jewelry, and foodstuffs were generally tax-exempt. Tax rates were annually fixed by the city council and fluctuated in the late Middle Ages. In the sixteenth century, real estate was usually taxed at 0.25 per cent and movable goods at 0.5 per cent. Individuals were assessed every three to seven years; thus profits garnered in long-distance trade or major losses manifested themselves in sudden leaps and drops in tax assessments. Propertyless inhabitants paid a head tax which was called the *Habnit-Steuer* ("have-not tax"). In the sixteenth and seventeenth centuries, this head tax, which was levied on all household heads, usually amounted to 30 pfennigs. Moreover, the council sought to attract wealthy immigrants by contracting with them for a fixed sum, which freed them from the obligation to disclose their property. Jakob Fugger the Rich was granted exemption from declaring his wealth in return for an annual lump sum (originally 1,200 gulden) in 1516. Other wealthy individuals and families followed suit, and in 1549 the city exempted all households who paid a "rich tax" of 600 gulden in gold from the obligation to declare their wealth.[1]

As this overview shows, several factors complicate the analysis of Augsburg's social structure: variations in assessment rates over time, the failure of tax officials to distinguish between immobile and mobile wealth in the registers, and privileges granted to wealthy individuals. Nonetheless, historians have been able to sketch a general picture of the city's social pyramid in certain years and identify developments over time.

For the late medieval period, Peter Geffcken has analyzed the ways in which property assessments were calculated and has reconstructed wealth assessments from 1396 to 1521. His aggregate data show that the total assessed wealth of Augsburg's inhabitants more than doubled from about 450,000 gulden in 1400 to 950,000 gulden in 1448. Subsequently, it fell to 725,000 gulden in 1466 before growing massively to roughly 3.2 million gulden in 1516. A severe economic crisis in the third quarter of the fifteenth century thus separated a period of significant growth in the first half of the century and a spectacular growth period during the late fifteenth and early sixteenth centuries, which coincided with Augsburg's emergence as a major commercial and financial center. Total wealth grew by 4 per cent per annum between 1492 and 1516. Taxpayers assessed at more than 500 gulden made up 5 per cent of all households in 1396, and their share rose to 10 per cent in 1516.

The rising number of relatively wealthy individuals, however, was not matched by an expansion of the middle ranks, defined by Geffcken as persons assessed for a property in the range of 100 to 500 gulden. Throughout the fifteenth and early sixteenth century, the share of the lower classes, i.e. taxpayers assessed below 100 gulden, never fell below 78 per cent. In other words, almost

---

1 Geffcken, "Steuern"; see also Clasen, *Die Augsburger Steuerbücher*.

four-fifths of the households in late medieval Augsburg belonged to the lower classes, about one-sixth to the middle classes and less than three per cent to the elite. During the crisis period from 1448 to 1472, the share of propertyless people, which had fluctuated between 35 per cent and 45 per cent in the first half of the century, rose to 60 per cent and remained high thereafter.[2]

What emerges from these figures is a highly polarized society. On the one hand, thousands of small artisans and day laborers found it difficult to make ends meet, let alone accumulate savings. In 1492, 85 per cent of Augsburg's taxpayers owned merely three per cent of the city's wealth.[3] On the other hand, several hundred families concentrated the lion's share of private property in their hands. The share of the richest five per cent of taxpayers rose from 60 per cent of the city's total wealth in 1396 to more than 85 per cent in 1516. In the latter year, two hundred taxpayers were assessed for at least 2,600 gulden. Jakob Fugger, whose wealth assessment Geffcken puts at 240,000 gulden, headed the list, followed by his nephews, Hans Baumgartner the elder, Sigmund Gossembrot's widow, and Philipp Adler, all of whom owned property in the range of 70,000 to 100,000 gulden. The list of Augsburg's largest taxpayers also included members of well-known patrician and merchant families such as the Honolds, Rehlingers, Granders, Hoechstetters, Herwarts, Imhofs, Laugingers, and Welsers. Long-distance commerce and mining ventures were the major sources of wealth at the dawn of the early modern era. In addition, rich families acquired landed property outside the city walls, and some of them imitated aristocratic lifestyles on their rural estates.[4] Moreover, wealth was strongly correlated with political influence: 94 per cent of the persons who held the most influential positions on the city council during the late medieval period belonged to the wealthiest three per cent of taxpayers.[5]

The sixteenth and early seventeenth centuries, Augsburg's "golden age" as a commercial and financial center, witnessed the further accumulation of wealth as well as the persistence of glaring social disparities. While the number of taxpayers rose from 5,351 in 1498 to 8,242 in 1554 (an increase of 54 per cent), the total volume of direct taxes more than tripled from 13,500 to 43,300 gulden. Both the elite and the lower classes grew faster than the middling ranks, however. While the latter grew by 17 per cent, the number of propertyless citizens increased by 88 per cent and the number of rich persons paying more

---

2 Geffcken, *Soziale Schichtung*, pp. 114–16, 119–22, 261. See also Jahn, "Augsburger Sozialstruktur".
3 Jahn, "Augsburger Sozialstruktur", p. 189.
4 Geffcken, "Soziale Schichtung", p. 127 and appendix 24, pp. 209–20; Kießling, "Augsburg zwischen Mittelalter und Neuzeit", pp. 245–46.
5 Geffcken, "Soziale Schichtung", pp. 199–202.

than 100 gulden in taxes almost doubled.[6] Despite the bankruptcy of dozens of merchant companies in the later sixteenth century, the number of very rich individuals who paid at least 100 gulden to the tax office (indicating at least 20,000 gulden in personal wealth) increased from 34 in 1516 to 80 in 1560 and reached an all-time high of 128 in 1618. Thus the number of large fortunes grew at a faster rate in the years around 1600 than the total number of taxpayers, which rose from 8,770 in 1558 to 10,069 in 1604, and faster than the number of propertyless households, which remained relatively stable (4,293 in 1604 compared to 4,161 in 1558).[7]

According to Bernd Roeck, about two per cent of Augsburg's taxpayers in 1618 belonged to the elite, 35 per cent can be grouped among the middle classes, and almost two-thirds lived near or below the poverty line. At the top of the social hierarchy, ten "super-rich" persons were taxed for properties in excess of 100,000 gulden. Wealth and professional status were closely correlated: patricians (members of the urban nobility) and merchants predominated in the upper ranks, while innkeepers, brewers, bakers, and goldsmiths were also doing comparatively well. The extreme concentration of wealth in Augsburg is underscored by the fact that the richest decile of taxpayers controlled almost 92 per cent of the total assessed property. Weavers and day laborers, by comparison, were disproportionately poor.[8] When the city council distributed cheap grain to several thousand needy Augsburgers during the economic crisis of the early 1620s, close to three-fifths of the recipients were working in the textile sector; about one-fifth of these needy households were headed by women.[9]

These disparities also shaped Augsburg's topography and social life. Whereas most patricians, merchants, goldsmiths, and prosperous innkeepers lived near the city center, poorer craftsmen and day laborers were concentrated in the peripheral quarters.[10] Patricians and merchants held lavish dinners in their exclusive drinking halls, while artisans and laborers met in a variety of beer and wine taverns scattered throughout the city.[11] Wealth and social status also influenced the choice of spouses, godparents, and guardians. Patricians, merchants, and artisans tended to marry among themselves: Only 5.5 per cent of the 652 marriages recorded for patricians and merchants between 1572 and 1618 involved a partner who did not belong to either of these groups. Social endogamy also led to the formation of tight kinship networks within particular

---

6   Kellenbenz, "Wirtschaftsleben der Blütezeit", p. 290; Safley, *Charity and Economy*, p. 32.
7   Hildebrandt, "The Effects of Empire", pp. 65, 75.
8   Roeck, *Eine Stadt in Krieg und Frieden*, vol. 1, pp. 398–433; see also Clasen, "Arm und Reich".
9   Roeck, "'Arme' in Augsburg", pp. 525–26, 532.
10   Roeck, *Eine Stadt in Krieg und Frieden*, vol. 1, pp. 489–510.
11   Tlusty, *Bacchus*, esp. chapters 2 and 3.

professions. Although it was possible to rise into the ranks of the merchants and gain acceptance into their drinking hall, only a limited number of physicians, lawyers, secretaries, wealthy innkeepers, and goldsmiths managed to do so. Dress regulations and other civic ordinances underscored the importance of rank and status.[12]

The Thirty Years' War truncated this elaborate social hierarchy, as a disproportionate number of poor inhabitants died and wealthy merchants and tradesmen lost much of their fortunes. Total property taxes paid by merchants plummeted from 18,680 gulden in 1618 to 3,056 gulden – less than one-sixth of the pre-war level – in 1646, and average tax payments of individual merchants fell from 77 to 30 gulden during the same period. The per capita decline in taxes was even more dramatic in the case of the patricians, dropping from over 111 gulden in 1618 to less than 24 gulden at the end of the war. While the population fell from 45,000 to 20,000, the 1646 tax register indicates that 8,000 to 9,000 people, roughly 45 per cent of Augsburg's inhabitants, belonged to the lower classes and were permanently or intermittently dependent on assistance. Another 10,000 persons – half of the population – paid low taxes and were able to make ends meet except in times of severe crisis. Only 1,000 to 2,000 persons, that is, five to ten per cent of the population, were living in fairly comfortable circumstances. Moreover, the number of wealthy individuals had declined to about one hundred (0.5 per cent) and the group of the "super rich" had completely evaporated.[13]

While the number of weavers shrank dramatically from more than 2,000 in 1610 to less than 400 in 1646, the situation for those who remained improved slightly after the Thirty Years' War: 38 per cent of the weavers paid no property taxes in 1646, compared to 67 per cent in 1618. By 1660, merely one-quarter of the 424 weavers were propertyless, and that share remained constant over the next half century. Thus the textile sector, which had suffered from overproduction before the war, obviously faced somewhat better prospects after 1648.[14] Nevertheless, artisans in the textile, leather, and construction branches remained relatively poor in the early eighteenth century compared to the food trades (butchers, bakers, innkeepers) and the metal-working crafts. Long-distance traders also gradually recovered during the postwar period: 148 individuals paid more than 100 gulden in property taxes between 1646 and 1717, the

---

12   See Mörke and Sieh, "Gesellschaftliche Führungsgruppen"; Reinhard, "Oligarchische Verflechtung"; Roeck, *Eine Stadt in Krieg und Frieden*, vol. 1, pp. 333–64; Häberlein, *Brüder, Freunde und Betrüger*, pp. 61–78.
13   Roeck, *Eine Stadt in Krieg und Frieden*, vol. 2, pp. 914–49.
14   Roeck, *Eine Stadt in Krieg und Frieden*, vol. 2, pp. 914–16; Clasen, *Textilherstellung*, vol. 1, p. 60.

vast majority of them Lutheran merchants.[15] 27 per cent of Augsburg's taxpayers were listed as propertyless in 1715, while 48 per cent were taxed for small amounts of property, 20 per cent belonged to the middle classes, and four per cent to the wealthy elite.[16] Although early eighteenth-century Augsburg still lagged far behind the levels of population and overall wealth it had attained in 1618, therefore, it had recovered from some of the worst losses incurred during the Thirty Years' War, and social inequality within the city walls had become less pronounced.

Statistical data are lacking for the remainder of the eighteenth century, but it is likely that wealth disparities once again became more pronounced during that period, as the mercantile and banking sectors grew and a group of wealthy cotton-printing manufacturers emerged.[17] On the other hand, large numbers of inhabitants remained dependent on poor relief: Close to 3,000 people – about 10 per cent of the population – received public support in the years around 1800. Numerous complaints about the plight of the weavers indicate that their profession was disproportionately affected by poverty.[18] The woes of this profession thus remained a constant feature of Augsburg's social history through the centuries.

2   The Organization of Craft Production

The two basic forms in which craft production was organized were the household and the guild. According to Lyndal Roper, "Augsburg's economy was dominated by a myriad of small household-based workshops", which she characterizes as spaces "where work-place and dwelling-place were the same". Master craftsmen oversaw the labor of journeymen, apprentices, and servants, most of whom were living in the household. The master artisan controlled all stages of the production process and ran his workshop as an independent tradesman.[19] In some professions like the construction trades, however, married journeymen lived in their own households. By the sixteenth century, even some master weavers employed married journeymen (so-called *Hausknappen*).[20]

---

15   Mayr, *Augsburger Vermögen*, pp. 115–23; François, *Die unsichtbare Grenze*, pp. 101, 106.
16   Fassl, *Konfession, Wirtschaft und Politik*, p. 95.
17   Ibid., pp. 42–51.
18   Ibid., pp. 96–106; Clasen, *Textilherstellung*, I, pp. 61–63.
19   Roper, *The Holy Household*, pp. 28–30.
20   Roper, *The Holy Household*, p. 42; Clasen, *Die Augsburger Weber*, p. 119.

While widows were generally allowed to continue their deceased husbands' workshops, women's involvement in the production process was sharply circumscribed by guild regulations that sought to prevent single and married women from learning and practicing the "secrets" of the trade. As research on the gender aspects of craft production has shown, however, master's wives and daughters did play important roles in workshops that ranged from preparing raw materials to selling the finished product.[21] Belt-makers were fined in 1558, for example, for setting "maids to do the work which it is fitting for journeymen to do".[22] In the seventeenth century, some master weavers even let servant maids work on their looms in defiance of legal norms.[23] The weaving of small ware (*Schmalweberei*) and veils was considered "practically just women's work" (*fast nur weyber arbeit*) and remained an unregulated trade (*freie Kunst*) until 1561.[24] Women also worked as spinners and in other preparatory stages of fustian- and, later, cotton-weaving. A 1795 source claims that it was the weavers' wives who oversaw most of the production process and were in control of spinning. Many women were in charge of submitting the finished cloth for quality control and selling it.[25] In the long run, however, the professionalization and corporate organization of craft production increasingly restricted the role of women in the marketplace.

Most sectors of urban craft production were organized in guilds, some of which comprised the members of a single trade while others grouped various crafts together. Apart from participating in urban government from 1368 to 1548,[26] the guilds collectively regulated the production and marketing of goods, the labor market, and the purchasing of raw materials. In addition, they defended their members against outside competition and acted as institutions of social and moral control which sought to protect the status and the collective honor of their members.[27] The guild-organized monitoring of product quality apparently originated in the food and textile sectors and subsequently spread to other crafts. According to Rolf Kießling, quality control was a significant factor promoting Augsburg's economic centrality.[28] Moreover, the lavishly decorated guildhalls were centers of sociability and collective pride. When

---

21 Roper, *The Holy Household*, pp. 40–55; Werkstetter, *Frauen im Augsburger Zunfthandwerk*. See also Chapter 13 in this volume.
22 Roper, *The Holy Household*, p. 44.
23 Clasen, *Textilherstellung*, vol. 1, p. 392.
24 Clasen, *Die Augsburger Weber*, pp. 131–32; Roper, The *Holy Household*, p. 49.
25 Clasen, *Textilherstellung*, vol. 1, pp. 135, 391.
26 See Chapter 6 in this volume.
27 Roper, *The Holy Household*, pp. 36–40 (quote on p. 36). See also Geffcken, "Zünfte".
28 Kießling, "Augsburgs Wirtschaft", pp. 171–74.

FIGURE 12.1   Goldsmith's workshop in Augsburg, copperplate by Etienne Delaune (1518/19–1583)
AUGSBURG, STÄDTISCHE KUNSTSAMMLUNGEN, G20955

Emperor Charles V abolished the guild regime in 1548 and ordered the dissolution of the guilds, many of their houses were sold and the craft corporations reduced to mere trades (*Handwerke*) controlled by the patrician-dominated city council.[29]

In early modern cities like Augsburg, guild notions of honor were of crucial importance to artisans' conceptions of themselves and others, and they exerted a decisive influence on processes of inclusion and exclusion. In a hierarchically organized society of estates, each corporation sought to maintain its particular rank and status by enforcing standards of admission and monitoring members' behavior. From the sixteenth century onwards, legitimate birth and descent from "honest" people were essential criteria for guild membership. In addition, journeymen and apprentices were expected to "behave honorably and uprightly," as the Augsburg goldsmith's ordinance spelled out in 1549. The ordinance continued to stipulate that "[n]o master shall employ those who are

---

29   Kellenbenz, "Wirtschaftsleben der Blütezeit", p. 263.

scoundrels, wastrels, gamblers, or who associate with disreputable women".[30] Early modern Augsburg experienced dozens of conflicts in which guilds either refused to accept persons born into the so-called dishonorable trades (e.g. executioners, skinners, grave-diggers, and associated trades) or expelled members who had tainted their own and their group's honor through sexual misconduct, criminal behavior, or association with dishonorable persons or trades. Thus a craftsman who drank with the executioner, touched the corpse of a suicide, or removed an animal cadaver "violated pollution prohibitions, thus dishonoring himself".[31]

The expansion of craft production from the late fifteenth century to the eve of the Thirty Years' War[32] was accompanied by a process of differentiation. By the second half of the sixteenth century, for example, the bakers' craft was divided into *Vorbäcker* and *Nachbäcker* ("pre-baker" and "after-baker"), with the latter subject to various restrictions and lacking their own ovens.[33] The baking of small cakes (*Küchlein, Krapfen*) was considered an unregulated trade.[34] The butchers' craft produced not only meat, but also entrails, horns, bones, and blood, which were subsequently processed by sausage-makers and related crafts.[35] Within the metal- and wood-working trades, the production of luxury objects for princely clients was accompanied by new forms of labor division. A luxury curiosity cabinet like the one commissioned for the Duke of Pomerania by the Augsburg merchant Philipp Hainhofer in the early seventeenth century testifies to the wide spectrum of specialized crafts concentrated in the city as well as to the superior skills and expertise of local artisans.[36] During the later seventeenth and eighteenth centuries, large-scale orders for luxury table services from princely courts were a mainstay of Augsburg's gold- and silver-working sector,[37] and the goldsmiths and jewelers who received these orders often enlisted the help of specialized fellow masters and related craftsmen such as gold-beaters and watchcase makers.[38] Similar patterns of specialization and

---

30   Quoted from Stuart, *Defiled Trades*, p. 201.
31   Stuart, *Defiled Trades*, p. 17. See also Stuart's extensive discussion of these issues at pp. 189–221.
32   See Chapter 5 in this volume.
33   Roeck, *Bäcker, Brot und Getreide*, pp. 135, 160, 186–87, 198.
34   Reith, *Arbeits- und Lebensweise*, pp. 74–75.
35   Dalhede, "Zur Erforschung".
36   Mundt, *Der Pommersche Kunstschrank*.
37   Seling, *Kunst der Augsburger Goldschmiede*, vol. 1, pp. 140–41.
38   Rathke-Köhl, *Geschichte*, p. 144; Bettger, *Handwerk in Augsburg*, pp. 182, 193; Reith, *Arbeits- und Lebensweise*, pp. 39–55; see also Fassl, "Wirtschaft, Handel und Sozialstruktur", pp. 473–74.

division of labor can be observed in the textile sector as well, which had a truly astonishing array of specialties.

The introduction of cotton-printing in the late seventeenth century likewise entailed new forms of labor organization. While the earliest printing establishments were little larger than craft workshops, successful cotton-printers substantially increased their workforce in the course of the eighteenth century. In 1739 the Neuhofer manufacture already employed 100 laborers. While printing took place in large central workshops, skilled workers like the block cutters worked on their own premises. Johann Heinrich Schüle, who established his own cotton-printing manufacture in 1759 and erected a "factory palace" outside the city near the Red Gate in the early 1770s, employed 350 workers by 1780.[39]

3   Labor Market and Labor Migration

As the preceding sections have shown, Augsburg was in need of a large supply of labor throughout the period covered in this volume. The following section considers where this labor force actually came from in order to highlight the city's role in networks of migration and socio-economic interaction.

For the fourteenth century, there is evidence that weavers immigrated to Augsburg from other Swabian towns and villages, from Bavaria and Franconia, and from parts of Bohemia and Austria.[40] Increasing numbers of foreign weavers were recorded in the book of new citizens (*Bürgerbuch*) from 1390 onward. After a slump in the early fifteenth century, which corresponds with an imperial trade ban against Venice (the most important supplier of cotton), the number of weavers admitted to citizenship rose sharply in the 1430s. Alongside those from Augsburg's rural environs, weavers from towns like Günzburg and Weißenburg also ranked among the new citizens. Following another decline during the economic depression of the 1450s and 1460s, the immigration of weavers picked up again during the 1480s.[41]

The origins of master weavers recorded between 1561 and 1575 and of journeymen weavers fined between 1578 and 1588 indicate that the central region of eastern Swabia extending from the Danube to the town of Mindelheim was their primary recruitment area.[42] Substantial evidence of the geographical

---

39   Dirr, "Augsburger Textilindustrie", p. 39.
40   Reininghaus, "Frühformen der Gesellengilden", p. 85.
41   Kalesse, *Bürger in Augsburg*, pp. 226–29.
42   Kießling, *Die Stadt und ihr Land*, p. 726.

origins of journeymen is provided by the military muster of 1619: the places of origin of 1,706 individuals – about 80 per cent of all journeymen listed in the register – can be identified. While 456 (26.7 per cent of those with known origins) were born in the imperial city, 24 per cent came from the region to the southwest of Augsburg, especially from the duchy of Württemberg. Immigration from the southeast, by contrast, accounted for only 9 per cent of the immigrants, and the duchy of Bavaria, the city's eastern neighbor, was hardly represented at all. Many journeymen came from regions that were more than 60 km distant from Augsburg, e.g. the Protestant electorate of Saxony.[43]

The muster registers also provide evidence that migration to the imperial city was highly branch-specific. Overall, 1,152 journeymen weavers were registered in 1615, and 755 were recorded in 1619.[44] The textile sector evinces a regionally circumscribed recruitment pattern, with almost half the journeymen coming from the surrounding countryside. In the year 1619, for which the origins of 594 journeymen are known, 35 per cent were born in Augsburg and small numbers came from Switzerland, Saxony, and the eastern parts of Habsburg Austria. Many hailed from the region between the rivers Iller and Lech, from the Allgäu, and from towns and villages on the banks of the Danube. The imperial cities of Biberach, Ulm, Kempten, Kaufbeuren, and Memmingen provided important recruitment pools, highlighting Augsburg's centrality within the Swabian textile region. Moreover, considerable numbers of journeymen had migrated from Catholic territories into a city where they worked for predominantly Protestant masters. It was only in the eighteenth century that Catholics came to dominate the weaving craft.[45]

While only eight of the 102 journeymen bakers listed in 1619 were natives of Augsburg, merely 24 were migrants from places more than 60 km away. Most journeymen bakers hailed from the western vicinity of Augsburg, from the Allgäu in the southern and the Ries in the northern part of eastern Swabia, from the duchy of Württemberg, and from smaller towns like Dillingen and Höchstädt. Of 96 journeymen goldsmiths with known origins, by contrast, only 24 (25 per cent) were native Augsburgers, and none came from a place within a 60 km radius. Many goldsmiths were migrants from Habsburg territories and ecclesiastical principalities. The migratory patterns among the goldsmiths in the early seventeenth century transcended confessional boundaries:

---

43 Roeck, *Eine Stadt in Krieg und Frieden*, vol. 2, pp. 791–829, 794.
44 Roeck, *Eine Stadt in Krieg und Frieden*, vol. 2, pp. 791–829; Clasen, *Die Augsburger Weber*, p. 106.
45 Roeck, *Eine Stadt in Krieg und Frieden*, vol. 2, pp. 796–800.

although Protestant masters dominated the craft, their journeymen came from both Catholic and Protestant regions.[46]

In the eighteenth century, Augsburg was integrated into regional and transregional migration systems, with different patterns for specific trades. Married local journeymen provided a permanent pool of labor in the construction sector, which was supplemented by commuters from nearby villages like Lechhausen, Haunstetten, and Oberhausen. Seasonal workers, especially from Tyrol, constituted another source of labor. Nearly 100 Tyrolean journeymen were employed in Augsburg during the 1790s, some of whom continued to return on a seasonal basis for decades.[47]

The large crafts of the shoemakers, tailors, joiners, and locksmiths mostly recruited their labor force from neighboring territories, but attracted some migrants from other regions as well. As these crafts were present in numerous places, however, journeymen did not have to wander long distances.[48] In the long run, the recruitment area of journeymen weavers contracted as immigration from other cities and towns dwindled. While Augsburg remained a center of cotton-weaving in the eighteenth century, it had by then lost its monopoly on employment because significant amounts of cotton were now processed in the countryside, where a number of guilds had newly been formed since the seventeenth century.[49] The textile-finishing trades recruited labor from a much wider area than the above-mentioned crafts. From 1579 to 1613, journeymen dyers hailed mainly from Nuremberg, Saxony, Thuringia, Silesia, Bohemia, and the Swabian imperial cities. In the later seventeenth and eighteenth century, they came to Augsburg from all over German-speaking central Europe.[50]

Another trade with a wide catchment area was the relatively new profession of the braid-makers, which had been introduced in the seventeenth century and counted 202 masters in 1750. By that time, Augsburg was a center of mechanized braid-making, attracting a large number of workers before a period of decline set in. By 1806, the number of masters was down to 64.[51] Numerous smaller, often highly specialized crafts likewise had strong interregional ties; these included gold-beaters, file-makers, bookbinders, and tinsmiths. The book-printers, who employed 83 journeymen in 13 workshops in

---

46   Roeck, *Eine Stadt in Krieg und Frieden*, vol. 2, pp. 800–04.
47   Reith, "Kommunikation und Migration", pp. 333–35.
48   Ibid., pp. 346–48.
49   Ibid., pp. 338–42; Sczesny, *Zwischen Kontinuität und Wandel*.
50   Clasen, *Textilherstellung*, vol. 2, pp. 205–06; Reith, "Kommunikation und Migration", pp. 343–44.
51   Reith, *Arbeits- und Lebensweise*, pp. 166–81.

the mid-eighteenth century, mainly drew migrants from other urban centers.[52] And corresponding to their far-flung marketing networks, the gold- and silversmiths in the eighteenth century attracted journeymen and laborers from all over central Europe, who may have hoped to perfect their skills in Augsburg and benefit from their masters' reputation.[53]

There is only scattered evidence on the geographical origins of female workers. As some immigrant women seem to have preferred wool-combing in their own households to domestic employment, some weavers reportedly were unable to hire maidservants in 1577. The city council therefore attempted to force these women to work in citizens' households. Concerns over the lack of female wool-combers, spinners, and maidservants were repeated in the seventeenth century.[54] Because most servants came from rural areas, a significant number of Catholic maidservants found employment in Protestant households. In the eighteenth century, the city council sought to muffle conflicts arising from masters' attempts to induce their servants to convert.[55]

The rise of cotton-printing shaped another highly differentiated labor market, which attracted male printing, dyeing, and bleaching assistants along with female wool-combers, block cleaners, and designers.[56] Some specialized cotton-printers worked in Augsburg on a seasonal basis and returned home during the winter. Many of the 52 cotton-printers who formed a mutual health insurance fund in 1783 came from urban centers of the printing industry.[57]

4   Poverty and Poor Relief

As noted above, a considerable segment of the city's population was temporarily or permanently dependent on poor relief. Assistance to the poor took two basic forms: public relief and private charity. The latter, which was originally more important, exhibited a bewildering variety in late medieval Augsburg. Wealthy individuals left bequests or established foundations for a number of purposes, including handouts of food and clothing to the indigent, the provision of dowries, the financing of apprenticeships and stipends, and the establishment of special houses for pilgrims, the elderly, invalids, or persons afflicted with contagious diseases. These bequests and foundations were

---

[52] Reith, "Buchdruckergesellen".
[53] Reith, "Fremde Goldschmiedegesellen".
[54] Clasen, *Die Augsburger Weber*, p. 133.
[55] François, *Die unsichtbare Grenze*, pp. 112–115.
[56] Clasen, *Textilherstellung*, vol. 2, pp. 472–500.
[57] Haertel, "Augsburger Weberunruhen", p. 191; Clasen, *Textilherstellung*, vol. 2, p. 477.

typically motivated by the dual aims of Christian charity towards the poor and good works for the sake of the benefactor's soul and memory. In addition, private charitable initiatives, which had long been a domain of the church, testify to citizens' growing self-consciousness and their emancipation from clerical dominance. Their administration was entrusted to guardians (*Pfleger*), usually wealthy citizens, while the city council increasingly sought to monitor private foundations.[58]

The largest of these projects was initiated by Augsburg's wealthiest man, Jakob Fugger the Rich. In 1511, he set aside 15,000 gulden for charitable purposes, and some years later he purchased real estate in St. Jacob's Suburb. A complex of uniform houses lined up along straight alleys was constructed on these premises: 52 houses, each with two apartments, were completed by 1522. Fugger stipulated that this settlement, later termed the Fuggerei, was meant for poor Catholic day laborers and artisans who were citizens of Augsburg, were not dependent on alms, and paid a yearly rent of one Rhenish gulden. As this sum equaled the monthly income of a day laborer at the time, it was not merely symbolic. The inhabitants were obliged to pray three times a day for the founder's family. Selectively adapting features of social housing projects in the Netherlands, northern Germany, and Italy, the Fuggerei exemplifies new approaches to poor relief that had emerged in the late Middle Ages: it assigned separate living quarters to individuals, giving them a degree of privacy, and catered to pious, honorable citizens who were willing to work but needed relief nonetheless (*Hausarme*). With its more than 100 apartments, the Fuggerei was the largest social housing project of its time. Although elderly people were admitted from the beginning, the settlement also housed younger families, and most household heads worked as craftsmen or day laborers. The Fuggerei survives to the present day as a residence for poor elderly Catholic Augsburgers who pay an annual rent of 0.88 Euros (the equivalent of one Rhenish gulden).[59]

Like many other German communities, Augsburg sought during the Reformation era to centralize poor relief and administer it more efficiently. While the city council had largely limited itself during the fifteenth century to publishing ordinances that sought to control begging,[60] it passed an alms ordinance in 1522 that put six councilors, the so-called alms lords (*Almosenherren*), in charge of collecting donations and distributing them to the needy. The

---

58 Kießling, *Bürgerliche Gesellschaft und Kirche*, pp. 215–40; Lengle, "Spitäler, Stiftungen und Bruderschaften"; Roeck, *Eine Stadt in Krieg und Frieden*, vol. 2, pp. 609–10; Safley, *Charity and Economy*, pp. 29–31.
59 Tietz-Strödel, *Fuggerei*; Scheller, *Memoria*, pp. 128–51; Häberlein, *The Fuggers of Augsburg*, pp. 156–59.
60 Kießling, *Bürgerliche Gesellschaft*, pp. 217–18; Clasen, "Armenfürsorge", 68–69.

city was divided into three districts, with two alms lords assigned to each district where they visited the poor, collected donations, and distributed alms. In 1541, another ordinance forbade begging in the streets and stipulated that relief should be handed out in kind (food, clothes, firewood) instead of cash. These measures, which were copied in other cities, exemplify an approach to relief that was not caused, but was certainly promoted by the Protestant Reformation: the distinction between deserving poor and unworthy beggars, and the corresponding attempt to monitor recipients in order to prevent waste and idleness. In the third quarter of the sixteenth century, the alms office supported an annual average of 1,260 persons, three to four per cent of the city's population. This number greatly increased during the economic crisis of the early 1570s, when up to 3,361 persons needed relief. Widows were disproportionately affected by poverty, accounting for 20–30 per cent of alms recipients.[61]

In the second half of the sixteenth century, Augsburg's alms office also took over private foundations like the pilgrim house, which was turned into a public hospital for the poor. An average of 459 individuals per year were treated there during the 1570s and 1580s. In 1572–73, the city established an orphanage for several hundred children of poor citizens; while boys were apprenticed to craftsmen, girls were taught sewing, spinning, and other domestic tasks. Foundlings were cared for in a separate institution, which was moved to a former monastery in 1536 and subsequently enlarged. The city's largest hospital for the elderly, the Hospital of the Holy Spirit, housed 250 to 300 people in the early seventeenth century. Meanwhile, wealthy citizens continued to make bequests for charitable and educational purposes in post-Reformation Augsburg: 91 such bequests have been counted for the century from 1548 to 1649.[62]

The Thirty Years' War caused a severe crisis in the local relief system. In 1607, the alms office had assets of slightly over 130,000 gulden; more than two-thirds were loaned at interest and yielded annual revenues of close to 4,000 gulden. Including collections and donations, the office's revenues amounted to almost 12,400 gulden in that year. But these revenues hardly sufficed to meet rising expenses, and after 1610 the office accumulated a growing deficit. Moreover, collections declined during the war and virtually dried up in some years, while obligations mounted and runaway inflation during the early 1620s

---

61 Kießling, *Bürgerliche Gesellschaft*, p. 234; Clasen, "Armenfürsorge", pp. 69–80, 86–90; Roeck, *Eine Stadt in Krieg und Frieden*, vol. 2, pp. 607–10, 618; Safley, *Charity and Economy*, pp. 33–35.

62 Clasen, "Armenfürsorge", pp. 100–07; Roeck, *Eine Stadt in Krieg und Frieden*, vol. 2, pp. 608–11; Safley, *Charity and Economy*, p. 34. After 1648, separate orphanages were set up for Catholic and Protestant children. On their history, see Safley, *Charity and Economy*; idem, *Children of the Laboring Poor*.

dramatically shrunk the capital stock. In 1624, the alms office's expenses of roughly 43,400 gulden exceeded its revenues (21,100 gulden) by more than 100 per cent. Under these circumstances the collection office (*Einnehmeramt*) had to transfer several thousand gulden to the alms office each year in order to balance its budget.[63]

In the later seventeenth century, the relative importance of voluntary charitable donations and testamentary bequests for the alms office and the institutions it funded (such as the orphanages) declined, while the importance of public subsidies increased. In 1670, public funds accounted for almost half of the alms office's revenues, whereas private donations made up merely two per cent. Expenditures for public charity continued to rise in the eighteenth century, and despite repeated efforts to reform the poor relief system and render it more efficient, the city ultimately had no choice but to transfer ever larger sums to the alms office in order to balance its budget.[64]

5 Social Conflict

Given the huge socio-economic disparities and high levels of poverty in late medieval and early modern Augsburg, the periodic outbreak of strikes and uprisings is hardly surprising. In 1360, 1397–98, 1466 and 1524, poor weavers, many of whom were dependent on the putting-out system, protested against the burdens imposed upon them by excise taxes. These protests targeted the city's highly unequal system of taxation: although the majority of Augsburg's householders paid no property taxes, excise taxes on beer and wine had to be paid by everyone (with the exception of clergy and certain city officials) and disproportionately fell on the poor.[65]

As early as the fourteenth century, two areas of conflict emerge which retained their significance in later periods: the formation of separate journeyman associations, and demands for higher wages. In 1358, several journeyman weavers were charged with forming an association to back up their demands,

---

63 Clasen, "Armenfürsorge", pp. 91–94, 99–100; Roeck, *Eine Stadt in Krieg und Frieden*, vol. 2, pp. 615–30.
64 Safley, *Charity and Economy*, pp. 79–107.
65 Kießling, "Augsburg im Aufstand", pp. 173–74; Rogge, *Für den Gemeinen Nutzen*, pp. 35–41. By the mid-sixteenth century, excise taxes were the most important source of revenue for Augsburg as for other German towns; see Tlusty, "Full Cups, Full Coffers", which points out how urban governments learned to manipulate excise taxes so as to maximize revenue without instigating unrest.

which was considered a severe breach of tradition.[66] In 1426, the council minutes record that journeyman smiths had committed the "sacrilege" of going on strike against their masters and reporting on them in letters to colleagues in other cities. According to Wilfried Reininghaus, this was merely one among a number of similar conflicts in south German cities and territories in which journeymen asserted their rights against masters and guilds.[67]

Several disputes within the textile sector are documented for the sixteenth century: journeymen weavers demanded raises in 1573 and 1592, and in the latter year, 35 of the 51 journeymen dyers left the city after being denied the right to assemble and discuss a dispute.[68] Most seventeenth-century conflicts relate to the textile sector as well. Journeyman dyers again left the city in 1661, 1681, and 1684, while the cloth-cutters and cloth-makers followed their example in 1668 after their wage demands had been rejected.[69] The journeyman weavers had obtained a raise in 1637 after complaints that prices for basic goods had more than doubled. In 1660, however, business was so bad that the journeymen were reportedly glad to find work at all and came "crawling back" to their masters (*kriechen sie anjetzo zum kreutz*). Seven years later, the journeyman weavers went on strike and left the city to protest the employment of artisans from Mattsee. In 1684–85, another weaver's strike was caused by the employment of a grave-digger.[70] The journeyman joiners' 1698 uprising shows how strikes were related to geographical mobility: the council proposed to employ "harsh measures" to bring them to order, but the masters cautioned that this would only entice them to take their leave. With the Frankfurt and Leipzig fairs approaching, this would have deprived the crafts of much-needed labor and been detrimental to the city's merchants as well.[71]

The above-mentioned conflict within the weavers' guild over the employment of a grave-digger in 1684–85 also highlights that journeymen were especially adamant when it came to enforcing guild standards of honor and averting the potential taint of corporate dishonor, which could also put its members in economic peril.[72] Kathy Stuart has noted "an explosion in the number of dishonor conflicts which Augsburg's guildsmen were called upon to arbitrate" in the eighteenth century, yet she also notes that most of these disputes occurred in other places, and their number actually decreased within the city

---

66   Reininghaus, "Frühformen der Gesellengilden", p. 73.
67   Reininghaus, "Frühformen der Gesellengilden", p. 81.
68   Clasen, *Textilherstellung*, vol. 2, pp. 115, 219.
69   Clasen, *Textilherstellung*, vol. 2, pp. 219–20, 222–23, 503–09.
70   Clasen, *Streiks und Aufstände*, pp. 24–25, 90–94, 94–101.
71   Reith, *Arbeits- und Lebensweise*, pp. 58, 123.
72   Stuart *Defiled Trades*, pp. 103–05, 209–13.

walls. While Stuart ascribes this development to the city council's policies, which sought to appease and placate the guilds,[73] other researchers have emphasized that Augsburg's artisans were becoming more concerned about economic issues. In total, 81 strikes have been documented for the eighteenth and the beginning of the nineteenth century by the commissioners for the weavers' guild-house (*Weberhausdeputation*) and the court of arts, trades, and crafts (*Kunst-, Gewerbs- und Handwerksgericht*), which had been established in 1719–21. While a number of conflicts did grow out of attacks on personal honor (involving issues like fornication, verbal insults, or debt), many more were primarily motivated by economic and corporate grievances.[74]

The latter category includes strikes about food and wages, working hours, masters' right of termination, control of the labor market, and competition from outsiders (such as soldiers, irregular workers, or women). Several labor protests addressed the lowering of wages and food allowances; in other cases, journeymen demanded raises in response to rising prices. Disputes about working hours revolved around the custom of showing up late (or not at all) for work on Mondays in the tradition of "good Monday" (also termed "blue Monday" in the eighteenth century), which agitated the furriers in 1748 and the locksmiths in 1805. Still others concerned the duration of so-called *Lichtarbeit* – work with artificial light during the winter months – about which the tailors argued in 1798. Compared with their seventeenth-century predecessors, eighteenth-century strikes appear to have been mostly defensive. Wage trends in the construction sector and wage levels in the textile crafts indicate that the position of journeymen on the labor market was deteriorating.[75] This resulted in numerous disputes about control of the labor market. In 1716, for example, journeyman weavers demanded a ban on three colleagues from Burgau because the Burgau guild had accepted a married journeyman as master in violation of Augsburg's rule prohibiting this.[76] In 1734, the journeyman braid-makers complained that masters' daughters were irregularly performing "journeymen's work".[77] In 1773, the first of several conflicts among the brewers was triggered by the employment of journeymen without proper certificates of apprenticeship.[78]

---

73 Stuart *Defiled Trades*, pp. 239–52 (quote on p. 239).
74 Clasen, *Textilherstellung*, vol. 1, pp. 89–122; Reith, Grießinger and Eggers, *Streikbewegungen*.
75 Reith, *Arbeits- und Lebensweise*, p. 222–25; Clasen, *Streiks und Aufstände*, pp. 24–29.
76 Clasen, *Streiks und Aufstände*, pp. 101–17.
77 Reith, Grießinger and Eggers, *Streikbewegungen*, pp. 102–103. See also Werkstetter, *Frauen im Augsburger Zunfthandwerk*.
78 Reith, Grießinger and Eggers, *Streikbewegungen*, pp. 192–93 (1793), 282–83 (1801), 398–99 (1805).

Numerous strikes centered on journeymen's corporate rights, e.g. their right to assemble, the autonomous administration of funds, or the right to correspond with colleagues in other cities. A case in point is the uprising of Augsburg's journeyman shoemakers. In response to strikes in Würzburg, Mainz, and Stuttgart, the city council had outlawed correspondence with outside craft associations in 1724. This led to an outbreak of massive protest in 1726, which dragged on for four months. The journeymen removed to the neighboring town of Friedberg, which was under Bavarian jurisdiction, and denied the council's authority to curtail their right of correspondence, which they claimed as a traditional liberty. After tense negotiations, the council eventually offered to grant the journeymen amnesty and rescind its 1724 decree until the emperor and the imperial diet had settled the matter. The journeymen, however, refused to pay for the costs incurred by their strike. It took 14 weeks before the strike broke down and a faction of the journeymen left. In September 1727, the masters still complained about a shortage of labor due to the boycott. After the imperial diet had initially dragged its feet, the local and imperial authorities finally began to cooperate in 1728, culminating in an imperial ordinance against grievances in the artisanal trades in 1731.[79]

As late as 1784, a temporary removal to Friedberg proved an efficient means for journeymen to force their cause. This conflict was triggered by one of the commissioners for the weavers' guildhall, a member of the patrician Langenmantel family. Langenmantel had responded to claims that the weaver's corporation court (*Ladengericht*) took bribes and misappropriated funds by ordering the arrest of seven journeymen, two of whom were put into the local workhouse. In reaction to this authoritarian measure, 200–300 Catholic journeymen weavers left the city for Friedberg. Following complaints by the masters, the council initially yielded to the journeymen's demands, who ceremoniously re-entered the city. The corporation court was eventually overhauled and the guildhall commissioners were sacked.[80]

Most strikes occurred between 1790 and 1806, when authorities in a number of cities, following the example of Frankfurt, sought to abolish the journeymen's associations. Augsburg had agreed to go along in 1802 on the condition that other important cities in the empire followed suit.[81] Resistance from journeymen against the abolition of their corporate autonomy ultimately proved

---

79 Grießinger, *Das symbolische Kapital der Ehre*, pp. 152–78; Clasen, *Streiks der Augsburger Schuhknechte*, pp. 30–184; Winzen, *Handwerk – Städte – Reich*.
80 Haertel, "Augsburger Weberunruhen", pp. 138–43; Clasen, *Streiks und Aufstände*, pp. 118–66.
81 Grießinger, *Das symbolische Kapital der Ehre*, pp. 272–85, 277.

unsuccessful.[82] Instead, more and more city councils summoned their legal counselors to deal with these conflicts, who often took a hardline stance against the artisanal corporations.[83]

The rise of cotton-printing opened up a new arena of conflict during the eighteenth century. After the Seven Years' War (1756–63) had temporarily interrupted the importation of East Indian cotton cloth to the advantage of Augsburg's weavers, imports picked up again in the early 1760s, triggering a dispute that continued until 1794. In 1785, the city council tied its permission of cotton imports from India, Switzerland, and Saxony to a guarantee that the cotton-printers would buy up the entire production of Augsburg's master weavers. The weavers' uprisings, which erupted in 1766, again in 1784–85, and culminated in 1794,[84] when the riots were quelled by several hundred soldiers, have accordingly been interpreted as reactions to economic and social disruptions, particularly the deteriorating position of the city's textile craftsmen.[85] Rolf Kießling convincingly argues that these conflicts in the final years of Augsburg's existence as a free imperial city did not aim at fundamental changes in the city's constitution.[86] Instead, they should be regarded as defensive measures by artisans who tried in vain to stem a tide of socio-economic forces that were largely beyond their control.

Bibliography

Secondary Literature

Bettger, R., *Das Handwerk in Augsburg beim Übergang der Stadt an das Königreich Bayern. Städtisches Gewerbe unter dem Einfluß politischer Veränderungen*, Augsburg, 1979.

Clasen, C.-P., "Arm und Reich in Augsburg vor dem Dreißigjährigen Krieg", in Gottlieb et al. (eds.), *Geschichte der Stadt Augsburg*, pp. 312–37.

Clasen, C.-P., *Die Augsburger Steuerbücher um 1600*, Augsburg, 1976.

Clasen, C.-P., "Armenfürsorge in Augsburg vor dem Dreißigjährigen Krieg", *Zeitschrift des Historischen Vereins für Schwaben* 78 (1986), pp. 65–115.

Clasen, C.-P., *Streiks und Aufstände der Augsburger Weber im 17. und 18. Jahrhundert*, Augsburg, 1993.

---

82   Reith, Grießinger and Eggers, *Streikbewegungen*, pp. 420–23.
83   Reith, Grießinger and Eggers, *Streikbewegungen*, pp. 400–01.
84   They are described in detail in Haertel, "Weberunruhen", and Clasen, *Streiks und Aufstände*.
85   Fassl, "Wirtschaft, Handel und Sozialstruktur", p. 476.
86   Kießling, "Augsburg im Aufstand", p. 171.

Clasen, C.-P., *Textilherstellung in Augsburg in der Frühen Neuzeit*, 2 vols., Augsburg, 1995.

Clasen, C.-P., *Streiks der Augsburger Schuhknechte. Freiheit und Gerechtigkeit*, Augsburg, 2002.

Dalhede, C., "Zur Erforschung des Augsburger Metzgerhandwerks im 16. Jahrhundert", *Scripta Mercaturae* 24 (1990), pp. 81–131.

Dirr, P., "Die Augsburger Textilindustrie im 18. Jahrhundert", *Zeitschrift des Historischen Vereins für Schwaben und Neuburg* 37 (1911), pp. 1–106.

Fassl, P., "Wirtschaft, Handel und Sozialstruktur", in Gottlieb et al. (eds.), *Geschichte der Stadt Augsburg*, pp. 468–80.

Fassl, P., *Konfession, Wirtschaft und Politik. Von der Reichsstadt zur Industriestadt. Augsburg 1750–1850*, Sigmaringen, 1988.

François, E., *Die unsichtbare Grenze. Protestanten und Katholiken in Augsburg 1648–1806*, Sigmaringen, 1995.

Geffcken, P., "Soziale Schichtung in Augsburg 1396 bis 1521. Beitrag zu einer Strukturanalyse Augsburgs im Spätmittelalter", Ph.D. diss., University of Munich, 1995.

Geffcken, P., "Steuern", in G. Grünsteudel, G. Hägele and R. Frankenberger (eds.), *Augsburger Stadtlexikon*, 2nd ed., Augsburg, 1998, pp. 854–57.

Geffcken, P., "Zünfte", in G. Grünsteudel, G. Hägele and R. Frankenberger (eds.), *Augsburger Stadtlexikon*, 2nd ed., Augsburg, 1998, pp. 949–50.

Gottlieb, G., Baer, W., Becker, J., Bellot, J., Filser, K., Fried, P., Reinhard, W. and Schimmelpfennig, B. (eds.), *Geschichte der Stadt Augsburg von der Römerzeit bis zur Gegenwart*, 2nd ed., Stuttgart, 1985.

Grießinger, A., *Das symbolische Kapital der Ehre. Streikbewegungen und kollektives Bewußtsein deutscher Handwerksgesellen im 18. Jahrhundert*, Frankfurt, 1981.

Häberlein, M., *Brüder, Freunde und Betrüger. Soziale Beziehungen, Normen und Konflikte in der Augsburger Kaufmannschaft um die Mitte des 16. Jahrhunderts*, Berlin, 1998.

Häberlein, M., *The Fuggers of Augsburg: Pursuing Wealth and Honor in Renaissance Germany*, Charlottesville and London, 2012.

Haertel, V., "Die Augsburger Weberunruhen von 1784 und 1794 und die Struktur der Weberschaft Ende des 18. Jahrhunderts", *Zeitschrift des Historischen Vereins für Schwaben* 64–65 (1971), pp. 121–268.

Hildebrandt, R., "The Effects of Empire: Changes in the European Economy after Charles V", in I. Blanchard, A. Goodman and J. Newman (eds.), *Industry and Finance in Early Modern History: Essays Presented to George Hammersley on the Occasion of his 74th Birthday*, Stuttgart, 1992, pp. 58–75.

Jahn, J., "Die Augsburger Sozialstruktur im 15. Jahrhundert", in Gottlieb et al. (eds.), *Geschichte der Stadt Augsburg*, pp. 187–93.

Kalesse, C., *Bürger in Augsburg. Studien über Bürgerrecht, Neubürger und Bürgen anhand des Augsburger Bürgerbuchs I (1288–1497)*, Augsburg, 2001.

Kellenbenz, H., "Wirtschaftsleben der Blütezeit", in Gottlieb et al. (eds.), *Geschichte der Stadt Augsburg*, pp. 258–301.

Kießling, R., "Augsburgs Wirtschaft im 14. und 15. Jahrhundert", in Gottlieb et al. (eds.), *Geschichte der Stadt Augsburg*, pp. 171–81.

Kießling, R., "Augsburg zwischen Mittelalter und Neuzeit", in Gottlieb et al. (eds.), *Geschichte der Stadt Augsburg*, pp. 241–51.

Kießling, R., *Bürgerliche Gesellschaft und Kirche in Augsburg im Spätmittelalter. Ein Beitrag zur Strukturanalyse der oberdeutschen Reichsstadt*, Augsburg, 1971.

Kießling, R., *Die Stadt und ihr Land. Umlandpolitik, Bürgerbesitz und Wirtschaftsgefüge in Ostschwaben vom 14. bis ins 16. Jahrhundert*, Cologne, 1989.

Kießling, R., "Augsburg im Aufstand. Ein systematischer Vergleich von Unruhen des 14./16. Jahrhunderts mit denen des 17./18. Jahrhunderts", in A. and E. Westermann (eds.), *Streik im Revier. Unruhe, Protest und Ausstand vom 8. bis 20. Jahrhundert*, St. Katharinen, 2007, pp. 153–75.

Kießling, R., "Aspekte der Lederbeschaffung und des Lederabsatzes in Oberdeutschland im 15./16. Jahrhundert", in A. Westermann and S. von Welser (eds.), *Beschaffungs- und Absatzmärkte oberdeutscher Firmen im Zeitalter der Welser und Fugger*, Husum, 2011, pp. 205–33.

Lengle, P., "Spitäler, Stiftungen und Bruderschaften", in Gottlieb et al. (eds.), *Geschichte der Stadt Augsburg*, pp. 202–08.

Mayr, A., *Die großen Augsburger Vermögen von 1618 bis 1717*, Augsburg, 1931.

Mörke, O. and Sieh, K., "Gesellschaftliche Führungsgruppen", in Gottlieb et al. (eds.), *Geschichte der Stadt Augsburg*, pp. 301–11.

Mundt, B., *Der Pommersche Kunstschrank des Augsburger Kaufmanns Philipp Hainhofer*, Munich, 2009.

Rathke-Köhl, S., *Geschichte des Augsburger Goldschmiedegewerbes vom Ende des 17. bis zum Ende des 18. Jahrhunderts*, Augsburg, 1964.

Reinhard, W., "Oligarchische Verflechtung und Klientel in oberdeutschen Städten", in A. Mączak (ed.), *Klientelsysteme im Europa der Frühen Neuzeit*, Munich, 1988, pp. 47–62.

Reininghaus, W., "Frühformen der Gesellengilden in Augsburg im 14. Jahrhundert", *Zeitschrift des Historischen Vereins für Schwaben* 77 (1983), pp. 68–89.

Reith, R., *Arbeits- und Lebensweise im städtischen Handwerk. Zur Sozialgeschichte der Augsburger Handwerksgesellen im 18. Jahrhundert, 1700–1806*, Göttingen, 1988.

Reith, R., "Buchdruckergesellen im Augsburg des 18. Jahrhunderts", in H. Gier and J. Janota (eds.), *Augsburger Buchdruck und Verlagswesen. Von den Anfängen bis zur Gegenwart*, Wiesbaden, 1997, pp. 517–38.

Reith, R., "Kommunikation und Migration: Der Arbeitsmarkt des Augsburger Handwerks im 17. und 18. Jahrhundert in räumlicher Dimension", in C.A. Hoffmann and R. Kießling (eds.), *Kommunikation und Region*, Constance, 2001, pp. 327–56.

Reith, R., "Fremde Goldschmiedegesellen in Augsburg im 18. Jahrhundert: Überlegungen zu Migration, Arbeitserfahrung und Wissenstransfer", in T. Meyer and M. Popplow (eds.), *Technik, Arbeit und Umwelt in der Geschichte. Günther Bayerl zum 60. Geburtstag*, Münster, 2006, pp. 7–25.

Reith, R., Grießinger, A., and Eggers, P., *Streikbewegungen deutscher Handwerksgesellen im 18. Jahrhundert. Materialien zur Sozial- und Wirtschaftsgeschichte des städtischen Handwerks 1700–1806*, Göttingen, 1992.

Roeck, B., "'Arme' in Augsburg zum Beginn des 30-jährigen Krieges", *Zeitschrift für Bayerische Landesgeschichte* 46 (1983), pp. 515–58.

Roeck, B., *Bäcker, Brot und Getreide in Augsburg. Zur Geschichte des Bäckerhandwerks und zur Versorgungspolitik der Reichsstadt im Zeitalter des Dreißigjährigen Krieges*, Sigmaringen, 1987.

Roeck, B., *Eine Stadt in Krieg und Frieden. Studien zur Geschichte der Reichsstadt Augsburg zwischen Kalenderstreit und Parität*, 2 vols., Göttingen, 1989.

Rogge, J., *Für den Gemeinen Nutzen. Politisches Handeln und Politikverständnis von Rat und Bürgerschaft in Augsburg im Spätmittelalter*, Tübingen, 1996.

Roper, L., *The Holy Household: Women and Morals in Reformation Augsburg*, Oxford, 1989.

Safley, T.M., *Charity and Economy in the Orphanages of Early Modern Augsburg*, Boston, 1997.

Safley, T.M., *Children of the Laboring Poor: Expectation and Experience among the Orphans of Early Modern Augsburg*, Leiden, 2005.

Scheller, B., *Memoria an der Zeitenwende. Die Stiftungen Jakob Fuggers des Reichen vor und während der Reformation (ca. 1505–1555)*, Berlin, 2004.

Sczesny, A., *Zwischen Kontinuität und Wandel. Ländliches Gewerbe und ländliche Gesellschaft im Ostschwaben des 17. und 18. Jahrhunderts*, Tübingen, 2002.

Seling, H., *Die Kunst der Augsburger Goldschmiede 1529–1868*, 3 vols., Munich, 1980.

Stuart, K., *Defiled Trade and Social Outcasts: Honor and Ritual Pollution in Early Modern Germany*, Cambridge, 1999.

Tietz-Strödel, M., *Die Fuggerei in Augsburg. Studien zur Entwicklung des sozialen Stiftungsbaus im 15. und 16. Jahrhundert*, Tübingen, 1982.

Tlusty, B.A., *Bacchus and Civic Order: The Culture of Drink in Early Modern Germany*, Charlottesville, 2001.

Tlusty, B.A., "Full Cups, Full Coffers: Tax Strategies and Consumer Culture in the Early Modern German Cities", *German History* 32 (2014), pp. 1–28.

Werkstetter, C., *Frauen im Augsburger Zunfthandwerk. Arbeit, Arbeitsbeziehungen und Geschlechterverhältnisse im 18. Jahrhundert*, Berlin, 2001.

Winzen, K., *Handwerk – Städte – Reich. Die städtische Kurie des Immerwährenden Reichstags und die Anfänge der Reichshandwerksordnung*, Stuttgart, 2002.

CHAPTER 13

Women, Family, and Sexuality

Margaret Lewis

As early modern Augsburg grappled with transformations in religion and governmental structure, the role of women, family, and sexuality received greater attention from city leaders than in previous centuries. Gender, familial, and sexual roles were sharply defined by the city's status as a center of Reformation-era religious transformation and as a leader in trade and production. Augsburg's highly patriarchal guild structure served as an early base for religious reform in the sixteenth century, and as such the city's guilds led the charge in enforcing increasingly strict gender segregation, more sharply defining masculine and feminine roles and characteristics. The early modern period in Augsburg saw women excluded from occupations and positions that they had held in previous centuries. Both brothels and, for a time, convents were shuttered in the name of religious reform and preserving proper social order, while women were also exiled from guild masterships and barred from skilled handicrafts. The family-based workshop with the father/master at the head was held to be the standard for proper, godly order, and any deviation from that order was increasingly seen as threatening to the community as a whole. While women often experienced harsher punishments and social repercussions for sexual impropriety, both women and men, married or single, and at all levels of society, were constricted by early modern behavioral standards. These standards were enforced both by law and by the community through pressure from guilds, employers, families, and neighbors, who were eager to protect their own honor and that of their associations. By the mid-sixteenth century, the people of Augsburg, despite continuing religious upheavals, had coalesced around a singular concept of proper roles for women, the makeup of family, and the purpose and place of sexuality.

1 Family

Family structure and the role of women in early modern Augsburg were deeply influenced by the religious reformation that took place in the 1520s and 1530s and the subsequent decades of sectarian unrest. Gender roles were also defined by the strict patriarchal structure of the powerful guilds who were early adopters of the new religion. In Augsburg, the institutionalization of the Reformation became official in 1537 with the election of two Protestant mayors, the establishment of the "discipline lords" and the marriage court, and the ushering in of a new discipline ordinance that addressed a wide range of behaviors from fornication to gambling. These measures allowed the city council to usurp oversight of marriage and sexuality from the church and exert stricter control over the personal lives of citizens than ever before. Reformation morality insisted on a strict code of sexual behavior and bolstered the patriarchal system, both in the home and at the municipal level. This process intensified pressure to conform on Augsburg's inhabitants while endeavoring to showcase the city as a godly, religiously reformed community.

Because of the strong guild influence in the city government, the discipline ordinance propagated guild values: the ideal of marriage and, as described by Lyndal Roper, the "hierarchy of discipline within the household – subordination of children to parents, servants to masters, and women to men".[1] This close watch over sexuality and marriage continued throughout the early modern period even after the guilds lost their predominance in city politics in 1548. Guild morality dictated that father and mother worked together as a peaceful, cohesive unit, both in matters pertaining to the household and in matters of business. The wife was held in her own high regard as nurturer and provider of sustenance, taking on a crucial role in the functioning of a craft workshop, yet this same ideology mandated a severely circumscribed role for women outside of marriage.[2]

In the Protestant ideal, marriage and motherhood remained the only acceptable path for women. Mothers in early modern Augsburg, like those elsewhere in Europe, usually experienced multiple pregnancies. Many women spent much of their child-bearing years pregnant or nursing. Heide Wunder, for example, presents the account of Elisabeth Störkerlin as representative of the early modern urban experience: the wife of Augsburg merchant Burkard Zink, she gave birth to a total of ten children over the course of their marriage. High birth rates were met with high child mortality rates, with about half of all children dying before reaching the age of ten.[3] Despite the likelihood of children dying young (and contrary to some modern claims about parents' lack of concern), mothers and fathers exhibited deep love for their children,

---

1   Roper, *The Holy Household*, pp. 21–27 (quotation from p. 22).
2   Roper, *The Holy Household*, p. 41.
3   Wunder, *He is the Sun, She is the Moon*, pp. 18–21, 71.

devoting significant energy to their moral and religious upbringing, education, and training.[4]

Children were immediately incorporated into everyday working life. Swaddled and kept out of the way during infancy, children were given tasks within the household and sent on errands around town as they grew. Children were tightly knit into the guild structure as well, with boys training in a specific craft or trade, progressing from apprentice to journeyman, while girls remained in the household, learning the duties of their future roles as wives and mothers, but not necessarily those that they might take on as the mistress in a craft workshop.[5] The raising of children in merchants' households was likewise marked by gender divisions, with boys being sent to European cities like Venice, Antwerp, and Lyons at a young age (usually 12 to 14), where they acquired foreign languages, the principles of book-keeping, and other aspects of trade.[6]

Despite the city's efforts, the institution of marriage in the reformed city faced many challenges and threats of disorder. As the only legal and honorable space for sex, marriage in early modern Augsburg could be threatened by any extra-marital sexual behavior, as examined below. Other threats to marital order were often interpreted through a sexual lens, seen as an inversion of the proper patriarchal system, the feminization of men or the masculinization of women. Frequently, marital discord spilled over the bounds of the domestic world and found its way to the courts, where spouses faced complaints and charges of disorderly behavior such as drinking, gambling, gossiping, and violence. Such complaints were more often leveled by women than by men: women had to look outside the family to assert their rights and gain support, while it could be a threat to a man's masculinity for him to acknowledge he had lost control of his household.[7]

Men and women ran into trouble when they acted in ways that undermined the expected marital order. Men most often faced complaints in court if their behavior interfered with their role as patriarch – i.e. if they drank or gambled so much that they could not provide for their family or if they treated their wives too severely. Women, on the other hand, were accused of behaviors that threatened masculine authority. Examples of both such accusations are provided in the 1592 court case of the rope-maker Ulrich Hemerle, whose wife

---

4   Wunder, *He is the Sun, She is the Moon*, pp. 11–12; for the classic argument that little genuine affection existed in the early modern family see Stone, *Family*.
5   Roper, *The Holy Household*, pp. 42–44.
6   Glück et al., *Mehrsprachigkeit*, pp. 55–92.
7   Tlusty (ed.), *Augsburg*, p. 93.

brought him to court and accused him of drinking heavily and then hitting and threatening to kill her, after she had given birth only a week earlier. Ulrich, in turn, accused his wife of "nasty talk", lying, and refusing to sleep with him, which he claimed drove him to drink.[8] Squabbles like this one, whether explicitly involving sexual issues or not, presented a threat to marital stability and thus implied dishonor and even crime. While not explicitly sexual from our perspective, for example, a man who undermined household stability by drinking away his family's money might have his masculinity called into question.

2   Sexuality

The anxiety surrounding sexual and marital order of course centered primarily on sexual acts themselves. The restriction of acceptable sexual behavior to the marital bed was not new to the Protestant faiths, nor to the renewed spirit of reformed Catholicism, but the enforcement of proper behavior had been more lax before the sixteenth century. Under the new order, improper sexuality threatened to undermine the patriarchal system, destroy families, and impugn the honor of guilds; thus it was tied not just to sexual acts, but also to ideas of honor and personal associations.

Both women's and men's behavior was governed by strict codes of honor, which dictated everything from sex to family to employment. Loss of honor, through criminal or otherwise questionable behavior, could result in the loss of social status or even one's employment. Thus, official punishment for criminal behavior was compounded by the effects on the criminal's honor.

Under the strict moral code ushered in by the Reformation, Augsburg city fathers perceived fornication as a far greater problem than it had been before. In the religious turmoil of the early sixteenth century, reformers stressed that individual behavior reflected on the morality of the entire community and that the community as a whole should fear the wrath of God in retribution for the sins of the few. Reformers focused heavily on ideas about sex, and illicit sexuality was perhaps their greatest concern. Augsburg was not alone in Reformation Germany in bringing sexual crimes formerly treated as a matter for penance, especially fornication, under the umbrella of criminal law. A fornicator could now be punished with time in jail or corporal punishment, or, if found to be a repeat offender, banishment from the city. Augsburg's court records are littered with cases of illicit sexual behavior. But as reformers attempted to counteract

---

8   "Interrogation of Ulrich Hemerle for poor householding, 1592", in Tlusty (ed.), *Augsburg*, pp. 115–17.

implicit acceptance of pre-marital sex in relationships that led to marriage, guild restrictions resulted in a later age of marriage for most young people, leading to an increased gap between sexual maturity and marriage.[9] This was a formula predestined to result in fornication.

Augsburg's new, tougher laws placed a greater share of the burden on women. Sexual offenses made up almost half of the crimes for which women were accused, but only 14 per cent of those for men.[10] This discrepancy can be partially explained by the fact that men were accused of more crimes in total: men were far more likely to be accused of theft and violent crimes than women. However, it was also far easier for men to dodge accusations of sexual misconduct, as they did not carry the physical evidence of pregnancy.

The respectable women of Augsburg thus followed an entirely different set of rules than did the men, and these boundaries were carefully delineated in public places, particularly in taverns. While public houses were the center of social life in early modern Augsburg, the role of women within their walls was strictly regulated by custom. On the one hand, drinking traditions were crucial not only to socialization, but also to conducting business in an early modern town. As such, women's participation in such rituals under certain circumstances was expected and even required. The tavernkeeper's wife and other women employed by the tavern were accepted as participating in their proper roles. Women accompanied by their husbands and those clearly conducting legitimate business were also perfectly acceptable. Yet, if a woman was found drinking under improper circumstances, especially in public, her reputation might be tarnished. It was entirely inappropriate for women to be clearly and publicly drunk, although this behavior was usually tolerated in men. A predominant underlying threat for a woman engaged in inappropriate drinking was suspicion of sexual license or even prostitution. Because drinking together implied a close social bond or business relationship, unaccompanied and unmarried women who drank with unrelated men were suspect and subject to accusations of illicit relationships or even prostitution.

Heavy drinking and habitual drunkenness were of course not acceptable for either men or women, especially if they negatively affected household finances or family position. However, the negative connotations of the drunken master of the house were different from those of the mistress. Female drunkenness indicated poor character and judgment and threatened to overturn the entire sexual order. Certain drinking rituals were firmly within the male sphere, and

---

9   Roper, *The Holy Household*, p. 15.
10 Roper, *The Holy Household*, p. 83.

female participation implied that the women were assuming masculine traits and roles.[11]

Women also suffered at the hands of abusive and drunken men. It is well known that a certain level of violence against women and children was tolerated in a familial context as acceptable paternal discipline, but this by no means implies that women subjected to serious abuse had no recourse. Court records reveal that women accused men of beating them *too severely*, not just of beating them. Rape, although difficult to prove, certainly did occur, and women could seek justice for it. A new Augsburg ordinance in 1537 reclassified the crime as a sexual offense, rather than a crime of violence, grouping rape with fornication and placing it on a level just slightly more severe than seduction. This change placed the burden on the female accuser to prove that she had physically resisted.[12] The difficulties of pursuing rape allegations likely account for how infrequently rape appears in the court records.

Sexual violence against women that did not get classified as rape also appears in the records. What might now be considered statutory rape – such as sex with a minor or someone otherwise unable to consent – was not labeled as rape in this period but as the crime of "seduction". The relationship between Anna Weilbächin and Jeremias Bair in the early seventeenth century provides an example of this situation. Bair was Weilbächin's employer and 20 years her senior. Weilbächin was said to be simple-minded. When he impregnated her, and subsequently helped her or coerced her into terminating the pregnancy, both were found guilty not only of abortion, but also of fornication.[13]

Fornication and adultery were of course not the only concerns of the reformed community preoccupied with the threat of illicit sexual behavior. Homosexual acts, like other forms of illicit sexuality, undermined early modern concepts of the orderly, acceptable household. Not only did homosexual acts necessarily occur outside of marriage, but they also subverted the patriarchal order of male domination over women. Early modern Europe did not recognize homosexuality as an identity in the modern sense, but regarded it as sinful behavior. As sex was by and large associated solely with the act of penetration, homosexuality among women was more difficult to define, and therefore to prosecute. Local court records reveal numerous investigations into acts of sodomy among men, but not into homosexual acts among women. These men were subject to intense interrogation, torture, and execution if

---

11 Tlusty, *Bacchus and Civic Order*, pp. 115–46.
12 Roper, *The Holy Household*, pp. 83–86.
13 Stadtarchiv Augsburg (StadtAA), Strafamt, Urgichten, Jeremias Bair, 4 September 1608; Strafbücher, Jeremias Bair, 4 September 1608.

found guilty. In 1532, for example, the bathhouse attendant Jacob Miller and the fruit seller Bernhart Wagner were both decapitated and their bodies burnt at the stake after they were found guilty of committing "the abominable evil and vice against nature". Further investigations revealed a small community of men who had engaged in homosexual acts centered at the three bathhouses located along the Singold Canal (*Senkelbach*) at the city's northwest corner, in some cases forming lasting relationships. Prosecutions of homosexual men declined by the seventeenth century, however, as economic woes and declining marriage prospects for journeymen led the authorities increasingly to deliberately keep accusations of sodomy from seeing the light of day. Little could have been more upsetting to the early modern mindset than the fear that interest in homosexual acts would spread.[14]

A more consistent concern for the city was prostitution, which was one of the most common illicit sexual acts. On the one hand, many recognized the inevitability, and even what they considered to be the necessity, of prostitution. On the other hand, by threatening the institution of marriage and the mandate of keeping sex within marriage, prostitution clearly ran counter to the fervent and renewed morality demanded by the new order. Prior to the Reformation, prostitution was legal within the confines of the official city brothel, which catered to male citizens as an outlet for their sexual energies, particularly before marriage. But a city-sanctioned brothel had no place in a godly community, and Augsburg closed its in 1532.

The closing of the brothel marked a revolution in attitudes toward prostitution. Throughout the late Middle Ages, the city brothel had played a central role in imperial visits to Augsburg;[15] but sex workers were now forced to the margins of society. The effect on the prostitutes and the brothel manager at the time was rather heartbreaking, for the city made no provision for where the occupants of the brothel should go. When the manager petitioned the council in hopes of eliciting some pity, they gave him no response.[16] Records indicate that city leaders did not believe that closing the brothel had the intended results; as with other efforts to reform sexuality, there was a gap between rhetoric and reality. When neighboring Nuremberg asked for advice about its own brothel, Augsburg replied that the city had experienced an increase in fornication, as young men, without the outlet of the brothel, instead seduced citizens'

---

14 Tlusty (ed.), *Augsburg*, pp. 94, 121–31.
15 Roper, *The Holy Household*, p. 90.
16 Wiesner-Hanks, *Gender, Church, and State*, p. 109.

daughters.[17] Illicit prostitution in any case continued, as evidenced by its frequent appearance in the court records.[18]

The criminalization of prostitution reflected the tightening morality of the period on multiple levels. The hiring of prostitutes had once been considered an acceptable outlet for the sexual energies of young, unmarried men. But as sexuality became more strictly controlled, association with dishonorable women grew more threatening to the reputations of their clients. Journeymen began discouraging each other from visiting prostitutes in order to preserve the honor of their station and their guilds, pushing prostitution even further outside the realms of acceptable society.[19]

Prostitution was not the only extramarital sexual outlet that faced criminalization or more intensive prosecution in the sixteenth century. City officials and citizens increasingly policed adultery and fornication as well. Fornication had been fairly widespread before the Reformation era, and indeed, continued to be so. Of course, it presented the threat of illegitimate pregnancy. Illegitimate children, who carried a taint of dishonor and were excluded from honorable guilds, endangered the patriarchal familial order, the community's system of honor, and the city's poor relief coffers. Their existence was also evidence of the rather widespread disregard of laws on fornication. Indeed, premarital sex was quite common, even in Reformation Augsburg. Jan de Vries finds evidence that four to ten per cent of the total population across Europe was illegitimate in the fifteenth and sixteenth centuries.[20] Augsburg records demonstrate that illegitimacy was no less common in this city than elsewhere. A high percentage of all brides in early modern Europe, perhaps as many as one-third, were pregnant at the time of marriage; fortunately for these women, marriage quickly legitimized their pregnancies.[21] The evidence suggests that most women pregnant out of wedlock did manage to marry the fathers of their children. So while there was a very high rate of pre-marital conception, there was a much lower rate of children born out of wedlock throughout early modern Germany.[22]

If an unwed mother was unable to marry before her child was born, she could potentially face severe consequences, including loss of employment, loss of honor, and even civil punishment handed down by the city council. Illegitimate childbirth could result in total destitution for a mother and child.

---

17   Wiesner-Hanks, *Gender, Church, and State*, pp. 109–10.
18   Roper, *The Holy Household*, p. 83.
19   Wiesner-Hanks, *Gender, Church, and State*, p. 131.
20   De Vries, "Population", p. 34.
21   Harrington, *The Unwanted Child*, p. 37.
22   Rublack, *The Crimes of Women*, pp. 135–36.

For this reason, some women went to extremes to escape their situations. These women might choose to hide their pregnancies and commit abortion or neonatal infanticide. Both were capital crimes; the fact that some women risked death to avoid the discovery of an illegitimate pregnancy indicates the severity of the potential repercussions. These crimes, although relatively infrequent, reveal much about societal expectations and pressures on women.

Reformed city officials saw these crimes as particularly cruel and horrific, as they not only violated norms in the act of illegitimate conception, but also indicated a rejection of the sacred bond of motherhood. Although the secrecy inherent in such offenses makes for incomplete records, the extent of the public outcry against them was surely out of proportion to the actual occurrence, as Augsburg witnessed a peak of only eight cases in the decade between 1600 and 1610.[23] Nevertheless, city chroniclers decried the crimes, and the city council repeatedly issued ordinances intended to curb infanticide and abortion, calling on midwives and the citizenry in general to help police unmarried women.[24] Over one hundred women were prosecuted for infanticide and abortion during the early modern era in Augsburg, numbers nowhere near the thousands claimed by some contemporaries, but significant nonetheless.[25]

Many more mothers tried abandoning their children, either simply in the streets or in the foundling house, which was established to deal with this growing problem by 1533.[26] The conditions of this institution were famously atrocious, which may testify to the desperation of the parents who abandoned their children there. Foundling homes across Europe were constantly criticized for their squalid conditions and horrifyingly low survival rates.[27] Mortality rates in such institutions were often two to three times the rates of the general population. In Augsburg, those who lived in the foundling house did not fare much better than elsewhere: five per cent of girls and just under seven per cent of boys survived until adulthood.[28] In response to an upsurge in the number of abandoned children and orphans during the economically difficult years of the late sixteenth century, the council founded an orphanage in 1572, making Augsburg the first city in Germany to build one.[29] The orphanage accepted only true orphans – children who had lost both parents – and only legitimate

---

23   Lewis, *Infanticide and Abortion*, p. 52.
24   Kölderer, *Chronik*, pp. 381, 455 and passim.
25   StadtAA, Urgichten and Strafbücher.
26   Obermeier, "Findel- und Waisenkinder", p. 142.
27   Ulbricht, "The Debate about Foundling Hospitals", p. 211–56; Boswell, *The Kindness of Strangers*, pp. 421–24.
28   Obermeier, "Findel- und Waisenkinder", p. 160.
29   Safley, *Charity and Economy*, p. 1.

children whose parents were citizens, while the foundling home continued to handle all others.[30] The fact that the city built separate institutions for legitimate and illegitimate children demonstrates the severe challenge that illegitimate children posed to the rigid standards of appropriate sexuality and proper familial structure. There was simply no room for sex or children outside of marriage.

3 Gender and Sexuality in the Workplace

Crucial to understanding the proper and acceptable familial structure of early modern Augsburg is the powerful system of guilds, which held tremendous political and social power in the city. The guilds not only shaped work life for urban men and women, but also strictly defined masculine and feminine behavior in and beyond the workplace. Early adopters of the new religious ideas as a whole, the guilds also played a crucial role in shaping and spreading Reformation ideas about family and morality. Marriage was the center not just of social life in early modern Augsburg, but of economic life as well. Guilds depended on a system of corporate honor to maintain respectability and collective legitimacy. All those connected to the guild were expected to be of legitimate birth and to avoid any taint of dishonor.[31] The guild hierarchy was defined by the structure of sexual maturity, so that guild honor was also shaped by appropriate sexual behavior. Journeymen, who were forbidden to marry in most trades before the eighteenth century, were banned from any sexual outlet, as the only appropriate arena for sexual relations was within marriage.[32] Threats to guild honor held journeymen to these expectations; likewise, the high stakes and expectations regulating sexuality threatened women's honor and position within society. Concepts of acceptable and unacceptable sexuality were central to the early modern family, and therefore, to the guild system and workplace.

Male-dominated guilds required strict divisions of labor between men and women; nevertheless, women in guild households worked in a staggering array of positions. In addition to the expected raising of children, cooking, and cleaning, they ran households, managed servants, worked market stalls selling goods, fed journeymen and apprentices, did piecemeal work, and served

---

30   Safley, *Children of the Laboring Poor*, p. 17.
31   Stuart, *Defiled Trades*, pp. 13–17.
32   Wiesner-Hanks, *Gender, Church and State*, pp. 170–71.

customers in taverns. These 'auxiliary' chores made an essential contribution to the well-being of guild households.[33]

Lyndal Roper points out that even though day-to-day labor within the workshop was likely shared in a more haphazard fashion, there remained a fundamental assumption that certain tasks were "not fitting" for women or not within the realm of men's work.[34] Guild structure was supposed to fit neatly within the ideal concept of the household. The workshop master and his wife filled a parental position for the journeymen and apprentices who worked for them. The guild life cycle was also supposed to reflect the sexual maturation of its young employees. Journeymen were to remain unmarried until the time they became masters and established their own workshop, a two-fold step in becoming sexually and economically mature adults.

Throughout the sixteenth and seventeenth centuries, however, this guild system began to deteriorate, resulting in the exclusion of women from skilled labor positions and the restriction of access to masterships for journeymen. As economic factors made the step from journeyman to master much more difficult, these young men became stuck in wage-labor positions, unable to marry, and needing to defend their quickly-diminishing rights and economic power. These struggling guilds became much more exclusive of women in skilled labor positions; journeymen were forced to bolster their own economic worth by labeling women's work and even that work done alongside women as inferior and potentially dishonoring. Merry Wiesner-Hanks has demonstrated how this devaluation continued through the age of industrialization, with skilled work denied to women and the work women did do construed as unskilled and less valuable.[35] Whereas there were specifically female guilds in other localities in Germany – though these too were declining in number and rights – Augsburg had none. The absence of women's guilds was a direct result of the perception that women's work required no specialized skill.[36]

As women were officially excluded from guilds, so too were their rights to manage money restricted. Widows, who had traditionally enjoyed considerable control over their property, faced increased restrictions in Augsburg and elsewhere in the sixteenth century. According to Merry Wiesner-Hanks, the city of Augsburg issued an order in 1578 that "all widows report to the official in charge (*Oberpfleger*) within one month of the death of their husband, make an appraisal of all goods and property, and choose two men who were not heirs to

---

33 See Werkstetter, *Frauen im Augsburger Zunfthandwerk*, pp. 54–143.
34 Roper, *The Holy Household*, pp. 44–46.
35 Wiesner-Hanks, *Gender, Church, and State*, pp. 178–96.
36 Roper, *The Holy Household*, pp. 47–48.

act as guardians. If the widow did not, the city council would choose these for her." The council claimed to be acting in the widows' best interests and that of their heirs, given their inherent 'stupidity' and naivety. The city found reason to re-issue this ordinance multiple times throughout the next century, as widows refused to comply.[37]

All of these trends of expanding restrictions are visible among Augsburg's weavers. Weaving was one of the city's largest industries, and one in which women initially participated at all levels. Most women in the cloth industry worked as spinners or carders, which were considered suitable female professions.[38] Women could do this work in their own homes, or in the home of their master weaver. According to Wiesner-Hanks, these women do not appear on the tax lists, and thus are not as readily associated with an occupation bringing in outside income.[39] Claus-Peter Clasen has found, however, that 15 per cent of master weavers in Augsburg in 1600 were women, presumably widows. While women tended to preside over much smaller workshops, women could, in some circumstances, work independently and as masters.[40] For the eighteenth century, Christine Werkstetter has found that widows continued to run their deceased husbands' workshops in many, if not all local trades. Whereas some craft ordinances required widows to hire journeymen, others contained no such requirement.[41] Masters' daughters could not be formally apprenticed in their fathers' workshops, to be sure, but there is considerable evidence that many acquired specific craft skills and were involved in production processes.[42]

New and growing restrictions on women's work often focused specifically on the weaving industry, as male guild members felt the pressure of competition from women. As was the case with other crafts, the weavers resented women in their profession and sought redress from the city council. In 1582, the council outlawed noncitizen women from living and working independently. The council grew increasingly strict with its mandates: it soon threatened to banish any woman who made demands of her employer, and forbade all unmarried women from heading their own households.[43] While these laws were written

---

37 Wiesner-Hanks, *Working Women*, p. 25.
38 Wiesner-Hanks, *Gender, Church, and State*, pp. 146–47.
39 Wiesner-Hanks, *Working Women*, p. 173.
40 Clasen, *Augsburger Weber*, p. 23. Brewers' widows also brewed independently but, as members of a more lucrative craft, their numbers were lower than that for weavers; StadtAA, Chroniken 10, Georg Siedeler, fols. 26–30, 101–07, 162.
41 Werkstetter, *Frauen im Augsburger Zunfthandwerk*, pp. 144–280.
42 Werkstetter, *Frauen im Augsburger Zunfthandwerk*, pp. 281–372.
43 Wiesner-Hanks, *Working Women*, pp. 176–77.

specifically with the weaving industry in mind, female weavers did not accept the new laws without protest, and in many instances ignored the laws and continued to work. Unmarried veil weavers, for instance, publicly protested a new law forbidding their trade.[44] Yet the restrictions kept coming: in the same vein, the city ordered that unmarried spinners could no longer live independently, but only with weavers, essentially demoting them to domestic servitude.[45] Unmarried women who continued to work often did so out of dire necessity and represented the most modest of incomes in the city. Wiesner-Hanks suggests that in some cases this work was allowed because it was cheaper for the city to ignore it than to provide the women with poor relief.[46]

Midwives were the natural exception to many of these trends and regulations. As midwifery involved questionably close contact with the female body, men were more hesitant to infringe on it than other professions. Yet, male medical professionals insisted on maintaining close oversight. Though the midwives of Augsburg did not work within an official guild, they were carefully regulated by the *Collegium Medicum*, a medical board made up of official physicians, which licensed and regulated them. Midwives completed intensive training in apprenticeships before undergoing thorough examination in order to obtain their licenses. Despite these regulations, midwives' day-to-day work was fairly independent of male influence and authority. For most of the early modern period, physicians were only consulted by midwives in extreme circumstances, such as situations requiring surgical intervention. Because midwives were excluded from those tasks considered to be more highly skilled and because they were women, midwives' work was underestimated as a specific and difficult skill set. The city appointed respectable, upper-class married women to supervise the midwives, with their only qualifications being their natural abilities as women and their circumspection and knowledge as wives.[47] Midwives were also undercompensated for their work because of their gender. The city routinely paid them less than male medical professionals, even barber-surgeons, who were also craftsmen without university training.[48] Midwives could supplement their income with private clients, whom they could charge more. Nevertheless, midwives on the whole were not well off, remaining among the lower-paid workers in the city.[49]

---

44 Clasen, *Augsburger Weber*, pp. 130–32.
45 Wiesner-Hanks, *Gender, Church, and State*, p. 100.
46 Wiesner-Hanks, *Working Women*, pp. 177–78.
47 Roper, *The Holy Household*, p. 48.
48 See Chapter 3 in this volume.
49 Wiesner-Hanks, "Midwives of South Germany", pp. 79–80, 83. Most midwives in Augsburg were the wives of craftsmen, rather than self-supporting; thus their income was likely viewed as supplemental: Roeck, *Eine Stadt in Krieg und Frieden*, vol. 1, p. 299.

By the late seventeenth and early eighteenth centuries, however, midwives faced the growing threat of attempts to professionalize the field of medicine. More and more of their practices were brought under direct physician oversight.[50] The midwives of early modern Augsburg faced the same trends that boxed women out of guild work: the classification of their labor as highly skilled, leading to an insistence on formal education and the subsequent disqualification of female midwives from the profession.

Many more women worked in unskilled and often temporary positions. The most common profession for an unmarried woman of the lower classes in Augsburg was domestic service in someone else's household. As the largest and most economically active city in the region, Augsburg drew both men and women seeking employment from a wide swath of southern Germany. Most young women who came looking for jobs ended up as domestic servants, often in guild workshops doing menial tasks such as laundry and cleaning. Serving maids often had multiple employers over the course of their working years, which could last from their early teens to their mid-to-late twenties. Some lucky women were able to save up a small dowry during their service; others never married, remaining servants for decades.[51]

Augsburg court records reveal some of the difficulties of life in domestic service. Maids complained about unpaid wages and slander, as well as more serious mistreatment such as beating, starvation, and rape at the hands of their employers. Although women could bring their employers to court over such abuses, many opted to stay in uncomfortable circumstances rather than try to find another position and risk losing honor.[52]

City magistrates were continuously suspicious of serving maids, viewing them as potentially destabilizing to the patriarchal structure of the community because of their lack of familial connections and their tendency to switch employers and housing frequently. In an effort to promote stability, governments attempted various strategies to control maidservants, including placing limits on when and how they could change positions.[53] In cities like Augsburg, servants could only switch employers on certain days, once or twice a year, or not at all; they were sometimes bound to a position for a set period, often six months or a year.[54]

At the upper end of the scale, merchant wives enjoyed greater freedoms than women in other occupations. They occasionally traveled with their

---

50   Wiesner-Hanks, "Midwives of South Germany", p. 83.
51   Hufton, *The Prospect Before Her*, pp. 78–89. See also Werkstetter, *Frauen im Augsburger Zunfthandwerk*, pp. 373–437.
52   Wiesner-Hanks, *Working Women*, p. 90.
53   Roper, *The Holy Household*, p. 55.
54   Wiesner-Hanks, *Working Women*, pp. 83–92.

husbands, sometimes ran their husbands' business affairs in their absence, and continued to operate businesses into widowhood. In the fifteenth century, the wives of the wealthy Fuggers were exemplary of this practice: Elisabeth Gefattermann, Hans Fugger's wife, and Barbara Bäsinger, their son Jakob's wife, both worked to double their taxable wealth in their widowhoods. It was only in the sixteenth century that Jakob Fugger the Younger – called "the Rich" on account of his fabulous wealth – enforced the exclusion of women from the management of the family firm. Although increasingly restricted in their ability to engage directly in business, the wives and widows of some merchant families, such as the Gossembrot, Meuting, and Weiß families, remained highly involved in building their husbands' businesses and protecting their own wealth. In the case of her husband's bankruptcy, a merchant wife's dowry, legally remaining her personal property, could be essential for providing the family with a fresh start.[55] In the later eighteenth century, the widow Anna Barbara Gignoux successfully ran one of Augsburg's large-scale cotton-printing manufactories.[56] Throughout the early modern period, women from wealthy families were also important in cementing business alliances through their marriages. It was through marriage that the Welsers reached the highest levels of German society: in 1557, Philippine Welser clandestinely married an emperor's son, Archduke Ferdinand of Tyrol.[57]

4   Religious Women

Given the Reformation-era desire to model society on male-dominated family units, religious unrest presented peculiar challenges. Religious women in Augsburg faced unique struggles, especially as the Reformation resulted in the closing of convents and the entry into society of dozens of unmarried women. Augsburg witnessed the formal institution of Protestantism in the 1530s, a forced reconversion to Catholicism at the end of the Schmalkaldic War, biconfessionalism after 1555, and the slow but steady re-emergence of a Catholic majority in the eighteenth century.[58] This religious turmoil affected women in all parts of society, but local religious women felt it most acutely.

---

55   Häberlein, *The Fuggers of Augsburg*, pp. 12–20; idem, "Zwischen Vormundschaft und Risiko".
56   Werkstetter, "Anna Barbara Gignoux".
57   Wunder, *He is the Sun, She is the Moon*, p. 160.
58   See Chapters 10 and 11 in this volume.

Marjorie Plummer has nuanced the discussion of religious women in her examination of clerical marriage after the Reformation. The closure of religious houses of both sexes and reformers' approval of clerical marriage resulted in turmoil: ideas of marriage were reevaluated, and cities faced sudden influxes of unmarried monks and nuns (as well as reformed priests seeking wives). Unmarried women, suddenly free of the protection and restriction of cloistered life, threatened to undermine the desired, tidy familial order. In the 1530s, Augsburg debated closing its convents, but the city councilors worried deeply about the possibility of unleashing weak-willed and naturally sinful women on their good Christian community.[59]

In the case of former Catholic priests, Augsburg quietly accepted clerical marriage in the early years of the Reformation, despite imperial decrees against it.[60] This may not actually have been a tremendous change, given the frequency with which priests took concubines prior to the Reformation. Yet such a dramatic shift in official practice could not go unnoticed. The marriage of former Carmelite prior Johann Frosch in 1525 turned into a public spectacle, drawing crowds eager to see a priest's marriage.[61] With the official adoption of the Reformation in 1537, the local clergy and laity were held subject to the same moral laws as other citizens, and clergy were expected to fall into Luther's model of moral heads of households.[62]

The closing of convents across the Holy Roman Empire has led many historians to conclude that the Reformation cut women off from options outside the home, removed traditional positions of female authority, and pushed them into married subjugation. Lyndal Roper interprets these moves as based in the era's distrust of women's power and community outside of male influence and of women outside of the familial structure.[63] Yet others have tempered this analysis by pointing out that far more female convents remained open after the Reformation than did monasteries.[64] Half of the city's eight convents survived until the reintroduction of Catholicism in 1548, while none of the monasteries did.[65]

---

59 Plummer, *From Priest's Whore to Pastor's Wife*, p. 152.
60 Ibid., p. 6.
61 Ibid., p. 106.
62 Ibid., p. 258.
63 Roper, *The Holy Household*, pp. 206–51.
64 Leonard, *Nails in the Wall*, p. 5.
65 Roper, *The Holy Household*, p. 235.

5   Women and Education

Augsburg's position as a center of the Reformation was closely tied to its position as a hub of trade, printing, and education. Germany, especially its urban areas, had higher than average rates of literacy for both men and women. Gerald Strauss described literacy as being "regarded as normal among artisans", who accounted for a large percentage of Augsburg's population.[66] Artisan women, the lower urban classes, and peasants were less likely to be literate than male artisans in Germany, but still enjoyed much higher rates than the rest of Europe. Augsburg was second only to Nuremberg as a south German center of print production; the print industry and high literacy rates bolstered each other.[67] Hans-Jörg Künast argues that, in the early sixteenth century, at least 30 per cent of Augsburg's population could read and write. The sixteenth century saw a proliferation of local schools, as the population grew and rival religious groups jockeyed to catechize and convert.[68]

Reformers of all stripes pushed for greater access to basic education starting in the mid-sixteenth century, and Augsburg was a leader in this trend. During the sixteenth century, there were 34 local schools, the majority being Protestant.[69] By 1623, the numbers had fallen, but the city still boasted 20 Protestant and four Catholic schoolmasters. The number of primary-level pupils was relatively evenly divided between boys and girls (47 per cent of Protestant students and 51 per cent of Catholic students were female).[70]

In addition to attaining basic levels of schooling, elite women were involved in more learned pursuits as well. The women of wealthy patrician and merchant families in Augsburg played a vital role in supporting education and humanist learning. The daughters of such families were educated in Latin and Greek, to flaunt the high culture of their families and make them more attractive marriage prospects for other well-educated and wealthy families.[71] The Welser daughter Margarete was thus suitable for marriage to the humanist Conrad Peutinger, who continued to support her education as well as that of their daughters.[72] After the founding of a local *Institutum Mariae Virginum Anglicanarum* by followers of the English Catholic reformer Mary Ward in 1662,

---

66   Strauss, *Luther's House of Learning*, p. 200.
67   Wiltenburg, *Crime and Culture*, pp. 9–14.
68   Künast, *"Getruckt zu Augspurg"*, pp. 11–13.
69   Nießeler, *Augsburger Schulen*, pp. 15–17.
70   Hsia, *Social Discipline*, p. 114.
71   Robin, "Intellectual Women", p. 397.
72   Wunder, *He is the Sun, She is the Moon*, p. 43; Zäh, "Konrad Peutinger und Margarete Welser".

the convent's highly educated sisters, some of whom hailed from England and France in the early years, played an important role in the education of Catholic girls in Augsburg, including the teaching of foreign languages.[73]

6 Women and Political Life

Higher levels of education were necessarily closely connected with participation in urban political life. Throughout the early modern period, the women of Augsburg remained active in politics, despite decreasing opportunities for participation and declining access to the rights of citizenship they had enjoyed in the late Middle Ages. Like men, women could be granted access to citizenship by virtue of their occupation: midwives and seamstresses, among others, could purchase citizenship. Women could even purchase citizenship rights apart from their husbands or pass citizenship to their husbands. Like their male counterparts, female citizens were required to contribute to the city's defense through defense taxes and provision of armed guards for the night watch. But although women from local families retained the right to the title of citizen, from the sixteenth century the distinction between the rights held by a male citizen and a female citizen widened dramatically. As Merry Wiesner-Hanks has argued, women's power and authority as citizens became a derivative of their relationship to their families, and not of their own standing.[74]

Women's role in the political life of Augsburg was tightly intertwined with their occupations and especially their relationship to the city's guilds. As noted above, a crucial factor in Augsburg's sixteenth-century restrictions on women's rights was the series of attempts by the council to restrict women's work. Local women did not passively accept these restrictions. They fought continuously in the courts and in public to retain what they perceived as their rights. Protesting occupational restrictions was one of the most frequent ways in which women became involved in political life; the pushback of women in the weaving industry discussed above was typical of this political action.[75]

The involvement of women in politics was also particularly apparent during the early, tumultuous years of the Reformation in the 1520s and 1530s. Women were often on the front lines of religious reform and participated in religiously-motivated political unrest. To take a religious stance in this era was to make

---

73 Juhl, *Institutum Mariae Virginum Anglicanarum*; Glück, Häberlein and Schröder, *Mehrsprachigkeit*, pp. 230–33.
74 Wiesner-Hanks, *Gender, Church, and State*, pp. 117–24.
75 Clasen, *Augsburger Weber*, pp. 103–32.

an inherently political statement, as in the case of Anna Fassnacht, who was tortured and banished for "seditious talk" in the aftermath of major religious protests in 1524, and Sabina Preiss, interrogated in 1588 for singing a banned political song.[76] Women defied official decrees to assert their religious beliefs, for example by smuggling newborns out of town to have a Catholic baptism during the years in which Catholicism was banned.[77]

Anabaptism was particularly appealing to some women, and female Anabaptists were just as vocal and active, if not more, than their male coreligionists. Anabaptists faced persecution throughout the early modern period, with equal numbers of female and male Anabaptists appearing in the Augsburg court records. Several women were recorded as deciding to receive baptism either against their husbands' orders or without their knowledge. Others appear to have worked actively to spread their faith and organize prayer groups. Women served as central axes in the familial and social networks through which Anabaptism spread. These records also show local women actively seeking out religious answers. In the atmosphere of religious diversity in the early 1500s, Augsburg's inhabitants were uniquely exposed to the many new religious ideas proliferating in that era. Michele Zelinsky Hanson examines the extraordinary example of Agnes Vogel, who spoke openly and clearly about her search for religious guidance: she became frustrated after hearing conflicting religious opinions and decided to listen to preachers from several confessions. Agnes finally settled on Anabaptism, having listened to various takes on communion and baptism.[78] As has been demonstrated by Caroline Gritschke, a number of Augsburg women were also active in the Schwenckfelder movement.[79]

7 Conclusion

The women of Augsburg experienced many of the same tribulations as women across the Holy Roman Empire: shrinking opportunity, power, and independence, along with the increasing pressures of heightened morality, and tumultuous decades of religious strife and economic uncertainty. Reform-minded leaders pushed through stricter laws about behavior – laws that, by biological necessity, fell disproportionately on women. Economic pressure led men to

---

76 "The Interrogation of Anna Fasnacht", and "Interrogation of Sabina Preiss for the 'Müller Song', 1588", in Tlusty (ed.), *Augsburg*, pp. 15–16, 52–53.
77 Zelinsky Hanson, *Religious Identity*, p. 119.
78 Zelinsky Hanson, *Religious Identity*, pp. 79–100.
79 Gritschke, *"Via Media"*, pp. 29–30, 95.

box women out of careers that they had held for centuries and devalue the work they were still allowed to do. Men and women alike strained against a society which was in many ways far more restrictive than that of previous generations. Yet these dictates were not entirely handed down from on high: male and female Augsburgers also helped to create this same society in order to defend their own individual or group honor and economic power. And even if women were increasingly exiled from public life and from access to positions of power through exclusion from official positions in guilds and the shuttering of convents, they continued to participate in politics and civic life in unofficial ways, even if they faced consequences for it.

Bibliography

Unpublished Primary Sources
Stadtarchiv Augsburg (StadtAA)
    Chroniken 10, Georg Siedeler.
    Strafamt, Urgichten and Strafbücher.

Published Primary Sources
Kölderer, G., *Beschreibunng vnnd Kurtze Vertzaichnus Fürnemer Lob vnnd gedenckhwürdiger Historien. Eine Chronik der Stadt Augsburg der Jahre 1576 bis 1607*, ed. S. Strodel and W.E.J. Weber, 4 vols., Augsburg, 2013.

Stetten, P. von (the Elder), *Geschichte der Heil. Röm. Reichs Freyen Stadt Augspurg*, Frankfurt, 1743.

Tlusty, B.A. (ed.), *Augsburg During the Reformation Era: An Anthology of Sources*, Indianapolis, 2012.

Secondary Literature
Boswell, J., *The Kindness of Strangers: The Abandonment of Children in Western Europe from Late Antiquity to the Renaissance*, New York, 1988.

Clasen, C.-P., *Die Augsburger Weber. Leistungen und Krisen des Textilgewerbes um 1600*, Augsburg, 1981.

De Vries, J., "Population", in T. Brady, H.A. Oberman and J. Tracy (eds), *Handbook of European History 1400–1600: Late Middle Ages, Renaissance and Reformation, Volume 1: Structures and Assertions*, Leiden, 1994, pp. 1–50.

Glück, H., Häberlein, M. and Schröder, K., *Mehrsprachigkeit in der Frühen Neuzeit. Die Reichsstädte Augsburg und Nürnberg vom 15. bis ins frühe 19. Jahrhundert*, Wiesbaden, 2013.

Gritschke, C., *"Via Media": Spiritualistische Lebenswelten und Konfessionalisierung. Das süddeutsche Schwenckfeldertum im 16. und 17. Jahrhundert*, Berlin, 2006.

Häberlein, M., *The Fuggers of Augsburg: Pursuing Wealth and Honor in Renaissance Germany*, Charlottesville and London, 2012.

Häberlein, M., "Zwischen Vormundschaft und Risiko: Ökonomische Handlungsspielräume und Investitionen Augsburger Patrizier- und Kaufmannsfrauen des 16. und frühen 17. Jahrhunderts", in G. Signori (ed.), *Prekäre Ökonomien. Schulden in Spätmittelalter und Früher Neuzeit*, Constance, 2014, pp. 139–58.

Harrington, J., *The Unwanted Child: The Fate of Foundlings, Orphans, and Juvenile Criminals in Early Modern Germany*, Chicago, 2009.

Hsia, R.P., *Social Discipline in the Reformation: Central Europe, 1550–1750*, London, 1992.

Hufton, O., *The Prospect Before Her: A History of Women in Western Europe, 1500–1800*, New York, 1998.

Juhl, A., *Institutum Mariae Virginum Anglicanarum. Ein Beitrag zur Geschichte des Englischen Institutes (BMV) zu Augsburg von den Anfängen bis 1830*, Augsburg, 1997.

Künast, H.-J., *"Getruckt zu Augspurg". Buchdruck und Buchhandel in Augsburg zwischen 1468 und 1555*, Tübingen, 1997.

Leonard, A., *Nails in the Wall: Catholic Nuns in Reformation Germany*, Chicago, 2005.

Lewis, M., *Infanticide and Abortion in Early Modern Germany*, New York, 2016.

Nießeler, M., *Augsburger Schulen im Wandel der Zeit. Ein Beitrag zur Geschichte des Augsburger Schulwesens*, Augsburg, 1984.

Obermeier, A., "Findel- und Waisenkinder: Zur Geschichte der Sozialfürsorge in der Reichsstadt Augsburg", *Zeitschrift des Historischen Vereins für Schwaben* 83 (1990), pp. 129–62.

Plummer, M., *From Priest's Whore to Pastor's Wife: Clerical Marriage and the Process of Reform in the Early German Reformation*, London, 2012.

Robin, D., "Intellectual Women in Early Modern Europe", in A. Poska, J. Couchman and K. McIver (eds), *The Ashgate Research Companion to Women and Gender in Early Modern Europe*, Farnham, 2013, pp. 381–406.

Roeck, B., *Eine Stadt in Krieg und Frieden. Studien zur Geschichte der Reichsstadt Augsburg zwischen Kalenderstreit und Parität*, 2 vols., Göttingen, 1989.

Roper, L., *The Holy Household: Women and Morals in Reformation Augsburg*, Oxford, 1989.

Rublack, U., *The Crimes of Women in Early Modern Germany*, Oxford, 1999.

Safley, T.M., *Charity and Economy in the Orphanages of Early Modern Augsburg*, Boston, 1997.

Safley, T.M., *Children of the Laboring Poor: Expectation and Experience Among the Orphans of Early Modern Augsburg*, Leiden, 2005.

Stone, L., *The Family, Sex, and Marriage in England 1500–1800*, New York, 1977.

Strauss, G., *Luther's House of Learning: Indoctrination of the Young in the German Reformation*, Baltimore, 1978.

Stuart, K., *Defiled Trades and Social Outcasts: Honor and Ritual Pollution in Early Modern Germany*, Cambridge, 1999.

Tlusty, B.A., *Bacchus and Civic Order: The Culture of Drink in Early Modern Germany*, Charlottesville, 2001.

Ulbricht, O., "The Debate about Foundling Hospitals in Enlightenment Germany: Infanticide, Illegitimacy, and Infant Mortality Rates", *Central European History* 18 (1985), pp. 211–56.

Werkstetter, C., *Frauen im Augsburger Zunfthandwerk. Arbeit, Arbeitsbeziehungen und Geschlechterverhältnisse im 18. Jahrhundert*, Berlin, 2001.

Werkstetter, C., "Anna Barbara Gignoux (1725–1796), Kattunfabrikantin oder Mäzenin? Zur Entstehung einer Augsburger Legende", in J. Burkhardt (ed.), *Augsburger Handelshäuser im Wandel des historischen Urteils*, Berlin, 1996, pp. 381–99.

Wiesner-Hanks, M., *Working Women in Renaissance Germany*, New Brunswick, 1986.

Wiesner-Hanks, M., "The Midwives of South Germany and the Public/Private Dichotomy", in H. Marland (ed.), *The Art of Midwifery: Early Modern Midwives in Europe*, London, 1993, pp. 77–94.

Wiesner-Hanks, M., *Gender, Church, and State in Early Modern Germany: Essays*, London, 1998.

Wiltenburg, J., *Crime and Culture in Early Modern Germany*, Charlottesville and London, 2013.

Wunder, H., *He is the Sun, She is the Moon: Women in Early Modern Germany*, Cambridge, MA, 1998.

Zäh, H., "Konrad Peutinger und Margarete Welser – Ehe und Familie im Zeichen des Humanismus", in M. Häberlein and J. Burkhardt (eds.), *Die Welser. Neue Forschungen zur Geschichte und Kultur des oberdeutschen Handelshauses*, Berlin, 2002, pp. 449–509.

Zelinsky Hanson, M., *Religious Identity in an Early Reformation Community: Augsburg, 1517 to 1555*, Leiden and Boston, 2009.

CHAPTER 14

Sociability and Leisure

B. Ann Tlusty

1   Introduction

Although we are used to thinking of leisure as time to relax, socialize, and pursue entertainments according to personal choice, sociability and leisure have always had a political side as well. This was certainly true in early modern Europe, especially during the Reformation and its aftermath, with its powerful emphasis on moral living. Because leisure is by definition time not dedicated to work or worship, when one is able to pursue activities considered by many religious reformers to be idle, frivolous, or wasteful, the authorities in Augsburg as in other German towns took steps to eliminate what they understood as disorder by enforcing pious behavior. This included issuing a profusion of decrees and ordinances aimed at restricting how people spent their free time.

Some historians have characterized this attack on leisure time as the repression of popular culture by elite rulers suspicious of the unrestrained and playful world of the popular classes. On the basis of a model famously labeled by Peter Burke "the triumph of Lent", control of popular leisure activities by elites was a theme central to the theories of social disciplining, confessionalization, and the "civilizing process" that have dominated early modern historical studies since the 1970s.[1] More recently, scholars have identified a more nuanced relationship between the elite and popular classes, recognizing that social control could function laterally as well as top-down, and that elite culture was hardly more orderly than that of the populace at large. Many of Augsburg's most powerful citizens were themselves enthusiastic participants in a playful culture of sociability that made a virtue out of excess.[2] Early modern authorities also knew that not all popular leisure led to disorder; in fact, many forms of leisure and sociability had positive effects for the city. Thus civic leaders often found themselves at odds with the extremely moral tone of their own ordinances, not all of which were regularly enforced.

---

[1]   Burke, *Popular Culture*; Oestreich, "Strukturprobleme"; Elias, *The Civilizing Process*; idem, *Quest for Excitement*; Schilling, "Konfessionalisierung".
[2]   Grüber (ed.), *"Kurzweil viel ..."*; Deutsches Historisches Museum (ed.), *"Kurzweil viel ..."*

Efforts by historians to explore popular leisure activities and the relationship between elite and popular culture remain complicated by the lopsided nature of early modern sources, nearly all of which were produced by ruling elements in society. Leisure activities among the populace have thus usually been interpreted primarily through the lens of printed descriptions and decrees aimed at religious or social discipline. But the resulting conclusion that the upper classes before the eighteenth century viewed all popular games, dances, and tavern sociability as "reprehensible examples of 'idleness'"[3] does little to explain elite support for many of these very same activities.

The exploitation of newly-discovered sources that engage more directly with the day-to-day business of providing for the recreational needs of the popular classes has chipped away at the assumption that either leisure time or leisure activities were modern inventions, or were confined to the elite classes before the eighteenth or nineteenth centuries. Instead, these studies highlight the roles of early modern innkeepers, musicians, merchants, booksellers, sports instructors, peddlers, and even the city government itself as entrepreneurs of recreational pastimes specifically intended to amuse the populace during non-working hours. More recent debates about the "invention" of leisure have shifted to questions of definition, centering largely on the etymology of words such as "leisure" and "sports" and the question of whether the rigid work rhythms associated with industrialization were indeed necessary to the development of a construct of leisure time.[4]

Support from the authorities for some leisure activities, particularly those associated with what historians have termed "festival culture",[5] resulted from the fact that they served religious, political, and military ends quite directly. Events tied to the religious calendar both underscored the primacy of the church as social center and reinforced the position of town authorities tasked with enforcing God's law on earth. Competitive games that we would now define as sports, including shooting matches, horse and footraces, and sword-fighting matches, were also supported by local governments as preparation for war as well as a kind of civic self-fashioning. In addition, the visible division by social rank of sociable activities such as dances, weddings, carnival events, guild processions, and other celebrations reinforced notions of social hierarchy, lending additional legitimacy to dominion by those at the top.

But people from all walks of life also engaged in leisure pastimes that were not limited to any particular holiday, season, or event. Many of these were

---

3 Burke, "Reply", p. 195.
4 Burke, "Invention"; Marfany, "Invention"; Behringer, *Kulturgeschichte des Sports*, pp. 11–19.
5 Burke, "Invention", pp. 138–39; Marfany, "Invention", pp. 185–90.

simply allowed, either as unremarkable economic transactions (eating and drinking in taverns, visiting markets and fairs, viewing traveling shows, attending plays) or as harmless fun (swimming, taking walks, reading, singing, playing board and card games, etc.). Any of these could become a problem, though, if done at the wrong time, for example during church services or instead of working, or if pursued in a disorderly way.

Attempts to control leisure activities increased during periods of tension such as outbreaks of plague, economic depression, war, and famine, which the authorities represented as evidence of God's wrath. Decrees issued during such crises typically targeted gluttony, drunkenness, and activities considered frivolous such as sleigh-riding, gambling, dancing, and exuberant carnival celebrations, including the custom of "mumming" (wearing carnival masks). In Augsburg, leisure pastimes were also particularly targeted during the Zwinglian-influenced years of the 1530s and 1540s, when discipline ordinances not only threatened punishments for all of the above-mentioned frivolities, but also forbade music and dancing even at weddings.[6]

These laws tell us as much about how people actually spent their leisure time as they do about official attempts to control it, especially if examined in light of the treatment of defendants arrested for violating them. Augsburg's large judicial collections provide rich evidence of an urban population that knew how to enjoy themselves in myriad ways; within the limited space of this chapter we can examine only the tip of the iceberg. And while the act of issuing a decree made a clear point about who represented divine power on earth, enforcement was a different matter. In many or even most cases, arrest records for drinking, gambling, singing in the streets, or idleness reveal concerns that have less to do with idle or frivolous behavior per se than with economic or political problems such as running households into ruin, evading taxes, slander and sedition, or shunning work and thus threatening to burden the city's system of poor relief. As the early modern period progressed and leisure became increasingly privatized and commercialized, decrees reflected less concern with God's wrath over frivolity and more concern with control of provisions, collection of taxes, protection of commerce, and control of the poor.[7] Given what we now know about the treatment of defendants in these cases, this looks more like an adjustment of the decrees to fit practice than a real change in policy.

---

6 Stadtarchiv Augsburg (StadtAA), Ains Ersamen Rats der Stat Augsburg Beruff, zu pflantzung Christlichs, züchtigs und erbars Lebens, Augsburg, 1541.
7 Tlusty, *Bacchus*, pp. 86–87.

2 Church Holidays and Seasonal Amusements

Many official celebrations as well as unofficial leisure activities supported religious consciousness and civic order. Early modern life was punctuated by opportunities to engage in church-sponsored entertainments that emphasized the centrality of religion and accentuated hierarchies of wealth and power. Festivals, holidays, and the general rhythms of work and rest served as reminders that the relationship between work and leisure was part of God's plan. Work was forbidden on Sundays and holidays, which were ideally to be spent in religious devotion, in support of which the city council also forbade certain kinds of sociability during the morning sermon, including gambling, taking walks, visiting taverns, and gathering to gossip. Repeated complaints about these activities suggest that they continued unabated. Naturally, a lot of socializing also went on in church. Sunday afternoons were free for relaxation, with the pubs typically opening at 1:00 PM.

The church calendar also provided opportunities for combining religious celebrations with relaxation and sociability. Church processions and festivals, carnival rituals, harvest celebrations, and Christmas feasts were organized to combine religious rituals with entertaining spectacles in order to increase attendance and remind Christians of their place in a godly community. Leisure time then followed religious ceremony, as people gathered afterwards to socialize in pubs, dance halls, and private homes.[8] Some guild rituals also fall into this category, since annual guild processions and celebrations usually coincided with religious holidays and typically began with special church services. Guild processions could be joyous affairs, sometimes accompanied by celebratory gunfire and traditional dances and invariably followed by sociable gatherings.[9]

Holidays were not located on the church calendar randomly, but were carefully timed to support seasonal cycles of work and play. It is no coincidence that religious holidays were most frequent in December, when work was limited to short periods of sunlight, and were particularly sparse during the planting and harvest seasons.[10] Less formal holiday activities were of course also influenced by the season; the approach of new year and carnival, for example,

---

8 Marfany, "Invention", pp. 188–89.
9 Roeck, *Lebenswelt*, pp. 35–36; StadtAA, Urgicht Veit Hefner, 13–20 August 1592; Polizeiwesen 6, 1591; Strafbuch 101, fol. 232v, 3 Sep. 1587; Staats- und Stadtbibliothek Augsburg (SuStBA), 4° Aug. 1021, vol. 4/1, pp. 69, 73.
10 StadtAA, Schätze 16, fols. 347–349.

were often celebrated with sleigh-riding, sometimes in carnival masks.[11] Such events might also attend winter weddings in elite circles. Sleigh-riding parties at night were also popular, although potentially dangerous on dark, slippery streets, and at times rowdy. A complaint to the city council in 1744 accused late-night sleigh-riders of making such a racket that an elderly member of the imperial family currently visiting Augsburg had to be medicated as a result of the shock.[12] Thus regulations forbidding recreational sleigh-riding after 9:00 or 10:00 PM focused mainly on disturbances of the peace, specifically noting noisy sleigh-bells, yodeling, shouting, and gratuitous whip-cracking as well as the throwing of snowballs.[13] During the day, however, the joyful sounds and sights of sleigh-riding provided entertainment both for the participants and for spectators, particularly when nobles and patricians were involved. Such a scene is depicted in an etching produced by Wilhelm Peter Zimmermann in 1618, which shows decorated sleighs and masked patrician riders parading before crowds of spectators lining the sides of the present-day Maximilianstraße.[14]

Elite entertainments of all kinds served as public spectacles and drew significant crowds. As displays of wealth and power, they underscored social hierarchies, while the more playful elements presented civic leaders in a benevolent light, willing to go to considerable expense in order to entertain the general population.[15] Especially popular in Augsburg during the fifteenth and early sixteenth century were tournaments, which often coincided with carnival celebrations and offered aristocratic visitors a chance to display their family crests, martial skills, and chivalrous reputations. Some tournaments were held privately on palace grounds, but most took place in public spaces such as the Wine Market, the cathedral yard, or at the shooting grounds just outside the city walls, providing opportunities for large crowds of spectators to enjoy the competitions.[16] As the sixteenth century progressed and the dangers of jousting with lances began to draw criticism in elite circles, safer alternatives arose that met new standards for civilized competition. By the later sixteenth century, jousting was replaced with tilting at rings, or *Ringelrennen*, the object

---

11 Grüber (ed.), *"Kurzweil viel ..."*, pp. 252–57; Gullmann, *Geschichte*, vol. 5, pp. 505, 516; vol. 6, p. 151; StadtAA, Polizeiwesen 12, Schlittenfahrten 1622–1744.
12 StadtAA, Polizeiwesen 12, Schlittenfahrten 1622–1744, 1744.
13 Deutsches Historisches Museum (ed.), *"Kurzweil viel ..."*, p. 188: StadtAA, Ratsbuch 16, Ratsprotokolle 1529–1542, fol. 35; Preu, *Chronik*, p. 74.
14 The etching commemorates a sixteenth-century event. Deutsches Historisches Museum (ed.), *"Kurzweil viel ..."*, pp. 188–90; Grüber (ed.), *"Kurzweil viel ..."*, pp. 254–55; on sleigh-riding in Augsburg by members of the imperial family see Stetten, *Erläuterungen*, pp. 551–52.
15 Rosseaux, *Freiräume*, pp. 75–77.
16 Grüber (ed.), *"Kurzweil viel ..."*, pp. 200–11; Jachmann, *Kunst*, p. 63.

FIGURE 14.1   Sleigh ride in front of Augsburg's Gothic city hall, engraving by Wilhelm Peter Zimmermann, 1618
AUGSBURG, STÄDTISCHE KUNSTSAMMLUNGEN, G 1387

of which was to stick the lance into a small ring while riding at a gallop.[17] In order to maintain the entertainment value, flesh-and-blood opponents were replaced with mechanical figures, while opportunities for showing off horsemanship were augmented with amusing new trappings and props. Typical of this kind of public play was a carnival tournament organized by the Fuggers in 1590, for which a group of 26 young patricians appeared on the Wine Market, mounted and dressed in fine attire, and took turns running a spear at a mechanical target dressed as a Turk. If the rider was successful, the mannequin collapsed and then righted itself for the next contestant; if the jouster missed, however, the figure would spin and strike the rider with a wooden staff, a fate preventable only with remarkable horsemanship.[18]

Also certain to draw crowds were elite wedding festivities, which began with spectacular processions of arriving guests featuring hundreds of horses

17   Behringer, "Fugger", p. 118.
18   Gullmann, *Geschichte*, vol. 2, pp. 153–54, 156–57; Koutná, "Feste und Feiern".

accompanied by trumpets, pipes, and drums, and continued for days with tournaments, fireworks, horse races, and occasionally outdoor dances.[19] Crowds of spectators were not necessary for elite entertainments to serve a representative function, however. The extravagance of the banquets, dances, and other amusements that took place in the private drinking rooms and palaces of Augsburg's elite citizens was well-known throughout the Empire and has been immortalized in literary and artistic renditions.[20]

Augsburg's less wealthy inhabitants engaged in playful behavior of their own as well, especially during the carnival season. Mumming was widespread among all social groups, the protection of anonymity behind carnival masks allowing more freedom for unrestrained behavior, including courting rituals and even some social mixing. Restrictions on carnival customs, particularly mumming, were implemented during times of war, plague, and other disasters, including periods of mourning for important rulers; but such rules were often ignored and rarely enforced.[21] In the eighteenth century, it was traditional at carnival time for Jesuit school students to stage noisy sleigh-rides while dressed in costumes representing intellectual themes, sometimes with a satirical flair.[22] The wedding processions of ordinary citizens also provided opportunities for festive sociability to the accompaniment of pipes, drums, and cheers. Weddings were often held during periods of seasonal bounty, such as the spring slaughter or the fall harvest, increasing the potential for opulent feasting.[23]

Available to all citizens as well were the amusements that accompanied Augsburg's seasonal markets and fairs, the largest of which were the Easter Market and Michaeli Fair (*Sankt Michels Messe* or *Michaelimarkt*).[24] Aside from offering foreign luxury goods in addition to domestic foods and crafts, seasonal fairs provided opportunities for traveling showmen and entertainers, including musicians, theatrical players, and sword dancers, to attract paying

---

19 Gullmann, *Geschichte*, vol. 2, pp. 156–57; Kölderer, *Beschreibung*, vol. 2, p. 943; Deutsches Historisches Museum (ed.), *"Kurzweil viel ..."*, pp. 41–44.

20 Grüber (ed.), *"Kurzweil viel ..."*, pp. 31–144; Jachmann, *Kunst*, pp. 57–64; Schweinichen, *Denkwürdigkeiten*, pp. 154–59.

21 StadtAA, Urgichten, Mathes Arnold, 2 March 1594; Hieronymus Metz, 17 February 1592; Schätze 16, fols. 24r, 38r, 46r–v, 72v, 86v, 105v, 287v–88r, 293r, 370r–v; Stetten, *Geschichte*, vol. 1, pp. 360, 595, 733, 860.

22 Gullmann, *Geschichte*, vol. 5, pp. 505, 516; vol. 6, p. 151. The students of the Jesuit St. Salvator school were of mixed social status: Baer, "Gründung", p. 20; Layer, "Musik", p. 67.

23 Roper, "Going to Church and Street"; Tlusty, *Bacchus*, pp. 93, 123, 174–76; idem (ed.), *Augsburg*, p. 158.

24 Both Augsburg fairs are mentioned in sources dating from the tenth century and are still celebrated as the biannual *Dult*. Häußler, *Marktstadt Augsburg*, p. 129.

audiences. At Michaeli Fair in 1597, for example, a certain Peter Purst from Savoy was granted permission to display a collection of curiosities in a local brewery that included live animals with extra feet; half a "dragon's head"; a tiger pelt; a fish with two mouths; the jawbone of a giant whale; and various other exotic oddities.[25] In 1629, visitors to St. Ulrich's Kermis could watch a performance by a trained elephant in the Dance House for an admission fee of five kreuzer,[26] while a live rhinoceros was put on display for the amusement of spectators in 1748.[27]

3 Theater

Augsburg's citizens regularly enjoyed carnival plays as well as school and church plays, which, like other amusements, occasionally created controversy and underwent a process of secularization and professionalization as the early modern period progressed. Carnival plays were especially popular during the fifteenth and sixteenth centuries, often performed in public houses or in the open air and characterized by bawdy and satirical themes.[28] The Protestant school at St. Anna began presenting plays in German and Latin beginning in 1538, many of them original works penned by the schoolmaster. After the establishment of the Jesuit St. Salvator school in 1579, the Jesuits provided Catholic competition with musicals, carnival plays, and dramas in the humanist tradition, the first of which opened in 1583.[29] Regulations in bi-confessional Augsburg demanded more confessional restraint in theater performances than was the case in confessionally homogeneous cities, with strongly polemical pieces forbidden after 1555 in order to avoid further inflaming the already tense relations between the confessions. After 1648, theater companies in Augsburg were also subject to rules of confessional parity (*Parität*).[30]

More popular than the often very religious school plays were performances by the local Meistersinger guild, whose members included a number of

---

25 StadtAA, Chroniken 10, Georg Siedeler, p. 202. See also Roeck, *Eine Stadt in Krieg und Frieden*, vol. 1, p. 36.
26 StadtAA, Chroniken 32, Ludwig Hainzelmann (n.p.), 1629.
27 Thienemann, *Leben*, no. 295. The rhinoceros, named Clara, was the property of Dutch sea captain Douwe Mout van der Meer, who exhibited her throughout Europe during the 1740s and 1750s: Ridley, *Clara's Grand Tour*.
28 Roeck, *Lebenswelt*, p. 39.
29 Schnell, *Meistersingerschule*, p. 23; Layer, "Musik und Theater", pp. 69–71.
30 Roeck, *Lebenswelt*, p. 39; Schnell, *Meistersingerschule*, pp. 45–51; Creasman, *Censorship*, pp. 119–32; on rules of parity see Chapter 11 in this volume.

schoolmasters. The Meistersingers began in 1540 to perform both religious and worldly works, drawing increasingly enthusiastic audiences to view plays by Hans Sachs and the local Meistersinger Sebastian Wild. Initially, the Meistersingers presented their plays and also held singing competitions primarily in churches on Sundays and religious holidays. Towards the end of the sixteenth century, however, church officials began to resist these performances in church space, decrying them as "frivolous plays and carnival farces" and finally putting an end to church performances during the 1580s. For a time, the Meistersingers continued to perform in markets, open squares, private homes, and rented halls. The activities of the Augsburg Meistersinger guild slowed during the Thirty Years' War, after which singing competitions continued to decline while theater quickly gained in popularity. In 1650, the stage contingent of the Meistersingers gained official recognition as a theater company, with a portion of their earnings allocated to poor relief.[31] In order to increase these revenues, the civic Office of Poor Relief invested in the construction of a permanent theater (*Komödienstadel*) in 1665 for the use of both local and professional traveling theater companies. The repertoire in the *Komödienstadel* expanded to include ballet and opera performances in the later seventeenth century and remained the center of Augsburg's theater scene until the construction of the new theater in its current location in 1877.[32]

4   Sports

Although the term "sport" did not yet exist as a collective descriptor in early modern Germany, many activities that we would now identify as sports certainly did. Most early modern sports could be defended by their supporters as a kind of preparation for war, which made them politically acceptable as leisure activities. This also ensured primarily (and in most cases exclusively) masculine participation. Many competitions, however, also functioned as spectator sports, providing entertainment and sociability for audiences that included women and children as well as men from a broad social spectrum.

Although some modern historians have questioned whether early modern games can be defined as "sports", all of the elements associated with modern sports can be identified in early modern games of skill, including

---

[31]   Schnell, *Meistersingerschule*, pp. 29–30, 36–37; Witz, *Versuch*, pp. 7–15, 18.
[32]   The theater, located on Lauterlech, was rebuilt in 1776 and remained in service into the nineteenth century, when it was replaced with the current city theater, which opened in 1877: Stoll, "Stadttheater", p. 841; see also Chapter 22 in this volume.

clearly-defined rules designed to level the playing field and ensure fair play; tests of physical skill; multiple phases of competition; and prizes and recognition for the winners. The sixteenth century also saw the beginning of a process of professionalization through the employment of trainers, instructors, and referees, as well as the production of manuals for sports of all kinds. For these reasons, the Renaissance can be defined as a formative period in the development of the modern concept of sports.[33]

Most obviously related to war training were martial sports. During the Middle Ages, hunting and tournaments served as both entertainment and military training for aristocratic men. As martial sports competitions expanded to include new military technologies, they also encompassed a much larger segment of society. Throughout Europe during the early modern period, men in both urban and rural communities honed their martial skills in shooting and fencing matches that ranged from informal target shoots to large, interregional festivals. If ruling authorities indeed viewed many popular leisure activities as idle or frivolous, martial sports were a clear exception, supported as constructive pastimes. Sports aimed at sharpening martial skills encouraged the development of masculine values associated with Renaissance notions of civic virtue, including physical competence and strength, courage, fortitude, and a sense of fair play.[34] They were also entertaining for both participants and spectators.

Shooting matches were normally hosted by local shooting societies or clubs (*Schützengesellschaften*), which were burgher-dominated organizations formed on the guild model. Shooting societies were supported by grants from the city council and included both guildsmen and patricians among their members. Augsburg's shooting match tradition began in the fourteenth century with archer and crossbowman's guilds, expanding to include guns in the fifteenth.[35] Crossbow and gun societies remained active in Augsburg throughout the early modern period, holding regular matches at two civic shooting grounds (the *Rosenau* and *Schießgraben*), both of which were originally located outside the city walls west of town. Because of its vulnerable position some distance from the walls, the Rosenau shooting ground was abandoned during

---

33   Behringer, *Kulturgeschichte des Sports*, pp. 11–13, 137; idem, "Arena", pp. 331–32, 348–51; McClelland, "Einleitung"; Mallinckrodt and Schattner, "Introduction".
34   Tlusty, *Martial Ethic*, p. 190.
35   StadtAA, Schützen-Akten 1; Edelman, *Schützenwesen*, p. 68; Tlusty, *Martial Ethic*, pp. 191–92.

the Thirty Years' War and reestablished outside of the Jakober Gate some years later.[36]

Shooting matches occurred in a variety of forms, from small shoots open only to members of the local shooting club to large, inter-regional and even international festivals. Rules were enforced by an elected board of expert shooting masters and by the so-called "paddle-master" (*Pritschenmeister*), a combination referee and jester who entertained the company with clever rhymes and "punished" shooters for minor infractions or unusually poor shooting by giving them a public paddling. Shooting matches produced home-town sports heroes as well; in addition to supporting local matches, Augsburg's council also provided travel grants to the best shooters so that they could compete in other cities. Bringing home a winner's wreath enhanced the reputation of the shooters' home town and their local shooting club.

During their heyday in the long sixteenth century, large shooting matches were among the grandest entertainments available to commoners, both for shooters and for spectators. Illustrative is the well-documented Augsburg match of 1509, which was commemorated 60 years later in a richly illuminated chronicle commissioned by the mercenary officer and former Augsburg captain of the guard Sebastian Schertlin von Burtenbach. The chronicle describes participation by 916 gunners and 546 crossbowmen as well as opportunities for participants and spectators to compete for prizes by racing, jumping, swordfighting, knife- and stone-throwing, and playing various games of chance. Both shooters and spectators were entertained by musicians, displays of horsemanship, and a footrace pitting men against scantily dressed common women.[37] Larger shooting festivals also hosted bowling lanes, horse races, fireworks, and elaborate lotteries that offered the chance of winning cash prizes, silver and gold dishes, decorative swords and daggers, and other treasures. Rules against gambling for high stakes with cards and dice not only discouraged card sharping, but also supported interest in the official games and lotteries upon which the shooting clubs depended to help finance their matches and facilities.[38]

Women also actively participated in some athletic games at early sixteenth-century shooting matches, for example bowling and footraces. Images from the later sixteenth century and beyond, however, suggest that the role of women had become more circumscribed, limited to playing lotteries and other games

---

36 Sporadic evidence suggests that a bowman's guild also operated during the sixteenth and seventeenth centuries. StadtAA, Schützen-Akten 1; Stetten, *Erläuterungen*, p. 56.
37 Universitätsbibliothek Erlangen-Nürnberg (UBEN), Ms B213. Women from good families competed in a separate, all-female race (ibid., fol. 177r).
38 StadtAA, Schützen-Akten 5/1, 1586; Tlusty, *Martial Ethic*, pp. 195–96.

of chance.[39] Lists of winners suggest that women remained enthusiastic participants in the lotteries, and some prizes, such as scissors and women's belts, were clearly aimed at getting their attention.

Shooting festivals also offered other entertainments, including opulent processions, *Pritschenmeister* comedy and poetry, and dances for the winners. Elaborate mechanical targets put on shows of their own, for example a castle constructed for a bow-and-arrow match in 1572 that shot paper bullets through a window in response to a direct hit.[40] Food and drink were available in abundance and often provided to the marksmen free of charge in the so-called "shooting house", a permanent structure that housed the shooting society's private drinking room, while spectators could purchase refreshments from food and drink peddlers on the grounds.[41] Even those unable to pay for games or food were free to watch others compete and to enjoy the parades, music, fireworks, and *Pritschenmeister* shenanigans.

Because the largest shooting festivals were immortalized in chronicles, broadsheets, and commemorative poems, they have received considerable attention from folklorists and historians seeking the roots of modern festival traditions. But these large matches were only one of many forms of sociability provided by and for shooting clubs. Target-shooting opportunities for locals occurred regularly, even on a weekly basis during the summer, encouraging what shooting ordinances regularly described as "friendly burgher society".[42] Members also gathered to drink and gamble in the shooting house between shooting events as well as before and after matches and shooting practice.[43]

Another martial sport sporadically supported by the city government was sword-fighting, which could also function as a spectator sport, although it was never as popular as the grand shooting festivals. Men honed their skills in sword-fighting "schools" (*Fechtschulen*), which were not permanent institutions, but lessons or competitions offered by local or traveling sword-masters.

---

39   Noblewomen occasionally competed with each other or with male family members in private shooting matches or at court, and sometimes appeared at public shooting fairs to take a celebratory shot; there is also evidence that aristocratic women competed at open crossbow matches in their residence cities during the later eighteenth century. There is no evidence of women participating in shooting contests in Augsburg: Froning, *Frankfurter Chroniken*, pp. 368–69; Montagu, *Complete Letters*, vol. 1, pp. 268–69; Reintges, *Ursprung*, pp. 298–99; Guttmann, *Women's Sports*, pp. 61–62; Rosseaux, *Freiräume*, p. 169.

40   StadtAA, Schützen-Akten 5/1.

41   Mülich, *Chronik*, pp. 230–33; UBEN, Ms B213, fols. 159v–160r, 171r.

42   StadtAA, Schützen-Akten 8, 1569–1578; Schützen-Akten 5/4, 21 March 1673; Schätze 16, fols. 34v–35r; see also Rosseaux, *Freiräume*, pp. 161–62.

43   StadtAA, Urgichten, Georg Herb, 17 September 1593; Wolf Behaim, 19 November 1593; Schätze 16, fols. 34v–35r; Schützen-Akten 5/1.

Most sixteenth-century sword-masters taught primarily long-sword fighting techniques based on late medieval traditions, which by the sixteenth century could no longer be justified as military skills, since the heavy swords were not practical on battlefields dominated by firearms and siege warfare. But aficionados of sword-fighting argued that the sport maintained its martial value by building strength, requiring courage, and teaching the basic concepts of honorable fighting, thus contributing to civic virtue.[44] Sword-masters also taught other fighting techniques, including wrestling and combat with pikes, halberds, daggers, and knives. The Augsburg city council regularly approved stipends for sword-masters in support of sword-fighting schools, in some years every two to four weeks.[45] The entertainment value of the matches is underscored by the fact that some sword-masters sold tickets, while civic funding included fees for musicians to play at the competitions.

Interest in traditional sword-fighting schools rose and fell in tandem with the great shooting festivals, although on a smaller scale. Like jousting, fighting with heavy swords was dangerous and regularly caused injuries and even death, which was undoubtedly part of its appeal during the earlier sixteenth century. By the seventeenth century, however, the bloody sport was beginning to elicit disgust among elite spectators and theologians. As the century progressed, the burgher-dominated sport of long-sword fighting was reduced to a side-show event at markets and fairs and eventually disappeared, while elite fencers took up the safer and more "civilized" exercise of fencing with foils imported from Italy and France.[46]

Ball games constitute another category of popular sport enjoyed at least by members of Augsburg's upper classes. Patricians played a kind of handball imported from Italy that involved hitting an inflated ball (*pallone*) with the lower arm, protected by a wooden or leather armguard.[47] During his brief visit to Augsburg at Pentecost 1632, King Gustavus Adolphus of Sweden played the game with members of his noble entourage and a group of patrician's sons in the cathedral yard, followed by a banquet and dance in the Fugger palace; mention of this event in Augsburg chronicles may have been meant as a refreshing interlude, nestled as it was between less pleasant memories of the war, including public hangings and the destruction of the city's orchards.[48] Like many other Renaissance towns, Augsburg also financed the construction of a "ball

---

44   Tlusty, "Martial Identity", pp. 552–53; Schwendi, "Diskurs", pp. 175–80.
45   Meyer, *Literarische Hausbücher*, vol. 1, pp. 435–49.
46   Tlusty, *Martial Ethic*, pp. 215–17.
47   Behringer, "Fugger", pp. 119–21; idem, "Arena", p. 333.
48   StadtAA, Chroniken 32, Ludwig Hainzelmann (n.p.); Chroniken 27a, Jakob Wagner, p. 150.

house" in 1548–49, which likely provided facilities for an early form of tennis. This building was situated next to St. Anna and also served as a theater for the performance of school plays. In 1562, it was transformed into a city library and replaced with a new ball house located on the Katzenstadel.[49] The likelihood that these were tennis courts is supported by records of Augsburg patrician Hans Fugger providing the dukes of Bavaria with 50 tennis rackets and around 11,000 balls during the 1570s. Both the Augsburg and Munich ball houses were mentioned in Fugger's correspondence.[50]

5 Bathing and Swimming

Whether the word bathing (in German *baden*) refers to recreational swimming or to taking a bath for reasons of hygiene is not always clear in the records, but there was considerable overlap between these two activities during the medieval and early modern periods. Swimming and visiting bathhouses were sociable activities as well as serving health and hygiene.[51] Fifteenth- and sixteenth-century bathhouses often allowed mixed-sex bathing, which was also the case with swimming in streams or rivers, as can be seen in the May bath depicted in the Augsburg Month Paintings (*Monatsbilder*, from the workshop of Jörg Breu the Elder) in which men in briefs and nude women play together in the water.[52] In the later sixteenth century, however, mixed bathing became associated with prostitution, so that bathhouses were sometimes decried as disreputable.[53] By 1592, the Augsburg bathers' guild opposed mixed bathing.[54]

Bathers and their attendants sometimes ran afoul of the authorities for engaging in or allowing other restricted forms of sociability in bathhouses, including serving drinks or holding singing competitions, both of which were forbidden by bathhouse ordinances.[55] Based on testimony in a series of sodomy trials from 1532, the three bathhouses located along the Singold Canal

---

49 Stetten, *Erläuterungen*, p. 113; Kirstein, "Zwitzel".
50 Behringer, "Fugger", pp. 121–26.
51 Bathers and barbers were also medical professionals, meaning that bathhouses served as centers of health, hygiene, and recreation. Dieminger, *Bader*.
52 The Augsburg "Month Paintings" or "Labors of the Months" were painted around 1530, based on a cycle of drawings by Augsburg artist Jörg Breu the Elder, and depict local society at work and play: Langner, *Feste*, pp. 100–01; Deutsches Historisches Museum (ed.), *"Kurzweil viel ..."*, pp. 129–30.
53 Dieminger, *Bader*, pp. 80–82.
54 Ibid., p. 81.
55 Ibid., pp. 61, 80–81.

FIGURE 14.2   Bathing scene, detail from the *Augsburger Monatsbild* April–June, workshop of Jörg Breu the Elder
DEUTSCHES HISTORISCHES MUSEUM BERLIN, 1990/185.2

(*Senkelbach*) served as sites of sociability for a network of gay men, one of whom was a bath attendant;[56] and the bather at the so-called *Eselsbad* across from St. Jacob's church was accused by his wife of celebrating Shrovetide in 1593 by dancing naked in the bathhouse with a group of beggars.[57] Outdoor swimming before the invention of swimming suits could cause problems as well, particularly as sensibilities about nudity heightened. Representative is the uproar caused on a hot July day in 1707 when a group of young men cooling off in the *Schwalbach*, a canal in the Lech Quarter, swam to within viewing distance of the nuns of St. Ursula convent and then called to the nuns and exposed themselves. The act was apparently an intentional response to earlier complaints from the nuns about naked men in the canal. When a guard tried to take control of the situation, he, too, was met with bare behinds. Explanations from participants suggest that they understood jumping into a canal on a hot day to be a civic right for men. Given that the men questioned were all Protestant, however, the protest may have been confessionally motivated, providing them with a convenient opportunity to tease and provoke Catholic

56   Tlusty (ed.), *Augsburg*, pp. 121–26.
57   StadtAA, Urgicht Jonas Schmid, 17 March 1593.

nuns. In response to the incident, the council issued a decree limiting bathing in canals to the hours of darkness.[58]

6 Public Houses and Sociability

Public houses were the principal places of sociability for most men in early modern Europe and provided opportunities for women to socialize as well, although visits to taverns by women were subject to greater limitations.[59] The provision of food, drink, and space for sociability as a commercial enterprise put publicans in the vanguard of consumer culture during the sixteenth and seventeenth centuries. Recent scholarship has demonstrated that early modern publicans displayed considerable creativity and versatility in meeting the shifting demands of their customers. Publicans were among the first private entrepreneurs to offer organized forms of sociability, and their premises provided opportunities for public discourse and exchange to the lower and middling classes well before the development of the bourgeois "public sphere" defined by Jürgen Habermas.[60]

Visiting pubs was popular not only after church on Sundays and holidays, but also on Monday afternoons, when journeymen were traditionally allowed a drinking bout that was sometimes paid for by their masters.[61] About 58 per cent of pub visits in Augsburg between 1540 and 1645 took place on Sundays, Mondays, and holidays; the other 42 per cent were spread relatively evenly throughout the rest of the week.[62] Public houses in Augsburg varied greatly in type and size, but all of them sold alcoholic drinks, thus providing a primary lubricant for sociability. In all early modern drinking cultures, the act of sharing a drink implied a sense of social solidarity with the drinking partner, meaning that the makeup of drinking groups reflected the existence of social bonds among their members. These bonds could be constant, as among members of a family or a profession, or they could be as fleeting as a single evening's

---

58 StadtAA, Polizeiwesen 11, 17–21 July 1707.
59 Brennan, "General Introduction", p. vii.
60 Medick, "Plebejische Kultur"; Brennan, "General Introduction", p. xx; Kümin, *Drinking*, pp. 185–88.
61 In Augsburg called "Good Monday" (*Guter Montag*).
62 Based on a sample of just under 400 cases of tavern drinking, 106 of which noted the day on which drinking took place. Pub visits were roughly evenly split between Sunday and Monday: StadtAA, Urgichten 1540–44, 1590–94, and 1640–44. During the 1590s, craftsmen were theoretically required to limit their pub visits to Sundays, Mondays, and holidays, but there is no evidence that the rule was enforced: see also Tlusty, *Bacchus*, pp. 200–08.

entertainment, but they always implied social acceptance. Tavern sociability thus provided opportunities for men to transcend social and professional boundaries, creating and affirming neighborhood ties and other friendships that were not always homogeneous. In some cases, especially during the sixteenth century, these ties crossed the lines of the society of orders; more often, however, drinking together served to underscore social stratification rather than supporting social leveling. This was increasingly the case as the early modern period progressed.[63]

Of course, the same intoxicating qualities that enhanced bonds of trust and friendship among drinking companions also had the potential to create disorder. At certain times, particularly in association with pre-Reformation carnival customs, drinking as a portal to chaos and inversion was intentional and ritualized, and was supported by the church calendar even if condemned by clerics.[64] But even in the post-Reformation period, with its emphasis on social and moral discipline, tavern drinking provided opportunities to let off steam and violate norms. Fights and brawls over drinks were a daily occurrence in Augsburg as in other early modern cities, as alcohol reduced inhibitions and increased aggressions among the mostly male company of the public house. Fighting is recognized by sociologists as an important form of sociability, often adhering to ritual forms more likely to be enforced in a tavern setting, where witnesses both increased the stakes for the brawlers' reputations and exercised lateral social control.[65] Pubs provided spaces for courting as well, which under the influence of alcohol could lead to problematic sexual contact.[66]

Tavern sociability also encouraged the sharing of news, gossip, and reading material, including broadsheets and songs, which were read aloud, copied down, and passed from hand to hand. Some craftsmen made a hobby out of composing and collecting songs and rhymes, both revising existing works and producing original compositions, often as political satire or with sexually provocative overtones. Singing occurred spontaneously as well, particularly when musicians were available as accompanists, who were sometimes traveling professionals or members of the city's official piper corps, but might also be amateur players of bagpipes, violins, and lutes. Recent research has revealed lively networks of artisans who made a pastime out of sharing voices, songs, and lay compositions at weddings, private homes, in the streets, and in public houses.[67]

---

63 Brennan, "General Introduction", pp. xi–xix; Kümin and Tlusty, "Introduction", p. xxxvii; Tlusty, *Bacchus*, p. 151.
64 Burke, *Popular Culture*, pp. 207–43.
65 Brennan, "General Introduction", pp. xvi–xviii; Tlusty, *Bacchus*, pp. 126–33.
66 Kümin, *Drinking*, p. 71; Tlusty, "Drinking", pp. 266–68.
67 Graser and Tlusty (eds.), *Jonas Losch*, pp. 28–32.

Gambling with dice or cards was another common form of tavern entertainment, often with a round of drinks as the price for losing. Despite attacks by theologians, who saw such games as catalysts for blasphemy and greed, gambling was never illegal in Augsburg, but only limited to small stakes, usually one-pfennig bets. This supports the conclusion that the authorities' real concern was with ruinous gambling rather than playing for fun. Although high-stakes gambling, like chronic drunkenness, created serious problems for some men, most games of chance attained their essential meaning not through placing high-risk bets, but through their potential for social integration. Gambling for the price of a round of drinks was simply an entertaining way to pass the time and enhanced the potential for companionable sociability.[68]

Women and children undoubtedly played card and dice games as well, just as women also drank, although prior to the eighteenth century, they did so primarily in domestic or private settings. Sources on gambling among women and children are extremely scarce.[69] Images of women playing cards with men are not unusual in early modern prints and paintings, including the Augsburg Month Paintings already noted, which include two scenes in which men and women sit together during card games. Significantly, however, only cards bearing hearts are shown being held by a woman or lying on the table near one, suggesting that these scenes served as allegories for sexual play rather than realistic gambling scenes. Like similar scenes in the genre of the "Love Garden", the card games in these scenes represent the game of love, and the heart in the hand of the woman suggests that the man is bound to lose.[70]

This imagery underscores the fact that gambling, like drinking, was a form of socializing that created close personal bonds – and such bonds were considered appropriate between the sexes only in the context of marriage. Thus women regularly visited taverns to drink and socialize with their husbands, or in family groups for special celebrations, including weddings, which always involved groups of both single and married women. The innkeeper's wife and her female servants were also regularly present in public houses. But prior to the eighteenth century, single or married women who entered a tavern alone or drank publicly with men to whom they were not married always risked accusations of sexual impropriety.[71]

---

68 Tlusty, "Playing by the Rules", pp. 37–38.
69 Ibid., pp. 32–36. Young boys played at gambling using pebbles or nutshells.
70 Ibid., pp. 37–38; Lymant, "Die sogenannte Folge", p. 32; Zangs, "Glück beim Spielen", pp. 17–20.
71 Tlusty, "Drinking", p. 266; idem, *Bacchus*, pp. 133–45. With the eighteenth-century rise of more commercial forms of sociability, opportunities for women to participate in public

7   Country Pleasures

The attractions of the bucolic pleasures of the countryside were often noted in early modern literature, and Augsburg's authorities recognized as well that the city's tradespeople, "having spent all week in their shops and close quarters", benefited from getting out of the walled city to enjoy the exercise, green landscapes, and fresh air associated with the countryside.[72] While Augsburg's wealthiest citizens took their air in country palaces or private gardens, ordinary townspeople made a public pleasure garden out of the shooting grounds, which were easily accessible outside the city walls. These open areas attracted not only townspeople but also country-dwellers, beggars, and other passers-by, all of whom regularly gathered there to watch the shooters, gamble in the open air, or dance to the music of pipers.[73] By the later seventeenth century, amusements such as bowling lanes and gaming tables had become regular weekend events during the summer, so that Augsburg's shooting ranges were beginning to resemble modern fairgrounds.[74] In the eighteenth century, the shooting house in the Rosenau housed a dance floor, a billiard room, and a drinking room, while in the Schießgraben children were offered a chance to ring-joust on a wooden horse.[75] Augsburg residents also regularly walked or rode to neighboring villages for entertainment and sociability, just as villagers came to town on market days and to visit baths and urban taverns. Records of such visits provide evidence of the many ties of friendship, family, and sociable professional relationships that existed between the city and the surrounding countryside.[76]

8   Privatization, Commercialization, and the Colonization of the Night

The long eighteenth century was marked by a process of privatization and commercialization of formerly government-sponsored entertainments. In Augsburg, cross-bow shooting became a private enterprise in 1695, when the

---

social life increased as enterprising innkeepers offered space for balls, concerts, reading circles, and other organized social events (discussed below).

72   StadtAA, Ungeldamt MM XVII, 1596; see also Stewart, "Paper Festivals".
73   StAA, Urgichten, Joseph und Jakob Juden, 11 August 1573; Isaac Jud, 31 July 1587; Tlusty, "Playing by the Rules", pp. 25–26; idem (ed.), *Augsburg*, pp. 179–81.
74   StAA, Schützen-Akten 5/4, 1673.
75   Ringelrennen (see fn. 17 above): Schützen-Akten 4.
76   StadtAA, Reichsstadt Akten 811–16.

cross-bow society purchased the shooting grounds at the Schießgraben from the city and took over responsibility for maintaining the grounds and buildings. The Rosenau gun range was privatized half a century later under similar conditions. In other cities, sponsorship of shooting matches was often assumed by enterprising innkeepers, who profited from the opportunity to house guests and sell food and drinks. This process of commercialization was accompanied by a rise in the play function of shooting matches, which increasingly took on the character of modern folk festivals, offering beer and wine tents, food stands, puppet shows, and trained animal acts along with traditional games, dances, and music.[77]

Innkeepers in Augsburg were also savvy about finding ways to profit from commercial leisure. Exemplary in this regard was the Viennese innkeeper Josef Linay, who took over the exclusive Three Moors (*Drei Mohren*) hotel on the Wine Market in the mid-eighteenth century and began hosting commercial masked carnival balls (*Redouten*) in 1765. These events imitated Italian models and functioned as both participatory and spectator entertainment, with tickets for spectators available at half the price of those for masked guests and a portion of the profits earmarked for the Alms Office. Theoretically, the balls were open to anyone who could afford the entrance fee, allowing for a mix of people from different social strata. *Redouten* occurred several times each carnival season, with attendance typically totaling over 2,000 people, roughly split between participants and spectators. Thus they yielded handy profits for both the innkeeper and civic poor relief.[78] Eighteenth-century innkeepers also hosted musical events and reading circles.[79]

As participation in commercial balls, concerts, plays, operas, and reading circles became more socially inclusive, leisure time increasingly extended to the hours of darkness. Official closing times for public houses shifted from 9:00 PM to 10:00 PM as lights stayed on longer, eventually leading to citizen-led campaigns for the installation of public street lights beginning in 1760.[80] Ultimately, emancipation from dependence on daylight would be a major factor in increasing the time available for leisure.[81]

---

77   Tlusty, *Martial Ethic*, p. 210.
78   StadtAA, Polizeiwesen 25/2, Redouten; SuStBA, 2° Aug. Anschläge, 1. Abt., nos. 605, 633; Haupt, *Drei Mohren* (n.p.); Rousseaux, *Freiräume*, pp. 89–97. According to Gullmann, *Redouten* had been held in the *Drei Mohren* since at least 1730: Gullmann, *Geschichte*, vol. 5, pp. 4–6.
79   Rajkay, "Totentanz", p. 95; Dussler (ed.), *Reisen*, p. 369; Mančal, "Collegium musicum".
80   StadtAA, Polizeiwesen 25/3, 1761; Tlusty, *Bacchus*, p. 187.
81   Rousseaux, *Freiräume*, pp. 60–71.

9   Conclusion

A major challenge to scholarship on early modern leisure is balancing top-down views produced by elite writers with more elusive popular voices, the latter of which must be teased out of archival documents typically shaped by the interests of professional scribes and bureaucracies. Invariably, gaps in the records remain. In all fields of historical scholarship, this problem is most acute in the case of those actors whose voices were least likely to be recorded, including women, children, and members of ethnic minorities.

Historians agree, however, that people from all walks of life have always socialized and sought opportunities to enjoy whatever time away from work was available to them; and for most of Augsburg's residents, leisure pastimes of one kind or another fit easily into the rhythm of early modern life. Current debates center instead on definitions of leisure time and leisure activities, and on their relationships to larger historical developments. Time away from work or worship was highly politicized during the post-Reformation period, with some pastimes (particularly those practiced at the bottom of the social scale) being labeled as idleness, while others (often those engaged in by people of middling to higher status) supported as training grounds for civic virtue. Those at the top of the social scale obviously had more time and money to invest in lavish leisure pursuits, some of which also served a representational function as entertaining spectacles. But even the poorest of Augsburg's residents found occasional opportunities to entertain themselves with dancing, singing, storytelling, games, or simply engaging in conversation.

That most popular leisure pastimes were tolerated and some were supported by Augsburg's ruling elites, even during phases characterized by morally charged attacks on idleness, is hardly surprising given the importance of such activities to the city's political and economic life. Then as now, the urban environment offered greater social diversity and access to a larger variety of cultural experiences than did life in the countryside, which was part of the appeal to travelers, visitors, and those who came to town to seek their fortune. The fact that urban diversions often came at a cost made them part of the daily exchange of goods and services upon which the city and its residents depended. In early modern European cities, the ability of urban leaders as well as private entrepreneurs to remain flexible and creative in catering to increasingly diverse consumer interests and tastes was a defining factor in the formation of a distinctly urban identity, or what would eventually be understood as a sense of urbanity, among town-dwellers.

Bibliography

Unpublished Primary Sources

Stadtarchiv Augsburg (StadtAA)

Ains Ersamen Rats der Stat Augsburg Beruff, zu pflantzung Christlichs, züchtigs und erbars Lebens, Augsburg, 1541.

Chroniken 10, Georg Siedeler.

Chroniken 27a, Jakob Wagner.

Chroniken 32, Ludwig Hainzelmann.

Polizeiwesen 6, 11, 12, 25.

Ratsbuch 16.

Reichsstadt Akten 811–16.

Schätze 16.

Schützenakten.

Strafbuch 101.

Ungeldamt MM XVII.

Urgichten.

Staats- und Stadtbibliothek Augsburg (SuStBA).

2° Aug. Anschläge, 1. Abt., nos. 605, 633.

4° Aug. 1021.

Universitätsbibliothek Erlangen-Nürnberg (UBEN).

Ms B213.

Published Primary Sources

Breu, J., *Die Chronik des Augsburger Malers Georg Preu des Älteren 1512–1537* (*Die Chroniken der deutschen Städte vom 14. bis ins 16. Jahrhundert*, 29 [CDS 29]), Leipzig, 1906.

Dussler, H. (ed.), *Reisen und Reisende in Bayerisch-Schwaben und seinen Randgebieten in Oberbayern, Franken, Württemberg, Vorarlberg und Tirol*, vol. 2, Weißenhorn, 1974.

Froning, R. (ed.), *Frankfurter Chroniken und annalistische Aufzeichnungen des Mittelalters*, Frankfurt, 1884.

Graser, H. and Tlusty, B.A. (eds.), *Jonas Losch, Teutscher Dichter und Componist. Die Lieder- und Reimspruchsammlung eines Augsburger Webers aus den Jahren 1579–1583*, Regensburg, 2015.

Kölderer, G., *Beschreihunng Vnnd Kurtze Vertzaichnus Fürnemer Lob Vnnd Gedenckhwürdiger Historien. Eine Chronik der Stadt Augsburg der Jahre 1576 bis 1607. Vol. 2: 1584–1588*, ed. S. Strodel and W.E.J. Weber, Augsburg, 2013.

Montagu, M.W., *The Complete Letters of Lady Mary Wortley Montagu. Vol. I: 1708–1720*, ed. R. Halsband, Oxford, 1965.

Mülich, H., *Chronik des Hector Mülich 1348–1487* (CDS 22), Leipzig, 1892.
Schweinichen, H. von, *Denkwürdigkeiten*, ed. H. Oesterley, Breslau, 1878.
Schwendi, L. von, "Diskurs und Bedenken über den Zustand des hl. Reiches von 1570", in E. von Frauenholz (ed.), *Lazarus von Schwendi. Der erste deutsche Verkünder der allgemeinen Wehrpflicht*, Hamburg, 1939, pp. 161–91.
Stetten, P. von (the Elder), *Geschichte der Heil. Röm. Reichs Freyen Stadt Augspurg aus bewährten Jahr-Büchern und tüchtigen Urkunden gezogen*, 2 vols., Frankfurt, 1743–58.
Stetten, P. von (the Younger), *Erläuterungen der in Kupfer gestochenen Vorstellungen aus der Geschichte der Reichsstadt Augsburg*, Augsburg, 1765.
Tlusty, B.A. (ed.), *Augsburg during the Reformation Era: An Anthology of Sources*. Indianapolis, 2012.

Secondary Literature

Baer, W., "Die Gründung des Jesuitenkollegs St. Salvator", in idem and H.-J. Hecker (eds.), *Die Jesuiten und ihre Schule St. Salvator in Augsburg 1582*, Munich, 1982, pp. 17–22.
Behringer, W., "Fugger als Sportartikelhändler: Auf dem Weg zu einer Sportgeschichte der Frühen Neuzeit", in R. Dauser and W. Weber (eds.), *Faszinierende Frühneuzeit. Reich, Frieden, Kultur und Kommunikation 1500–1800. Festschrift für Johannes Burkhardt zum 65. Geburtstag*, Berlin, 2008, pp. 115–34.
Behringer, W., "Arena and Pall Mall: Sport in the Early Modern Period", *German History* 27, 3 (2009), pp. 331–57.
Behringer, W., *Kulturgeschichte des Sports. Vom antiken Olympia bis ins 21. Jahrhundert*, Munich, 2012.
Brennan, T., "General Introduction", in *Public Drinking in the Early Modern World: Voices from the Tavern, 1500–1800*, Vol. 1, London, 2011, pp. vii–xxii.
Burke, P., *Popular Culture in Early Modern Europe*, New York, 1978.
Burke, P., "The Invention of Leisure in Early Modern Europe", *Past & Present* 146 (1995), pp. 136–50.
Burke, P., "The Invention of Leisure in Early Modern Europe: Reply", *Past & Present* 156 (1997), pp. 192–97.
Dieminger, W., "Bader, Barbiere, Wund- und Zahnärzte in der Reichsstadt Augsburg von 1316 bis 1806", M.D. diss., University of Ulm, 1999.
Edelmann, A., *Schützenwesen und Schützenfeste der deutschen Städte vom 13. bis zum 18. Jahrhundert*, Munich, 1890.
Elias, N., *The Civilizing Process: The History of Manners and State Formation and Civilization*, Oxford, 1994.
Burke, P. and Dunning, E., *Quest for Excitement: Sport and Leisure in the Civilizing Process*, Oxford, 1986.
Grüber, P.M. (ed.), *"Kurzweil viel ohn' Mass und Ziel". Vol. 1: Augsburger Patrizier und ihre Feste zwischen Mittelalter und Neuzeit* (exhibition catalogue), Munich, 1994.

Grüber, P.M. (ed.), *"Kurzweil viel ohn' Mass und Ziel".* Vol. 2: *Alltag und Festtag auf den Augsburger Monatsbildern der Renaissance*, Munich, 1994.

Gullmann, F.K., *Geschichte der Stadt Augsburg seit ihrer Entstehung bis zum Jahre 1806*, 6 vols., Augsburg, [1808–22].

Guttmann, A., *Women's Sports: A History*, New York, 1991.

Haupt, K., *Die Drei Mohren zu Augsburg*, Augsburg, 1956.

Häußler, F., *Marktstadt Augsburg. Von der Römerzeit bis zur Gegenwart*, Augsburg, 1998.

Jachmann, J., *Die Kunst des Augsburger Rates 1588–1631. Kommunale Räume als Medium von Herrschaft und Erinnerung*, Berlin, 2008.

Kirstein, U., "Zwitzel", in G. Grünsteudel, G. Hägele and R. Frankenberger (eds.), *Augsburger Stadtlexikon*, 2nd ed., Augsburg, 1998, p. 953.

Koutná, D., "'Mit ainer sollichen kostlichkeit und allerley kurtzweil ...'. Feste und Feiern der Fugger im 16. Jahrhundert", in J. Burkhardt (ed.), *Anton Fugger (1493–1560)*, Weißenhorn, 1994, pp. 99–115.

Kümin, B., *Drinking Matters: Public Houses and Social Exchange in Early Modern Central Europe*, Basingstoke, 2007.

Kümin, B. and Tlusty, B.A., "Introduction", in idem (eds.), *Public Drinking in the Early Modern World: Voices from the Tavern. Vol. 2: Holy Roman Empire I*, London, 2011, pp. xxxv–l.

Langner, C., and Dormeier, H. (eds.), *Feste und Bräuche aus Mittelalter und Renaissance. Die Augsburger Monatsbilder*, Gütersloh, 2007.

Layer, A., "Musik und Theater in St. Salvator", in W. Baer and H.-J. Hecker (eds.), *Die Jesuiten und ihre Schule St. Salvator in Augsburg 1582*, Munich, 1982, pp. 67–75.

Lymant, B., "Die sogenannte Folge aus dem Alltagsleben von I.v. Meckenem. Ein spätgotischer Kupferzyklus zu Liebe und Ehe", *Wallraf-Richartz-Jahrbuch* 53 (1992), pp. 7–44.

Mallinckrodt, R. von and Schattner, A., "Introduction", in idem (eds.), *Sports and Physical Exercise in Early Modern Culture: New Perspectives on the History of Sports and Motion*, London, 2016, pp. 1–17.

Mančal, J., "Collegium musicum", in G. Grünsteudel, G. Hägele and R. Frankenberger (eds.), *Augsburger Stadtlexikon*, 2nd ed., Augsburg, 1998, p. 335.

Marfany, J.-L., "The Invention of Leisure in Early Modern Europe", *Past & Present* 156 (1997), pp. 174–91.

McClelland, J., "Einleitung", in A. Krüger and idem (eds.), *Die Anfänge des modernen Sports in der Renaissance*, London, 1984, pp. 9–18.

Medick, H., "Plebejische Kultur, plebejische Öffentlichkeit, plebejische Ökonomie: Über Erfahrungen und Verhaltenswesen Besitzarmer und Besitzloser in der Übergangsphase zum Kapitalismus", in R. Berdahl, A. Lüdtke and H. Medick (eds.), *Klassen und Kultur. Sozialanthropologische Perspektiven in der Geschichtsschreibung*, Frankfurt, 1982, pp. 157–204.

Meyer, D.H., *Literarische Hausbücher des 16. Jahrhunderts*, 2 vols., Würzburg, 1989.

Oestreich, G., "Strukturprobleme des europäischen Absolutismus", *Vierteljahrschrift für Sozial- und Wirtschaftsgeschichte* 55 (1968), pp. 329–47.

Rajkay, B., "Totentanz oder Maskenbälle? Geschichte Augsburgs im 18. Jahrhundert", in D. Schiersner, A. Link, B. Rajkay and W. Scheffknecht (eds.), *Augsburg, Schwaben und der Rest der Welt. Neue Beiträge zur Landes- und Regionalgeschichte. Festschrift für Rolf Kießling zum 70. Geburtstag*, Augsburg, 2011, pp. 85–109.

Reintges, T., 1963. *Ursprung und Wesen der spätmittelalterlichen Schützengilden*, Bonn, 1963.

Ridley, G., *Clara's Grand Tour: Travels with a Rhinoceros in Eighteenth-Century Europe*, New York, 2004.

Roeck, B., *Lebenswelt und Kultur des Bürgertums in der Frühen Neuzeit*, Munich, 1991.

Roper, L., "'Going to Church and Street': Weddings in Reformation Augsburg", *Past & Present* 106 (1985), pp. 62–101.

Rosseaux, U., *Freiräume. Unterhaltung, Vergnügen und Erholung in Dresden (1694–1830)*, Cologne, 2007.

Schilling, H., "Die Konfessionalisierung im Reich. Religiöser und gesellschaftlicher Wandel in Deutschland zwischen 1555 und 1620", *Historische Zeitschrift* 246 (1988), pp. 1–45.

Schnell, F., *Zur Geschichte der Augsburger Meistersingerschule*, Augsburg, [1958].

Stewart, A., "Paper Festivals and Popular Entertainment the Kermis Woodcuts of Sebald Beham in Reformation Nuremberg", *Sixteenth Century Journal* 24, 2 (1993), pp. 301–50.

Stoll, P., "Stadttheater", in G. Grünsteudel, G. Hägele and R. Frankenberger (eds.), *Augsburger Stadtlexikon*, 2nd ed., Augsburg, 1998, p. 841.

Thienemann, G.A., *Leben und Wirken des unvergleichlichen Thiermalers und Kupferstechers Johann Elias Ridinger*, Leipzig, 1856.

Tlusty, B.A., *Bacchus and Civic Order: The Culture of Drink in Early Modern Germany*, Charlottesville, 2001.

Tlusty, B.A., "Drinking, Family Relations and Authority in Early Modern Germany", *Journal of Family History* 29 (2004), pp. 253–73.

Tlusty, B.A., "Playing by the Rules: Gambling and Social Identity in Early Modern German Towns", *Memoria y Civilización* 7 (2004), pp. 7–38.

Tlusty, B.A., *The Martial Ethic in Early Modern Germany: Civic Duty and the Right to Bear Arms*, Basingstoke, 2011.

Tlusty, B.A., "Martial Identity and the Culture of the Sword in Early Modern Germany", in D. Jaquet, K. Verelst and T. Dawson (eds.), *Late Medieval and Early Modern Fight Books: Transmission and Tradition of Martial Arts in Europe (14th–17th Centuries)*, Leiden, 2016, pp. 547–70.

Witz, F.A., *Versuch einer Geschichte der theatralischen Vorstellungen in Augsburg von den frühesten Zeiten bis 1876*, Augsburg, 1876.

Zangs, C., "Glück beim Spielen, Pech in der Liebe", in idem and S. Bieder (eds.), *"Mit Glück und Verstand". Zur Kunst- und Kulturgeschichte der Brett- und Kartenspiele* (exhibition catalogue), Aachen, 1993, pp. 17–20.

CHAPTER 15

The Experience of War

Andreas Flurschütz da Cruz

1   "Experience" as a Historical Category

The historiography on wars and the military has undergone a major shift in recent decades, as historians have moved beyond the political consequences of warfare, accounts of major battles, and military leaders, and have begun to study the everyday dimensions of war. Scholars nowadays approach military conflicts by including the experiences and perceptions of ordinary soldiers and civilians, which are viewed as essential for a comprehensive understanding of the history of war. In accordance with this historiographical trend, this chapter focuses on the actions and perceptions of those who lived in wartime, exploring the ways in which Augsburg's inhabitants experienced the many armed conflicts that made the early modern period a notoriously bellicose era, in order to emphasize a "key category for social history."[1]

In general, "experience" as a category is located at the intersection of power structures and social forces on the one hand and individual responses on the other. Social scientists understand experience as "the linguistically shaped process of weighing and assigning meaning to events as they happen".[2] How did people in early modern Augsburg experience and cope with war, and how did they interpret events? This chapter is concerned with the ways in which groups and individuals lived through wars and reacted to them, how they thought and wrote about them, and how they visualized their own role and those of their contemporaries. From the fifteenth to the eighteenth century, Augsburg was the site of a number of large-scale battles, sieges and military occupations, and while some of them – especially the horrific siege of 1634–35 – had a major impact on urban development, here we will look beyond spectacular manifestations of military violence and also consider the phases preceding and following actual military campaigns.

---

[1] Forrest et al., "Introduction", p. 6; Medick and Marschke, *Experiencing the Thirty Years War*, pp. vii, 17.
[2] Scott, "The Evidence of Experience"; Sewell, *Gender, History, and Deconstruction*, p. 19; Canning, "Feminist History", p. 72.

The chapter begins by pointing out some central aspects of how Augsburg's residents conceived of themselves. Chroniclers did not write down their experiences in a void; their writings mirror the dominant discourses and cultural constraints of their time and place. In a second step, the armed hostilities in which the city was involved during the period covered in this volume will be surveyed, focusing on people's understanding of and behavior in these events: warfare did not only happen on the battlefields, but also in people's heads.[3] In so-called ego-documents – personal accounts, letters, diaries, and chronicles – literate individuals wrote about what they deemed important in their lives, both in their everyday existence and in extraordinary situations. These accounts are among the closest we can get to immediate personal experiences and responses, but they mainly represent the views of elites. Supplementing information from literate writers are the many petitions from ordinary, in some cases illiterate, residents complaining via a scribe about various aspects of war, notably quartering. These sources have already been studied very well.[4]

2 A City of God in Times of War

As explored elsewhere in this volume, the majority of Augsburg's population turned Protestant during the Reformation era and remained so until the eighteenth century, when immigration from Catholic territories turned the confessional balance in favor of the latter.[5] Lutherans in the imperial city evinced a strong, occasionally excessive historical consciousness. Many viewed their city as a "City of God",[6] emphasizing its status as an important place in the Christian world and a central site of occidental history. They shared a growing sense of respect for the spiritual dignity of laypeople, a worldview that was widespread in the free imperial cities.[7] According to this worldview, everything that happened had a special meaning. Pre-modern sciences like astrology were integrated into this concept, and printed works, of which Augsburg was a major production center, helped to promote it.[8] This providential worldview, which

---

3 Schindling, "Kriegserfahrung", p. 17; Rutz, "Westen des Reiches", p. 12.
4 Tlusty, "The Public House".
5 See Chapters 10 and 11.
6 Pronk, "A City of God"; Roeck, *Geschichte Augsburgs*, p. 91.
7 Amberg, *A Real Presence*, p. 255.
8 Staats- und Stadtbibliothek Augsburg (SuStBA), Wilhelm Peter Zimmermann [?], Der Komet von 1618 über Augsburg, [1618?]; Mohrmann, "Alltag in Krieg und Frieden", p. 319; Zillhardt, *Zeytregister*, pp. 86–87; see Chapter 19 in this volume.

was a continuation and extension of pre-Reformation concepts,[9] was shared by chroniclers, Lutheran ministers, and schoolteachers. The popular practice among Lutherans of naming their children after Old Testament figures is further evidence of their adherence to this vision.[10]

Facing Counter-Reformation pressure during the Thirty Years' War, Augsburg's Lutherans considered themselves to be the "true" community of Christ, the "Chosen People" and rightful successors of the ancient people of Israel. They viewed their city as the counterpart of the Heavenly Jerusalem, an "artificial Protestant Utopia in the midst of a hostile environment".[11] The apocalyptic events of the war years further strengthened these convictions.[12]

This response was not unusual, if we take into account studies of medical trauma as applied to persons facing martial events or other radical breaks with the past, who tend to see themselves as completely subject to blind fate. Survivors of such events were inclined to consider their survival as an act of divine favor, while warfare and suffering were interpreted as punishments for the sinful life of the community or as a trial "because the Lord disciplines the one He loves, and He chastens everyone He accepts as His son" (Heb. 12:6). Early modern Augsburgers thus viewed their own destiny as part of a larger historical process.

Religious events contributed to Augsburg's (self-)glorification. As a result of the *Confessio Augustana* of 1530 and the Religious Peace of Augsburg in 1555, the city bore great symbolic significance to Lutherans throughout the Holy Roman Empire, who gave it the unofficial title "Lutheran Rome".[13] Moreover, a number of imperial diets took place within the city walls, making it the "secret capital" of the Empire.[14]

But the city's political, economic, and cultural centrality and its symbolic prominence as one of the cradles of Protestantism could become a liability in times of confessional conflict. Although Augsburg was spared from attack during the Peasants' War of 1525,[15] subsequent conflicts did not bypass it. The following sections will elucidate Augsburg's experiences in the Schmalkaldic

---

9   Augsburg's fifteenth-century chronicles already tended to focus on external conflicts, constructing a stable image of the city's internal conditions; Kießling, "Augsburg-Bild", p. 215.
10 François, *Die unsichtbare Grenze*, pp. 167–79.
11 Roeck, *Als wollt die Welt schier brechen*, p. 268.
12 SuStBA, 4° Cod. Adl. 22: Samuel Heiland, *Augspurgisches Erlösung Jahr vom Päpstlichen gewissens Zwang* [1632], fol. 5r.
13 Pronk, "A City of God", p. 452; François, *Die unsichtbare Grenze*, p. 157.
14 Kießling, *Kleine Geschichte Schwabens*, p. 71.
15 Werlich, *Chronica*, vol. 3, p. 10.

War (1546–47), the Thirty Years' War (1618–48), the War of Spanish Succession (1701–14), and the French Revolutionary and Napoleonic Wars (1792–1815), stressing the differences and commonalities in people's perceptions, behavior, and interpretation of these conflicts and what war meant for their lives.

3 Pride and Humiliation: the Schmalkaldic War (1546–47)

In order to protect their Protestant faith, a number of German princes and cities joined the Schmalkaldic League in 1531.[16] When Charles v banished its leaders, Landgrave Philip of Hesse and the Saxon Elector John Frederick I, the League's south German members mobilized their troops, numbering up to 57,000 soldiers, against him.[17] The predominantly Protestant city of Augsburg joined the League in 1536. As early as 1545, the city council initiated preparations for a possible military conflict, culminating in a splendid review of troops to demonstrate its determination and power.[18] About 3,600 armed people, including 470 horsemen, took part in the parade. Grain supplies were hoarded and the fortifications reinforced, with remarkable popular support.[19] Daily public morning prayers for the victory of the Schmalkaldic League became mandatory in all churches.[20] Augsburg's inhabitants seemed to long for battle in order to prove their patriotism and loyalty to the city, God, and their "true Protestant faith".

War broke out in the summer of 1546, and upper Germany soon became the center of action. When the Schmalkaldic League's army initially achieved considerable gains,[21] Augsburgers celebrated what they understood as a judgement of God in their favor by composing and printing polemical treatises, poems, and songs about the events.[22] Landgrave Philip of Hesse was equated with his namesake, the Macedonian king, as well as with the biblical prophet Joshua, and was called "father to the fatherland".[23] The emperor, meanwhile,

---

16 Lenz, *Rechenschaftsbericht*, p. 41, no. 9: Landgrave Philip to Bullinger, 8 Aug. 1546; Stetten, *Geschichte*, vol. 1, p. 392; Schmidt, "Libertät", p. 166.
17 Whaley, *Heiliges Römisches Reich*, vol. 1, pp. 382, 399–400.
18 Werlich, *Chronica*, vol. 3, p. 56; Zorn, *Augsburg*, p. 185.
19 Hecker, "Jacob Herbrot", pp. 52–53; Paulus, "Schertlin von Burtenbach", p. 54.
20 Roth, *Augsburgs Reformationsgeschichte*, vol. 3, pp. 389–90; Werlich, *Chronica*, vol. 2, pp. 58–61.
21 Kießling, "Eckpunkte", pp. 36–37.
22 Liliencron, *Volkslieder*, vol. 4, p. 269, no. 514; Roth, *Augsburgs Reformationsgeschichte*, vol. 3, p. 305; Lenz, *Briefwechsel*, pp. 444–47: Sailer to Landgrave Philip, 8 Aug. 1546.
23 Lenz, *Briefwechsel*, pp. 522–26: Fröhlich to Schertlin, 21 June 1546; Krämer, "Kunstzentrum", p. 523.

was compared to Herod. The conflict and its protagonists were thus interpreted in biblical and historical terms. In addition, Augsburg's troops, led by the city's military captain Sebastian Schertlin von Burtenbach (1496–1577), initially succeeded in conquering surrounding Catholic towns and territories, which were immediately staffed with Protestant clergy.[24] Spreading the "true faith" in the countryside was one of the city fathers' main goals. Augsburg units carried battle flags bearing the biblical words *Verbum Domini manet in aeternum* (Is. 40:8: "the Word of the Lord endures forever"), and Zwinglian ministers from Zurich and Basel filled the gaps left by the deposed Catholic priests.[25]

The city's aggressively Protestant stance in the Schmalkaldic War was mainly devised by the patrician mayor Georg Herwart, the guild mayor Jakob Herbrot,[26] city physician Gereon Sailer, city secretary Georg Frölich,[27] and the already mentioned Schertlin.[28] On 1 July 1546, Herwart gave a speech in the council that had strong anti-imperial and bellicose overtones and was probably written by Fröhlich. The Protestant clergy was also in favor of war, reminding the laity of the wars of the Old Testament and God's personal intervention in them. But it was not just Augsburg's exiled bishop Otto Truchsess von Waldburg who disagreed with the course the city was taking; the council members as well were not unanimously in favor of Augsburg's aggressive policy, and many Protestant patricians and merchants argued in favor of neutrality. Augsburg's Catholic community strongly disagreed with the council's politics, of course. Some of the wealthiest Catholic merchants, including members of the Fugger, Welser, and Baumgartner families, emigrated, but soon this option was forbidden by municipal decree, and those who had already left had to pay high fees to prevent their expatriation.[29] Rich merchant-bankers such as Anton Fugger secretly supported Charles V with large loans – ultimately employed against the city – while refusing to lend money to "Schmalkaldic Augsburg".[30]

The victorious atmosphere did not last long: in mid-September 1546, imperial forces gained the upper hand. Stories about Spanish troops plundering and

---

24   Close, *Negotiated Reformation*, p. 210; Kießling, "Augsburg in der Reformationszeit", p. 36.
25   Maissen, "Eidgenossen", p. 82.
26   On his influential network as well as on the Welser and Fugger networks, see Sieh-Burens, *Oligarchie*, pp. 109–16.
27   Roth, *Augsburgs Reformationsgeschichte*, vol. 3, appendix 2, p. 522; Paulus, "Schertlin von Burtenbach", p. 55; Häberlein, *Brüder*, pp. 199–224.
28   Kießling, "Augsburg in der Reformationszeit", p. 33.
29   Stetten, *Geschichte*, vol. 1, pp. 392–93; Roth, *Augsburgs Reformationsgeschichte*, vol. 3, pp. 351, 362.
30   Zelinsky Hanson, *Religious Identity*, p. 11; Roeck, *Geschichte Augsburgs*, p. 115. In June and July 1546, the Fugger Company transferred 600,000 gulden to the emperor and his brother, King Ferdinand. See Kirch, *Fugger*.

setting fire to neighboring cities worried the populace. Following the surrender of other cities including Ulm, Augsburg capitulated in early 1547.[31] Although a few days earlier, the city's leaders had declared that capitulation to the emperor would be considered equal to apostasy, the inhabitants' propensity to suffer was limited. Elaborating a strategy to defend the city, Schertlin warned that this disgrace would be remembered forever.[32] Pride, however, now gave way to forced humility. Augsburg not only had to pay a fine of 150,000 gulden to the emperor and even higher sums to King Ferdinand and Bishop Otto, but also had to open its doors to an imperial garrison.[33] The city's keys were handed over, in a highly symbolic act. However, the council refused to extradite the outlawed Schertlin to the emperor's authority.[34] The hardliner[35] Bishop Otto, whose predecessor had been expelled from his residence in 1537, triumphantly returned from his exile in Dillingen and entered Augsburg in a victory parade. The city council had long suspected him of conspiring with the emperor and Catholic princes such as William IV of Bavaria. Five days later, Emperor Charles V himself arrived.[36] Catholicism now celebrated its rebirth in Augsburg, and the major churches were restored to the bishop and his clergy, while Protestant ministers and schoolteachers were forced to leave, to be replaced by compliant successors.[37]

There had always been significant opposition – mainly, but not exclusively Catholic – to the political course taken by the city. When their religiously motivated politics failed, many Protestants found a scapegoat in Herbrot, who, in alliance with the Schmalkaldians, had allegedly led them along the road to disaster.[38] Whereas the leaders of the pro-Schmalkaldic movement had formerly been praised in heroic and biblical hymns, Herbrot was now called a Judas and denigrated in songs and libels.[39]

31　Creasman, *Censorship*, p. 100; Roth, *Augsburgs Reformationsgeschichte*, vol. 3, p. 465.
32　Hecker, "Jacob Herbrot", p. 65. On Schertlin's historical conscience see Herberger, *Schertlin von Burtenbach*, pp. 115–17, no. 29.
33　Roth, *Augsburgs Reformationsgeschichte*, vol. 3, p. 474; vol. 4, p. 6; Werlich, *Chronica*, vol. 2, p. 65.
34　Hecker, "Correspondenz", pp. 274–75.
35　Roeck, *Geschichte Augsburgs*, p. 115; Ansbacher, "Otto Truchseß von Waldburg", p. 2; Zoepfl, *Bistum Augsburg*, pp. 210–11.
36　*Chroniken* 33 (Mair), pp. 325–27; Mameranus, *D. Caroli V. Roma. Imp. Avg. Iter*; Zelinsky Hanson, *Religious Identity*, p. 17.
37　*Chroniken* 32 (Mair), p. 248, 328; Kießling, "Evangelisch St. Ulrich", pp. 213, 225, 227; Creasman, *Censorship*, pp. 103–04.
38　Hecker, "Jacob Herbrot", pp. 39, 52–53; *Chroniken* 32 (Mair), p. 84.
39　Wagner Oettinger, *Music*, pp. 327–78; Sieh-Burens, *Oligarchie*, p. 156.

The Schmalkaldic War's most momentous effect on Augsburg's Protestants was not the military conflict itself, which took place far from the city, but its aftermath. The emperor imposed a severe penalty on the city, above all on its Protestant inhabitants. Catholics benefited from the new situation, as the Mass was reinstated and the constitution revised in favor of a Catholic- and patrician-dominated regime.[40] The emperor's imposition of a new constitution on the rebellious city was interpreted as a warning to the rest of the Empire. The Augsburg *Interim*, which Charles V proclaimed in May 1548, forced Protestants to observe Catholic traditions in their services and was undoubtedly the greatest humiliation for the downcast majority of Augsburg's inhabitants.[41] Charles also compelled the city to host the next imperial diet, the so called "Armored Diet" of 1547–48, which looked to the people more like a tribunal.[42] Again, worries and fears were expressed in poems and hymns. Ulrich Holtzman's "I cry out from my heart" is the epitome of the anti-*Interim* song, bemoaning its enforcement on the city.[43] Over the next seven years, Protestant Augsburg saw itself as the successor to the exiled people of Israel. The events strengthened solidarity inside the Protestant parishes and aided the development of a Lutheran confessional culture.[44]

But the *Interim* remained only an episode, as the Princes' Revolt in 1552 brought the emperor into grave difficulties, and the Religious Peace of Augsburg (1555) finally established the city's status as a bi-confessional community, fully recognizing both confessions and challenging the medieval identity of the city as a united civil and spiritual community.[45]

4   A Dying City: The Thirty Years' War (1618–48)

While the Schmalkaldic War was short-lived, the Thirty Years' War turned out to be a lasting traumatic experience. Following the eruption of tensions in the 1580s, religious coexistence had returned to a carefully-orchestrated state of peace,[46] and by the beginning of the seventeenth century, the city had long since overcome the financial strains of the Schmalkaldic War. But the Thirty Years'

---

40   Kraus, *Militärwesen*, p. 34; Häberlein, *Brüder*, p. 36.
41   See Chapter 10 in this volume.
42   Zelinsky Hanson, *Religious Identity*, p. 17; Roeck, *Geschichte Augsburgs*, p. 116.
43   Original German title: "Von hertzen thü ichs klagen"; Wagner Oettinger, *Music*, pp. 169, 362–67.
44   Kießling, "Otto Truchseß von Waldburg", pp. 71–73.
45   Warmbrunn, *Zwei Konfessionen*; Kießling, "Augsburg in der Reformationszeit", p. 40.
46   See Chapter 11 in this volume.

War would not only be a demographic and economic disaster for Augsburg; it would also fortify the "invisible boundary" between the confessions and create two separate socio-religious communities.[47] The Thirty Years' War was also the first modern war in which printed mass media played a major role by defining and publicly commenting on events. In particular, numerous printed sermons and pamphlets produced by Lutheran ministers put the pastors into the role of political actors capable of influencing a significant audience.

War did not come immediately to the city, as the military actions during its first decade took place far away. Nevertheless, the atmosphere in Augsburg was tense from the beginning, as the mustering of troops, the stockpiling of supplies, and negotiations for alliances had already begun in 1614.[48] A comet over Augsburg seemed to announce upcoming disaster in 1618. The hyperinflation of the early 1620s known as the "Kipper and Wipper period" brought the city's finances to ruin and caused the number of alms recipients to rise significantly.[49] Food prices rose, and commerce, the backbone of Augsburg's wealth, stagnated as Duke Maximilian I of Bavaria prohibited grain from his territory being supplied to the city.[50] Moreover, the period of cooling temperatures and poor harvests known as the "Little Ice Age" adversely affected central European agriculture and was widely interpreted as God's punishment for sinful lives and ingratitude.[51] In Augsburg, bakeries were pillaged, and the city leaders had to organize the central distribution of essential goods.

Bernhard Heupold, a schoolteacher, interpreted this period as a "prelude to apocalypse",[52] but the real suffering did not start until 1628, when the plague hit and 9,611 mostly poor inhabitants died – five times the number of an ordinary year. Broadsheets and penance ordinances interpreted this as another divine punishment for the city's sins.[53] As the community was collectively responsible for war and misery, it could only redeem itself by heeding God's commands.[54]

In the following year, Augsburg became the focus of the emperor's Counter-Reformation politics. In his chronicle, the merchant Jakob Wagner referred to

---

47 François, *Die unsichtbare Grenze*, p. 33; Roeck, "Totentanz", pp. 223–24.
48 Kraus, *Militärwesen*, pp. 85, 176; Simmet, *Reichsstadt Augsburg*, pp. 4–5.
49 Herz, "Tagebuch", p. 195.
50 Roeck, *Bäcker*, chapter 3.2.
51 Staatsbibliothek zu Berlin Preußischer Kulturbesitz, Ms. germ. qu. 1125; SuStBA, 2° Cod. S 66, p. 371; Zillhardt, *Zeytregister*, p. 113. On the Little Ice Age, see Parker, *Global Crisis*, pp. 3–25.
52 Cited in Roeck, *Als wollt die Welt schier brechen*, p. 182.
53 Raphael Custos, Print 1628. Reprinted in Roeck, *Als wollt die Welt schier brechen*, p. 210.
54 Gantet, "Wahrnehmung des Friedens", p. 363.

1629 as the point "where this city's nemesis begins".[55] On 6 March, Emperor Ferdinand II issued the Edict of Restitution, ordering all churches that had become Protestant after 1552 to revert to Catholicism. The city council, aware of significant opposition to its execution, forbade citizens to leave their houses on the day it went into effect (8 August) to prevent a public uprising. Nowhere was the Edict of Restitution executed as severely as in Augsburg. Protestants such as the architect Elias Holl[56] and the city physician Philipp Hoechstetter[57] were dismissed, and Lutheran ministers were forbidden to preach. Those who were not citizens had to leave the city – an event which Protestant clergymen later compared to the biblical exodus. Protestant churches were closed and in some cases damaged, and Lutherans were not allowed to leave the city on Sundays to attend services in neighboring communities. Protestant poor were even excluded from the distribution of alms and public hospitals. To enforce these measures, about 1,000 soldiers were stationed inside the city walls, and a gallows was erected in the city center as a general warning.[58]

These events gained wide publicity in the Empire. Once again, it was a bishop, Heinrich V von Knöringen, who cooperated with the Bavarian duke to repress Protestantism in the city. Heinrich, "a prominent advocate of Catholic restoration", understood the city's significance as the birthplace of the Augsburg Confession and therefore considered it as a model case in the Holy Roman Empire.[59] He was the driving force behind the proclamation of the Edict in Augsburg, envisioning the city's complete return to Catholicism.[60] All church buildings had to be returned to the Catholics. Augsburg became a frontline, as its re-catholization in 1629 turned into "one of the war's most conspicuous 'media events'".[61]

In the wake of these events, Augsburg's Lutherans continued to see themselves as a "chosen people" facing the trials of war, sickness, and suffering sent by God to turn the war into a test of faith. It was this sense that enabled them to survive physically and psychologically. The war triggered not only apocalyptic fears, but also millenarian hopes for a kingdom of peace that would arise from the fall of the "Roman antichrist", as they called the pope.[62] Lutheran preachers and theologians interpreted the excessive violence and unprecedented

---

55   Cited in Roeck, "Totentanz", p. 224.
56   Meyer (ed.), *Hauschronik Holl*, p. 87.
57   Herz, "Tagebuch", pp. 202–03.
58   Simmet, *Reichsstadt Augsburg*, p. 11; Zorn, *Augsburg*, p. 214.
59   Pronk, "A City of God", pp. 451–52; Zillhardt, *Zeytregister*, pp. 125–26.
60   Stetten, *Geschichte*, vol. 2, p. 36; Kießling, "Eckpunkte", p. 40; idem, "St. Anna", p. 242.
61   Pronk, "A City of God", p. 452.
62   Kaufmann, "Predigt", p. 247.

human suffering, the advance of Catholicism, and the breakdown of the city's legal and political structure as part of a universal struggle between the forces of good and evil. This tendency to interpret political and religious events in religious terms was a strategy that ensured social stability in times of crisis. It demonstrates an inclination to identify divine signs in this world and thus wrest meaning from chaotic circumstances.[63]

The political situation completely changed with the arrival of Swedish troops under King Gustavus II Adolphus in 1632, who was now integrated into the interpretation of current events. The Protestant monarch appeared to fulfill biblical prophecies by fighting for God and, like the heroes of the ancient people of Israel and the Messiah himself, overcoming his enemies.[64] Gustavus Adolphus' name was read as an anagram of the city's Latin name (AVGVSTA–GVSTAVA), and his arrival endowed the community with a sense of higher purpose. Thus, when the Swedish army approached Augsburg in April 1632, the city council unanimously decided to surrender the city. The occupying Bavarian troops withdrew peacefully and were promptly replaced by the Swedes, who were welcomed and even greeted as "God's angels" by the Lutheran population. The new lord was showered with presents.[65] Despite mounting war burdens, the people's image of the soldiers was initially positive, as the Swedes were not occupying citizens' houses but initially sleeping in the open air, singing hymns and psalms, and reading the gospel, albeit in a foreign language.[66] While the imperial and Bavarian occupying forces had been seen as uncivilized enemies, the Swedish Lutheran foreigners seemed to be educated and pious fellow Christians, not unlike the way the majority of the Lutheran population viewed themselves. Churches were reopened to Protestant services, and Lutherans such as Holl regained their offices.[67] Now Protestant families were promoted into the city's elite as patricians and councilors.

A huge number of panegyrical pamphlets, songs,[68] and Lutheran sermons indulged in a virtual sanctification or even deification of the Swedish king,[69] creating a veritable cult about his person and propagating the glorious events

---

63   Roeck, *Eine Stadt in Krieg und Frieden*, vol. 1, p. 35; vol. 2, p. 978.
64   Meyer (ed.), *Hauschronik Holl*, p. 88; Tschopp, *Heilsgeschichtliche Deutungsmuster*, p. 46.
65   SuStBA, 2° Cod. S 68, fol. 14v; Roos (ed.), *Chronik Jakob Wagner*, p. 9; Roeck, *Als wollt die Welt schier brechen*, pp. 247–48.
66   SuStBA, 2° Cod. S 68, fol. 1r; Emmendörffer, "Wunde Welt", p. 467; Roos (ed.), *Chronik Jakob Wagner*, p. 13.
67   Stetten, "Philipp Hainhofer", pp. 11–12; Meyer (ed.), *Hauschronik Holl*, pp. 12, 88.
68   On Augsburg's importance as a center of printing songs, see Nehlsen, "Liedpublizistik", p. 434.
69   Anon., *Augusta Angustiata, a Deo per Deum liberate*, 1632; Heyde, "Kunstpolitik und Propaganda", p. 108.

as "the final apocalyptical battle against the forces of the Antichrist".[70] When the preacher Samuel Heiland returned to Augsburg,[71] the entire political establishment, including the newly installed Lutheran city council (the "Swedish council") attended his sermon, which stressed once again the parallels between the suppressed Lutheran community of Augsburg and the exiled people of Israel. The sermon was printed immediately afterwards, informing an even larger number of recipients about the recent events and their significance as representing an end of Babylonian Captivity and the rebuilding of the modern Jerusalem and its temple in Augsburg.[72]

Gustavus Adolphus fit into this concept very well, and he exploited it to his own advantage.[73] Soon his portrait could be seen on every wall in Augsburg. Local men appeared in Swedish dress, songs of gratitude were composed, coins were minted, and some babies were baptized in the king's name.[74] While the mood among Protestants brightened, Catholic Augsburgers – at least after Gustavus Adolphus' death, when the situation dramatically deteriorated – were suppressed and prohibited from leaving their homes.[75] Some who did not obey were imprisoned in the city hall. The new regime distrusted Catholics, suspecting them of a kind of a "popish plot" to undermine Protestantism. Catholics were thus forbidden to ascend church spires, supposedly to prevent them from communicating with the enemy outside the city, and for the same reason, their windows looking outward from the city were bricked up. The Catholic clergy was forced to leave Augsburg.

In due course, Protestants also found that life under Swedish rule was not that different from what it had been before. Citizens had to labor on the fortifications and received military training to protect Augsburg, while Swedish soldiers were replaced by 4,000 German mercenaries. They were not as

---

70 E.g. Universitätsbibliothek Frankfurt am Main, Collection G. Freytag, nos. 5496, 3: anon., *Evangelischer Auffwecker*.
71 SuStBA, 4° Cod. Adl. 22: Samuel Heiland, *Augspurgisches Erlösung Jahr vom Päpstlichen gewissens Zwang* (1632), fol. 5r.
72 Tschopp, *Heilsgeschichtliche Deutungsmuster*, pp. 142–82; Pronk, "A City of God", pp. 463–65.
73 Recalling other events believed to be presaged by heavenly signs, Gustavus Adolphus arrived in Augsburg and addressed the citizens with the following words: "Dear good friends! I have no doubt that God has sent me forth on this long journey to save you from your plight in answer to your devoted and diligent prayers and your commendable persistence": Roos (ed.), *Chronik Jakob Wagner*, p. 9.
74 Simmet, *Reichsstadt Augsburg*, p. 21; Heyde, "Kunstpolitik und Propaganda", p. 108.
75 SuStBA, 2° Cod. S 68, fols. 34r, 50r; Emmendörffer, "Wunde Welt", pp. 497–99; Roos (ed.), *Chronik Jakob Wagner*, pp. 18–19, 25; Zorn, *Augsburg*, p. 216; Häberlein, "Vom Augsburger Religionsfrieden", p. 86.

disciplined as their predecessors, but indulged in gluttony and heavy drinking, often causing damage to their host quarters. The Catholic housing project known as the Fuggerei, for example, was left in ruins. Moreover, the occupying soldiers required 20,000–30,000 gulden per month in contributions.[76] When imperial troops started to lay siege to the city in the fall of 1634 and cut it off from the countryside and even the water supply, people became increasingly desperate and war-weary. The Protestant chronicler Jakob Wagner describes a world turned upside down, as food supplies from outside virtually ceased around Christmas 1634, and disease spread again. Many peasants from nearby villages fled inside the city walls, thus worsening Augsburg's economic, logistic, and hygienic situation. Horses, cats and dogs, and even human bodies were eaten. One of the refugees from the surrounding villages, the priest Johann Georg Mayr, wrote that "the bodies of the living turned into graves of the dead".[77] According to Bernd Roeck, these horrific tales testify to the citizen's tenacious struggle for survival.[78]

But things got even worse: The plague returned, killing 4,664 people in 1634 and another 6,243 in 1635. Grave-diggers complained about a lack of space in the cemeteries, and bodies decayed in the streets. In the Lutheran churches, the sacrament began to be celebrated as a kind of public last rite. It seemed that the city was dying. The Benedictine chronicler Reginbald Moehner informs us about Augsburg's "Swedish Carnival" in February 1635, when people were walking the streets looking like ghosts and living dead.[79] Comedies, music, and even sleigh-rides had long been forbidden to save the city from God's wrath in a desperate attempt to ward off disaster.

Jakob Wagner at some point wondered if it might have been better to agree with the Catholic emperor,[80] and so did the city and its inhabitants. In March 1635, after six months of siege and much hesitation by the council and the Swedish officers, Augsburg surrendered.[81] A militant Lutheran wing, however, was convinced that capitulation would mean the rescue of bodies, but the loss of souls.[82] Some still viewed the city as an image of Jerusalem,

---

76 Roos (ed.), *Chronik Jakob Wagner*, pp. 29, 36, 42. Augsburg's annual income amounted to 390,000 gulden on average between 1631 and 1635 and 201,000 gulden between 1636 and 1640: Stadtarchiv Augsburg (StadtAA), Einnehmerbücher 1631–1640.
77 Roeck, "Totentanz", p. 227.
78 Roeck, *Eine Stadt in Krieg und Frieden*, vol. 2, p. 751.
79 SuStBA, 2°Cod. S 65, pp. 266–67.
80 SuStBA, Chroniken 27a, p. 195.
81 Roos (ed.), *Chronik Jakob Wagner*, p. 56; Paulus, "Sebastian Schertlin von Burtenbach", p. 80.
82 Herz, "Tagebuch", pp. 205–07.

potentially "a world free from suppression, tyranny, injustice, violence, illness and sorrow".[83]

After the garrison had capitulated, imperial and Bavarian forces took possession of Augsburg once more. These events were accompanied by the appearance of a rainbow, in the eyes of the many a sign of God's approval of the contentious decision to surrender.[84] Things now returned to the state during the years 1629–32; Catholic ascendancy was restored, and once again people had to pay high contributions and provide supplies to the soldiers and their lords. In contrast to 1629, however, Protestants were now allowed to practice their faith, although not inside churches. For 14 years, Augsburg's Lutherans held their services in the open air in St. Anna's churchyard, a "traumatic experience" for the community. The Protestant patrician Paul von Stetten the Elder would later describe the period from 1628 to 1649 as the worst in Augsburg's history.[85]

Although the 1640s were more peaceful and even the climate seemed to improve, the city had lost much of its former splendor. Alvise Contarini, a Venetian traveler, reported in the summer of 1643 that the formerly proud and crowded city appeared run-down and dilapidated. According to Contarini, 100 years might not be enough to restore the city's former grandeur.[86] In 1646, war returned to Augsburg as an allied French-Swedish army appeared outside the city walls, but this time Catholics and Protestants successfully collaborated to prevent another conquest. The enemy now was the war itself.

In the end, less than half of Augsburg's pre-war population of approximately 45,000 people survived the war.[87] Peace was initially accompanied by hardship, as the city had to pay high contributions to the remaining troops. In addition, people were afraid of the soldiers' behavior once they were dismissed.[88] Therefore, the first months after the declaration of the Peace of Westphalia in 1648 were not really perceived as any different from wartime, although relations between the confessions were eventually stabilized through the implementation of a system of parity.[89]

Meanwhile, some individuals profitably cooperated with the troops. When soldiers plundered houses and churches in Augsburg's hinterland, citizens

---

83 Pronk, "A City of God", p. 474.
84 SuStBA, 2° Cod. S 68, fol. 47r; Emmendörffer, "Wunde Welt", p. 528.
85 Stetten, *Geschichte*, vol. 2, Preface, A2r; Simmet, *Reichsstadt Augsburg*, pp. 5–6.
86 Roeck "Venedigs Rolle", p. 161.
87 See Chapter 2 in this volume for population figures.
88 Gantet, "Wahrnehmung des Friedens", pp. 370, 373.
89 See Chapter 7 in this volume.

bought up the booty at low prices;[90] otherwise the plundering system would not have lasted long. This indicates that Augsburgers were not mere passive victims of the war. Moreover, aside from Suhl (Thuringia) and Nuremberg, Augsburg was one of the few southern German towns that profited from the mass production of military weapons.[91]

5   History Repeated? The War of the Spanish Succession (1701–14)

The War of the Spanish Succession involved all of Europe. Originally the Bavarian Prince Joseph Ferdinand was to succeed the childless Spanish Habsburg King Charles II, but Joseph Ferdinand, only six years old, died in 1699. When Charles also died on All Saints' Day of the following year, the arena was open for the competing claims of Charles' closest relatives, the Habsburgs of Austria and the Bourbons of France. In the ensuing conflict, Bavaria sided with France against the Habsburg emperor. So the early events of the war took place far from Spain, with Augsburg becoming the center of military operations in southern Germany in the fall of 1703.

Its territory bordering on the city, Bavaria had long been a relevant political and economic factor for Augsburg. The war for the Spanish crown now seemed to provide the Bavarian elector with a long-sought opportunity to subdue the independent imperial city and incorporate it into his territory.[92] Supported by troops of his French ally, Elector Maximilian II Emanuel ordered the siege and occupation of the city in 1703.

The Bavarian occupation had grave financial consequences for Augsburg, as the total cost for supplying the occupation forces, paying the enforced taxes, and repairing the destroyed city walls amounted to four million gulden.[93] The cultural and psychological consequences were equally grave. The rector of St. Anna school, Philip Jacob Croph, wrote a detailed eyewitness account. Once more, the martial events were interpreted in religious and historical terms, culminating in a "miraculous rescue" of the city and the "consolation" of its people.[94]

When the city of Ulm was taken by Bavarian troops in September 1702, Augsburgers were shocked and frightened. As in former wars, people from the

---

90   SuStBA, 4° Cod. Aug. 238, fol. 17v: Bartholomäus Beyer, *Diarium Rerum Augustanarum à m. Mayo, 1648. ad m. 7br. 1651*, p. 163.
91   Langer, "Heeresfinanzierung", p. 297.
92   Bátori, *Reichsstadt Augsburg*, p. 193; Faulmüller, *Reichsstadt Augsburg*, p. 21.
93   Köberlin, "Jac. Crophius", p. 5; Croph, *Das mit Krieges-Last gedrückte [...] Augspurg*, p. 42.
94   Croph, *Das mit Krieges-Last gedrückte [...] Augspurg*, p. 3.

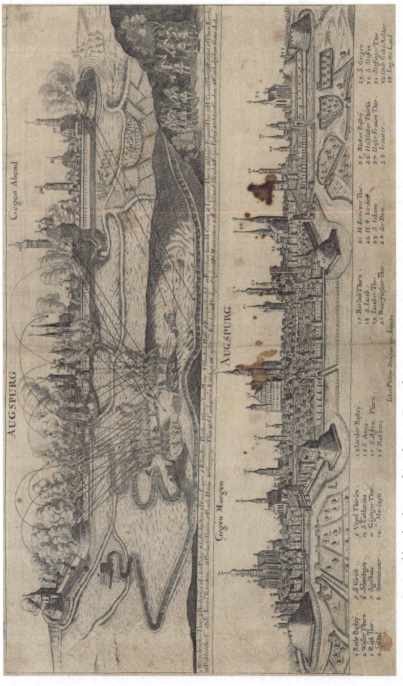

FIGURE 15.1 Siege and bombardment of Augsburg in December 1703
STAATS- UND STADTBIBLIOTHEK AUGSBURG, GRAPH 56/109/9

surrounding countryside fled into the city and commerce came to a standstill, which meant a disaster for the mercantile metropolis.[95] Immediately, measures reminiscent of the Thirty Years' War were introduced, including the prohibition of blasphemy, disputing, and even public music; the establishment of days of penance; and a clothing ordinance that allowed only black clothes to be worn.[96] People once more saw the events as a divine punishment for their sins, but with one big difference; this war was no longer viewed as a religious conflict. Thus the aggressor, the Bavarian elector, did not primarily represent a confessional party, but a political force. Instead of mistrusting each other, Catholics and Protestants now cooperated to defend their city.

Initially, an imperial garrison entered Augsburg to protect it, but in the early morning of 3 December 1703, drums announced the arrival of the Bavarian-French enemy. Croph describes the sound as a "wake-up call to penitence".[97] Five days later, the artillery fire began, killing some people and setting fire to over 100 buildings. The ringing of bells and clocks was stopped, so time literally stood still for the inhabitants. Destruction, fire, and chaos continued for another five days, causing despair and fear that the final judgment was imminent. The imperial forces were unable to hold the city and had to surrender it after ten days of bombardment on 16 December 1703, when 13,000 French soldiers with 7,000 horses entered Augsburg. The strength of the occupying forces by far exceeded the number of citizens.[98]

According to Croph, the Augsburgers accepted their destiny, mindful of the biblical words of punishment for sins at the hands of strangers (Jer. 5:15). The symbol of imperial liberty, the eagle, was either removed from official buildings or painted over. The city officially became Bavarian on 13 March 1704. By then, Augsburg hardly resembled its former self, the walls having been razed and the dung of war horses turning the streets into a cesspit. The Bavarian occupation was short-lived, however, ending at Christmas 1704, when Augsburg regained its status as a free imperial city in the wake of the defeat of French and Bavarian forces at the Battle of Blenheim. This battle not only turned the tide in southern Germany in favor of the Emperor and his allies, but was a major media event as well, celebrated by Augsburg printers in numerous publications.[99]

---

95 Köhler, "Wolfgang Jakob Sulzer", p. 136.
96 Faulmüller, *Reichsstadt Augsburg*, pp. 24–25.
97 Croph, *Das mit Krieges-Last gedrückte [...] Augspurg*, p. 30.
98 Köberlin, "Jac. Crophius", p. 3.
99 Weißbrich, *Höchstädt 1704*.

6 The End of Imperial Augsburg: The French Revolutionary and Napoleonic Wars (1792–1815)

The Seven Years' War (1756–63) did not affect the city directly, and the eighteenth century generally was a peaceful period for Augsburg. Its status as a free imperial city, however, continued to be threatened by its powerful neighbor Bavaria. When Napoleon Bonaparte invaded the Holy Roman Empire at the beginning of the nineteenth century in a kind of early "total war",[100] Elector Maximilian IV of Bavaria sided with him. In return for his support, Maximilian would be elevated to the rank of king in 1806, and was given the opportunity to expand his territory by incorporating secularized church property as well as former imperial cities and other estates as compensation for losses on the left bank of the Rhine.[101] The city of Augsburg was at the top of Maximilian's wish list, but it managed to be among the last of the approximately 50 imperial cities to lose their independence, holding out like an island in the midst of the Bavarian territory until 1805.[102]

But incorporation into Bavaria was only the end of a decade of hardship that had begun in 1796, when Augsburg was occupied by French and Bavarian troops. In the following years, up to 30,000 soldiers needed to be provisioned and quartered, turning Augsburg into a large garrison.[103] Depending on the military situation, imperial and even Russian troops entered the city as well. Augsburg was an important provisioning station and served as a detention center and military hospital. Even the cathedral became a lazaretto. The financial burdens were gigantic: in 1800, the city council had to charge citizens with a quintuple tax in order to pay the requested contributions. Furthermore, Augsburg had to deliver huge payments in kind.[104] Costs for the entire period from 1792 to 1806 are estimated at ten million gulden. Augsburg never recovered from the financial collapse that resulted.[105]

Shortly before Christmas 1805, the city was officially handed over to Bavaria. Once more, and now for good, all signs of imperial liberty were obliterated.[106] After more than 500 years, Augsburg's history as a free imperial city had come to an end; according to Paul von Stetten the Younger, the poor had become

---

100   Planert, *Mythos*, pp. 96–97, 107.
101   Dotterweich, "Mediatisierung", p. 541; Zorn, *Augsburg*, p. 235; Roeck, *Geschichte Augsburgs*, pp. 153–54.
102   Kießling, *Kleine Geschichte Schwabens*, p. 124; Pahnke, "Patriotismus ohne Nation", p. 203.
103   Häberlein, "Vom Augsburger Religionsfrieden", p. 96; Zorn, *Augsburg*, p. 234.
104   Planert, *Mythos*, p. 219.
105   Fassl, *Konfession, Wirtschaft und Politik*, pp. 173–74.
106   Roeck, *Geschichte Augsburgs*, p. 155.

beggars and the rich had become poor during the 15 years leading up to the city's incorporation into Bavaria.[107]

Not everybody in Augsburg was as unhappy about the city's loss of independence as were the members of old patrician families, such as Stetten, who had long controlled the city council. Before and during the war, some citizens advocated the voluntary surrender of imperial liberty and even petitioned the Bavarian elector to take care of the city.[108] Even the Secret Council, the city's inner circle of leadership, included a pro-Bavarian faction that hoped for more security and stability as part of a larger territory. Social tensions in the city erupted in a series of artisan uprisings during the late eighteenth century that culminated in a major weavers' revolt in 1794. Artisan discontent, however, did not usually center on political grievances, but on the unequal distribution of the huge financial commitments caused by warfare.[109]

The strained relations within the city also resulted from a conflict between patricians and merchants about participation and financial control.[110] One day after the regime change in 1805, the merchants held a lavish ball, and Protestants seemed to welcome their new Catholic ruler more than did their Catholic counterparts. Excitement about these changes subsided, however, when people became aware that their new lord would not treat them much better than their old ones. Popular discontent in Augsburg after 1805 often centered on Bavaria's bureaucratic absolutism, which disregarded local traditions and resulted in an unpopular administrative shakeup. Augsburg became just one among many Bavarian municipal cities, neglected and exploited, and its population emerged from the war as subjects of a distant king.[111]

7   Conclusion

The four military conflicts considered here affected the imperial city in strikingly different ways. Correspondingly, war was experienced in diverse forms. In 1546–47, Augsburg had just been transformed by the Reformation, and the majority of inhabitants felt that it was following the way of the Gospel. Fired by messianic hopes and under the guidance of leaders who were compared

---

107   Pahnke, "Patriotismus ohne Nation", p. 203; Zorn, *Augsburg*, p. 241.
108   Kießling, *Kleine Geschichte Schwabens*, p. 124; Bátori, *Reichsstadt Augsburg*, p. 194.
109   See Chapter 12 in this volume.
110   See Chapter 7 in this volume.
111   See Bitterauf, "Geschichte", p. 62.

with ancient heroes and even the Saviour himself, Augsburg hurled itself into a military conflict with the emperor and its bishop, only to suffer defeat.

But even in defeat, the Bible offered Augsburg's Protestant majority a plausible basis for identifying themselves with the people of Israel and the city with devastated Jerusalem. This remained a central aspect of Augsburg's identity over the following centuries. This view was promoted by politicians and ministers who found meaning in traumatic wartime experiences. People consequently accepted even the horrors of the Thirty Years' War as the result of their sins, and therefore their suffering made sense as another chapter in an ongoing story of ordeal and redemption. At the same time, criticism of warfare emerged as a genre during the Thirty Years' War, and its experiences contributed to the emergence of a more secular attitude towards war.

Later wars were no longer defined in confessional terms, although faith still mattered in Augsburg. The War of the Spanish Succession was interpreted in the same biblical way as earlier wars, but the enemy forces were not primarily seen as agents of a particular confessional party, as had been the case with Charles V or Gustavus Adolphus. Instead, they came to be perceived as political actors. Catholics and Lutherans in Augsburg now collaborated and suffered together.

If the city's cession to Bavaria in 1805–06 once more aroused confessional hopes and fears, they were now of secondary importance. Some welcomed their new Bavarian lord while others did not, but most shared concerns about the unequal distribution of financial obligations among the city's inhabitants. To some extent, this diversity of interests characterized all early modern wars, corresponding with different ways of experiencing political and social changes. Religion was not the only category that mattered, and the confessional parties did not constitute homogeneous groups.[112] Merchants emphasized other aspects than did patricians, and rich citizens may have suffered less during wartime crises than did poorer inhabitants.[113] Older people did not experience hard times as did younger people, who were more likely to be hopeful and to lack knowledge about previous conflicts. And men, who often had to support the occupation forces and guard the fortifications, experienced wars differently from women who had to cater to foreign soldiers in their houses. The experiences of war in Augsburg must therefore be understood as diverse. For those who lived through these events, they undoubtedly were formative experiences shaping their careers, ambitions, and identities.[114]

---

112 Gößner, "Zwischen Religionsfrieden", p. 219.
113 See Chapter 12 in this volume.
114 See Medick and Marschke, *Experiencing the Thirty Years' War*, p. viii.

Bibliography

Unpublished Primary Sources

Staats- und Stadtbibliothek Augsburg (SuStBA)

4° Cod. Adl. 22: Samuel Heiland, *Augspurgisches Erlösung Jahr vom Päpstlichen gewissens Zwang* [1632].

Ordnungen, Decreten, Verrüffe und Anschläge, 1522–1677.

2° Cod. S 66.

2° Cod. S 68: *Diarium. Die Schwedische Occupation der Statt Augsp: beschr: 1632*–[1634].

4° Cod. Aug. 238: Bartholomäus Beyer, *Diarium Rerum Augustanarum à m. Mayo, 1648. ad m. 7br. 1651.*

Wilhelm Peter Zimmermann [?], *Der Komet von 1618 über Augsburg* [1618?].

Stadtarchiv Augsburg (StadtAA), Einnehmerbücher 1631–1640.

Universitätsbibliothek Frankfurt am Main, Collection G. Freytag, no. 5496, 3: Anon., *Evangelischer Auffwecker*.

Published Primary Sources

Die Chroniken der schwäbischen Städte: Augsburg

Vol. 7, ed. F. Roth (*Die Chroniken der deutschen Städte vom 14. bis ins 16. Jahrhundert*, 32 [DCS 32]), Leipzig, 1917 (repr. Stuttgart, 1966).

Vol. 8, ed. F. Roth (DCS 33), Stuttgart, 1928 (repr. Stuttgart, 1966).

Creide, H., *Danckh- Buß und // Bet-Altar // Das ist // Zehen underschiedliche Predigten* [...]. Frankfurt am Main, [1650].

Croph, P.J., *Das mit Krieges-Last gedrückte Und durch Wunder-Hülff erquickte Augspurg/ Oder Wahrhaffte und unpartheyische Erzehlung/ Was sich Vor/ in und nach der Belagerung und Bombardirung/ ... in diser deß H.R. Reichs Freyen Stadt Augspurg zugetragen*, Augsburg, 1710.

Emmendörffer, C., "Wunde Welt: Hainhofers Diarium der Schwedischen Besatzung Augsburgs", in idem and C. Trepesch (eds.), *Wunder Welt. Der Pommersche Kunstschrank* (exhibition catalogue), Augsburg, 2014, pp. 467–539.

Hecker, P., "Die Correspondenz der Stadt Augsburg mit Karl V. im Ausgang des schmalkaldischen Krieges", *Zeitschrift des Historischen Vereins für Schwaben und Neuburg* 1 (1874), pp. 257–309.

Herberger, T., *Sebastian Schertlin von Burtenbach und seine an die Stadt Augsburg geschriebenen Briefe*, Augsburg, 1852.

Herz, J., "Das Tagebuch des Augsburger Arztes und Stadtphysicus Dr. Philipp Hoechstetter 1579–1635", *Zeitschrift des Historischen Vereins für Schwaben* 70 (1976), pp. 180–224.

Lenz, M., *Der Rechenschaftsbericht Philipps des Grossmüthigen über den Donaufeldzug 1546 und seine Quellen*, Marburg, 1885.

Lenz, M. (ed.), *Briefwechsel Landgraf Philipp's des Großmüthigen von Hessen mit Bucer*, vol. 3, Berlin, 1891.

Liliencron, R. von, *Die historischen Volkslieder der Deutschen vom 13. bis 16. Jahrhundert*, vol. 4, Leipzig, 1869.

Mameranus, N., *D. Caroli V. Roma. Imp. Avg. Iter ex inferiore Germania ab Anno 1545*, Augsburg, 1548.

Meyer, C. (ed.), *Die Hauschronik der Familie Holl (1487–1646), insbesondere die Lebensaufzeichnungen des Elias Holl, Baumeisters der Stadt Augsburg*, Munich, 1910.

Roos, W. (ed.), *Die Chronik des Jakob Wagner über die Zeit der schwedischen Okkupation in Augsburg vom 20. April 1632 bis 28. März 1635*, Augsburg, 1902.

Stetten, P. von (the Elder), *Geschichte der Heil. Roem. Reichs Freyen Stadt Augspurg, Aus Bewährten Jahr=Büchern und Tuechtigen Urkunden gezogen*, 2 vols., Frankfurt am Main, 1743–58.

Stetten, P. von (the Younger), "Philipp Hainhofer", in idem (ed.), *Lebensbeschreibungen zur Erweckung und Unterhaltung bürgerlicher Tugend*, Augsburg, 1778, pp. 267–88, repr. in C. Emmendörffer and C. Trepesch (eds.), *Wunder Welt. Der Pommersche Kunstschrank* (exhibition catalogue), Augsburg, 2014, pp. 11–19.

Werlich, E., *Chronica Der Weitberuempten Keyserlichen Freyen vnd deß H. Reichs Statt Augspurg* [...], vol. 3, Frankfurt am Main, 1595.

Zillhardt, G., *Der Dreißigjährige Krieg in zeitgenössischer Darstellung. Hans Heberles "Zeytregister" (1618–1672). Aufzeichnungen aus dem Ulmer Territorium. Ein Beitrag zu Geschichtsschreibung und Geschichtsverständnis der Unterschichten*, Stuttgart, 1975.

Secondary Literature

Amberg, J. van, *A Real Presence: Religious and Social Dynamics of the Eucharistic Conflicts in Early Modern Augsburg 1520–1530*, Leiden, 2012.

Ansbacher, W., "Kardinal Otto Truchseß von Waldburg (1514–1573) und die Glaubensspaltung: Ein Leben für Kaiser und Kirche", in T. Groll (ed.), *Kardinal Otto Truchseß von Waldburg (1514–1573)*, Neustadt an der Aisch, 2015, pp. 1–47.

Bamji, A., Janssen, G.H. and Laven, M. (eds.), *The Ashgate Research Companion to the Counter-Reformation*, Farnham, 2013.

Bátori, I., *Die Reichsstadt Augsburg im 18. Jahrhundert. Verfassung, Finanzen, Reformversuche*, Göttingen, 1969.

Bitterauf, T., "Zur Geschichte der öffentlichen Meinung im Königreich Bayern im Jahre 1813 bis zum Abschluss des Vertrags von Ried", *Archiv für Kulturgeschichte* 11 (1914), pp. 31–69.

Canning, K., "Feminist History after the Linguistic Turn: Historicizing Discourse and Experience", in idem (ed.), *Gender History in Practice: Historical Perspectives on Bodies, Class, and Citizenship*, Ithaca, 2006, pp. 62–100.

Close, C., *The Negotiated Reformation: Imperial Cities and the Politics of Urban Reform, 1525–1550*, Cambridge, 2009.

Creasman, A.F., *Censorship and Civic Order in Reformation Germany, 1517–1648: "Printed Poison and Evil Talk"*, Farnham, 2012.

Dotterweich, V., "Die Mediatisierung der Reichsstadt", in G. Gottlieb, W. Baer, J. Becker, J. Bellot, K. Filser, P. Fried, W. Reinhard and B. Schimmelpfennig (eds.), *Geschichte der Stadt Augsburg von der Römerzeit bis zur Gegenwart*, Stuttgart, 1984, pp. 541–47.

Fassl, P., *Konfession, Wirtschaft und Politik. Von der Reichsstadt zur Industriestadt, Augsburg 1750–1850*, Sigmaringen, 1988.

Faulmüller, A., *Die Reichsstadt Augsburg im Spanischen Erbfolgekrieg*, Augsburg, 1933.

Forrest, A., Hagemann, K. and Rendall, J., "Introduction: Nations in Arms – People at War", in idem (eds.), *Soldiers, Citizens and Civilians: Experiences and Perceptions of the Revolutionary and Napoleonic Wars, 1790–1820*, Basingstoke, 2009, pp. 1–19.

François, E., *Die unsichtbare Grenze. Protestanten und Katholiken in Augsburg 1648–1806*, Sigmaringen, 1991.

Gantet, C., "Die ambivalente Wahrnehmung des Friedens: Erwartung, Furcht und Spannungen in Augsburg um 1648", in B. von Krusenstjern and H. Medick (eds.), *Zwischen Alltag und Katastrophe. Der Dreißigjährige Krieg aus der Nähe*, Göttingen, 1999, pp. 357–73.

Gößner, A., "Zwischen Religionsfrieden und Dreißigjährigem Krieg: Die Prädikanten im Spannungsfeld der theologischen Orientierungen", in R. Kießling (ed.), *St. Anna in Augsburg – eine Kirche und ihre Gemeinde*, Augsburg, 2013, pp. 219–38.

Häberlein, M., *Brüder, Freunde und Betrüger. Soziale Beziehungen, Normen und Konflikte in der Augsburger Kaufmannschaft um die Mitte des 16. Jahrhunderts*, Berlin, 1998.

Häberlein, M., "Vom Augsburger Religionsfrieden bis zum Ende der Reichsfreiheit", in G. Grünsteudel, G. Hägele and R. Frankenberger (eds.), *Augsburger Stadtlexikon*, 2nd ed., Augsburg, 1998, pp. 75–96.

Hecker, P., "Der Augsburger Bürgermeister Jacob Herbrot und der Sturz des zünftischen Regiments in Augsburg", *Zeitschrift des Historischen Vereins für Schwaben und Neuburg* 1 (1874), pp. 34–98.

Heyde, A., "Kunstpolitik und Propaganda im Dienste des Großmachtstrebens: Die Auswirkungen der gustav-adolfinischen 'repraesentatio maiestatis' auf Schweden und Deutschland bis zum Ende des Nordischen Krieges (1660)", in K. Bußmann and H. Schilling (eds.), *1648. Krieg und Frieden in Europa*, Munich, 1998, vol. 2, pp. 105–11.

Kaufmann, T., "Predigt im Krieg und zum Friedensschluss", in K. Bußmann and H. Schilling (eds.), *1648. Krieg und Frieden in Europa*, Munich, 1998, vol. 2, pp. 245–50.

Kießling, R., "Zum Augsburg-Bild in der Chronistik des 15. Jahrhunderts", in J. Janota and W. Williams-Krapp (eds.), *Literarisches Leben in Augsburg während des 15. Jahrhunderts*, Tübingen, 1995, pp. 183–215.

Kießling, R., "Augsburg in der Reformationszeit", in J. Kirmeier, W. Jahn and E. Brockhoff (eds.), "... wider Laster und Sünde". Augsburgs Weg in der Reformation (exhibition catalogue), Augsburg, 1997, pp. 17–43.

Kießling, R., *Kleine Geschichte Schwabens*, Regensburg, 2009.

Kießling, R., "Eckpunkte der Augsburger Reformationsgeschichte", in idem, T.M. Safley, and L.P. Wandel (eds.), *Im Ringen um die Reformation. Kirchen und Prädikanten, Rat und Gemeinden in Augsburg*, Epfendorf, 2011, pp. 29–42.

Kießling, R., "Evangelisch St. Ulrich: Die Entstehung und Etablierung der protestantischen Kirchengemeinde", in M. Weitlauff (ed.), *Benediktinerabtei St. Ulrich und Afra in Augsburg (1012–2012). Geschichte, Kunst, Wirtschaft und Kultur einer ehemaligen Reichsabtei. Festschrift zum tausendjährigen Jubiläum*, Augsburg, 2011, vol. 1, pp. 200–31.

Kießling, R., "St. Anna im Dreißigjährigen Krieg: Die Geburt eines Traumas", in idem (ed.), *St. Anna in Augsburg – eine Kirche und ihre Gemeinde*, Augsburg, 2013, pp. 239–69.

Kießling, R., "Kardinal Otto Truchseß von Waldburg und das Augsburger Interim von 1548", in T. Groll (ed.), *Kardinal Otto Truchseß von Waldburg (1514–1573)*, Augsburg, 2015, pp. 49–74.

Kirch, H.J., *Die Fugger und der Schmalkaldische Krieg*, Munich, 1915.

Köberlin, K., "M. Phil. Jac. Crophius, Rektor des St. Annagymnasiums in Augsburg 1704–1742", *Blätter für das Gymnasial-Schulwesen* 41 (1905), pp. 1–16.

Köhler, R., "Wolfgang Jakob Sulzer der Jüngere (1685–1751): Erlebnis- und Erfahrungsräume eines evangelischen Patriziers in Augsburg", in R. Kießling (ed.), *Neue Forschungen zur Geschichte der Stadt Augsburg*, Augsburg, 2011, pp. 121–63.

Krämer, G., "Das Kunstzentrum Augsburg während des Dreißigjährigen Krieges: Malerei und Zeichnung", in K. Bußmann and H. Schilling (eds.), *1648. Krieg und Frieden in Europa*, Munich, 1998, vol. 2, pp. 227–34.

Kraus, J., *Das Militärwesen der Reichsstadt Augsburg 1548–1806. Vergleichende Untersuchungen über städtische Militäreinrichtungen in Deutschland vom 16.–18. Jahrhundert*, Augsburg, 1980.

Langer, H., "Heeresfinanzierung, Produktion und Märkte für die Kriegführung", in K. Bußmann and H. Schilling (eds.), *1648. Krieg und Frieden in Europa*, Munich, 1998, vol. 2, p. 293–99.

Maissen, T., "Die Eidgenossen und das Augsburger Interim: Zu einem unbekannten Gutachten Heinrich Bullingers", in L. Schorn-Schütte (ed.), *Das Interim 1548/50. Herrschaftskrise und Glaubenskonflikt*, Heidelberg, 2005, pp. 76–104.

Medick, H. and Marschke, B., *Experiencing the Thirty Years War: A Brief History with Documents*, Boston, 2013.

Mohrmann, R.-E., "Alltag in Krieg und Frieden", in K. Bußmann and H. Schilling (eds.), *1648. Krieg und Frieden in Europa*, Munich, 1998, vol. 2, pp. 319–27.

Nehlsen, E., "Liedpublizistik des Dreißigjährigen Krieges", in K. Bußmann and H. Schilling (eds.), *1648. Krieg und Frieden in Europa*, Munich, 1998, vol. 2, pp. 431–37.

Pahnke, G., "Patriotismus ohne Nation: Die patriotische Ideenwelt des Augsburger Patriziers Paul von Stetten d. J. (1731–1808)", in R. Kießling (ed.), *Neue Forschungen zur Geschichte der Stadt Augsburg*, Augsburg, 2011, pp. 165–230.

Parker, G., *Global Crisis: War, Climate Change and Catastrophe in the Seventeenth Century*, New Haven, 2013.

Paulus, C., "Sebastian Schertlin von Burtenbach im Schmalkaldischen Krieg", *Zeitschrift für bayerische Landesgeschichte* 67, 1 (2004), pp. 47–84.

Planert, U., *Der Mythos vom Befreiungskrieg. Frankreichs Kriege und der deutsche Süden: Alltag – Wahrnehmung – Deutung 1792–1841*, Paderborn, 2007.

Pronk, T., "A City of God. Augsburg during the Thirty Years' War", in V. Wieser, C. Zolles, C. Feik, M. Zolles and L. Schlöndorff (eds.), *Abendländische Apokalyptik. Kompendium zur Genealogie der Endzeit*, Berlin, 2013, pp. 451–74.

Roeck, B., *Bäcker, Brot und Getreide in Augsburg. Zur Geschichte des Bäckerhandwerks und zur Versorgungspolitik der Reichsstadt im Zeitalter des Dreißigjährigen Krieges*, Sigmaringen, 1987.

Roeck, B., *Eine Stadt in Krieg und Frieden. Studien zur Geschichte der Reichsstadt Augsburg zwischen Kalenderstreit und Parität*, 2 vols., Göttingen, 1989.

Roeck, B., *Als wollt die Welt schier brechen. Eine Stadt im Zeitalter des Dreißigjährigen Krieges*, Munich, 1991.

Roeck, B., "Venedigs Rolle im Krieg und bei den Friedensverhandlungen", in K. Bußmann and H. Schilling (eds.), *1648. Krieg und Frieden in Europa*, Munich, 1998, vol. 2, pp. 161–68.

Roeck, B., *Geschichte Augsburgs*, Munich, 2005.

Roeck, B., "Totentanz am Lech", in D. Pieper and J. Saltzwedel (eds.), *Der Dreißigjährige Krieg. Europa im Kampf um Glaube und Macht 1618–1648*, Munich, 2012, pp. 222–34.

Roth, F., *Augsburgs Reformationsgeschichte*, 4 vols., Munich, 1901–11.

Rutz, A., "Der Westen des Reiches als Kriegsschauplatz und Erfahrungsraum im langen 17. Jahrhundert", in idem (ed.), *Krieg und Kriegserfahrung im Westen des Reiches 1568–1714*, Göttingen, 2016, pp. 11–30.

Schindling, A., "'Ikonen' der Kriegserfahrung: Eine Bilderauswahl zur Einführung", in idem and G. Schild (ed.), *Kriegserfahrungen, Krieg und Gesellschaft in der Neuzeit. Neue Horizonte der Forschung*, Paderborn, 2009, pp. 17–39.

Schmidt, G., "'Teutsche Libertät' oder 'Hispanische Servitut': Deutungsstrategien im Kampf um den evangelischen Glauben und die Reichsverfassung (1546–1552)", in L. Schorn-Schütte (ed.), *Das Interim 1548/50. Herrschaftskrise und Glaubenskonflikt*, Heidelberg, 2005, pp. 166–91.

Scott, J.W., "The Evidence of Experience", *Critical Inquiry* 17 (1991), pp. 773–97.

Sewell, W.H., *Gender, History, and Deconstruction: Joan W. Scott's Gender and the Politics of History* (CSST Working Paper, 34), Ann Arbor, 1989.

Sieh-Burens, K., *Oligarchie, Konfession und Politik im 16. Jahrhundert. Zur sozialen Verflechtung der Augsburger Bürgermeister und Stadtpfleger 1518–1618*, Munich, 1986.

Simmet, L., *Die Reichsstadt Augsburg in der ersten Hälfte des dreissigjährigen Krieges*, Augsburg, 1901.

Spindler, J., *Heinrich V. von Knöringen, Fürstbischof von Augsburg (1598–1646). Seine innerkirchliche Restaurationstätigkeit in der Diözese Augsburg*, Dillingen, 1911.

Tlusty, B.A., "The Public House and Military Culture in Germany, 1500–1648", in B. Kümin and idem (eds.), *The World of the Tavern: The Public House in Early Modern Europe*, Ashgate, 2002, pp. 136–56.

Tschopp, S.S., *Heilsgeschichtliche Deutungsmuster in der Publizistik des Dreißigjährigen Krieges. Pro- und antischwedische Propaganda in Deutschland 1628 bis 1635*, Frankfurt am Main, 1991.

Wagner Oettinger, R., *Music as Propaganda in the German Reformation*, Aldershot, 2001.

Warmbrunn, P., *Zwei Konfessionen in einer Stadt. Das Zusammenleben von Katholiken und Protestanten in den paritätischen Reichsstädten Augsburg, Biberach, Ravensburg und Dinkelsbühl von 1548 bis 1648*, Wiesbaden, 1983.

Weißbrich, T., *Höchstädt 1704. Eine Schlacht als Medienereignis. Kriegsberichterstattung und Gelegenheitsdichtung im Spanischen Erbfolgekrieg*, Paderborn, 2015.

Whaley, J., *Das Heilige Römische Reich deutscher Nation und seine Territorien*, 2 vols., Darmstadt, 2014.

Zelinsky Hanson, M., *Religious Identity in an Early Reformation Community: Augsburg, 1517 to 1555*, Leiden and Boston, 2009.

Zoepfl, F., *Das Bistum Augsburg und seine Bischöfe im Reformationsjahrhundert* (Geschichte des Bistums Augsburg und seiner Bischöfe, 2), Munich, 1969.

Zorn, W., *Augsburg. Geschichte einer deutschen Stadt*, 2nd ed., Augsburg, 1972.

CHAPTER 16

Jews as Ethnic and Religious Minorities

Sabine Ullmann

Jews were one of the longstanding ethnic and religious minorities in a premodern estate-based society that was otherwise dominated by the Christian religion. Unlike the Romany, who are identifiable as an itinerant group within western Christianity only from the fifteenth century, the Jews were present in society from the early Middle Ages. From the very beginning, Jews preferred to settle in cities, where they were able to shape their own religious communities and were provided with special rights. Their distinct cultural and social identity was based upon a self-definition that understood the people of Israel not only as a religious community, but also as an ethnic community based on lineage. Whereas the Romany, as traveling people, integrated themselves through their own legends and narratives into Christian salvation history, Judaism competed with the majority religion's claim to truth. From the perspective of the Gentile environment, therefore, a crucial criterion of Jews' otherness was their faith and their ritual way of life. The perception of "otherness" that arose from religious difference and the competition between Christianity and Judaism led to a situation in which the conditions of Jewish existence within Christian society were subject to manifold restrictions and recurring outbursts of violence.

The history of the Jews in Augsburg is in many respects representative of these developments. If in the following account Jews are emphasized over other minorities, this is due to the comparatively good state of research and source material as well as an understanding of the distinctiveness of Jewish history. Although the discrimination and mechanisms of exclusion to which Jews were submitted were also experienced by other minorities,[1] there are unique features in the relationship between Christians and Jews that cannot entirely be grasped within a comparative history of marginalized groups.

1   The Fifteenth Century: Processes of Marginalization and the Expulsion of 1438–40

Like most imperial cities in southern Germany, Augsburg in the late Middle Ages housed a Jewish community that was an intrinsic part of urban life. After

---

1   Graus, "Randgruppen"; Roeck, *Außenseiter*, passim.

the Black Death persecutions of November 1348, new residence privileges under the protection of Emperor Charles IV were granted to Jews as early as 1355. The near-complete tax lists that have survived for Augsburg document a continual growth of the Jewish community up to a total of 65 taxpayers in 1385. Due to this rapid increase after resettlement, Augsburg in 1400 housed one of the largest Jewish communities in the Holy Roman Empire. The families lived in Jews Lane (*Judengasse*, near what is today *Karlsstraße*) and had established their most important municipal-religious facilities, i.e. a synagogue, a cemetery, a dance hall, and a mikvah (ritual bath).[2] The community's religious services thereby attracted Jews living in the surrounding region. The importance of Augsburg's Jewish community is apparent, for example, in the fact that Rabbi Jakob b. Juda Weil, one of the most famous rabbinic authorities in the Holy Roman Empire, lived there until the expulsion of 1438–40, serving on the secular parish council and running a Talmud school in his house. The cemetery, which was located at the northwestern edge of Our Lady's Suburb (*Frauenvorstadt*), was also of regional significance and was used by Jewish families from the surrounding area.[3]

The late medieval Jewish community's main branch of trade was collateral-based moneylending, for which the economic boom that the city underwent during this phase provided fertile soil. Jewish creditors played a crucial role as financiers for Augsburg's city council and the bourgeoisie as well as for regional potentates, albeit on a smaller scale than before the Black Death persecutions of 1348. However, some Jews were still able to extend credit in the range of 600–900 gulden.[4]

As in other cities of the Holy Roman Empire, the Jews' legal status was determined by the imperial laws of serfdom (*Kammerknechtschaft*) and by Jewish civil statutes. The emperor also claimed protective authority over Jews in the Empire, which he deployed as an instrument of power and, particularly, of taxation. From a legal standpoint, the Jews thus became a special group within the city whose conditions of life were subject to the standards of imperial law. The imperial grant of protection offered prospects for greater legal security; at the same time, their status as imperial serfs carried an extra financial burden. On the part of the city, Jews were granted citizenship and were registered together with Christians in the "burgher-book" (*Bürgerbuch*), Augsburg's list of new citizens.[5] Augsburg's city council thus claimed regulatory power over

---

2   Seitz, "Topographie der älteren Judengemeinde", pp. 19–35.
3   Maimon, *Germania Judaica*, pp. 45–48.
4   Schimmelpfennig, "Christen und Juden", p. 34.
5   Mütschele, *Juden in Augsburg*, pp. 180–96; Haverkamp, "Concivilitas", pp. 126, 132.

the Jews, which manifested itself in a series of edicts that determined their living conditions. The implementation of Jewish citizenship varied from town to town, but the underlying tendencies were the same everywhere. At base was a guaranteed legal status that provided for temporary protection and included obligations for tax contributions and military service. In addition, a variety of limitations signified the Jews' inferior status, including interdictions against holding office or participating in the municipal assembly. Of course, Jewish citizens were also forbidden to join the merchants' and crafts' guilds.[6]

These were – roughly speaking – the general conditions of Jewish existence in Augsburg around 1400: a religious community that was highly respected within the Jewish world; whose members could still engage in quite profitable financial transactions; and who had gained a certain degree of legal protection within the context of the civic constitution, via Jewish citizenship on the one hand and imperial protection on the other. But developments in the first third of the fifteenth century show how precarious this situation ultimately was. To begin with, the city intensified its enforcement of protection laws, extending its claim to authority and power over the Jews. In 1401, 1415, and 1431, the council had its residential rights for Jews (*Judenschutzrechte*) confirmed by the Empire, each time for a period of 12 years. As of 1419, admittance to citizenship also became obligatory for those Jews who had thus far been bound only by a chartered entrance agreement. At the same time, restrictive edicts multiplied. At first these focused on Jewish commercial activity: in 1404, Jews were prohibited from extending credit to grocers who sought to pawn their merchandise; in 1435, they were forbidden to trade in cattle. In 1433, the council increased customs charges for funerals of non-local Jews at the local cemetery from 20 pfennigs to one gulden.[7] Further regulations were aimed at separating Christian and Jewish living spaces. In line with these council policies, Jews became an increasingly segregated and marginalized religious group that was also perceived as such by the populace.

Significantly, at the same time as civic authority was newly implemented in the form of the *Ratsregiment* ("ruling council", a board of Christian overseers), Augsburg's religious self-definition as a commune that perceived itself as "holy" intensified as well.[8] The local Jewish community became a victim of both this new sacred self-definition and the expansion of municipal authority. The growing concentration of religious life within the urban environment through foundations, fraternities, and the rise of lay spirituality along with

---

6 Toch, *Juden*, pp. 51–53.
7 Maimon, *Germania Judaica*, pp. 42–44.
8 See generally Rogge, *Für den gemeinen Nutzen*; Kießling, *Bürgerliche Gesellschaft*.

the council's authoritarian interests brought the Jews' religious difference and their special legal status more clearly into view. Their intensified perception as a "foreign body" now led to efforts to increase their visibility by means of stigmatizing symbols. In 1432, Augsburg was one of the first cities in the Holy Roman Empire to apply for King Sigismund's permission to require Jews to wear a yellow ring on their clothing within the city's public spaces.

This request was justified by asserting that one could not tell the difference between Jews and Christians, since the former also dressed in costly and priest-like garments. Thus, a difference that apparently had not always been obvious in daily life was now considered significant enough to be made evident.[9] In this the city council followed a general tendency to emphasize the lesser status of marginal groups by means of stigmatizing symbols. Not only Jews, but also beggars or prostitutes were affected, for example.[10]

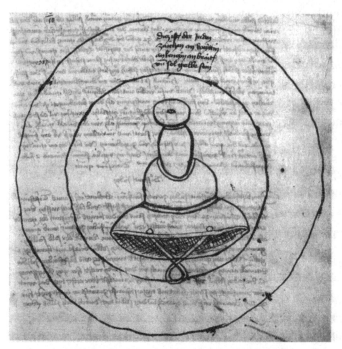

FIGURE 16.1 Drawing from the letterbook (*Missivbuch*) of the Augsburg city council depicting the proposed designation of Jews, 1434
STADTARCHIV AUGSBURG, MISSIVBUCH III (1429–1435), NO. 1387, F. 334R

9   Mütschele, *Juden in Augsburg*, pp. 158–63.
10 Jütte, "Stigma-Symbole", pp. 65–89.

As a further step, in 1436 the council abolished the *Judengericht*, the special court that had settled disputes between Christians and Jews, which consisted of 12 Christians and 12 Jews and met in the synagogue. It was replaced by a board consisting solely of Christians and based in the city hall. This measure not only eliminated the religious parity of the court; the change of venue to a spatial domain controlled by Christian authority also consolidated the council's claim to power over the Jews.

Parallel to these internal restrictions, the monarchy pursued an exploitative fiscal policy. The use of imperial serfdom for tax benefits climaxed under Sigismund, who sought to recoup the high expenses caused in part by the Hussite Wars and the Council of Constance. Apart from collection of regular taxes on the Jews (*Judensteuer*) and the additional *Goldener Opferpfennig* (a head tax on propertied Jews), he repeatedly made special demands between 1414 and 1433, in the last instance 1,500 gulden on the occasion of his coronation as emperor. The Jews of Augsburg vetoed these demands with the support of the council, which had an interest in fiscal levies of its own on the Jewish community – but their attempts met with no success.[11] Sigismund continued to pursue a policy that undermined the imperial protective relationship and increasingly demoted the Empire's Jews to the status of fiscal objects. This course of action was legitimized both by denouncing Jewish creditors for their ethically reprehensible accumulation of capital and based on the assumption that the protector had a legitimate claim to Jewish assets.[12]

Although the Jewish community of Augsburg had experienced rapid demographic and economic recovery after its resettlement in 1355, this fiscal policy now resulted in the decline of its financial power. Tax payments to the city radically diminished and remained below 100 gulden total from 1400 onwards. Another reason for this drop in revenues was a decrease in Jewish taxpayers to approximately 30 families around 1430. Subsequently, their function as creditors also declined, undermining an essential motive for the city to offer its guarantee of protection and admit Jews as citizens. Meanwhile, urban economic life boomed between 1420 and 1440 and the population increased. Augsburg appears to have attained a degree of economic independence that made Jewish credit expendable. In July 1438, the council consequently decided to expel the Jews, giving them two years to leave the city. The buildings and facilities that were left behind became city property. In 1449, the Jewish cemetery was defiled; the gravestones were used to build an extension to the city hall, and the site was incorporated into the fortifications. Carrying

---

11   Steinthal, *Geschichte der Augsburger Juden*, pp. 40–67.
12   Battenberg, *Das europäische Zeitalter*, vol. 1, pp. 147–50.

out the expulsion enactment, however, proved to be difficult under imperial law: the imperial *Erbmarschall* ("hereditary marshal") von Pappenheim, to whom Jewish taxes were pledged, initially intervened against the planned expulsion with the support of King Albrecht II. Royal permission was therefore delayed, so that Emperor Frederick III was able to demand 13,000 gulden from Augsburg's council in 1456 in exchange for a retroactive privilege to expel the Jews.[13]

The arguments for expulsion mentioned in the city chronicles point to further motives: Besides charges of violating council decrees, there were sermons against the Jews in the churches. A crucial element was the preaching activity of mendicant orders in the cities, which had a clear anti-Jewish thrust. Debates about imperial and ecclesiastical reform culminated in the restrictive decree *De Judaeis et Neophitis* ("On Jews and Converts") at the Council of Basel in 1434, which, among other things, forced Jews to attend Christian sermons aimed at converting them to Christianity. Moreover, the period from 1432 to 1438, during which the exclusionary measures in Augsburg were mounting, saw a wave of inflation and severe famine that in turn led to outbreaks of epidemic diseases. This allowed a causal connection to be drawn so that Jews could be scapegoated in response to a sense of threat. Additionally, political motives existed on the part of the city council, which resisted claims of imperial authority in order to retain its communal autonomy. Having Jews in their midst who were under imperial protection repeatedly provoked external interventions, be they taxation demands or the granting of privileges, and thus undermined the council leaders' claim to exclusive authority. Hence, the reasons for the expulsion of Augsburg's Jews must be sought in a range of different economic, religious, social, and political motives.[14]

The council's decision to expel the Jews was certainly no isolated case; rather, it was part of a series of expulsions of Jewish communities from imperial cities in southern Germany between 1430 and 1520. The process began with Lindau in 1430, followed by Constance in 1448, Ulm and Nuremberg in 1499, Nördlingen in 1506–07, and Donauwörth and Regensburg in 1518, among others. Additionally, Jews were evicted from the larger territories, including the Bavarian duchies in 1442–50, Württemberg in 1498, and the margravates of Brandenburg-Ansbach and Kulmbach.[15] Significantly, following a decision by the imperial diet in 1498, the Romany were also expelled from several cities

---

13 Wenninger, *Man bedarf keiner Juden mehr*, pp. 116–19, 123–34, 251–62.
14 Jörg, "Basler Konzil", pp. 63–92.
15 Burgard et al., *Judenvertreibungen*, passim.

around 1500. Thus these exclusionary procedures targeted not only Jews but extended to ethnic-religious minorities more broadly.[16]

2 Jews at the Gates of Augsburg in the Sixteenth Century

Although protection and residency within the city walls remained prohibited to Jews, they were present in urban life once again by the second half of the sixteenth century after finding protection in a number of villages just outside the gates. The migrations resulting from the expulsion of 1438–40 can only be fragmentarily reconstructed, which for a long time resulted in the erroneous assumption among scholars that Jews had moved directly from the city to the surrounding villages.[17] But the sources point to more complex migration processes. Some of the Jews expelled from Augsburg initially migrated to those southern German cities that still offered them residential protection – for instance to Bamberg, Günzburg, Nördlingen, Rothenburg ob der Tauber, or Ulm.[18] When these cities also ceased to tolerate Jews, they emigrated to northern Italy, Bohemia, Poland, Lithuania, or the Balkans, along with many more of their coreligionists. Not until the second half of the sixteenth century do we find the earliest evidence of Jewish settlements in the city's environs: for Oberhausen, for example, in 1553; for Kriegshaber around 1560; for Steppach in 1570; for Pfersee in 1583; and for Schlipsheim not until 1700–01. Although the sporadic presence of individual Jews in Augsburg can be documented prior to 1550, it took more than a century after the expulsion for permanent Jewish communities to appear in the region around Augsburg. Urban Jews (*Stadtjuden*) thus did not become rural Jews (*Landjuden*) within a single generation; instead the process in Swabia, as elsewhere, was characterized by a series of fluid transitions.[19]

As a result, new ways of life developed in niches of existence in the countryside, which resulted in an adaptation to rural economies as well as a dispersed habitat that impeded compliance with religious traditions. The rural Jewry of the early modern period evolved from the urban Jewry of the Middle Ages in discrete regional population centers, primarily situated on the Rhine and in Alsace, Franconia, and Swabia. Around Augsburg a pattern of settlement emerged that is similar to what can be observed in Fürth near Nuremberg, in Heidingsfeld near Würzburg, or in Weißenau near Mainz.

---

16   Schubert, "Existenz der Zigeuner", p. 185.
17   Straus, *Regensburg and Augsburg*, p. 193.
18   Maimon, *Germania Judaica*, p. 49.
19   Kießling, "Einführung", pp. 15–16; Rohrbacher, "Ungleiche Partnerschaft", pp. 192–94.

The Jewish settlements in the immediate rural environs of the urban centers were no longer under municipal rule, but under the protection of foreign princes. Oberhausen, for instance, belonged to the domain of Augsburg's bishop, who housed Jews only for a short time up until 1574.

Settlements in Kriegshaber, Pfersee, and Steppach were more successful, developing into large and stable communities. Decisive for this was an active policy of protection for Jews on the part of the margravate of Burgau, which belonged to the house of Habsburg's Swabian domain and bordered directly on Augsburg's territory. The Habsburgs used their territorial sovereignty for fiscal exploitation of their prerogative over Jews, generally in the face of resistance from local lords from the ranks of the urban bourgeoisie, such as Bartholomäus Sailer and Martin Zobel in Pfersee or the Baumgartners in Steppach. All three villages were conveniently situated just outside the gates of Augsburg, but were free from direct governmental influence by the city.[20] At the same time, these villages were part of a network of Jewish settlements extending across large parts of the Habsburg territories south of the Danube between the Lech and the Iller Rivers claimed by the margravate of Burgau. From the Jewish perspective, this area constituted "Medinat Swabia", a loose association of Jewish communities connected by the vibrancy of the rabbinates and their own *minhag Swabia*, a regionally distinct religious tradition.[21]

In this situation, the imperial city of Augsburg – rimmed on the west side by a group of Jewish settlements – pursued a vehement anti-Jewish policy during the sixteenth century that aimed at excluding the Jews from urban markets and allowing them only short visits to the city under difficult conditions. Numerous council decrees have survived from the first half of the sixteenth century onwards that were aimed at controlling entrance to the city and the business activities of Jewish traders. In 1538, 1541, and 1553, prohibitions were enacted against townspeople engaging in "usurious dealings" with Jews. Starting in 1536, Jews were allowed to enter the city only in the company of a civic guard. In 1599, this policy acquired a new legal and conceptual dimension through a comprehensive privilege issued by Emperor Rudolf II that secured these measures under imperial law as well. Financial transactions with Jews were forbidden without the previous knowledge and permission of civic authorities; ongoing contracts had to be reported to the council; and pawning to Jews was entirely prohibited. Parallel to the sanctions on Christian – Jewish dealings, the council intensified its control over Jews' access to the city and saw

---

20   Ullmann, *Nachbarschaft und Konkurrenz*, pp. 66–73.
21   Rohrbacher, "Medinat Schwaben", pp. 80–109.

to it that the escort requirement was more strictly enforced.[22] Surviving local court cases document that these regulations were indeed enforced and violations were prosecuted: numerous Jews were arrested and brought before the courts during the late sixteenth and early seventeenth centuries because they were caught in the city without the escort of the city watch, and Christians were jailed for forbidden loan transactions with Jews.[23]

These measures were justified with the accusation that the Jews were fleecing and cheating their Christian customers, reducing them to a state of financial dependency. The stereotype of "Jewish usury" (*Judenwucher*) complemented religious rebukes and underscored the minority's otherness by implying a moral and ethical inferiority vis-à-vis the Christian majority. Like restrictions on carrying weapons in Christian jurisdictions and the mandatory requirement for an identifying symbol, the escort requirement also had a stigmatizing effect, for it showed quite plainly that a Jewish trader needed special supervision when transacting business. All these measures underscored the Jews' questionable legal and social status in the city.[24]

The years around 1600 also marked the peak of an economic crisis in Augsburg. A rise in the price of corn along with a decline in real wages caused a progressive deterioration in the financial situation of lower and middle income groups. The council therefore initiated some measures to better provide for the inhabitants. Apart from controlling the grain trade and the production of bread, these also included restrictions on Jewish trade classified as damaging. This turned out to be neither a wise nor an effective move. The privilege of 1599 already included the stipulation that Jewish traders at the city market could continue to offer all goods necessary for the citizens' nourishment. Jewish traders of rural goods fulfilled important roles in supplying the city, as did Jewish pawnbrokers, who served as a lifeline for the middle and lower classes in emergency situations by providing cash even for poor household articles or worn clothing. In times of crisis, even better-off artisan households pawned their objects of value to Jews. Shortages originating from cyclical downturns in the urban economy could thus be contained.

In addition to serving as pawnbrokers and providing credit, Jews earned a living in suburban villages by offering a wide variety of goods closely targeted to urban needs. Since Jews were excluded from owning land and breeding

---

22 Ullmann, "Leihen umb fahrend Hab und Gut", pp. 304–35.
23 Roeck, *Eine Stadt in Krieg und Frieden*, vol. 1, pp. 471–75; Stadtarchiv Augsburg (StadtAA), Urgichten 1553–1614, passim.
24 Bearing arms was a symbol of citizenship and the right of resistance for Christian men: Tlusty, *The Martial Ethic*, pp. 177–78.

cattle, they developed livelihoods that concentrated on trade but encompassed a complex range of commercial activities. Jewish merchants from suburban settlements supplied Augsburg's market with agrarian products from the countryside while influencing intra-urban economic cycles and participating in the distribution of artisan products in the surrounding villages. At the center was trade in foodstuffs, scrap and precious metals, as well as clothes and textiles.[25] Regardless of the council's restrictions, the presence of Jewish traders thus remained an important element of the urban economy. As a result, although Jews no longer lived *in* the city, they definitely lived *from* the city.

Augsburg's policy of exclusion, which in the sixteenth century considerably hindered the ability of Jews from rural communities to earn a living, was an expression of hostility against the Jews in the early modern period that had much in common with the late Middle Ages but also introduced new accents. The vast majority of the ecclesiastical and political elite shared the belief that Jews were inferior, based on a specific theological perception. Because Jews rejected the prophecies of the Old Testament regarding Christ and denied Christ as the Messiah and the son of God, thus rejecting the doctrine of the Trinity – and were even responsible for crucifying him – they had to answer to grave allegations of blasphemy and deicide. According to this view, the Jews' allegedly willful adherence to false doctrines and their supposed enmity to Christians legitimized exclusionary measures and their confinement to a life at the margins of society. In the Middle Ages, anti-Jewish legends that derived from this theological assumption, such as those of the ritual murder of Christian children or the desecration of the host, were institutionalized as literary stereotypes and graphic images that remained influential during the early modern period. The Protestant Reformation and the confessionalization process exacerbated the anti-Judaism of Christian society in the sixteenth century, as both Catholics and Protestants intensified their polemics and demarcations against Judaism in an effort to fortify their respective dogmas. Both the followers of Luther and those who remained loyal to the pope used similar tactics to distance themselves more strongly from dissenting non-Christian doctrines. As part of Catholic reform policy, the papal bull *Cum nimis absurdum*, issued by Paul IV in 1555, demanded the mandatory identification of Jews and a tightened control of trade, among other things. By comparison, the Protestants drew upon the anti-Semitic teachings of Luther, who demanded a stronger dissociation from the Jews after attempts at converting them had failed, and who further

---

25   Ullmann, *Nachbarschaft und Konkurrenz*, pp. 243–54, 321–27.

intensified the existing anti-Jewish stereotypes with his tract *Von den Juden und ihren Lügen* ("On the Jews and Their Lies"), published in 1543.[26]

The Holy Roman Empire was now in fact denominationally mixed, but the idea of a confessionally homogeneous *corpus Christianum* was pursued all the more vigorously in individual territories and cities. In the bi-confessional imperial city of Augsburg too, Protestants and Catholics increasingly segregated themselves from each other during the second half of the sixteenth century and became embroiled in severe confessional conflicts, for instance over the calendar reform introduced by Pope Gregory XIII in 1583–84, which was rejected by Protestants.[27] The urban self-conception by this time was characterized by the ideal of a holy commune in which urban-secular and religious-confessional ideas and values coalesced. Consequently, the council authorities were not only entrusted with peacekeeping and representing economic and political interests, but also had to assume responsibility for the citizens' salvation. According to contemporary mentalities, this task included protecting and defending God's glory against defilement in the city. Within this worldview, the very presence of Jews represented a potential danger. Confessional differentiation and the ostracism of "the other", Jewish, religious group thus appeared as parallel processes.[28]

While Jews' living conditions worsened in the sixteenth century in individual domains – cities hindered access to their markets and numerous principalities no longer granted protection – opposing tendencies can be observed at the imperial level. At the instigation of Josel von Rosheim, who served as spokesman of the Jewish community leaders, Emperor Charles V granted the Speyer Privilege in 1544, which provided Jews with protection against expulsion and prosecution, safe conduct, and even freedom from the mandatory identification requirement. This privilege, which was prolonged time and again down to 1717, represented an important token of the persistence of imperial protection, leading to close relations between resident Jews and their respective emperors, especially in the region of Swabia.[29] At the same time, following the views of the German humanist and Hebraist Johannes Reuchlin (1455–1522), the opinion prevailed among sixteenth-century jurists that as *cives Romani*, Jews were subject to Roman law and therefore had the same rights and duties before the courts as Christians. With the increasing reception of Roman law, the Jews of

---

26 Battenberg, *Das europäische Zeitalter*, vol. 1, pp. 190–207.
27 See Chapter 11 in this volume.
28 Roeck, *Außenseiter*, pp. 13–22.
29 Kießling, "Zwischen Schutzherrschaft und Reichsbürgerschaft".

the Empire thus attained a legal status that implied equality in legal process and gave them access to the imperial courts, which they repeatedly employed.

Altogether, the position of the Jews is therefore characterized by considerable ambivalence. Early modern society was steeped in ideological thinking that rested on stereotypes labeling Jews as inferior and represented them as the antithesis of the Christian ideal. The idea of the *civis Romanus* thus competed with a sense of justice among the majority of the population based on stereotypes of religious enmity that were in turn reflected in the policies of the imperial cities. At the same time, the sources provide evidence of everyday contacts and pragmatic interaction between Jews and Christians in Augsburg. The itinerant Jewish printer Chajim Schwarz, for example, produced several Hebrew publications there between 1533 and 1544. Schwarz was housed by the preacher and theologian Bonifacius Wolfart and was able to use Silvan Otmar's workshop for his work.[30] Jews received special dispensations to serve wine and meals during imperial diets in the sixteenth century[31] and were regular visitors at local inns and coffeehouses during the eighteenth; and they occasionally ran afoul of the authorities for gambling, drinking, or having sex with Christians in and around Augsburg.[32] These tendencies in social interaction with the ethnic-religious minority – a dialectics of polemics and confrontation on the one hand, mutual cooperation and frequent contacts on the other – intensified during the following two centuries.

3 Economic Presence and Competition in the Seventeenth and Eighteenth Centuries

From the beginning of the seventeenth century, a certain degree of stabilization in the relations between Christian authorities and Jewish communities in the Empire can be observed: expulsions decreased, communities slowly grew, and new settlements appeared. As these developments mainly applied to rural areas, Jewish culture could not yet consistently establish itself as an urban element. But changes occurred even where Jews still lacked the right of abode, as was the case in most larger towns. In Augsburg, this shift is apparent during the Thirty Years' War, when the city granted refuge to Jews from the suburban

---

30 Künast, "Hebräisch-jüdischer Buchdruck", pp. 277–303.
31 Most likely catering kosher meals to visiting court Jews: StadtAA, Urgicht Haim and Hanna Juden, 9 September 1566.
32 StadtAA, Judenakten 15, no. 21; Urgicht Joseph and Jacob Juden, 10 August 1573; Urgicht Joachim Jud, 21 January 1553; Urgicht Seligman Jud, 9 May 1590. I thank Ann Tlusty for these references.

villages. Likewise, the council granted a temporary right of abode to specific groups as protection against troops passing through during the War of Spanish Succession (1701–14) and the War of Austrian Succession (1740–48). Thus in the summer of 1704, 62 Jewish families resided in Augsburg during the Battle of Blenheim. In 1699, when an insurrection was directed against the Jews due to the rise in grain prices in the bishopric of Bamberg, Jewish communities turned to the city authorities on the basis of their imperial protections, requesting that the imperial decree they had obtained as protection against plunder and violence be posted at the city gates as well.[33]

The willingness to extend protection and the temporary right of abode led to the establishment of proper "war communities" in the city in the eighteenth century, which also had a certain communal infrastructure at their disposal. In 1741, the council granted the right of abode to the Mändle family and their trading company. One year later, complaints emerged in the council because the Jews had moved to houses in a prime location and were now practicing their rites in the city as well. There are reports about the establishment of kosher cook shops, the building of sukkahs for the Succoth, and even the establishment in 1744 of a synagogue in a Jewish dwelling in present-day Philippine Welser Street.[34]

The Jews who were permitted to stay longer often belonged to the elite group of so-called court Jews (*Hofjuden*), which had emerged from the late sixteenth century onwards at the wealthiest pinnacle of Jewish society. Due to royal privileges and the functions they served at several courts, some Jews managed a spectacular economic and social ascent. They acted as army suppliers, bullion traders, court financiers, political agents, and suppliers for the court societies' manifold needs for luxury and consumer goods. Their exceptional status was based on a whole range of special rights that made them stand out from the crowd of protected Jews. These included customs and tax exemptions, special protection privileges, rights of abode in cities (especially in princely residences), and titles. The process of Jewish social differentiation was triggered after the crisis of the Thirty Years' War, as a result of mercantile and fiscal policies on the part of the princely states aimed at advancing the development of their principalities. Since they often lacked the necessary administrative apparatus, the princes relied on the knowledge and networks of Jewish merchants and financiers. Even if members of this group tended towards assimilation and acculturation with their Christian-aristocratic environment, many remained

---

33   Ullmann, *Nachbarschaft und Konkurrenz*, pp. 74, 145.
34   Joisten-Pruschke, "Juden in Augsburg", pp. 292–95.

deeply rooted in the Jewish community, where they held executive positions and supported religious and social institutions.[35]

This Jewish elite could be found not only at the princely courts and residence towns, but also in the suburban villages. Among the group of court Jews in the Augsburg region were members of the Ulman, Landau, Oppenheimer, and Kitzinger families in Pfersee as well as the Mändle and Neuburger families in Kriegshaber. They exploited their advantageous location at the gates of Augsburg both for commercial activities on behalf of their princely employers and for contacts with Augsburg's trading community. Samuel Ulman, who worked closely with the Oppenheimer trading company in Vienna, organized the supply of the Austrian troops in the War of Spanish Succession from his base in Pfersee. His son Löw Simon Ulman (the Younger) maintained business contacts with Augsburg's most important bankers and silver traders, such as Markus von Schnurbein (1671–1746) and Johann Adam Liebert von Liebenhofen (1697–1766). The assets of the Mändle and Neuburger families from Kriegshaber were instead based on their services for the courts of the Bavarian elector and the Duke of Württemberg. Particularly notable in this context was the Mändle trading company, which was among the most important suppliers of the Bavarian army in the second half of the eighteenth century.[36]

The villages closest to the imperial city were not only situated strategically, they also provided a comparatively good religious and communal infrastructure for Jewish court factors. The communities in Kriegshaber, Pfersee, and Steppach had experienced a substantial demographic boom after 1648. In Steppach, a 1732 tax list documents 32 families; 40 families lived in Pfersee around 1700; and 68 families resided in Kriegshaber in 1730. Hence the Jewish segment of the population had increased to 16.6 per cent in Pfersee, to almost 30 per cent in Steppach, and to 57 per cent in Kriegshaber. Large and stable communities with synagogues and comprehensive Jewish real estate holdings had developed in all three villages.[37]

The steady growth of Jewish communities in the suburban villages was accompanied by an increasing presence of Jewish merchants in the city. More and more often they appeared in Augsburg's commercial life, be it as court factors, pawnbrokers, or retail merchants. The many Jewish retailers in particular now faced considerable competitive pressure. Their imposed resettlement in villages and small towns had limited the Jews to only a few lines of

---

35 Battenberg, *Juden in Deutschland*, pp. 41–45.
36 Ullmann, *Nachbarschaft und Konkurrenz*, pp. 330–38.
37 Hetzer, "Anmerkungen", passim.

business, mainly the trading of cattle, agricultural products, consumer goods, and credit.[38] Even when the population was dense, as it was in the environs of Augsburg, not all Jewish retailers had sufficient opportunities to make a living. As a way out of this precarious situation, specializations in trade evolved among the Jewish settlements in the immediate vicinity. These become apparent if one moves away from the level of the court Jews and focuses on the retail trades, from which the majority of Jewish families lived. Whereas the Jews in Kriegshaber developed a focus on the cattle trade with peasants from the surrounding villages despite their close proximity to the city, the Pfersee Jews were represented more strongly in the trade in goods and particularly in pawnbroking, where they apparently managed to maintain an actual monopoly.[39] Meanwhile, the affluent Jewish merchants and the elite court Jews engaged in Augsburg's gold and silver trade as well as the textile trade and financial services. Diversification took place only in connection with princely courts; otherwise the flourishing urban market offered them sufficient profit opportunities. They were thus active precisely in those sectors of commercial life that were important in Augsburg at that time: banking, trading in precious metals, and textile production.[40]

On the whole, the council's restrictions were aimed less at the Jewish elite than at the microcredit sector. Nevertheless, Augsburg's citizens found ways and means to pawn their goods with the Jewish pawnbrokers of Pfersee. Christians acted as intermediaries, and an unofficial market was established in the shooting grounds (*Schießgraben*) just outside the city gates, where Christian customers and Jewish merchants made their transactions. The council tried to abolish this practice, in April 1732 for example, but with little success – this branch of trade was too lucrative and necessary for both sides. After 1648, the city no longer sought to establish a general trade ban, but instead took account of the important role Jewish salesmen played in supplying the urban market and in granting small-scale credit. At the same time, however, a clear boundary was drawn with the Christian grocers' guild by prohibiting Jews from selling their wares in public shops. Disparate interests thus appealed to the council. The grocers' guild as well as members of the merchant and patrician societies still pushed for limits on Jewish trade in the city. These groups were primarily interested in eliminating annoying competition, and relied on perpetrating anti-Jewish stereotypes of the "Jewish usurers" or harnessing convenient religious arguments. Yet those citizens who were active in trade and commerce

---

38   Battenberg, *Das europäische Zeitalter*, vol. 2, pp. 4–5.
39   Ullmann, "Erwerbsprofile", pp. 79–98.
40   Fassl, *Konfession, Wirtschaft und Politik*, pp. 123–70; see Chapter 5 in this volume.

and themselves had business connections with Jews advocated their continued presence in the urban market. For example, a group of goldsmiths argued in 1720 that they could not survive without Jewish clients, and in 1732 the Lairische Company asked the council to grant their Jewish customers access to the city because their wares would be left unsold otherwise. The disputes about Jewish commerce in Augsburg generated a plethora of reports and regulations, which reveal the maneuverings of different economic interest groups that ultimately resulted in large contradictions within the council's policies.[41]

Meanwhile, the implementation of restrictive admittance conditions was becoming increasingly difficult. Although the forced escort regulation remained nominally valid until the end of the eighteenth century, more and more exceptions were allowed. The court Jews could usually produce letters of reference from their princely employers requesting exemption from the degrading escort by a city guard, which, due to political considerations, the council could hardly refuse. Ultimately this rule would be applied only to foreign Jews, whereas Jews from Kriegshaber, Pfersee, and Steppach remained exempt. Another factor was awareness of the inefficiency of this method of surveillance. According to a report on this practice by the local guard captain, city soldiers usually accepted bribes from the Jews and neglected their task. Wealthy Jews for their part now self-confidently ridiculed the escorts, thus defusing on their own the defamatory impact of the mandatory escorts.[42]

The collection of admission fees, which were charged collectively at the Gögginger Gate, which was the only legal entry point for Jews, proved more effective. At the beginning of the eighteenth century, the council modernized payment by concluding so-called general contracts (*Akkordverträge*) with the suburban communities. Under these agreements, the fees were no longer demanded from individual Jews, but paid by each Jewish community in an annual lump sum. In this way the council lightened the burden of the administrative apparatus and eliminated the ability of individual traders to avoid this fee.[43]

All of this points to the existence of frequent and manifold trading contacts between citizens of Augsburg and Jews in the rural communities. Reading between the lines of the sources reveals the extent of social contacts and affiliations as well. Jews, particularly wealthy ones, were highly visible in daily life. We know that they visited local taverns and, in the eighteenth century, coffeehouses as well. In doing so, they likely sat with Christians after business deals.

---

41   Ullmann, *Nachbarschaft und Konkurrenz*, pp. 251–54.
42   Ullmann, *Nachbarschaft und Konkurrenz*, pp. 245–46.
43   Joisten-Pruschke, "Juden in Augsburg", pp. 288–91.

When 37 Jewish families found refuge from the impending passage of troops in 1741, they lived as tenants in the homes of Augsburg citizens for several weeks. Augsburgers also visited Jewish homes in Pfersee to borrow money or engage in trade.

Nevertheless, anti-Jewish stereotypes continued to have an effect: Jewish trade was still forbidden in the city on Sundays and holidays to protect its inhabitants from alleged Jewish blasphemy. But the stereotypes could be overcome on a situational and individual basis, not least for economic reasons. Thus, in Augsburg as elsewhere, a dynamic interdependence in economic life can be observed at the end of the early modern period that, although by no means on an equal footing, led to mutual cooperation and to companionable everyday contacts between Christians and Jews.

4   The Path Back into the City: 1803–13

The year 1803 marked a change of course in municipal policy. For the first time since the expulsion in 1438–40, Jews were granted a permanent right of abode. The immediate cause was the imperial city's financial crisis, which brought the council to the brink of insolvency. The city's creditors included a number of Jewish banking houses, such as the Munich bankers Westheimer and Strassburger and the Kaula house in Kriegshaber. In 1803, the Kaula bank refused to roll over its credit and insisted on repayment. Meanwhile, in February of the same year, several Jewish banking families petitioned for permanent rights of abode. A vigorous and contentious debate now arose within the council. Should Augsburg get rid of its indebtedness by granting an appropriate privilege while negotiating a favorable a line of credit from the Jewish bankers in order to alleviate the disastrous budgetary situation? Simultaneously, the council sought alternative possibilities for refinancing among Christian bankers, ultimately without success. This resort failed because the loan offers were less attractive and the Christian bankers were extremely hesitant, well aware of the high risk they would be taking. In November 1803, therefore, a decree was issued to the banking and exchange companies of Westheimer and Straßburger, Henle Ephraim Ulmann and Jakob Obermayer-Kaula, conceding them and their families unlimited rights of residence in Augsburg in exchange for the granting of loans. Despite protest from the Merchant Society and the grocers' guild, the Jewish families were granted the status of legal residents, which permitted them to live in the city and open their banking houses but did not include citizenship. The three financially powerful banking families thus purchased their move to the city – but at a high price.[44] Some members of this Jewish elite eventually trod the path of assimilation and acculturation taken by many Jews in Germany during the later eighteenth century. They converted to Christianity and in many cases obtained noble titles, as did Arnold Seligmann in Augsburg (Baron of Eichthal as of 1814).[45]

At base, of course, this was just another step along the already well-worn path of specially privileging individual wealthy Jews. In the 1780s and 1790s, a successive relaxation of the restrictions on granting admission for Jews can be observed. More and more often, longer stays were approved without specific grounds, and the general contracts with the Jewish communities of Kriegshaber, Pfersee, and Steppach were signed for periods of six years. This demonstrates increasing routine in pragmatic dealings with Jewish commerce in Augsburg. The contractual agreements reveal that Jewish tradesmen also brought their wives, children, and servants into the city during the day. They rented taverns to prepare kosher food and were allowed to establish branch offices to store their merchandise and transact business. Only at night and on Jewish holidays did they still have to return to their homes in the villages. Trade in the city on Sundays and Christian holidays also remained forbidden to them, but sporadic special permissions were granted for this as well.[46]

The return of Jews to Augsburg took place gradually: in a process spanning several decades, they gained ever greater privileges. Since a considerable part not only of their business but also their everyday and family life took place in the city, Jews became an increasingly visible part of urban society. Whether and to what extent Jewish retailers – who made their way through Augsburg with vendors' trays – also benefited from these easing measures is still open to question. The other side of the coin was increasing hostility toward Jews on the part of the Merchant Society and the grocers' guild, which becomes obvious in the council discussions of 1803. In June of this year the council's legal consultant (*Ratskonsulent*) Hoscher was charged with preparing an opinion about the controversial question of readmission. Ultimately, he spoke in favor of it, but only under strict stipulations – he demanded that Jewish applicants for admission to the city be in possession of at least 40,000 gulden in assets and pay markedly higher taxes than other residents. Despite these rigid conditions, which once again underlined the inferior status of the Jews, most of the council's members voted against it.

---

44 Baer, "Zwischen Vertreibung und Wiederansiedlung", p. 125.
45 Volkov, *Juden in Deutschland*, pp. 8–13.
46 Joisten-Pruschke, "Juden in Augsburg", pp. 287–91.

Augsburg's policy was finally overtaken by political events. In 1806, the imperial city was integrated into the newly formed Kingdom of Bavaria. The laws issued by what was now the royal city council abolished the general contracts, made petitions for access to the city obsolete, and abrogated the degrading toll levied for personal protection (*Leibzoll*) along with other admission fees.[47] Initially this was a great relief for Jewish tradesmen from the surrounding villages. In a counter move, however, the Jewish policy put in place by the kingdom of Bavaria, with its *Matrikelparagraph* (registration paragraph) of 1813 limiting the number of Jewish families in a particular location, again entailed significant constraints.[48] The Bavarian edict once more restricted further Jewish immigration to Augsburg for many decades. Thus, only 13 families could initially live in Augsburg, most of whom ran banks and exchange offices.[49] Only the abolition of the edict on Jews in 1861 led to the growth of Augsburg's Jewish community and subsequently to the gradual dissolution of the former rural communities.

5 Conclusion

Augsburg and its environs formed a significant center of Jewish life between 1400 and 1800. As elsewhere, Jews were confronted with the stereotype of "Jewish usurers", religious legends of ritual murder and host desecration, and accusations of blasphemy. The resulting inferior status led to a series of exclusionary and discriminatory measures, which escalated during the first third of the fifteenth century. Other fringe groups such as the Romany or foreign beggars were affected by similar ostracism. For the Jews, it ultimately led to banishment from the city in 1438–40. This policy of expulsion, which took place in most larger cities at the end of the Middle Ages, led to the disruption of Jewish life in this area for several generations. Only in the second half of the sixteenth century do Jews again appear, now outside the city walls rather than inside and under the protection of the margravate of Burgau. In the transitional phase of rural Jewish life during the early modern period, settlements in suburbs and nearby villages played a crucial role. Augsburg was typical in this respect: Jews continued to participate in urban markets and acted as intermediaries between urban and agrarian economies. But their commerce in the city was subject to strict constraints and complicated by the many restrictions imposed

---

47 Schwarz, *Juden in Bayern*, pp. 124–26.
48 Kießling, "Gab es einen pragmatischen Weg", pp. 175–99.
49 Hirsch, "Zur Situation der Juden", pp. 307–12.

by a council policy shaped by mercantile competition and religious prejudices. Nevertheless, Jews were present in Augsburg's commercial and daily life. During the seventeenth and eighteenth centuries, increasingly pragmatic attitudes toward Jewish trading activities prevailed, and temporary permission to reside in the city was occasionally granted during times of war. But only at the beginning of the nineteenth century were certain wealthy individual families granted a permanent right of abode in Augsburg.

Bibliography

Unpublished Primary Sources
Stadtarchiv Augsburg (StadtAA)
  Judenakten 15.
  Urgichten 1553–1614.

Secondary Literature
Baer, W., "Zwischen Vertreibung und Wiederansiedlung: Die Reichsstadt Augsburg und die Juden vom 15. bis zum 18. Jahrhundert", in R. Kießling (ed.), *Judengemeinden in Schwaben im Kontext des Alten Reiches*, Berlin, 1995, pp. 110–26.
Battenberg, J.F., *Das europäische Zeitalter der Juden. Zur Entwicklung einer Minderheit in der nichtjüdischen Umwelt Europas*, 2 vols., Darmstadt, 1990.
Battenberg, J.F., *Die Juden in Deutschland vom 16. bis zum Ende des 18. Jahrhunderts*, Munich, 2001.
Burgard, F., Haverkamp, A. and Mentgen, G. (eds.), *Judenvertreibungen in Mittelalter und früher Neuzeit*, Hannover, 1999.
Fassl, P., *Konfession, Wirtschaft und Politik. Von der Reichsstadt zur Industriestadt. Augsburg 1750–1850*, Sigmaringen, 1988.
Graus, F., "Randgruppen in der städtischen Gesellschaft im Spätmittelalter", *Zeitschrift für Historische Forschung* 8 (1981), pp. 385–437.
Haverkamp, A., "'Concivilitas' von Christen und Juden in Aschkenas", in R. Jütte and A.P. Kustermann (eds.), *Jüdische Gemeinden und Organisationsformen von der Antike bis zur Gegenwart*, Vienna, 1996, pp. 103–36.
Hetzer, G., "Anmerkungen zur Geschichte der Judensiedlungen in Steppach und Schlipsheim", in M. Nozar and W. Pötzl (eds.), *Neusäß. Die Geschichte von acht Dörfern auf dem langen Weg zu einer Stadt*, Neusäß, 1988, pp. 239–62.
Hirsch, H.K., "Zur Situation der Juden in Augsburg während der Emanzipationszeit", in R. Kießling (ed.), *Judengemeinden in Schwaben im Kontext des Alten Reiches*, Berlin, 1995, pp. 306–23.

Jörg, C., "Zwischen Basler Konzil, Königtum und reichsstädtischen Interessen: Kennzeichnung und Ausweisung der Augsburger Juden in europäischen Zusammenhängen", in M. Brenner and S. Ullmann (eds.), Die Juden in Schwaben, Munich, 2013, pp. 63–92.

Joisten-Pruschke, A., "Die Geschichte der Juden in Augsburg während der Emanzipationszeit 1750–1871", in R. Kießling (ed.), Neue Forschungen zur Geschichte der Stadt Augsburg, Augsburg, 2011, pp. 277–349.

Jütte, R., "Stigma-Symbole: Kleidung als identitätsstiftendes Merkmal bei spätmittelalterlichen und frühneuzeitlichen Randgruppen (Juden, Dirnen, Aussätzige, Bettler)", Saeculum 44 (1993), pp. 65–89.

Kießling, R., Bürgerliche Gesellschaft und Kirche in Augsburg im Spätmittelalter. Ein Beitrag zur Strukturanalyse der oberdeutschen Reichsstadt, Augsburg, 1971.

Kießling, R., "Einführung", in idem (ed.), Judengemeinden in Schwaben im Kontext des Alten Reiches, Berlin, 1995, pp. 11–22.

Kießling, R., "Zwischen Schutzherrschaft und Reichsbürgerschaft: Die schwäbischen Juden und das Reich", in idem and S. Ullmann (eds.), Das Reich in der Region während des Spätmittelalters und der Frühen Neuzeit, Constance, 2005, pp. 99–122.

Kießling, R., "Gab es einen pragmatischen Weg zur Emanzipation? Die jüdischen Gemeinden in Schwaben an der Schwelle zur Moderne", in M. Brenner and S. Ullmann (eds.), Die Juden in Schwaben, Munich, 2013, pp. 175–99.

Künast, H.-J., "Hebräisch-jüdischer Buchdruck in Schwaben in der ersten Hälfte des 16. Jahrhunderts", in R. Kießling and S. Ullmann (eds.), Landjudentum im deutschen Südwesten während der Frühen Neuzeit, Berlin, 1999, pp. 277–303.

Maimon, A. and Guggenheim, Y. (eds.), Germania Judaica. Vol. 3/1: 1350–1519, Tübingen, 1987.

Mütschele, S., Juden in Augsburg, 1212–1440, Stuttgart, 1996.

Roeck, B., Eine Stadt in Krieg und Frieden. Studien zur Geschichte der Reichsstadt Augsburg zwischen Kalenderstreit und Parität, 2 vols., Göttingen, 1989.

Roeck, B., Außenseiter, Randgruppen, Minderheiten. Fremde im Deutschland der frühen Neuzeit, Göttingen, 1993.

Rogge, J., Für den gemeinen Nutzen. Politisches Handeln und Politikverständnis von Rat und Bürgerschaft in Augsburg im Spätmittelalter, Tübingen, 1996.

Rohrbacher, S., "Medinat Schwaben: Jüdisches Leben in einer süddeutschen Landschaft in der Frühneuzeit", in R. Kießling (ed.), Judengemeinden in Schwaben im Kontext des Alten Reiches, Berlin, 1995, pp. 80–109.

Rohrbacher, S., "Ungleiche Partnerschaft. Simon Günzburg und die erste Ansiedlung von Juden vor den Toren Augsburgs in der Frühen Neuzeit", in R. Kießling and S. Ullmann (eds.), Landjudentum im deutschen Südwesten während der Frühen Neuzeit, Berlin, 1999, pp. 192–219.

Schimmelpfennig, B., "Christen und Juden im Augsburg des Mittelalters", in R. Kießling (ed.), *Judengemeinden in Schwaben im Kontext des Alten Reiches*, Berlin, 1995, pp. 23–38.

Schubert, E., "Die verbotene Existenz der Zigeuner", in R. Erb (ed.), *Die Legende vom Ritualmord. Zur Geschichte der Blutbeschuldigung gegen Juden*, Berlin, 1993, pp. 179–200.

Schwarz, S., *Die Juden in Bayern im Wandel der Zeiten*, Munich, 1963.

Seitz, R.H., "Zur Topographie der älteren Judengemeinde in Augsburg und Lauingen (Donau)", in P. Fassl (ed.), *Geschichte und Kultur der Juden in Schwaben*, Sigmaringen, 1994, pp. 19–35.

Steinthal, F.L., *Geschichte der Augsburger Juden im Mittelalter*, Berlin, 1911.

Straus, R., *Regensburg and Augsburg*, Philadelphia, 1939.

Tlusty, B.A., *The Martial Ethic in Early Modern Germany: Civic Duty and the Right of Arms*, Basingstoke, 2011.

Toch, M., *Die Juden im mittelalterlichen Reich*, Munich, 1998.

Ullmann, S., *Nachbarschaft und Konkurrenz. Juden und Christen in Dörfern der Markgrafschaft Burgau 1650 bis 1750*, Göttingen, 1999.

Ullmann, S., "Leihen umb fahrend Hab und Gut. Der christlich-jüdische Pfandhandel in der Reichsstadt Augsburg'", in R. Kießling and idem (eds.), *Landjudentum im deutschen Südwesten während der Frühen Neuzeit*, Berlin, 1999, pp. 304–35.

Ullmann, S., "Regionale und lokale Erwerbsprofile jüdischer Händler in den ländlichen Ökonomien des 17. und 18. Jahrhunderts", in J. Ebert and W. Troßbach (eds.), *Dörfliche Erwerbs- und Nutzungsorientierungen (Mitte 17. bis Anfang 19. Jahrhundert). Bausteine zu einem überregionalen Vergleich*, Kassel, 2016, pp. 79–98.

Volkov, S., *Die Juden in Deutschland 1780–1918*, Munich, 1994.

Wenninger, M., *Man bedarf keiner Juden mehr. Ursachen und Hintergründe ihrer Vertreibung aus den deutschen Reichsstädten im 15. Jahrhundert*, Vienna, 1981.

PART 4

Communication, Cultural and Intellectual Life

∴

CHAPTER 17

The Dissemination of News

Regina Dauser

In many respects, the second half of the fifteenth century was a key period in the premodern history of Augsburg. This is also true for the "news market". Due to topographical, economic, educational, and infrastructural factors, Augsburg emerged as one of the major early modern German news centers. News centers can be characterized either by their political relevance, "producing" news in the form of important political decisions, or by their position as news brokers, which was often based on mercantile activities, especially in long-distance trade.[1] Augsburg actually was an important political arena of the Holy Roman Empire, especially regarding crucial imperial decisions that were negotiated at sixteenth-century diets (notably the Religious Peace of Augsburg in 1555). But above all, it was the local merchants who turned Augsburg into a communication hub. This chapter surveys the major written and printed forms of news media available to citizens of Augsburg in the late medieval and early modern periods and examines the city's role in the development of both local and international markets for news reports.

1 Commercial Transactions and the Communication of News

The history of early modern news communication is closely intertwined with the informational needs of European merchants, who had been increasingly engaged in long-distance trade since the late Middle Ages. Merchants trading abroad were highly dependent on current information about supply and demand in the major European markets; about the political situation, which might either restrict or promote trade; about new economic opportunities emerging with overseas discoveries; or about natural catastrophes or epidemics affecting travel and the transport of goods. Therefore, they regularly sought channels for current information and forwarded it to others as well. Due to this need for news, at least in terms of numbers, merchants are considered the main pioneers of intensified communication and especially the dissemination

---

[1] For general observations on communication and news centers, with a focus on Italy, see Infelise, "Merchants' Letters", esp. pp. 40–43.

of news, albeit policy makers (in cities or at courts), scholars, and clergymen were also avid recipients and to some extent brokers of news as well.[2]

In the second half of the fifteenth century, when Augsburg was rapidly catching up with its major economic competitor in the Empire, Nuremberg, and Augsburg's merchants were laying the foundation for the city's status as a European commercial metropolis, written communication regarding banking, trade, and mining was mainly organized "on demand" by courier services or messengers. By this time, Augsburg merchants, like those in Nuremberg and other commercial cities, had a more or less regular courier system at their disposal. It was organized and controlled by the city council, which needed couriers for communication with other political entities, in close collaboration with the merchants' guild.[3] Sources from the last quarter of the fifteenth century indicate real competition between the Nuremberg and Augsburg courier services on the route to Venice.[4]

Merchants thus managed to maintain long-distance business relations not only by travelling in person or sending their employees to make direct contact with their offices and business partners, but also by sending letters to partners and clerks in their branch offices in commercial or production centers inside and outside of Germany.[5] In the final quarter of the fifteenth century, a number of Augsburg merchant companies, including the Fuggers, Welsers, Meutings, and Hoechstetters, had well-established trading connections with the major commercial cities of Europe, especially Venice, Antwerp, and Lyons.[6]

For a long time, travel – which also served as a means of exerting control through personal presence – and correspondence were complementary activities. A good example is provided by the autobiographical notes of the merchant Lukas Rem (1481–1541), who was employed by the Welser Company before starting his own business with his brothers. Rem worked for and regularly visited different branch offices and agents of the Welser Company in Italy, Switzerland, Portugal, Spain, France, and the Netherlands, constantly sending

---

2 Infelise, "Merchants' Letters"; Böning, "'Gewiss ist es'", p. 209. For scholars' correspondence networks, see Mauelshagen, "Netzwerke des Nachrichtenaustauschs".
3 See Lankes, "Postgeschichte der Reichsstadt Augsburg"; Kränzler, "Augsburger Botenanstalt"; Wüst, "Reichsstädtische Kommunikation". On courier systems before the institutionalization of postal relay systems, especially in the Holy Roman Empire, see Heimann, "Brievedregher".
4 Helbig, *Postvermerke*, p. 105.
5 For the interrelation of business communication and transport systems, see Veluwenkamp, "International Business Communication Patterns".
6 For an overview of Augsburg's economic development, see Chapter 5 in this volume; for business relations with Venice, see Häberlein, "Fondaco dei Tedeschi"; for Antwerp, see Trauchburg-Kuhnle, "Kooperation und Konkurrenz".

and receiving letters, and sometimes complaining about *heftig brief* ("severe letters" in an authoritarian tone) from the head office in Augsburg.[7]

At the end of the fifteenth century, King Maximilian (who would become emperor in 1508) sought to improve his communications infrastructure by establishing regular information exchanges between his Tyrolean and Burgundian territories in present-day Austria and Belgium. From 1490 onwards, he commissioned professional couriers from the north Italian Tassis family (later known as Taxis) to build up a courier system with regular relay stations (postal stations) for changing the courier's horse. This opportunity to switch to a fresh horse tremendously accelerated the speed of delivery. Thus Maximilian created a postal axis across the Empire, connecting not only his territories, but also the major economic regions of Europe, the Netherlands and northern Italy, by a single route. The relay system also provided important connecting points for other courier services. Augsburg became a relay station on this route around 1520 and was the first imperial city with a permanent post office by 1549, clearly giving it an advantage over other cities without direct links to the new communication flow.[8]

As the postal organization was expensive, Maximilian needed financial supplies. These he obtained by credit, which was provided by merchant-bankers like the Fuggers, and by opening the postal system to paying customers with fixed rates for the transport of letters. Those who could afford the postal service could now make use of a courier system that provided regular weekly services with fixed days for the arrival and departure of the mail.[9]

This innovation also promoted the communication of news; western and northern Europe were provided with a model for the development of a communication infrastructure. The new, publicly accessible, regular postal services are commonly seen as the "essential spine to news networks".[10] But at least in the Holy Roman Empire, they remained dependent for decades on supplementary, often traditional courier services that covered destinations beyond the main routes, thus serving as the "nerves" of the European "news organism".[11]

---

7   Greiff (ed.), *Tagebuch des Lucas Rem*, quote on p. 11.
8   The establishment of the Taxis post is comprehensively covered by Behringer, *Im Zeichen des Merkur*, esp. pp. 59–98. On Augsburg, see esp. pp. 68, 97.
9   Behringer, *Im Zeichen des Merkur*, p. 68.
10 Schobesberger et al., "European Postal Networks", p. 19.
11 At least for the later sixteenth century, the impact of the new postal system should not be overestimated, as the need for alternative courier systems during the "postal crisis" (including a horsemen's strike in the late 1560s) and the "postal reformation" in the Holy Roman Empire show. See Behringer, *Im Zeichen des Merkur*, pp. 136–76; Dauser, *Informationskultur*, pp. 121–30.

Augsburg merchants benefited from these innovations and, like other European merchants, disseminated the incoming news reports within their social networks – to relatives, city councilors, or customers, including princes of the Empire. The exclusivity and reliability of the news they spread depended on the quality of their personal and business networks.

The forms of transferring written information by mail or courier ranged from accidental remarks in a letter to entire news paragraphs, usually at the end of a letter, and even to separate newssheets enclosed with a letter.[12] From the latter type emerged the so-called *Newe Zeit[t]ungen* ("current tidings"), in Italy usually called *avvisi* ("notices"), a specific form of handwritten newsletter that became all but universal in Europe. The term *Newe Zeitungen* thus became the label for a new genre, characterizing these newsletters merely by the place where they had been written and the date of writing. Thus, news could be fed into an anonymous news flow for a wider audience, not restricted to specific news brokers and readers.[13] These types of written news coexisted from the sixteenth until the end of the eighteenth century and were tailored to the needs of news recipients. It took some time before printed news would be able to meet more specific information needs.[14]

Based on evidence from other European news centers,[15] Augsburg merchants regularly acted as news brokers. Some of them delivered news for payment, while others passed them on as a gratuitous service, expecting (more or less explicitly) some service in return, be it valuable information, prospects of a good business deal, or merely the strengthening of an important network relationship.[16] Examples of the origins of regular merchant news services in the early sixteenth century include Jakob Fugger's letters to members of the Wettin dynasty of Saxony (1519–25) and Anton Welser's letters to his business partner Lienhart Tucher in Nuremberg (1536–39).[17]

---

12   For the different types, see Werner, "Das kaufmännische Nachrichtenwesen".
13   In communication history research, anonymization is considered a characteristic trait of a "more modern news and information network"; see Infelise, "Merchants' Letters", p. 38.
14   Böning, "'Gewiss ist es'", p. 220.
15   See Infelise, *Prima dei giornali*.
16   Sporhan-Krempel explored the intense relationships between Nuremberg authors of newsletters to princes and city councils: Sporhan-Krempel, *Nürnberg als Nachrichtenzentrum*, chapter E.
17   Pölnitz, "Jakob Fuggers Zeitungen"; Welser, *Welser*, pp. 136–38.

2 Written and Printed News from Augsburg: Characteristics, Producers, Recipients

From the beginning of the sixteenth century, Augsburg emerged as a leading news center, consolidating and professionalizing news transfer from a growing range of sources. This was true for handwritten as well as printed news, which both relied primarily on merchants' business relations.[18] Handwritten news from Augsburg mainly met the needs of the political, economic, and scholarly elites. However, local printers also turned select news items from letters into a publicly available resource – admittedly with some restrictions. Newsprints and specific practices of oral dissemination were combined in the genre of news songs, which dealt with both political and "sensational" news and which were written and sung by individuals like the Augsburg newsvendor Thomas Kern in the early seventeenth century.[19]

For local printers specializing in marketable works in German, news broadsheets became an important sideline business; their production entailed low risk and little financial investment.[20] Together with Nuremberg, Augsburg was the major production site for early modern broadsheets and pamphlets in the Empire, as least those whose origins can be traced.[21] Newsprints have been identified for prominent local printers like Erhard Öglin, Philip Ulhart, and Hans Zimmermann.[22] One of the earliest German newsprints was a pamphlet about the exploration of Brazil entitled *Copia der Newen Zeitung aus Presilg Landt* ("Copy of the Current Tidings from Brazil", published around 1515), which was printed in two editions by Erhard Öglin and was certainly based on a handwritten report. Handwritten letters about Spanish and Portuguese overseas expeditions had reached Augsburg via Spain and Italy since 1493 and were repeatedly transformed into locally printed works.[23]

The practice of mentioning letters in broadsheet titles became common, and occasionally even the writers and recipients were noted, thus

---

18 Schilling, "Augsburger Einblattdruck", pp. 388–89.
19 See Brednich, *Liedpublizistik im Flugblatt*; Schilling, *Lieder des Augsburger Kolporteurs*.
20 Schilling, "Augsburger Einblattdruck", p. 387; see also Chapter 18 in this volume.
21 With detailed figures: Schilling, "Stadt und Publizistik", p. 349.
22 See the list of newsprints in Dresler, *Augsburg und die Frühgeschichte der Presse*, pp. 16–29.
23 For the transfer of written news about the Americas to Augsburg, see Pieper, *Die Vermittlung einer Neuen Welt*, pp. 131–33. For different accounts of the origins of the aforementioned print, see ibid., pp. 131–32 (suggesting a Fugger employee from Lisbon) and Häberlein, "Monster und Missionare", pp. 353–55.

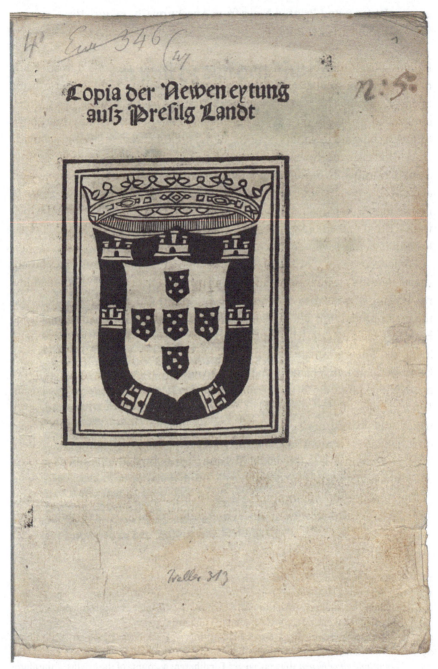

FIGURE 17.1 *Copia der Newen [Z]eitung aus Presilg Landt*, c. 1515, title page
BAYERISCHE STAATSBIBLIOTHEK MÜNCHEN, RAR. 614, FOL. 1R

underscoring their timeliness and authenticity.[24] The term *Newe Zeitung* referred to both written and printed news.[25] While we do not know exactly how printers obtained the material for written news, the forwarding of information by merchants or their employees is proven by textual comparisons. Political and military news, mainly from the European theaters of war, and reports of miraculous appearances and catastrophes such as earthquakes, floods, and fires, were the mainstays of Augsburg's broadsheet and pamphlet printers, providing for the growing "news hunger" of the urban (and, albeit to a lesser degree, rural) population with affordable products.[26] Prints relating to the events of the Reformation represent a special genre, as they were mainly concerned with theological and religious issues; therefore they are omitted here. But the control exerted by the censorship office established in the early sixteenth century as a result of the proliferation of these polemical prints (the first censorship decree dates from 1515) likewise furthered the production of newsprints about foreign wars, miracles and catastrophes, as the censors intervened when prints threatened to disturb the peace with religious or political propaganda.[27]

As recent research has shown, news gathered from letters or handwritten newsletters were not printed without revisions; instead, they were adapted to the format of broadsheets and pamphlets as well as to the expectations and reading customs of a wider supra-regional audience. This becomes obvious when we compare printed works to the handwritten newspapers upon which they were based. Prints could summarize or combine several handwritten newsletters; they could also include additional comments in order to provide an interpretation of events in a particular, often religious, sense.[28]

---

24 Böning, "'Gewiss ist es'", p. 219. Dresler, *Augsburg und die Frühgeschichte der Presse*, provides numerous examples in his list of printers and news printings, such as "Copia ains briefs" (p. 22), "Abschrift Ains Briefs" (p. 27) or "Zeittung Copeya Zwaier Schreiben" (p. 28).
25 On terminology, see Arblaster et al., "Lexicons of Early Modern News", pp. 70–73.
26 For a general overview, see Barbarics and Pieper, "Handwritten Newsletters", p. 57. For a list of printers and their news production, see Dresler, *Augsburg und die Frühgeschichte der Presse*. The interplay between news demand and supply is explored in Infelise, "Merchants' Letters", p. 51.
27 For this assumption see Schilling, "Augsburger Einblattdruck", p. 388. On local censorship, see Büchler, "Zensur im frühneuzeitlichen Augsburg"; Costa, "Rechtseinrichtung der Censur".
28 Michael Schilling, Zsusza Barbarics and Renate Pieper undertook such comparative research on the basis of the so-called "Fuggerzeitungen" (a collection of handwritten newspapers; for details see below) and prints based on them. Schilling, "Stadt und Publizistik", pp. 356–57; Barbarics and Pieper, "Handwritten Newsletters", pp. 62–67.

The most detailed and significant sources for Augsburg's position in an increasingly professionalized news market date from the later sixteenth century. By this time, the city had gained the position of a "news hub", especially for news from Italy.[29] However, in spite of the considerable number of identifiable local news brokers, the richest sources focus on a small group of persons, with several members of the Fugger family standing out.

With the growing demand for news in the Empire, a new type of news broker appeared, collectively called *Novellanten* or *Avisenschreiber* (gazetteers). The origins of these news agents can be traced to Italy. Benefiting from their proximity to merchant companies, foreign diplomats, and local officials, these professional newsgatherers, who were not necessarily associated with merchant firms, began to copy news obtained by others; combine news from different places in newssheets; and regularly sell or send them to customers (mainly noblemen and diplomats) on a subscription basis. Such early news agencies developed in the first half of the sixteenth century; their *avvisi* became a commodity in great demand.[30] There is clear evidence that Augsburg merchants were clients of these Italian gazetteers from the mid-sixteenth century onwards.[31] They also adopted the model of writing *avvisi* and passing them on to noble clients, as we know for several members of the Fugger family and their scribes, who from the 1560s regularly sent newssheets to the Duke of Bavaria and the Count of Pfalz-Neuburg.[32]

The new profession of the gazetteer was established in Augsburg by the 1580s. Sources are fragmentary and disparate: traces of the gazetteers' work can be found in the bills and correspondence of their customers, tax and muster registers, marriage and court records, and registers of deceased residents.[33] Estimates of their numbers from the late sixteenth to the mid-seventeenth century are difficult, since there was no single term for a professional newsgatherer, who might be called a *Novellant*, scribe, secretary, or courier.[34] Gazetteers could earn considerable sums working for distinguished customers – between 30 and 40 gulden per subscription and year on average. Handwritten

---

29   Infelise, "News Networks between Italy and Europe"; Raymond, "News Networks", pp. 116, 120–21.
30   See Infelise, *Prima dei giornali*.
31   Bauer, *Zeitungen vor der Zeitung*, pp. 101–02; Dauser, *Informationskultur*, p. 150.
32   Zwierlein, *Discorso und Lex Dei*, p. 592; idem, "Fuggerzeitungen"; Dauser, *Informationskultur*, p. 173. Zwierlein's hypothesis of a cultural transfer of the *avvisi* model to Germany was confirmed by Bauer, *Zeitungen vor der Zeitung*, p. 154–55.
33   On the current state of research, see Bauer, *Zeitungen vor der Zeitung*, pp. 103–05.
34   Behringer, *Im Zeichen des Merkur*, p. 332 estimates the number of *novellanti* at about 40 in 1610.

newspapers were still an elite medium around 1600.[35] To all appearances, however, many newswriters led a precarious existence, whereas only the owners of proper news agencies earned fortunes.[36] Still, some *Novellanten* managed to run their own news bureaus or agencies successfully for decades; Jeremias Schiffle (1561–1626), for example, whose handwritten newspapers can be traced back to 1596, worked at least until 1619, when he was listed in a muster register as one of four professional *Zeitungsschreiber* ("news scribes").[37]

As far as we know, the new profession of full-time newsgathering within a mercantile context was more prevalent in Augsburg than in other commercial cities or princely residences of the Holy Roman Empire. Wolfgang Behringer states that handwritten newspapers from Augsburg became an early modern "brand" – the origins of the news serving as an advertising argument for potential customers, as can be seen in the correspondence between Albrecht Reiffenstein and Elector August of Saxony in 1579. In order to underline his ability to gather the latest news, Reiffenstein not only stressed the regular postal services supplying Augsburg with news from Italy, France, Spain, Portugal, and the emperor's court in Vienna each week, but also emphasized his contacts with the city's most distinguished gentlemen (*den fürnembsten Herren*).[38] Nevertheless, before the late sixteenth century, German elite customers could not do without *avvisi* received directly from the major Italian news centers, Venice and Rome.[39]

3 News and Networks: Hans Fugger's Correspondence as a Case Study

As noted by Reiffenstein, social relationships with well-informed news brokers were indispensable for gathering detailed up-to-date news. Due to this fact,

---

35 The shared acquisition of handwritten newspapers by commoners, like teachers or parish priests, is seen as an exception in the seventeenth century; see Böning, "'Gewiss ist es'", p. 216.

36 Bauer, *Zeitungen vor der Zeitung*, pp. 107–09; Behringer, *Im Zeichen des Merkur*, pp. 331–39.

37 Schiffle was already mentioned in the 1610 register; in the 1645 register, a news scribe named Jeremias Schiffle is noted for the first time, obviously a member of the next generation. Stadtarchiv Augsburg (StadtAA), Reichsstadt, Censuramt 1649–1753; Schätze 37. It is unknown how many news scribes were hidden in other columns of the register merely as scribes or in similar terms, because news scribes in the 1610 register were listed only as scribes in 1615: Behringer, *Im Zeichen des Merkur*, p. 332–33. For information about Schiffle and his supposed Augsburg partner Crasser, see Bauer, *Zeitungen vor der Zeitung*, pp. 103–04.

38 Behringer, *Im Zeichen des Merkur*, p. 330–31.

39 For the evaluation and use of German handwritten newspapers and Italian *avvisi*: Keller and Molino, *Fuggerzeitungen im Kontext*.

even members of the noble and patrician elites were constantly searching for reliable news partners. The sums that were sometimes spent on subscriptions of handwritten newsletters from reliable sources are astonishing.[40]

The correspondence of the patrician and wealthy landowner Hans Fugger (1531–98) provides us with the rare opportunity to study the scope, organization, social dimensions, and practices of an elite news network. More than 4,800 of his letters have survived, mainly in copy books, for the period from 1566 to 1594 (with some gaps).[41] Hans' father, the merchant-banker Anton Fugger (1493–1560), who was elevated to the ranks of the hereditary nobility in 1526, provided his sons with a scholarly and elite education, sending them not only to universities, but also to the imperial court in Vienna and other princely courts. This provided them with numerous opportunities for networking.[42]

From the mid-1560s, Hans Fugger acted as the deputy of his elder brother Marx (or Marcus, 1529–97), the manager of the Fugger family firm. His correspondence, though, was no business correspondence in the usual sense. Instead, it is characterized by his preoccupation with the firm's representation and the family's social advancement. Hans acted as a kind of "foreign secretary" of the family enterprise,[43] maintaining commercial and patron-client relationships, providing diverse gratuitous services for noble customers, and disseminating news, mainly from theaters of war. About 20 per cent of his letters deal with European news events.

Undoubtedly, the weekly postal connections with the Fugger Company's branch offices, including those in Spain, Italy, the Netherlands, Austria, and Bohemia, formed the backbone of the Fugger news system. Via this system, weekly information became available for the company's management and for handwritten newspapers, which were regularly sent to select members of the Fugger network – especially to princely customers like Duke Albrecht V of Bavaria and his eldest son Wilhelm, but also to high-ranking officials at several courts of the Empire. Fugger's letters reveal that scribes in the head office had to copy incoming news and pass these handwritten newspapers on to certain customers. While these enclosures were omitted from the copy books, Fugger

---

40 The elector of Saxony offered the Augsburg gazetteer 100 gulden for newsletters sent three times a month in 1579: Behringer, *Im Zeichen des Merkur*, p. 331.
41 The Fuggers had been elevated to the imperial nobility in 1526–30 by Emperor Charles V: Dauser and Ferber, *Fugger und Welser*.
42 For a short biography, see Dauser, *Informationskultur*, pp. 13–16. For both family and company, see Häberlein, *The Fuggers of Augsburg*.
43 Karnehm used the term *Außenminister* to characterize Fugger's role as a correspondent: Karnehm, *Korrespondenz Hans Fuggers*, vol. 1, p. 14.

often mentioned news events in his letters and commented on them for select correspondents.

The news that Fugger discussed and disseminated by letter was certainly of high interest for his correspondents and was indispensable for the Fugger firm, especially on financial markets, as the company was an important creditor of the Spanish and Austrian branches of the Habsburg dynasty. At war in the Netherlands, the Mediterranean, and Eastern Europe, Habsburg rulers were in constant need of fresh money. Therefore the Fugger Company had to carefully calculate the risks of further loans. The political situation in the Holy Roman Empire, where confessional conflict was increasing, was another major topic affecting business and even family life in the bi-confessional imperial city.

In the case of high-ranking correspondents, the news exchange was one-sided: the Fugger Company delivered news, which was accepted as a gratuitous service, but received no news in return. Regarding correspondents who were not company employees – mainly officers in imperial or Spanish service and officeholders at the imperial or princely courts – Fugger not only acted as a news broker, but was also a recipient of news reports, albeit not as regularly as was the case with employees in the branch offices. All of these letters provided him with fresh information from various places of interest. With this benefit, Fugger could offer other correspondents a surplus of detailed information that the gazetteers and *Novellanten* usually could not match. The fact that most of these expert correspondents were not only connected with Fugger by news exchange, but also by ties of credit, kinship, and other forms of social contact provided further opportunities for mutual news transfer, participation in which was a kind of unwritten law in correspondence relationships. In addition, opportunities for obtaining insider information increased when the correspondents were connected in multi-layered networks. Contacts with high-ranking officials provided particular occasions for obtaining certain types of news that were important for Fugger business.[44]

Hans Fugger's comments on the reports that he sent and received also highlight the differences between printed and handwritten news. The trimming of facts for commercial or propaganda purposes was not necessary in personal correspondence, whereas information about military losses and their possible consequences for Fugger loans were undoubtedly more important news items than the enemy stereotypes or wartime atrocities that were typical fodder for printed broadsheets. Uncertain news and doubtful assessments were clearly

---

44   Dauser, *Informationskultur*, pp. 300–02. Some information which Fugger transferred can be connected with creditors' interests, e.g. news about insufficient war funds sent to princely officials who were supposed to be financially engaged; ibid., pp. 248–51.

pointed out. The tailoring of news to meet the recipients' special interests seems to have been another special feature of news transfer in an elite network such as Fugger's: the news noted in his letters as supplementary enclosures did not represent the whole spectrum of handwritten newspapers, but concentrated on areas of specific interest to his correspondents.[45]

Additional factors characterizing Hans Fugger's practices of disseminating news were the timeliness and reliability of information. Fugger was keen on receiving and spreading high-quality news. Therefore, he consistently exhorted employees in the branch offices to give weekly accounts of the news situation in accordance with the rhythms of the postal and courier services. If nothing noteworthy had happened, this fact still had to be mentioned in the letter to the head office to make sure that no piece of information had been lost or omitted by chance.[46] Furthermore, information was carefully assessed, and gazetteers who repeatedly delivered false news were no longer engaged.[47]

The reward for these efforts was the high quality of news, which was well-known and acknowledged by the fact that recipients included those at the top of the social ladder. Fugger newsletters were even sent to the imperial court, presumably by Hans' brother Marx.[48] The low rate of evidently false news is surprising: only 30 of 515 analyzed news reports mentioned in Fugger's letters can be classified as false. Hans Fugger knew that nobody was safe from hoax or outright deception, but he demonstrated confidence in the news that he passed on without reserve.[49] Thus Fugger was able to act as a dependable news broker, providing a German-speaking elite with highly reliable, regular news from the most important European theaters of action.

There is little evidence about the transfer of incoming news from the Fugger houses to other places in the city, aside from Fugger's occasional remarks about reporting some news to friends.[50] Employees of the merchant companies almost certainly contributed to the (oral) dissemination of news, as Georg Kölderer's chronicle shows. Kölderer (c. 1550–1607) was a clerk of the Weiß

---

45   Ibid., pp. 152–58. For differences between handwritten news and printings, see also Barbarics and Pieper, "Handwritten Newsletters".
46   Dauser, *Informationskultur*, p. 144.
47   Ibid., p. 153.
48   Ibid., p. 147; Bauer, *Zeitungen vor der Zeitung*, pp. 352–53.
49   In a letter to his nephew Anton von Montfort, who was in the cardinal of Trento's service, Fugger pointed out in 1583 that news transferred by the Fugger Company were particularly detailed and carefully revised. Dauser, *Informationskultur*, p. 154.
50   Dauser, *Informationskultur*, pp. 148–49.

Company who benefited from the firm's incoming newsletters, which provided him with fresh items for his chronicle.[51]

Regarding the relationship between handwritten and printed newsletters, one example of potential links between elite news brokers and printers dates from 1585. In that year, the Fugger employee Hans Mehrer, who sent weekly news to his brother-in-law Stefan Fugger, treasurer of the imperial city of Regensburg in the 1580s and 1590s, enclosed in one of his missives a broadsheet depicting a pontoon bridge built by Spanish soldiers in the Dutch War. His employers Marx and Hans Fugger had commissioned the print, as Mehrer told his addressee.[52] The broadsheet is nearly identical with a drawing found among the so-called *Fuggerzeitungen* ("Fugger newsletters"), a collection of handwritten newspapers gathered by two cousins of Hans Fugger, Philipp Eduard (1546–1618) and Octavian Secundus Fugger (1549–1600). In many cases, it is obvious that members of the various branches of the Fugger family received the same news – according to Oswald Bauer, their communication networks were largely independent from each other but frequently drew on the same sources. As the Fugger newsletters with their more than 16,000 items are the most important handwritten newspaper collection for Augsburg and one of the most famous such collections in Europe,[53] they will be considered in a second case study.

4 The *Fuggerzeitungen*: A News Collection in Its European Context

The collecting history of the Fugger newsletters provides important information about the status of news for the European patrician and noble elites. The chronologically organized collection, bound in annual volumes, comprises handwritten newsletters from professional newsgatherers, economic agents, clerks of the imperial court, and officers in the Habsburg armies. The surviving 27 volumes cover the period from 1568–69 to 1604–05. The earliest of these yearly volumes, which Octavian Secundus ordered to be bound together, were not assembled by active merchants, but by young men who had not yet even inherited their family fortune.[54] Collecting news therefore was not necessarily

---

51 Kölderer, *Beschreibunng*; Tschopp, "Wie aus Nachrichten Geschichte wird".
52 The broadsheet was printed by Hans Schultes in Augsburg. For more information about this case, see Bauer, *Zeitungen vor der Zeitung*, pp. 349–50. Georg Kölderer also bought the broadsheet; see the image in Kölderer, *Beschreibunng*, vol. 2, p. 627.
53 See Pettegree, *Invention of News*, pp. 113–16.
54 For their biographies, see Hildebrandt, *Die "Georg Fuggerischen Erben"*.

associated with economic interests, even if Octavian Secundus and Philipp Eduard Fugger founded a company of their own in the late 1570s.

Obviously, the brothers deemed it necessary to be informed about current events in Europe and beyond. It was part of their self-conception as members of a well-informed elite. They perceived themselves as participants in a kind of competition with members of their social network and took a strong interest in topics not directly related to their own economic pursuits.[55] The range of news was mainly of a European scope – correspondingly, the handwritten newsletters mostly came from news centers like Venice, Rome, Antwerp, and Cologne.[56] The diligent collection and annual binding of handwritten newspapers from all over Europe also reveals their view that newsletters were important repositories of events worthy of storing and memorizing. We also find news collections of various extents in a number of European libraries and archives, usually as part of princely, urban, or scholarly collections, indicating a comparable interest in their preservation.[57] Beyond that, the economic benefits derived from the information conveyed by handwritten newspapers should not be neglected, as underscored by recent work on the Fugger newsletters.[58]

Current research does not consider the Fugger newsletters as a medium of dissemination to a wider audience, but rather as an indicator for the existence and quality of news-gathering and long-distance communication in Augsburg.[59] By comparison, Marx and Hans Fugger seem to have sent news to many more people than their cousins Octavian Secundus and Philipp Eduard, mainly to members of the noble elite.[60]

---

55 In a letter to their agent in Venice in 1590, they complained about the quality of the news sent by a Venetian gazetteer, noting that others had received more detailed information. Furthermore, the Fugger newsletters present a wide thematic range, including reports about miracles, spectacular executions, etc. Bauer, *Zeitungen vor der Zeitung*, pp. 134–35, 142–46, 196–201. For further references, see Bauer's bibliography, and Keller and Molino, *Fuggerzeitungen im Kontext*.

56 Recent research stresses the "pan-European" character of early modern news networks: Zwierlein, *Discorso und Lex Dei*, p. 600; Bauer, *Zeitungen vor der Zeitung*, p. 367; Raymond, "News Networks". Cologne attained its status not only because of its importance as an imperial city and a commercial center, but also because direct communication with Antwerp was severely affected by warfare during the Dutch Revolt. In this context, Cologne served as an alternative place of communication. For the consequences concerning courier routes, see Dauser, *Informationskultur*, pp. 126–27.

57 See the list of German collections in Keller and Molino, *Fuggerzeitungen im Kontext*, pp. 184–96.

58 Bauer, *Zeitungen vor der Zeitung*, pp. 141–42.

59 Bauer, *Zeitungen vor der Zeitung*, p. 360.

60 Zwierlein, *Discorso und Lex Dei*, p. 599. Both Zwierlein (pp. 595–97) and Bauer (*Zeitungen vor der Zeitung*, pp. 354–58) stress that German princes exchanged newsletters and often received news which they had earlier obtained from the Fugger Company.

By comparing certain news mentioned in both Hans Fugger's letters and the Fugger newsletters, Oswald Bauer gained important insights into the sources available to the Augsburg elite. In order to acquire a full picture of political events like the contested election of the king of Poland in the 1570s, several sources had to be combined. Hans Fugger's excellent sources at the imperial court provided detailed reports about the emperor's view, whereas Italian newspapers, which were more systematically collected in the Fugger newsletters, contained better information about the intentions of the Hungarian magnate Báthory. Handwritten newspapers did not necessarily present fewer details. It was the quality of the sources that mattered – the more diverse and reliable the sources, the more complete the information. On the whole, both branches of the family – Marx and Hans Fugger on the one side, and Philipp Eduard and Octavian Secundus Fugger on the other – often benefited from identical sources; they even ordered newspapers from the same Italian *gazzettieri*, who obviously enjoyed a good reputation. Handwritten newsletters identical in content with some Fugger newsletters can also be identified in other contemporary collections.[61] Yet personal relationships with experts, which had to be maintained by social interaction and exchange (as revealed in Hans Fugger's correspondence) remained important.[62] This continued to be true in the seventeenth century, when the Augsburg art broker Philipp Hainhofer (1578–1647) tried to establish contacts with high-ranking customers. Maintaining social relations was clearly facilitated by the regular transfer of handwritten news.[63]

Handwritten news provided by gazetteers and printed news were closely intertwined. In a number of cases, Octavian Secundus and Philipp Eduard Fugger must have drawn their information from the same sources as printers; Michael Schilling has identified more than 20 printed news broadsheets whose content was nearly identical with that of the Fugger newsletters. As research on the history of the press emphasizes, the form of handwritten newspapers that we find in the Fugger newsletters was directly adopted by the first weekly printed newspapers. In the late sixteenth century, the first steps toward the printing of news periodicals were undertaken, for example the so-called *Messrelationen* (collections of news published on the dates of important fairs) by Michael von Eitzing in Cologne[64] or the monthly news collection *Annus Christi*, compiled by Samuel Dilbaum (1530–c. 1618) of Augsburg in 1597. By that time Dilbaum was already known for newsprints produced in Rorschach

---

61   Bauer, *Zeitungen vor der Zeitung*, pp. 227–31, 353–65.
62   See Bauer, *Zeitungen vor der Zeitung*, p. 349.
63   Behringer, *Im Zeichen des Merkur*, pp. 338–39.
64   Rosseaux, "Entstehung der Messrelationen"; Körber, *Messrelationen*, esp. pp. 41–90.

(near Lake Constance).[65] Michael Manger, an Augsburg printer with a wide production range, began to edit enumerated news pamphlets about the war against the Ottoman empire in the 1590s, but this enterprise was as short-lived as the other mentioned publication projects.[66] The production of broadsheets and printed news pamphlets continued, however, and the business of professional newsgathering is documented at least until the 1680s. The handwritten *Wochendliche Staats Zeitung* (Weekly State Newspaper), for example, was sold supra-regionally, as evidence from Saxony shows.[67]

5   News Media in the Seventeenth and Eighteenth Century

Given the excellent supply of information from all major European news centers and its status as one of the most important printing locations of the Empire, it appears astonishing that Augsburg was not among the places of publication for the first weekly printed newspapers. So far, we can only speculate about the reasons. At the beginning of the seventeenth century, the local printing business underwent a severe crisis,[68] intensified by the economic consequences of the Thirty Years' War, which ravaged Augsburg and devastated its economy. In the post-war Empire, the major economic centers were clearly no longer in the south, but in the northwest, with maritime trade becoming increasingly important. While Augsburg never regained the economic status it had held during the "golden age" of the sixteenth century, the city gradually began to recover from the wartime crisis in the later seventeenth century, partly because of immigration by entrepreneurs from other regions.[69]

In the 1670s, Jakob Koppmayer (1640–1701) opened a new chapter of news dissemination in Augsburg by obtaining the city council's permanent permission to print a weekly newspaper.[70] After several of his earlier publications had been prohibited, Koppmayer finally succeeded in convincing the censorship committee and the council that the community could only benefit from his

---

65   On Dilbaum, see Schilling, "Augsburger Einblattdruck", p. 384 (including further references).
66   Hans-Jörg Künast provided me with information about Michael Manger's printings on the "Turkish" war. See also Dresler, *Augsburg und die Frühgeschichte der Presse*, pp. 36–39.
67   Mančal, "Augsburger Zeitungen", p. 685.
68   See Chapter 18 in this volume.
69   See Chapter 5 in this volume.
70   On local newspapers, see Mančal, "Augsburger Zeitungen"; idem, "München-Augsburger Abendzeitung".

newspaper and that public order would not be endangered.[71] Thus, Augsburg caught up with a development that had begun nearly 70 years before: In 1605, the first weekly printed newspaper (*Relation*) had been founded in Strasbourg, and in 1650 the first daily newspaper (with six editions a week) was being published in Leipzig.[72]

One of the rare early printed local newspapers that has survived, an issue of Koppmayer's *Fried-bringende Neue Avisen* ("Peace-Bringing News Reports") from February 1679, demonstrates that its editor and printer had managed to build up a correspondence network in order to deliver news from the most important European theaters of action. On four pages in quarto format, Koppmayer gathered political and court news from Paris, Brussels, Nijmegen, various places in the Empire, Danzig, Copenhagen and – with broad coverage – Vienna. He combined several news items in short sentences under each city's name. The newsletter style, including references to time and place ("today", "tomorrow", "here"), was preserved, as was typical for contemporary newspapers.[73]

Koppmayer's newspaper soon experienced heavy competition, as his former assistant August Sturm applied for permission to print another weekly newspaper and for the prohibition of further editions of Koppmayer's paper in 1686. The appeal for confessional equality in the printing sector between the Protestant Koppmayer and the Catholic Sturm – an important, sometimes abused argument in the bi-confessional city[74] – obviously exacerbated competition. The struggle for an exclusive printing privilege went on for years and included petitions to Emperor Leopold I. During this time, both newspapers, regardless of the conflicting privileges each of the two printers had obtained, continued to be published under nearly identical titles: Koppmayer sold his as the *Wochentlich-Ordinari-Post-Zeitung*, whereas the successors of Sturm (who died in 1695) printed the *Wochentliche Ordinari-Post-Zeitung* (both translate roughly as "Weekly Regular Postal Newspaper"). The two papers, which were issued daily from 1718 onwards,[75] presented the usual range of European political news without editorial comments.

---

71   StadtAA, Reichsstadt, Censuramt 1649–1753, Bl. 109; Mančal, "Augsburger Zeitungen", p. 693. Publication bans for newspapers were frequent, as rulers regarded politics as an *arcanum*, which should not be available to the common man; see Weber, "Kontrollmechanismen".
72   For a concise early history of the printed newspaper, see Weber, "Early German Newspaper".
73   Staats- und Stadtbibliothek Augsburg, Rar 70.
74   The bi-confessional character of Augsburg has been explored by François, *Die unsichtbare Grenze*; on confessional parity, see Chapter 11 in this volume.
75   Both newspapers underwent several changes in title, like other Augsburg periodicals of the eighteenth and nineteenth centuries. A useful overview, including title variants, can be found in Mançal, "Augsburger Zeitungen", pp. 721–32; for a similar index, published

Two of Sturm's successors, the printer and editor Joseph Anton Moy (1727–1813) and the editor Tobias Brandmüller, oversaw the emergence of the *Ordinari-Post-Zeitung* as the leading south German newspaper and one of the most widely read dailies in the Empire. At its peak around 1800, it had a print run of 11,000 to 13,000 copies, more than two-thirds sold out of town. By this time, Augsburg had successfully regained a predominant position on the German news market. Its timeliness and the high quality of its correspondence network are demonstrated by news about the French Revolution, with decisions of the national assembly in Paris appearing in the *Ordinari-Post-Zeitung* within only a few days.[76]

The local competitor was less successful: neither Koppmayer's son-in-law, Andreas Maschenbauer (1660–1727), printer and editor of the *Wochentlich-Ordinari-Post-Zeitung* since 1701, nor his son, could compete with Sturm's and his successors' newspaper. It was not until the grandson Johann Andreas Erdmann Maschenbauer (1719–73) assumed control that the print run increased, reaching at least 950 copies in 1754, when Maschenbauer sold his printing office to Johann Michael Wagner.[77]

Besides these two newspapers, a whole range of periodical news journals were printed and edited in Augsburg from the late seventeenth century onwards – most of them short-lived, which was a common phenomenon on the German printing market. One of these was the *Monatliche Staats-Spiegel* ("Monthly State Mirror"), printed by Andreas Maschenbauer from 1698 to 1709, a collection of select European news items and official documents (such as resolutions of the imperial diet at Regensburg or extracts from European peace treaties) arranged country by country. Such publications were relatively easy to compile from various sources – *aus besonders guten Correspondentzen und Nachrichten*[78] ("from especially good correspondents and new reports"), as the title tells us – and official publications. They gave a comprehensive overview of important events and decisions and – in contrast to newspapers – commented on them as well.

These printed newspapers, much like their written predecessors, usually did not include local news. For Augsburg – as for many other contemporary cities and towns – this gap was at least partly filled by a special weekly periodical

---

online by the Universitätsbibliothek Augsburg, see https://www.uni-augsburg.de/de/organisation/bibliothek/nutzen-leihen/augsburg-zeitungen/ [09.12.2019].

76   See, for example, the issue of 9 September 1789 (on the French constitution). I thank Barbara Rajkay for this reference. For online access, see http://digital.bib-bvb.de/R?func=collections&collection_id=2677&local_base=UBA [09.12.2019].

77   Mančal, "Augsburger Zeitungen", p. 703.

78   Staats- und Stadtbibliothek Augsburg, Stw 7312.

or "intelligencer" (*Intelligenzblatt*), called *Augspurgischer Intelligenz-Zettel* ("Augsburg Intelligence Note"). It was Johann Andreas Erdmann Maschenbauer who started to print this information leaflet in 1745, on the model of a widely adopted media type that had been around since the first German intelligencer was published in 1722 in Frankfurt based on French and English examples.[79] Thus far, research on the *Augspurgische Intelligenz-Zettel* has mainly focused on Maschenbauer's enlightened intentions, displayed in his articles on morality, frugality, nutrition, housekeeping, scientific (especially technical) findings and innovations, and similar topics of "practical" enlightenment.[80] But news in the *Intelligenz-Zettel* also included information about the city and its inhabitants, intertwined with the intelligencers' original function as an advertising paper (developing out of the so-called intelligence bureaus[81]). The first columns were always dedicated to private and professional purchases and sales. They were followed by rental offers and requests; incidents of theft; information about lost and found property; the labor market; price lists for grain, bread, and meat; lottery draws; information about people who had lately arrived and found accommodation in a local hotel; incidents of birth and death; and some (very short and irregularly inserted) news about local events. The latter information does not entirely conform to the modern idea of local news, but Maschenbauer did present interesting insights into everyday social and economic life in Augsburg, an area that needs to be further explored.

Maschenbauer, who died in 1777, and his successors never tried to include news from places beyond Augsburg on a regular basis. From an economic point of view, this was probably a reasonable decision, in light of the problematic position of Maschenbauer's daily newspaper. The main characteristics of an intelligencer were preserved when the *Intelligenz-Zettel* was turned into an official information leaflet of the now royal Bavarian city in 1806–07. Step by step, the articles with enlightened intentions were reduced in number and replaced primarily by official announcements.[82] The *Wochentliche Ordinari-Post-Zeitung* likewise continued to be published in the nineteenth century, although it could not compete with Johann Friedrich Cotta's *Allgemeine Zeitung*, which was transferred from Ulm to Augsburg in 1810. Cotta's newspaper opened a further chapter in the history of Augsburg news publications with a European

---

79 Böning has dedicated a series of publications to this long-neglected form of periodicals, e.g. Böning, "Intelligenzblatt".
80 See Doering-Manteuffel et al. (eds.), *Pressewesen der Aufklärung*; for the items of interest here, see Mančal, "Wissensorganisation und Wissensvermittlung"; Künast, "Maschenbauer".
81 See Tantner, *Die ersten Suchmaschinen*.
82 Mančal, "Augsburger Intelligenzblatt".

reputation. By 1800, Augsburg had become a major news center again, and it was able to stabilize this position after its era as a free imperial city had come to an end.

Bibliography

Unpublished Primary Sources
Stadtarchiv Augsburg (StadtAA)
  Reichsstadt, Censuramt 1649–1753.
  Schätze 37.

Published Primary Sources
Fried-bringende Neue Avisen, February 1679 (Staats- und Stadtbibliothek Augsburg, Rar 70).
Greiff, B. (ed.), *Tagebuch des Lucas Rem aus den Jahren 1494–1541. Ein Beitrag zur Handelsgeschichte der Stadt Augsburg*, Augsburg, 1861.
Karnehm, C. (ed.), *Die Korrespondenz Hans Fuggers von 1566–1594. Regesten der Kopierbücher aus dem Fuggerarchiv*, 3 vols., Munich, 2003.
Kölderer, G., *Beschreibunng vnnd Kurtze Vertzaichnus Fürnemer Lob vnnd gedenckhwürdiger Historien. Eine Chronik der Stadt Augsburg der Jahre 1576 bis 1607*, ed. S. Strodel and Wolfgang E.J. Weber, 4 vols., Augsburg, 2013.
Monatlicher Staats-Spiegel 1698–1709 (Staats- und Stadtbibliothek Augsburg, Stw 7312).

Secondary Literature
Arblaster, P., Belo, A., Espejo, C., Haffemayer, S., Infelise, N., Moxham, N., Raymond, J. and Schobesberger, N., "The Lexicons of Early Modern News", in J. Raymond and N. Moxham (eds.), *News Networks in Early Modern Europe*, Leiden, 2016, pp. 64–101.
Barbarics, Z. and Pieper, R., "Handwritten Newsletters as a Means of Communication in Early Modern Europe", in F. Bethencourt and F. Egmond (eds.), *Cultural Exchange in Early Modern Europe. Vol. 3: Correspondence and Cultural Exchange in Europe, 1400–1700*, Cambridge, 2007, pp. 53–79.
Behringer, W., *Im Zeichen des Merkur. Reichspost und Kommunikationsrevolution in der Frühen Neuzeit*, Göttingen, 2003.
Böning, H., "Das Intelligenzblatt", in E. Fischer, W. Haefs, and Y.-G. Mix (eds.), *Von Almanach bis Zeitung. Ein Handbuch der Medien in Deutschland 1700–1800*, Munich, 1999, pp. 89–104.
Böning, H., "'Gewiss ist es/dass alle gedruckten Zeitungen erst geschrieben seyn müssen': Handgeschriebene und gedruckte Zeitung im Spannungsfeld von Abhängigkeit, Koexistenz und Konkurrenz", *Daphnis* 37 (2008), pp. 203–42.

Brednich, R.W., *Die Liedpublizistik im Flugblatt des 15. bis 17. Jahrhunderts*, 2 vols., Baden-Baden, 1974–75.

Büchler, V., "Die Zensur im frühneuzeitlichen Augsburg 1515–1806", *Zeitschrift des Historischen Vereins für Schwaben* 84 (1991), pp. 69–128.

Costa, G., "Die Rechtseinrichtung der Zensur in der Reichsstadt Augsburg", *Zeitschrift des Historischen Vereins für Schwaben und Neuburg* 42 (1916), pp. 1–82.

Dauser, R., *Informationskultur und Beziehungswissen. Das Korrespondenznetz Hans Fuggers (1531–1598)*, Tübingen, 2008.

Dauser, R. and Ferber, M.U., *Die Fugger und Welser. Vom Mittelalter bis zur Gegenwart*, Augsburg, 2010.

Doering-Manteuffel, S., Mančal, J. and Wüst, W. (eds.), *Pressewesen der Aufklärung. Periodische Schriften im Alten Reich*, Berlin, 2001.

Dresler, A., *Augsburg und die Frühgeschichte der Presse*, Munich, 1952.

François, E., *Die unsichtbare Grenze. Protestanten und Katholiken in Augsburg 1648–1806*, Sigmaringen, 1991.

Häberlein, M., "Monster und Missionare: Die außereuropäische Welt in Augsburger Drucken der frühen Neuzeit", in H. Gier and J. Janota (eds.), *Augsburger Buchdruck und Verlagswesen. Von den Anfängen bis zur Gegenwart*, Wiesbaden, 1997, pp. 353–80.

Häberlein, M., "Der Fondaco dei Tedeschi in Venedig und der Italienhandel oberdeutscher Kaufleute (ca. 1450–1650)", in H.-M. Körner and F. Schuller (ed.), *Bayern und Italien. Kontinuität und Wandel ihrer traditionellen Bindungen*, Lindenberg, 2010, pp. 124–39.

Häberlein, M., *The Fuggers of Augsburg: Pursuing Wealth and Honor in Renaissance Germany*, Charlottesville and London, 2012.

Heimann, H.-D., "Brievedregher: Kommunikations- und alltagsgeschichtliche Zugänge zur vormodernen Postgeschichte und Dienstleistungskultur", in H. Hundsbichler (ed.), *Kommunikation und Alltag in Spätmittelalter und früher Neuzeit*, Vienna, 1992, pp. 251–92.

Helbig, J., *Postvermerke auf Briefen, 15.–18. Jahrhundert. Neue Ansichten zur Postgeschichte der frühen Neuzeit und der Stadt Nürnberg*, Munich, 2010.

Hildebrandt, R., *Die "Georg Fuggerischen Erben". Kaufmännische Tätigkeit und sozialer Status 1555–1600*, Berlin, 1966.

Infelise, M., *Prima dei giornali. Alle origini della pubblica informazione*, Rome, 2002.

Infelise, M., "From Merchants' Letters to Handwritten Political *Avvisi*: Notes on the Origins of Public Information", in F. Bethencourt and F. Egmond (eds.), *Cultural Exchange in Early Modern Europe. Vol. 3: Correspondence and Cultural Exchange in Europe, 1400–1700*, Cambridge, 2007, pp. 33–52.

Infelise, M., "News Networks between Italy and Europe", in B. Dooley (ed.), *The Dissemination of News and the Emergence of Contemporaneity in Early Modern Europe*, Aldershot, 2010, pp. 51–67.

Keller, K. and Molino, P., *Die Fuggerzeitungen im Kontext. Zeitungssammlungen im Alten Reich und in Italien*, Vienna, 2015.

Körber, E.-B., *Messrelationen. Geschichte der deutsch- und lateinischsprachigen "messentlichen" Periodika von 1588 bis 1805*, Bremen, 2016.

Kränzler, P., "Die Augsburger Botenanstalt", *Archiv für Post und Telegraphie* 4 (1876), pp. 658–62.

Künast, H.-J., "Johann Andreas Erdmann Maschenbauer, sein Augsburger Intelligenz-Zettel und der Buchmarkt in der zweiten Hälfte des 18. Jahrhunderts", in S. Doering-Manteuffel, J. Mančal, and W. Wüst (eds.), *Pressewesen der Aufklärung. Periodische Schriften im Alten Reich*, Berlin, 2001, pp. 337–55.

Lankes, O., "Zur Postgeschichte der Reichsstadt Augsburg", *Archiv für Postgeschichte in Bayern* 2 (1926), pp. 39–49, 68–81.

Mančal, J., "Zu Augsburger Zeitungen vom Ende des 17. bis zur Mitte des 19. Jahrhunderts: Abendzeitung, Postzeitung und Intelligenzzettel", in H. Gier and J. Janota (eds.), *Augsburger Buchdruck und Verlagswesen. Von den Anfängen bis zur Gegenwart*, Wiesbaden, 1997, pp. 683–733.

Mančal, J., "Wissensorganisation und -vermittlung im Augsburger Intelligenzblatt: Aspekte einer praktischen Enzyklopädie", in W.E.J. Weber and T. Stammen (eds.), *Wissenssicherung, Wissensordnung und Wissensverarbeitung. Das europäische Modell der Enzyklopädien*, Berlin, 2004, pp. 413–31.

Mauelshagen, F., "Netzwerke des Nachrichtenaustauschs: Für einen Paradigmenwechsel in der Erforschung der 'neuen Zeitungen'", in J. Burkhardt and C. Werkstetter (eds.), *Kommunikation und Medien in der Frühen Neuzeit*, Munich, 2005, pp. 409–25.

Pettegree, A., *The Invention of News: How the World Came to Know about Itself*, New Haven, 2014.

Pieper, R., *Die Vermittlung einer neuen Welt. Amerika im Nachrichtennetz des Habsburgischen Imperiums, 1493–1598*, Mainz, 2000.

Pölnitz, G., "Jakob Fuggers Zeitungen und Briefe an die Fürsten des Hauses Wettin in der Frühzeit Karls V. 1519–1525", *Nachrichten von der Akademie der Wissenschaften in Göttingen. Philosophisch-Historische Klasse* 2 (1941), pp. 89–160.

Raymond, J., "News Networks: Putting the 'News' and 'Networks' Back in", in idem and N. Moxham (eds.), *News Networks in Early Modern Europe*, Leiden, 2016, pp. 102–29.

Rosseaux, U., "Die Entstehung der Messrelationen: Zur Entwicklung eines frühneuzeitlichen Nachrichtenmediums aus der Zeitgeschichtsschreibung des 16. Jahrhunderts", *Historisches Jahrbuch* 124 (2004), pp. 97–123.

Schilling, M., "Der Augsburger Einblattdruck", in H. Gier and J. Janota (eds.), *Augsburger Buchdruck und Verlagswesen. Von den Anfängen bis zur Gegenwart*, Wiesbaden, 1997, pp. 381–404.

Schilling, M., "Zwischen Mündlichkeit und Druck: Die Fuggerzeitungen", in H.-G. Roloff (ed.), *Editionsdesiderate zur Frühen Neuzeit. Beiträge zur Tagung der Kommission für die Edition von Texten der Frühen Neuzeit*, Amsterdam, 1997, vol. 2, pp. 717–27.

Schilling, M., "Die Lieder des Augsburger Kolporteurs Thomas Kern aus den Anfangsjahren des Dreißigjährigen Krieges", in N.-A. Bringéus (ed.), *Popular Prints and Imagery*, Stockholm, 2001, pp. 49–68.

Schilling, M., "Stadt und Publizistik in der Frühen Neuzeit", in idem and W. Harms (eds.), *Das illustrierte Flugblatt der Frühen Neuzeit: Traditionen – Wirkungen – Kontexte*, Stuttgart, 2008, pp. 347–70 (first publication in K. Garber, S. Anders and T. Elsmann (eds.), *Stadt und Literatur im deutschen Sprachraum der Frühen Neuzeit*, Tübingen, 1998, pp. 112–41).

Schobesberger, N., Arblaster, P., Infelise, M., Belo, A., Moxham, N., Espejo, C. and Raymond, J., "European Postal Networks", in J. Raymond and N. Moxham (eds.), *News Networks in Early Modern Europe*, Leiden, 2016, pp. 19–63.

Sporhan-Krempel, L., *Nürnberg als Nachrichtenzentrum zwischen 1400 und 1700*, Nuremberg, 1968.

Tantner, A., *Die ersten Suchmaschinen. Adressbüros, Fragämter, Intelligenz-Comptoirs*, Berlin, 2015.

Trauchburg-Kuhnle, G., "Kooperation und Konkurrenz: Augsburger Kaufleute in Antwerpen", in J. Burkhardt (ed.), *Augsburger Handelshäuser im Wandel des historischen Urteils*, Berlin, 1996, pp. 210–23.

Tschopp, S.S., "Wie aus Nachrichten Geschichte wird: Die Bedeutung publizistischer Quellen für die Augsburger Chronik des Georg Kölderer", *Daphnis* 37 (2008), pp. 33–78.

Veluwenkamp, J.W., "International Business Communication Patterns in the Dutch Commercial System, 1500–1800", in H. Cools, M. Keblusek and B. Noldus (eds.), *Your Humble Servant: Agents in Early Modern Europe*, Hilversum, 2006, pp. 121–34.

Weber, J., "Kontrollmechanismen im deutschen Zeitungswesen des 17. Jahrhunderts: Ein kleiner Beitrag zur Geschichte der Zensur", *Jahrbuch für Kommunikationsgeschichte* 6 (2004), pp. 56–73.

Weber, J., "The Early German Newspaper – A Medium of Contemporaneity", in B. Dooley (ed.), *The Dissemination of News and the Emergence of Contemporaneity in Early Modern Europe*, Aldershot, 2010, pp. 69–79.

Welser, J.M., *Die Welser*, vol. 1, Nuremberg, 1917.

Werner, T.G., "Das kaufmännische Nachrichtenwesen im späten Mittelalter und in der frühen Neuzeit und sein Einfluß auf die Entstehung der handschriftlichen Zeitung", *Scripta Mercaturae* 2 (1975), pp. 3–51.

Wüst, W., "Reichsstädtische Kommunikation in Franken und Schwaben: Nachrichtennetze für Bürger, Räte und Kaufleute im Spätmittelalter", *Zeitschrift für bayerische Landesgeschichte* 62 (1999), pp. 681–707.

Zwierlein, C., *Discorso und Lex Dei. Die Entstehung neuer Denkrahmen im 16. Jahrhundert und die Wahrnehmung der französischen Religionskriege in Italien und Deutschland*, Göttingen, 2006.

Zwierlein, C., "Fuggerzeitungen als Ergebnis von italienisch-deutschem Kulturtransfer", *Quellen und Forschungen aus italienischen Archiven und Bibliotheken* 90 (2010), pp. 169–224.

Electronic Resources

Mančal, J., "Augsburgischer Intelligenz-Zettel/ Amtsblatt der Stadt Augsburg", in *Historisches Lexikon Bayerns*, URL: http://www.historisches-lexikon-bayerns.de/Lexikon/Augsburgischer Intelligenz-Zettel / Amtsblatt der Stadt Augsburg (published on 17 September 2012; accessed on 7 October 2016) [30.04.2018].

Mančal, J., "München-Augsburger Abendzeitung", in *Historisches Lexikon Bayerns*, URL: http://www.historisches-lexikon-bayerns.de/Lexikon/München-Augsburger Abendzeitung (published on 30 January 2009; accessed on 7 October 2016) [30.04.2018].

Universitätsbibliothek Augsburg, digitized copies of the *Ordinari-Post-Zeitung*, 1768–1848: http://digital.bib-bvb.de/R?func=collections&collection_id=2677&local_base=UBA [09.12.2019].

Universitätsbibliothek Augsburg, list of newspapers published in Augsburg: https://www.uni-augsburg.de/de/organisation/bibliothek/nutzen-leihen/augsburg-zeitungen/ [09.12.2019].

CHAPTER 18

Book Production and Trade

Hans-Jörg Künast
Translated by Christine R. Johnson

The printing, bookselling, and publishing industries, along with the production of graphic arts, belong alongside textiles and gold- and silversmithing to the formative branches of trade in the imperial city of Augsburg.[1] The first printed work in Augsburg, published on 12 March 1468 in the printing house of Günther Zainer (1468–78),[2] appeared at an opportune moment: beginning around 1470, southern Germany experienced a long period of economic growth, innovation, and vitality, from which Augsburg in particular profited.[3] The invention of movable type printing was one of the most significant technological innovations, introducing a production process with a multi-step workflow that represented a turning point in the history of technology.[4] Marking the onset of industrial mass production and resulting in the first mass media in history,[5] printing qualitatively and quantitatively transformed political and social developments. The Reformation, for example, would have been unthinkable without the printing press.[6]

Augsburg held a unique position among German printing centers in the early modern period. From the fifteenth to the seventeenth centuries, it was the only city in Europe in which more vernacular than Latin books were published. In the eighteenth century, when the production of vernacular books increased elsewhere under the influence of the popular Enlightenment, Augsburg once again went in the opposite direction, publishing a growing number of Latin-language texts. The reasons for these developments will be explored in the following chapter. A noteworthy aspect of Augsburg publishing that unfortunately cannot be examined in depth here is the printing of

---

1 Augsburg has correctly been characterized as an "image factory" (*Bilderfabrik*) in light of its importance for the German-speaking lands in the field of graphic reproduction: Paas (ed.), *Augsburg*.
2 Date ranges associated with individual printers indicate period active.
3 See Chapter 5 in this volume.
4 Wolfgang von Stromer emphasizes that the invention of movable type was the result of technological innovation in a variety of industries ranging from metallurgy to papermaking: Stromer, "Große Innovationen".
5 Werfel, "Einrichtung und Betrieb", pp. 97–124; Reske, "Drucken", pp. 16–29.
6 Martin Luther's influence on Wittenberg's rise to an important printing center is explored in Pettegree, *Brand Luther*.

illustrated books, for which printers, woodblock cutters (*Formschneider*), and engravers collaborated particularly closely and symbiotically to adorn books in all genres with woodblock prints and copper engravings.[7]

1 State of the Scholarship

Bibliographers and historians began researching the early history of Augsburg printing at the end of the eighteenth century, beginning by cataloguing extant book collections and gathering information about the printers. These efforts produced pioneering work by Georg Wolfgang Panzer and Georg Wilhelm Zapf on Augsburg printing in the fifteenth and early sixteenth centuries.[8] Carl Wehmer's 1933 study used archival sources to show that, in the fifteenth century, the prominence of a printer's shop correlated strongly with the level of taxes he paid and the number of times he appeared in Augsburg's archival records, thus demonstrating the necessity of studying printers in their social and economic environments.[9] Other studies examined individual printers, publishing programs, and specifics about the development of the printing process before 1500, of which only the highlights can be outlined here.[10]

Albert Schramm demonstrated the importance of Augsburg's first printer, Günther Zainer, in setting the stage for the future direction of local publishing, and provided evidence of Zainer's increasing emphasis on illustrated vernacular books.[11] The Benedictine monastery of Sts. Ulrich and Afra and its abbot, Melchior von Stammheim, were also of central importance in the first decade of Augsburg book publishing. Almost all of Augsburg's significant printers working during the fifteenth century had a relationship with the Benedictines. From 1472 to 1476/77, the monastery even ran its own press in the service of the reform movement associated with the monastery at Melk.[12]

A study of Erhard Ratdolt (1486–1522), who worked in Venice from 1476 to 1485 before moving to Augsburg, describes a significant but atypical local printer, as Ratdolt published only limited numbers of German-language texts.

---

7   Overviews in König, "Augsburger Buchkunst"; Ott, "Frühe Augsburger Buchillustration"; Appuhn-Radtke, "Augsburger Buchillustration"; Augustyn, "Augsburger Buchillustration".
8   Panzer, *Ausführliche Beschreibung*; Zapf, *Annales*; Zapf, *Augsburgs Buchdruckgeschichte*.
9   Wehmer, "Zur Beurteilung des Methodenstreits".
10 A bibliography of older literature (up to 1992) on the incunabula period is available in Corsten and Fuchs, *Buchdruck*; important work since 1992 is described in Hägele and Thierbach, *Augsburg macht Druck*.
11 Schramm, "Günther Zainer".
12 Hägele, "Top oder Flop?"; Eisermann, "A Golden Age?"; see also Chapter 20 in this volume.

Instead, he worked closely with the church to supply a number of bishoprics with liturgical literature. He also published astronomical-astrological works, spurred by his personal interests and contacts.[13]

Johannes Bämler, another early printer, who also engaged in book trading and illumination as well as owning a paper mill, has likewise received scholarly attention.[14] Of particular interest has been his vernacular output and its language usage, which demonstrate Bämler's efforts to transmit knowledge to new audiences.[15] Research on Bämler emphasizes that Augsburg rose as a center of German-language book culture by redefining the relationship between author and public through the mediating editorial work of printers.

As a result of their many publications in German, the first printers in Augsburg contributed substantially to the unification of the German language. For Johannes Rynmann (1489–1522), the most significant publisher and bookseller before the Reformation, the Augsburg dialect was the most intelligible in all of Germany, leading him to have almost all of his German-language publications printed there.[16] Over a quarter (27.3 per cent) of all German-language incunabula (books published before 1500) came from Augsburg presses, according to the calculations of Manfred Sauer.[17] It is not surprising, therefore, that linguists have long been interested in the printed language of Augsburg, agreeing on the city's central role in the publication of High German texts from the earliest years of printing to at least the 1540s.[18]

The period after 1500 has been less intensively examined than the fifteenth century. A series of more or less exhaustive studies of individual printers had appeared by the 1980s which, although helpful in themselves, did not paint a complete picture. The most important portrayals are those of the workshops of Hans Gegler (1554–60), Hans von Erfurt (1518–20), and Alexander Weissenhorn (1528–39/40), as well as the early history of the printing shop of Philipp Ulhart the Elder (1523–67).[19] Josef Bellot's research on vernacular humanist writing, which formed an important component in the publishing program of Heinrich

---

13   Geissler, "Erhard Ratdolt".
14   Edmunds, "New Light on Johannes Bämler"; Beier, "Missalien massenhaft".
15   Leipold, "Das Verlagsprogramm", p. 243.
16   Tauler, *Predigten*, fol. 222r.
17   Sauer, *Die deutschen Inkunabeln*, p. 69. After Augsburg came Nuremberg with 11.5 per cent; Strasbourg with 9.3 per cent; Leipzig with 7.7 per cent; Ulm with 7.5 per cent; and Basel with 4.8 per cent.
18   Stopp, "Das in Augsburg gedruckte Hochdeutsch", p. 152; Fujii, *Günther Zainers druckersprachliche Leistung*; Mihm, "Druckersprachen".
19   Schottenloher, "Hans Werlich"; idem, "Hans Gegler"; idem, *Philipp Ulhart*; Eiden and Müller, "Alexander Weißenhorn".

Steiner (1522–47), is also worth noting.[20] For the second half of the sixteenth century, biographical treatments appeared only for Michael Manger (1570–1603) and the Schönig printing family (1572–1753),[21] to which must be added the overview of the first significant scholarly publisher in Augsburg, founded and financed by the humanist and mayor Marcus Welser under the name of *Ad insigne pinus* (1594–1614).[22]

The year 1997 marked a turning point in the scholarship on Augsburg printers and publishing. While earlier work had concentrated on the early history, that year saw the publication of a monograph based on archival sources and covering the period from the beginnings to the 1555 Religious Peace of Augsburg; an overview of Augsburg publishing in the seventeenth century; and a wide-ranging collection of essays that examined aspects of the Augsburg book trade up to the present day.[23] This research clarified the key factors and larger contexts that continued to shape Augsburg's publishing and book trade sectors into the modern era. Building on this work, additional scholarly publications on the history of local newspaper and magazine publishing[24] and on seventeenth- and eighteenth-century publishing houses appeared in the years following,[25] as well as more specialized studies on Jewish book printing,[26] the production and trade of printed musical materials,[27] modern foreign-language publishing,[28] printed maps,[29] and Augsburg's dominance in the book trade within the Habsburg dynastic lands.[30]

In comparison with other important German publishing centers, Augsburg's history in printing and publishing is thus well studied. Considerable lacunae remain, however, particularly for the eighteenth century (a period that is also under-researched for Augsburg more generally). This is especially the case for the large Catholic printers and publishers, which had their own distribution networks independent of the great book fairs in Frankfurt am Main and Leipzig.[31]

---

20   Bellot, *Augsburger volkssprachliches humanistisches Schrifttum*.
21   Rogister, "Michael Manger"; Wohnhaas, "Die Schönig".
22   Bellot, "Ad insigne pinus".
23   Künast, *"Getruckt zu Augspurg"*; idem, "Augsburg's Role"; idem, "Konfessionalität und Buchdruck"; Gier and Janota, *Augsburger Buchdruck*.
24   Künast, "Maschenbauer"; Fischer, *Johann Friedrich Cotta*.
25   Gier, "Augsburger Buchwesen"; idem, " Verlagslandschaft"; idem, "Stapelstadt".
26   Künast, "Hebräisch-jüdischer Buchdruck".
27   Lodes (ed.), *Niveau – Nische – Nimbus*; Künast, "Buchdruck und -handel".
28   Künast, "Augsbourg".
29   Ritter, "Augsburger Landkartenproduktion"; Ritter and Lotter, *Die Welt aus Augsburg*.
30   Künast, "Bücher für Tirol".
31   With the exception of Matthäus Rieger and the Bencard family, larger studies of important Catholic printers and publishers of the eighteenth century are lacking: Pörnbacher,

2   The Legal Framework for Augsburg Printing

Between the fifteenth and seventeenth centuries, any man who possessed the necessary capital and technical capabilities could open a print shop in Augsburg – there was no obligation to join a guild nor any other limitation, not even a citizenship requirement.[32] Someone like Heinrich Steiner, who was of illegitimate birth, could only operate independently as a printer because printing belonged to the "free trades". Although Steiner's dishonorable birth prevented him from being accepted into any of the local guilds, they could not stop him from practicing his profession.[33] Because the city council did not impose admission restrictions, established printers, who were concerned that substantial competition could threaten their survival, clashed regularly with bookbinders, illuminators (*Briefmaler*), and woodblock cutters, who hoped to find in printing another lucrative field of endeavor. Economic downturns in particular produced lengthy rows before the council.

Even before the Reformation, printers in Augsburg were required to swear an oath not to print defamatory material and to preserve the city's peace.[34] When the Reformation was officially introduced in 1537, so was a censorship office, although the Council still did not deem it necessary to pass a formal censorship law or to regulate printers. Instead, it based individual decisions on imperial law, which began with the decrees of the 1521 Diet of Worms and culminated with the Imperial Police Ordinance of 1577.[35]

In particular after 1585, both the censorship office and the council had to contend with repeated complaints by printers against illuminators,[36] finally leading them to issue Augsburg's first printer ordinance in 1614.[37] The ordinance, although never officially passed by the council, was drafted by the Catholic mayor Bernhard Rehlinger, and required prior review of planned publications and inclusion of a complete printer's imprint. For the first time, illuminators were prohibited from printing if they had not been properly trained. This restriction on illuminators was officially published only on 29 October 1648, after

---

"Matthäus Rieger"; Heitjan, "Bencard". On the Protestant printers and music publishers Johann Jakob Lotter the Elder and Younger, see Reinfurth, *Musikverlag Lotter*.

32   Johann Otmar (1502–14) and Erhard Öglin (1505–20/22) never obtained citizenship, and Alexander Weißenhorn, Heinrich Steiner, and Philipp Ulhart the Elder did so only after a decade or more in Augsburg: Künast, *"Getruckt zu Augspurg"*, pp. 42, 44, 47, 50.

33   Stadtarchiv Augsburg (StadtAA), Reichsstadt, Ratsbuch 16, fol. 46r (17 June 1530).

34   On censorship see Creasman, *Censorship*; Costa, "Rechtseinrichtung der Zensur"; Büchler, "Zensur"; Künast, *"Getruckt zu Augspurg"*, pp. 197–216.

35   On imperial censorship see Eisenhardt, *Die kaiserliche Aufsicht*.

36   StadtAA, Censuramt, Valentin Schönig (1572–1613) vs. Hans Schultes the Elder (1577–1619), 31 December 1585; Michael Manger vs. Hans Schultes the Elder, 21 July 1592.

37   This ordinance is published in Schilling, *Bildpublizistik*, pp. 393–95.

which they could print no more than one full sheet or four quarto pages, which in effect limited them to producing broadsheets and pamphlets.[38]

In 1649, new censorship regulations governing theological works appeared based on the principle of parity, so that two Protestant censors oversaw Protestant publications and two Catholic censors Catholic publications. When the printing ordinance was reissued on 29 January 1682, it included the requirement that before publication, all texts must be submitted for review by the four censors (or the relevant two in the case of religious material). This stipulation applied not only to new publications, but also to those which had already passed censorship review when they were published elsewhere.[39]

The age of printing as a "free trade" in Augsburg ended at the beginning of the eighteenth century. By 1709, after several new shop openings, there were 14 printers in business; only the trade fair city of Leipzig boasted more. In the face of this perceived threat to their livelihood, the established printers agreed privately among themselves to limit the total number of print shops to ten.[40] When this decision proved unenforceable, they petitioned the city council to transform their private agreement into a legal standard.[41] As a result, the printing trade was restructured along the same lines as other crafts. It was led by two guild principals (*Vorgeher*), selected from the master printers, and two assessors (*Assessoren*) from the journeymen who had completed their training. These positions were filled according to the principle of parity, and those selected had to be confirmed by the city censors. The printers were also placed under the jurisdiction of the newly established court of arts, trades, and crafts (*Kunst-, Gewerb- und Handwerks-Gericht*), finally putting them in the same position as all other local crafts.

A sizable gap could exist between legal norms and their application in specific circumstances, especially as the office of censor was unpaid. Augsburg's city council, in contrast to neighboring Bavaria, evinced little interest in strictly controlling print production or in interfering with the book trade, as most of the output was exported.[42] Only when the city's domestic peace appeared endangered, or in response to complaints from the emperor or powerful neighbors such as Bavaria or the bishop of Augsburg, was the council moved to act. The situation in 1547–48, for example, was particularly delicate for the printing trade. After his defeat of the Schmalkaldic League, Emperor

---

38   StadtAA, Handwerksgericht (uncatalogued collection).
39   Staats- und Stadtbibliothek Augsburg (SuStBA), 2° Cod. Aug. 324, no. 88, fols. 269f.
40   StadtAA, Reichsstadt, Handwerkerakten, Buchdrucker, Fasc. 1, fols. 123–26.
41   Decretum in Senatu, Augsburg, 12 October 1709; published in the printer ordinance of 1713. See SuStBA, 4° Cod. Aug. 1020, no. 64.
42   Büchler, "Zensur", pp. 121–26.

Charles V nullified Augsburg's existing guild constitution and imposed a new one on the city, which guaranteed the Catholics a clear majority on the council, thus positioning a nervous, Catholic-dominated authority against the exclusively Protestant producers of printed texts and graphics.[43] Between 1560 and 1630, supervision of the book trade on the part of the council was once again relatively loose; however, as the tensions of the Thirty Years' War reached their peak, the council's intrusions became onerous, simply enforcing the wishes of whichever power was currently occupying the city. Thus the Catholic printer Andreas Aperger (1617–58) was expelled from the city at the start of the Swedish occupation in 1632 because he was widely known as a Jesuit and Counter-Reformation printer.[44]

Finally, a continuing and consequential problem for the early modern book trade was the absence of a modern copyright law to prevent the unauthorized reprinting of successful publications. While one could seek a printing privilege guaranteeing exclusive publishing rights from the territorial ruler or from the emperor, such privileges were expensive, usually limited to ten years, and offered very limited protection against pirating.[45]

3   The Cultural Context

A decisive difference between Augsburg and other publishing hubs such as Cologne or Basel was the absence of a university.[46] The existence of Latin monastery schools since the late Middle Ages, the founding of the St. Anna *Gymnasium* (high school) and the city library in the 1530s, and the establishment of the Jesuit school St. Salvator in 1582 with financial support from the Fugger family could not make up for the lack of a university. Apparently, Augsburg's political and economic elites simply did not perceive a need for

---

43   For examples of harsh punishments for violating censorship laws before 1547, see Künast, "*Getruckt zu Augspurg*", pp. 211–16. Punishments even in this period were generally limited to confiscations, fines, and brief incarceration, although the pamphlet printer Hans Zimmermann was banished in 1571 after multiple infractions (which also included adultery). On the guild constitution and constitutional change in 1547–48, see Chapters 6 and 7 in this volume.

44   Künast, "Konfessionalität und Buchdruck", p. 108.

45   Koppitz, *Die kaiserlichen Druckprivilegien*; idem, "Kaiserliche Privilegien"; see also the conflict over printing privileges between 1635 and 1652, described below.

46   The advantages of a university town for printers are outlined in Guggisberg, "Reformierter Stadtstaat".

such an institution of higher learning,[47] and the council repeatedly rejected requests by learned men to found private Latin schools.[48]

The local market for academic literature therefore remained restricted to a small circle of literati. Of even greater consequence were the difficulties experienced by printers and publishers in finding suitable help to prepare material for publication by adapting, editing, correcting, and proofreading texts. For this reason, Augsburg authors such as Hieronymus Wolf preferred to entrust their Latin and Greek works to the larger publishing houses in Basel, where the necessary assistance was readily available. Such a favorable combination of well-capitalized printers or publishers with learned communities occurred in Augsburg only rarely, for example for a brief period in the decade before the Reformation, when the humanist circle that developed around the city secretary Conrad Peutinger included several printers in its ranks.[49] Even more productive was the cooperation between the *Ad insigne pinus* publishing house founded by Marcus Welser and the instructors at the St. Anna *Gymnasium*.[50]

Despite the absence of a university, the rich literary culture that flourished in Augsburg from the fifteenth century testifies to a self-confident lay public.[51] Even before the arrival of movable type printing, the manuscripts written in the Augsburg area included a higher percentage of vernacular texts than in other regions. Printers looked to this available pool for publishing ideas, selecting works already favored by urban elites.[52] Moreover, the formative Augsburg printers (with the exception of Günther Zainer) came from families with deep roots in the city and from crafts linked to the fine arts or the reproduction of illustrations and texts.[53] Thus they were familiar with the local cultural landscape.

In addition, German schools teaching reading, writing, and arithmetic were in operation from the fifteenth century and became increasingly numerous in the sixteenth century. In 1543, a year for which accurate records survive, there were twenty-four boys' and nine girls' schools, with individual teachers instructing up to a hundred pupils or more. A literacy rate of 30 per cent for

---

47 The Jesuit school was approved only with the assurance that it would not be turned into a university: Baer and Hecker (eds.), *Die Jesuiten*.
48 StadtAA, Evangelisches Wesensarchiv, no. 1042, vol. 1.
49 Künast, *"Getruckt zu Augspurg"*, pp. 95–100; on Peutinger's circle see Chapter 20 in this volume.
50 Bellot, "Ad insigne pinus".
51 Janota and Williams-Krapp (ed.), *Literarisches Leben*.
52 Micus, "Handschriftenproduktion".
53 Künast, *"Getruckt zu Augspurg"*, pp. 72–77.

Augsburg is therefore a realistic estimate, with most households including at least one person who could read aloud from the Bible or a pamphlet.[54]

4 Printing and the Confessions

Whether a person was Lutheran or Catholic does not appear to have played a role in training or work relationships in the print shops of sixteenth- and seventeenth-century Augsburg. Thus both David Franck (1603–25), Michael Manger's Protestant stepson, and the Catholic Christoph Mang (1601–24) learned the printing trade under Manger. Later in the seventeenth century, both the Protestant Jakob Koppmayer (1667–1703) and the Catholic August Sturm (1685–95) served as apprentices in the workshop of Hans Schultes the Younger (1623–67). The fact that no sources have survived describing disputes between Catholic and Protestant journeymen working in the same shop suggests that different confessional affiliations did not create problems. On the other hand, the "invisible barrier" between confessions does appear to have affected marriage connections, which only very rarely crossed confessional lines.[55]

Michael Manger's print shop passed to the Catholic Christoph Mang on Manger's death, and then to Andreas Aperger, who ran the business for the next 41 years. This single Catholic press in the first half of the seventeenth century had to compete with four or five Protestant presses,[56] which at first glance might appear an unfavorable ratio for the Catholic side. The perspective changes, however, when one examines the production figures, which show that the Catholics possessed by far the most productive presses and their output accounted for around 40 per cent of total Augsburg book production.[57]

The most significant confessional conflict within the local publishing industry took place during the Thirty Years' War, sparked by the sole Catholic printer, Andreas Aperger, on his return from exile in 1635. A confluence of factors, including a desire for profits along with local and imperial power struggles on top of confessional tensions, caused a furor about a printing privilege which

---

54 Künast, *"Getruckt zu Augspurg"*, pp. 11–13.
55 François, *Die unsichtbare Grenze*; Reith, "Buchdruckergesellen"; Künast, "Konfessionalität". Christoph Mang married a sister of the Protestant printer David Franck: Künast, "Dokumentation", pp. 1233–34. See also Chapter 11 in this volume.
56 Between 1608 and 1614, there was a second Catholic print shop under the direction of Chrysostomus Dabertzhofer, which printed almost exclusively Jesuit material: Künast, "Dokumentation", p. 1235.
57 Künast, "Konfessionalität", p. 113.

occupied the printers, the Augsburg civic court, and the Imperial Aulic Council in Vienna for more than twenty years. The disagreement began when Aperger received an exclusive privilege to print almanacs from Emperor Ferdinand II, guaranteeing him a monopoly on this lucrative market which his Protestant competitors refused to accept. The resulting conflict between Aperger and his chief rival, Hans Schultes the Younger, escalated after the Peace of Westphalia in 1648, when Schultes was able to unite all of Aperger's opponents behind him. A petition to the city council accused Aperger, with the backing of the Fuggers, of selfishly seeking to ruin the local printing industry and with it many venerable Augsburg families. When Schultes continued to print almanacs undisturbed, Aperger responded by suing Schultes in 1652 for damages amounting to 1,070 gulden, a sum that would have ruined Schultes had he been required to pay it. This conflict, which was decided in Schultes' favor, confirms the importance of almanac printing to the success of Augsburg printers.[58]

Confessional relations in the book trade would be fundamentally altered by immigration after the Thirty Years' War, and especially after 1670. Numerous Catholic printers settled in the city, along with well-capitalized publishers and booksellers, turning Augsburg into a center of Catholic publishing by the middle of the eighteenth century at the latest.[59]

5   Trajectories in Book Production

Printing in Augsburg began with a bang, with nine presses opening between 1468 and 1478 and using their considerable printing capacity to publish 287 works, some of them of considerable length. We know that Augsburg's first printer, Günther Zainer, received intellectual and financial support from influential clerical circles, but it quickly became clear that the market could not sustain such high levels of output. This excessive boom phase ended a few years later when the combination of insufficient demand and underdeveloped and untried distribution systems caused the collapse of undercapitalized print shops.[60] As support from the church faded, printers reoriented their businesses. The publication of Latin books fell sharply, with the decline driven as well by increasing competition from imports from the Rhenish cities of Basel,

---

58   This conflict is described in detail in Künast, "Konfessionalität", pp. 100–11, 116–17; idem, "Entwicklungslinien", pp. 19–21. A decision against Aperger was recorded in 1653.
59   Gier, "Buchdruck und Verlagswesen"; idem, "Stapelstadt".
60   Künast, *"Getruckt zu Augspurg"*, pp. 86–91, 295, diagram 2.

Cologne, and Strasbourg and from Venice. The future direction of Augsburg printing thus was evident from a very early point.

This phase was also marked by deliberate collaboration among printers. An association of around ten printers and booksellers shaped the local book market for more than 20 years, producing between 30 and 40 editions per year. 75 per cent of the books published in Augsburg between 1480 and 1500 were in German, with an emphasis on light fiction and advice manuals in fields such as medicine. In this respect Augsburg diverged from the rest of fifteenth-century Europe, a point that can also be illustrated by examining printed Bibles. Out of 14 vernacular editions of the complete Bible printed before the appearance of Luther's translation, nine were printed in Augsburg, whereas not a single Latin edition appeared in Augsburg during the entire fifteenth and sixteenth centuries. The focus on just a few authors and titles was also a characteristic of Augsburg's printers that had been established in the 1480s, with bestsellers and perennial favorites republished multiple times.[61] Around 1,300 incunabula are currently identified as Augsburg publications.[62]

This early phase of the city's printing history did not end with the century, however, but with the arrival of Martin Luther. Not only did the reformer's appearance on the scene coincide with the demise of the first generation of Augsburg printers,[63] but it completely transformed the content coming off the presses. The early years of the Reformation unleashed such a demand that it not only ended the market slump of the previous two decades, but also enabled new print shops to gain a foothold in the city.[64] In the period between 1518 and 1530, about 3,000 Reformation prints appeared in Augsburg (over 90 per cent of them in German). With nearly a third of all pamphlets appearing there during this period, Augsburg became the most important printing center for Reformation literature.[65] The peak occurred in 1524, when 277 publications flooded the market.[66] The fact that Luther's writings could be republished in Augsburg within two to three weeks after their initial

---

61   Künast, "*Getruckt zu Augspurg*", pp. 89, 91–95, 222–23, 234.
62   A complete list of fifteenth-century prints is available online in *Gesamtkatalog der Wiegendrucke* <http://www.gesamtkatalogderwiegendrucke.de>. Approximately 70 per cent of Augsburg's incunabula are currently available digitally.
63   Künast, "Dokumentation", pp. 1211–13.
64   Künast, "Dokumentation", pp. 1218–21. Six new print shops were established between 1517 and 1528.
65   Köhler, "Flugschriften", p. 170. On Augsburg printing of Luther's work, see Künast, "Martin Luther".
66   Künast, "Augsburg's Role", p. 331; idem, "Augsburger Buchproduktion," pp. 69–70. For a chart showing Augsburg pamphlet production between 1515 and 1530, see Künast, "Entwicklungslinien", p. 15.

appearance in Wittenberg was due to the city's position as a mail and news distribution center, which was a major advantage.[67] After the German Peasants' Revolt of 1524–25, output stabilized at around 60 publications a year. Along with pamphlets, printers churned out editions of Luther's vernacular Bible and resumed publication of the previous standbys: advice manuals and light fiction.

The political fallout from being on the losing side in the Schmalkaldic War of 1546–47 had significant consequences for the printing business. Not only did book production collapse because of the war, but after Emperor Charles V imposed his new constitution on the city, the printers and book merchants, all of whom by now were affiliated with one or another of the reformed movements,[68] had to come to terms with the new Catholic authorities. To avoid fines and imprisonment, as well as confiscations due to censorship infractions, Augsburg printers ceased almost entirely to publish controversial theological literature or politically dangerous writings.[69]

After 1570, enterprising printers again settled in Augsburg. Publishers and book dealers such as Georg Willer the Elder (1548–93) and his sons Elias (1594–1611) and Georg the Younger (1594–1632) increased the city's book production figures substantially.[70] A further impetus was provided in the 1590s by *Ad insigne pinus*, which in addition to a quantitative increase in output produced high-quality Latin editions and, for the first time in Augsburg, Greek texts.[71] Although this publishing house would continue to employ Protestants until it closed in 1615, it increasingly directed its efforts to Counter-Reformation channels. The fact that the Catholic printer Christoph Mang dared to open a print shop in 1601 was likely related to the resurgence of the Catholic church.[72]

In the sixteenth century, around 6,500 works were printed and published in Augsburg, although about 600 of them were broadsheets[73] and over 4,000 were pamphlets.[74] More than 70 per cent of this output was in the German language, and thus accessible to lay publics. Because of the brisk business cre-

---

67 See also Chapter 17 in this volume.
68 The last of the Catholic printers, Alexander Weißenhorn, had moved to the university town of Ingolstadt: Künast, "Dokumentation", p. 1221.
69 An exception was Hans Gegler, who continued to publish works by Schwenckfeld and other provocative Protestant texts: Schottenloher, "Hans Gegler".
70 Künast, "Georg Willer d. Ä."; idem and Schürmann, "Johannes Rynmann", pp. 31–40; Künast, "Bücher für Tirol", pp. 39–45.
71 Bellot, "Ad insigne pinus".
72 Künast, "Konfessionalität".
73 Schilling, *Bildpublizistik*.
74 The VD16 lists around 90 per cent of Augsburg's titles (excepting broadsheets, which are not included). About 60 per cent of these are currently available digitally.

ated by the Reformation, around 4,500 of these prints appeared in the first half of the century and only 2,000 in the second half. In addition to Reformation propaganda, news pamphlets and printed songs played an important role; additional strengths included light fiction, advice manuals, and almanacs along with school books for Augsburg's two high schools.

The Thirty Years' War devastated the local book trade. With the Swedish army's arrival in 1632, book publication declined dramatically and remained at a greatly reduced level until the end of the war and beyond. In addition, a series of bankruptcies and deaths spelled the end for a number of printing and publishing houses. The printing infrastructure, however, remained largely intact, as did Augsburg's advantages as a center of news and commerce, making the recovery that began around 1670 possible.

In the seventeenth century, Augsburg experienced a decline in its importance relative to other German printing centers as well as relative to its status in the fifteenth and sixteenth centuries. The century produced no printer to rival the production numbers of a Heinrich Steiner or Philipp Ulhart the Elder, who produced more than 1,000 works each. In total, about 4,000 works were printed during the seventeenth century.[75] At first glance, it would appear that Catholic printers had a greater attachment to Latin-language publications than their Protestant counterparts, as German-language texts made up only 47 per cent of Christoph Mang's production and 46 per cent of Andreas Aperger's output. But closer inspection reveals that these Latin publications were actually commissioned and financed by the *Ad insigne pinus* publishing house and the local Jesuits. Comparison with the Protestant printers Hans Schultes the Elder and David Franck, for whom German-language texts also comprised under or just over half of their output, confirms that the outside financing of Latin publishing was the decisive factor: both Schultes and Franck received commissions from *Ad insigne pinus*. When this publisher ceased operations, German-language printing increased for Catholic as well as Protestant printers.

Two further characteristics of seventeenth-century Augsburg printing are also noteworthy: first, the less significant the print shop, the smaller the Latin output; and second, the longer a printer had been in business, the greater the proportion to German texts. Thus the longstanding preference for vernacular publication in Augsburg continued throughout the seventeenth century.

---

75 A catalogue called *Druckerdatei* of the Augsburg State and City Library documents around 3,700 prints. A search of the VD17, which is still incomplete for Augsburg, currently returns 3,400 hits.

During the eighteenth century, Augsburg regained its position as a leading printing and publishing center.[76] The first indication of this development is in the production numbers, estimated to be well over 10,000 works. Primarily responsible for this output were the Catholic printers and publishers who had settled in Augsburg from the late seventeenth century onwards.[77] This development can be readily traced in the sermon literature. During the seventeenth century, the Protestant city of Nuremberg had played the leading role in the production of this genre. Over the course of the following century, however, Augsburg not only surpassed Nuremberg to move into first place; it achieved a near monopoly in this market.[78] The Berlin Enlightenment author and publisher Friedrich Nicolai in his 1781 travelogue referred to the Catholic book dealers in Augsburg as "true tycoons", describing the bookshops of the Veith brothers and Joseph Wolf as "among the biggest and wealthiest in Germany, perhaps even Europe".[79] This success was only possible because Augsburg booksellers no longer limited themselves to their traditional markets in southern Germany and the Alpine regions, but sent Latin publications for distribution to France, Italy, and Spain.[80]

The Catholic book market was so significant and profitable that even Protestant printers, engravers, and publishers increasingly produced works for it out of economic necessity. While important Catholic Enlightenment texts were published in Augsburg, the city remained largely a bastion of Catholic conservatism. As confessional tensions eased, demand for controversial theological works of the type published in Nuremberg, Cologne, and Munich waned, while interest in illustrated devotional literature increased. Augsburg's position as the leading producer of graphic arts in this case proved an advantage.[81] The city's bi-confessional status eventually proved to be another locational advantage, allowing it to serve both Catholic and Protestant markets.

6 The Book Trade

The significance of Augsburg for the German and European book trade can only be fully understood by examining the structure of the book market, which

---

76 Gier, "Stapelstadt".
77 More precise numbers are currently unavailable. The Augsburg State and City Library documents around 9,600 prints, and a search of the VD18, also still incomplete, currently returns 3,450 hits.
78 Eybl, "Konfession und Buchwesen".
79 Cited in Gier, "Buchdruck und Verlagswesen", p. 480.
80 Ibid., p. 483.
81 Ibid., pp. 488–94, 501–03.

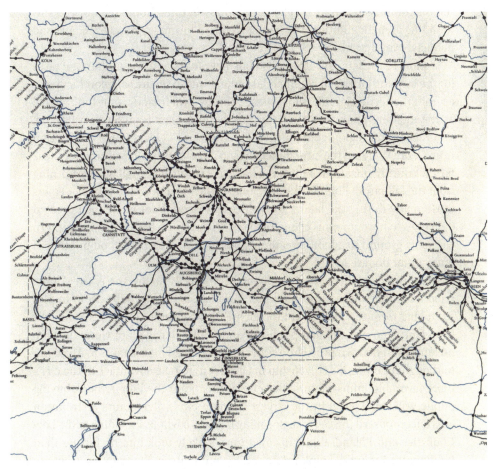

FIGURE 18.1 Map of trade routes from Jörg Gail's "Reisebüchlein der vornehmsten Lande und Städte", printed in Augsburg in 1563

was organized around long-distance and luxury trade. In contrast to the stationary Italian model,[82] the book trade in the German lands overwhelmingly depended on traveling merchants and seasonal fairs, the most important of which were the spring and fall fairs in Frankfurt am Main and in Leipzig.[83]

Augsburg printers and book dealers can be documented attending these fairs from the 1480s onward.[84] The timing of major fairs then guided the schedules for smaller fairs and local markets. Book fairs provided book dealers the opportunity not only to sell their own new publications, but also to buy and

82 Nuovo, *Book Trade*.
83 Grimm, "Buchführer".
84 Künast, *"Getruckt zu Augspurg"*, p. 122.

sell on commission from smaller print shops in one's hometown or the surrounding area. In addition, the fairs served as a forum for news exchange and financial transactions.

Visitors to the fairs traveled by established routes, and one of the chief tasks for the city authorities in commercial centers was to secure safe-conduct passes from the territorial rulers for passage through their lands. Augsburg served as the meeting point for merchants and book dealers from Swabia, Bavaria, and the Alpine region going to the Frankfurt and Leipzig fairs.[85] A petition from Georg Willer to the city council in 1559 illustrates the importance of these fairs for the organization of the book trade as a whole. Arrested when returning from the fall fair in Frankfurt, Willer, one of the most prominent book dealers in Germany during the later sixteenth century, could not make the expected deliveries to his numerous clients; as a result, the entire book trade in southern Germany ground to a halt, threatening not only Willer's livelihood but that of many other booksellers.[86]

Augsburg's significance in supplying southern Germany, the entire Alpine region, and beyond with printed literature can be illustrated with examples stretching from the fifteenth to the eighteenth centuries. Johannes Rynmann from Öhringen was the first publisher and bookseller in all of Germany who no longer ran his own print shop.[87] In 1489, he moved his business to Augsburg (although retaining his citizenship in Öhringen) to take advantage of the city's more favorable infrastructure. Because at this point the literate book-buying public was small, even in the largest German cities, Rynmann's distribution area encompassed the German-speaking lands as a whole, including in the Low Countries and Poland. While his own travels likely took him no further than Freiburg im Breisgau, Frankfurt am Main, and Leipzig, Rynmann was able to conduct trade along the Rhine river and in the Low Countries from Frankfurt, and in northern Germany and eastern Europe from Leipzig. He maintained important outposts in university towns such as Freiburg, Tübingen, Heidelberg, and Ingolstadt, and published using printers in Basel, Nuremberg, Strasbourg, Venice, and Hagenau. The most important of these for Rynmann was the Hagenau printer Heinrich Gran (1489–1527), to whom he entrusted over 200 Latin works, mostly on theological subjects. Rynmann's German-language works were of course printed in Augsburg.

---

[85]   Rautenberg, "Buchhändlerische Organisationsformen". The book dealer Leonhard Stegmann traveled during the 1550s from Laibach (today Ljubljana, the capital of Slovenia) to Augsburg to stock up on books: Grimm, "Buchführer", no. 993.
[86]   Künast, *"Getruckt zu Augspurg"*, p. 167.
[87]   Künast and Schürmann, "Johannes Rynmann", pp. 23–29.

Georg Willer the Elder rose from modest beginnings through his bookselling and publishing enterprises to become one of the wealthiest inhabitants of the city.[88] Contributing to his success was undoubtedly his invention of a "fair catalogue", which made available for the first time a complete list of books offered for sale. From 1564, Willer was thus able to make known all the new publications he had on offer at the Frankfurt fair. This represented a new standard in book advertising that had since the fifteenth century depended on fliers and placards.[89] Like Rynmann, Willer was a regular visitor to the Frankfurt and Leipzig fairs. Beginning in the 1590s, the firm's interests in Frankfurt were permanently represented by Willer's son Elias, who settled in the city on the Main.

The elder Willer also maintained branches in the university cities of Ingolstadt, Freiburg, and Tübingen, and had a notable presence in the Habsburg lands. Less significant as a publisher than Rynmann, Willer still provided commissions to printers in Augsburg, Lauingen, Dillingen, and Nuremburg. Vienna, capital of the Habsburg Empire, served as Willer's shipping and payment center for books printed in Croatian in the Württemberg town of Urach and sent to the Protestant Slavic populations in Carniola and Carinthia. Despite being (at least in his younger years) sympathetic to the teachings of the reformer Kaspar Schwenckfeld, in the era of growing confessional division Willer remained neutral in his business dealings. In Tyrol, he supplied both the Jesuit establishments and the surrounding mining communities where the evangelical message retained its hold. So dominant were Augsburg book dealers in the Alpine region that even in cities such as Innsbruck, Salzburg, and Graz, it was nearly impossible for local booksellers to establish a foothold.[90]

Matthias Rieger (1734–75) is a further example of the social mobility provided by the book trade. Born in 1705 as the son of a farmer in Seehausen on the Staffel lake, Rieger began his publishing business in Seehausen in 1731 before settling in Augsburg in 1734, where he became one of the most prominent Catholic book dealers and publishers.[91] Aside from trading at the important book fairs, Rieger developed direct sales into another significant source of profit, employing an army of peddlers to sell books and other printed materials door-to-door in every city, village, and monastery in southern Germany and the Alps.[92] Their wide-ranging assortment included sermons, catechisms, de-

---

88   Künast and Schürmann, "Johannes Rynmann", pp. 31–40.
89   Vorderstemann, "Augsburger Bücheranzeigen".
90   Künast, "Bücher für Tirol".
91   Seehausen is about 80 km southeast of Augsburg, and during Rieger's lifetime was the property of the Ettal monastery.
92   Pörnbacher, "Matthäus Rieger", p. 623. Although books were the mainstay of their trade, the peddlers also dealt in colored paper, jewelry, and other trinkets.

votional literature and prayer books, treatises on theology and church history, textbooks, medical tracts, and other advice literature. The authors of the theological works marketed by Rieger came from all the Catholic orders, from the Jesuits to the mendicant friars.[93] He also enthusiastically oversaw the translation and printing of works by Italian and French authors, which he published in both German and Latin.[94]

7 Conclusion

This overview of the printing industry and book trade in the imperial city of Augsburg from the fifteenth to the eighteenth century is necessarily limited to the most crucial developments. After an energetic introductory phase, Augsburg established itself as the only significant printing center in Europe where more German than Latin works were printed. In the 1520s, the city was the most important location for the publication of Reformation literature in the German lands and, until the 1540s, the most important producer of Luther's vernacular Bible. From 1540 through the end of the sixteenth century, no Augsburg printer publicly professed the Catholic faith.

The evolution of Augsburg's book trade was regularly interrupted by wars and external political interference, but its advantageous location enabled it to recover from these crises. The Schmalkaldic War and resulting revisions to the city's constitution in 1547–48 resulted in the elimination of controversial theological literature from the printers' repertoire. The decades around 1600 saw the return of Catholic publishing and Catholic printers to Augsburg; the printing trade would thenceforth remain bi-confessional. Although in the seventeenth century there was only one Catholic print shop in the city, it was always the most active.

The Thirty Years' War also had tremendous consequences for Augsburg's book trade. Book production collapsed at the beginning of the 1630s, and many firms closed due to the death or bankruptcy of the owners. It took until about 1680 for book printing and selling in Augsburg to begin to recover from the effects of the war. A crucial factor in this rebound was the arrival of well-capitalized Catholic printers and publishers, who made Augsburg a center of Catholic printing and distribution. The production of Latin-language materials rose in the second half of the eighteenth century, largely due to the presence of Catholic printers and publishers who supplied the book market with hefty

---

93   Gier, "Stapelstadt".
94   Pörnbacher, "Matthäus Rieger", pp. 625–26.

amounts of theological literature, even as Latin-language printing shrank in other German printing centers as a result of the influence of the learned and popular Enlightenment. Of particular importance to the Catholic publishing programs were Latin translations of French, Italian, and Spanish authors, whose books reached an international Catholic audience. Thus, in the eighteenth century as in the sixteenth, Augsburg once again occupied a unique position among printing centers in the German-speaking lands.

The book trade was thus a crucial aspect affecting economic and cultural dynamics in the imperial city of Augsburg. When employees and suppliers of the printing firms are included, between 100 and 200 families, depending on the period, made their living in this industry. As a capital-intensive, loosely regulated sector, the publishing business created opportunities for upward economic and social mobility. At the same time, the numerous bankruptcies testify to the riskiness of these ventures: hardly any publishing firm survived more than two or three generations. Overall, Augsburg was not renowned for publishing great works of science or philosophy, but made its mark distributing news,[95] information, and knowledge to broader audiences who had neither knowledge of Latin nor university educations.

Bibliography

Unpublished Primary Sources
Staats- und Stadtbibliothek Augsburg (SuStBA)
    2° Cod. Aug. 324, no. 88.
    4° Cod. Aug. 1020, no. 64.
Stadtarchiv Augsburg (StadtAA)
    Censuramt.
    Evangelisches Wesensarchiv, no. 1042, vol. 1.
    Handwerksgericht.
    Reichsstadt, Handwerkerakten, Buchdrucker.
    Reichsstadt, Ratsbuch 16.

Published Primary Sources
Panzer, G.W., *Ausführliche Beschreibung der ältesten Augspurgischen Ausgaben der Bibel mit literarischen Anmerkungen*, Nuremberg, 1780 (repr. Amsterdam, 1971).
Tauler, J., *Predigten*, Augsburg, 1508 (SuStBA, 2° Th.Pr. 226).

---

95   See Chapter 17 in this volume.

Zapf, G.W., *Annales typographicae Augustanae ab eius origine MCCCCLXVI usque ad annum MDXXX*, Augsburg, 1778.

Zapf, G.W., *Augsburgs Buchdruckgeschichte nebst den Jahrbüchern derselben. Vol. 1: Vom Jahre 1468 bis auf das Jahr 1500. Vol. 2: Vom Jahre 1501 bis auf das Jahr 1530*, Augsburg, 1786–91.

Secondary Literature

Appuhn-Radtke, S., "Augsburger Buchillustration im 17. Jahrhundert", in Gier and Janota (eds.), *Augsburger Buchdruck und Verlagswesen*, pp. 735–90.

Augustyn, W., "Augsburger Buchillustration im 18. Jahrhundert", in Gier and Janota (eds.), *Augsburger Buchdruck und Verlagswesen*, pp. 791–861.

Baer, W. and Hecker, H.J. (eds.), *Die Jesuiten und ihre Schule St. Salvator in Augsburg 1582*, Munich, 1982.

Beier, C., "Missalien massenhaft: Die Bämler-Werkstatt und die Augsburger Buchmalerei im 15. Jahrhundert", *Codices Manuscripti. Zeitschrift für Handschriftenkunde* 48–49 (2004), vol. 1, pp. 55–72 (text), vol. 2, pp. 67–78 (illustrations).

Bellot, J., "Ad insigne pinus: Kulturgeschichte der Reichsstadt Augsburg im Spiegel eines Verlages an der Wende des 16./17. Jahrhunderts", *Buchhandelsgeschichte* 14 (1978), pp. 697–709.

Bellot, J., *Augsburger volkssprachliches humanistisches Schrifttum und seine Illustration von 1520 bis 1550*, Augsburg, 1982.

Büchler, V., "Die Zensur im frühneuzeitlichen Augsburg 1515–1806", *Zeitschrift des Historischen Vereins für Schwaben* 84 (1991), pp. 69–128.

Corsten, C. and Fuchs, R.W. (eds.), *Der Buchdruck im 15. Jahrhundert. Eine Bibliographie*, 2 vols., Stuttgart, 1988–93.

Costa, G., "Die Rechtseinrichtung der Zensur in der Reichsstadt Augsburg", *Zeitschrift des Historischen Vereins für Augsburg und Neuburg* 42 (1916), pp. 3–129.

Creasman, A., *Censorship and Civic Order in Reformation Germany, 1517–1648: "Printed Poison and Evil Talk"*, Farnham, 2012.

Edmunds, S., "New Light on Johannes Bämler", *Journal of the Printing Historical Society* 22 (1993), pp. 29–53.

Eiden, I. and Müller, D., "Der Buchdrucker Alexander Weißenhorn in Augsburg 1528–1540", *Archiv für Geschichte des Buchwesens* 11 (1971), pp. 527–92.

Eisenhardt, U., *Die kaiserliche Aufsicht über Buchdruck, Buchhandel und Presse im Heiligen Römischen Reich 1496–1806. Ein Beitrag zur Geschichte der Bücher- und Pressezensur*, Karlsruhe, 1970.

Eisermann, F., "A Golden Age? Monastic Printing Houses in the Fifteenth Century", in B.R. Coastas (ed.), *Print Culture and Peripheries in Early Modern Europe: A Contribution to the History of Printing and the Book Trade in Small European and Spanish Cities*, Leiden and Boston, 2013, pp. 37–67.

Eybl, F.M., "Konfession und Buchwesen: Augsburgs Druck- und Handelsmonopol für katholische Predigtliteratur, insbesondere im 18. Jahrhundert", in Gier and Janota (eds.), *Augsburger Buchdruck und Verlagswesen*, pp. 633–52.

Fischer, B., *Johann Friedrich Cotta. Verleger, Entrepreneur, Politiker*, Göttingen, 2014.

François, E., *Die unsichtbare Grenze. Protestanten und Katholiken in Augsburg 1648–1806*, Sigmaringen, 1991.

Fujii, A., *Günther Zainers druckersprachliche Leistung. Untersuchungen zur Augsburger Druckersprache im 15. Jahrhundert*, Tübingen, 2007.

Geissler, P., "Erhard Ratdolt", *Lebensbilder aus dem Bayerischen Schwaben* 9 (1966), pp. 97–153.

Gier, H., "Buchdruck und Verlagswesen in Augsburg vom Dreißigjährigen Krieg bis zum Ende der Reichsstadt", in idem and Janota (eds.), *Augsburger Buchdruck und Verlagswesen*, pp. 479–516.

Gier, H., "Augsburger Buchwesen und Kunst der Druckgraphik im zweiten Jahrzehnt des 17. Jahrhunderts: Der Verlag von Stephan Michelspacher, sein Gönner Philipp Hainhofer und der Kupferstecher Lucas Kilian", in Paas (ed.), *Augsburg, die Bilderfabrik Europas*, pp. 55–78.

Gier, H., "Die ostschwäbische und altbayerische Verlagslandschaft in der Epoche des Späthumanismus: Augsburg, Dillingen, Lauingen, Ingolstadt, München, Tegernsee und Thierhaupten", in A. Schmid (ed.), *Justus Lipsius und der europäische Späthumanismus in Oberdeutschland*, Munich, 2008, pp. 143–64.

Gier, H., "Die Stapelstadt der katholischen Buchhandlung in Deutschland: Augsburg als Verlagsort jesuitischen Schrifttums vor und nach der Aufhebung der Gesellschaft Jesu", *Zeitschrift des Historischen Vereins für Schwaben* 101 (2008), pp. 151–70.

Gier, H. and Janota, J. (eds.), *Augsburger Buchdruck und Verlagswesen. Von den Anfängen bis zur Gegenwart*, Wiesbaden, 1997.

Grimm, H., "Die Buchführer des deutschen Kulturbereichs", *Archiv für Geschichte des Buchwesens* 7 (1967), pp. 1153–1772.

Guggisberg, H.R., "Reformierter Stadtstaat und Zentrum der Spätrenaissance: Basel in der zweiten Hälfte des 16. Jahrhunderts", in A. Buck (ed.), *Renaissance – Reformation. Gegensätze und Gemeinsamkeiten*, Wiesbaden, 1984, pp. 197–216.

Hägele, G., "Top oder Flop? Zur Produktion der Klosterdruckerei St. Ulrich und Afra in Augsburg", *Wolfenbütteler Notizen zur Buchgeschichte* 39 (2016), pp. 133–52.

Hägele, G. and Thierbach, M. (eds.), *Augsburg macht Druck. Die Anfänge des Buchdrucks in einer Metropole des 15. Jahrhunderts* (exhibition catalogue), Augsburg, 2017.

Heitjan, I., "Die Buchhändler, Verleger und Drucker Bencard 1636–1762", *Archiv für Geschichte des Buchwesens* 3 (1960), pp. 613–980.

Janota, J. and Williams-Krapp, W. (eds.), *Literarisches Leben in Augsburg während des 15. Jahrhunderts*, Tübingen, 1995.

Köhler, H.-J., "The Flugschriften and their Importance in Religious Debate: A Quantitative Approach", in P. Zambelli (ed.), *Astrologi hallucinati: Stars and the End of the World in Luther's Time*, Berlin and New York, 1986, pp. 153–75.

König, E., "Augsburger Buchkunst an der Schwelle zur Frühdruckzeit", in Gier and Janota (eds.), *Augsburger Buchdruck und Verlagswesen*, pp. 173–200.

Koppitz, H.-J., "Kaiserliche Privilegien für das Augsburger Druckgewerbe", in Gier and Janota (eds.), *Augsburger Buchdruck und Verlagswesen*, pp. 41–53.

Koppitz, H.-J., *Die kaiserlichen Druckprivilegien im Haus-, Hof- und Staatsarchiv Wien. Verzeichnis der Akten vom Anfang des 16. Jahrhunderts bis zum Ende des Deutschen Reichs (1806)*, Wiesbaden, 2008.

Künast, H.-J., "Georg Willer d.Ä. von Augsburg und die Erstausgabe des Gesamtwerks von Hans Sachs", in D. Merzbacher (ed.), *500 Jahre Hans Sachs. Handwerker – Dichter – Stadtbürger* (exhibition catalogue), Wiesbaden, 1994, pp. 63–66.

Künast, H.-J., "Martin Luther und der Buchdruck in Augsburg, 1518–1530", in H. Gier and R. Schwarz (eds.), *Reformation und Reichsstadt – Luther in Augsburg* (exhibition catalogue), Augsburg, 1996, pp. 65–77.

Künast, H.-J., *"Getruckt zu Augspurg". Buchdruck und Buchhandel in Augsburg zwischen 1468 und 1555*, Tübingen, 1997.

Künast, H.-J., "Entwicklungslinien des Augsburger Buchdrucks von den Anfängen bis zum Ende des Dreißigjährigen Krieges", in Gier and Janota (eds.), *Augsburger Buchdruck und Verlagswesen*, pp. 3–21.

Künast, H.-J. and Schürmann, B., "Johannes Rynmann, Wolfgang Präunlein und Georg Willer – Drei Augsburger Buchführer des 15. und 16. Jahrhunderts", in Gier and Janota (eds.), *Augsburger Buchdruck und Verlagswesen*, pp. 23–40.

Künast, H.-J., "Dokumentation: Augsburger Buchdrucker und Verleger", in Gier and Janota (eds.), *Augsburger Buchdruck und Verlagswesen*, pp. 1205–1340.

Künast, H.-J., "Konfessionalität und Buchdruck in Augsburg, 1600–1700", *Wolfenbütteler Barock-Nachrichten* 24 (1997), pp. 103–19.

Künast, H.-J., "Hebräisch-jüdischer Buchdruck in Schwaben in der ersten Hälfte des 16. Jahrhunderts", in R. Kießling and S. Ullmann (eds.), *Landjudentum im deutschen Südwesten während der Frühen Neuzeit*, Berlin, 1999, pp. 277–303.

Künast, H.-J., "Johann Andreas Erdmann Maschenbauer, sein Augsburger Intelligenz-Zettel und der Buchmarkt in der zweiten Hälfte des 18. Jahrhunderts", in S. Doering-Manteuffel, J. Mančal and W. Wüst (eds.), *Pressewesen der Aufklärung: Periodische Schriften im Alten Reich*, Berlin, 2001, pp. 337–55.

Künast, H.-J., "Buchdruck und -handel des 16. Jahrhunderts im deutschen Sprachraum. Mit Anmerkungen zum Notendruck und Musikalienhandel", in Lodes (ed.), *Niveau – Nische – Nimbus*, pp. 149–65.

Künast, H.-J., "Augsburg's Role in the German Book Trade in the First Half of the Sixteenth Century", in M. Walsby and G. Kemp (eds.), *The Book Triumphant: Print in Transition in the Sixteenth and Seventeenth Centuries*, Leiden and Boston, 2011, pp. 320–33.

Künast, H.-J., "Augsbourg, ville des diètes d'empire: la production en langues étragères au XVIe siècle. – Reichsstadt und Reichstage. Moderne Fremdsprachen in Augsburg im 16. Jahrhundert", in E. Kammerer and J.-D. Müller (eds.), *Imprimeurs et libraires de la Renaissance. Le travail de la langue. Sprachpolitik der Drucker, Verleger und Buchhändler der Renaissance*, Geneva, 2015, pp. 237–52.

Künast, H.-J., "Bücher für Tirol – Die Literaturversorgung Tirols durch den Augsburger Buchhandel im 15. und 16. Jahrhundert", in R. Sila (ed.), *Der frühe Buchdruck in der Region. Neue Kommunikationswege in Tirol und seinen Nachbarländern*, Innsbruck, 2016, pp. 29–46.

Künast, H.-J., "Die Augsburger Buchproduktion des 16. Jahrhunderts – Stand der Erfassung im Verzeichnis der im deutschen Sprachbereich erschienenen Drucke des 16. Jahrhunderts (VD16)", *Wolfenbütteler Notizen zur Buchgeschichte* 40 (2015/16), pp. 65–78.

Leipold, I., "Das Verlagsprogramm des Augsburger Druckers Johann Bämler: Zum Funktionstyp 'Frühe deutschsprachige Druckprosa'", *Bibliotheksforum Bayern* 4 (1976), pp. 236–52.

Lodes, B. (ed.), *Niveau – Nische – Nimbus. Die Anfänge des Musikdrucks nördlich der Alpen*, Tutzing, 2010.

Micus, R., "Augsburger Handschriftenproduktion im 15. Jahrhundert", *Zeitschrift für deutsche Philologie* 104 (1985), pp. 411–24.

Mihm, A., "Druckersprachen und gesprochene Varietäten: Der Zeugniswert von Bämlers 'Melusine'-Druck (1474) für eine bedeutende Frage der Sprachgeschichte", in U. Rautenberg, H.-J. Künast, M. Habermann and H. Stein-Kecks (eds.), *Zeichensprachen des literarischen Buchs in der Frühen Neuzeit. Die 'Melusine' des Thüring von Ringoltingen*, Berlin and Boston, 2013, pp. 161–203.

Nuovo, A., *The Book Trade in the Italian Renaissance*, Leiden and Boston, 2013.

Ott, N.H., "Frühe Augsburger Buchillustration", in Gier and Janota (eds.), *Augsburger Buchdruck und Verlagswesen*, pp. 201–41.

Paas, J.R. (ed.), *Augsburg, die Bilderfabrik Europas. Essays zur Augsburger Druckgraphik der Frühen Neuzeit*, Augsburg, 2001.

Pettegree, A., *Brand Luther: 1517, Printing, and the Making of the Reformation*, New York, 2015.

Pörnbacher, H., "Matthäus Rieger – Landbuchhändler in Augsburg", in Gier and Janota (eds.), *Augsburger Buchdruck und Verlagswesen*, pp. 621–32.

Rautenberg, U., "Buchhändlerische Organisationsformen in der Inkunabel- und Frühdruckzeit", in Vorstand der Maximilian-Gesellschaft and B. Tiemann (eds.), *Die Buchkultur im 15. und 16. Jahrhundert*, Hamburg, 1999, pp. 339–76.

Rheinfurth, H., *Der Musikverlag Lotter in Augsburg (ca. 1719–1845)*, Tutzing, 1977.

Reith, R., "Buchdruckergesellen im Augsburg des 18. Jahrhunderts", in Gier and Janota (eds.), *Augsburger Buchdruck und Verlagswesen*, pp. 517–38.
Reske, C., "Drucken in der Handpressenzeit", in Hägele and Thierbach (eds.), *Augsburg macht Druck*, pp. 16–29.
Ritter, M., "Augsburger Landkartenproduktion im 18. Jahrhundert: Die Verleger Seutter, Lotter und Probst", in Paas (ed.), *Augsburg, die Bilderfabrik Europas*, pp. 153–162.
Ritter, M., Lotter, A. and Trepesch, Ch. (eds.), *Die Welt aus Augsburg. Landkarten von Tobias Conrad Lotter (1717–1777) und seinen Nachfolgern* (exhibition catalogue), Munich, 2014.
Rogister, L. von, "Michael Manger, ein Alt-Augsburger Buchdrucker", *Familienblatt der Manger* 3–4 (1934), pp. 50–57; 3–4 (1936), pp. 23–26.
Sauer, M., "Die deutschen Inkunabeln, ihre historischen Merkmale und ihr Publikum", Ph.D. diss., University of Cologne, 1956.
Schilling, M., *Bildpublizistik der frühen Neuzeit. Aufgaben und Leistungen des illustrierten Flugblatts in Deutschland bis um 1700*, Tübingen, 1990.
Schottenloher, K., "Hans Werlich, genannt Hans von Erfurt: Der Drucker des Wormser Edikts (1518–1532)", *Gutenberg-Jahrbuch* 2 (1927), pp. 53–67.
Schottenloher, K., "Der Augsburger Winkeldrucker Hans Gegler: Ein Beitrag zur Schwenckfeld-Bibliographie", *Gutenberg-Jahrbuch* 14 (1939), pp. 233–42.
Schottenloher, K., *Philipp Ulhart. Ein Augsburger Winkeldrucker und Helfershelfer der "Schwärmer" und "Wiedertäufer" 1523–1529*, München and Freising, 1921.
Schramm, A., "Günther Zainer: Augsburgs erster Drucker", in M. Breslauer and K. Koehler (eds.), *Werden und Wirken. Ein Festgruß Karl W. Hiersemann zugesandt am 3. September 1924 zum 70. Geburtstag und 40-jährigen Bestehen seiner Firma*, Leipzig, 1924, pp. 363–93.
Stopp, H., "Das in Augsburg gedruckte Hochdeutsch: Notwendigkeit, Stand und Aufgaben seiner Erforschung", *Zeitschrift für deutsche Philologie* 98 (1979), pp. 151–72.
Stromer, W. von, "Große Innovationen der Papierfabrikation in Spätmittelalter und Frühneuzeit", *Technikgeschichte* 60 (1993), pp. 1–6.
Vorderstemann, J., "Augsburger Bücheranzeigen des 15. Jahrhunderts", in Gier and Janota (eds.), *Augsburger Buchdruck und Verlagswesen*, pp. 55–71.
Wehmer, C., "Zur Beurteilung des Methodenstreits in der Inkunabelkunde", *Gutenberg-Jahrbuch* 8 (1933), pp. 250–325.
Werfel, S., "Einrichtung und Betrieb einer Druckerei in der Handpressenzeit (1460 bis 1820)", in Gier and Janota (eds.), *Augsburger Buchdruck und Verlagswesen*, pp. 97–124.
Wohnhaas, T., "Die Schönig, eine Augsburger Druckerfamilie", *Archiv für Geschichte des Buchwesens* 5 (1964), pp. 1473–84.

Electronic Resources

GW = *Gesamtkatalog der Wiegendrucke*: www.gesamtkatalogderwiegendrucke.de [30.04.2018].

VD16 = Bayerische Staatsbibliothek München/Herzog August Bibliothek Wolfenbüttel, *Verzeichnis der im deutschen Sprachbereich erschienenen Drucke des 16. Jahrhunderts (VD16)*: www.vd16.de [30.04.2018].

VD17 = Bayerische Staatsbibliothek München/Staatsbibliothek zu Berlin – Preußischer Kulturbesitz/Herzog August Bibliothek Wolfenbüttel (eds.), *Das Verzeichnis der im deutschen Sprachraum erschienenen Drucke des 17. Jahrhunderts*: www.vd17.de [30.04.2018].

VD18 = Niedersächsische Staats- und Universitätsbibliothek Göttingen et al., *Digitalisierung und Erschließung der im deutschen Sprachraum erschienenen Drucke des 18. Jahrhunderts*: www.vd18.de [30.04.2018].

CHAPTER 19

Dress and Material Culture

Victoria Bartels and Katherine Bond

> Nobody can bring me a part of dress that is too adventurous; for the stranger someone cuts hose, doublet, and shoes, the more I like wearing it.[1]
>
> VEIT KONRAD SCHWARZ

∴

1 Introduction

For those who could afford it, much thought, time, and energy went into dressing oneself in early modern Augsburg. In the introduction of his 1561 *Klaidungsbüchlein* or "little book of clothes", Augsburg bookkeeper Veit Konrad Schwarz confessed his love for fashion and for pushing sartorial boundaries (figure 19.1). Following his father Matthäus Schwarz, who famously compiled an album recording a lifetime of fashionable ensembles, Veit Konrad commissioned 41 images displaying his likeness and costume from newborn to 19 years of age. While his fondness for fashion might seem extreme, other sources from the period consistently reveal the prominent position of dress and bodily adornment in the hearts and minds of contemporaries. References to purchasing, displaying, repairing, tailoring, lending, and/or gifting clothing frequently appear in account books, letters, inventories, and wills. Moreover, painstakingly-created illustrations of leading fashions and goods can also be found in hundreds of extant sketch and design books, commemorative programs, costume albums, portraits, and figurative scenes.

Although levels of disposable income varied, early modern Augsburgers invested a fair amount of household earnings into the making and maintenance of clothing. This was especially true for elites, as exhibited in 1516 when Ulrich Fugger the Younger ostentatiously gave his bride Veronika Gassner 3,000 gulden worth of clothing and jewelry, equivalent to what his uncle Jakob Fugger

---

[1] Translated in Rublack, Hayward and Tiramani (eds.), *First Book of Fashion*, pp. 331–32.

DRESS AND MATERIAL CULTURE 441

FIGURE 19.1   "From summer until September this was my usual dress to walk the streets …",
Book of Clothes (*Klaidungsbüchlein*), Veit Konrad Schwarz, 1560
HERZOG ANTON ULRICH-MUSEUM, HS 27 N.67B, ILL. 36R

the Rich had spent on the construction of a new castle four years earlier.[2] This sum was on top of the "silk clothing, and velvet, and sateen, and other sorts of clothes" bestowed upon family members and servants for Fugger's extravagant nuptials.[3]

This practice of conspicuous consumption could wreak havoc on the pocketbooks of the wealthy. Lisa Jardine and Ulinka Rublack have shown that elite families in Renaissance Italy and Germany keenly felt the pressure to maintain their status through tidy and fashionable dress, yet the threat of debt and downward mobility brought on by overspending loomed large.[4] Among both the upper and lower classes, clothing and textiles were stocked as investments as they often retained their value and could be sold, gifted, pawned, rented, and in some instances used in place of cash itself.[5] Apparel was one of the most frequently pawned categories of goods, and for some from the lowest rungs of society, basic clothing and simple household goods were the only items in their dowries.[6]

Augsburg had a particular stake in the fashion industry, as the city owed its first economic boom in the fifteenth and sixteenth centuries to fustian, a coarse cloth made from linen and cotton. In fact, the first Fugger ancestor to settle in Augsburg famously was a weaver who moved there in 1367 for work.[7] In addition to textile manufacture, Augsburg was one of Europe's most prominent centers for the production and distribution of luxury goods, excelling in the making of arms and armor, for example. The city's central location on the trade route from Italy to northern Europe also contributed to its commercial success. This allowed Augsburg to become a center of consumption as well, as a host of international products made their way to this southern German city, including more exotic items like Mediterranean silks, gems, and spices, in addition to familiar mainstays including Hungarian livestock, Tyrolean silver and copper, and Bavarian salt.[8] As Lee Palmer Wandel points out, "Augsburg was a city in motion: people and things moved, within, through, to and from Augsburg. A network of goods linked Augsburg to Venice and Rome, Lyons and

---

2 Häberlein, *The Fuggers of Augsburg*, pp. 177, 201.
3 Translated and quoted in Häberlein, *The Fuggers of Augsburg*, p. 177.
4 Jardine, *Worldly Goods*, p. 93; Rublack, *Dressing Up*, p. 229.
5 Rublack, *Dressing Up*, pp. 5–6. As Ann Rosalind Jones has shown, servants' wages were often paid with clothing and cloth (in addition to food and shelter), commoditizing the "liveried body" into an object of ownership. For more, see Jones and Stallybrass, *Renaissance Clothing*, p. 11.
6 For more on weddings and dowries, see Roper, *The Holy Household*, pp. 132–64.
7 Häberlein, *The Fuggers of Augsburg*, p. 25; Stuart, *Defiled Trades*, p. 36.
8 Pieper, "Trading with Art and Curiosities", p. 87; Wandel, *Eucharist*, p. 49.

Lisbon, Amsterdam and Brussels, Frankfurt and Leipzig, points south, west, north, and east."[9]

Enjoying a prominent position under the Habsburg emperors, the free imperial city of Augsburg hosted numerous imperial diets and other high-profile stately events during its zenith in the sixteenth century. These occasions drew thousands of foreign visitors, giving the city – along with its agents, merchants, craftsmen, and markets – increased visibility in the global market, causing chronicler Clemens Sender to proclaim in connection with the Diet of Augsburg in 1530, "[a]s long as Augsburg has existed, there has never been so many foreign folk from so many nations".[10] By the same token, artists and skilled craftsmen from outside the region such as the painter Christoph Amberger (*c.* 1505–62) and the portrait medalist Christoph Weiditz (*c.* 1500–59) entered the city in the hopes of attracting new commissions. Sumptuary ordinances – legislation that restricted residents' consumption of luxuries based on their social class – were temporarily suspended so inhabitants could use consumer goods as a way of displaying the city's honor, wealth, and prestige on an international stage.[11]

Many southern German cities in the sixteenth century experienced an increase in the production and acquisition of material goods. This period witnessed European exploration of the Americas and Asia, facilitating globalization and trade on an unprecedented scale. New commercial opportunities, along with the growth of cities and bourgeois communities, concentrated consumer markets and drove industrial productivity. Jardine, Rublack, and Evelyn Welch, among others, have demonstrated how consumption among the upper classes skyrocketed in the sixteenth and seventeenth centuries, generating a "material Renaissance".[12] With the right materials, techniques, and/or adornment, everyday items, once considered banal, were painted, gilded, and fashioned into collectible objects. Artisans, craftsmen, specialists, and subspecialists manufactured their wares in a range of qualities and prices to satisfy increasing consumer demand across all classes.

To highlight the dramatic surge in consumption in Augsburg during the "material Renaissance", this chapter focuses on sixteenth- and seventeenth-century examples. The first section investigates how sartorial items were used to label, identify, and negotiate Augsburg's civic spaces and social structures.

---

9   Wandel, *Eucharist*, p. 49.
10 Translated and quoted in Rublack, "Renaissance Dress", p. 16.
11 Rublack, "Renaissance Dress", p. 15.
12 Jardine, *Worldly Goods*; Rublack, *Dressing Up*; idem., "Matter in the Material Renaissance"; Welch, *Shopping in the Renaissance*.

Clothing as a financial investment is discussed in the next section, followed by an investigation into the city's gendered dress practices, additionally exploring the personalization of dress as a means of self-expression. The final section looks at armor in Augsburg and its close relationship to clothing, exploring both the commissioning and production processes involved in adorning the early modern male body.

2   Clothing the Commune

The streets of Renaissance Augsburg were visually alight with expressive clothing cultures mediating social hierarchies, measuring prosperity, and demonstrating aesthetic imagination. Vocabularies of color, texture, and form were harnessed by dressers to express alignment to social communities and group identities which might revolve around age, gender, social or professional distinction, religious belief, or political commitment. The last two categories were especially contested in the sixteenth century, as the Reformation shook the city's confessional loyalties and Augsburg had to negotiate relations with its Catholic Habsburg sovereigns.

Following the hierarchical social order that Augsburg adhered to and that characterized early modern urban landscapes in general, dress was expected to anticipate identity and organize dressed bodies. The city's social stratification distinguished the patrician class from merchants, artisans from journeymen, and servants from beggars. Both patricians and allied families (*Herren*) and merchants founded "societies" in the fifteenth century with the purpose of affirming their rank and privilege through exclusive membership. While the patricians and merchants maintained collective private drinking halls, commoners forged social bonds and maintained prestige of varying degrees through membership in a guild or trade and socializing in public houses.[13] Augsburg's governing council made efforts to control the publicly displayed dressed bodies of these groups. Managing social legibility through clothing, they set apart those considered dishonorable, legislated against degrees of sumptuousness, and administered livery for daily wear and ceremonial display.

The most marginal groups of society were required to identify themselves through prescribed clothing and symbols. Jews had to pin a yellow ring to their clothes, a measure enforced in Augsburg from 1432.[14] Before the city closed down its brothels in 1532, the council attempted to prevent prostitutes from

---

13   Tlusty (ed.), *Augsburg*, pp. 67–68, 159.
14   Stuart, *Defiled Trades*, p. 29. See also Chapter 16 in this volume.

being mistaken for "pious and honorable women" by issuing a number of decrees beginning in 1438, prohibiting them from wearing silk clothing and rosaries and forcing them to wear an identifiable broad green stripe.[15] Wearing Augsburg's pinecone emblem (the *Stadtpyr*) in the civic colors of red, green, and white was a requirement for impoverished citizens receiving urban welfare or licensed to beg. When a poor watchmaker was arrested in 1602 for receiving welfare without wearing the *Stadtpyr*, he told civic authorities that he had refused to wear it because he feared it would damage his reputation and his relationship with customers.[16]

The body was not merely marked by these worn symbols, but was profoundly invested with the stigma they denoted because of the sense that *wearing* something injurious penetrated the skin and left an enduring stain on one's character. Kathy Stuart documents the example of the "thief's fur coat", a garment appearing in the 1660 inventory of Augsburg's dungeon where it was forced upon the imprisoned.[17] Such was the affective, psychological power of the coat to imbue its wearer with dishonor that local authorities were compelled to offer honorable citizens arrested for non-capital offenses the opportunity to wear their personal furs in the dungeon to protect against the cold.[18]

In 1582, the city issued a comprehensive sumptuary ordinance specifying rules for each of its recognized social tiers. Attempting to curb "unnecessary expenses" and see its residents "behaving in accordance with their estate[s]", the council regulated quantities of luxury velvets, silks, damasks, furs, and precious stones and metals following class divisions.[19] As Rublack documents, German proto-nationalist ideology and Lutheran values fueled the mistrust of excessive luxury in dress, particularly costly imported fabrics associated with Catholic Italy and Spain that were deemed not only a burden on local economies but symbols of popish decadence.[20] Decorous dress reflected well on the city as a whole, however, and thus in 1582 the members of the patrician society (*Herrenstube*) were entitled to wear velvet, silk, and damask, although not embroidered in any way. Members of the merchant society were allowed to wear silk or damask doublets and hose, but were not permitted to use such lavish fabrics for their outer garments. While merchants' wives were permitted to wear up to one-and-a-half ell of velvet trim on their bodices, artisans' wives

---

15 Stuart, *Defiled Trades*, p. 30; Roper, *The Holy Household*, p. 89.
16 Roeck, *Eine Stadt in Krieg und Frieden*, vol. 1, pp. 464–65.
17 Ibid., p. 130.
18 Ibid.
19 Translated and quoted in Tlusty (ed.), *Augsburg*, p. 69.
20 Rublack, *Dressing Up*, pp. 107–12, 129–39.

and other female commoners were restricted to only half an ell.[21] This was reduced to an eighth of an ell for maidservants. Nevertheless, some fairly generous concessions were made as well, and even maidservants were permitted to wear a silk cape and a velvet hair-band.[22] Still, the council had "noted for some time now that luxury in clothing and adornments among some people has so taken the upper hand that one can hardly tell one estate from the other", a concern that resurfaced in 1663, 1668, and 1735.[23] Discussing sumptuary legislation in Renaissance Italy, Welch points out that "the desire for luxuries could cut across social boundaries".[24] Indeed, sumptuary legislation reacted to aspirational dressing, and, in one case, craftsmen including knife-makers and butchers appeared before the Nuremberg court for having worn velvet doublets.[25] Although the maintenance of perceptible sartorial distinctions between the classes continued to be stressed, sumptuary legislation was nonetheless sporadically implemented and selectively enforced.[26]

The Augsburg council also exercised control over the bodies of the city's employees, distributing livery to workers as diverse as the city's fishermen and government staff.[27] In this practice they were no different from princely courts and aristocratic households across early modern Europe, who used apparel to incorporate retainers and servants into a visible social body.[28] In February 1537, it was decreed that clothing must be sent to the timber officials, the craft-work assessors, and the four city bailiffs, made "solely with the city's three colors, red, green, and white".[29] Although these colors were imbued with collective civic pride and were adopted into livery to impart municipal authority, their official purpose could be corrupted and devalued, as the example of the welfare *Stadtpyr* demonstrated. This potential is also seen in a case from 1666, when a group of weavers, protesting one of their own marrying a bailiff's daughter, recounted: "So that they may immediately be recognizable to all, especially to strangers, such beadles and bailiffs must always wear special liveries ... This shows that they are not equal to other honorable people, and

---

21 Rublack, *Dressing Up*, p. 71. A unit of measurement for cloth, the Augsburg long ell was equivalent to 24 inches, while the short ell was 23½ inches: Rublack, Hayward and Tiramani (eds.), *First Book of Fashion*, p. 399.
22 Tlusty (ed.), *Augsburg*, p. 72.
23 Translated and quoted in Tlusty (ed.), *Augsburg*, p. 69; see also Stuart, *Defiled Trades*, p. 41.
24 Welch, *Shopping in the Renaissance*, p. 13.
25 Rublack, *Dressing Up*, p. 253.
26 Chapuis, "Juges et Jupons", pp. 209–11.
27 Seidl, "Einspännigerbuch", p. 112.
28 Jones and Stallybrass, *Renaissance Clothing*, pp. 11, 17.
29 Staats- und Stadtbibliothek Augsburg (SuStBA), Aug. 2° Cod. S 228, fols. 32v–33r.

do not participate in civic affairs."[30] Despite being important officials, the city bailiffs were considered by the public at large to retain a dishonorable social status because of their handling of malefactors. Civic livery was intended to be prestigious, not defamatory. However, its capacity to be devalued with social stigma shows, Stuart argues, that meanings associated with color could not be imposed by authorities but "remained fluid and emerged in everyday interactions".[31]

In addition to evoking emotional responses, color enacted and enlivened social bonds and group identities.[32] Political allegiances and affective symbolism determined sartorial color choices at the Augsburg imperial diet of 1530, for instance, with the opposing Catholic and Protestant parties signaling their loyalties and determinations through their choice of fabric colors.[33] Rublack draws attention to Matthäus Schwarz's outfits for this event, one of which was expressly designed to "please Ferdinand [I of Habsburg]".[34] This ensemble included a doublet of brilliant gold-yellow damask, a color aligning him to the imperial Habsburg cause. A color of joyous resplendence, yellow livery was worn by the bodyguards of Emperor Charles V (1500–58) and the retainers of his brother Ferdinand (1503–64), while Charles himself was recorded to have worn a "golden" riding coat.[35]

Preserving livery designs for a branch of the Augsburg civic militia, the *Einspännigerbuch* of Augsburg council officer Paul Hektor Mair (1517–79) underscores the material interplay of color and allegiance.[36] The album collates records of clothing commissions for the so-called "one-horse" (*Einspänniger*) soldiers, tasked with defense duties including service as armed escorts and messengers.[37] Pasting in original clothing designs by the artist Christoph Weiditz from the years 1542–65, Mair documented the occasions for which new uniforms were issued along with the color, type, and amount of fabric they required. In the 1547 design, the patterns of nine potential shoulder bands using heraldic red, green, and white are tested before the eighth is selected (figure 19.2). The requirement for municipal fashion to convey authority and dignity was no more pronounced than at this very moment, when the city was

---

30 Translated and quoted in Stuart, *Defiled Trades*, p. 38.
31 Stuart, *Defiled Trades*, p. 139.
32 Rublack, Hayward and Tiramani (eds.), *First Book of Fashion*, p. 38.
33 Rublack, "Renaissance Dress", pp. 18–20.
34 Ibid., p. 18.
35 Translated and quoted in ibid., p. 20.
36 SuStBA, Aug. 2° Cod. S 228.
37 Seidl, "Einspännigerbuch", p. 112.

FIGURE 19.2 *Einspänniger* soldiers' livery, 3 July 1547, *Einspännigerbuch* (*Memorybuch über die ausgabe der Kleidung*), Paul Hektor Mair with illustrations by Christoph Weiditz, c. 1569
STAATS- UND STADTBIBLIOTHEK AUGSBURG, 2° COD S 228, FOL. 13R

DRESS AND MATERIAL CULTURE 449

FIGURE 19.3   "This is a Castilian peasant as he goes into a city to market or rides upon an ass", Christoph Weiditz, *Trachtenbuch*, ca. 1529
GERMANISCHES NATIONALMUSEUM, HS. 22474, ILL. 19R

forced to submit to the imperial authorities following Charles v's defeat of the Schmalkaldic League.[38]

Deemed worthy of historical memory, these pictorial records of local uniforms are another example of the social capital of garments in early modern Augsburg. In fact the city cultivated a unique fascination for visualizing clothing and transformed it into a principal subject of its pictorial culture, which gazed not only inward, but also outward to identify, appraise, and compare local and global dress cultures. One of the most formative of these projects was Christoph Weiditz's costume album (*Trachtenbuch*), comprised of 154 watercolor drawings documenting the diverse clothing habits of Iberia, Italy, France, Germany, and the Low Countries.[39] Assembled from material that Weiditz compiled on a journey to the Spanish court in 1529, the album enthusiastically portrays regional varieties of clothing, often depicting outfits from different angles to better capture design, cut, and color (figure 19.3). Weiditz's deployment of dress as the lens through which to compare and contrast foreign cultures and customs was subsequently developed by the printed costume book, a popular sixteenth-century genre that offered curious owners "armchair access" to people and fashions abroad.[40]

3 Investing in Clothing

Articles of dress were investments for Augsburgers of all social classes, and their value could be measured materially, financially, or emotionally according to the owner and wearer. Clothes were of crucial value to those who fell on hard times. The Augsburg pawn trade was long maintained by Jewish communities living in villages near the city. Such was the scale of the "ruin and poverty" that frequently accompanied pawnbroking that in 1538 the council forbade citizens from dealing with Jewish brokers.[41] These measures did not stifle the trade, however, and in 1547, the tailor Michael Gigel was reprimanded for his spendthrift ways because he pawned his wife's clothing to Jews.[42] Sabine Ullmann has shown that while wealthier Augsburgers in need of cash normally pawned jewelry and household valuables made of precious metal, poorer borrowers mostly bargained with clothes, often their most valuable

---

38   Häberlein, *The Fuggers of Augsburg*, pp. 189–90.
39   See Weiditz, *Trachtenbuch*.
40   Jones, "Habits, Holdings, and Heterology", p. 94.
41   Tlusty (ed.), *Augsburg*, p. 189. See also Chapter 16 in this volume.
42   Tlusty (ed.), *Augsburg*, p. 118.

items. These articles – typically bodices, skirts, doublets, jackets, hose, and mantles – could vary considerably in value. In 1602, Maria Pembold received just one gulden for pawning a fustian petticoat and a woolen bodice. By contrast, Anna Kugelmann received 14 gulden for a mantle, bodice, and doublet of assumedly superior quality. These items were not necessarily as unremarkable as their simple descriptions suggest. In a transaction recorded in the same year with greater detail, the silk embroiderer Martin Beltzer pawned a bodice trimmed with silk braids, a woolen bodice embellished with three velvet cords, a yellow-embroidered doublet, and a black buttoned doublet. Beltzer joined the high proportion of cloth-workers pawning clothing at this time, a reminder that the textile trade employed a large number of low-income artisans who were especially susceptible to economic downturns and for whom garments represented the most valuable and expendable items in their household.[43]

As well as being frequently pawned, clothing was also gambled, and in September 1537, to the dismay of the Augsburg council, the unfortunate weaver Bartholme Tagwercker managed to gamble away all his clothes. Dress articles were also a common target for theft. In 1593 and again in 1642, gypsy women faced the Augsburg court charged with stealing and reselling clothing and linen.[44] Garments were not disposable items, and the loss of clothing could result in extreme distress. In 1566, the Jewish doctor Andreas Salomon and his sons were attacked and stripped of their clothes by a city guard. Salomon's complaint did not merely protest his violent treatment, but beseeched the council "to deliver and turn over to me unharmed the clothes that were taken from me".[45] The fear of losing a coat even caused a sword-fight at a wedding in 1600. When the guard Georg Siber could not find his coat, his drunken accusations of theft led to a bloody fight, which Siber justified before the council authorities by claiming that he "couldn't afford to leave it behind".[46]

Due to its financial worth, clothing was also presented as prizes at civic shooting matches. In Augsburg and other towns, winning marksmen at local matches were often rewarded with cloth or articles of clothing, including hose and doublets. The practice was so common that contemporaries regularly used the terms "pants money" (*Hosengeld*) or "winning the pants" (*die Hosen gewinnen*) to refer to any sort of prize money, regardless of the competition.[47]

---

43 Ullmann, "'Leihen umb fahrend Hab und Gut'", pp. 315–17, 325–28.
44 Tlusty (ed.), *Augsburg*, pp. 164, 200–4.
45 Ibid., pp. 193–94.
46 Ibid., pp. 178–79.
47 Tlusty, *The Martial Ethic*, p. 204; on shooting matches, see Chapter 14 in this volume.

Clothing provisions were a principal concern for the city orphanage as well, which managed to reduce expenditures on clothing and footwear by nearly two-thirds of what was projected when it opened its doors in 1572, freeing up money to spend on meat and vegetables.[48] As Thomas M. Safley argues, the orphanage operated a clever regime of "disciplined consumption that emphasized efficiency through standardization and routinization".[49] It contracted regular services from a tailor, a seamstress, and a cobbler, who were supplied with durable materials such as fustian, woolen cloth, leather, and linen to provide homogeneous apparel in bulk. In 1577, Michael Eberhart and his wife tailored 24 blouses, eight aprons, and one petticoat as a monthly order for the orphanage, while Michael Frey supplied 73 pairs of new shoes and repaired 51 pairs.[50] Although the orphanage's measures resulted in practical, uniform garments, the orphans were not necessarily appareled in drab, monotonous outfits and could in fact appear quite colorful. In 1638, for instance, the orphan girls were to be given black woolen aprons and dresses of red and green cloth, while the boys would receive dark blue cloaks.[51]

Affording the maintenance of one's wardrobe was not only a concern for the poor. Aspiring to appear decorous and fashionable also put pressure on wealthy members of the elite and burgher folk to spend outrageous sums on dress. Thus the purchase of new clothing was a regular topic of correspondence between the young patrician Friedrich Endorfer and his father in the years 1620–27, when he was stationed in Lucca and Lyons. Endorfer the Younger repeatedly compared his appearance to other young elite Germans such as Hans Jakob Knopf, who in January 1621 spent a small fortune on a silk mantle with satin braids and a silk doublet made in three colors.[52] Endorfer justified his own spending by insisting he made new purchases only when necessary. The changing of the seasons provided a convenient time to impress such a need upon his father: In January 1621, for instance, he insisted that he required new winter clothing and a proper woolen coat, as until then he had been walking around wearing his summer clothes and a small, black coat that did not even reach his knees.[53]

---

48   Safley, *Charity and Economy*, p. 193. The projected cost was 22 per cent of their annual budget. By 1595 this was down to just 8.7 per cent.
49   Ibid., p. 180.
50   Ibid., pp. 190–91.
51   Ibid., p. 182.
52   Häberlein, Künast, and Schwanke (eds.), *Korrespondenz*, pp. 40, 81.
53   Häberlein, Künast, and Schwanke (eds.), *Korrespondenz*, p. 107.

DRESS AND MATERIAL CULTURE   453

4   Identity and Sartorial Expression

As well as expressing taste and refinement, acts of dressing up negotiated the wearer's relationship to prescribed gender and sexual norms. Contemporary notions of gender could be emphasized by codified accessories and embellishments. Arguably, the most pivotal accessories bedecking men's dress in sixteenth- and seventeenth-century Germany were weapons. In contemporary

FIGURE 19.4   Portrait of Christoph Fugger: oil on wood, Christoph Amberger, 1541, 97,5 × 80,4 cm, Munich, Bayerische Staatsgemäldesammlungen, Alte Pinakothek
PHOTO: BPK | BAYERISCHE STAATSGEMÄLDESAMMLUNGEN

portraiture, sword hilts were frequently emphasized by placing the sitter's hand on his hip or unabashedly gripping the sword's hilt, as seen in the 1541 portrait of Christoph Fugger by Christoph Amberger (figure 19.4).

As arms became regular fixtures in men's dress, swords and daggers (or any other items routinely worn together) were commonly fashioned in sets. Hilts, scabbards, and sword belts were customized to complement the metalwork found on a patron's dress, including rings, pendants, earrings, buttons, and buckles.[54] Making no mention of blade type, size, or length, Augsburg's sumptuary legislation designated the approved metals and levels of embellishment on weapons worn by the city's social classes. For instance, several ordinances issued throughout the period concerned the prohibition of gold ornamentation on the swords and scabbards of craftsmen and journeymen.[55] Elaborately adorned arms, created by enamellers and gold- and silversmiths, were treasured objects. The multi-talented Christoph Weiditz skillfully manipulated gold, silver, steel, and ivory to create an ornamental dagger and knife set featuring the allegorical figure Fortuna (figure 19.5).[56]

The more ornate a sword was, the less useful it was as a weapon of defense. Only hilts constructed from iron or steel were effective for fighting, assuming any additional decoration had not compromised their effectiveness.[57] Martial ability aside, men who donned arms were displaying their readiness to defend themselves and their honor at a moment's notice.[58]

As B. Ann Tlusty demonstrates, male heads of households in Augsburg, as in other towns, had a civic responsibility to keep and bear arms in the public defense. Violators risked a host of penalties for failing to comply, including monetary fines, incarceration, and even exile. In fact, weapons were so inherently connected to notions of public male identity that as a form of punishment the Augsburg council commonly prohibited men from carrying bladed weapons. After breaking an oath in 1551, for instance, a peasant was banned from carrying all weapons except for a blunted bread knife.[59] In 1585, the cloth finisher Matheis Koch was banned from carrying weapons after he had been locked up for public drunkenness and urinated in his cell-mate's food bowl. Thus, to don a sword was to perform a masculine act, signaling that its wearer was a

---

54 Capwell and Anglo, *The Noble Art*, p. 30.
55 Tlusty, *The Martial Ethic*, p. 126.
56 Although most celebrated for his bronze portrait medals, Weiditz worked with various media and crafts, making "pictures from wood, iron, marble and other stone, clay, and gilder's mass": Weiditz, *Trachtenbuch*, p. 15.
57 Capwell and Anglo, *The Noble Art*, p. 83.
58 Tlusty, *The Martial Ethic*, pp. 1, 124.
59 Ibid., p. 1.

FIGURE 19.5
Dagger with sheath, cased in gold, silver, ivory, and steel, Christoph Weiditz, c. 1560, Staatliche Kunstsammlungen Dresden, Rüstkammer, inv. no. p203
PHOTO: RICHARD ANDRICH, SLUB / DEUTSCHE FOTOTHEK

"free and honorable citizen" who successfully and competently managed his personal, financial, and domestic affairs.[60]

Lyndal Roper's critical studies on male honor and early modern German craftsmen reveal how fighting and violence were intertwined with cultural concepts of masculinity. The "group" milieu, which could include guilds, societies, or participants at a particular event, provided a public environment where men could substantiate both individual and collective worth through bellicose acts.[61] Paradoxically, the very same patterns of behavior that established male honor (such as fighting for sport) could also threaten social order

---

60   Ibid., pp. 6, 75, 124 (quote).
61   Roper, *Oedipus and the Devil*, pp. 108–10, 113–16.

if taken to extremes in unregulated contexts (such as brawling in the streets).[62] "Symbolically, masculinity was guaranteed when a man took up weapons and defended his city."[63]

Femininity was constructed around defined classifications of womanhood, determined above all by age and marital status.[64] The passage from maiden to matron was encoded in hair-styling and veiling practices that reflected contemporary notions of female hair and sexuality. A wedding ordinance released by the Augsburg council in 1599 illustrates these ideals and outlines how female guests' hair ought to be dressed, ornamented, or concealed to visually perform their stage of life as they entered the wedding procession.[65] Following custom, young, unmarried women could wear their hair uncovered, while those who were married were expected to conceal their hair with bonnets. The ordinance then mentions old women, who "normally wear veils", and lastly the bride, who wore her hair loose and bare with a bridal crown or wreath on top signifying her virginal status.[66] In spite of these prescribed standards, which were applicable in everyday practice, women nevertheless achieved creative expression through the rich variety of headwear on offer.

Women's embroidered hair-caps, coifs, and bonnets were supplemented by the sixteenth-century fashion for berets, which allowed more hair to be on display.[67] When going to church, however, both married and unmarried women were to conceal their hair under veils and hoods made of linen or cotton.[68] These could be folded, wired, padded, steamed, and starched. Artful shapes were achievable through the skillful manipulation of fabric and careful application of pins. *Zöpfe* – artificial, dyed hair braids – were an especially popular trend across Germany in the second half of the sixteenth century. These colorful, padded ribbons were supplied by specialist vendors in a striking range of hues.[69] An Augsburg costume book from the last quarter of the sixteenth century shows them variously woven into women's hair, color-coordinated with other garments (figure 19.6). Certain colors were adopted for their symbolic value, too, and in one case a woman chose to wear a green pair on her wedding

---

62 Roper discusses this observation in relation to both fighting and drinking in ibid., pp. 107–24.
63 Ibid., p. 108.
64 See Chapter 13 in this volume.
65 Tlusty (ed.), *Augsburg*, p. 76.
66 Roper, *The Holy Household*, p. 143.
67 Rublack, *Dressing Up*, p. 248.
68 For more on women's veiling practices see Burgartz, "Covered Women?", and Zander-Seidel, "'Haubendämmerung'".
69 Rublack, *Dressing Up*, p. 252.

DRESS AND MATERIAL CULTURE 457

FIGURE 19.6   An Augsburg bride going to church on her wedding day, *Kostüme der Männer und Frauen in Augsburg und Nürnberg, Deutschland, Europa, Orient und Afrika*, late 16th century
MUNICH, BAYERISCHE STAATSBIBLIOTHEK, BSB-HSS COD.ICON. 341, FOL. 2V

day because it signaled hope.[70] Like many other decorative hair pieces, *Zöpfe* were relatively inexpensive and enabled women of diverse social rank and wealth to participate in the stylization of the self. Costume books show the braids being worn by women ranging from maidservants to patricians.[71]

The impact of the Reformation upon domestic lives overturned the social expectations of women who fell outside of the marital continuum. As Roper has explored, nuns, prostitutes, and widows were challenged by the city's reformed evangelical moralism.[72] A reformist campaign to abolish Augsburg's seven convents gained momentum in the 1530s and aimed to reintegrate the city's nuns into the lay community.[73] In 1537, the reformed council forced its nuns to put aside their convent habits and supplied at their own expense "honorable worldly clothing" for those at St. Katherina's convent, the largest and most prestigious in the city. Because wearing distinctive habits internalized the nuns' unique feminine identity and membership in a particular religious order, the decree met with resistance. The women were subsequently granted the freedom to wear their habits underneath their new, secular clothing. However, the reformers' attempts destabilized a category of female identity that, as Roper points out, resisted the sexualization of women "in a society in which marital and social status were coded in clothing".[74]

As seen in the case of the nuns of St. Katherina's, the act of dressing, and undressing for that matter, were vehicles of personal expression and individual agency. As Rublack suggests, dressing was akin to the act of creation, using a visual vocabulary rooted in cultural understanding and technical fluency.[75] Collaboration between consumers, agents, and artisans bound urban citizens into networks of material knowledge. Elite Augsburgers in particular were involved in rather than detached from the production and acquisition of goods in their city, and nowhere was this more pronounced than in the creative fashioning of the body.[76] The locating of materials was often the first step, which for more prosperous consumers was assisted by access to networks of international agents and a solid understanding of regional products and merchandising practices.[77] The Fugger and Welser families took advantage of

---

70 Ibid.
71 Ibid., p. 265.
72 See Roper, *The Holy Household*.
73 Ibid., p. 211.
74 Ibid., pp. 209, 239–40 (quotes from p. 240).
75 Rublack, "Renaissance Dress", p. 7.
76 Rublack, "Matter in the Material Renaissance", p. 84.
77 For more on agents and traders, see Pieper, "Trading with Art and Curiosities", pp. 94–96.

their commercial networks to pursue high-quality goods and raw materials.[78] Hans Fugger (1531–98), for instance, spent nine months in correspondence with agents abroad seeking out 60 of the finest lynx pelts for a winter coat. His agents shopped for the pelts in places as diverse as Sweden, Spain, Prague, and Venice, to balance cost against quality.[79] However, the penchant for purchasing high-quality goods was not exclusive to the upper classes. Even peasants living in the countryside of southwestern Germany in the seventeenth century were recorded to have searched for fine quality leather shoes, and sometimes traveled far and wide on foot visiting specific craftsmen at various markets.[80]

Once materials were located, wealthy clients searched for the most skilled craftsmen, including tailors, dyers, tanners, and furriers, who stayed current with the latest trends and emerging technologies.[81] Veit Konrad Schwarz appears to have collaborated with specialist makers across the city to construct "all cuts of hose, doublet, shoes, and bonnets", many of which he proudly proclaimed to have "invented" himself.[82] Depending on the number of specialists needed, craftsmen's fees could surpass the value of materials. The "little book of clothes" of Veit Konrad's father, Matthäus Schwarz, depicts its owner in 137 images during the span of his life wearing a variety of garments and accessories. In the entry dated 1 August 1529, when the Fugger bookkeeper was "32 years, five months, and eight days old", he explains that the craftsmen's fees for his billowy, silk-trimmed, knee-length cape cost more than the material itself.[83]

Material knowledge gained through wearing items could also influence the customization of designs. One such case occurred when Hans Fugger ordered six pairs of white porsequine shoes in Antwerp from his agent Hans Keller. In his correspondence, Fugger states the need to replace his worn-out shoes with new ones. However, he requests that the leather be pinked with small incisions or holes instead of slashed with longer cuts, as the latter method caused the leather to tear easily and look shabby.[84] Veit Konrad Schwarz even noted that he "several times slashed the shoes myself", boldly applying his material know-how and creative taste to his shoes' leather.[85] The vogue for slashing swept across early modern Europe and appeared in a wide variety of materials

---

78 Pieper, "Trading with Art and Curiosities", p. 93.
79 Rublack, *Dressing Up*, p. 52.
80 Rublack, "Matter in the Material Renaissance", p. 77.
81 Rublack, "Matter in the Material Renaissance", p. 77.
82 Translated in Rublack, Hayward and Tiramani (eds.), *First Book of Fashion*, p. 332.
83 Translated in Rublack, Hayward and Tiramani (eds.), *First Book of Fashion*, p. 299.
84 Rublack, "Matter in the Material Renaissance", pp. 53–54.
85 Translated and quoted in Rublack, Hayward and Tiramani, *First Book of Fashion*, p. 331.

FIGURE 19.7 "In March 1523. The doublet of fustian, which has 4,800 slashes with velvet rolls all in white," Book of Clothes (*Klaiderbüchlein*), Matthäus Schwarz, 1520–60
HERZOG ANTON ULRICH-MUSEUM, HS 27 N. 67A, ILL. 61V

used for both men's and women's dress. In 1523, Matthäus Schwarz notoriously ordered a fustian doublet with 4,800 slashes, permitting an underlayer of white velvet to peek through the slits (figure 19.7).[86] However, since the irreversible nature of cutting fabric prevented a garment from being reused or handed down, slashing was often deemed lavish, ostentatious, or wasteful by more ascetic contemporaries.[87]

5 Clothing the Body in Steel

In addition to linen, wool, leather, velvet, and silk, steel was another material called upon to outfit the male body. Armor served as the outfit *de rigeur* for a variety of civic functions, including diplomatic entries, tournaments, parades, and carnivals. One such case occurred at the 1547–48 Diet of Augsburg, where the emperor's son Philip, later King Philip II of Spain (1527–98), represented his ambitions for the title of Holy Roman Emperor fully outfitted in steel.[88] In 1559, Paul Hektor Mair recorded that citizens were instructed by Emperor Ferdinand I to don armor and bear arms for his first imperial entry into Augsburg.[89] Clothing and armor were inextricably linked in the minds of male contemporaries, further demonstrating how masculinity appeared almost synonymous with martial ability in this period. In addition to their own bodies, men were expected to defend and protect their state, household, and familial honor. Clothing and accessories with martial influences – whether fashioned from cloth or steel – promoted these abilities, simultaneously emboldening wearers and tacitly warning onlookers.

In 1538, Mair authored a *Geschlechterbuch* (genealogy book) consisting of a woodcut series illustrating male representatives of Augsburg's leading patrician families adorned in fantastic, historicizing armor.[90] The book commemorates the council's addition of 38 families into the patriciate after their numbers had dwindled to a mere seven families.[91] It demonstrates medieval varieties of armor including houndskull bascinets and visored sallets, while other pieces of garniture incorporate lions' heads and foliate motifs harking back to antiquity (figure 19.8).[92] The book's deployment of classical and Gothic

---

86 Grancsay and Pyhrr, *Arms and Armor*, p. 369.
87 Currie, "Diversity and Design", p. 163.
88 Springer, *Armour and Masculinity*, p. 123.
89 Tlusty (ed.), *Augsburg*, pp. 226–27.
90 Mair, *Bericht und anzeigen*.
91 Häberlein, *The Fuggers of Augsburg*, p. 173.
92 Forgeng and Bauer, "Arms, Armor, and the Artist", pp. 51–52.

FIGURE 19.8 "Langenmantel vom R.", *Bericht und Anzeigen aller Herren Geschlecht der loblichen Stadt Augspurg*, Paul Hektor Mair, 1538, Strasbourg: Christoph Weiditz and David Kannel

MUNICH, BAYERISCHE STAATSBIBLIOTHEK, RAR. 641, FOL. 8

armor granted the patricians, including those newly added, the sense of being from ancient, noble stock. This lineage was to stretch not just backward but forward as well, because otherwise "five hundred or more years from now no one will know and can learn who dwelt there [in Augsburg]".[93] The patricians' armored bodies, set into "manly" poses, are ennobled with an aura of chivalry borrowed from imagined knightly ancestors and classical heroes.[94]

In addition to conjuring up classical associations, armor could also serve as a marker of modernity, demonstrating the latest technological advances in the manipulation of metal. Elaborate harness commissions for elite patrons required multiple craftsmen to work collaboratively, and the combined efforts of armorers, goldsmiths, etchers, engravers, and painters led to increasingly complex aesthetic designs. Plate armor could be etched, embossed, engraved, blued, gilded, and/or damascened, allowing for the addition of awe-inspiring embellishments. Despite the more rigid configuration of its materiality, contemporary trends in menswear were also fashioned in steel, including slashing, pinking, billowing sleeves and breeches, and peascod bellies. For instance, the Augsburg armorer Kolman Helmschmied often incorporated imitative slashing into his high-spec, customized armor designs. In 1523, Helmschmied teamed up with local armor-etcher (and his son-in-law) Daniel Hopfer (c. 1471–1536) to create a *Kostümharnisch* (dress armor) for Wilhelm Freiherr zu Rogendorf, an officer of the Landsknecht mercenaries.[95] The impressively fashioned parade armor, housed in the Kunsthistorisches Museum in Vienna, has been worked to mimic the exaggerated puffed-and-slashed costume worn ubiquitously by German and Swiss mercenaries in this period (figure 19.9). Marina Belozerskaya equates sixteenth-century parade armor to "a kind of wearable sculpture", linking it to "modern-day haute couture, which is similarly intended to communicate the wearer's exclusivity and wealth and not be a practical everyday ware".[96] Even low-grade, mass-produced armor followed basic contemporary trends, and many extant breastplates from the period reflect the latest doublet styles.[97]

Augsburg was a city particularly renowned for its production of armor, due to its ability to source high-quality raw materials and its talented pool of local craftsmen. All suits of armor produced in the city were inspected by the armorers' guild before receiving the Augsburg's maker's mark (the *Stadtpyr* or

---

93   Mair, *Bericht und anzeigen*, p. i.
94   Mair, *Bericht und anzeigen*, p. i.
95   Hale, *Artists and Warfare*, p. 65; Krause, "Daniel Hopfer", p. 67; Grancsay and Pyhrr, *Arms and Armor*, p. 233.
96   Belozerskaya, *Luxury Arts of the Renaissance*, p. 158.
97   Patterson, *Fashion and Armour*, p. 47.

FIGURE 19.9   Costume harness of Wilhelm of Rogendorf (1481–1541): steel and leather, Kolman Helmschmied (German, Augsburg 1471–1532) and Daniel Hopfer (German, Kaufbeuren-Augsburg 1471–1536), 1523
KUNSTHISTORISCHES MUSEUM VIENNA, COURT HUNTING AND ARMORY, NO. A 374

DRESS AND MATERIAL CULTURE 465

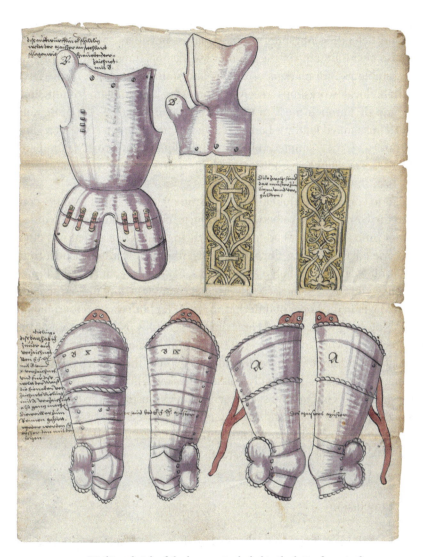

FIGURE 19.10   Working sketch of the harness included in the letter from Andreas
Brenker to Archduke Ferdinand II, Augsburg, 11 July 1557
INNSBRUCK, TIROLER LANDESARCHIV, VGL. ANHANG, DOKUMENT 2

pinecone), thus guaranteeing the level of craftsmanship on locally produced goods and defending Augsburg's trades against outsiders.[98] Finished pieces would also bear the stamp of the armorer's workshop, transforming these site-specific emblems into markers of wealth and status. As a result of the city's reputation, local workshops received domestic and foreign commissions from some of Europe's most prominent men. For instance, the aforementioned Helmschmied family – Lorenz (ca. 1445–1516), Kolman (1470–1532) and Desiderius (1513–79) – counted Habsburg Holy Roman Emperors Maximilian I and Charles V as clients, in addition to Philip II of Spain and various princely members of the Italian courts.[99]

Similar to commissions for clothing, adornment and fit dominated the concerns in the correspondence between patron, armorer, and agent when ordering armor from afar. Armor had to fit properly to be effective, so patrons often sent precise measurements, along with items from their wardrobe (most commonly arming doublets) when placing orders. For instance, in 1562, the Prince of Florence and Siena Francesco I de' Medici (1541–87) wrote to Fugger agent Michael Mayer in the hopes of ordering an armor for both war and tournament from an Augsburg workshop.[100] For sizing, he sent sheepskins for each of the pieces requested with measurements "written in Italian and German", along with a jacket and a pair of hose. In order to express the armor's design and adornment, Francesco additionally sent along a sketch illustrating the requested appearance. A comparable sketch sent in 1557 illustrates the armor commission of Archduke Ferdinand II of Tyrol, who worked with his local agent, Andreas Brenker, to create a suit of armor made in Augsburg intended as a gift for Augustus of Saxony (1526–86) (figure 19.10).[101]

6   Conclusion

The study of dress and material culture in early modern Augsburg allows historians to further understand the city's cultural, social, and behavioral landscape. These inanimate objects tell a lively, multifaceted story and reveal key themes contributing to the city's growth, success, and development. The city's

---

98   De Munck, "Artisans, Products, and Gifts", p. 48.
99   Williams, *The Knight and the Blast Furnace*, p. 363.
100 Archivio di Stato di Firenze, Mediceo del Principato, Filza 215, fol. 20rv, in *Documentary Sources for the Arts and Humanities* (The Medici Archive Project, Inc.), doc. ID 9030.
101 For more on these letters, see Krause, "Arbeitsskizze"; for more on the use of sketches for armor commissions, see Terjanian, "The Art of the Armorer".

inhabitants were conversant in the technical processes of making and the sensorial, communicative powers of dressing. Elite patrons sought out Augsburg's luxury commodities, connecting agents, merchants, and artisans into networks of aesthetic taste and material knowledge. Nevertheless, the example of Augsburg stresses that, across the social spectrum, dress practices negotiated shared identities and allegiances, class and prosperity, gender, religion, and aesthetic creativity. Given its pivotal role in constituting memories, identities, and emotional sensibilities, it is no wonder that dress dominated the lives and minds of many Augsburgers in this period.

Bibliography

Unpublished Primary Sources
Archivio di Stato di Firenze, Mediceo del Principato, Filza 215.
Staats- und Stadtbibliothek Augsburg (SuStBA), 2° Cod. S 228.

Printed Primary Sources
Häberlein, M., Künast, H.-J. and Schwanke, I. (eds.), *Die Korrespondenz der Augsburger Patrizierfamilie Endorfer 1620–1627. Briefe aus Italien und Frankreich im Zeitalter des Dreißigjährigen Krieges*, Augsburg, 2010.
Mair, P.H., *Bericht und anzeigen aller Herren Geschlecht der loblichen Statt Augspurg ...*, Strasbourg, 1538.
Rublack, U., Hayward, M. and Tiramani, J. (eds.), *The First Book of Fashion: the Book of Clothes of Matthäus and Veit Konrad Schwarz*, London, 2015.
Tlusty, B.A. (ed.), *Augsburg During the Reformation Era: An Anthology of Sources*, Indianapolis, 2012.
Weiditz, C., *Trachtenbuch,* ed. T. Hampe, Toronto, 1994.

Secondary Literature
Belozerskaya, M., *Luxury Arts of the Renaissance*, London, 2005.
Burghartz, S., "Covered Women? Veiling in Early Modern Europe", *History Workshop Journal* 80 (2015), pp. 1–32.
Capwell, T. and Anglo S., *The Noble Art of the Sword*, London, 2012.
Chapuis, S., "Juges et Jupons: Les lois vestimentaires et les femmes à Augsbourg au XVIe siècle", in M. Viallon (ed.), *Paraître et se vêtir au XVIe siècle. Actes du XIIIe Colloque du Puy-en-Velay*, Saint-Étienne, 2006, pp. 193–212.
Currie, E., "Diversity and Design in the Florentine Tailoring Trade, 1550–1620", in M. O'Malley and E. Welch (eds.), *The Material Renaissance*, Manchester, 2007, pp. 154–73.

De Munck, B., "Artisans, Products and Gifts: Rethinking the History of Material Culture in Early Modern Europe", *Past and Present* 224 (2014), pp. 39–74.

Forgeng, J.L. and Bauer, C., "Arms, Armor, and the Artist", in I. Sinkević (ed.), *Knights in Shining Armor: Myth and Reality 1450–1650* (exhibition catalogue), Piermont, 2006, pp. 36–55.

Frieder, B.K., *Chivalry and the Perfect Prince: Tournaments, Art, and Armor at the Spanish Habsburg Court*, Kirksville, 2008.

Grancsay, S. and Pyhrr, S., *Arms and Armor: Essays*, New York, 1986.

Häberlein, M., *The Fuggers of Augsburg: Pursuing Wealth and Honor in Renaissance Germany*, Charlottesville and London, 2012.

Hale, J.R., *Artists and Warfare in the Renaissance*, New Haven, 1990.

Hayward, J., *Virtuoso Goldsmiths and the Triumph of Mannerism*, London, 1976.

Hess, D. and Hirschfelder, D., *Renaissance, Barock, Aufklärung. Kunst und Kultur vom 16. bis zum 18. Jahrhundert* (exhibition catalogue), Nuremberg, 2010.

Jardine, L., *Worldly Goods: A New History of the Renaissance*, London, 1996.

Jones, A.R., "Habits, Holdings, Heterologies: Populations in Print in a 1562 Costume Book", *Yale French Studies* 110 (2006), pp. 92–121.

Krause, S., "Der Augsburger Druckgraphiker Daniel Hopfer (1471–1536) als Waffendekorateur," *Jahrbuch des Kunsthistorischen Museums Wien* 13–14 (2011–12), pp. 53–75.

Krause, S., "Eine Arbeitsskizze zu einem Küriss für Kurfürst August von Sachsen (1526–1586)", *Waffen- und Kostümkunde. Zeitschrift für historische Waffen- und Kleidungsgeschichte* 1 (2015), pp. 1–18.

Patterson, A., *Fashion and Armour in Renaissance Europe: Proud Lookes and Brave Attire*, London, 2009.

Pieper, R., "Trading with Art and Curiosities in Southern Germany before the Thirty Years War", in M. North and D. Ormrod (eds.), *Markets for Art, 1400–1800*, Seville, 1998, pp. 87–99.

Roeck, B., *Eine Stadt in Krieg und Frieden. Studien zur Geschichte der Reichsstadt Augsburg zwischen Kalenderstreit und Parität*, 2 vols., Göttingen, 1989.

Roper, L., *The Holy Household: Women and Morals in Reformation Augsburg*, Oxford, 1989.

Roper, L., *Oedipus and the Devil: Witchcraft, Sexuality, and Religion in Early Modern Europe*, London, 1994.

Rublack, U., *Dressing Up: Cultural Identity in Renaissance Europe*, Oxford, 2010.

Rublack, U., "Matter in the Material Renaissance", *Past and Present* 219 (2013), pp. 41–85.

Rublack, U., "Renaissance Dress, Cultures of Making, and the Period Eye", *West 86th* 23 (2016), pp. 6–34.

Safley, T.M., *Charity and Economy in the Orphanages of Early Modern Augsburg*, Boston, 1997.

Seidl, E., "Einspännigerbuch (Memorybuch über die ausgabe der Kleidung)", in C. Emmendörfer and H. Zäh (eds.), *Bürgermacht & Bücherpracht. Augsburg Ehren- und Familienbücher der Renaissance* (exhibition catalogue), Lucerne, 2011, vol. 1, pp. 112–15.

Springer, C., *Armour and Masculinity in the Italian Renaissance*, Toronto, 2010.

Stuart, K., *Defiled Trades and Social Outcasts: Honor and Ritual Pollution in Early Modern Germany*, Cambridge, 1999.

Terjanian, P. "The Art of the Armorer in Late Medieval and Renaissance Augsburg: The Rediscovery of the Thun Sketchbooks, in *Jahrbuch des kunsthistorischen Museums Wien*, Part I, vol. 13/14 (2013), pp. 298–395; Part II, vol. 17/18 (2016), pp. 153–292.

Tlusty, B.A., *The Martial Ethic in Early Modern Germany: Civic Duty and the Right of Arms*, Basingstoke, 2011.

Ullmann, S., "'Leihen umb fahrend Hab und Gut': Der christlich-jüdische Pfandhandel in der Reichsstadt Augsburg", in R. Kießling and S. Ullmann (eds.), *Landjudentum im deutschen Südwesten während der Frühen Neuzeit*, Berlin, 1999, pp. 304–35.

Wandel, L.P., *The Eucharist in the Reformation: Incarnation and Liturgy*, Cambridge, 2006.

Welch, E., *Shopping in the Renaissance: Consumer Cultures in Italy 1400–1600*, New Haven, 2005.

Williams, A.R., *The Knight and the Blast Furnace: A History of the Metallurgy of Armour in the Middle Ages and the Early Modern Period*, Leiden, 2003.

Zander-Seidel, J. "'Haubendämmerung': Frauenkopfbedeckungen zwischen Spätmittelalter und Früher Neuzeit", in R.C. Schwinges, R. Schorta and K. Oschema (eds.), *Fashion and Clothing in Late Medieval Europe*, Riggisberg, 2010, pp. 37–43.

CHAPTER 20

Learned Culture

Wolfgang E.J. Weber
Translated by Mark Häberlein and B. Ann Tlusty

1   Late Medieval Christian and Secular Knowledge

Learned culture begins to develop when individuals and groups start to cope with knowledge in a reflective manner that goes beyond mere everyday knowledge, i.e. skills and abilities necessary for the maintenance of basic processes of material and social reproduction. In Augsburg – an ecclesiastical, political, and economic center of European significance – a learned culture in that sense emerged at an early date, but the existing sources provide detailed information only from the mid-fifteenth century onward.

In the later Middle Ages, the higher clergy constituted a local elite that was universally literate and was therefore particularly capable of receiving, adapting, producing, and transmitting learned knowledge. This group was essentially made up of the top leaders of the diocese (including the cathedral chapter) and the city's numerous monasteries, above all the imperial abbey of Sts. Ulrich and Afra. The higher clergy's specific needs and interests shaped the kinds of knowledge it required. These included legal and administrative knowledge for the efficient management of their respective institutions, both internally and externally, vis-à-vis the Roman Curia and various secular powers; theological knowledge in order to represent the prevailing Christian dogma as completely and confidently as possible; and knowledge about Christian piety and morality in order to deepen their faith, diligently perform their pastoral duties, and adequately represent the church as the unerring, venerable and singular guardian of God's truth and destiny. In accordance with these general aims, ecclesiastical institutions and individual clerics collected manuscripts and (from the later fifteenth century onward) prints; produced copies, excerpts, and commentaries; wrote sermons and organized discussions; and, in addition, developed and recorded ideas of their own and put them to print.

These efforts intensified when Peter von Schaumberg (1388–1469) became bishop in 1424 and when, beginning during his tenure in about 1440, the monastic reform originating in the monasteries of Melk and Tegernsee gained a foothold in Augsburg. The well-educated new bishop was determined to bring his diocese to new heights. Accordingly, he initiated internal reforms such as examinations to ensure that priests possessed certain minimal standards of learning before they were ordained. Moreover, Schaumberg instigated a lengthy lawsuit against the imperial city aimed at restoring ancient episcopal rights. An important precondition for the success of these efforts was the growing dependence on the written word for administrative processes, including the collection, registration, and indexing of existing documents; the acquisition of necessary but locally unavailable knowledge, mainly in written form; and the purposeful, methodologically refined processing of knowledge. The result of these efforts was a more scholarly approach, especially regarding legal matters. Schaumberg also placed the first orders for printed works and initiated the short-lived establishment of a printing press in the imperial abbey of Sts. Ulrich and Afra, from 1472 to 1474. According to Klaus Unterburger, the abbey supported the bishop's efforts to reform learned culture in three respects: it "promoted the collection, writing, illuminating, and printing of books"; it worked for "the diffusion of a specific monastic theology [...] aimed at Christianization, internalization, and religious experience"; and it effected "a turn towards history" in order to strengthen the monastic community's identity, self-awareness, and dedication to its purpose through the study and knowledge of its past. In this context, Sigismund Meisterlin (1435–97) compiled the monastic chronicle *Index monasterii Sanctorum Udalrici et Afra*, while the monk Wilhelm Wittwer penned a *Catalogus abbatum* which also contains information on the abbey's library and on monastic practices of knowledge.[1]

A second elite group that required advanced forms of knowledge in the context of its demarcation from and competition with the church was the urban ruling class. The patrician core of this group focused on the accumulation of legal and administrative knowledge in order to govern, and also for the purpose of defending against the potentially dangerous ambitions of external rivals and social climbers. These efforts went hand in hand with the growing use of written records for governance, which had begun in the twelfth century. The growth in administrative business and record-keeping, as well as concerns such as lawsuits with clerical institutions, accelerated the introduction of council protocols, the systematic registration of the city's correspondence, and the growing use of marginal notes, cross-references, commentaries, graphical marks, and indexes, which may be regarded as preconditions and evidence of

---

1 Unterburger, "Zwischen freier Reichsstadt und monastischer Reform", quotes on pp. 161–62; Hägele and Thierbach (eds.), *Augsburg macht Druck*; Schmidt, "Klosterdruckerei"; Augustyn, "Historisches Interesse".

new forms of knowledge management. These processes must largely be inferred, however, from related traces in the records, such as the employment of lawyers and scribes, or the establishment of the urban chancellery and archives. A "little memorial book" (*Denckbuechlin*) in which the city council recorded its conflicts, "particularly with the clergy" (*sonderlich wider die gaistlichen*), for example, has apparently been lost. On the other hand, members of the political elite also sought to acquire the necessary educational knowledge to position themselves culturally and historically and support their claims to social precedence, superior reputation, and authority. These developments continued throughout the early modern era.[2]

The demand for knowledge was essentially similar among the second tier of the political elite, the non-patrician merchants, whose influence relied on their financial clout and far-reaching networks. As the merchants' position was crucially dependent on their knowledge of changing market circumstances, however, business information was of even more fundamental importance for them than political expertise. The relevance of commercial knowledge increased in tandem with the accelerating expansion of Augsburg's commercial and financial activities. This included advanced techniques of bookkeeping and internal information management; the gathering of accurate information on current tariffs and prices, supply and demand, and the activities of competitors; as well as access to the most recent news about relevant political and military events and developments. Thus business-related documents also began to accumulate in the houses and offices of the large family companies. Increasingly rigorous attention was devoted to the collection and evaluation of information, even though the need for immediate practical application would impede its more general value. This was true for the acquisition of foreign languages as well, which was initially confined to business-related communication skills. Those written documents, commentaries, and perhaps also expert opinions thus produced were also liable to loss, as many documents were thrown away when they were considered outdated. Research on the fifteenth century consequently has to rely on scant data, with only business correspondence surviving to a somewhat greater extent. For the sixteenth century, the sources on practices of business management become much more plentiful.[3]

---

[2] Kluge, *Macht des Gedächtnisses*, passim (on the *Denckbuechlin*, see p. 247); Weber, "Herrschafts- und Verwaltungswissen".

[3] Kluge, *Macht des Gedächtnisses*, pp. 293–305; idem, "Kaufmann und die Schrift"; Schmidt, "Einführung: Stagnation oder Revolution?", esp. pp. 17–18; Häberlein, "Aneignung"; Kießling, "Spannungsfeld".

A third elite group which established itself in fifteenth-century Augsburg were the secular jurists. Legal scholars owed not merely their exalted position but their very existence to their handling of complex, highly specialized knowledge. They also began at an early stage to collect relevant textual repositories (manuscripts and printed works), discuss their contents, and compose texts of their own. Moreover, they likewise sought to acquire a comprehensive education in order to gain recognition within the upper echelons of urban society.

Finally, the existence of an early lay *Bildungsbürgertum* (literate bourgeoisie), which cut across these elite groups and even included some craftsmen, was one of Augsburg's peculiarities. Indeed, both manuscripts and early printed works evince a sustained interest in German-language prose literature and the performance of plays. These partly imported, partly self-composed texts point to a literate milieu which may be regarded as the base layer of the imperial city's learned culture.[4]

It should be noted, however, that the acquisition of a general and professional education by members of the above-mentioned elites, as well as by some people of middling rank, largely took place outside the city. There was no university in Augsburg before 1970, and we know little about the existence, activities, and impact of diocesan and monastic schools. Even less is known about the structure and influence of the imperial city's school system in the late medieval period. As a rule, patricians' and merchants' sons probably enjoyed domestic tutoring and other kinds of private instruction in their early years. Their later studies took them mostly to Italy, but also to French and eventually to German university towns like Ingolstadt, located about 45 miles northwest of Augsburg, which opened its gates in 1472. Studying the liberal arts provided young men with basic linguistic, methodological, and socio-cultural skills, while the higher faculties of law, theology, and – to a lesser extent – medicine supplied them with in-depth general and specialized knowledge. The scions of Augsburg's business elite often underwent a commercial apprenticeship, with Venice being the preferred location as early as the fifteenth century. These stays abroad, and the contacts that were acquired there, provided an essential infrastructure for the import of knowledge into Augsburg.[5]

On the whole, Augsburg's late medieval learned culture, with its characteristic mix of Christian and secular influences, appears to have satisfied the various underlying demands for knowledge and education. Yet it initially lacked

---

4   See Janota and Williams-Krapp (eds.), *Literarisches Leben*.
5   Kintzinger, "Schulen"; Glück, Häberlein, and Schröder, *Mehrsprachigkeit*; Kießling, "Das gebildete Bürgertum"; idem, "Ansatzpunkte".

innovative impulses, and its significance hardly extended beyond the local and regional sphere. What was missing was a novel concept of knowledge, education, and scholarship that combined and integrated the various approaches in a comprehensive and appealing way. This concept reached the city in the later fifteenth century with the advent of humanism.

2   Humanism

News from Italy that an intense search had begun for ancient texts, whose study promised a substantial enrichment of knowledge, as well as support for claims of cultural ascendancy, initially came to Augsburg with returning travelers, above all students from the universities of Bologna, Padua, and Pavia. Augsburg clerics attending the Council of Constance (1414–18) confirmed reports about the new movement, which intensified as Greek scholars fleeing before and after the fall of Constantinople in 1453 joined its ranks. The local political and ecclesiastical elites soon responded to these impulses – not merely out of curiosity, but because it promised to satisfy their quest for education and cultural orientation.

From about 1450 onward, a circle of interested individuals led by the patrician mayor Sigmund Gossembrot the Elder (1417–93) formed the city's first humanist *sodalitas* or *congregatio*. The circle included the jurist and city recorder Valentin Eber (1420–96), the theologian Thomas Ödenhofer (1430–80), the vicar-general Leonhard Gessel (1400–65), and the reform-minded pastor and later diocesan secretary Heinrich Lur (1410–after 1476). Moreover, Laurentius Blumenau (1415–84), a legal scholar who served as counselor to the Order of the Teutonian Knights in Prussia and subsequently to Bishop Peter von Schaumberg, formed close relations with this circle, as did the Nuremberg physician Hermann Schedel (1410–85), who was in the service of Augsburg until 1467. Contacts of varying intensity also existed with other clerics: Benedictines from the abbey of Sts. Ulrich and Afra; some Dominicans like Johann Faber (1470–1522); and above all, cathedral canons like Bernhard von Waldkirch (1470–1523). A temporary associate of the *sodalitas* was Josef Grünpeck (1470–1532), professor of rhetoric at the University of Ingolstadt and author of numerous historical tracts as well as two humanist plays, whom the emperor had crowned as *poeta laureatus*.[6]

---

6   For this and the following paragraph, see Gier, "Bernhard von Waldkirch"; idem, "Italien rezeption im Augsburger Humanismus"; and the contributions in Müller (ed.), *Humanismus*

Most members and associates of this circle had studied in Italy. They provided for the acquisition of original works by Italian humanists, some of which were translated into German and printed in Augsburg. Before long, the circle moved from the mere discussion of these works and the canon of ancient texts to the production of original texts in a humanist spirit. Commissioned by Gossembrot, the above-mentioned Benedictine Sigismund Meisterlin finished the *Cronographia Augustensium*, a chronicle of Augsburg, in 1456. This account, which was not very polished by humanist or literary standards, sought to endow the imperial city with a glorious history of its own in accordance with Italian models of patriotic communal historiography. The aim was to place the German city of Augsburg on an equal footing with metropolises like Florence and Milan.[7] It is revealing that Meisterlin's humanist pursuits earned him a rebuke from the leadership of his convent and prompted him to leave the monastic community after 1457.

In 1488, when his older relative Sigmund Gossembrot was still alive, the 23-year-old merchant's son Conrad Peutinger returned to his native Augsburg after several years of studying the humanist liberal arts and Roman law in Padua and Bologna, and of travelling to Rome and Florence. Peutinger not only became the leading figure of the imperial city's internal and external politics as city secretary (from 1497) and legal counselor,[8] but also stood at the center of another humanist circle, which would eventually outshine Gossembrot's group and soon became known as the *sodalitas Augustana*. Crucially, from 1491 onward Peutinger gained the favor of King Maximilian (who became emperor in 1508). Peutinger's 1498 marriage with Margarete Welser, the daughter of one of Augsburg's pre-eminent patrician merchants, provided him with substantial financial means.[9] Moreover, he managed to build a far-flung scholarly and political network, membership in which was coveted due to its exclusivity and prestige. Consequently, humanism became enshrined at the very core of Augsburg's politics and culture and allowed the imperial city to claim the position of a cultural capital within upper Germany.

Peutinger himself concentrated on building extensive collections in a humanist and antiquarian spirit, as well as on the transmission of contacts, news, and artifacts. He also applied his humanist knowledge and skills to his legal and political work, playing an essential role in the reordering of the city's

---

und Renaissance.
7   See Chapter 4 in this volume.
8   See Lutz, *Conrad Peutinger*.
9   See Zäh, "Konrad Peutinger und Margarethe Welser".

repositories and archives around 1540 and making improvements in accordance with humanist principles in the style and arguments employed in the city's correspondence and diplomatic efforts. Peutinger undoubtedly sought to enhance his own reputation through these activities as well, for he did not hail from a patrician family and, as a mere public official, belonged only to the second tier of the political elite.

Particularly noteworthy are Peutinger's inventory of Augsburg's Roman inscriptions (*Romanae vetustatis fragmenta in Augusta Vindelicorum*), published in 1505 and again in 1520 as a humanist urban topography based on Italian models; his acquisition of a late Roman road map in 1507, which has been named *Tabula Peutingeriana* after him and which he intended to publish; and the establishment of his library from the 1480s onward. The latter eventually comprised almost 6,000 identifiable titles bound in 2,200 separate volumes, probably the largest contemporary private library north of the Alps. That Peutinger actually worked with this collection is evident from comprehensive entries in his own hand in two library catalogues along with numerous marginal notes, commentaries, and other traces he left in the texts themselves.[10]

While he was able to complete only a small fraction of his ambitious plans for editing texts, Peutinger often patronized other humanist activities, and his elevation to the rank of imperial counselor involved him in significant financial, political, and diplomatic affairs of the Holy Roman Empire. Examples include compiling materials for Emperor Maximilian's memoir and advising the ruler on the composition and execution of pertinent historical and panegyrical works. He was also involved in the preparations and realization of an expedition to India initiated by the Welser family (to whom, as noted above, Peutinger was related by marriage) in 1504–07. Peutinger's library and artifact collections evince a sustained interest in the Ottoman Empire as well, for Augsburgers were keenly aware of the danger posed by the Ottomans to Christian Europe after the fall of Constantinople. In the 1520s, Peutinger penned important legal opinions on behalf of Augsburg's large merchant companies, which repudiated the rigid regulation of interest payments and the prohibition of monopolies. This was followed by an equally significant, humanistically and irenically inspired opinion on the religious conflict that had broken out in the city in the 1520s.[11] Peutinger's pleas for a "middle way" of compromise, however, remained unheeded.

---

10 Künast and Zäh, *Bibliothek Konrad Peutingers*.
11 See Chapter 10 in this volume as well as Kießling and Müller (eds.), *Konrad Peutinger*.

Among Peutinger's humanist correspondents and friends were such well-known figures as Sebastian Brant, Konrad Celtis, Erasmus of Rotterdam, Thomas More, Willibald Pirckheimer, Johannes Reuchlin, and Juan Luis Vives. Further contacts, for example with Ulrich von Hutten, were forged on the occasion of Augsburg's imperial diets, in which Peutinger took an active part. Among the local humanists associated with his circle, worth mentioning are Johannes Pinicianus (1477/78–1542), sometime private instructor of Peutinger's children, translator of Latin works, and author of textbooks and poems; Johann Mader (d. 1534/35), a local teacher who likewise translated and edited Latin texts; and Johannes Böschenstein (1472–1550), editor of Augsburg's first Hebrew textbook. Also noteworthy is Veit Bild (1481–1529). Of humble background, Bild had studied at the University of Ingolstadt, which had already come under the influence of humanism at the time. In 1504, he entered the abbey of Sts. Ulrich and Afra, where he studied Latin, Greek, and Hebrew, along with mathematical and astronomical topics. His writings sought to deepen the Christian faith (according to the teachings of the Roman Church) in a humanist spirit, making him a typical example of the learned monk.[12]

By the time Peutinger died in 1547, the local humanist scene had undergone significant change. In terms of membership it had become much stronger. The St. Anna high school (*Gymnasium*), founded in 1531, now provided it with an institutional foundation.[13] Other local schools, whose founding had been inspired by the Protestant Reformation and the ensuing confessional rivalry, were also shaped by humanist teachers and programs. Studying ancient texts, learning the requisite languages, editing manuscripts according to new, critical, philological standards, and imitating or even surpassing the ancient and humanist classics had become central concerns for many scholars. Within urban society, humanist scholars became recognizable by their polished language and were in demand as keynote speakers, composers of texts, and students of history and current problems like the "Turkish danger". Imperial diets witnessed acclaimed appearances by humanist poets and the dissemination of humanist-inspired historical texts.

At the same time, the Reformation split the humanist community into Protestant and Catholic camps. A third group, which sought to maintain a neutral position and harmonious relations in the spirit of Erasmus of Rotterdam, was temporarily represented by men like Bishop Christoph von Stadion

---

12   Zäh, "Einführung"; Laube and Zäh (eds.), *Gesammeltes Gedächtnis*; Lutz, *Conrad Peutinger*; Müller, "Konrad Peutinger und die sodalitas Peutingeriana"; Biehler-Praxl, "Eigennutz".
13   See Kießling, "'und also ein newe Liberey anzurichten'".

(1478–1543), but it remained small and nearly invisible in times of confessional strife. Connections with Italy were largely severed, and relations between the divided confessions became increasingly strained. The original goals of the followers of humanism were modified accordingly, as the confessional parties were forced to curtail their efforts to apply pre-Christian norms and insights towards the improvement of the present. The church fathers now moved to the foreground as crucial historical links between antiquity and Christianity, while pre-Christian authors were considered heathens who had little to teach to true Christians. Irenic scholars who distanced themselves from confessional allegiances were particularly susceptible to charges of being lukewarm Christians. Nonetheless, all confessions remained interested in acquiring pedagogical, didactic, and rhetorical skills, and in the philological, historical, theoretical, and critical instruments conferred by humanism, for these were the advanced skills that were indispensable for strengthening one's own confession and destabilizing rivals.[14]

Already during the early stages of the Reformation, Urbanus Rhegius (1489–1541), who had studied in Ingolstadt, been crowned as *poeta laureatus* by Maximilian I in 1517, and originally served as cathedral preacher, had successfully applied these techniques as preacher in St. Anna. Opposing him was Luther's main antagonist Johannes Eck (1486–1543), a noted humanist and professor of theology in Ingolstadt. The St. Anna *Gymnasium* incorporated humanism in this religious context during the tenure of Sixt Birck (1501–54), its headmaster from 1536 on. Birck also oversaw the establishment of the city library, which began in 1537 with the identification and acquisition of suitable works from abandoned monastic libraries. In 1543–44, the library managed to acquire 99 Greek manuscripts, which had been purchased in Venice and were mainly related to the early Christian period. Hieronymus Wolf (1516–80) served as headmaster and librarian from 1557 until his death; his private library eventually comprised 650 volumes containing 1,200 titles, and he is regarded as the founder of Byzantine studies in Germany. Both Wolf and his successor David Höschel (1556–1617), who compiled an additional 35 Greek editions, strengthened this specific humanist approach. Höschel, however, remained hesitant to reveal his confessional allegiance.[15]

On the other side of the confessional divide, the Fugger family, almost all of whom remained faithful to the Roman Church, supported Catholic efforts to match Protestant achievements in education and scholarship. Family members patronized humanist scholars, and the brothers Hans Jakob, Ulrich,

---

14   See Unterburger, "Zwischen Irenik und Kontroverstheologie".
15   Roeck, *Als wollt die Welt schier brechen*, pp. 134–41, 148–53.

and Georg Fugger built up extensive libraries. With the help of the above-mentioned Hieronymus Wolf, the Vatican's librarian Onophrio Panvinio, and the bibliophile and art expert Jacopo Strada, Hans Jakob Fugger purchased numerous books and manuscripts in Italy, commissioned manuscript copies, and in 1552 acquired the acclaimed library of the Nuremberg physicians Hartmann and Hermann Schedel. After Hans Jakob moved to Munich, he sold his collection to Duke Albrecht of Bavaria for the latter's court library in 1571. Hans Jakob's brother Ulrich Fugger had 250 Greek codices in his possession in 1555 and financed the printing of more than 20 Latin and Greek editions by the Paris printer Henri Estienne (Henricus Stephanus) between 1558 and 1568. When he moved to Heidelberg in 1567, Ulrich Fugger took several thousand books with him – a collection which was incorporated into the Palatine court library and eventually transferred to Rome when troops of the Catholic League occupied Heidelberg during the early years of the Thirty Years' War.[16]

The opening of the Jesuit college of St. Salvator in 1582, which was largely financed by members of the Fugger family as well, marked a further step in the establishment of a decidedly Roman Catholic version of learned culture in Augsburg.[17] Even earlier, the Jesuit order had taken over the diocesan university, founded in nearby Dillingen in 1549–51. One of its early professors, the noted Latin scholar Jakob Pontanus (1542–1626), taught at Augsburg's Jesuit college from 1582 onward. For Pontanus' fellow Jesuit Matthäus Rader (1561–1634), humanist scholarship primarily served to highlight the order's capacity to serve the Roman Church. Still, Rader compiled the first edition of Martial's epigrams, which confessional fundamentalists considered too obscene to merit serious attention as an ancient literary document.[18]

Financed by the Catholic humanist, merchant, and mayor Marcus (Marx) Welser (1558–1614), Augsburg from 1594 to 1614 housed the scholarly publishing enterprise *Ad Insigne Pinus* (a reference to the city's emblem, the pine cone, which humanists had rediscovered in their studies of the city's Roman past). Its output mainly consisted of original Greek editions of church fathers as well as historiographical and hagiographical works. Although the Protestant David Höschel was one of Welser's main collaborators, the publishing house failed to evolve into a trans-confessional enterprise with a broad appeal to scholars in Augsburg and beyond. Instead, individual humanists remained tied to confessionally circumscribed scholarly communities. Only members of the highest

---

16   Weber, "Vermächtnis des 'Wassermanns'"; Häberlein, *The Fuggers of Augsburg*, pp. 166–69.
17   Baer and Hecker (eds.), *Jesuiten*.
18   Kießling (ed.), *Universität Dillingen*; Schmid, "Korrespondenz"; Marschler and Müller (eds.), *Jesuitische Gelehrsamkeit*.

social stratum could afford to break with this pattern. Marcus Welser, for example, who also distinguished himself as a historian of Augsburg's and Bavaria's ancient past, could afford to maintain close ties with all confessional camps. Evidence that the humanist ideal of peaceful scholarly debate continued to exert any influence otherwise exists only in the relatively mild, objective tone which characterized at least occasional controversies.[19]

The humanist impulse eventually surrendered to the forces of confessionalism in the early seventeenth century. Due to the educational and scholarly work of the Jesuits, who among other methods successfully employed the theater to advance their agenda,[20] the Catholics increasingly gained the upper hand. But the achievements of this now fading concept of education and learning were impressive. The humanist movement had stimulated the urban culture of writing and debate, as is evident in the spread of literacy, the introduction of new writing styles and languages, the enhanced quality of expression, and the establishment of new circles of local debate. Humanism had endowed the city with historical and cultural knowledge and set processes in motion by which it continued to be acquired and improved. This included knowledge about antiquity and early Christianity; contemporary Europe and the non-European world; the meaning, course, and driving forces of history; secular concepts of identity, such as patriotism; the causes and consequences of human action; and ways to apply this knowledge to increase its practical usefulness. Moreover, the humanist movement was an important source of Augsburg's global expansion, manifested in expeditions, voyages, and the collection and printing of news about the Old and New Worlds,[21] including the expanding Ottoman Empire. A key example is provided by the physician Leonhard Rauwolf, who traveled in the Syrian and Mesopotamian provinces of the Ottoman Empire during the 1570s, collecting hundreds of botanical specimens, and published an account of his voyage in 1582.[22] In sum, humanism helped the imperial city to acquire a specific identity and to preserve an irreplaceable historical record that would otherwise have been lost.

These accomplishments in many ways implied a diminution of the position of the church. In this respect, humanism also helped Augsburg's elites to secure their positions of leadership and distinguish themselves from those below them. An exemplary case is the command of Latin, which the

---

19   Ferber, "Cives vestros"; idem, *'Scio multos te amicos habere'*; Roeck, "Geschichte, Finsternis und Unkultur".
20   See Gier (ed.), *Jakob Bidermann*. On related Protestant efforts, see Tschopp, "Protestantisches Schultheater".
21   See Johnson, *German Discovery of the World*, pp. 47–87.
22   Walter, "Reise ins (Un-)Bekannte"; Häberlein, "Botanisches Wissen".

population at large lacked. During the final phase of humanism, the city witnessed a progressive political and rhetorical refinement of urban correspondence and diplomacy, and improvement of legal and political record-keeping in the city archives and library. Other indicators of progress are the exactitude of the city's topographical measuring in 1598, along with the creation of a city plan and city model, and the reception of late-humanist political theories like the *Politica* (1589) of Justus Lipsius, one of Marcus Welser's correspondents. The Italian Hieronymus Sirturus, who compiled a handbook version of this enormously influential tract, the *Compendium Politicum ex universi civili Doctrina Justi Lipsii*, dedicated it to Hans Ernst Fugger, who had hosted him in Augsburg during his travels in 1614. These late humanist achievements had several advantages for the rulers, providing them with a knowledge base that the common citizens did not command; a modern construct of politics as a concept and practice of success-oriented rule; and relevant instruments of governance. All these aspects found their way into the Religious Peace of Augsburg (1555), which would hardly have been conceivable without the impact of humanism.[23]

After the Thirty Years' War had temporarily stifled the progress of learned culture, the Peace of Westphalia (1648) offered renewed opportunities. The dramatic experience of war diminished the impact of confessionalism and encouraged religiously neutral approaches.[24] The tract *Abbild- und Beschreibung des Türckischen Haupt-Fahnens*, for example, which the Protestant orientalist (and noted translator of the Quran) Matthias Friedrich Beck (1649–1701) wrote in 1686 about a Turkish flag captured in Hungary, described the war against the Turks as a joint enterprise of Catholics and Protestants. The extent to which the two confessional camps actually converged remains to be systematically researched: despite evidence of increasing contacts between Catholic and Protestant scholars, it is also clear that they continued to prefer citing authors from their own confession in their publications.[25] But from about 1700 onward, a new local configuration of science, education, and learning began to emerge which was at least partly shaped by Enlightenment impulses. This development was influenced by the new science, which had also been present in the imperial city for some time.

---

23   Weber, "Humanismus und reichsstädtische Politik".
24   See Chapter 15 in this volume.
25   Hamilton, "Lutheran Translator".

3   New Science

The term "new science" applies to the study of natural empirical phenomena. Its adherents sought to grasp these as precisely as possible through measurement, experiment, and description, based on the assumption that their origins and manifestations were primarily due to natural causes rather than divine intervention. Our modern concept of science is closely related to the emergence of the "new science" of the early modern period, which now moved beyond scholarship, in the sense of adopting, processing, and disseminating existing knowledge, and towards empirical research and the generation of new exact knowledge.[26]

In late medieval learned culture, measurement, calculation, and the search for precision were already important within certain fields of knowledge, especially mathematics, astronomy, astrology, medicine, and chemistry. In this context, not only contemporary classics in Arabic and Persian, but also Mediterranean texts were translated and printed in Augsburg. In addition, locally available instructions for pilgrimages to the Holy Land demonstrate an effort to render exact distances, even though the rather imprecise average day trip remained the dominant unit of measurement.

Nor did local humanism neglect the empirical sciences. In 1514, Johannes Böschenstein published a textbook on arithmetic for children with Indo-Arabic numbers (*Ain new geordnet Rechen biechlein mit den zyffern*), and Veit Bild studied astronomy not merely theoretically, but also constructed fairly exact calendars and numerous sundials. In 1518, for example, during the Imperial Diet of Augsburg, Bild made sixteen sundials for the Elector of Saxony. The patrician Paul Haintzel (1527–81), a former student of Sixt Birck who had studied in Italy, took a sustained interest in astronomy and contacted the renowned Danish astronomer Tycho Brahe (1546–1601), who apparently came to Augsburg in 1569 in order to consult local instrument-makers and was on friendly terms with Hieronymus Wolf. In 1570, Haintzel and Brahe constructed the so-called Augsburg quadrant, a new type of large instrument for taking precise astronomical measurements.[27] Unfortunately, in 1574 a storm destroyed the instrument in Haintzel's garden property in Göggingen, just outside the city walls. Twenty years later, the physician Georg Henisch, who taught mathematics at the St. Anna *Gymnasium*, did the complicated calculations for a large astronomical clock that was temporarily set up in Augsburg's cathedral.

---

26   See Shapin, *Scientific Revolution*.
27   Keil and Zäh, "Tycho Brahe".

In 1569, the compass-maker Christoph Schissler the Elder delivered an up-to-date *Quadratum geometricum* to the Dresden court, and in 1598, Augsburg's city government entrusted him with a topographical survey of the city bailiwick (*Stadtvogtei*) according to the latest methods, making his results available for a new city plan completed in 1606. In 1605, Schissler also completed an armillary sphere of almost two meters in height. While his models were based on the Ptolemaic system, they were executed to scale with unprecedented technical precision, presenting the old geocentric worldview in a way that made it easier to call it into question. The St. Anna *Gymnasium* had its own observatory well before 1600, apparently the first of its kind in Germany. Another observatory, commissioned by a member of the Fugger family, may have been constructed even earlier.[28]

The learned interests of Marcus Welser, the key figure of late humanism in Augsburg, included the natural sciences from the beginning. In 1603, Welser expertly edited the celestial atlas *Uranometria* of Johann Bayer (1572–1625), a Catholic and later city counselor. This atlas, which incorporated the latest findings, went through seven editions into the eighteenth century, thus remaining the most important work of its kind for more than a century. It introduced a system of using Greek letters to consecutively identify stars within the constellations in accordance with their apparent brightness, starting with alpha for the brightest star – a practice that is still in use today. In 1612, Welser published three letters from the Jesuit mathematician and astronomer Christoph Scheiner (1573–1650), who had been educated in Augsburg and Dillingen and worked at the nearby University of Ingolstadt. These letters reported the solar spots Scheiner had observed through a telescope in early March 1611 (*Tres epistolae de maculis solaribus*). Welser did not reveal the author's name, however, for the Jesuits had commanded Scheiner to remain silent about the discovery, since Aristotle's work contained no information about it. Welser sent a copy of this work to a member of the *Accademia dei Lincei,* an academy of sciences founded in Rome in 1603 that counted Galileo Galilei among its members. Another copy was sent to Johannes Kepler, whose path-breaking *Dioptrice seu Demonstratio eorum quae visui et visibilius propter conspicilla non ita pridem inventa accidunt*, a discussion of the possibilities associated with the discovery of the telescope in 1608, had been printed in Welser's publishing house the year before. Galileo commented on the results of Scheiner's observations in an epistle to Welser, partially rejecting them. Later on he accused Scheiner

---

28 For this and the following paragraph, see Keil, "Augsburger Hersteller"; idem and Gier, *Himmelsbeobachtung*; Keil, *Augustanus Opticus*, pp. 26–37.

of plagiarism, claiming the discovery of the phenomenon for himself. In fact, Galileo seems to have made the same observation as early as January 1610. It is thus possible that Scheiner may have joined Galileo's opponents during the latter's trial in 1632–33, but conclusive evidence is lacking. In 1612, Welser himself became a member of the renowned *Accademia dei Lincei*, while Scheiner did further pioneering astronomical and optical work, which was debated in Augsburg.[29]

The new scientific principles also began to influence local medicine from early on.[30] The first edition of Paracelsus' *Große Wundarznei*, which explicitly distanced itself from the old, Galenic medicine and introduced new chemical substances, was printed in Augsburg in 1536. The city physician Karl Widemann (1555–1637) apparently collected all available works by Paracelsus, hand-copying some that have subsequently been lost. He is therefore regarded as a central figure within early modern Paracelsism.

In 1620, the optician Johann Wiesel (1583–1662) took up residence in Augsburg. He initiated the local production of technically advanced telescopes, microscopes, eyeglasses, and other optical instruments, which remained important well into the eighteenth century and became another hallmark of local scientific culture. Wiesel and his successors continually improved their products through technical experiments and collaboration with mathematicians and related experts. Like Karl Widemann, they also collected relevant manuscripts and prints for their private libraries; at least some of the insects studied under Wiesel's microscopes, for example, were recorded as paper drawings. It is not surprising, therefore, that Wiesel became a figure of European renown and that Augsburg's specialized opticians were able to market their products throughout Europe.[31]

Yet the Protestant Reformation and confessional strife exacted their price in this field as well, retarding the careers and professional activities of many scientists and technicians, including those of the Protestants Johann Wiesel and Karl Widemann. The latter had to resign from his post as city physician during the Thirty Years' War. There were other setbacks as well. When Julius Schiller published a new edition of Johann Bayer's 1603 *Uranometria* under the title *Coelum stellatum christianum* in 1627, its interpretation according to Counter-Reformation principles significantly reduced the work's appeal despite the fact that it represented the latest in science, with a third of the stars it described

---

29 Daxecker, *Scheiner*; Ferber, *'Scio multos te amicos habere'*, pp. 292–300.
30 See Chapter 3 in this volume.
31 Keil, *Augustanus Opticus*; idem, *Von Ocularien*.

previously unknown. The same applies to geographical, topographical, ethnological, and other insights gained by members of particular confessional parties, which were often ignored in the opposing camp and hardly acknowledged or debated. And it holds true for printed works about the non-European world as well, published by Catholics from 1610 onward with the support of the Jesuits and Marcus Welser. These included translations and summaries of travelogues and voyages of discovery from Catholic countries, reports on Catholic overseas missions as far as China, and related cosmographies and encyclopedias. Although the goal of these works was primarily moral edification and the strengthening of religious convictions, their convincing depictions of alterity and the exotic conveyed new and often rather exact knowledge. Examples included not only reports about China, which were highly regarded by scholars such as Gottfried Wilhelm Leibniz (1646–1716) and were received by patrons like Maria Theresia von Fugger-Wellenburg (1690–1762), but also accounts of the so-called Orient, now increasingly differentiated as the Near Orient and Far Orient, with their diverse cultures and peoples. By 1700, therefore, a scientific branch of learned culture had taken root in Augsburg, where it was poised either to form new alliances with the scholarly mainstream, or to emancipate itself as an independent field of inquiry.[32]

4   Enlightenment

Competition between the two major confessions impregnated the imperial city of Augsburg with a particularly intense Christian identity. In addition, Augsburg's Protestant majority was shrinking by the later seventeenth century, while the Catholics, who became a majority by around 1750, were under tighter ecclesiastical control than their Protestant counterparts, with the Jesuits exerting a profound cultural and intellectual dominance. In the face of this growing Catholic pressure, the Protestant elite turned inward and closed its ranks.[33] Under these conditions, the Enlightenment critique of the ecclesiastical establishment and its ideology of reordering the world according to the principles of reason, nature, and utility progressed slowly and rather belatedly. Insofar as the Enlightenment was also a movement for unshackling the quest for knowledge and initiating practical reforms in natural history, economic

---

32   Häberlein, "Monster und Missionare"; Blaufuss, "Korrespondenten von G.W. Leibniz"; Hsia, *Noble Patronage*.

33   See François, *Die unsichtbare Grenze*, pp. 44–64.

improvement, scientific invention, and technical innovation, however, the confessional rivalry actually strengthened its impulses, as new insights and advances could be interpreted and propagated as proofs of the superiority of one's own confession.

Augsburg's contribution to the Enlightenment merged seamlessly with that which the local brand of the new science had begun. Particularly important in this regard was the field of medicine, which also made pioneering contributions to chemistry and pharmacology. The Protestant city physician Lukas Schroeck (1646–1730) received his doctorate in Jena in 1671 with a dissertation on musk as a narcotic substance. His success in supplementing his medical practice by conducting experiments and publishing the results earned him election in 1677 to the Academy of Scientists (*Leopoldina*) in Jena. In 1693, he became the academy's president, a post he held until his death. In this position, Schroeck promoted the election of other renowned Augsburg physicians to the *Leopoldina*.[34]

Among the Catholics, printing and discussion of missionary reports and travelogues, cosmographies, and geographical encyclopedias continued up to the mid-eighteenth century. In 1728, the Austrian Jesuit Joseph Stöcklein (1676–1733) began to publish *Der Neue Welt-Bott* ("The New World Messenger"), a collection of missionary letters that was innovative in its systematic, scholarly approach to the subject.[35] At the University of Dillingen and the St. Salvator college, Jesuit and non-Jesuit teachers alike devoted substantial energy to natural history, physics, and mathematics. On the Protestant side, the calendars, tracts on comets, and geographical accounts of the Nuremberg-born theologian and astrologer Johann Christoph Wagner (1640–1703) initially stood out; his aim, however, was not only to improve the precision of astronomical measurements, but also to pursue the very traditional concern of "purifying" astrology from heathen influences.[36]

From 1731–32 onward, the involvement of the Pietist Augsburg pastor Samuel Urlsperger (1687–1772) in the migration of Lutheran exiles from the archbishopric of Salzburg to the North American colony of Georgia contributed to the dissemination of knowledge about the New World and intense debates about the conditions there, for Urlsperger published accounts of the Salzburger settlement and never tired of collecting goods and funds for the emigrants.[37] Contemporary Protestant publishers in Augsburg also printed

---

34   Rajkay, "Totentanz oder Maskenbälle", pp. 101–02.
35   Dürr, "Der 'Neue Welt-Bott'".
36   Pfeuffer, *Von der Natur fasziniert*, pp. 14–16; Herbst, "Johann Christoph Wagner".
37   Freudenberger, "Samuel Urlsperger"; Pyrges, *Kolonialprojekt EbenEzer*, passim.

works on architectural theory and technical subjects. Meanwhile, the printing of maps, city plans, and urban prospects, which the publishing houses Bodenehr and Seutter successfully pursued throughout the eighteenth century, transcended narrow confessional boundaries. Although most of their output was based on external models, they also produced works that relied on the gathering of fresh information, original surveys, comparison, or the calculation of scale. Most of these tasks were carried out locally, which highlights the availability of a pool of practical scientific experts.[38]

The same holds true for economic handbooks and practical guides, which Augsburg printers turned out in large numbers. These texts aimed at improving agriculture, transport, hygiene, and public health. Major works of Enlightenment economic theory like Adam Smith's *The Wealth of Nations* were imported, however, and did not stimulate the production of original works in that vein, although the translation and publication of an important physiocratic work, François Quesnay's *Analyse du tableau économique* (1758), as *Die Kunst sich geschwinde durch den Ackerbau zu bereichern* (1763), which was followed by several texts of moral admonition, demonstrated that the new conception of economics as a sustained quest for profit had at least reached Augsburg.[39]

Enlightenment philosophy was introduced to the city through book purchases, conversations within interested elite circles, and the reading of enlightened journals. Attempts to establish a stable basis for these pursuits in a learned society, a permanent reading circle, or a publisher's gazette were ultimately unsuccessful. Still, the work of the Protestant pastor, theologian, and philosopher Johann Jacob Brucker (1696–1770) made a substantial local contribution to the spread of Enlightenment thought. Brucker's five-volume *Historia critica philosophiae* (1747), based on a preliminary German version published in eight volumes from 1731 to 1737, provided an innovative understanding of the history of philosophy. It treated its subject critically and based as much as possible on primary sources rather than secondary accounts; represented it as a history less concerned with the discovery, rise, and progress of truth than with reflective positions and opinions; as independent of Christian chronology, following its own historical dynamics; and as a repository of ideas and concepts from which contemporary philosophers might draw according to their own interests. The influence of this new concept extended even to the French Enlightenment. Brucker was elected to the Berlin Academy of Sciences, the German Academy in Göttingen, and further learned societies. He also published extensively on other topics, consistently demonstrating his command of recent methods and

---

38 Ritter, "Landkartendruck".
39 Burkhardt, "Altökonomik und Handelsliteratur".

approaches. Brucker was no atheist, however; he remained convinced that philosophy was theology's handmaid. Instead, he tried to reconcile reason and revelation by extending the sphere of human liberty to history. But liberty had to be applied reasonably and modestly, ultimately remaining the preserve of rational and moral individuals and groups. These, Brucker assumed, would be found among Catholics as well as Protestants, leading him repeatedly to initiate inter-confessional debating circles.[40]

In the second half of the eighteenth century, though, the local scene became less receptive to the influence of these larger questions. When individual Dillingen professors began to raise fundamental doubts about belief in witchcraft, as Joseph von Weber did in 1787, and to discover laudable aspects in Christian Wolff's and Immanuel Kant's philosophies, the ex-Jesuits (who continued to teach at St. Salvator after the order's dissolution in 1773) and their followers protested vociferously, styling themselves as guardians of Catholic orthodoxy. From 1787 to 1796, orthodox ex-Jesuits published the perceptive, yet vigorously anti-Enlightenment journal *Kritik über gewisse Kritiker, Rezensenten und Broschürenmacher* ("Critical Views on Certain Critics, Reviewers and Pamphleteers"), which stimulated a number of controversies within the Catholic camp around 1790. Eventually, Enlightenment's opponents intervened with the bishop and managed to suppress this rapprochement with its philosophical positions.[41]

One major reason for this was that established scholars and political elites had to cope with a new and much graver threat: the French Revolution. Local unrest and opposition to the patrician regime, which sporadically adopted enlightened political demands for more transparency, participation, and liberty, proved increasingly difficult to suppress. A profound constitutional discussion about the modernization of the city's government failed to materialize, however. In politics and administration as in many other areas, Augsburg's eighteenth-century learned culture lagged far behind other, more enlightened German centers, such as Halle, Göttingen, and Berlin.

---

40 Schmitt-Biggemann and Stammen (eds.), *Jacob Brucker*.
41 Hochadel, "Physiker, Volksaufklärer und 'Experte'"; Gier, "Stapelstadt"; Rajkay, "Sarkasmen Schlözers"; Spehr, "Gegen Protestantismus, Aufklärung und Toleranz"; Weber, "St. Moritz und die katholische Reform".

Bibliography

Published Primary Sources

Künast, H.-J. and Zäh, H. (eds.), *Die Bibliothek Konrad Peutingers. Edition der historischen Kataloge und Rekonstruktion der Bestände*, 2 vols., Tübingen, 2003–05.

Secondary Literature

Augustyn, W., "Historisches Interesse und Chronistik in St. Ulrich und Afra in Augsburg im Umfeld von monastischer Reform und städtischem Humanismus: Wilhelm Wittwer und sein 'Catalogus abbatum'", in Müller (ed.), *Humanismus und Renaissance in Augsburg*, pp. 329–87.

Baer, W. and Hecker, H.J. (eds.), *Die Jesuiten und ihre Schule St. Salvator in Augsburg 1582*, Munich, 1982.

Biehler-Praxl, B., "Der Eigennutz als Garant des Gemeinwohls beim Augsburger Stadtschreiber Dr. Konrad Peutinger", in idem, *Der Eigennutz – Feind oder "Wahrer Begründer" des Gemeinwohls?*, Epfendorf, 2011, pp. 209–346.

Blaufuss, D., "Korrespondenten von G.W. Leibniz: Georg Spizel aus Augsburg", *Studia Leibnitiana* 5 (1973), pp. 116–44.

Burkhardt, J., "Altökonomik und Handelsliteratur in den Augsburger Druckmedien", in H. Gier and J. Janota (eds.), *Augsburger Buchdruck und Verlagswesen. Von den Anfängen bis zur Gegenwart*, Wiesbaden, 1997, pp. 423–46.

Daxecker, F., *Der Physiker und Astronom Christoph Scheiner*, Innsbruck, 2006.

Doering-Manteuffel, S., Mancal, J. and Wüst, W. (eds.), *Pressewesen der Aufklärung. Periodische Schriften im Alten Reich*, Berlin, 2001.

Dürr, R., "Der 'Neue Welt-Bott' als Markt der Informationen? Wissenstransfer als Moment jesuitischer Identitätsbildung", *Zeitschrift für historische Forschung* 34 (2007), pp. 441–66.

Ferber, M.U., "'Cives vestros sine controversia habeo pro Germaniae cultissimis'. Zum Verhältnis von Späthumanismus und Konfessionalisierung am Beispiel der bikonfessionellen Reichsstadt Augsburg", in Müller (ed.), *Humanismus und Renaissance in Augsburg*, pp. 409–20.

Ferber, M.U., *'Scio multos te amicos habere'. Wissensvermittlung und Wissenssicherung im Späthumanismus am Beispiel des Epistolariums Marx Welsers d.J. (1558–1614)*, Augsburg, 2008.

Ferber, M.U., "Zwischen Lipsius und Galilei: Der Briefwechsel Marx Welsers als Spiegel der geistesgeschichtlichen Umwälzung zu Beginn des 17. Jahrhunderts", in A. Schmid (ed.), *Justus Lipsius und der europäische Späthumanismus in Oberdeutschland*, Munich, 2008, pp. 37–54.

François, E., *Die unsichtbare Grenze. Protestanten und Katholiken in Augsburg 1648–1806*, Sigmaringen, 1991.

Freudenberger, R., "Samuel Urlsperger und die Salzburger in Georgia: Eine pietistische Beziehung Augsburgs nach Nordamerika im 18. Jahrhundert", in P. Gassert, G. Kronenbitter, S. Paulus and W.E.J. Weber (eds.), *Augsburg und Amerika. Aneignungen und globale Verflechtungen in einer Stadt*, Augsburg, 2013, pp. 81–102.

Gier, H., "Der Augsburger Domherr Bernhard von Waldkirch und der Beginn der Blütezeit des Humanismus in Augsburg", *Jahrbuch des Vereins für Augsburger Bistumsgeschichte* 36 (2002), pp. 109–23.

Gier, H., "Die Stapelstadt der katholischen Buchhandlung in Deutschland – Augsburg als Verlagsort jesuitischen Schrifttums vor und nach der Aufhebung der Gesellschaft Jesu", *Zeitschrift des Historischen Vereins für Schwaben* 101 (2007), pp. 151–70.

Gier, H., "Italien rezeption im Augsburger Humanismus", *Zeitschrift des Historischen Vereins für Schwaben* 102 (2010), pp. 223–38.

Gier, H. (ed.), *Jacob Bidermann und sein "Cenodoxus". Der bedeutendste Dramatiker aus dem Jesuitenorden und sein erfolgreichstes Stück*, Regensburg, 2005.

Glück, H., Häberlein, M. and Schröder, K., *Mehrsprachigkeit in der Frühen Neuzeit. Die Reichsstädte Augsburg und Nürnberg vom 15. bis ins frühe 19. Jahrhundert*, Wiesbaden, 2013.

Häberlein, M., "Botanisches Wissen, ökonomischer Nutzen und sozialer Aufstieg im 16. Jahrhundert: Der Augsburger Arzt und Orientreisende Leonhard Rauwolf", in Müller (ed.), *Humanismus und Renaissance in Augsburg*, pp. 101–16.

Häberlein, M., "Monster und Missionare: Die außereuropäische Welt in Augsburger Drucken der frühen Neuzeit", in H. Gier and J. Janota (eds.), *Augsburger Buchdruck und Verlagswesen: Von den Anfängen bis zur Gegenwart*, Wiesbaden, 1997, pp. 353–80.

Häberlein, M., "Aneignung, Organisation und Umsetzung von Kaufmannswissen in Süddeutschland im 16. und 17. Jahrhundert", in M. North (ed.), *Kultureller Austausch. Bilanz und Perspektiven der Frühneuzeitforschung*, Cologne, 2009, pp. 273–88.

Häberlein, M., *The Fuggers of Augsburg: Pursuing Wealth and Honor in Renaissance Germany*, Charlottesville and London, 2012.

Hägele, G., and Thierbach, M. (eds.), *Augsburg macht Druck. Die Anfänge des Buchdrucks in einer Metropole des 15. Jahrhunderts*, Augsburg, 2017.

Hamilton, A., "A Lutheran Translator for the Quran: A Late Seventeenth Century Quest", in idem, M. van den Boogert and B. Westerweel (eds.), *The Republic of Letters and the Levant*, Leiden, 2005, pp. 197–222.

Herbst, K.-D., "Johann Christoph Wagner (1640–1703)", in *Biobibliographisches Handbuch der Kalendermacher von 1550 bis 1750*. URL: https://www.presseforschung.uni-bremen.de/dokuwiki/doku.php?id=wagner_Johann_Christoph [05.09.2017].

Hochadel, O., "Physiker, Volksaufklärer und 'Experte': Joseph Weber an der Universität Dillingen", in Kießling (ed.), *Die Universität Dillingen*, pp. 729–52.

Hsia, R.P., *Noble Patronage and Jesuit Missions: Maria Theresia von Fugger-Wellenburg (1690–1762) and Jesuit Missionaries in China and Vietnam*, Rome, 2006.

Janota, J. and Williams-Krapp, W. (eds.), *Literarisches Leben in Augsburg während des 15. Jahrhunderts*, Tübingen, 1995.

Johnson, C.R., *The German Discovery of the World: Renaissance Encounters with the Strange and Marvelous*, Charlottesville, 2008.

Keil, I., *Augustanus Opticus. Johann Wiesel (1583–1662) und 200 Jahre optisches Handwerk in Augsburg*, Berlin, 2000.

Keil, I., *Von Ocularien, Perspicillen und Mikroskopen, von Hungersnöten und Friedensfreuden, Optikern, Kaufleuten und Fürsten. Materialien zur Geschichte der optischen Werkstatt von Johann Wiesel (1583–1662) und seiner Nachfolger in Augsburg*, Augsburg, 2003.

Keil, I., "Augsburger Hersteller von wissenschaftlichen Instrumenten: Beziehungen zu Italien", in W. Wüst (ed.), *Schwaben und Italien. Zwei europäische Kulturlandschaften zwischen Antike und Moderne*, Augsburg, 2010, pp. 337–50.

Keil, I. and Gier, H. (eds.), *Himmelsbeobachtung mit dem Fernrohr in der Frühen Neuzeit. Eine Ausstellung aus den Schätzen der Staats- und Stadtbibliothek Augsburg*, Augsburg, 2009.

Keil, I. and Zäh, H., "Tycho Brahe (1546–1601) und seine Beziehungen zu Augsburg", *Zeitschrift des Historischen Vereins für Schwaben* 97 (2004), pp. 139–93.

Kießling, R., "Das gebildete Bürgertum und die kulturelle Zentralität Augsburgs im Spätmittelalter", in B. Moeller, H. Patze, and K. Stackmann (eds.), *Studien zum städtischen Bildungswesen des späten Mittelalters und der frühen Neuzeit*, Göttingen, 1983, pp. 553–85.

Kießling, R. (ed.), *Die Universität Dillingen und ihre Nachfolger. Stationen und Aspekte einer Hochschule in Schwaben. Festschrift zum 450jährigen Gründungsjubiläum*, Dillingen, 1999.

Kießling, R., "Ansatzpunkte und Entwicklungstendenzen in den spätmittelalterlichen Schullandschaften Schwabens", in idem and H. Flachenecker (eds.), *Schullandschaften in Altbayern, Franken und Schwaben*, Munich, 2005, pp. 247–80.

Kießling, R., "Im Spannungsfeld von Markt und Recht: Die Augsburger Wirtschaft im 15. und 16. Jahrhundert", in C. Becker and H.G. Hermann (eds.), *Ökonomie und Recht. Historische Entwicklungen in Bayern*, Berlin, 2009, pp. 73–99.

Kießling, R., "'und also ein newe Liberey anzurichten': Zur Gründung der Augsburger Stadtbibliothek im Kontext der Reformationsgeschichte", in M. Häberlein, S. Paulus and G. Weber (eds.), *Geschichte(n) des Wissens. Festschrift für Wolfgang E.J. Weber zum 65. Geburtstag*, Augsburg, 2015, pp. 303–20.

Kießling, R. and Müller, G.M. (eds.), *Konrad Peutinger. Ein uomo universale zwischen Mittelalter und Früher Neuzeit*, Berlin, 2018.

Kintzinger, M., "'Ich was auch ain schueler': Die Schulen im spätmittelalterlichen Augsburg", in Janota and Williams-Krapp (eds.), *Literarisches Leben in Augsburg*, pp. 58–81.

Kluge, M.F., "Der Kaufmann und die Schrift: Risiken der Globalisierung des Handels im Spätmittelalter", in M. Kaufhold (ed.), *Städtische Kultur im mittelalterlichen Augsburg*, Augsburg, 2012, pp. 71–90.

Kluge, M.F., *Die Macht des Gedächtnisses. Entstehung und Wandel kommunaler Schriftkultur im spätmittelalterlichen Augsburg*, Leiden, 2014.

Laube, R. and Zäh, H. (eds.), *Gesammeltes Gedächtnis. Konrad Peutinger und die kulturelle Überlieferung im 16. Jahrhundert*, Lucerne, 2016.

Lutz, H., *Conrad Peutinger. Beiträge zu einer politischen Biographie*, Augsburg, 1958.

Marschler, T. and Müller, M.C. (eds.), *Jesuitische Gelehrsamkeit in Büchern des 16. und 17. Jahrhunderts aus dem Bestand der Universitätsbibliothek Augsburg* (exhibition catalogue), Augsburg, 2015.

Müller, J.-D., "Konrad Peutinger und die Sodalitas Peutingeriana", in S. Füssel and J. Pirozywski (eds.), *Der polnische Humanismus und die europäischen Sodalitäten*, Wiesbaden, 1997, pp. 167–86.

Müller, G.M. (ed.), *Humanismus und Renaissance in Augsburg. Kulturgeschichte einer Stadt zwischen Spätmittelalter und Dreißigjährigem Krieg*, Berlin, 2010.

Pfeuffer, E. (ed.), *Von der Natur fasziniert ... Frühe Augsburger Naturforscher und ihre Bilder*, Augsburg, 2003.

Pyrges, A., *Das Kolonialprojekt EbenEzer. Formen und Mechanismen protestantischer Expansion in der atlantischen Welt des 18. Jahrhunderts*, Stuttgart, 2015.

Rajkay, B., "Totentanz oder Maskenbälle? Anmerkungen zur Geschichte Augsburgs im 18. Jahrhundert", in D. Schiersner, A. Link, B. Rajkay and W. Scheffknecht (eds.), *Augsburg, Schwaben und der Rest der Welt. Neue Beiträge zur Landes- und Regionalgeschichte. Festschrift für Rolf Kießling zum 70. Geburtstag*, Augsburg, 2011, pp. 85–110.

Rajkay, B., "Die Sarkasmen Schlözers in Göttingen: Süddeutsche Reichsstädte als Prügelknaben der Aufklärer", in K. Becher and D. Schiersner (eds.), *Aufklärung in Oberschwaben. Barocke Welt im Umbruch*, Stuttgart, 2016, pp. 357–78.

Ritter, M., "Der Augsburger Landkartendruck", in H. Gier and J. Janota (eds.), *Augsburger Buchdruck und Verlagswesen. Von den Anfängen bis zur Gegenwart*, Wiesbaden, 1997, pp. 405–22.

Roeck, B., "Geschichte, Finsternis und Unkultur: Zu Leben und Werk des Marcus Welser (1558–1614)", *Archiv für Kulturgeschichte* 72 (1990), pp. 115–41.

Roeck, B., *Als wollt die Welt schier brechen. Eine Stadt im Zeitalter des Dreißigjährigen Krieges*, Munich, 1991.

Schmid, A., "Die Korrespondenz zwischen P. Matthäus Rader SJ und Marcus Welser", in Müller (ed.), *Humanismus und Renaissance in Augsburg*, pp. 421–42.

Schmidt, R., "Die Klosterdruckerei von St. Ulrich und Afra in Augsburg (1472 bis kurz nach 1474)", in H. Gier and J. Janota (eds.), *Augsburger Buchdruck und Verlagswesen. Von den Anfängen bis zur Gegenwart*, Wiesbaden, 1997, pp. 141–52.

Schmidt, S., "Einführung: Stagnation oder Revolution? Kaufmännisches Praxiswissen im 16. Jahrhundert", in idem (ed.), *Das Gewerbebuch der Augsburger Christoph-Welser-Gesellschaft 1554–1560. Edition und Kommentar*, Augsburg, 2015, pp. 11–22.

Schmitt-Biggemann, W. and Stammen, T. (eds), *Jacob Brucker (1696–1770). Philosoph und Historiker der europäischen Aufklärung*, Berlin, 1998.

Shapin, S., *The Scientific Revolution*, Chicago, 1996.

Spehr, C., "Gegen Protestantismus, Aufklärung und Toleranz: Die Kontroverspredigten des Augsburger Dompredigers Aloys Merz", in A. Beutel, V. Leppin and U. Sträter (eds.), *Christentum im Übergang. Neue Studien zu Kirche und Religion in der Aufklärungszeit*, Leipzig, 2006, pp. 237–50.

Tschopp, S.S., "Protestantisches Schultheater und reichsstädtische Politik: Die Dramen des Sixt Birk", in Müller (ed.), *Humanismus und Renaissance in Augsburg*, pp. 187–215.

Unterburger, K., "Zwischen Irenik und Kontroverstheologie: Der Einfluss des Humanismus auf die Ausbildung konfessioneller Wissenskulturen", in Müller (ed.), *Humanismus und Renaissance in Augsburg*, pp. 61–85.

Unterburger, K., "Zwischen freier Reichsstadt und monastischer Reform: Leben und Gelehrsamkeit in St. Ulrich und Afra im 15. Jahrhundert", in M. Weitlauff (ed.), *Benediktinerabtei St. Ulrich und Afra in Augsburg (1012–2012). Geschichte, Kunst, Wirtschaft und Kultur einer ehemaligen Reichsabtei. Festschrift zum tausendjährigen Jubiläum*, vol. 1, Augsburg, 2011, pp. 147–65.

Walter, T., "Eine Reise ins (Un-)Bekannte: Grenzräume des Wissens bei Leonhard Rauwolf (1535–1596)", *N.T.M. – Zeitschrift für Geschichte der Wissenschaften, Technik und Medizin* 17 (2009), pp. 359–85.

Weber, W.E.J., "Humanismus und reichsstädtische Politik", in Müller (ed.), *Humanismus und Renaissance in Augsburg*, pp. 87–100.

Weber, W.E.J., "Herrschafts- und Verwaltungswissen in oberdeutschen Reichsstädten der Frühen Neuzeit", *Jahrbuch für Europäische Verwaltungsgeschichte* 15 (2003), pp. 1–28.

Weber, W.E.J., "St. Moritz und die katholische Reform des 18. Jahrhunderts: Giovanni Battista Bassi (1713–1776)", in G.M. Müller (ed.), *Das ehemalige Kollegiatstift St. Moritz in Augsburg*, Lindenberg, 2006, pp. 259–72.

Weber, W.E.J., "Das Vermächtnis des 'Wassermanns': Hans Jakob Fugger und die Münchener Hofbibliothek", in A. Schmid (ed.), *Die Anfänge der Münchener Hofbibliothek unter Herzog Albrecht V.*, Munich, 2009, pp. 132–45.

Zäh, H., "Konrad Peutinger und Margarete Welser – Ehe und Familie im Zeichen des Humanismus", in M. Häberlein and J. Burkhardt (eds.), *Die Welser. Neue Forschungen zur Geschichte und Kultur des oberdeutschen Handelshauses,* Berlin, 2002, pp. 449–509.

Zäh, H., "Einführung: Zur Person Konrad Peutingers und zur Geschichte der Bibliothek", in idem and H.-J. Künast (eds.), *Die Bibliothek Konrad Peutingers. Edition der historischen Kataloge und Rekonstruktion der Bestände,* vol. 1, Tübingen, 2003, pp. 1–24.

CHAPTER 21

The Arts

Andrew Morrall

In the introduction to his comprehensive history of the arts and crafts of Augsburg, the *Kunst-, Gewerb- und Handwerks-Geschichte der Reichs-Stadt Augsburg*, published in 1779, the Augsburg antiquarian and historian Paul von Stetten the Younger praised his city's prominence and international standing relative to other cities, attributing its reputation to the city's 300-year tradition of excellence in the production of high quality art and craft. This was by virtue of Augsburg's own artists and those who had been drawn to the city, as well as a tradition of enlightened patronage by the civic authorities and the most prominent citizens, who regarded it a civic duty to protect and encourage them. He included in his history practitioners of the fine arts, the "mechanical and chemical arts", and "those craftsmen who were engaged not only with the things of daily need but principally with objects of external trade and luxury goods".[1] His definition of art (*Kunst*) was accordingly broad and included such tradespeople as cabinet makers, instrument makers, dyers, paper makers, metal stampers, and bell founders, as well as painters, sculptors, and goldsmiths. Stetten's history, framed within the convention of the *Städtelob* (praise for one's native city), was predicated upon an Enlightenment belief in the civilizing power of art, and praised Augsburg, by virtue of its artists and cultural policy, as one of the first cities to raise Europe out of "the darkness of ignorance and barbarity".[2] It was a vision of the arts based on a longstanding ideal of urban community that had grown up around craft production, the product of a culture based on a model of household workshops and organized by a guild system, and infused with an idea of citizenship founded upon the mastery of practical skills.

Stetten looked back over a tradition of artistic flowering spanning three centuries with a pleasure (*Entzuecken*) tinged with regret (*Wehmuth*), to those times when the arts were allegedly in their highest bloom. He was referring to the period of the late fifteenth and early sixteenth centuries, the first great flourishing of art during the *Maximilianzeit*, when a coherent sense of a local

---

1 Stetten, *Kunst-, Gewerb- und Handwerks-Geschichte*, "Vorrede", fol. 3v.
2 Ibid., fol. 2v.

style began to emerge in the city.³ In the preceding centuries, a rich artistic life had revolved around the large ecclesiastical institutions: stained-glass workshops were established in the twelfth century at the cathedral, and an equally vibrant school of manuscript illumination flourished at the Benedictine monastery of Sts. Ulrich and Afra. As early as 1276, a class of lay craftsmen and artists had also established itself into a form of guild organization. A rebellion by these craftsmen in 1368 secured them a degree of representation within the city's government, which they maintained until 1548, when they were stripped of their political rights during the religious conflicts of the Reformation. Throughout, the craftsmen's guilds, which included the artistic trades (painters, goldsmiths, sculptors, and glaziers) remained central to the economic and cultural life of the city. The systems of training, strict divisions of labor, and the quality controls they established over time contributed greatly to the city's success as an artistic center. They were also central to urban social life. Only after long years of training and journeyman experience in a specific trade could the aspiring apprentice attain full mastership and the right to run his own workshop. Only established masters, moreover, were permitted to marry or participate in public office. The family workshop thus formed the kernel of an economic system in which the familial and political bonds of the community were integrally bound to professional expertise.⁴

1 From the Late Gothic to the Renaissance

Family-based artist workshops are traceable in Augsburg from the beginning of the fifteenth century. Names of painter families, passing from fathers to sons, such as Kron, Zan, Giltlinger, Knoder, and Mauermüller, occur in the guild and tax records, though little of their work has survived. Archival records show that the workshop of Gumpolt Giltlinger worked in various media, including painting, sculpture, and glass painting, under the aegis of a single enterprise, possessing the largest number of apprentices of any workshop in the 1480s. Yet not a single work is firmly attributable to them today.⁵ Individuals from other family workshops such as Apt, Breu, and Burgkmair come into focus as discrete artistic personalities only at the end of the fifteenth century.

---

3   Ibid.
4   Roper, *The Holy Household*, pp. 31–33.
5   Huth, *Künstler und Werkstatt*; Beutler and Thiem, *Hans Holbein der Ältere*, pp. 163–64; Wilhelm, *Augsburger Wandmalerei*.

A prevailing late Gothic style of religious art emerges in a series of altarpiece commissions of the 1490s and early 1500s by a group of identifiable painters that includes Ulrich Apt the Elder, Thoman Burgkmair, Hans Holbein the Elder, and the sculptor Michael Erhart, as well as a number of talented younger artists such as Hans Burgkmair the Elder, Jörg Breu the Elder, and Leonhard Beck. These works included Holbein's Weingartner Altarpiece of 1490 for the cathedral; the Holbein and Burgkmair "Basilica Series" for the convent of St. Katharina between 1499 and 1504 (Augsburg, Städtische Sammlungen); and Ulrich Apt's altarpiece of 1510 for the church of the Holy Cross, of which two panels remain, in Karlsruhe and in the Louvre, Paris. Collectively, these works affirmed a local idiom that drew mainly from the conventions of Flemish art. It was a style distinguished by material richness, preciousness of detail, gravity, and restrained emotion.

Broadly representative of this style, while intensely individual in forging new, forward-looking tendencies, was the art of Hans Holbein the Elder. His rich palette drew from Netherlandish examples, notably the work of Rogier van der Weyden, which he may have encountered first-hand while traveling as a journeyman. He succeeded in injecting into a pattern-book workshop practice a vivid power of observation in his handling of details, a wide range of convincing physiognomic types, and moments of unforced naturalism in poses and facial features. These qualities are evident in his scene of the martyrdom of St. Paul in his painting of 1504 of San Paolo Fuori le Mura (figure 21.1), part of the so-called Basilica cycle, a series of seven works that he painted, together with Hans Burgkmair the Younger and a "Master L.F.", for the Dominican convent of St. Katharina. Depicting seven different pilgrimage basilicas in Rome, the paintings were used by the nuns, who were unable to travel to Rome, as surrogates for the actual pilgrimage sites through which they could obtain indulgences.[6] Holbein's centrally-placed figure of St. Thecla, seated on a cushioned chair and drawn incongruously from behind, injects into the scene a vivid observation from life. The drawing upon which it is based is one of more than 200 surviving drawings of head and figure studies, mostly in silverpoint, whose qualities of naturalism were carried on in the work of Holbein's sons, Ambrosius and especially Hans Holbein the Younger, as well as by the emerging generation of artists that included Hans Burgkmair the Younger and Leonard Beck.[7]

---

6   Gärtner, *Römische Basiliken*.
7   Staatliche Museen zu Berlin, Preußischer Kulturbesitz, Kupferstichkabinett. See Krause, *Hans Holbein der Ältere*, pp. 191–222, 290–99.

FIGURE 21.1 Hans Holbein the Elder, *The Basilica of San Paolo fuori le mura*, oil on panel
AUGSBURG, STÄDTISCHE KUNSTSAMMLUNGEN

These tendencies were part of a larger movement of artistic innovation. The powerful influence of Albrecht Dürer and an increasing knowledge of Italian art, mediated primarily through prints, provided enormous stimulus for change. This was further encouraged by a growing humanist culture, exemplified by Conrad Peutinger (1465–1547), legal adviser to the city council and city secretary, a significant collector of antique marbles, Italian prints, medallions, plaques, books and manuscripts, and a keen patron of literary humanist enterprises. Peutinger's role from 1491 onwards as literary and artistic advisor to Emperor Maximilian I gave him a pivotal position of influence in the encouragement of humanist taste. Indeed, the emperor's attachment to Augsburg, his frequent visits there, and his employment – via Peutinger's agency – of local artists and craftsmen gave enormous impetus to the revival of the sense of the city's Roman past (retained in its Latin name *Augusta*) and to the formation of an "imperial" style, appropriate to the emperor's propagandist ambitions.[8]

Equally important for the spread of humanist values and taste was the early printing press. In 1471, the printer Günther Zainer introduced an early *antiqua* typeset. Fifteen years later, the Augsburg printer Erhard Ratdolt (1442–1538), returning from a ten-year sojourn in Venice where he had worked in the circle of Aldus Manutius, introduced new typographical layouts, inventive typesets, and color printing techniques that he applied to an impressive array of classical editions and humanist texts. Among his most ambitious projects was his *Romanae Vetustatis Fragmenta* of 1505, a record of a collection of Roman inscriptions, taken from Peutinger's own collection and those of his fellow humanists, which reproduced the epigraphy of the Roman originals.[9] A luxury edition of this text, printed in red, black and gold, demonstrates Ratdolt's other notable innovation of printing in multiple colors.

The strong influence of Italian prints extended to other media. It is visible, for instance, in the etched *grotesque* decoration of fantastic hybrid forms on suits of armor made by the city's leading armorer, Kolman Helmschmied (1471–1532). As a member of an internationally renowned armorer dynasty, Helmschmied provided suits of armor for the archdukes of Austria and Tyrol, the Holy Roman Emperor, and the German and European nobility. Certain of these etched designs are attributed to Daniel Hopfer (c. 1470–1536), a painter and metal etcher who since 1493 had become the leading armor decorator in the city.[10] His expertise in etching iron and steel, in which a design is etched into the metal by the corrosive action of acid, led in all likelihood to

---

8   See Chapter 20 in this volume.
9   Wood, *Forgery, Replica, Fiction*, pp. 70, 292–94.
10   See e.g. Jecmen and Spira, *Imperial Augsburg*, p. 82, cat. 92, p. 110.

his experimenting with printing on paper from an inked etched plate, making him the first to specialize exclusively in this new printing technique. From 1500 until his death in 1536, Hopfer produced an estimated 150 etched prints.[11]

Ratdolt's experiments in book printing stimulated important artistic innovations in the field of printmaking. Hans Burgkmair, who early in his career provided Ratdolt with woodcut decorations, began making his own independent woodcut prints – itself an innovation in artistic practice – around 1507, after a probable trip to Italy. From then on, his work displayed an intense interest in *all'antica* forms and Italian compositional and formal modes. His woodcut, "St Luke Painting the Virgin" (B.24) of that year portrays the Virgin and Child, seated beneath a classical, columned portico that is adapted from contemporary Venetian altarpiece design. A year later, inspired by Italian large format woodcuts such as the Venetian Jacopo de Barbari's multi-block map of Venice, he created a woodcut frieze stretching over six woodblocks almost two meters in length, illustrating the inhabitants of Africa, Arabia, and East India, based on Balthasar Springer's report of a 1505–06 trading expedition sponsored by the Welser Company.[12]

Working under Peutinger's direction, Burgkmair developed a new technique of chiaroscuro woodblock printing. The use of multiple blocks inked in different colors and then printed separately onto a single sheet allowed him to produce a range of richly toned, colored prints. A St. George appeared in 1508, followed by a companion equestrian figure of Maximilian I in armor.[13] Working with the woodblock cutter Jost de Negker, a Fleming who settled in Augsburg at some point between 1508 and 1512, Burgkmair produced a series of further chiaroscuro prints, including the macabre "Lovers Surprised by Death", in which a skeleton violently assaults the lovers in a fancifully exotic setting, at once classicizing and Venetian. De Negker was a key figure in the development of fine woodcut printing and, together with Burgkmair and other Augsburg artists like Jörg Breu the Elder and Younger and Leonard Beck, was central to the production of the emperor's often grandiose autobiographical and propagandist publishing projects.[14] Through their early efforts, printmaking became one of the most important fields of artistic production in Augsburg, a tradition maintained until the end of the eighteenth century and rivaled only perhaps by the related field of goldsmithing.

---

11 Metzger (ed.), *Daniel Hopfer*; see also Chapter 19 in this volume.
12 Parshall and Landau, *The Renaissance Print*, p. 178; Silver and Wykoff (eds.), *Grand Scale*, pp. 17–18, 135.
13 Parshall and Landau, *The Renaissance Print*, pp. 185–89.
14 See Silver, *Marketing Maximilian*.

FIGURE 21.2   Hans Burgkmair the Elder, The Emperor Maximilian I on Horseback, chiaroscuro woodcut, 1508

FIGURE 21.3   Fugger Funerary Chapel, St. Anna, Augsburg

The patronage and internationalism of taste of the powerful merchant families, especially the Fuggers and the Welsers, were also crucial in developing a modern *all'antica* style. Their strong business links and cultural ties with Italy stimulated an interest in Italianate forms. The most complete monument to this Italian taste is the funerary chapel in the Carmelite monastery of St. Anna, which Jakob Fugger "the Rich" built for himself and his brothers, Ulrich and Georg (built 1509–12; consecrated in 1518) (figure 21.3). The chapel's plan, the types and disposition of piers and windows, and the ornamental details and materials all recall the repertoire of the Italians Mauro Codussi and Pietro Lombardo. The chapel's interior walls are clad in an arrangement of diverse marbles and honestone, integrated into a subtly-colored, harmonious space, perhaps inspired by Pietro Lombardo's delicate marble wall facings of Santa Maria dei Miracoli in Venice. The overall concept of the chapel has been attributed to Albrecht Dürer. A freestanding sculptured "Corpus Christi" group stands at the center, with carved epitaphs of Georg and Ulrich Fugger, who died in 1506 and 1510 respectively, behind. The forms of the statuary are so strongly Venetian that scholars are still divided over whether to attribute them to northern artists (Adolf and Hans Daucher) or an Italian hand.[15] Dürer certainly made the designs for the epitaphs, which depict the resurrection of Christ and Samson's fight with the Philistines. A monumental organ, built by Jan von Dobrau, seemingly hovering overhead, dominates the space. Jörg Breu's two painted sets of organ shutters, twin Assumptions of the Virgin and of Christ – key intercessors for the souls of the interred – are closely dependent upon Filippino Lippi's "Assumption of the Virgin" fresco in the Caraffa Chapel in Santa Maria Minerva in Rome and an engraving by Francesco Rosselli respectively. The theme of the shutters of a secondary, small organ is "Musica", the liberal art, and incorporates both the classical and biblical accounts of the invention of music, showing Pythagoras and Jubal at their respective anvils. They are unique in German art at this time in conflating biblical and classical themes within a religious context, reconciling two traditions and thus realizing in visual form one of the chief ambitions of Renaissance humanism.[16]

Sculptors also responded to a developing humanist interest in small-scale works of classical or allegorical subjects, suitable for a study or private collection, by creating a genre of small relief sculptures, carved in fine-grained honestone, limestone, or wood. Hans Daucher (1486–1538), the son of the talented Ulm sculptor and wood carver Adolf Daucher and perhaps the greatest Augsburg sculptor of this period, made this genre a specialty. He created

---

15   For an exhaustive account, see Bushart, *Fuggerkapelle*, pp. 115–42.
16   Morrall, *Jörg Breu the Elder*, pp. 103–10.

FIGURE 21.4 Hans Daucher, The Holy Family and Angels, honestone limestone, c. 1520
AUGSBURG, STÄDTISCHE KUNSTSAMMLUNGEN, MAXIMILIANMUSEUM,
NO. 5703

numerous small, crisply carved honestone reliefs of devotional and allegorical subjects, often for noble patrons. His "Allegory of Virtues and Vices at the Court of Charles V", executed around 1522, shows the emperor on horseback, leading members of his family across a bridge, surrounded by his enemies.[17] Daucher's exquisitely carved relief of the Virgin and child with angels of *c.* 1520 situates the holy family beneath a classical triumphal arch, with an elaborately carved barrel vault framed by columns and pilasters (figure 21.4). This classical edifice, a popular motif among advanced artists in Augsburg, derived ultimately from Venetian altarpiece painting and stands in very close relation to a similar edifice in Holbein the Elder's late Virgin and child with the saints Margaret and Barbara of 1519.[18]

The culmination of these manifold activities was that by the 1520s, the fusion of intense artistic experimentation and technical innovation with a receptiveness to new stylistic possibilities, a new humanist sensibility, and engaged elite patronage collectively produced an original, modern idiom: an entirely new and recognizable "Augsburg Renaissance style".

2   The Reformation and the Arts

Ironically, the Fugger Chapel was completed only a few years before the onset of the Reformation in Augsburg, and St. Anna was to become one of the first churches to come under Lutheran sway, stimulated by the presence in the city of Luther himself in 1518, brought to answer charges of heresy at the imperial diet. Popular disturbances throughout the 1520s prompted the removal of a number of altarpieces and epitaphs from the cathedral, and a comprehensive reformation of the church, administered by the city authorities, was effected in 1537 with the abolition of Catholicism.[19] Radical "cleansings" of the cathedral, Sts. Ulrich and Afra, Holy Cross, St. Moritz, and St. Georg followed. Significant works of art such as Holbein the Elder's altarpiece for the high altar of the cathedral were destroyed and tombs and epitaphs were defaced, while many other sculptures and paintings were simply removed.

An immediate consequence for artists was a severe decline in commissions for religious works. Many left the profession; others left the city, following artists like Holbein the Elder and his sons, who had left in 1515, lured by better prospects elsewhere. As the Reformation took hold within the city, those

---

17   Metropolitan Museum of Art, inv. no. 17.190.745. Eser, *Hans Daucher*, pp. 106–14.
18   Lisbon, Museu Nacional de Arte Antiga.
19   Broadhead, *Internal Politics*, pp. 86–95. See Chapter 10 in this volume.

FIGURE 21.5   Hans Burgkmair the Elder, Esther before Ahasuerus, oil on panel, 1528
MUNICH, ALTE PINAKOTHEK, NO. 689

who stayed looked to an increasingly buoyant market for secular forms of art. Domestic silver-stain painted glass roundels, for example, which had emerged in the later fifteenth century as a popular form of household decoration, enjoyed a marked flourishing under these conditions.[20] Jörg Breu the Elder (c. 1475–1537), in particular, intensified his activity as a designer of domestic glass roundels in the 1520s, precisely during the period of popular unrest.[21] Among his most influential designs was a series of stained-glass roundels depicting the "Labors of the Months", commissioned by the merchant Georg Hoechstetter around 1521. They show Augsburg patricians enjoying pastoral pursuits as well as scenes of interior feasting – the traditional pleasures of the aristocracy, transposed to suit the lifestyle of urban elites. The unusually large number of workshop copies of these designs testifies to their popularity.[22]

Artists also found work outside the city. Hans Burgkmair the Elder and Jörg Breu the Elder were commissioned to execute paintings for a twin series of "Famous Battles" and "Famous Women" for the Munich Residence of (the Catholic) Wilhelm IV, Duke of Bavaria, between 1528 and 1535. Burgkmair's "Esther before Ahasuerus" represents the artist at the apogee of his powers, combining borrowed Italianisms for his architectural forms with orientalizing figures, bejeweled and turbaned amid Turkish carpets and richly patterned textiles, to conjure a strikingly exotic vision of ancient Babylon, executed in a palette of glowing tonalities and *sfumato* transitions inspired by Venetian painting.

Portraiture, for which there was a steady demand from wealthy patrons, also provided a lucrative aspect of production in a meager market. Hans Schwarz (1492–after 1521) was one of several trained sculptors, including Friedrich Hagenauer and Hans Daucher, who began specializing in portrait medals of Augsburg's leading citizens and visiting dignitaries. The subjects of the medals were usually shown in profile and with an inscription, and were cast in bronze or lead from a carved wooden model. In a brief career of merely five years between c. 1516 and 1521, Schwarz produced 149 medals and wooden models for medals. Some 137 bust-length portrait drawings that served as preparatory sketches for medals survive.[23]

While a tradition of painted portraiture had developed over the first quarter of the century in the hands of Holbein the Elder and his younger

---

20 Butts and Hendrix (eds.), *Painting on Light*.
21 Morrall, *Jörg Breu the Elder*, pp. 53–72, 196–217.
22 Grüber (ed.), *"Kurzweil Viel, ohn' Mass und Ziel"*, vol. 2, pp. 154–63.
23 Bernhart, "Augsburgs Medailleure"; Alsteens and Spira, *Dürer and Beyond*, pp. 53–55, no. 23.

contemporaries, only the highly gifted Christoph Amberger, who arrived in the city in 1530, made portraiture a professional specialism. His portraits, particularly in the 1540s, drew heavily upon the conventions of Venetian Renaissance portraiture, becoming larger in size and adopting three-quarter formats and a repertoire of dignified poses and expressions that spoke to the aristocratic pretensions of the various members of the Fugger, Welser, and other patrician families.[24]

Protestant domination of Augsburg was to last only 11 years. Following the decisive victory of Emperor Charles V over the Protestant Schmalkaldic League at Mühlberg in 1547, the emperor convened an imperial diet in Augsburg between September 1547 and May 1548 and began the restitution of Catholic worship in the city. Churches converted to Protestantism between 1534 and 1537 were returned to Catholic use, and civic reimbursements and replacements for destroyed church ornaments were ordered. In 1554, Christoph Amberger was commissioned to paint a new high altar for the cathedral, carefully replicating the essential traits of Holbein the Elder's former high altar of 1508–09. In the Benedictine abbey of Sts. Ulrich and Afra, the reforming abbot Jakob Köpplin (1548–1600) commissioned in 1571 a monumental high altar from the local sculptor, Paulus II Mair, which was intentionally modeled to the design of late fifteenth-century Gothic altarpieces, with a predella, corpus, and superstructure. In both cases, artistic style was employed as a means to maintain continuity with Catholic tradition. Indeed, for some Catholic patrons, the older, Gothic style remained an important vehicle of affective devotion. Hans Fugger rejected a painting of the Resurrection in a 1568 letter to his agent David Ott in Venice because it was "too much *à la italiana*, flashy [*frech*]". His demand for "something devout and beautiful and not this kind of thing, where the painter is showing off his skill and nothing else", well expresses this surviving conservative taste in religious art.[25]

Protestant worship was nonetheless allowed to continue in the city, an accommodation to a status quo further ratified by the Religious Peace of Augsburg of 1555 for the entire Holy Roman Empire. As the century progressed and new artistic commissions were given to redecorate the Catholic churches, considerable care was given to select themes that would be acceptable to Protestants as well as Catholics.[26]

Nonetheless, Mair's Mary Altar at Sts. Ulrich and Afra was replaced as the high altar only a generation later by a set of dramatic new altars, executed in

---

24 Kranz, *Christoph Amberger*, pp. 27, 44–46, 54–62, 233–38, 243–47; see also figure 19.4 in this volume.
25 Cited in Baxandall, "Hubert Gerard", pp. 127–44.
26 Rasmussen, "Bildersturm", pp. 95–114.

a modern, Counter-Reformation style by Hans Degler: the St. Narcissus (or "Adoration of the Shepherds") Altar and the Pentecost and the Resurrection Altars dedicated in 1604 and 1607, respectively.[27] These monumental altarpieces dominate the eastern nave of the church with a sense of dramatic action that extends from the grand rhetorical gestures of the figures in the central narrative scenes to the broken silhouettes and open forms of their frames, creating a sense of restless, upward-aspiring movement. The overt emotionalism registered in these forms brilliantly expresses the resurgent spirit of the Council of Trent and the Catholic Counter-Reformation. Thereafter, the wealthy Catholic families began anew to commission religious works in their churches.

3   Civic Monuments and Spaces

Parallel with new ecclesiastical monuments, a series of artistic and architectural projects were commissioned by the civil authorities between 1588 and 1631 which radically transformed the city center and made it one of the great civic spaces of the late Renaissance in Germany. These included the redesigning and rebuilding of public buildings, including replacing the old Gothic city hall with a new building by the architect Elias Holl between 1615 and 1620; the renovation of the numerous gate towers that transformed the city's skyline; the re-modeling of the main squares and thoroughfares; and the erection of three great public monuments – the Augustus Fountain designed by Hubert Gerhard, and the Mercury and Hercules Fountains by Adriaen de Vries. Each provided an artistically impressive and powerfully symbolic accent to the newly articulated main axes of the city center.[28]

Such reorganizations provided a symbolic means for the ruling authorities to express their relationship to the citizenry and the larger political world of the Empire.[29] The three fountains, for instance, conveyed in their subject matter, heroic medium, and Italianate style the city's Roman heritage and its enduring imperial associations, as well as the contemporary political and commercial standing of its citizenry.[30] Hubert Gerhard's bronze statue of the Emperor Augustus, after whom the Roman settlement of Augusta was named, stands imperiously above personifications of Augsburg's four rivers and streams: the Lech, Brunnenbach, Singold, and Wertach, whose attributes collectively sum up the city's natural resources and economic and commercial strengths. The

---

27   Chipps Smith, *German Sculpture*, pp. 113–14.
28   See Chapter 22 in this volume.
29   See Jachmann, *Kunst des Augsburger Rates*.
30   Bushart, "Augsburger Brunnen und Denkmale", pp. 82–94.

FIGURE 21.6   Adriaen de Vries, Hercules Fountain, 1602, bronze. Augsburg

emperor's commanding pose and outward gesture along with the stylistic concinnity of his forms with the city hall's classical façade directly opposite created a continuum that both bolstered the current ruling authority by association with the Roman past and suggested the continuing relationship of the imperial city to the present emperor.

The Mercury Fountain, designed by the Dutch sculptor Adriaen de Vries and cast by Wolfgang Neidhart of Augsburg in the years 1596 and 1599, was erected on what is today the Maximilianstraße.[31] De Vries, who like Hubert Gerhard had received his training in the circle of Giambologna in Florence, adapted that master's characteristic serpentine stance for his Mercury and included a small Cupid who fastens Mercury's winged sandal. The god of commerce is thereby sent forth by "love of what is right", as an inscription reads, directed perhaps, as Bushart suggests, to the common good.[32] If the Augustus Fountain was a monument to Augsburg's enduring government and political authority, Mercury represented the mercantile power and benefits of its merchant class.

31   Friedel, *Bronzebildmonumente*, p. 125, Doc. 25.
32   Bushart, "Augsburger Brunnen und Denkmale", p. 85. The inscription reads: "Industriae / Recti Amore / Temperatae" ("Industry tempered by love of what is right").

The third great sculptural monument of this same period, commissioned in 1602, was the Hercules Fountain, also by Adriaen de Vries, destined for a place on the Wine Market (figure 21.6). A study in late Renaissance monumental dramatic form, also inspired by Giambologna, the theme of Hercules subduing a water dragon with a firebrand has been interpreted as a reference to the city's third estate, the craftsmen, whose Promethean energies lay in harnessing the powers of the rivers' waters, and triumphing in their endeavors by the fire of the forge.[33]

Two further large bronze commissions, a monumental St. Michael overcoming Lucifer above the entrance of the city arsenal, or *Zeughaus*, designed by another pupil of Giambologna, Hans Reichle (*c.* 1570–1642), and an eagle for the *Siegelhaus* (seal house, where wine was measured and taxed), as well as a stone column with the *Stadtpyr* (pinecone), placed before the Protestant church of St. Ulrich, were all in place by 1610.

Elias Holl's city hall façade is impressive in its classical proportions and in the ascending progression of the simple yet variegated forms of the window enclosures. It is complemented by a geometrically ordered series of interior spaces: a succession of rooms leading to the final splendor of the "Golden Hall" (*Goldener Saal*), where the council deliberated and entertained. This scheme mirrored the logical ordering of the governmental offices they contained and thus symbolically evoked an ordered microcosm of good government. Such symbolism was underscored by the painted imagery, most spectacularly in the Golden Hall (which was destroyed during World War II and has since been restored in fragments and facsimile). Conceived and designed by the artist Peter Candid (1548–1628) and the Jesuit priest Matthäus Rader, and carried out by the Augsburg painter Matthias Kager (1575–1634), the frescoed walls and painted allegories, set into a carved and gilded wood and stucco ceiling, depict the virtues of good government. A central oval panel representing Wisdom, accompanied by the inscription from Proverbs 8:15, *Per Me Reges Regnant*, proclaims the central theme: that the authority to rule devolves from God. Taken together, the city hall's architectural layout and visual program thus reify an ideal of oligarchic government, a climax to a broader conception of Renaissance urban planning, by which the public monuments, buildings, and spaces collectively created an effective environment that worked as a medium for civic identity and public memory.

These works were largely commissioned from celebrated foreign artists who worked in an international court style that was popular throughout Europe, from Antwerp to Prague and Florence. This influx of foreigners was due in part to a dearth of artists of the first rank in Augsburg after the disruptions

---

33   Bushart, "Augsburger Brunnen und Denkmale", pp. 87–90.

of the mid-sixteenth century, a situation from which the city's painters never fully recovered. As Gode Krämer has pointed out, these foreign painters' sojourns in the city were too brief to leave any lasting impact upon locally trained practitioners. This is true of Titian, who resided in the city during the imperial diets in 1547–48 and again in 1551–52, at the behest of Emperor Charles V, whose equestrian "Portrait of the Emperor at the Battle of Mühlberg" (Prado, Madrid) he painted there in 1548. It is equally true of other Venetians, including Bernardino Licinio, Lambert Sustris (a native of Amsterdam), and later in the century Friedrich Sustris (c. 1540–1599), who decorated the house of Hans Fugger on the Zeugplatz and won commissions for altarpieces in the cathedral and in the Jesuit church; and of Flemish-trained painters like Hans von Aachen (1552–1616) and Peter Candid (c. 1548–1628), who won commissions for altars in Sts. Ulrich and Afra.[34]

The commitment to an internationalism of style and the ability to command commissions from celebrated foreign artists was largely possible because of the pan-European connections of the Fugger family and their highly sophisticated tastes. Prodigious builders and collectors, they had early on decorated the exteriors of their expanded, Italianate urban palace on the Wine Market with fresco cycles of historical and allegorical subjects, known today only partially from prints.[35] Further commissions for frescoed mural decorations followed the numerous building projects of other members of the Fugger family from mid-century onwards.[36] These essentially private projects, which gave public face to the wealth and prestige of their owners, were complemented and eventually superseded by the public commissions of the later century.

The Fuggers were also prodigious collectors. As Mark Meadow has shown, the city's wealthy burghers and merchants were the first – well before princes and the nobility – to develop a new form of encyclopedic collection, the *Kunst- und Wunderkammer*, which comprised antiquities, contemporary works of art, technical and mechanical instruments, and a range of natural rarities.[37] Most notable was Raymund Fugger, nephew of Jakob the Rich, who owned an extensive collection of paintings by a range of Italian and German artists, collections of rare books and manuscripts, and musical, mathematical, and horological instruments as well as *selzamkhayten* (rarities) and *naturalia*. He is also credited with the most sophisticated Central-European collection of antiquities of

---

34   Krämer, "Malerei in Augsburg", p. 32.
35   Lieb, *Die Fugger und die Kunst*, vol. 1, pp. 92–100; vol. 2, pp. 71–73, 155–56, 158–96, 204–05; Häberlein, *The Fuggers of Augsburg*, pp. 150–51.
36   For a list, see Lieb, "Augsburger Baukunst der Renaissance", p. 245.
37   Meadow, *First Treatise on Museums*, pp. 4–5; Lieb, *Die Fugger und die Kunst*, vol. 2, pp. 42–51, 61–63.

his day, and is remembered on his epitaph as *rerum antiquarum amantissimus*.[38] Such collectors were important for the development of art and craft production not just by virtue of their own commissioning and buying of art and of luxury goods. Their families' extended trade networks within Europe also afforded Augsburg craftsmen access to an international clientele, while their mercantile power and wealthy patronage gave Augsburg an unrivalled position as an entrepôt of both precious metals and exotic woods that in turn stimulated the growth of specific luxury crafts – notably goldsmithing, cabinet-making, and mechanical instruments – that set it apart from other cities.

Such habits of secular collecting gave rise to new artistic forms such as the *Kunstschrank* (art cabinet). A characteristic type was decorated with surface patterns made of wood inlays, or intarsia work.[39] Originating in fifteenth-century Italy, this art flourished in Augsburg, which had a long tradition of woodworking and where an equally technologically advanced metalworking industry was able to produce wire saws of a sufficient thinness for the fashioning of thin veneers of wood. From about 1560 onwards, a taste for these cabinets, with surfaces covered in elaborate landscapes of ruins and complicated geometric forms, often incongruously rendered as startling showpieces of perspectival construction, gathered the momentum of a European-wide fashion. The so-called *Wrangelschrank*, dated 1566 and executed by an unknown Augsburg master, possibly for a member of the Fugger family, is one of the first examples specifically made to house works of art and curiosities.[40] Its iconography of decay and transience was partly influenced by the woodcuts of Lorenz Stöer (active 1555–99), a Nuremberg artist and designer who had moved to Augsburg and whose pattern book, the *Geometria et Perspectiva* of 1567, was explicitly aimed at intarsia workers.[41]

A second type of cabinet, decorated with dark ebony veneers and silver mounts, gradually overtook the taste for intarsia. Such cabinets often possessed complex iconographical programs showing the virtues, the liberal arts, or figures drawn from biblical or classical history or myth, expressive of themes such as the virtues of good rulership. They found their place in the *Kunstkammern* and *studioli* of the high nobility. The magnificent "Hercules" cabinet, once almost certainly in the collection of Archduke Ferdinand of

---

38   Kellenbenz, "Augsburger Sammlungen", pp. 77–78; Häberlein, *The Fuggers of Augsburg*, pp. 159–60.
39   Chastel, "Marquetrie et perspective", pp. 141–54.
40   It takes its name from its seventeenth-century owner, the Swedish *Reichsmarschall* and Governor General of Pomerania, Carl Gustav Wrangel (1613–76), who, it is believed, acquired it on campaign during the Thirty Years' War. See Möller, *Wrangelschrank*, p. 13.
41   Stoer, *Geometria et Perspectiva*.

FIGURE 21.7 Philipp Hainhofer, Ulrich Baumgartner, The Kunstschrank of Gustavus Adolphus, 1625–31 (240 cm high × 120 cm wide)
GUSTAVIANUM, UNIVERSITY OF UPPSALA

Tyrol and now in the Kunsthistorisches Museum in Vienna, is a characteristic example.[42] The exceptional significance of such cabinets to a trade that in 1568 counted 130 independent local cabinet makers is shown by the fact that in 1575 the cabinet maker's guild made the completion of a *Schreibtisch* (writing desk) the required masterpiece for guild membership.[43]

The key figure in the development of the *Kunstschrank* in the seventeenth century was Philipp Hainhofer (1578–1647), an Augsburg merchant, dealer, diplomat, and art collector. Through his own trading and collecting activities, he became an art adviser and agent in acquiring objects and works of art. His role, anticipating the *marchands-merciers* of eighteenth-century Paris, was to bring together many different craftsmen on a single project that was often many years in the making, and to arrange its sale to wealthy clients. Of Hainhofer's surviving curiosity cabinets, the best-preserved is a cabinet presented by the city of Augsburg to King Gustavus Adolphus of Sweden in 1632. It has survived with most of its original contents of over a thousand pieces (figure 21.7).[44] Made under the direction of the cabinet maker Ulrich Baumgartner between 1625 and 1631, it employed some 30 independent craftsmen. The outer doors, veneered mostly in ebony, are inset with an array of hard stones, many painted with biblical and other moralizing subjects. Many of these came from Florence, where Hainhofer's brother Christoph, who lived there between 1609 and 1626, bought *pietre dure* panels and other carved and uncarved stones for the Augsburg firm. The cabinet is crowned by a magnificent display of *naturalia* – rocks, corals, and crystals – surmounted by a Seychelles nut fashioned into a goblet in the form of a sea chariot, surmounted by a reclining Venus. The interior drawers and compartments contained manmade and natural objects, including an array of small paintings, many on stone; portraits in wax; small-scale sculptures; eating and drinking vessels; writing implements; surgical and toiletry sets; mathematical instruments; mechanical dolls; and board games and entertainments, including a mechanical music box. The cabinet could also be revolved at will and contained a small collapsible ladder that unfolded to allow easy access to the upper tiers.

Hainhofer's conception of the *Kunstschrank* was thus much more than a piece of furniture for securing valuables and curios: it was a theater of wisdom, intended to encapsulate knowledge of the world through the products of newly discovered worlds and the achievements of contemporary European art and science. Hainhofer's indefatigable cultural and intellectual ambition transformed the collector's cabinet into an art form in its own right.

---

42   Vienna, Kunsthistorisches Museum, Slg. für Plastik und Kunstgewerbe, inv. no. 883.
43   Himmelheber, "Augsburger Kabinettschränke".
44   Boström, "Philipp Hainhofer"; idem, *Det Underbara Skåpet*.

4   Instrument Making

Augsburg became internationally famous for another equally intellectual branch of production: that of mechanical and scientific instruments. Over the course of the sixteenth and seventeenth centuries, the clockmakers, long since established among Augsburg's incorporated crafts, and the instrument makers, a new subset

FIGURE 21.8   Christoph Schissler, *Horologium Achaz Hydrographicum*, 1578, gilded brass, 12 cm diam
PHILADELPHIA, AMERICAN PHILOSOPHICAL SOCIETY, INV. NO. 58.66

of artisans who remained unincorporated, produced a dazzling array of measuring instruments, whether for marking time, mapping the heavens, or surveying the land. Small portable sundials, mostly of brass but sometimes of gilded silver, were a speciality of the Augsburg workshops. The city was especially well known for equatorial sundials, which were accompanied by a table of between 30 and 60 different cities, each with its respective latitude, from Jerusalem to Corfu, from Bergen to Lisbon, from London to Krakow.[45]

---

45   Bobinger, *Alt-Augsburger Kompassmacher*.

A letter from Christoph Schissler the Elder (c. 1531–1608), one of the most gifted of the instrument makers, addressed to Augustus I, Duke of Saxony, in 1572 in the hope of receiving orders, provides a glimpse of the range of specialized instrument production.[46] It referenced terrestrial and astronomical globes, astrolabes, "planispheres", "unusual and wonderful" clocks, as well as sundials and compasses that could tell the hours of the day and night. One item, the so-called "Horologium Achaz Hydrographicum", a sundial in the form of a drinking vessel, could, Schissler claimed, make time move backwards (figure 21.8).[47] Surviving letters between himself and Augustus of Saxony record their mutual engagement in the ongoing development of a prototype odometer – the first to be built in the Latin West since antiquity – and are testimony to a remarkable collaboration between nobleman and artisan.[48]

Similar creations, such as two extraordinary celestial globes by Georg Roll (c. 1546–92) and Johann Reinhold (c. 1550–96), which could set in motion the entire movement of the heavens, the sun, and its encircling planets by means of a single clockwork, went hand in hand with the production of accurate astronomical instruments. They attest to a strong local interest in astronomy, especially among the rectors of the city's Latin School that had been founded in 1531 as the *Gymnasium* of St. Anna. The rector Hieronymus Wolf developed a friendship with the Danish astronomer Tycho Brahe, who spent the year 1569–70 in the city and used the time to acquaint himself with the instrument makers' workshops. The burgomaster Paul (or Paulus) Hainzel had what was then the largest quadrant in Europe erected in his garden in Göggingen to Brahe's specifications.[49] In the seventeenth century, Johann Wiesel (1583–1662), a lens and optical instrument maker from the Palatinate who settled in Augsburg in 1621, developed a new type of telescope in collaboration with a Capuchin monk, Anton Maria Schirle de Rheita, by adding two additional lenses to the by then well-established Keplerian telescope. This extended the range and "righted" the inverted image of the Keplerian prototype. Two examples of this type are preserved in Skokloster Castle in Sweden.[50]

---

46   Hauptstaatsarchiv Dresden, Loc. 8679, fols. 44–45. See Bobinger, *Christoph Schissler*, p. 34.
47   See Sadler, "An Ancient Time Machine", pp. 211–16.
48   See Morrall, "Urban Craftsmen and the Courts", pp. 231–37.
49   Keil, "Augsburger Instrumentenmacher", p. 33. See also Chapter 20 in this volume.
50   Keil, "Augsburger Instrumentenmacher", p. 34.

5 The Luxury Trades

The influx of foreign artists and craftsmen, a lack of notable local fine artists, and the collaborative nature of art-making of the kind established by Philipp Hainhofer produced a highly effective system of production by which Augsburg's luxury art market flourished throughout the seventeenth century, surviving the deprivations of the Thirty Years' War, and continuing well into the eighteenth century. It provided for many individualized practitioners – silver engravers, gem cutters, ivory carvers, cabinet makers and case makers, even embroiderers and braid makers – much of whose livelihood came from collaborations on complex larger works with furniture makers, clockmakers, goldsmiths, and builders of automata and organs. Sculptors prepared models for the figurative elements incorporated into these luxury projects. The important Baroque sculptor and specialist ivory carver Georg Petel (1601–35), who had left his native Bavaria at the outset of the Thirty Years' War and travelled to Italy, where he became acquainted with Rubens and van Dyck, before settling in Augsburg in 1624, contributed in this way, as did later sculptors like Egid Verhelst (1696–1749) and Johann Michael Feichtmayr (1709–79). Of considerable significance was Augsburg's continuing position as a leading centre of print-making and publishing. Prominent draughtsmen active in the city would supply goldsmiths with designs for their work that were in keeping with the ornamental forms currently in fashion.

6 Gold- and Silver-Working

Within this very intensive artistic ambience, the craft of the goldsmith was pre-eminent. The goldsmiths had a long and prominent history within the city. They were documented as early as 1276; they had their own association from 1368, a meeting room from 1447, and a funerary chapel, the *Goldschmiedekapelle* in St. Anna's, from 1485, founded by the goldsmith Konrad Hirn. By 1420, the association had a system of control and an inspection mark of a pinecone. Buoyed by the mining and trading interests of the merchant patriciate and by their own extremely high standards of quality, the goldsmiths ranked highly within the city's guild hierarchy throughout the early modern period. Between the time of the Thirty Years' War (1618–48) and the demise of the Holy Roman Empire (1806), Augsburg was the preeminent European center of gold- and silver-working.[51] This was made possible in part by the religious tolerance following the Religious Peace of Augsburg in 1555, which encouraged talented workers of

---

51   Seling, *Kunst der Augsburger Goldschmiede.*

THE ARTS 519

FIGURE 21.9   Joachim Friess (ca. 1579–1620) Automaton in the form of Diana and the stag, ca. 1620. Partially gilded silver, enamel, jewels (case); iron, wood (movement), 14 3/4 × 9 1/2 in. (37.5 × 24.1 cm) Metropolitan Museum of Art, Gift of J. Pierpont Morgan, 1917, acc. no. 17.190.746

both confessions – Catholic and Protestant alike – to move to Augsburg from other cities, although the resurgent Catholic Church remained a major source of patronage. The traditional mining and international trading interests of the local merchant houses, meanwhile, ensured a ready supply of raw precious materials and rapid access to foreign markets, orienting the Augsburg goldsmiths' trade mainly towards export.

These circumstances encouraged the emergence of specialist silver dealers, who had often begun as goldsmiths but now acted as middlemen. They sought out commissions and advised on the large orders required for dynastic festivities and assemblies at European courts. In this way, silver artefacts were exported throughout Germany, to Scandinavia, Poland, Russia, Bohemia, Austria, Hungary, Switzerland, and Italy. They included an array of products ranging from ecclesiastical plate to courtly regalia, ambassadorial gifts, display plate, drinking vessels in the form of human figures and animals that were used as table decoration, writing cabinets, jewel boxes, and cabinets with silver ornaments. By the eighteenth century, Augsburg took the lead from Nuremberg in producing large numbers of fashionable services – tea services, silver-gilt travel and toilet sets, and, from about 1680 to 1730, silver furniture.[52]

The extraordinary success of the goldsmiths' trade also lay in a system of production that divided commissions between several workshops and which, by standardizing labor, allowed the fast completion of large commissions. The dealers also relieved the individual workshops of the often burdensome financial responsibility of large orders by taking them on themselves. As tastemakers, alert to the newest fashionable trends, and with an extraordinary pool of local expertise at their disposal, dealers could introduce new designs into the market quickly and effectively, such as the incorporation, after 1710, of Meissen porcelain into the objects produced by the goldsmiths' workshops.

The collaborative structures of production described above continued to characterize the arts in Augsburg throughout the eighteenth century. In 1730, as a leading center for the production of high-quality printmaking, Augsburg was host to 61 engravers and 23 publishers of engravings.[53] Just as in the early sixteenth century, artistic innovation had been generated by local responses to external influence from Italy, mediated in large part by prints, so it was in the engravers' workshops of the eighteenth century that designers responded to printed designs emanating from Paris, the new dominant European cultural center. Copies were routinely made and fresh designs generated that amalgamated a German late-Baroque with the French idiom to produce a distinctive and wonderfully vibrant version of the Rococo that was taken up and ex-

---

52 Baumstark and Seling (eds.), *Silber und Gold*.
53 Seitz, "The Engraving Trade", pp. 116–27.

THE ARTS

FIGURE 21.10 Gregorio Guglielmo, Ballroom, Schaezler Palace, Augsburg, 1765

tended by artists in other media. The Augsburg Academy of Art, an institution founded in 1670 with the help of Joachim von Sandrart, became a fulcrum for the style.[54] Its director in 1730, the painter Johann Georg Bergmüller (1698–1762), published six suites of proto-Rococo ornament in the late 1720s. He counted among his pupils several artists who were to become outstanding exponents of the Rococo manner, including Jeremias Wachsmuth (1712–71), whose many suites of Rococo ornaments served as models across a gamut of different media. Franz Xaver Habermann (1721–96), trained as a sculptor, was a prolific designer of Rococo ornament and furniture in this distinctive German style.[55] Another director of the Academy, Matthäus Günther (1705–88), executed more than 60 fresco cycles between the 1720s and the 1780s, working in collaboration with sculptors and local decorators for churches around Bavaria and Swabia. In many churches throughout the region, exquisite architectural and ornamental design was combined with paintings on ceilings, in side chapels, and on nave walls. Typically, painters like Günther or his predecessor as director of the Augsburg Academy, Johann Georg Bergmüller, would spend the summer months executing frescoes in the surrounding area.[56]

Today, the best-preserved secular Rococo monument in the city is the Schaezler Palace, built in 1765 by the banker and silver dealer Baron Benedikt Adam Liebert von Liebenhofen (1731–1810) (figure 21.10). The magnificent, double-storied ballroom that forms its centerpiece houses a massive ceiling painting of the four continents by the Italian artist Gregorio Guglielmi (1714–73), supported by exceptionally skilful and delicate stucco work on the ceilings and walls by the local artisans Franz Xaver Feichtmayr the Younger and Simpert Feichtmayr, and with woodcarving and panelling executed by Placidus Verhelst.

7 Conclusion

The works of this era form the last distinctive artistic climax in the city. Production and trade in luxury goods continued unabated throughout the eighteenth century: the metalworking and printing industries remained buoyant; calico-printing had been successfully introduced in 1689 and colored paper-making from *c.* 1690; and there were various attempts to establish porcelain and faience factories. Yet from the 1770s onwards, as Paul von Stetten's history of the arts registered, Augsburg's significance as an artistic center was

---

54 Bushart, "Augsburger Akademien", pp. 332–47.
55 Thornton, *Form and Decoration*, pp. 142–44.
56 Epple (ed.), *Johann Georg Bergmüller*.

on the wane, relying increasingly on its former greatness. The secularization of ecclesiastical territories in 1802–03 heralded the end of a long tradition of church patronage; and when Augsburg lost its status as a free imperial city and was incorporated into the state of Bavaria in 1805–06, the city's influence as a cultural center, tied for so long to the court ethos of the *ancien régime*, fell into ineluctable decline, unable to prevail against the forces of industrialization.

Bibliography

Unpublished Primary Source
Hauptstaatsarchiv Dresden, Loc. 8679.

Published Primary Sources
Stoer, L., *Geometria et Perspectiva. Hierinn Etliche// Zerbrochene Gebew/ den Schreinern// in eingelegter Arbeit dienstlich/ auch vil andern Liebhabern zusondern // gefalen geordent unnd // gestalt / Durch // Lorenz Stoeer // Maller Burger inn Augspurg* […], 1567.

Stetten, P. von (the Younger), *Kunst-, Gewerb- und Handwerks-Geschichte der Reichs-Stadt Augsburg*, Augsburg, 1779.

Secondary Literature
Alsteens, S. and Spira, F., *Dürer and Beyond: Central European Drawings Before 1700 in the Metropolitan Museum of Art* (exhibition catalogue), New York and New Haven, 2012.

Baumstark, R. and Seling, H. (eds), *Silber und Gold. Augsburger Goldschmiedekunst für die Höfe Europas*, 2 vols, Munich, 1994.

Baxandall, M., "Hubert Gerard and the Altar of Christoph Fugger: The Sculpture and its Making", *Münchener Jahrbuch der bildenden Kunst* 17 (1966), pp. 127–44.

Bernhart, M., "Augsburgs Medailleure und Bildnisse Augsburger Kunsthandwerker auf Schaumünzen des 16. Jahrhunderts", *Mitteilungen der Bayerischen Numismatischen Gesellschaft* 55 (1937), pp. 41–98.

Beutler, C. and Thiem, G., *Hans Holbein der Ältere. Die spätgotische Altar- und Glasmalerei*, Augsburg, 1960.

Bobinger, M., *Christoph Schissler der Ältere und Jüngere*, Augsburg, 1954.

Bobinger, M., *Alt-Augsburger Kompassmacher*, Augsburg, 1966.

Boström, H.-O., "Philipp Hainhofer and Gustavus Adolphus' *Kunstschrank* in Uppsala", in O. Impey and A. MacGregor (eds), *The Origins of Museums: the Cabinet of Curiosities in Sixteenth- and Seventeenth-Century Europe*, Oxford, 1985, pp. 121–36.

Boström, H.-O., *Det Underbara Skåpet: Philipp Hainhofer och Gustav II Adolfs konstskåp*, Stockholm, 2001.

Broadhead, P., *Internal Politics and Civic Society in Augsburg during the Era of the Early Reformation, 1518–1537*, London, 1981.

Bushart, B., "Die Augsburger Brunnen und Denkmale um 1600", in *Welt im Umbruch. Augsburg zwishen Renaissance und Barock* (exhibition catalogue), Augsburg, 1980, vol. 3, pp. 82–94.

Bushart, B., "Die Augsburger Akademien", in A.W.A. Bonschloo (ed.), *Academies of Art between Renaissance and Romanticism* (*Leids kunsthistorisch jaarboek* 5–6), The Hague, 1989, pp. 332–47.

Bushart, B., *Die Fuggerkapelle bei St. Anna in Augsburg*, Augsburg, 1994.

Butts, B. and Hendrix, L. (eds.), *Painting on Light: Drawings and Stained Glass in the Age of Dürer and Holbein*, Oxford, 2001.

Chastel, A., "Marquetrie et perspective au XVe Siecle", *Revue des Arts* 3 (1953), pp. 141–54.

Chipps Smith, J., *German Sculpture of the Later Renaissance, c. 1520–1580: Art in an Age of Uncertainty*, Princeton, 1994.

Cornet, C., *Die Augsburger Kistler des 17. Jahrhunderts*, Petersberg, 2016.

Epple, A. (ed.), *Johann Georg Bergmüller 1688–1762: Zur Wiederkehr seines Geburtjahres* (exhibition catalogue), Weißenhorn, 1988.

Eser, T., *Hans Daucher. Augsburger Kleinplastik der Renaissance*, Munich, 1996.

Friedel, H., *Bronzebildmonumente in Augsburg 1589–1606. Bild und Urbanität*, Augsburg, 1974.

Gärtner, M., *Römische Basiliken in Augsburg. Nonnenfrömmigkeit und Malerei um 1500*, Augsburg, 2002.

Grüber, P.M. (ed.), *"Kurzweil Viel ohn' Mass und Ziel". Vol. 1: Augsburger Patrizier und ihre Feste zwischen Mittelalter und Neuzeit* (exhibition catalogue), Munich, 1994.

Grüber, P.M. (ed.), *"Kurzweil Viel ohn' Mass und Ziel". Vol. 2: Alltag und Festtag auf den Augsburger Monatsbildern der Renaissance*, Munich, 1994.

Häberlein M., *The Fuggers of Augsburg: Pursuing Wealth and Honor in Renaissance Germany*, Charlottesville and London, 2012.

Himmelheber, G., "Augsburger Kabinettschränke", in *Welt im Umbruch. Augsburg zwischen Renaissance und Barock* (exhibition catalogue), Augsburg, 1980, vol. 2, p. 58–62.

Huth, H., *Künstler und Werkstatt der Spätgotik*, 2nd ed., Darmstadt, 1967.

Jachmann, J., *Die Kunst des Augsburger Rates 1588–1631. Kommunale Räume als Medium von Herrschaft und Erinnerung*, Munich, 2008.

Keil, I., "Augsburger Instrumentenmacher", in P. Plaßmeyer and W. Dolz (eds.), *Weltenglanz. Der Mathematisch-Physikalische Salon Dresden zu Gast im Maximilianmuseum Augsburg*, Berlin, 2009, pp. 32–36.

Kellenbenz, H., "Augsburger Sammlungen", in: *Welt im Umbruch. Augsburg zwischen Renaissance und Barock* (exhibition catalogue), Augsburg, 1980, vol. 1, pp. 76–88.

Krämer, G., "Malerei in Augsburg 1560–1610", in *Welt im Umbruch. Augsburg zwischen Renaissance und Barock* (exhibition catalogue), Augsburg, 1980, vol. 2, pp. 31–35.

Kranz, A., *Christoph Amberger, Bildnismaler zu Augsburg. Städtische Eliten im Spiegel ihrer Porträts*, Regensburg, 2004.

Krause, K., *Hans Holbein der Ältere*, Munich, 2002.

Lieb, N., *Die Fugger und die Kunst*, 2 vols., Munich, 1952–58.

Lieb, N., "Augsburger Baukunst der Renaissance", in *Augusta 955–1955*, Augsburg, 1955, pp. 229–247.

Meadow, M., *The First Treatise on Museums: Samuel Quiccheberg's Inscriptiones 1565*, Los Angeles, 2013.

Metzger, C. (ed.), *Daniel Hopfer. Ein Augsburger Meister der Renaissance* (exhibition catalogue), Munich, 2009.

Möller, L., *Der Wrangelschrank und die verwandten süddeutschen Intarsienmöbel des 16. Jahrhunderts*, Berlin, 1956.

Morrall, A., *Jörg Breu the Elder. Art, Culture and Belief in Reformation Augsburg*, Aldershot, 2001.

Morrall, A., "Urban Craftsmen and the Courts in Sixteenth-Century Germany", in D. Eichberger and P. Lorentz (eds), *The Artist between Court and City (1300–1600)*, Petersberg, 2017, pp. 231–37.

Parshall, P. and Landau, D., *The Renaissance Print*, New Haven, 1988.

Rasmussen, J., "Bildersturm und Restauratio", in *Welt im Umbruch. Augsburg zwischen Renaissance und Barock* (exhibition catalogue), Augsburg, 1980, vol. 3, pp. 95–114.

Roper, L., *The Holy Household: Women and Morals in Reformation Augsburg*, Oxford, 1989.

Sadler, P.M., "An Ancient Time Machine: The Dial of Ahaz", *American Journal of Physics* 63, 211 (1995), pp. 211–16.

Seitz, W., "The Engraving Trade in Seventeenth- and Eighteenth-Century Augsburg: A Checklist", *Print Quarterly* 3, 2 (1986): 116–27.

Seling, H., *Die Kunst der Augsburger Goldschmiede, 1529–1868. Meister, Marken, Werke*, 3 vols., Munich, 1980.

Silver, L., *Marketing Maximilian: The Visual Ideology of a Holy Roman Emperor*, Princeton, 2008.

Silver, L., and Wykoff E. (eds.), *Grand Scale: Monumental Prints in the Age of Dürer and Titian*, New Haven, 2008.

Thornton, P., *Form and Decoration Innovation in the Decorative Arts, 1400–1870*, New York, 1998.

Wilhelm, J., *Augsburger Wandmalerei. Künstler, Handwerker und Zunft*, Augsburg, 1983.

Wood, C.S., *Forgery, Replica, Fiction: Temporalities of German Renaissance Art*, Chicago, 2008.

CHAPTER 22

Architecture

Dietrich Erben

This chapter focuses on the social and cultural conditions of architectural production in Augsburg between the late fourteenth century and the end of the eighteenth century. Augsburg's architecture and urban development in this period are characterized not only by an abundance of building activities, but also by significant dynamics of modernization. Two factors are noteworthy: competition between patrons, and reception of the Renaissance style. These factors simultaneously characterize the city's specific historical situation.

On the one hand, three formally independent, yet interconnected political entities in the city effectively coexisted in productive competition for architectural patronage: the municipality and the wealthier citizens of the free imperial city; the prince-bishopric; and the imperial abbey of Sts. Ulrich and Afra. These developments were evidently due to competing intentions, which were not necessarily accompanied by economic prosperity or stable internal and external political circumstances. In fact, the opposite was occasionally true.

On the other hand, the city's early modern building culture was greatly influenced by the reception of the stylistic principles of Renaissance architecture. To begin with, this refers to the acceptance of a classical canon of form, in which the humanist discovery of the city's ancient history through cultural contacts with Italy interacted with the accompanying transfer of Renaissance architecture. A study of Augsburg thus shows that a purely formal understanding of architecture is insufficient for capturing the dynamics of modernization. Simply put, until the middle of the sixteenth century, building was taking place simultaneously in both Gothic and Renaissance styles. It is thus important to enquire into the semantically connoted building typologies and the formal repertoire. Attention should also be paid to the basic communicational and functional relationships in which the architecture of this era is embedded.[1]
A study of Augsburg's history and art history in the early modern period can rely on an impressive body of research, which has been inspired by the city's historical significance, the abundance of material documentation, and the collective efforts of several local institutions such as the university, the museums,

---

1   On Renaissance architecture as a research problem, see Nussbaum et al. (eds.), *Wege zur Renaissance*; Günther, *Was ist Renaissance?*; Châtenet et al. (eds.), *Le Gothique de la Renaissance*. For a methodological sketch see Erben, "Architektur".

ARCHITECTURE

FIGURE 22.1   City map of Augsburg from Braun und Hogenberg, *Civitates orbis terrarium* …, colored woodcut, 1572
AUGSBURG, STÄDTISCHE KUNSTSAMMLUNGEN, G30

and the archives. This body of research provides an excellent basis for an overview such as the present one, but its breadth also limits us to a strict selection of material and choice of method.[2]

1   Urban Development and Competitive Patronage

Augsburg's early modern urban development did not take the form of an outward expansion but rather of an inward modernization. Since the High Middle Ages, a city wall had enclosed the triad of secular and ecclesiastical forces with the municipality in the center, the cathedral district in the north, and the abbey region in the south (figure 22.1). Extensions to Our Lady's Suburb (*Frauenvorstadt*) north of the cathedral and to the east with the neighborhood

---

2 In this chapter, the relationship between confessional policy, art and architecture will be omitted for reasons of space and content; for discussion, see Hoffmann et al. (eds.), *Als Frieden möglich war*.

of artisans who had settled around the parish church of St. Jacob (donated in 1348) had already been completed during the fourteenth century, thus establishing Augsburg's spatial extent and street pattern. In the succeeding centuries, buildings were only occasionally constructed outside the city walls, and large-scale residential and industrial areas were added only in the course of the nineteenth century.[3] The changes that did take place from the late Middle Ages took the form of new building structures and modifications within a generally fixed framework of streets and squares. The continuity of urban architecture, which had been established with the Roman founding of the city around 15 BC, was respected, while the dynamics arising from the desire of various builders for innovation evolved within these set boundaries.

The new construction of the east chevet (*Ostchor*) of Augsburg's cathedral was the largest building project of the fourteenth and fifteenth centuries (figure 22.2). Construction on the east end of the Romanesque basilica began around 1340. The year 1343 is mentioned in a building inscription on the north portal, and a chronicle from 1356 records construction on the long chancel. Thereafter, building proceeded extremely sluggishly, due among other things to several changes in plans. Only after the turn of the century could the vaults be constructed, and three more decades passed until consecration in 1431.[4] The east chevet was constructed adjacent to the two Romanesque church towers as a long choir with five aisles, an ambulatory, and an apse chapel. Two portals to the north and south served as main entrances. The addition of the *Ostchor* not only gave the existing bishop's church, which already contained a west chancel, an orientation in the opposite direction, but also increased the cathedral's dimensions within the city's new alignment. Although the road that followed the magisterial Roman *Via Claudia* as it cut through the center of the city was forced to swerve around the new building, the old rights of way were still visible. In fact, the right of way remained in effect until 1821, for citizens had the formal right to use the old Roman road via the newly built ambulatory of the cathedral.

Due to its exposed site and sheer size within the city topography, the cathedral's east chevet remains a prominent structure to the present day. The exterior design underscores this dominance through the monumental dimensions of the portals, the splendor of their sculptures, the porches which extend

---

3   The city's most important early modern buildings and ensembles are examined in numerous individual studies. A survey of the entire period is not available. For partial accounts, see Zimmer, "Veränderungen im Augsburger Stadtbild"; Bushart, "Kunst und Stadtbild"; Jachmann, *Kunst des Augsburger Rates*; for specific buildings see von Hagen and Wegener-Hüssen, *Stadt Augsburg*.
4   On the construction, see Chevalley, *Dom zu Augsburg*, pp. 68–141; Kayser, "Der Ostchor".

FIGURE 22.2　View from the south of the east chancel of Augsburg Cathedral, constructed 1340–1431. Photo from 1990, Eberhard Lantz
BAYERISCHES LANDESAMT FÜR DENKMALPFLLEGE MÜNCHEN

into public space, and the striking battlements above the chapels. The restored church towers, with their original white walls and red tile roofs, also served as a distinctive color element in the city – Augsburg's heraldic city colors of red, white, and green were introduced around 1370.

The interplay of various interests can already be discerned in the positioning of the new structure, blocking the old Roman road. They can also be seen in the development of the structure and its interior space.[5] The floor plan of the chevet exactly replicates a layout that took its example from existing cathedral chancels of the thirteenth century (in particular Amiens, Beauvais, and Cologne). The insistence on constructing this venerable building type in Augsburg nearly a century later, by which time it had already become uncommon, hints at the political intentions of the building's patron, the bishop, which lay behind this deliberate invocation of tradition. Contemporary events, however, showed little regard for the bishop's claims to status and ecclesiastical

---

5　See Himmelheber, *Ostchor*, pp. 36–42; Chevalley, *Dom zu Augsburg*, pp. 114–16.

power. An in-depth analysis of the chevet's construction reveals through innumerable details that the architectural systems of floor plan, elevation, and vaulting are not exactly compatible. These apparent "construction errors" imply that, as the building progressed, the original concept was successively revised. Intermittently the planned basilica had even been abandoned in favor of a modern-style hall church which, however, given the already completed building elements, was ultimately considered undesirable.

These conflicts over form can be seen as an ongoing struggle over usage rights to the building, as they document the occasionally bitter fights between the bishop and the cathedral chapter on the one hand, and the patricians and common citizens on the other. The latter were able to assert their interests in the spatial arrangement of the church beyond their already existing financial contributions. Significantly, after the guild rebellion of 1368[6] the clergy was forced to accept citizenship and pay taxes, while at the same time certain local patrician families including the Öfelin, Dachs, Ilsung, and Schweingen, and eventually also the guilds, were required to contribute funds for the construction of the chevet. The coats of arms on the keystones in the east chevet confirm this commitment. Ultimately, local political circumstances were also resolved through the spatial relationships in the newly constructed east chancel: the cathedral chapter retreated behind the high walls of the interior high chancel; the civic community asserted its right of way through the ambulatory; and the chapels provided the patrician families with spaces for endowing altars, tombs, and the reading of holy masses.

While the enormous structure of the cathedral's east chevet was slowly rising, the city hall (*Rathaus*) was rebuilt approximately 500 meters further south on the Roman road. The new stone structure, begun in 1385, replaced a previous wooden building. The core building was enlarged with two additions to form a three-gabled complex in 1449. The late medieval city hall, which was replaced in 1615 by a new construction still in existence today (figure 22.7), was documented as a wooden model probably produced when a new design for the Perlach Tower was planned in 1518 (figure 22.3).[7] The entire building complex comprised three parallel gabled houses which together formed a relatively unified main façade. A continuous canopy construction above the ground floor and molding above the main floor helped to create the appearance of unity. Furthermore, the main floor on all three buildings was united by grandly framed tracery windows and generously provided with light. Behind

---

6 See Chapter 6 in this volume.
7 Hilbich, *Das Augsburger spätgotische Rathaus*; Baer et al. (eds.), *Elias Holl*, cat. no. 217.

FIGURE 22.3   Late Gothic city hall, built 1385, expanded 1449 and 1515–1516. Wooden model, c. 1515–16
AUGSBURG, STÄDTISCHE KUNSTSAMMLUNGEN, GRAPHISCHE SAMMLUNG, NO. 3453

the windows were the halls for the Great and Small Councils as well as the courtroom (*Gerichtsstube*). In addition to the functional elements, the main façade was adorned with numerous symbols of the imperial city's sovereignty. These included the pillory, which consisted of a balcony with metal bars and handcuffs attached to the wall, upon which condemned delinquents were displayed to the public; the oriel with its tracery ornamentation, which was used to announce oaths and decrees; the large clock on the front of the main gable that served as a civil counterpart to the clocks on the church towers; and a slender polygonal tower with an open belfry rising out of the divide between the gabled roofs. The tower bells also served as an important proclamation tool of the council. The significance of the city hall was thus not merely restricted to the function of the interior rooms, but also lay in its central position on the imperial road at the core of the city, which broadened out into the market area.

FIGURE 22.4 View from the north of the former abbey church of Sts. Ulrich and Afra, built from 1467 onwards, with the Protestant church of St. Ulrich in the foreground
PHOTO: ISABEL MÜHLHAUS, LEHRSTUHL FÜR THEORIE UND GESCHICHTE VON ARCHITEKTUR, KUNST UND DESIGN, TU MÜNCHEN

The abundance of structural symbols on the building's exterior also served to proclaim the municipality's political sovereignty.

The southern part of the city was occupied by the extensive property of the Benedictine abbey of Sts. Ulrich and Afra (figure 22.4). Settlement of this area extends back to the ancient necropolis once situated here at the southern end of the road, with tombs on either side, along which people settled over the centuries. A Christian burial site had already existed in the area of the necropolis in late antiquity. A monastery was later established here and was presumably taken over by the Benedictine order around 1000 AD. By the end of the twelfth century, an unusual double-naved Romanesque church had been constructed to house the sepulchres of the holy patrons, the early Christian martyr Afra and the medieval bishop Ulrich (canonized in 993). Beginning in

1467, this structure was replaced by the currently existing basilica, which had been largely completed under various builders by the sixteenth century.[8]

The institution of the abbey and its building history were closely associated with the interests of the city. The church provided one of the noblest local burial sites, and the tomb of the patron saints of the diocese functioned as a pilgrimage site. The abbey consequently constructed its own preaching hall (*Predigthaus*) for parish church services in 1458 (it was converted after 1536 into the Protestant church of St. Ulrich) and evolved into a center of humanist scholarship with its own printing office. At the same time, the Benedictine congregation clearly searched for ways to establish a degree of independence from the city and form an alliance with the emperor. Emperor Maximilian I joined the monastic community in 1502 and acted as a donor who supported the construction of the church. He was present at the dedication of the nave in 1500 and laid the foundation stone for the chevet. In this context, he commissioned an equestrian monument for himself, designed by Hans Burgkmair the Elder and already begun by Gregor Erhard in 1501, which was to be placed on the northern (city) side of the chancel.[9] The support that the Benedictine abbey traditionally received from the Empire ultimately resulted in its independence from the city, which had existed *de facto* since 1541 and was formally legalized in 1577, when the abbey was placed directly under the emperor's sovereignty.

The architecture of the church of St. Ulrich documents the dialectic interplay between urban integration and institutional autonomy. In drafting the design, everything possible was done to create a structure of monumental unity that corresponded to the contemporary principles of modern architecture. Great emphasis was placed on simplicity in the basilica's interior, highlighted in the strict serial reticulated vaults and reduced elevation. The open triforium was replaced by a flat wall relief of tracery framings. The northern façade of the basilica offers the city a grandiose view. The imperial road, which until the nineteenth century was divided into two lanes by low structures in the center, (see figure 22.1) parts to turn both west and east at the front of the building. Both the size of the construction, which is monumentally tiered toward the east, and the construction details were rigorously calculated with a distant viewpoint in mind. The buttresses on the nave and the transept were moved against the wall in order to avoid optical overlapping of the individual façade elements and to create a clear and readable façade by alternating stucco walls and ashlar structuring. This was further achieved through the complex framework and

---

8 For a recent work on the building history, see Bischoff, *Burkhard Engelberg*.
9 On this project, which was abandoned in 1510, see Erben, "Krise des Reiterdenkmals", pp. 278–80.

the open silhouette of the transept's windowed gable. A remarkable special solution was applied on the east side of the church: facing the city, the eastern section consists of the main apse and a large sacristy with a huge chapel on its upper floor. The church tower is positioned between these two structures. The main chapel and sacristy, parallel to one another, allude to the Romanesque double church that once stood on this site, but without actually reconstructing the two-choir structure. The city's architectural façade is thus enriched by a noteworthy work of structural historical fiction.

The basilica of Sts. Ulrich and Afra owes its status as one of the most important late Gothic churches in the Empire both to the history of its commissioning in the context of competitive patronage within the city of Augsburg and to the stylistic history of a significant claim to modernization in building design. The relevant innovations do not relate to the formal repertoire but rather to the basic conditions of the design concept. In other words, the traditional forms of the late Gothic period (particularly the ribbed vaults and the tracery structures of the windows and walls) continued to be applied, but were structurally integrated into a spatial design that was nearly simultaneously developed in Italian Renaissance architecture from the beginning of the fifteenth century. Sts. Ulrich and Afra is exemplary of this process of architectural modernization using traditional formal resources. This applies firstly to the overall concept, which differentiates between basic architectural elements and wall sections and endows the building with tectonic expression; secondly, to the unity and, ideally, immediately recognizable clarity of the interior space and the façade; and thirdly, a new emphasis on accentuating the building itself within the overall urban context.[10]

The basilica of Sts. Ulrich and Afra, together with the cathedral's prominent chevet and the city hall, completed the triad of major buildings in late medieval Augsburg. The three buildings not only correspond to distinct political powers, but also encompass the entire topography of the Roman city *Augusta Vindelicorum*. Following their completion, it was left to the sixteenth-century humanists to draw attention to the cultural capital provided by the city's ancient tradition, before the municipality could in turn exploit it as a self-assertive political strategy through the construction of monumental public buildings.

---

10 Erben, "Architektur". Analogous considerations are applicable for the new parish church of St. Georg (1490) and the Dominican church of St. Magdalena (1513–15).

2   Civic Construction, Learned Culture, and the Reception of Antiquity

From the beginning of the sixteenth century, the Fugger family secured its political position in Augsburg not only through its legendary wealth and far-flung international networks, but also through its patronage of art and architecture. The family thus achieved a special status within local society. It is symptomatic that the family's patronage was highlighted in Norbert Lieb's groundbreaking works well before the focus on patronage became an established research direction in art history. This focus has since continued to be applied in more recent research on the Fugger family.[11] In the present context, special attention will be paid to the spatial order created in each of the three large Fugger building foundations as well as in the overall urban structure.

Around 1506, the Fuggers endowed a funeral chapel in St. Anna's church and acquired properties for the family palace on the Wine Market. Starting in 1514, Jakob Fugger the Rich began purchasing real estate for an urban housing project for the poor, known as the Fuggerei, in St. Jacob's Suburb (*Jakobervorstadt*), and construction commenced in 1516. The Fuggers' architectural patronage followed a highly expansive strategy, evident both in the close temporal sequence of the three projects and their various functions, which serve a broad spectrum of sacred and profane purposes.[12] This aspiration is also illustrated by the exorbitant amount of surface area occupied by the buildings and by their topographical positions within the city.

The family mausoleum was constructed as an addition to the west side of the late Gothic Carmelite church of St. Anna (figure 21.3), thus competing with the friar's choir in the east.[13] Although there were local models for such additions (such as the Hirn family chapel, also in St. Anna, from 1420), they do not account for the exposed location of the Fugger Chapel in the nave and its central design plan. Italian buildings served as models for the wall elevation and the choice of precious materials. All of the conceptual decisions for the construction undeniably reflected the wishes of the patrons, who sought to demonstrate the breadth of their cultural horizons and their economic potency, in turn derived from commerce and monetary transactions. The combination of architectural features of the Renaissance in the design of the walls with

---

11   Lieb, *Die Fugger und die Kunst*; Scheller, *Memoria an der Zeitenwende*; Wölfle, *Kunstpatronage der Fugger*; see also Chapter 21 in this volume.
12   For an overview, see Häberlein, *Fuggers of Augsburg*, pp. 149–59.
13   Important recent studies on the Fugger Chapel include Bushart, *Fuggerkapelle*; Eser, *Hans Daucher*, pp. 39–49 and cat. nos. 26, 27, 35, 36; and Bellot, "Fuggerkapelle".

an intricate late Gothic web of ribbed vaults in the Fugger Chapel illustrates, as in the basilica of Sts. Ulrich and Afra, that the cultural force of tradition was in no way considered inferior to innovation. This can also be seen in the family's residence: remarkably, the complex of Fugger houses in the city center took up an entire quarter. Local residential forms were applied to the allocation of space, while the rooms surrounding the courtyards were grouped around ambulatories with column arcades whose Renaissance forms also extended to the original façade paintings.[14] With its social housing project, the family ultimately expanded its sphere of influence beyond the patrician uptown (*Oberstadt*) to the peripheral artisan's suburb around St. Jacob's church.[15] The term *Fuggerei* for the settlement is documented as early as 1531. Once again, the housing project took up an extraordinary amount of space, for which an appropriate building design had to be devised. The patron and the master builder Thomas Krebs adopted a row house building style for the settlement, which was enclosed with its own wall. This building type had already been developed in various forms elsewhere.[16] The Fuggerei implemented a high level of social discipline within a framework of social welfare.

The Fugger family was decidedly interested in promoting cultural imports through its architectural patronage. This cultural transfer clearly favored the "modern" elements of early Italian Renaissance architecture and had no connections to older local traditions. In this sense, the Fugger buildings represent a "Renaissance without Augsburg".[17] The Fuggers as patrons differ significantly in this respect from other members of the political and intellectual elite, who were more likely to tap into existing cultural resources with an ancient heritage.

An example of the latter approach is provided by the humanist Conrad Peutinger, who initiated a particular view of the city's Roman history with a collection of inscriptions that he displayed in his own home. Peutinger played a significant role both in Augsburg as city secretary (1497–1534) and at the emperor's court as an imperial counselor (beginning in 1506). He moved into

---

14   Hascher, "Auftragslage"; on the reception of Italian art in the context of Fugger patronage, see Tönnesmann, "Anfänge der Renaissancearchitektur", pp. 301–06.
15   Ropertz, "Wohnstiftungen", pp. 210–13; Tietz-Strödel, *Fuggerei*; Scheller, *Memoria*, pp. 225–34.
16   In addition to German *Stiftungshöfe*, the Beguine houses of Flanders, college buildings in England, and Venetian social settlements should be mentioned. Subsequent housing projects in Augsburg were the *Herrnhäuser* of St. Georg (1529) and the *Zinshäuser* near the city wall on the *Oberer Graben* (1560–63).
17   This term suggests that the local Renaissance need not be based on a prior classical heritage; see Herselle Krinsky, "Renaissance Without Rome".

his house on the Cathedral Square (*Domhof*) in 1499 and began to furnish it with Roman inscriptions salvaged from the city and its environs or, in some cases, purchased as "building refuse". He documented his collection along with other known examples in published catalogues of Roman inscriptions (1505 and 1520). Some of these artifacts were integrated into the entrance gate and courtyard of his house and are still *in situ* today. In displaying the inscriptions in his home, the humanist transmitted a practice already established in Italy in the mid-fifteenth century, and which Peutinger had encountered during his studies there.[18]

Almost a century later, the humanist mayor (*Stadtpfleger*) Marcus Welser also erected his garden house (the so-called *Wieselhaus*; see figure 22.5) in the center of the ancient Roman city.[19] In 1583, Welser bought a typical garden property in a sparsely settled quarter in which numerous ancient relics had been found in the course of the century. A Roman floor mosaic had already been discovered in 1571 on Welser's property, but could not be recovered due to its size. According to Welser, he had it excavated again and subsequently documented it with an illustration and description in his chronicle of Augsburg's history, throughout which ancient artifacts were recorded as historical sources.[20] Welser's house closely corresponded to its immediate environment. The house front is graced by a loggia portico, whose system of supports becomes increasingly narrower from floor to floor according to the rule of superposition. From the balconies, the resident owner enjoyed a panoramic view over the site of the ancient garden. Welser's garden house resembles a *villa suburbana* set in rural surroundings, and which has been adapted to local circumstances.

By the time Welser commissioned his garden house, elements of Italian Renaissance architecture had already been adopted in inner-city buildings like the palace of the merchant and imperial counselor Lienhard Böck von Böckenstein, built in 1543–46 (today the *Maximilianmuseum*). The ornamentation of ancient reliefs depicting the busts of Roman emperors and German

---

18   On the inscription collection and its presentation, see Busch, *Antikensammlungen*, pp. 11–16; Ott, *Entdeckung des Altertums*, pp. 92–93, 165–66; for Peutinger's catalogue, see Ferber and Müller (eds.), *Augsburger Humanist*. For the examples of Venice and Padova, see Fortini Brown, *Venice & Antiquity*. For the political context, see Chapter 20 in this volume.

19   No research has been published on this recently renovated building. A documentation of the restoration can be found in the brochure [anon.], *Wieselhaus*; on Welser's archeological activities, see Ott, *Entdeckung des Altertums*, pp. 223–29; Mauer, "Patrizier als Archäologe".

20   Welser, *Chronica*, pp. 35–36 and appendix: *Antiqua Monumenta: Das ist Alte Bilder, Gemählde, unnd Schrifften, so wol deren zu Augspurg etc.*, pp. 44–46.

FIGURE 22.5 Marcus Welser's former garden house in the *Frauenvorstadt*, built after 1583, restored in 2013
PHOTO: DIETRICH ERBEN

rulers extends over both oriels and the façade painting and testifies to the city's historical continuity.

Augsburg's most significant *antiquarium* was within the Fugger palace and became known, misleadingly, as *Badstuben* (bath chambers).[21] In 1569, Hans Fugger commissioned the Florence-trained sculptor and painter Friedrich Sustris, together with a team of international artists, to decorate a series of palace rooms designated to house the library and the collection of antiquities which Fugger had acquired on the international market. Thus the *Badstuben* combine two types of exhibition rooms, the *antiquarium* and the *studiolo*. Both main halls, preserved only rudimentarily, are richly decorated with grotesque figures on the vaults, illusionistic architectural paintings and ancient stucco figures on the walls, and a series of imperial busts in the large exhibition hall. The epochal significance of Augsburg's *antiquarium* lies not only in its status as the first adaptation of contemporary Florentine ornamental mannerist art in Germany; it also laid the foundations for Munich's court art of the late sixteenth century. The artists working for Fugger were taken into the service of the Bavarian Duke Wilhelm V, and Hans Fugger himself acted as a sort of artistic consultant to the duke. This transfer of personnel and cultural objects from Augsburg's patrician milieu to a neighboring court is also indicative of the long-term shift of political power from the imperial cities to the princes of the Empire.

3   Municipal Buildings since the Late Sixteenth Century

The influence of individual intellectual endeavors like Welser's on the city's representational culture is particularly evident in the comprehensive urban modernization program which began in the final decade of the sixteenth century. Its origins can be traced to the design of monumental fountains, with numerous new communal buildings being constructed over the course of the next three decades. The alliance between humanism and communal representation had in fact been signaled many years previously. Not only did the itineraries of foreign travelers to Augsburg include visits to private buildings in order to bear witness to the city's renown, as the example of Michel de Montaigne prominently shows,[22] but the municipal institutions of higher learning also promoted

---

21   An extensive literature is available on the *antiquarium* and on the art historical context: Diemer, "Hans Fuggers Sammlungskabinette"; idem, *Hubert Gerhard*; von Hagen, "Fuggersche Antikenrezeption"; see also Wölfle, *Kunstpatronage der Fugger*, pp. 107–11.

22   For his stay in Augsburg on his journey to Italy in 1580, see Montaigne, *Journal de voyage*.

humanist studies. Against this background of personal and institutional connections, a policy developed that connected municipal self-representation to references to antiquity and especially to Augsburg's Roman foundation; this agenda became the focus of the self-confidence of the free imperial city.

The city library was a monument of exceptional importance for the municipality's culture of humanism and education (figure 22.6).[23] Work on the building began in 1562 in the courtyard of St. Anna's church, based on the plans of the city architect Bernhard Zwitzel, and was completed within only one year. In the early seventeenth century, Elias Holl, the city architect of the time, built a new high school (*Gymnasium*) at the front side of the square and elevated the porch of the library by an octagonal upper story which housed an observatory. The extensive book collection of the city library, founded in 1537, had been enriched by a large number of Greek manuscripts during the sixteenth century, with the main body of the collection dating back to the acquisition of church property by the Lutheran city government during the Reformation. The building itself was constructed on the site of the defunct Carmelite convent of St. Anna, which housed the high school after the Reformation.

Augsburg's municipal library is considered the earliest independent, freely accessible library in Europe used exclusively for this purpose. The building was a simple two-story hall. The library was housed in the upper story. A curious symbolic message adorned the roof: seven pyramids protruded in a row of separate roof constructions above the building's eaves and imparted to the library a special position in the immediate surroundings of the square and in the urban landscape. The significance of the roofs is hinted at in the Latin donor's inscription, which was placed below the upper double window on the narrow side and is also rendered in an etching by Wolfgang Kilian. Translated, the inscription reads: "This library was erected in 1562 by the Council and the citizens of Augsburg for the study of the liberal arts and for the use of scholars" (*Bibliothecam hanc S(enatus) P(opulusque) / Augustanus bonarum artium / studiis et doctorum hominum / usui extruxit MDLXII*). The term *bonae artes* in the inscription points to the meaning of the curious roof design, which had already prompted discussion among contemporaries. The inscription reveals that the row of canopy roofs can be seen as an architectural symbol for the canon of the "seven liberal arts". That this interpretation is only one of many, however, is documented in the introductory poem to the book catalogue composed by library director Georg Henisch and published in 1600. This eulogy to the building places the *septum turres* next to the *septem artes liberales* in further analogies – to the seven hills of Rome, the seven wonders of the world,

---

23 On the building, see Erben, "Pluralisierung des Wissens", pp. 176–79.

the seven estuaries of the Nile, and the seven-part shield of the Argonaut Telamon.[24] Such historical references follow a unique humanist and historical rationale and obey the rules of contemporary rhetoric, which the eulogy to the library naturally observes as well. It demonstrates the desire to connect the building to the tradition of the antique *exempla* while at the same time singling it out as unique.

The innovative role of Augsburg's library applies not only to its formal design and structure, but is also validated by its internal organization.[25] The library director also served as rector of the St. Anna high school, a joint function that guaranteed extraordinary continuity and a highly qualified library leadership. The founding director, the prominent humanist Hieronymus Wolf, transformed the *Gymnasium* and the library into a center of *studia humanitatis* in the Holy Roman Empire. The city provided the library director with his own legal advisor and allocated a permanent budget for the acquisition of books, which were systematically purchased at the Frankfurt book fair. Augsburg's library ultimately played a pioneering role in the professional indexing of the collection via catalogues which, beginning with Hieronymus Wolf's catalogue of Greek manuscripts, were published in a close sequence starting in 1575.

In its architectural and functional originality, the city library heralded one of the most ambitious and comprehensive municipal building programs of early modern Europe. Parallels can be found only at the highest level: Venice's urban renewal under the city architect Jacopo Sansovino (beginning in 1529), the construction of the canal belt in Amsterdam (from 1585 onwards), or the building program around the main axes connecting the pilgrimage churches in Rome under Pope Sixtus V (also starting in 1585). In Augsburg, the designs for the major municipal buildings and for the new fortifications constructed during this campaign originated with the city architect Elias Holl.[26]

The Augustus Fountain, erected on City Hall Square in 1594, provided the initial impulse for the entire urban renewal project. Two additional magnificent fountains, decorated with the bronze statues of Mercury and Hercules, were positioned on the main city axis. The monumental fountains created a new spatial order on material, technical, visual, and symbolic levels, which radiated out from the urban center toward larger territorial dimensions.[27] The

---

24   Henisch, *Bibliothecae inclytae reipublicae Augustanae*, p. 3. The building was torn down in 1893.
25   See Lenk, *Augsburger Bürgertum*, pp. 153–82.
26   Essential: Roeck, *Elias Holl*; Baer et al. (eds.), *Elias Holl*; Jachmann, *Kunst des Augsburger Rates*; Haberstock, *Elias Holl*; see also Erben, *Kunst des Barock*, pp. 66–68.
27   There is a considerable literature on Augsburg's fountains. Recent studies include Merz, "Skulptur im öffentlichen Raum", and Jachmann, *Kunst des Augsburger Rates*, pp. 102–21;

FIGURE 22.6   City library in the *Annahof*, built in 1562. Etching by Wolfgang Kilian, 1623
AUGSBURG, STÄDTISCHE KUNSTSAMMLUNGEN, G274

fountains were supplied with water by means of numerous newly constructed and modernized water towers containing technically complex pumps.[28] They pumped the water into the city quarters located at higher elevations, including the municipal center, important churches, and the residences of patrician families. The traditional fountains of the late Middle Ages, which had been ornamented with heraldic figures or statues of saints, had already at the beginning of the sixteenth century been replaced by free-standing fountains adorned with bronze statues depicting ancient mythological figures (e.g. the Neptune Fountain, c. 1537). The three splendid fountains of the 1590s, however, were conceived in much larger dimensions and occupied positions of urban prominence.

---

for a lucid, largely forgotten analysis of urban development, which includes the fountains, see Schürer, *Augsburg*.

28   The technical aspects are covered in Ruckdeschel, "Wasser", and Kluger, *Augsburgs historische Wasserwirtschaft*.

The political dimension of the fountain triad is anchored in the classical program which underlies the statues and reliefs. The iconography of the Augustus Fountain confidently emphasizes the city's Roman origins under the government of the Emperor Augustus and thus underscores Augsburg's historic status as a free imperial city in the Holy Roman Empire. The Mercury and Hercules fountains likewise recall the city's ancient beginnings while confirming the wealth-promoting virtues of the merchant patricians (cf. figure 21.6 on page 510). Viewed in light of the political events around 1600, this recourse to Augsburg's Roman imperial origins on all three fountains was directed against the growth of territorial states such as neighboring Bavaria. Specifically, the Munich historiographer Johannes Aventin had denied the city's ancient founding under Emperor Augustus and thus contested its water rights. The images on the Augustus Fountain were used to counter this claim by dedicating the fountain's four personifications to the rivers and streams running through Augsburg. The river gods were thus symbolically placed under the protection of the Emperor Augustus. Whereas the Roman emperor serves to preserve the political independence of the imperial city, the river personifications highlight the city-state's territorial integrity.

Situated in front of the city hall, the Augustus Fountain marks the beginning of a succession of architectural renewal projects. The fountain not only accentuates the square but is located on a magisterial axis which, together with the two other monumental fountains, extends southwards. Instead of serving merely as a form of street ornamentation, the individual monuments are, in the words of Oskar Schürer, "acknowledged and utilized as functional elements in the overall structure. The gentle turns and meanderings of the city's grand main artery, which had until then remained completely blurred, are brought into focus by the fountains; thresholds are created, and physical energy is set against spatial movement."[29]

In close succession, an impressive array of stylistically unified public buildings were erected, many of which still define the cityscape today. They included the bakers' guildhall, the arsenal (*Zeughaus*), the hallmark house (*Siegelhaus*), the city hall, the city bell tower, a slaughterhouse, a Protestant high school, a guild dance hall (*Neuer Bau*), and a hospital. The city hall is perhaps the most magnificent example of this building type in the entire era. The building looms over City Hall Square next to the *Neuer Bau*, the Augustus Fountain, and the municipal *campanile* of the Perlach Tower. The massive and awe-inspiring structure is organized with strict regularity in the rhythm and framing of the windows and a distinctive roof silhouette. The use of significant

---

29 See Schürer, *Augsburg*, p. 29.

FIGURE 22.7 City hall square with Augustus fountain and city hall. Etching by Wolfgang Kilian, 1623
AUGSBURG, STÄDTISCHE KUNSTSAMMLUNGEN, G12069

doric columns is limited to the portal, on whose balcony the city authorities presented themselves, as well as to the framing pilaster of the tympanum with the double eagle, symbol of the imperial city. The building's sheer mass has its closest parallels in the monumental buildings of the Jesuit College in Munich (dating from 1574) and the Collegio Romano in Rome (1582). The double towers are a reminder of castle architecture but can also be traced back to the reconstruction of the ancient *basilica* style of Vitruvius, as suggested by Bernardino Baldi in his commentary on Vitruvius' *De architectura*, published in Augsburg in 1612. According to Baldi, the Roman halls of justice must have appeared similar to Christian churches in that they also possessed towers.[30] Moreover, in a comprehensive commentary in his German translation of Vitruvius, Walter Ryff equated the ancient forum, as described by the Roman author, with the marketplace, whereas he saw the basilica – a "heavenly large palace" and "royal

---

30   Baldi, *De verborum Vitruvianorum significatione*, p. 26.

building" – as a building appropriate for assemblies at the imperial diets.[31] Inside the city hall, the rooms are arranged according to a highly functional, cross-symmetrical floor plan. The enormous council hall cuts through the entire structure and extends up to the ceiling. The construction of the building on the eve of the Thirty Years' War may indicate that the builders played with the ambition to continue the powerful tradition of hosting imperial diets. This gamble ultimately failed; nevertheless, it was crucial that the historical legitimization of the city's political status not be forgotten. This is important for understanding the building and the iconographic program of its halls. Two cycles showing emperors attest to the continuity of the Empire's history: a series of bronze busts in the entrance foyer of the ground floor and a painted emperor gallery in the "Golden Hall". The story of the city's founding by the Romans also finds reference elsewhere in the building. In the inscription on the southern portal of the Golden Hall, the council hall is referred to as a *praetorium*,[32] and the acting representatives of the city regiment are identified with the titles of the Roman constitution (DVVM VIRI PRAEFECTI – *Stadtpfleger* [mayors]; QVINQVE VIRI – *Geheime Räte* [secret councilors]; and AEDILES – *Baumeister* [chief financial officers]).

In the course of urban modernization, distinct measures to ensure public welfare and security were constantly accompanied by such ideological pronouncements: symbolic politics fused with real politics. The renovated and expanded arsenal (*Zeughaus*), completed in 1607, provides one example. The bronze statue of the Archangel Michael who, as patron saint of the Holy Roman Empire, conquers the devil, appears on the façade above the entrance portal used for heavy artillery. Storage rooms in the steep attic, which is equipped with ventilation devices in the intermediate floors, provided for the storage of grain. The supplies were needed in order to stabilize bread prices and ensure a municipal supply policy that could be stylized as a reenactment of the ancient political ritual of distributing grain, the so-called *annona*. Throughout the entire building campaign, the city was also comprehensively modernized along the outer boundary of its city walls through the construction of new gates and the expansion of the fortifications according to contemporary methods of military technology.[33] The entire early modern city was

---

31 Rivius, *Vitruvius Teutsch*, chapter 5.2.
32 "FERDINANDO II / IMPERATORE AVG(usto) / PRAETORIVM HOC / PERFECTVM EST" – the dedicatory inscription to Emperor Ferdinand II during the Thirty Years' War specifically refers to the importance of the *praetorium* as imperial headquarters during the war.
33 On fortifications, see Baer et al. (eds.), *Elias Holl*, pp. 265–72.

thus restructured in a form which, in its general outlines and major features, still exists today.

4 Residential, Commercial and Industrial Buildings

To be sure, the public buildings of the community and the church form only part of the architectural substance of a city, which mainly consists of residential buildings and workspaces for artisans. It is noteworthy that in the case of Augsburg the substantial growth in population was not accompanied by expansion but by concentration. From 1512 to the early seventeenth century, the population doubled in size, whereas the number of new residential structures increased by only about 200 (from roughly 2,300 to 2,500).[34] As a result, daily life and the urban environment in early modern Augsburg were shaped by countless building alterations, including horizontal or vertical additions and the building-over of courtyards, gardens, and even cemeteries. The municipality also encouraged the separation of residential and commercial functions. This resulted in the partial merging of shopping areas into markets or granaries (e.g. around St. Moritz and St. Peter on Perlach Square), while commercial sites like sawmills and fulling mills were moved to the periphery with its dense network of canals. Similar processes of concentration can be observed in the construction of residential buildings, in which small housing units were joined to create larger residential palaces (in the area of the *Maximilianstraße*). A series of 24 etchings by Karl Remshart published in 1725 depicts the city's building density at the time. The etcher was not interested in isolated monuments, but rather in the closely packed, multi-storied residential structures that lined the main streets and squares.[35]

As natural stone was unavailable in the immediate vicinity, most buildings were constructed of stuccoed brick, with more elaborate houses adorned with façade paintings. In general, residential building activity observed the late medieval boundaries of spatial concentration, so that no additional administrative regulations were required. Significantly, the building ordinance of 1391 remained in force with minor alterations into the early seventeenth century. The responsibilities of the master builder and the mason reflect this traditional practice. Most buildings were planned and completed by master masons, who were members of the masonry guild and signed contracts with

---

34 Still fundamental: Buff, *Augsburg in der Renaissancezeit*; see also Zimmer, "Veränderungen", pp. 42–44, and Baer et al. (eds.), *Elias Holl*, pp. 257–58.

35 Schmidt, *Augsburger Ansichten*, pp. 144–48.

FIGURE 22.8   Johann Heinrich von Schüle's cotton-printing manufacture, 1770–1772, demolition of the wings and modern rebuilding in 1996
PHOTO: DIETRICH ERBEN

their clients. Their knowledge was often transmitted orally, based on the conventions and experience of artisanal training. This did not exclude constructive new developments, of course, such as complicated vaultings for staircases or the adaptation of new ornamental forms based on printed pattern books (*Vorlagenbücher*), which were a specialty of Augsburg as a publishing center.[36]

Along with the textile, metal-working, and printing sectors, the masonry, carpentry, and locksmithing trades made up part of a local production economy in which the early phase of industrialization of the second half of the eighteenth century was rooted. Within the building sector, this was particularly true for the technically sophisticated, scientifically-based construction of water systems, including canals and fountains with corresponding systems of

---

36   On the local situation, see Roeck, *Elias Holl*, pp. 43–47; Valeriani, "Behind the Façade"; and more generally Erben, "Architektur als öffentliche Angelegenheit", pp. 106–07, 116–17.

pumps, and for large-scale fortifications.[37] Both areas achieved a high standard beginning in the sixteenth century, thus ensuring the existence of a level of technical know-how. Also at hand were energy resources provided by hydraulic power generated via the canal system; moreover, commercial profits and social networks generated the necessary investment and social capital. All of these factors set the stage for early industrialization.[38]

The most impressive monument to Augsburg's development into an early manufacturing city is the cotton-printing factory of Johann Heinrich von Schüle, parts of which still exist.[39] The construction of the factory, which employed up to 350 workers, outside the eastern city wall testifies to the need for more industrial space. At the same time, this heretofore sparsely developed, yet spacious area was already provided with canals. Schüle obtained a factory privilege from the emperor in Vienna in 1772 against local guild resistance, along with a patent of nobility, and the factory building was completed in the same year based on the plans of Leonhard Christian Mayr. Its functions as a production site and as a demonstration of the owner's social ascent are both symbolized in the triple-winged "factory palace". Schüle's residence, with its slightly curving, classicistic façade, mirrors the course of the road to the east. At the rear of the building, the two long, three-storied wings of the workshops (demolished in 1996) flanked the inner yard, which was part garden and part factory yard and was at one time enclosed by a magnificent wrought-iron fence (parts of which are exhibited in the local Textile and Industrial Museum).

Along with other companies which established themselves in the eastern sector of the city, Schüle's cotton-printing enterprise was a forerunner of local industrialization. In 1806, Augsburg became incorporated into the administrative district of Swabia, part of the new Kingdom of Bavaria, and, alongside Nuremberg, developed into one of the two major industrial cities of the region in the early nineteenth century. The policies regulating the establishment of the textile and manufacturing industries in both cities represented the explicit will of the Bavarian government and the Wittelsbach dynasty. The example of Augsburg illustrates, however, that successful industrialization was often based upon existing structures of the *ancien régime*. Once again, we can see a dialectical relationship between urban history and the history of architecture in Augsburg, as patrons and planners followed the imperatives of a culture that fostered innovation as well as continuity.

---

37 For an overview, see Schütte (ed.), *Architekt und Ingenieur*.
38 On Augsburg's development in this period, see Möller, *Bürgerliche Herrschaft*, pp. 63–78.
39 The most detailed study of the building is Nerdinger (ed.), *Klassizismus in Bayern*, cat. no. 83.

Bibliography

Published Primary Sources

Baldi, B., *De verborum Vitruvianorum significatione sive perpetuus in M. Vitruvium Pollionem commentarius*, Augsburg, 1612.

Ferber, M. and Müller, G.M. (eds.), *Ein Augsburger Humanist und seine römischen Inschriften. Konrad Peutingers ROMANAE VETUSTATIS FRAGMENTA IN AUGUSTA VINDELICORUM ET EIUS DIOECESI. Faksimile-Edition der Ausgabe von 1505 mit Übersetzung, epigraphischem Kommentar und kulturgeschichtlichen Essays*, Paderborn, 2014.

Henisch, G., *Bibliothecae inclytae reipublicae Augustanae utriusque tum Graecae tum Latinae librorium & impressorum & manu exaratorum Catalogus*, Augsburg, 1600.

Montaigne, M. de, *Journal de voyage*, ed. F. Garavini, Paris, 1983.

Rivius, W., *Vitruvius Teutsch etc.*, Nuremberg, 1548 (repr. Hildesheim and New York, 1973).

Welser, M., *Chronica Der Weitberuempten Keyserlichen Freyen vnd deß H. Reichs Statt Augspurg in Schwaben etc.*, Frankfurt, 1595 (repr. Augsburg, 1984).

Secondary Literature

[anon.], *Das Wieselhaus im Äußeren Pfaffengässchen in Augsburg*, Augsburg, 2013.

Baer, W., Kruft, H.-W. and Roeck, B. (eds.), *Elias Holl und das Augsburger Rathaus*, Regensburg, 1985.

Bellot, C., "Auf welsche art, der zeit gar new erfunden: Zur Augsburger Fuggerkapelle", in G.M. Müller (ed.), *Humanismus und Renaissance in Augsburg. Kulturgeschichte einer Stadt zwischen Spätmittelalter und Dreißigjährigem Krieg*, Berlin, 2012, pp. 445–90.

Bischoff, F., *Burkhard Engelberg, "der vilkunstreiche Architector und der Statt Augspurg Wercke Meister". Burkhard Engelberg und die süddeutsche Architektur um 1500. Anmerkungen zur sozialen Stellung und Arbeitsweise spätgotischer Steinmetzen und Werkmeister*, Augsburg, 1999.

Buff, A., *Augsburg in der Renaissancezeit*, Bamberg 1893.

Busch, R. von, "Studien zu deutschen Antikensammlungen des 16. Jahrhunderts", Ph.D. diss., Tübingen, 1973.

Bushart, B., "Kunst und Stadtbild", in: G. Gottlieb, W. Baer, J. Becker, J. Bellot, K. Filser, P. Fried, W. Reinhard and B. Schimmelpfennig (eds.), *Geschichte der Stadt Augsburg von der Römerzeit bis zur Gegenwart*, Stuttgart, 1984, pp. 225–33, 363–85.

Bushart, B., *Die Fuggerkapelle bei St. Anna in Augsburg*, Munich, 1994.

Châtenet, M., De Jonge, K., Kavaler, E.M. and Nussbaum, N. (eds.), *Le gothique de la Renaissance. Actes des quatrième Rencontres d'architecture européenne*, Paris, 12–16 juin 2007, Paris, 2011.

Chevalley, D.A., *Der Dom zu Augsburg*, Munich, 1995.
Diemer, D., "Hans Fuggers Sammlungskabinette", in R. Eikelmann (ed.), *"lautenschlagen lernen und ieben". Die Fugger und die Musik. Anton Fugger zum 500. Geburtstag*, Augsburg, 1993, pp. 13–40.
Diemer, D., *Hubert Gerhard und Carlo di Cesare del Palagio. Bronzeplastiker der Spätrenaissance*, Berlin, 2004.
Erben, D., "Die Krise des Reiterdenkmals und das Wachstum der Staatsgewalt im 16. Jahrhundert", in J. Poeschke, T. Weigel, and B. Kusch-Arnhold (eds.), *Praemium Virtutis III. Reiterstandbilder von der Antike bis zum Klassizismus*, Münster, 2008, pp. 269–92.
Erben, D., *Kunst des Barock*, Munich, 2008.
Erben, D., "Architektur als öffentliche Angelegenheit – Ein berufssoziologisches Porträt des Architekten im Barock", in W. Nerdinger (ed.), *Der Architekt. Geschichte und Gegenwart eines Berufsstandes*, Munich, 2012, vol. 1, pp. 105–19.
Erben, D., "Die Pluralisierung des Wissens: Zum Bibliotheksbau zwischen Renaissance und Aufklärung", in W. Nerdinger (ed.), *Die Weisheit baut sich ein Haus. Architektur und Geschichte von Bibliotheken*, Munich, 2013, pp. 169–94.
Erben, D., "Architektur", in M. Landfester (ed.), *Der Neue Pauly. Supplemente 9: Renaissance-Humanismus*, Stuttgart, 2014, cols. 41–54.
Eser, T., *Hans Daucher. Augsburger Kleinplastik der Renaissance*, Munich, 1996.
Fortini Brown, P., *Venice and Antiquity*, New Haven, 1997.
Günther, H., *Was ist Renaissance? Eine Charakteristik der Architektur zu Beginn der Neuzeit*, Darmstadt, 2009.
Haberstock, E., *Der Augsburger Stadtwerkmeister Elias Holl (1573–1646). Werkverzeichnis*, Petersberg, 2016.
Häberlein, M., *The Fuggers of Augsburg: Pursuing Wealth and Honor in Renaissance Germany*, Charlottesville and London, 2012.
Hagen, B. von, "Fuggersche Antikenrezeption im 16. Jahrhundert: Zum Bildungsgut des Humanismus in Augsburg", in: idem, J. Pursche and E. Wendler (eds.), *Die "Badstuben" im Fuggerhaus zu Augsburg*, Munich, 2012.
Hagen, B. von and Wegener-Hüssen, A., *Stadt Augsburg. Ensembles, Baudenkmäler, archäologische Denkmäler*, Munich, 1994.
Hascher, D., "Die Auftragslage für Fassadenmalerei in Augsburg im frühen 16. Jahrhundert", in K. Bergdolt and J. Brüning (eds.), *Kunst und ihre Auftraggeber im 16. Jahrhundert*, Berlin, 1997, pp. 95–110.
Herselle Krinsky, C., "Cesariano and the Renaissance Without Rome", *Arte Lombarda* 16 (1971), pp. 211–18.
Hilbich, E.P., *Das Augsburger spätgotische Rathaus und seine Stellung unter den süddeutschen Rathausbauten*, Augsburg, 1968.

Himmelheber, G., *Der Ostchor des Augsburger Doms. Ein Beitrag zur Baugeschichte*, Augsburg, 1963.

Hoffmann, C.A., Johanns, M., Kranz, A., Trepesch, C. and Ziedler, O. (eds.), *Als Frieden möglich war. 450 Jahre Augsburger Religionsfrieden*, Regensburg, 2005.

Jachmann, J., *Die Kunst des Augsburger Rates 1588–1631. Kommunale Räume als Medium von Herrschaft und Erinnerung*, Munich, 2008.

Kayser, C., "Der Ostchor des Augsburger Doms", *Jahrbuch der bayerischen Denkmalpflege* 68/69 (2014–15), pp. 21–78.

Kluger, M., *Augsburgs historische Wasserwirtschaft. Der Weg zum UNESCO-Welterbe. Wasserbau und Wasserkraft, Trinkwasser und Brunnenkunst in Augsburg (um 1400–1921)*, Augsburg, 2015.

Lenk, L., *Augsburger Bürgertum im Späthumanismus und Frühbarock (1580–1700)*, Augsburg, 1968.

Lieb, N., *Die Fugger und die Kunst*, 2 vols., Munich, 1952–58.

Mauer, B., "Der Patrizier als Archäologe: Markus Welser und Augsburgs römische Vergangenheit", in B. Kirchgässner and H.-P. Becht (eds.), *Stadt und Archäologie*, Stuttgart, 2000, pp. 81–100.

Merz, J.M., "Skulptur im öffentlichen Raum: Der Fall Augsburg um 1600", *Zeitschrift des deutschen Vereins für Kunstwissenschaft* 51 (1997), pp. 9–42.

Möller, F., *Bürgerliche Herrschaft in Augsburg 1790–1880*, Munich, 1998.

Nerdinger, W. (ed.), *Klassizismus in Bayern, Schwaben und Franken. Architekturzeichnungen 1775–1825*, Munich, 1980.

Nussbaum, N., Euskirchen, C. and Hoppe, S. (eds.), *Wege zur Renaissance. Beobachtungen zu den Anfängen neuzeitlicher Kunstauffassung im Rheinland und den Nachbargebieten um 1500*, Cologne, 2003.

Ott, M., *Die Entdeckung des Altertums. Der Umgang mit der römischen Vergangenheit Süddeutschlands im 16. Jahrhundert*, Kallmünz, 2002.

Roeck, B., *Elias Holl. Architekt einer europäischen Stadt*, Regensburg, 1985.

Ropertz, H.-P., "Die Wohnstiftungen des 15. bis 18. Jahrhunderts: Eine besondere Form 'anstaltsmäßigen Wohnens'", *Zeitschrift für Stadtgeschichte, Stadtsoziologie und Denkmalpflege* 4 (1977), pp. 183–214.

Ruckdeschel, W., "Wasser für die schöne, publique Springbrunnen", in B.R. Kommer (ed.), *Adriaen De Vries 1556–1626. Augsburgs Glanz – Europas Ruhm* (exhibition catalogue), Heidelberg, 2000, pp. 113–19.

Scheller, B., *Memoria an der Zeitenwende. Die Stiftungen Jakob Fuggers des Reichen vor und während der Reformation (ca. 1505–1555)*, Berlin, 2004.

Schmidt, A., *Augsburger Ansichten. Die Darstellung der Stadt in der Druckgraphik des 15. bis 18. Jahrhunderts*, Augsburg, 2000.

Schürer, O., *Augsburg*, Burg b.M., 1934.

Schütte, U., (ed.), *Architekt und Ingenieur. Baumeister in Krieg und Frieden*, Wolfenbüttel, 1984.

Tietz-Strödel, M., *Die Fuggerei in Augsburg. Studien zur Entwicklung des sozialen Stiftungsbaus im 15. und 16. Jahrhundert*, Tübingen, 1982.

Tönnesmann, A., "Anfänge der Renaissancearchitektur in Deutschland: Interesse und Intention der Auftraggeber", in B. Guthmüller (ed.), *Deutschland und Italien in ihren wechselseitigen Beziehungen während der Renaissance*, Wolfenbüttel, 2000, pp. 299–317.

Valeriani, S., "Behind the Façade: Elias Holl and the Italian Influence on Building Techniques in Augsburg", *Architectura* 38 (2008), pp. 97–108.

Wölfle, S., *Die Kunstpatronage der Fugger 1560–1618*, Augsburg, 2009.

Zimmer, J., "Die Veränderungen im Augsburger Stadtbild zwischen 1530 und 1630", in *Welt im Umbruch: Augsburg zwischen Renaissance und Barock. Wende zur Neuzeit* (exhibition catalogue), 3 vols., Augsburg, 1980, vol. 3, pp. 25–65.

CHAPTER 23

Music

Alexander J. Fisher

By the sixteenth century, Augsburg enjoyed a musical culture worthy of one of the Empire's great cities. Music in early modern Augsburg was shaped largely by two circumstances: the city's central position in imperial politics; and an economic vitality spurred by a vibrant textile industry, Augsburg's favorable position astride continental trade routes, and the cultural ambitions of a wealthy patriciate.[1] Emperor Maximilian I's frequent presence during his reign (1486–1519) helped to catalyze local music and musical culture, and the convening of no less than 12 imperial diets there during the sixteenth century guaranteed a healthy circulation of international music and musicians. Augsburg's importance as a musical center arguably peaked in the sixteenth century, but it was significantly inflected by the process of confessionalization following the Religious Peace of Augsburg (1555), which led to gradually diverging Protestant and Catholic musical institutions and cultures. The economic stagnation that set in by the late sixteenth century, combined with the devastating consequences of the Thirty Years' War, brought an end to Augsburg's leading musical role in Europe. Although its musical culture did recover considerably in the later seventeenth and eighteenth centuries, it receded in importance relative to other German cities and courts.

1   Music in Late Medieval Augsburg

After 1400, evidence increases for a local upswing in sophisticated musical activity, driven by the city's increasing economic prosperity as a center for textile manufacture; its favorable position along long-distance trade routes linking northern Italy with the Low Countries; and its significant political role as a host of imperial diets – and indeed, of the emperor himself. Liturgical music in Augsburg was dominated on the one hand by the cathedral in the northern

---

1   Some of the foundational literature on Augsburg's music history includes Krautwurst, "Musik im Mittelalter"; idem, "Musik der Blütezeit"; idem, "Musik nach dem Dreißigjährigen Krieg"; and Layer, *Musik und Musiker der Fuggerzeit*. See also the thorough encyclopedia entries by Layer and Brusniak, "Augsburg"; Brusniak and Mančal, "Augsburg".

quarter of the city and on the other by the well-endowed Benedictine monastery of Sts. Ulrich and Afra in the southern quarter, both of which had enjoyed organs for several centuries and cultivated rich traditions of plainchant and liturgical drama.[2] The earliest indications of a fixed ensemble of cathedral musicians are found during the reign of Bishop Peter von Schaumberg (reg. 1424–69), while the church of Sts. Ulrich and Afra already enjoyed an outstanding tradition of manuscript music copying by the late fifteenth century, especially by the scribe Leonhard Wagner (1457–1522).[3] Wagner participated in a broader culture of humanistic learning that flourished in the convent around the turn of the sixteenth century, represented most prominently in the musical field by Veit Bild's treatise on liturgical monophony, the *Stella musicae*.[4]

Augsburg's increasing prosperity during the fifteenth century, enriched by musical exchange facilitated by trade networks, heightened the sophistication of civic and bourgeois music-making. A firmly established group of city musicians expressed a rising sense of civic identity and pride: the fiddle players, pipers, and organist that constituted the *Stadtpfeifer* at the end of the fourteenth century were augmented by lutenists and other musicians for more intimate or *stille Musik*.[5] In addition, Emperor Sigismund granted Augsburg the right to engage civic trumpeters in 1426, the first imperial city to enjoy such a privilege.[6] By mid-century, a sophisticated culture of song was cultivated by the *Meistersinger*, a guild-like organization of singers that represented the oldest such school in the Empire.[7] Several extant manuscript collections of song texts, moreover, testify to an active reception of late medieval secular lyric and *Minnesang*, including the so-called *Augsburger Liederbuch* (c. 1454) and the songbook of Clara Hätzlerin (c. 1470–71).[8] To these we can add a notable collection – completed in 1513 by the Augsburg piper Jakob Hurlacher and later found in the library of the patrician Johann Heinrich Herwart – of polyphonic

---

2   On organs in the cathedral, see Fischer and Wohnhaas, "Miscellanea", p. 125; and idem, *Augsburger Domorgeln*. See also Krautwurst, "Musik im Mittelalter", pp. 234–35.
3   Krautwurst, "Musik im Mittelalter", p. 234. On Wagner, see Pötzl, *Leonhard Wagner*.
4   Röder and Wohnhaas, "Die Stella musicae".
5   Krautwurst, "Musik im Mittelalter", p. 235; see also Layer, "Augsburger Musikpflege im Mittelalter".
6   Schuler, "Musik in Konstanz", p. 168, n. 145.
7   For a general overview see Schnell, " Augsburger Meistersinger".
8   See Bayerische Staatsbibliothek München Cgm 379, and Prague, National Museum, Cod. x A 12, respectively. See also Krautwurst, "Musik im Mittelalter", pp. 235–36; Knor, "Liederbuch der Clara Hätzlerin"; and Rettelbach, "Lied und Liederbuch". Further patrician interest in music may be seen in the musical handbook compiled for his own use by Ulrich Fugger the Elder (1441–1510), the *Commentarius de notis* (1463). See Layer, "Augsburger Musikpflege im Mittelalter", p. 26.

music in mensural notation by luminaries such as Josquin des Prez, Alexander Agricola, Heinrich Isaac, Ludwig Senfl, and Paul Hofhaimer, a testament to Augsburg's connections with the circle of Maximilian I.[9]

Augsburg established itself at an early stage as an important center for music printing, although Nuremberg would overtake it in importance by the mid-sixteenth century.[10] The earliest known printer of music, the Reutlingen native Günter Zainer, arrived in Augsburg in 1468 and may have printed the first extant book of music using movable type, the *Graduale Constantiense* (c. 1473).[11] The period from the 1480s to 1520 was especially rich for the local production of musical incunabula: notable are the liturgical service books of Erhard Ratdolt (1447–1527/28), featuring musical notation printed by woodblocks and movable type,[12] and the works of Erhard Öglin (d. 1520), including the first book of mensural music printed with movable type north of the Alps (*Melopoeiae sive Harmoniae tetracenticae*, 1507), the treatises *Stella musicae* by Veit Bild (1508) and *Musica getutscht* by Sebastian Virdung (1511), as well as song collections (1512, 1513) featuring musicians of Maximilian's chapel, including Paulus Hofhaimer, Heinrich Isaac, Adam Rener, and Ludwig Senfl.[13] Perhaps the most impressive is the *Liber selectarum cantionum, quas vulgo mutetas appellant*, printed at Augsburg in 1520 by the firm of Sigismund Grimm and Marcus Wirsung.[14] This first Latin motet anthology published in Germany is especially notable for the music of Josquin des Prez, but also contains numerous works by the imperial musicians Heinrich Isaac and Ludwig Senfl; the latter appears to have been directly involved with the volume's preparation for printing.[15] The *Liber* was evidently prompted by the wealthy humanist Conrad Peutinger

---

9   Staats- und Stadtbibliothek Augsburg [hereafter: SuStBA], 2° Cod. 142a. See Taricani, "A Renaissance Bibliophile"; Jonas, *Augsburger Liederbuch*; Martinez-Göllner, "Die Augsburger Bibliothek Herwart"; and Slim, "Music Library".
10 For the early sixteenth century, see Röder, "Innovation and Misfortune". A thorough survey of music printing to the end of the Thirty Years' War may be found in Röder and Wohnhaas, "Augsburger Musikdruck". See also Layer, "Augsburger Musikdrucker".
11 British Library London, I. B: 15154. See Layer, "Augsburger Musikdrucker", p. 124.
12 See Wohnhaas, "Notizen zu Druck und Verlag", p. 152; Röder and Wohnhaas, "Augsburger Musikdruck", pp. 292–93.
13 See Répertoire International des Sources Musicales [hereafter: RISM], 1512^1 and c. 1513^3; Röder and Wohnhaas, "Augsburger Musikdruck", pp. 294–97. Imperial connections are also evident in an undated Cologne print (c. 1512–20; RISM [1519]^5) of 77 anonymous songs, a number of which are attributable to Hofhaimer, Isaac, and Rener: Krautwurst, "Musik im Mittelalter", p. 236.
14 *Liber selectarum cantionum quas vulgo mutetas appellant sex quinque et quatuor vocum* (Augsburg, 1520) [RISM 1520^4]. See Röder and Wohnhaas, "Augsburger Musikdruck", pp. 297–99.
15 Picker, "Liber selectarum cantionum".

(1465–1547), who provided an afterword; its dedication to the Augsburg native Cardinal Matthäus Lang may originally have been intended for Maximilian himself, but the latter's death in 1519 led to its rededication to the cardinal, who had long served both Maximilian and his predecessor Frederick III.[16]

2 From the Reformation to the Thirty Years' War (1517–1648)

Martin Luther's disputation with the papal legate Cardinal Thomas Cajetan, which took place at Augsburg in October 1518 in the aftermath of the imperial diet, helped to set in motion religious changes that would fundamentally transform musical institutions and networks in the city and throughout the Empire. The center of Protestant activity in Augsburg was the Carmelite church of St. Anna, which by the 1520s already enjoyed a rich musical tradition. In 1512, Jakob Fugger the Rich had donated a superb organ for his family's chapel, an instrument built by Jan Behaim von Dobrau and with wings painted by Jörg Breu the Younger; the famed Paulus Hofhaimer was among those who performed on it (1512–18).[17] Dramatic change came through the efforts of the prior Johann Frosch, who had hosted Luther during the 1518 disputation and began to preach evangelical ideas from 1523 onward, eventually introducing the communion service according to the Wittenberg liturgy in 1525. Frosch likely had a role in the preparation of the first evangelical hymnal printed in Augsburg, the *Form und Ordnung gaystlicher Gesang und Psalmen*, printed by Jakob Dachser in 1529.[18] The establishment of a Protestant high school (*Gymnasium*) in 1531 was a crucial step for Protestant church music in the city: by around 1538 school dramas with music were being produced, and from 1552 the school began sending student choirs into the streets of the city (the so-called *Kurrendengesang*), a practice that would continue with some interruptions until the beginning of the nineteenth century.[19]

The Reformation exerted a major influence on music printing and publishing as well, as the leading figures in this field before mid-century were

---

16 Giselbrecht and Upper, "Glittering Woodcuts", pp. 50–52.
17 See Fischer and Wohnhaas, "Die Fugger-Orgel"; Lieb, *Die Fugger und die Kunst*, p. 137; Krautwurst, "Musik der Blütezeit", p. 386. Five codices, copied by the organists Hans and Bernhart Rem between 1510 and 1519, survive from the estate of Bishop Johann Egolph von Knöringen (Universitätsbibliothek München, 2° Cod. ms. 153, 4° Cod. 168–171); see Gottwald, *Musikhandschriften*, pp. 6–7, 45–48.
18 Krautwurst, "Musik der Blütezeit", p. 387.
19 Krautwurst, "Musik der Blütezeit", p. 387. On the regulation of *Kurrendengesang* at St. Anna see also Fisher, *Music and Religious Identity*, pp. 73–74.

directly or indirectly tied to the movement.[20] Sigmund Salminger (c. 1500–62/3), a former Franciscan monk from Munich, became a leader of Augsburg's Anabaptists in 1527. After a period of imprisonment, he renounced the sect and eventually became a prolific editor of music printed by Philipp Ulhart (himself an Anabaptist sympathizer) and Melchior Kriesstein (Kriegstein).[21] The products of these men were aimed in part toward Lutheran and Reformed practice: Ulhart printed Dachser's aforementioned Psalter in 1529, as well as Salminger's *Der gantz Psalter* [...] *in gsangweiss gestelt* in 1537, the first complete Psalter in German with melodies. In 1540 Kriesstein printed the Augsburg native Johann Kugelmann's *Concentus novi*, an important early document of German-texted Protestant polyphony commissioned by Duke Albrecht of Prussia and the Fuggers.[22] Nevertheless, an ecumenical repertory of Latin motets in the Franco-Flemish tradition remained a strong focus for Salminger, Ulhart, and Kriesstein, who issued four anthologies of these works in the 1540s. A representative example is the *Cantiones selectissimae* printed by Ulhart in 1548 and dedicated to the Fugger family, devoted entirely to Latin motets in four voices by the imperial musicians Cornelius Canis, Thomas Crecquillon, Nicolas Payen, and Jean Lestainnier.[23] This print and others like it testify not only to the ongoing musical connections between Augsburg and the imperial court, but also to the flexibility of the Latin motet across confessional lines.

The political disruptions in the wake of Emperor Charles V's victory in the Schmalkaldic War, leading to the uncertain period of the Interim (1548) and finally to the stabilizing arrangement of the Religious Peace of Augsburg (1555), marked a point of inflection for musical life in Augsburg, as a formalized confessional divide gradually led to diverging musical institutions and practices. The initial impetus for the revitalization of Catholic music came from Cardinal-Bishop Otto Truchsess von Waldburg (reg. 1543–73), whose musical interests were legion.[24] The dedicatee of Heinrich Glarean's famed treatise *Dodecachordon* (1549) and a major protagonist in the discussions surrounding Catholic church music at the Council of Trent, Waldburg founded a chapel of ten musicians at his Dillingen residence in 1562, headed by Jacobus de Kerle (c. 1531–91), whose *Preces speciales* of that year were written and performed for the Council. By this time the bishop had already engaged for the cathedral

---

20 Röder and Wohnhaas, "Augsburger Musikdruck", pp. 299–301.
21 Krautwurst, "Musik der Blütezeit", p. 387; on Salminger's editions see Röder and Wohnhaas, "Augsburger Musikdruck", pp. 301–6.
22 Krautwurst, "Musik der Blütezeit", p. 387.
23 *Cantiones selectissimae. Quatuor Vocum. Ab eximiis et praestantibus Caesareae Maiestatis Capellae musicis* [...] (Augsburg, 1548) [RISM 1548²].
24 Layer, "Musikpflege", pp. 199–207.

a permanent chapelmaster, Anton Span, and may have had a hand in a new singing ordinance (*Ordnung der Singerei*) of 1561 that called for a chapelmaster, organist, and 24 additional singers, and specified a range of feast days on which polyphonic and organ music would be heard.[25] The cardinal's former chapelmaster Kerle (the episcopal chapel at his Dillingen residence had been dissolved in 1565) remained at the cathedral as vicar-choral and organist until 1575, during which time he composed and published numerous motets blending Netherlandish traditions with Italian clarity.[26] It was under Truchsess von Waldburg, furthermore, that instrumentalists began to be regularly engaged to support the vocalists. Among the most prominent of these around and after the turn of the century would be the cornettists Jakob Paumann (fl. 1600) and Philipp Zindelin (c. 1570–1622). The latter distinguished himself in several publications of original music, notably the Magnificats of the *Symphonia Parthenia* (Augsburg, 1615).[27]

Waldburg's successors made further efforts to enhance the prestige of the cathedral's music.[28] Although choirbooks or other musical sources from the cathedral are sadly lost, the repertory must have been extensive, given the large amount of music donated to the bishop and the cathedral chapter by the early seventeenth century.[29] Heinrich von Knöringen's (reg. 1598–1646) initiative to formally introduce the Roman Rite in the cathedral after 1600, along with distinctive celebrations for Marian feasts, the Guardian Angels, and St. Michael, led to opportunities for more regular polyphonic performances.[30] A painting (dated 1616) of the cathedral's interior during Knöringen's episcopal synod of 1610 shows a large group of musicians positioned in the west choir, including choirboys, adult singers, wind and string instruments, and a regal, a type of organ sounded by brass reeds.[31] Absent since the wave of iconoclastic destruction that took place between 1537 and 1548, organs were now built or purchased, beginning with an instrument completed by Eusebius Ammerbach

---

25   On the origins of the 1561 ordinance and Span's biography, see Schmidmüller, "Augsburger Domkapellmeister", pp. 69–74. On the cathedral music more generally, see Fischer and Wohnhaas, "Miscellanea" (pp. 127–28 on the 1561 ordinance). Ursprung, "Chorordnung", discusses the 1616 revision of the ordinance, which clearly lays out the hierarchy of feasts and their musical embellishment.
26   Krautwurst, "Musik der Blütezeit", p. 387. For a major recent study of Kerle, see Leitmeir, *Jacobus de Kerle*.
27   RISM Z239. See Krautwurst, "Musik der Blütezeit", p. 387, and, on Zindelin's compositions, Fisher, *Music and Religious Identity*, pp. 149–52.
28   Layer, "Musikpflege", pp. 208–11.
29   Fischer and Wohnhaas, "Miscellanea", p. 130.
30   Fisher, *Music and Religious Identity*, pp. 90–103.
31   Fischer and Wohnhaas, "Miscellanea", pp. 129–30.

in 1579 that served for festal occasions in the cathedral as well as for the celebration of the liturgical hours in the choir.[32] By 1621, there were also two regals available, instruments that could support divided choirs distributed throughout the cathedral's space.[33]

The engagement of Bernhard Klingenstein (c. 1546–1614), a native of Peiting near Schongau, as chapelmaster in 1574 marked the beginning of a dramatic upswing in musical culture at the cathedral, which peaked during Heinrich von Knöringen's tenure.[34] Much of the extant music of composers connected to the cathedral flows directly or indirectly from the spirit of Catholic reform and Counter-Reformation championed by Knöringen. Notable in this regard is Klingenstein's anthology *Rosetum Marianum* (Dillingen, 1604), offering 33 polyphonic settings of the traditional song *Maria zart* by a variety of local and regional contemporaries.[35] Gregor Aichinger (c. 1564–1628), a vicar-choral at the cathedral, organist at Sts. Ulrich and Afra, and a former student of the famed Giovanni Gabrieli in Venice, published over two dozen collections of music in a wide array of contemporary, Italianate styles, much of which embraces the Marian and Eucharistic imagery that helped to deepen the confessional divide in the city.[36] Most of the keyboard music of his fellow organist Christian Erbach (c. 1570–1635) is lost, but the latter's extant vocal repertory features Latin motets, sacred canzonettas, German religious songs, and large-scale Proper cycles (*Modorum sacrorum sive cantionum*, Augsburg and Dillingen, 1604–05) that addressed the increasing need for regular polyphonic music as an embellishment of the Catholic Mass.[37]

The cathedral musicians helped to build musical networks with Augsburg's other Catholic institutions. Klingenstein, for example, was engaged as music director at the new Jesuit church of St. Salvator in 1584. Little is known about the church music repertory cultivated there, but the school soon became an active site for Jesuit dramas penned by Matthäus Rader, Jakob Bidermann,

---

32 Ibid., pp. 127–28.
33 Ibid., p. 129. On organs generally in the cathedral, see Fischer and Wohnhaas, *Augsburger Domorgeln*.
34 On Klingenstein's biography see Schmidmüller, "Augsburger Domkapellmeister", pp. 74–78; Singer, "Leben und Werke".
35 RISM 1604[7]. See edition by Hettrick (ed.), *Bernhard Klingenstein: Rosetum Marianum*. On his fragmentary anthology *Triodia sacra* (RISM 1605[1]) see also Leitmeir, "Catholic Music".
36 See for example the *Solennia augustissimi Corporis Christi* (Augsburg, 1606; RISM A533); and the Marian devotional canzonettas of the *Virginalia* (Dillingen, 1607; RISM A539). On Aichinger's music see Fisher, *Music and Religious Identity*, pp. 129–49. See also Kroyer, "Aichingers Leben und Werke".
37 RISM E728–E730. On Erbach's music see Fisher, *Music and Religious Identity*, pp. 99, 127–29.

Jeremias Drexel, and others, some of which were surely accompanied by music.[38] At the Benedictine monastery of Sts. Ulrich and Afra, Aichinger had already served as the organist for the Fugger Chapel since 1584, and likely aided the transmission of the modern, Venetian music he encountered during his studies. But the flourishing musical culture there owed itself also to the musical interests of abbots Jakob Köpplin (1548–1600) and Johann Merck (1600–32), as well as to the copyist Johannes Dreher (c. 1543–c. 1614), whose 22 manuscript choirbooks for the monastery's use – featuring the music of Orlando di Lasso (1532–94) in particular – demonstrate a clear effort to systematically build up the repertory available for regular performance.[39] The lavish, polychoral music of Giovanni Gabrieli was likely also cultivated there after the turn of the century, for Gabrieli's famed second book of *Symphoniae sacrae* (Venice, 1615), containing a series of brilliant, modern works for multiple choirs of voices and instruments, was in fact dedicated posthumously by his pupil Alvise Grani to Abbot Merck, while the latter's coat of arms is also printed in a copy of Gabrieli's *Canzoni et sonate* (Venice, 1615) that was in the monastery's library. Appended to this print is a manuscript copy, dated 1616, of Gabrieli's first book of *Symphoniae sacrae* (Venice, 1597) by the Augsburg music publisher Caspar Flurschütz.[40]

A similar openness to modern music was evident at St. Anna, the leading Protestant musical institution in the city. Here it was Adam Gumpelzhaimer (1559–1625), a former student at the school of Sts. Ulrich and Afra, who as cantor of St. Anna was chiefly responsible for compiling a magnificent music collection and developing a large and capable musical ensemble among the students of the Latin school.[41] Gumpelzhaimer was chiefly famous for his *Compendium musicae* (1591), a pedagogical manual that was reissued numerous times over the following century, but he also assembled an impressive collection of

---

38 Layer, "Musik und Theater in St. Salvator". See also Fisher, *Music and Religious Identity*, pp. 116–22, 157–63.

39 See Gottwald, *Musikhandschriften*, pp. 56–99, 102–57, 163–64. Recent studies of this repertory include Galle, "Liturgische Musik", and especially Rimek, *Das mehrstimmige Repertoire*. On the hymn repertory see Zager, "Liturgical Rite and Musical Repertory". Burn, "Mass-Propers by Henricus Isaac" discusses the role of Isaac's music in two of the monastery's choirbooks, SuStBA Tonk. Schl. 7 and 23.

40 SStBA, Tonk. Schl. 39. On the reception of Gabrieli's music at Sts. Ulrich and Afra see Charteris, "Newly Discovered Works", p. 349, n. 17; idem, "Manuscript Discovery", pp. 44–45; and Fisher, *Music and Religious Identity*, pp. 106–08.

41 On the cantorate of St. Anna see Krautwurst, "Musik der Blütezeit", pp. 389–90; Cuyler, "Musical Activity"; Städtler, "Kantorei und Kantoreien"; Pittroff, "Aus vier Jahrhunderten". For detailed commentary on Gumpelzhaimer's career, see also Otto Mayr's introduction to *Adam Gumpelzhaimer. Ausgewählte Werke*, pp. 9–36.

contemporary, international music in both Latin and German that is as notable for its confessional ecumenism as for its quality; the content was recorded in several manuscript inventories and score-books.[42] Gumpelzhaimer was remarkably prolific as a composer as well, bringing out several collections of German sacred lieder in the fashionable idioms of the Italian canzonetta and villanella, as well as books of Latin motets in the Venetian double-choir style that was becoming increasingly popular in the more ample German churches of the time.

The presence of so many talented musicians in Augsburg before the war was a testament to the interests of the Fuggers, many of whom were keen amateur musicians (particularly on lute and keyboard), music collectors, and patrons.[43] Jakob III Fugger (1542–98) donated organs to Sts. Ulrich and Afra (1580) and St. Moritz (1587), instruments that would be played by Gregor Aichinger, Hans Leo Hassler, and Christian Erbach.[44] Jakob's cousin Octavian Secundus Fugger (1549–1600) engaged Hassler as his personal chamber organist by 1586 and patronized the famed lutenist Melchior Neusidler (*c.* 1531–*c.* 1591), among whose compositions is a "Lady Fugger Dance" (*Fuggerin dantz*) printed in his *Teütsch Lautenbuch* (Strasbourg, 1574).[45] In the early modern era, the Fugger house received the dedications of some 50 printed collections of music, a remarkable number that testifies to the family's prestige and influence. As early as 1545, the Augsburg printer Sigmund Salminger dedicated a motet collection to Hans Jakob Fugger (1516–75), a connoisseur who facilitated the engagement of Orlando di Lasso at the Bavarian court in 1563;[46] Lasso, in turn, would go on to dedicate three collections of music to various members of the family.[47] Jakob III Fugger, who had financed Aichinger's studies in Venice, received the

---

42 Fisher, *Music and Religious Identity*, pp. 71–84. The contents of this repertory are transmitted in several extant manuscript inventories and score-books: see Schletterer, *Katalog der Musikwerke*, pp. 11–16; Schaal, *Inventar der Kantorei Sankt Anna*; Charteris, *Adam Gumpelzhaimer's Little-Known Score Books*; idem, "An Early Seventeenth-Century Collection".

43 On the Fuggers and music generally see Layer (ed.), *Musik und Musiker*; Eikelmann (ed.), *Die Fugger und die Musik*.

44 Schaal, "Musikpflege", p. 5.

45 On Neusidler's connections to the family see Krautwurst, "Melchior Neusidler". On Hassler's biography and his connections to the Fuggers see Schmid, "Hans Leo Haßler"; Sandberger, "Bemerkungen zur Biographie", pp. xi–cxii. See also Krautwurst, "Musik der Blütezeit", pp. 389–90.

46 *Cantiones septem, sex et quinque vocum* (Augsburg: Melchior Kriesstein, 1545) [RISM 1545³].

47 The *Viersprachendruck* (Munich, 1573) to the sons of Anton Fugger, his *Motetta sex vocum* (Munich, 1582) to Jakob III Fugger, and his *Sacrae cantiones* (Munich, 1585) to Alexander Secundus Fugger, provost of Freising cathedral. See RISM L860, L939, and L955.

dedication of the splendid *Concerti* (1587) by Giovanni and Andrea Gabrieli.[48] Further dedications to members of the dynasty would be offered by such prominent musicians as Carl Luython, Philippe de Monte, and Jakob Regnart. Some Fuggers, moreover, amassed impressive collections of music and instruments. Raymund Fugger (1489–1535) created the basis of the family's music library: his collection of musical incunabula and manuscripts was expanded by his son Hans Jakob, and, together with the former library of the Nuremberg humanist Hartman Schedel, was purchased by Duke Albrecht V of Bavaria in 1571.[49] Raymund's son Raymund II Fugger (1528–69) owned a superior collection of music (much of which ended up in the *Biblioteca Palatina* at the Vatican after 1622) and over 200 musical instruments, including lutes, keyboards, strings, and winds.[50]

The patriciate's entrenchment in the structures of city governance – Hans Jakob Fugger, for example, served as burgomaster (1548–50), while Octavian Secundus Fugger served as mayor (*Stadtpfleger*, 1594–1600) – encouraged the development of instrumental music, given that many of the musicians they patronized were also engaged by the city. Both Hans Leo Hassler and Christian Erbach, for example, would be installed as leaders of the *Stadtpfeifer*, and the cornettist Philipp Zindelin, who had served Maximilian Fugger, also performed regularly for civic functions. This group of instrumentalists, which had expanded to up to seven members by the end of the sixteenth century, was anchored by the continuous service of certain families across several generations, and performed not only for the festivals and observances of the city and patriciate, but were also hired for special occasions by other cities and territories.[51] Instrumental music was bolstered by the local manufacture of musical instruments, notably lutes (by Laux Boss, Paul Sturm, Sixt Rauwolff, and the Bossard family), organs (by Eusebius Ammerbach, Samuel Bidermann the Elder, and Marx Güntzer), and automatic musical instruments for the delectation of wealthy elites: the so-called *Pommerscher Kunstschrank* (1617), for example, was constructed by Marx Güntzer and Achilles Langenbucher in Augsburg, and presented to the Pomeranian court by local merchant, art dealer and collector Philipp Hainhofer (1578–1647).[52]

Nuremberg displaced Augsburg as the principal German center for music printing by the mid-sixteenth century, but a local industry continued after

---

48 Andrea and Giovanni Gabrieli, *Concerti di Andrea, et di Gio[vanni] Gabrieli* (Venice, 1587) [RISM G58].
49 Häberlein, *The Fuggers of Augsburg*, p. 167.
50 Häberlein, *The Fuggers of Augsburg*, pp. 167–68.
51 Krautwurst, "Musik der Blütezeit", p. 388.
52 Fischer and Wohnhaas, *Historische Orgeln in Schwaben*, pp. 289, 301.

the Religious Peace of Augsburg, especially in the hands of the Ulhart family, father and son.[53] By the end of the century, music printing was established on a firmer basis by printers like Valentin and Johann Ulrich Schönig and Hans Schultes (Praetorius). Before the Thirty Years' War, music printing tended to split along confessional lines, with Protestant music printed largely by the Schönig family and Catholic music produced either locally by Johann Schultes or by printers in the episcopal residence of Dillingen, where the press of Adam Meltzer was closely linked to the Jesuit university.[54] In Augsburg itself, an international array of printed music was made available by the bookseller Georg Willer (1548–93), who enjoyed close relations with the Fugger dynasty and served both the Catholic and Protestant book markets; his 1622 catalogue shows a remarkable array of 355 musical titles, including sacred and secular music by German and Italian composers.[55] A younger contemporary of Willer was Caspar Flurschütz, who sold musical instruments as well as printed editions; the first of his printed catalogues from 1613 prominently advertises the latest music from Milan, Venice, and Rome, pointing to Flurschütz's role as a conduit for transalpine musical fashions.[56]

The vibrancy of Augsburg's musical culture suffered as confessional tensions in the Empire boiled over into open conflict after 1618. Musical culture had played no small role in the rise of these tensions, particularly in the wake of the calendar conflict (*Kalenderstreit*) of 1583–84, when the introduction of the Gregorian calendar led to confessional controversy and violence. Vernacular songs critical of the city government, the Catholic party, and the emperor were circulated and performed, their singers and disseminators facing prosecution by city officials keen to avoid religious tensions.[57] Augsburg's Catholic composers, notably Gregor Aichinger, had helped to sharpen the confessional divide in the city's musical culture by their tendency to set texts representing divisive confessional symbols, such as the Virgin Mary and the Eucharist. Furthermore, a sense of Catholic space was projected effectively within the city through the sights and sounds of religious processions, some of which were accompanied

---

53 Röder and Wohnhaas, "Augsburger Musikdruck", pp. 306–09.
54 Wohnhaas, "Notizen zu Druck und Verlag", pp. 154–55; Röder and Wohnhaas, "Augsburger Musikdruck", pp. 310–19.
55 Schaal, "Georg Willers Augsburger Musikalien-Lagerkatalog"; see also Röder and Wohnhaas, "Augsburger Musikdruck", pp. 319–20.
56 Röder and Wohnhaas, "Augsburger Musikdruck", pp. 320–21. See also Schaal, *Kataloge*.
57 Fisher, *Music and Religious Identity*, pp. 24–70. See also Fisher, "Song, Confession, and Criminality"; Creasman, *Censorship*, esp. pp. 147–84; Graser and Tlusty (eds.), *Jonas Losch*, pp. 14–32.

by strikingly militaristic music.[58] Although Augsburg was initially spared direct military violence and destruction, disastrous bouts of inflation (1622–23) and pestilence (1627–28) severely affected its economic and cultural vitality. Ferdinand II's Edict of Restitution (1629) returned most Protestant properties to Catholic hands, bringing an end to the formerly elaborate church music of St. Anna. With the occupation of Augsburg by Swedish troops in April 1632 and the subsequent, ruinous siege of the city by imperial and Bavarian troops in 1634–35, the golden age of music in Augsburg came to a definitive close.[59]

3   Baroque and Classical Music in Augsburg (1648–1800)

Following the Peace of Westphalia, Augsburg's musical life underwent a slow recovery, thanks to the stability guaranteed by a system of confessional parity and the persistence of a strong sense of civic identity. Nevertheless, musical culture would not achieve its previous heights, given the city's weakened economic position and the concentration of talented composers and performers in wealthier courts and cities.[60] The first signs of recovery were evident at the cathedral, the music of which would express an openness to the Italian influences previously cultivated under earlier figures like Aichinger and Klingenstein.[61] A critical move was the engagement of Philipp Jakob Baudrexel (1627–91) at the cathedral in 1651, following his studies at the Collegium Germanicum in Rome with its famed music director Giacomo Carissimi.[62] Although Baudrexel may have introduced Carissimi's affective *concertato* idiom into the cathedral music, it is evident that he faced numerous practical difficulties there and departed in 1654.[63] His successor Johann Melchior Gletle (1626–83) was the first to combine the posts of chapelmaster and cathedral organist. Having possibly studied with Carissimi in Rome as well, Gletle is known to have composed over two hundred sacred compositions, many of which thoroughly embrace

---

58   Fisher, *Music and Religious Identity*, pp. 154–278.
59   See Chapter 15 in this volume.
60   On music in Augsburg after the Peace of Westphalia, see Krautwurst, "Musik nach dem Dreißigjährigen Krieg"; Göthel, "Das reichstädtische Musikleben"; Layer, "Augsburger Musik im Barock"; Valentin, "Augsburger Musik".
61   On the cathedral music of this period see Hoyer and Tremmel, "Musik am Augsburger Dom"; Krautwurst, "Musik nach dem Dreißigjährigen Krieg", pp. 504–05, 510–11; Fischer and Wohnhaas, "Miscellanea", pp. 130–35.
62   Archival records are unclear as to whether Baudrexel was formally appointed to the post of chapelmaster. See Schmidmüller, "Augsburger Domkapellmeister", pp. 85–86.
63   Schmidmüller, "Augsburger Domkapellmeister", p. 86. On Baudrexel's studies in Rome see also Culley, *Jesuits and Music*, pp. 207–08.

the Italian *concertato* idiom requiring virtuosic singers and independent instrumental timbres.[64] The two volumes of Gletle's *Musica genialis Latino-Germanica* (Augsburg, 1675 and 1684) show a different side of the composer's achievement, providing jocular and moralizing *Gesellschaftslieder* for student and amateur singers and instrumentalists, a so-called "Quodlibet" tradition also pursued by his successor Johann Melchior Caesar (chapelmaster 1685–92) in his *Musicalischer Wendunmuth* (Augsburg, 1688).[65] The level of musical talent at the cathedral remained rather uneven through the eighteenth century, with prominent exceptions in Johann Andreas Joseph Giulini (chapelmaster 1755–72), who wrote dramatic music for the Jesuits, symphonies, and sacred music in a style mixing Baroque counterpoint with early Classical melody and harmony, and in the organist and violin virtuoso Johann Michael Demmler (1748–85), who performed together with Johann Andreas Stein and Wolfgang Amadeus Mozart in the latter's Concerto for Three Pianos (KV 242) at the Fugger residence in October 1777.[66] The Mozart family, in fact, was well connected with the nearby Augustinian canons of Holy Cross, which had already developed an important musical tradition by the late seventeenth century in the hands of the organists and composers Ludwig Hölzl and Octavian Panzau.[67] Following his 1777 concerts, Wolfgang Amadeus Mozart sent compositions to the prelate Bartholomäus Christa (1740–78) in thanks for his hospitality. Ludwig Zöschinger (1731–1806), a composer of keyboard and sacred music, had close relations both with Wolfgang and his father Leopold (who was a native of Augsburg); and the convent organist Matthäus Fischer (1763–1840) was an active promoter of Mozart's music locally into the early nineteenth century.[68]

The postwar period also saw a renewed interest in music among Augsburg's prince-bishops, notably Johann Christoph Freiherr von Freyberg und Eisenberg (reg. 1665–90), who enjoyed a private musical chapel of 11 musicians by the end

---

64   See especially the five-volume *Expeditionis musicae classis* (Augsburg, 1667–81; RISM G2616–2618, G2620–2621) and intabulations in the Düben collection at Uppsala. On Gletle see Layer, "Gletles Leben und Wirken"; Schmidmüller, "Augsburger Domkapellmeister", pp. 87–90; Krautwurst, "Ein unbekanntes Briefautograph".

65   RISM C18. On Caesar generally see Schmidmüller, "Augsburger Domkapellmeister", pp. 91–92. The popular song tradition would reach its pinnacle with the *Augsburger Tafel-Confect* (Augsburg, 1733–46; RISM R318, R319, R320, S2877), comprising four volumes of humorous songs by Johann Valentin Rathgeber and Johann Kaspar Seyfert. See Krautwurst, "Musik nach dem Dreißigjährigen Krieg", p. 506.

66   Schmidmüller, "Augsburger Domkapellmeister", pp. 100–01; Hoyer and Tremmel, "Musik am Augsburger Dom", pp. 49–50; Krautwurst, "Musik nach dem Dreißigjährigen Krieg", pp. 510–11.

67   Krautwurst, "Musik nach dem Dreißigjährigen Krieg", p. 511.

68   Krautwurst, "Musik nach dem Dreißigjährigen Krieg", pp. 511–12.

of his reign, and Alexander Sigismund von der Pfalz (reg. 1690–1737), whose familial connections led to some especially lavish performances in Augsburg on the occasion of the crowning of his sister Eleonora as empress (19 January 1690) and the election and crowning of her son Joseph I as King of the Romans (24 and 26 January 1690).[69] These events were also celebrated by a newly-composed Jesuit drama penned by the imperial organist Tobias Richter; two operas (*Il Telemaco* and *La regina de' Volschi*) staged at the Fugger residence by the imperial chapelmaster Antonio Draghi; and the performance of the *Coronatio Augusta* by the Passau chapelmaster Georg Muffat, later to be published in the latter's *Florilegium* (Augsburg, 1695).[70] Joseph I Ignaz Philipp Landgraf von Hessen-Darmstadt (reg. 1740–68) expanded his musical chapel to 22 musicians by 1766. He also sourced modern music from Vienna, Innsbruck, and Bologna, and engaged a series of virtuoso musicians, including the Brescian native Pietro Pompeo Sales (1729–97), a versatile composer of operas, oratorios, intermezzi, and orchestral music.[71]

At St. Anna, the legacy established by Gumpelzhaimer in the early seventeenth century persisted after the Peace of Westphalia, as the new cantor Tobias Kriegsdorfer (1607–86) was explicitly instructed by the city council to perform "nothing other than the traditional motets, and especially those of Herr Adam Gumpelzhaimer".[72] Neither Kriegsdorfer nor his successors into the eighteenth century would match Gumpelzhaimer's ambition as composers, but they did introduce into the church's repertory some of the latest trends from the central and north German Protestant traditions of the high Baroque. The cantor Philipp David Kräuter (1690–1741), a former student of Johann Sebastian Bach in Weimar, introduced at St. Anna the church cantata in the mold of Bach and Telemann, and founded a local *Collegium musicum* in 1713 after the model established by Georg Philipp Telemann in Leipzig. This ensemble would be the seed of the *Musikliebende und -übende Gesellschaft* (Society of Music Lovers and Practitioners, 1752), which produced public concerts for the city's growing bourgeois class.[73] Through their training of young musicians,

---

69 On the court music for the prince-bishops of this time see especially Layer, "Musikpflege am Hofe der Fürstbischöfe von Augsburg in der Barockzeit".

70 On the coronation festivities see Wanger, *Kaiserwahl und Krönung*, p. 140.

71 Layer, "Musikpflege am Hofe des Augsburger Fürstbischofs Joseph I. Landgraf von Hessen-Darmstadt". See also Brusniak and Mančal, "Augsburg", col. 1002; Krautwurst, "Musik nach dem Dreißigjährigen Krieg", p. 511.

72 Pittroff, "Aus vier Jahrhunderten", pp. 139–44; see also Krautwurst, "Musik nach dem Dreißigjährigen Krieg", p. 505.

73 Pittroff, "Geschichte evangelischer Kirchenmusik", pp. 170–74; see also Krautwurst, "Musik nach dem Dreißigjährigen Krieg", pp. 509–10.

both St. Anna and the Jesuit church of St. Salvator actually generated considerable activity in the realm of secular and instrumental music. A distinctive tradition of instrumental music in the style of Jean-Baptiste Lully, for instance, was established in part by Kriegsdorfer's students Johann Fischer (1646–1716) and Jakob Scheiffelhut (1647–1709), both of whom served at the Franciscan church (1677–83 and 1697–1707, respectively) and published sets of instrumental dance suites in the French manner.[74]

The vibrant culture of amateur and domestic music-making in Baroque Augsburg was supported by a local industry in the manufacture of musical instruments, which recovered quickly after the war. Augsburg emerged as a center for violin production, especially under Gregor Ferdinand Wenger (c. 1679–1767), who also constructed bass lutes (the *mandora* or *calichon*) for the accompaniment of singers and ensembles.[75] Most conspicuous among Augsburg's makers of keyboard instruments was Johann Andreas Stein (1728–92), a leading member of the *Musikliebende und -übende Gesellschaft* who enjoyed connections with the Mozart family.[76] Stein, who learned his craft from Johann Andreas Silbermann and Franz Joseph Späths, built new organs for the Franciscan church (1755–57), where he served as organist, and for the Catholic church of Holy Cross (1766), but he became chiefly famous for developing a new escapement action for the fortepiano (the so-called "Viennese action"), which was widely praised and became standard in the nineteenth century. In 1777 Wolfgang Amadeus Mozart praised Stein's pianos for the superiority of their action and for their inclusion of knee levers for lifting the dampers, and it is known that Mozart owned one of Stein's clavichords.[77]

Local demand for music and hymnals led to a revival of music printing after the conclusion of the war, led by printers like Andreas Erfurt, Johann Jakob Schönig, Johann Christoph Wagner, Jakob Koppmayer, and Andreas Maschenbauer.[78] Although these printers published both sacred and instrumental music by local composers, the music of more regional and international figures appeared as well, such as the orchestral suites of the *Florilegium primum* by Georg Muffat (1695), the *Concerti musicali* of Giuseppe Torelli (1698), and

---

74 Krautwurst, "Musik nach dem Dreißigjährigen Krieg", p. 505–06. See, for example, Scheiffelhut's *Musicalischer Gemüths-Ergötzungen* (1681), the *Lieblicher Frülings-Anfang, oder Musicalischer Seyten-Klang* (1685), and the *Musicalisches Klee-Blut* (1707) [RISM S1369, S1370, S1373], all published at Augsburg.
75 Krautwurst, "Musik nach dem Dreißigjährigen Krieg", p. 506.
76 Krautwurst, "Musik nach dem Dreißigjährigen Krieg", p. 507.
77 Layer and Brusniak, "Augsburg"; Maunder, "Mozart's Keyboard Instruments".
78 Mančal, "Augsburger Druck-, Verlags-, und Handelswesen". See also Wohnhaas, "Geschichte des Gesangbuchs"; Layer, "Augsburger Notendrucker und Musikverleger".

FIGURE 23.1 Portrait of Johann Andreas Stein (1728–1792), maker of keyboard instruments, by an anonymous artist, 1755/57
AUGSBURG, STÄDTISCHE MUSEEN, MOZARTHAUS

keyboard and sacred music of Johann Caspar Ferdinand Fischer (1695–1711). A dominant position in music publishing was established by Johann Jakob Lotter (c. 1683–1738), who, despite his Protestant background, specialized in the printing of Catholic sacred music. The firm reached a peak under his son Johann Jakob Lotter the Younger (1726–1804), a friend of Leopold Mozart and the publisher of the first edition of the latter's famed *Violinschule* (1756). During this period, the Lotter firm published the works of over 100 composers and was arguably the most influential publisher in the south German orbit.[79]

A local tradition of opera was slow to establish itself, although foundations were laid in the tradition of school drama as well as by the *Meistersinger*, who formed themselves into a privileged theater company (*Privilegierte Schauspielergesellschaft*) in 1650.[80] Until the eighteenth century, operas were largely private initiatives and were mounted for the celebration of auspicious occasions, such as the aforementioned operas by Antonio Draghi for the crowning of Eleonore of Pfalz-Neuburg and Joseph I in 1689 and 1690. The prominent French musical influence in the city around 1700 was reflected in the performance of several operas by Lully's disciple Johann Sigismund Kusser (1660–1727), including his *Julia* and *Erindo*. Local composers such as Johann Georg Mayr and Johann Georg Widmann also tried their hand at the genre.[81] A more international repertory only established itself in Augsburg in the later eighteenth century, as the playhouse (*Komödienstadel*) of the *Meistersinger* was rebuilt as the city theater (*Schauspielhaus*) in 1776, subsequently hosting German musicals (*Singspiele*) by Adam Hiller as well as *opere buffe and opéras comiques* by Niccolò Piccinni, André Grétry, Christoph Willibald Gluck, and François-André Danican Philidor. Mozart's operas arrived in Augsburg in 1777 with his *Bastien und Bastienne*, followed by *La finta giardiniera* in 1780 and *Die Zauberflöte* in 1793.[82] Thanks to the efforts of Augsburg's last prince-bishop, Clemens Wenzeslaus (reg. 1768–1812), who as Elector of Trier was forced by French military advances to return to Augsburg in 1802, the city saw a late flowering of concert and theatrical music in the bishop's residence after 1803: highlights included symphonies by Haydn and Mozart as well as performances of Haydn's grand oratorios *The Creation* and *The Seasons*. However, the secularization of Augsburg's religious institutions in 1802–03 and the permanent loss of its imperial status in 1805 would channel the city's musical life into entirely different directions.

---

79 Krautwurst, "Musik nach dem Dreißigjährigen Krieg", pp. 507–08.
80 Ibid., p. 509.
81 Ibid.
82 Ibid., pp. 509–10.

Bibliography

Unpublished Primary Sources

Staats- und Stadtbibliothek Augsburg (SuStBA)
  2° Cod. 142a.
  Tonk. Schl. 7, 23 and 39.
Bayerische Staatsbibliothek München, Cgm 379.
National Museum Prague, Cod. X A 12.
British Library London, I. B: 15154.
Universitätsbibliothek München, 2° Cod. ms. 153, 4° Cod. 168–171.

Published Primary Sources

Graser, H. and Tlusty, B.A. (eds.), *Jonas Losch, Teutscher Dichter und Componist. Die Lieder- und Reimspruchsammlung eines Augsburger Webers aus den Jahren 1579–1583*, Regensburg, 2015.

Hettrick, W. (ed.), *Bernhard Klingenstein. Rosetum Marianum*, Madison, WI, 1977.

Jonas, L., *Das Augsburger Liederbuch. Die Musikhandschrift 2° Codex 142a der Staats- und Stadtbibliothek Augsburg*, 2 vols., Munich, 1983.

Répertoire International des Sources Musicales (RISM)

Schletterer, H.M. (ed.), *Katalog der in der Kreis- und Stadt-Bibliothek, dem Staedtischen Archive und der Bibliothek des historischen Vereins zu Augsburg befindlichen Musikwerke*, Berlin, 1878.

Secondary Literature

Brusniak, F. and Mancal, J., "Augsburg", in L. Finscher (ed.), *Die Musik in Geschichte und Gegenwart*, Sachteil 1, Kassel, 1994, pp. 997–1027.

Burn, D.J., "Mass-Propers by Henricus Isaac Not Included in the *Choralis Constantinus*: The Case of Two Augsburg Sources", *Archiv für Musikwissenschaft* 60 (2003), pp. 186–220.

Charteris, R., "Newly Discovered Works by Giovanni Gabrieli", *Music & Letters* 68 (1987), pp. 343–63.

Charteris, R., *Adam Gumpelzhaimer's Little-Known Score Books in Berlin and Kraków*, Neuhausen, 1996.

Charteris, R., "An Early Seventeenth-Century Collection of Sacred Vocal Music and Its Augsburg Connections", *Music Library Association Notes* 58 (2002), pp. 511–35.

Creasman, A.F., *Censorship and Civic Order in Reformation Germany, 1517–1648: "Printed Poison and Evial Talk"*, Farnham, 2012.

Culley, T.D., *Jesuits and Music. Vol. 1: A Study of the Musicians connected with the German College in Rome during the 17th Century and of their Activities in Northern Europe*, Rome and St. Louis, 1970.

Cuyler, L., "Musical Activity in Augsburg and Its Annakirche, ca. 1470–1630", in J. Riedel (ed.), *Cantors at the Crossroads: Essays on Church Music in Honor of Walter E. Buszin*, St. Louis, 1967, pp. 33–43.

Eikelmann, R. (ed.), *Die Fugger und die Musik. Lautenschlagen lernen und ieben. Anton Fugger zum 500. Geburtstag* (exhibition catalogue), Augsburg, 1993.

Fischer, H. and Wohnhaas, T., *Historische Orgeln in Schwaben*, Munich, 1982.

Fischer, H. and Wohnhaas, T., "Die Fugger-Orgel von St. Anna in Augsburg – ein Strukturmodell schwäbischer Renaissanceprospekte", in F. Hellwig (ed.), *Studia Organologica. Festschrift für John Henry van der Meer*, Tutzing, 1987, pp. 127–41.

Fischer, H. and Wohnhaas, T., "Miscellanea zur Augsburger Dommusik", in F. Brusniak and H. Leuchtmann (eds.), *Quaestiones in musica. Festschrift für Franz Krautwurst zum 65. Geburtstag*, Tutzing, 1989, pp. 123–45.

Fischer, H. and Wohnhaas, T., *Die Augsburger Domorgeln*, Sigmaringen, 1992.

Fisher, A.J., "Song, Confession, and Criminality: Trial Records as Sources for Popular Musical Culture in Early Modern Europe," *Journal of Musicology* 18 (2001), pp. 616–57.

Fisher, A.J., *Music and Religious Identity in Counter-Reformation Augsburg, 1580–1630*, Aldershot, 2004.

Galle, D., "Liturgische Musik aus dem Benediktinerkloster St. Ulrich und Afra nach dem Tridentinum: Gregor Gastels Officium 'In Festo Conceptionis Beatae Mariae Virginis' aus dem von Johannes Dreher geschriebenen Chorbuch Tonk. Schl. 7 (1576)", M.A. thesis, Universität Augsburg, 2003.

Giselbrecht, E. and Upper, E., "Glittering Woodcuts and Moveable Music: Decoding the Elaborate Printing Techniques. Purpose and Patronage of the *Liber selectarum cantionum*", in S. Gasch, B. Lodes, and S. Tröster (eds.), *Senfl-Studien* 1, Tutzing, 2011, pp. 17–67.

Göthel, F., "Das reichstädtische Musikleben Augsburgs im 17. und 18. Jahrhundert", in F. Göthel (ed.), *Musik in Bayern, vol. 2* (exhibition catalogue), Tutzing, 1972, pp. 221–42.

Gottlieb, G., Baer, W., Becker, J., Bellot, J., Filser, K., Fried, P., Reinhard, W. and Schimmelpfennig, B. (eds.), *Geschichte der Stadt Augsburg von der Römerzeit bis zur Gegenwart*, 2nd ed., Stuttgart, 1985.

Gottwald, C., *Die Musikhandschriften der Staats- und Stadtbibliothek Augsburg*, Wiesbaden, 1974.

Gottwald, C., *Die Musikhandschriften der Universitätsbibliothek München*, Wiesbaden, 1968.

Häberlein, M., *The Fuggers of Augsburg: Pursuing Wealth and Honor in Renaissance Germany*, Charlottesville and London, 2012.

Hoyer, J. and Tremmel, E., "Musik am Augsburger Dom in der Barockzeit", in M. Thierbach (ed.), *Der Augsburger Dom in der Barockzeit* (exhibition catalogue), Augsburg, 2009, pp. 46–53.

Knor, I., *Das Liederbuch der Clara Hätzlerin als Dokument urbaner Kultur im ausgehenden 15. Jahrhundert. Philologische Untersuchung zum Textbestand in den Handschriften Prag Nationalmuseum, X A 12, der Bechsteinschen Handschrift (Halle/S. 14 A 39) und Streuüberlieferung*, Halle (Saale), 2008.

Krautwurst, F., "Musik im Mittelalter", in Gottlieb et al. (eds.), *Geschichte der Stadt Augsburg*, pp. 233–37.

Krautwurst, F., "Musik der Blütezeit", in Gottlieb et al. (eds.), *Geschichte der Stadt Augsburg*, pp. 386–91.

Krautwurst, F., "Musik nach dem Dreißigjährigen Krieg bis zum Ende der reichsstädtischen Zeit", in Gottlieb et al. (eds.), *Geschichte der Stadt Augsburg*, pp. 504–15.

Krautwurst, F., "Ein unbekanntes Briefautograph Johann Melchior Gletles," *Musik in Bayern* 43 (1991), pp. 79–86.

Krautwurst, F., "Melchior Neusidler und die Fugger", *Musik in Bayern* 54 (1997), pp. 5–24.

Kroyer, T. "Gregor Aichingers Leben und Werke: mit neuen Beiträgen zur Musikgeschichte Ingolstadts und Augsburgs", in T. Kroyer (ed.), *Ausgewählte Werke von Gregor Aichinger (1564–1628)*, Leipzig, 1909, ix–xcv.

Layer, A., *Johann Melchior Gletles Leben und Wirken*, Basel, 1959.

Layer, A., (ed.), *Musik und Musiker der Fuggerzeit. Begleitheft zur Ausstellung der Stadt Augsburg 1959*, Augsburg, 1959.

Layer, A., "Augsburger Musikdrucker der frühen Renaissancezeit", *Gutenberg-Jahrbuch* 40 (1965), pp. 124–29.

Layer, A., "Augsburger Musikpflege im Mittelalter", in L. Wegele (ed.), *Musik in der Reichsstadt Augsburg*, Augsburg, 1965, pp. 11–26.

Layer, A., "Augsburger Musik im Barock", in K. Arndt and C. Thon (eds.), *Augsburger Barock* (exhibition catalogue), Augsburg, 1968, pp. 453–68.

Layer, A., "Augsburger Notendrucker und Musikverleger der Barockzeit", *Gutenberg-Jahrbuch* 44 (1969), pp. 150–53.

Layer, A., "Musikpflege am Hofe der Fürstbischöfe von Augsburg in der Renaissancezeit", *Jahrbuch des Vereins für Augsburger Bistumsgeschichte* 10 (1976), pp. 199–211.

Layer, A., "Musikpflege am Hofe der Fürstbischöfe von Augsburg in der Barockzeit", *Jahrbuch des Vereins für Augsburger Bistumsgeschichte* 11 (1977), pp. 123–47.

Layer, A., "Musikpflege am Hofe des Augsburger Fürstbischofs Joseph I. Landgraf von Hessen-Darmstadt(1740–1768)",*Jahrbuch des Vereins für Augsburger Bistumsgeschichte* 13 (1979), pp. 128–59.

Layer, A. "Musik und Theater in St. Salvator", in W. Baer and H.J. Hecker (eds.), *Die Jesuiten und ihre Schule St. Salvator in Augsburg 1582*, Munich, 1982, pp. 67–75.

Layer, A. and Brusniak, F., "Augsburg", *Grove Music Online*, URL: www.oxfordmusiconline.com (accessed 23 January 2017).

Leitmeir, C.T., "Bernhard Klingensteins Triodia Sacra (1605): Ein rekonstruierter Sammeldruck als Schlüsselquelle für das Musikleben der Spätrenaissance in Süddeutschland", *Musik in Bayern* 63 (2002), pp. 23–55.

Leitmeir, C.T., *Jacobus de Kerle. Komponieren im Spannungsfeld von Kirche und Kunst*, Turnhout, 2009.

Lieb, N., *Die Fugger und die Kunst im Zeitalter der Spätgotik und frühen Renaissance*, Munich, 1952.

Mančal, J., "Zum Augsburger Druck-, Verlags-, und Handelswesen im Musikalienbereich am ausgehenden 17. und im 18. Jahrhundert", in H. Gier and J. Janota (eds.), *Augsburger Buchdruck und Verlagswesen. Von den Anfängen bis zur Gegenwart*, Wiesbaden, 1997, pp. 873–907.

Martinez-Göllner, M.L., "Die Augsburger Bibliothek Herwart und ihre Lautentabulaturen". *Fontes artis musicae* 16 (1969), pp. 29–48.

Maunder, R., "Mozart's Keyboard Instruments", *Early Music* 20 (1992), pp. 207–09.

Picker, M., "Liber selectarum cantionum (Augsburg: Grimm & Wirsung, 1520): A Neglected Monument of Renaissance Music and Music Printing", in M. Staehelin (ed.), *Gestalt und Entstehung musikalischer Quellen im 15. und 16. Jahrhundert*, Wiesbaden, 1998, pp. 149–67.

Pittroff, K., "Aus vier Jahrhunderten evangelischer Kirchenmusik in Augsburg", *Zeitschrift für evangelische Kirchenmusik* 9 (1931), pp. 31–36, 39–44, 59–61, 70–75, 87–94, 115–20.

Pötzl, W., *Der Kalligraph Leonhard Wagner aus Schwabmünchen (1454–1522). Leben und Werk*, Augsburg, 1973.

Przywecka-Samecka, M., "Problematik des Musiknotendruckes in der Inkunabelzeit", *Gutenberg-Jahrbuch* 53 (1978), pp. 51–56.

Rettelbach, J., "Lied und Liederbuch im spätmittelalterlichen Augsburg", in J. Janota and W. Williams-Krapp (eds.), *Literarisches Leben in Augsburg während des 15. Jahrhunderts*, Tübingen, 1995, pp. 281–307.

Rimek, T., *Das mehrstimmige Repertoire der Benediktinerabtei St. Ulrich und Afra in Augsburg (1549–1632)*, Stuttgart, 2015.

Röder, T., "Innovation and Misfortune: Augsburg Music Printing in the First Half of the Sixteenth Century", in E. Schreurs and H. Vanhulst (eds.), *Music Fragments and Manuscripts in the Low Countries – Alta Capella – Music Printing in Antwerp and Europe in the 16th Century*, Peer, 1997, pp. 465–77.

Röder, T. and Wohnhaas, T., "Der Augsburger Musikdruck von den Anfängen bis zum Ende des Dreißigjährigen Krieges", in H. Gier and J. Janota (eds.), *Augsburger Buchdruck und Verlagswesen. Von den Anfängen bis zur Gegenwart*, Wiesbaden, 1997, pp. 291–331.

Röder, T. and Wohnhaas, T., "Die Stella musicae des Benediktiners Veit Bild: Eine spätmittelalterliche Musiklehre aus Augsburg", *Jahrbuch des Vereins für Augsburger Bistumsgeschichte* 32 (1998), pp. 305–25.

Sandberger, A., "Bemerkungen zur Biographie Hans Leo Hasslers und seiner Brüder, sowie zur Musikgeschichte der Städte Nürnberg und Augsburg im 16. und zu Anfang des 17. Jahrhunderts", in idem (ed.), *Werke Hans Leo Hasslers*, vol. 2 (Denkmäler der Tonkunst in Bayern 5.1), Leipzig, 1904, xi–cxii.

Schaal, R., "Zur Musikpflege im Kollegiatstift St. Moritz zu Augsburg", *Die Musikforschung* 7 (1954), pp. 1–24.

Schaal, R., "Georg Willers Augsburger Musikalien-Lagerkatalog von 1622", *Die Musikforschung* 16 (1963), pp. 127–39.

Schaal, R., *Das Inventar der Kantorei Sankt Anna in Augsburg. Ein Beitrag zur protestantischen Musikpflege im 16. und beginnenden 17. Jahrhundert*, Kassel, 1965.

Schaal, R., *Die Kataloge des Augsburger Musikalien-Händlers Kaspar Flurschütz, 1613–1628*, Wilhelmshaven, 1974.

Schmid, E.F., "Hans Leo Haßler und seine Brüder", *Zeitschrift des Historischen Vereins für Schwaben* 54 (1941), pp. 60–212.

Schmidmüller, M., "Die Augsburger Domkapellmeister seit dem Tridentinum bis zur Säkularisation", *Jahrbuch des Vereins für Augsburger Bistumsgeschichte* 23 (1989), pp. 69–107.

Schnell, F., "Die Augsburger Meistersinger", in L. Wegele (ed.), *Musik in der Reichsstadt Augsburg*, Augsburg, 1965, pp. 27–42.

Schuler, M., "Die Musik in Konstanz während des Konzils 1414–1418", *Acta musicologica* 38 (1966), pp. 150–68.

Singer, A., "Leben und Werke des Augsburger Domkapellmeisters Bernhardus Klingenstein 1545–1645", Ph.D. diss., University of Munich, 1921.

Slim, H.C., "The Music Library of Hans Heinrich Herwart", *Annales musicologiques* 7 (1964–77), pp. 67–109.

Taricani, J., "A Renaissance Bibliophile as Musical Patron: The Evidence of the Herwart Sketchbooks", *Music Library Association Notes* 49 (1993), pp. 1357–89.

Ursprung, O., "Die Chorordnung von 1616 am Dom zu Augsburg: Ein Beitrag zur Frage der Aufführungspraxis", in *Studien zur Musikgeschichte. Festschrift für Guido Adler zum 75. Geburtstag*, Vienna, 1930, pp. 137–42.

Valentin, E., "Augsburger Musik zwischen dem Dreißigjährigen Krieg und dem Ende der Reichsstadt", in L. Wegele (ed.), *Musik in der Reichsstadt Augsburg*, Augsburg, 1965, pp. 103–48.

Wanger, B.H., *Kaiserwahl und Krönung im Frankfurt des 17. Jahrhunderts*, Frankfurt am Main, 1994.

Wegele, L. (ed.), *Musik in der Reichsstadt Augsburg*, Augsburg, 1965.

Wohnhaas, T., "Zur Geschichte des Gesangbuchs in der Diözese Augsburg", *Jahrbuch des Vereins für Augsburger Bistumsgeschichte* 10 (1976), pp. 212–20.

Wohnhaas, T., "Notizen zu Druck und Verlag katholischer Kirchenmusik in Augsburg", *Jahrbuch des Vereins für Augsburger Bistumsgeschichte* 31 (1997), pp. 152–63.

Zager, D., "Liturgical Rite and Musical Repertory: The Polyphonic Latin Hymn Cycle of Lasso in Munich and Augsburg", in I. Bossuyt, E. Schreurs and A. Wouters (eds.), *Orlandus Lassus and His Time: Colloquium Proceedings, Antwerpen 24.–26.08.1994*, Peer, 1995, pp. 215–31.

Index

Aachen, Hans von 512
abortion 299, 302
Academy of Arts 164, 522
ad insigne pinus (publishing house) 418, 422, 426–427, 479
Adler, Philipp 273
administration 2, 8, 23, 46, 48–52, 56, 61, 67, 71, 73, 78, 89, 133, 150, 154, 171–172, 174, 178, 183, 191, 197, 206, 208, 210, 284, 289, 359, 379, 382, 470–471, 488, 505, 546, 548
advertising 62–63, 399, 409, 431, 536, 563
Africa 105, 110, 500
agents 8, 11, 129, 360, 379, 392, 398, 403, 443, 458–459, 466–467, 508, 515
Agricola, Alexander 555
Agricola, Stephan 226, 231, 236
Ahorner von Ahornrain, Joseph 57
Aichinger, Gregor 559–561, 563–564
Albrecht II of Prussia, Duke 372, 557
Albrecht V of Bavaria, Duke 400, 562
Alexander Sigismund von der Pfalz 566
Almadén 108
Almanacs 424, 427
alms 113, 133, 284–286, 349–50; Alms Office 163–164, 285–286, 335; see also Fuggerei, poor relief, workhouses
Alps 4, 20, 24, 72, 105, 109, 114, 130, 159, 201, 209, 428, 430–431, 476, 555, 563
altars 81, 222, 250, 497, 500, 505, 508–509, 512, 530
Altenstetter, David 260
Amberger, Christoph 443, 453–454, 508
America 118, 221, 443
Ammerbach, Eusebius 558, 562
Amsterdam 112, 118, 183, 443, 512, 541
Anabaptism, Anabaptists 136, 221–222, 232–233, 243, 247, 250, 254, 312, 557
anatomy 54, 62
anti-Judaism, anti-Semitism 162, 367, 369–386; see also Jews
antiquities 512, 539
Antwerp 105, 108, 110–111, 258, 296, 392, 404, 459, 511
Aperger, Andreas 421, 423–424

apocalypse 344, 349–350, 352
apprentices 12, 61, 158, 183, 276, 278, 283, 285, 288, 296, 303–306, 423, 473, 496
Apt family 496–497
Apt, Ulrich 497
architects, architecture 7, 35, 38, 47, 49, 51, 53, 69, 78, 114–115, 221–222, 263–264, 350, 487, 507, 509, 511, 522, 526–548
archives 6, 8–9, 12–13, 64, 73, 78, 82, 209, 404, 472, 476, 481, 527
Argon, Peter von 76, 86
armor 82, 88, 146, 240, 251, 264, 348, 442, 444, 461, 463, 466, 499–500
arms, see weapons
artisans 20–21, 89, 103, 113, 115, 123, 152, 156, 162, 164, 224–225, 257–258, 264–265, 273–276, 278–279, 284, 287–290, 310, 332, 359, 375–376, 443–445, 451, 458, 467, 517–517, 522, 528, 536, 546–547; see also craftsmen
artists 7, 36, 38, 83, 88, 263, 266, 322, 443, 447, 495–525, 535, 539
Artzt family 102
Asia 101, 105, 110, 443
Aspruck, Franz 35
astrology 55, 61, 343, 417, 482, 486
astronomy 55, 417, 477, 482–484, 486, 517
Augsburg Confession 234–235, 241–242, 247, 279–280, 252–255, 350; see also Lutheranism, Lutherans
Augsburg Interim 142, 146–147, 240–242, 251–253, 348, 557
Augspurgischer Intelligenz-Zettel 409
August I of Saxony, Elector 399
Austria 24, 280–281, 355, 379–380, 393, 400–401, 486, 499, 520
autobiography 4, 12, 38, 81, 83, 86, 392, 500
Aventin, Johannes 544

Bach, Johann Sebastian 566
Bächlin, Johann 253
Bair, Jeremias 299
bakers 9, 104, 113, 125, 199, 274–275, 279, 281, 349, 543
Baldi, Bernardino 544

Baldinger, Gottfried   47
Baltic   105
Bamberg   373, 379
Bämler, Johannes   74, 86, 417
Banat   116
banishment   179, 183–184, 190, 252, 255, 260, 262, 297, 385
bankers   25, 38, 46–47, 105, 107, 109, 148, 159, 224–225, 346, 380, 383, 393, 400, 522; see also banking
banking   7, 101, 105, 107–108, 112, 116–118, 125, 130, 132, 157, 162, 204, 221, 225, 276, 381, 383–384, 392
bankruptcy   101, 109, 111–112, 114, 118, 150, 274, 308, 427, 432–433; bankruptcy law   203–206, 208, 209–211
Barbari, Jacopo de   500
barber-surgeons   51, 53, 58–62, 65, 306, 329
barbican houses   27
Baroque   7, 518, 520, 564–567
Basel   69, 346, 372, 421–422, 424, 430
Bäsinger, Barbara   308
Bass, Laux   562
bathing, bathhouses   55, 60, 300, 329–331, 334, 368, 539; see also swimming
Baudrexel, Philipp Jakob   564
Bauer, Oswald   403
Baumgartner family   105, 109, 230, 240, 346, 374
Baumgartner, Hans   147, 273
Baumgartner, Ulrich   514–515
Bavaria   3, 5, 13, 21, 24, 27, 30, 33, 47–48, 57–58, 63, 65, 69, 79, 86, 103–104, 111, 116, 129, 131–132, 139, 148, 151, 161, 203, 211, 221, 230, 233, 235, 258, 265, 280–281, 289, 329, 347, 349–351, 353, 355, 357–360, 372, 380, 385, 398, 400, 409, 420, 430, 442, 472, 480, 507, 518, 522–523, 539, 544, 549, 561–562, 564
Bayer, Johann   483–484
Beck, Leonhard   497
Beck, Matthias Friedrich   481
beggars   163, 183, 284–285, 330, 334, 445, 359, 370, 385, 444
Behringer, Wolfgang   399
Bellot, Josef   417
Beltzer, Martin   451
Benz, Philipp Adam   116

Bergmüller, Johann Georg   38, 522
Berlin   428, 487–488
Bertermann, Samuel   116
Biberach an der Riß   102, 116, 154, 281
Bidermann, Jakob   559
Bidermann, Samuel   562
bi-confessionalism   10, 31, 46, 48, 51, 55, 142, 154, 221, 243, 247–267, 308, 323, 348, 377, 401, 407, 428, 432; see also confessions, confessionalization, religious coexistence, parity
Bild, Veit   77, 223, 477, 482, 554–555
bills of exchange   111, 204–205, 208–209
Bimmel family   83, 109, 236
Bimmel, Anton   236
Birck, Sixt   478, 482
Benheim, Battle of   357, 379
Blumenau, Laurentius   474
Böck von Böckenstein, Lienhard   537
Bodenehr family   487
Bohemia   280, 282, 373, 400, 520
Bologna   474–475, 566
book production   4, 74, 79, 117, 282–283, 415–428
book trade   317, 418, 420–421, 424, 415–433, 563
Böschenstein, Johannes   477, 482
Bossard family   562
Brahe, Tycho   482, 517
Brandenburg-Ansbach, margravate   372
Brandmüller, Tobias   408
Brant, Sebastian   477
Brazil   395
Brenker, Andreas   465–466
Brentano-Mezzegra family   117
Breu, Jörg   7, 78, 87–88, 329, 496–497, 500, 503, 507, 556
brewers, breweries   78, 80, 104, 274, 288, 305n, 323
broadsheets   70, 78, 259, 327, 332, 349, 395, 397, 401, 403, 405–406, 420, 426
Brucker, Johann Jakob   487–488
Bruges   104
Brussels   407, 443
Bucer, Martin   139, 147, 238, 250
builders   32, 78, 161, 263, 511, 518, 528, 533, 536, 545, 547
Burgau, margravate   23, 265, 288, 374, 385

Burgkmair family 496
Burgkmair, Hans the Elder 497, 500–501, 506–507, 533
Burgkmair, Hans the Younger 83, 497
Burgkmair, Thoman 497
burgomaster 77, 205, 208, 517, 562
Burkhart family 114
butchers 104, 113–114, 152, 164, 275, 279, 446

cabinet makers 279, 495, 513–515, 518
Caesar, Johann Melchior 564
Cajetan, Thomas de Vio, Cardinal 223–224, 556
calendar, calendar reform, calendar conflict 55, 151–153, 257–258, 260, 262, 317, 319, 332, 377, 482, 486, 563
calico printing, see cotton printing
canals 161, 300, 329–331, 541, 546–548
Candid, Peter 511–512
Canis, Cornelius 557
Canisius, Petrus 255–256
canon law 174, 204, 206, 211
Carissimi, Giacomo 564
Carli, Tomaso 117
Carmelites 222–224, 226, 236–237, 309, 503, 535, 540, 556; see also St. Anna
carnival 164, 185, 317–324, 335, 353, 461
catastrophes 27–28, 391, 397
catechism 139, 431
cathedral 20, 25, 33, 76, 222, 224, 226–227, 231, 237, 240, 255, 263, 320, 328, 358, 478, 482, 496–497, 505, 508, 512, 528–530, 534, 553–554, 557–559, 564–565
cathedral chapter 146, 159, 222–226, 470, 474, 530
Catholicism, Catholics 3, 10, 25, 27, 29–31, 36, 46–47, 49–51, 54–55, 57, 116–117, 128, 133–140, 142, 146–149, 151–155, 157–159, 183, 221, 229–241, 243, 248–249, 251–267, 281–284, 289, 308–312, 323, 330, 343, 346–348, 350, 352–354, 357, 359–360, 376–377, 418–421, 423–424, 426–428, 431–432, 444–445, 447, 477–481, 483, 485–486, 488, 507, 508–509, 520, 553, 557, 559, 563–564, 567, 569

Celtis, Conrad 477
censorship 175, 253, 261–262, 397, 406, 419–420, 426
chapelmasters 558–559, 564–566
Charles II of Spain, King 355
Charles IV, Emperor 368
Charles V, Emperor 25, 50, 88, 107, 110–111, 132, 136–137, 141–142, 146–149, 157, 174, 230, 233–232, 240, 242, 251, 278, 345–348, 360, 377, 421, 426, 447, 450, 466, 505, 509, 512, 557
chemistry 54, 482, 484, 486, 495
children 60, 81, 158, 190, 200, 239, 257, 264–266, 285, 295–296, 299, 301–303, 324, 333–334, 336, 344, 355, 376, 384, 477, 482, 500, 505
China 485
Christa, Bartholomäus 565
chronicles 3–5, 11, 32–33, 69–90, 153, 302, 326–328, 343–344, 349, 353, 372, 402–403, 443, 471, 475, 528, 537
churches and convents, see cathedral; Franciscan church; Holy Cross; Maria Stern; St. Anna; St. Clara; St. Georg; St. Katharina; St. Margaret; St. Moritz; St. Nicholas; St. Peter; St. Salvator; St. Sebastian; St. Servatius; St. Stephan; Sts. Ulrich and Afra; St. Ursula; St. Wolfgang
city council 5, 23, 26–29, 31–32, 35–38, 49–53, 55, 59–63, 71–73, 76–78, 86–87, 89, 104, 112–114, 123, 125, 127–143, 147–159, 161–165, 171–172, 174–177, 180, 182–186, 190, 202–203, 205–207, 210, 221–222, 225–226, 228–231, 235–242, 247–248, 251–260, 263, 272–276, 278, 283–284, 287–290, 295, 300–302, 305, 309, 311, 319–320, 325–326, 328, 331, 341, 345–347, 350–353, 358–359, 368–372, 374–377, 379, 381–386, 392, 394, 406, 419–422, 424, 430, 444–447, 450–451, 454, 456, 458, 461, 471–472, 499, 511, 531, 545, 557, 566; see also Council of Thirteen; Large Council; Secret Council; Small Council
city gates 20, 32, 37, 114, 152, 184, 238, 373–374, 379–381, 545; see also fortifications

city hall 33, 35, 37, 87, 114, 123, 127, 134, 152, 157, 179, 185, 228, 258, 352, 371, 509–511, 530–531, 534, 541, 543–545
city secretary 7, 132, 140, 157, 202, 223, 230, 239, 346, 422, 475, 499, 536
city walls 20, 21, 29, 22, 35–36, 38, 49, 63, 123, 143, 151, 222, 224, 226, 229, 273, 276, 287–288, 320, 325, 334, 344, 350, 353–355, 357, 373, 385, 482, 527–528, 545–548; see also fortifications
Clasen, Claus-Peter 8–9
Clemens Wenzeslaus von Sachsen, Bishop 569
clergy 10, 24–25, 30, 32–33, 35, 72, 87–88, 128–129, 134, 137–139, 141, 146–147, 151–153, 154, 158, 172, 182, 185, 196–197, 222–242, 248, 251–256, 258, 260, 266, 286, 309, 312, 338, 346–347, 349–350, 352, 360, 372, 374, 378–379, 392, 416–417, 420, 432, 470–472, 474, 477–478, 486–488, 508, 526, 528–530, 532, 554, 556–558, 560, 565, 569; see also monks, nuns, rabbis
clocks, clockmakers 357, 482, 516–518, 531; see also watchmakers
cloth makers 287; see also textile production, weavers
clothing, see dress
Cobres Company 117
Codussi, Mauro 503
collecting, collectors 58, 73–74, 78–79, 82–83, 90, 323, 332, 403–405, 408, 416, 443, 470–473, 475–476, 479–480, 484, 486, 499, 503, 512–513, 515, 536–537, 539–540, 541, 554–555, 559–562
Collegium Medicum 47–48, 57–59, 61–65, 164, 306
Cologne 13, 102, 404, 421, 425, 428, 529
Colombia 110
commemoration 34, 72, 266, 326–327, 440, 461; see also memory
commerce 5, 101–102, 108, 112, 135, 157, 159, 235, 273, 318, 349, 357, 381–382, 384–385, 427, 510, 535; see also trade
commercial law 204
common law 201–202, 204, 207, 211
communication 11, 69–73, 81, 90, 127, 391–394, 403–404, 467, 472, 526; see also media

composers 76, 78, 87, 260, 252, 473, 477, 558–559, 561, 563–567, 569
Comunero Revolt 146
concertos 565
confessions, confessionalization 3, 10, 29–32, 51, 55, 78, 142, 148, 150–158, 165, 173, 180–181, 207, 221, 230, 234–235, 241–243, 247–267, 281, 312, 316, 323, 343–344, 348–350, 354, 357, 360, 376–377, 401, 407, 423–424, 428, 431, 444, 477–488, 520, 553, 557, 559, 561, 563–564, 571; see also bi-confessionalism
Constantinople 474, 476
constitution 3–4, 29, 36, 46, 83, 87, 89, 125–126, 128, 146, 149–150, 155–157, 159, 162, 165, 174, 177n, 221, 290, 348, 369, 421, 426, 432, 488, 545
consumers 11, 59, 63, 104, 113, 331, 336, 379, 381, 442–443, 452, 458
Contarini, Alvise 354
contract law 199, 204
convents 9, 222, 226, 236–237, 241, 248–249, 252, 308–309, 311, 313, 330, 458, 475, 497, 540, 554, 565; see also monks, nuns
conversion 30, 232–233, 254, 256–257, 264–266, 283, 308, 310, 372, 376, 384
Copenhagen 407
copper trade 24, 101, 105, 108–109, 116, 442
corporate law 203–204
correspondence 5–6, 60, 127, 132–133, 223, 289, 329, 392, 398–402, 405, 407–408, 452, 459, 466, 471–472, 476–477, 481
costume books 12, 440, 450, 456, 458
Cotta, Johann Friedrich 409
cotton 101–103, 112–113, 117–118, 159, 277, 282, 442, 456; cotton printing 4, 117–118, 276, 280, 283, 290, 522, 547–548
Council of Basel 372
Council of Constance 74, 371, 474
Council of Thirteen 126
Council of Trent 147, 255, 509, 557
Counter-Reformation 241, 344, 349, 421, 426, 484, 509, 559
courier system 392–394, 398, 402
court Jews 379–382
courts 9, 72, 74, 86–87, 104, 116, 133, 140, 150, 152, 156, 164, 174, 178, 182, 185, 197, 202,

INDEX 579

206–211, 239, 247, 251–253, 279,
288–289, 295–297, 299, 301, 307,
311–312, 322, 329, 332, 371, 375, 377–382,
392, 398–403, 405, 407, 420, 424, 446,
450–451, 466, 473, 483, 505, 511, 520,
523, 531, 536–537, 539–540, 546, 553,
557, 561–562, 564; see also Imperial
Aulic Court; Imperial Chamber Court
craftsmen   8–9, 31, 118, 123, 152–153, 262, 271,
274, 276, 279, 284–285, 290, 306, 332,
443, 446, 454–455, 459, 463, 466, 473,
495–496, 499, 511, 513, 515, 518
credit   101–102, 109, 111–112, 114–116, 149, 210,
368–369, 371, 375, 381, 383, 393, 401
Crequillon, Thomas   557
crime   171–191, 197, 208, 210, 231, 254, 279,
297–299, 301–302
Croph, Philip Jacob   355, 357
Curaçao   118
curiosity cabinets   279, 513, 514–515

Dachs family   530
damask   445, 447
dance   317–319, 322, 327–328, 330, 334–336,
368, 561, 567
dance house/hall   323, 543
Danube   31, 102, 280–281, 374
Danzig, see Gdánsk
Daucher, Adolf   503
Daucher, Hans   503–505, 507
decrees   53, 57, 61, 132, 138–139, 146, 150, 157,
165, 174–176, 203, 205–207, 210, 251–254,
257, 265, 289, 309, 312, 316–318, 331, 346,
372, 374, 379, 383, 397, 419, 445–446,
458, 531; see also ordinances
Degler, Hans   509
Demer, Jörg   78
Demmler, Johann Michael   565
Denmark   111
des Prez, Josquin   555
Dilbaum, Samuel   405
Dillingen an der Donau   222–223, 252, 281,
347, 431, 479, 483, 486, 488, 557–559,
563
diplomacy   58, 127, 221, 398, 461, 476, 481, 515
Dirr, Pius   4
disarmament   263–264
domestic servitude   224, 256, 276–277, 283,
306–307

Dominicans, Dominican church   222, 231,
474, 497, 534n
Donauwörth   102, 141, 372
Draghi, Antonio   566, 569
Dreher, Johannes   560
Dresden   116, 483
dress   200, 252, 271, 275, 283, 285, 321–322,
326, 352, 357, 370, 375–376, 440–467
Drexel, Jeremias   560
drinking   36, 87, 157, 159, 175, 179, 199, 266,
274–275, 296–299, 318, 322, 327, 329,
331–335, 353, 378, 444, 451, 454, 515, 517,
520
Dürer, Albrecht   499, 503
dyers   113, 282, 287, 459, 495

Eber, Valentin   474
Eberhart, Michael   452
Eberstein, Sibilla von   256
Eck, Johannes   225–226, 478
economy   3–7, 9–10 23–24, 26, 29, 31–32, 36,
50, 53, 56, 58–59, 70, 72, 74, 79, 81,
101–119, 123, 125, 127, 129, 132, 134,
149–151, 153–154, 157–159, 161–163, 165,
176, 184, 187, 208–209, 221, 225, 228, 230,
235, 237, 243, 258–259, 264n, 265–266,
271–272, 276–277, 280, 285, 287 –288,
290, 300, 302–304, 307, 312–313, 318,
336, 344, 349, 353, 355, 368, 371–372,
375–379, 382–383, 385, 391–393, 395,
403–404, 406, 409, 415–416, 419, 421,
428, 433, 442, 451, 470, 485, 487, 496,
509, 526, 535, 547, 553, 564
Edict of Restitution   154, 262, 350, 564
ego-documents   12, 81, 343
Ehrenberg, Richard   5–6, 104
Eichthal, Arnold Seligmann Baron von   384
Eisleben   116
Elias, Norbert   188
Endorfer family   12, 158, 452
Endorfer, Friedrich   12, 158, 452
Endorfer, Hans   12
England   88, 117, 211
Enlightenment   3, 46–48, 63, 79, 90, 164,
188–189, 267, 409, 415, 428, 433, 481,
485–488, 495
entertainment   70, 316–336, 511, 515; see also
under individual entertainments
Erasmus von Rotterdam   223, 231, 477

Erbach, Christian 559, 561–562
Erfurt 417, 567
Erfurt, Andreas 567
Erfurt, Hans von 417
Erhard, Gregor 533
Estienne, Henri 479
Evans, Richard 178
excise tax (*Ungeld*) 102–103, 240, 286
execution, executioner 62–63, 77, 129, 135, 178, 181–190, 228, 233, 261, 265, 279, 299

Faber, Johann 474
fairs 102, 104, 112, 115, 157, 287, 318, 322–323, 328, 334, 405, 418, 420, 429–431; see also markets
family 3, 5–6, 11, 28, 30, 49, 53, 60, 63, 69, 78–83, 86–88, 102, 108, 114, 132, 147–149, 151, 153–159, 161, 184, 197, 200–201, 203–206, 208–210, 222, 225, 230–231, 233, 240, 249, 256, 265, 271–273, 284, 289, 294–299, 301, 303, 307–312, 320, 331, 333–334, 346, 351, 359, 368, 371, 379–381, 383–386, 393, 398, 400–401, 403, 405, 418, 421, 442, 458–459, 461, 466, 472, 476, 478–479, 483, 496, 503, 505, 508–509, 512–513, 530, 535–536, 542, 556–557, 561–563, 565–567
family books, family chronicles 11, 69, 80–87
family law 203, 205, 208
famine 27, 31, 162–163, 248, 318, 372
fashion 12, 81, 89, 132, 164, 304, 317, 440, 442–443, 447, 450, 452, 454, 456, 458, 461, 463, 513, 515, 518, 561, 563
Fassnacht, Anna 312
Feichtmayr family 518, 522
Ferdinand I, Emperor 149, 461
Ferdinand II, Emperor 154, 350, 424, 564
Ferdinand II of Tyrol, Archduke 308, 465–466, 513
Fernpass 24
finances 3, 5–7, 13, 23, 25, 28, 31, 35, 50–52, 60, 62, 101, 104–105, 107, 110, 112, 114, 118, 130–132, 137, 148, 150–151, 157–158, 161–165, 209, 221, 224–225, 231, 233, 239–240, 263, 271–273, 283, 298, 326, 328, 348–349, 355, 358–360, 368–369, 371, 374–375, 379, 381, 383, 393, 395, 401, 418, 421, 424, 427, 430, 444, 450–451, 455, 472, 475–476, 479, 520, 530, 545, 561
Fischer, Matthäus 565
Flemish 112, 497, 512, 557
Florence 466, 475, 510–511, 515, 539
Flurschütz, Caspar 560, 563
fornication 288, 295, 297–301
fortifications 21, 24, 29, 36–38, 114, 161, 239, 345, 352, 360, 371, 541, 546–547; see also city gates, city walls
Foucault, Michael 188
fountains 21, 34–35, 37–38, 70, 509–511, 539, 541–543, 547
France 12, 27, 38, 46, 75, 80, 104, 111–112, 116, 118, 160, 162, 165, 255, 311, 328, 345, 354–355, 357–358, 392, 399, 408–409, 428, 450, 473, 488, 569
Franciscans, Franciscan church 134, 140, 222, 226–229, 231, 235, 237, 241, 557, 567
Franck, David 423, 427
François, Etienne 10, 30, 47, 264
Franconia 280, 373
Frank, Johannes 77
Frankfurt am Main 79, 102, 115–116, 176, 176, 186, 203, 287, 289, 409, 418, 429–431, 443, 541
Frederick I, Emperor 172, 196, 345
Frederick III, Emperor 174, 372, 556
Freiburg im Breisgau 201, 430–431
French pox, French pox house 49, 52–54, 56
Frey, Johann Michael 38, 452
Freyberg und Eisenberg, Christoph Freiherr von 565
Friedberg (Bavaria) 25, 289
Friess, Joachim 519
Fröhlich, Georg 137, 140, 239, 346
Frosch, Johann 223–224, 226, 231, 236, 309, 556
Fugger family 5–7, 11–12, 49, 53, 64, 83, 86–87, 101, 104–105, 107–111, 115, 130, 140, 147–149, 151, 153–154, 157, 209, 222, 224–225, 230, 233, 240, 242, 248–249, 256, 272–273, 284, 308, 321, 328–329, 346, 392–394, 398, 400–405, 421, 424, 440, 442, 454, 458–459, 466, 478–479, 481, 483, 485, 503, 505, 509, 512–513,

535–536, 539, 556–557, 560–563, 565–566
Fugger, Anna Jacobäa   248
Fugger, Anton   6, 107–108, 148, 346, 400
Fugger, Christoph   453–454
Fugger, Georg   111, 256, 479, 503
Fugger, Hans   11, 256, 308, 329, 399–405, 459, 508, 512, 539
Fugger, Hans Ernst   481
Fugger, Hans Jakob   87, 147–148, 561–562
Fugger, Jakob   5–6, 105–107, 224–225, 284, 308, 384, 440, 503, 535, 556, 561
Fugger, Marcus (Marx)   151, 256, 404
Fugger, Maximilian   562
Fugger, Octavian Secundus   403, 405, 561–562
Fugger, Ott Heinrich   154
Fugger, Philipp Eduard   404–405
Fugger, Raymund   512, 562
Fugger, Stefan   403
Fugger, Ulrich   104, 222, 248, 440, 479, 503
Fugger-Wellenburg, Maria Theresia von   485
Fuggerei   28, 49, 263, 284, 353, 535–534
Furriers   104, 111, 239, 242, 260, 288, 459
Fürth   373
Füssen   24
fustian   101–103, 112–113, 117, 277, 442, 451–452, 461

Gabrieli, Andrea   562
Gabrieli, Giovanni   559–560
Gail, Jörg   429
Galilei, Galileo   483–484
gambling   175, 279, 295–296, 318–319, 326–327, 333–334, 378, 451, 545
games   63, 162, 317–318, 324, 326–328, 333, 335–336, 515
Gasser, Achilles Pirmin   55–56, 60–61, 77
Gassner, Veronika   440
gazetteers   398, 400–402, 405
Gdánsk   105, 407
Gefattermann, Elisabeth   308
Geffcken, Peter   272–273
Gegler, Hans   417
gender   9, 51, 80, 177–178, 183, 205, 248, 277, 283, 294–313, 326–327, 332–333, 444, 446, 453–458, 461, 467; see also women, families

genealogy   33, 71, 81, 87, 158, 461
Genoa   102, 104
geography   28, 31–32, 77, 280, 283, 287, 485–486
Gerhard, Hubert   509–510
Gessel, Leonhard   474
Ghent   146
Giambologna   510–511
Gigel, Michael   450
Gignoux, Anna Barbara   118, 308
Giltlinger family   496
Giulini, Johann Andreas Joseph   565
Gletle, Johann Melchior   564
globes   517
Gluck, Christoph Willibald   569
Goa   111
Göggingen   482, 517
goldsmiths   4, 35, 113–114, 117–118, 248, 260, 274–275, 278–279, 281, 328, 382, 463, 495–496, 500, 518–519, 544
Gossembrot family   33, 76, 82, 86, 105, 308, 474–475
Gossembrot, Hans   82
Gossembrot, Sigmund (Sigismund)   33, 76, 86, 273, 474–475
Gothic   461, 497, 508–509, 526, 534–536
Gran, Heinrich   430
Grander family   273
graphic arts   36, 81, 376, 415, 421, 428, 471, 499, 513, 517, 545
grave-diggers   279, 287, 353
Greek   54, 310, 422, 426, 474, 477–479, 483, 540, 541
Gregory XIII, Pope   151, 257, 377
Greiff, Benedikt   4, 116
Greiff, Gerhard   161
Greiff-Köpf Company   116
Grétry, André   569
Grimm, Sigismund   555
Grimm, Simon   37
Gritschke, Caroline   312
Grünpeck, Josef   474
Gugliemi, Gregorio   522
guilds   9, 35, 50, 87, 89, 102–104, 111, 113, 123, 125–131, 135, 137–140, 142–143, 147–150, 174–176, 178, 224, 228–229, 231, 236–237, 239–242, 251, 271, 276–279, 282, 287–289, 294–298, 301, 303–307, 311,

guilds (cont.)
    313, 317, 319, 323–326, 329, 346, 369, 381,
    383–384, 392, 419–421, 444, 455, 463,
    495–496, 515, 518, 530, 544, 547–548,
    554
guildhalls   113, 148, 175, 277, 289, 544
guild processions   317, 319
Gullmann family   116
Gumpelzhaimer, Adam   560–561, 566
Gumpolt family   496
Günther, Matthäus   38, 522
Güntzer, Marx   562
Günzburg   117, 280, 373
Gustavus II Adolphus of Sweden, King   154,
    263, 328, 351–352, 360, 514–515

Haas/Hase, Hans Heinrich   149, 252
Habermann, Franz Xaver   522
Habsburg dynasty   33, 88, 105, 107, 117,
    130–131, 230, 240, 281, 355, 374, 401, 403,
    418, 431, 443, 447
Hagenau   430
Hagenauer, Friedrich   507
Halder, Joseph   116
Hall (Tyrol)   117
Hamburg   112, 165
Hämmerlin family   102
Hainhofer family   82, 515
Hainhofer, Christoph   515
Hainhofer, Philipp   112, 279, 405, 514–515,
    518, 562
Haintzel, Paul (Paulus)   482, 517
Hainzelmann, Ludwig   78
Hartmann, Susanna   265
Hassler, Hans Leo   561–562
Hätzlerin, Clara   554
Haug family   109, 231
Haug, Wolfgang   231
Haug-Langnauer Company   109
Haunstetten   23, 282
Haydn, Joseph   569
headwear   456
health care institutions   23, 37, 46–65, 115,
    256, 285, 350, 358, 543; see also
    barber-surgeons, midwives, Holy
    Ghost hospital, Pilgrim's House
Hebrew   378, 477
Hefelin, Apollonia   80

Heidelberg   430, 479
Heidingsfeld   373
Heiland, Samuel   352
Hel, Konrad   237
Helmschmied, Desiderius   466
Helmschmied, Kolman   463–464, 466, 499
Helmschmied, Lorenz   466
Hemerle, Ulrich   296
Henisch, Georg   482, 540
Henry II of France, King   111
Henry VIII of England, King   88
Herbrot, Jakob   87–88, 111, 141, 149, 239, 242,
    346–347
Hermann, Hans Jakob   248
Herwart family   87, 105, 109, 112, 140–141, 155,
    273, 346, 554
Herwart, Georg   87, 140–141, 346
Herwart, Hans David   155
Herwart, Johann Heinrich   554
Heupold, Bernhard   349
Hildebrandt, Reinhard   6
Hirn, Konrad   518
Hispaniola   110
historiography   3–13, 53, 69–80, 86, 88–90,
    247, 342, 475, 479, 543
Höchstädt   281
Hoechstetter family   109–110, 273, 350, 392,
    507
Hoechstetter, Ambrosius   109
Hoechstetter, Daniel   109
Hoechstetter, Georg   507
Hoechstetter, Philipp   350
Hofhaimer, Paul   555–556
Hohenkirchen   105
Holbein, Ambrosius   497
Holbein, Hans the Elder   497–498, 505,
    507–508, 509
Holbein, Hans the Younger   497
holidays   151–152, 257, 266, 317, 319, 324, 331,
    383–384
Holl, Elias   35, 49, 78, 115, 161, 263, 350–351,
    509, 511, 540, 541
Hölzl, Ludwig   565
Holy Cross church   222, 231, 255, 497, 505,
    565, 567
Holy Ghost hospital   49, 51
Holy Roman Empire   4, 8, 23, 34–35, 46, 48,
    75, 79, 88–89, 103, 107, 132, 135, 138, 155,

162, 165, 172, 176, 181, 186–187, 189, 191, 206, 208, 221, 223, 232–233, 235, 242–243, 248, 252, 260–261, 264, 289, 309, 312, 322, 344, 348, 350, 358, 368–371, 377–378, 391–395, 398–401, 406–408, 476, 508–509, 518, 533–534, 539, 541, 544–546, 553–554, 556, 563
Homann, Johann Baptist 36
Honold family 102, 273
Honold, Hans 102
honor 9, 79, 83, 87, 107, 111, 150, 165, 178, 182–184, 186, 209, 230, 257, 265, 277–279, 284, 287–288, 294, 296–297, 301, 303–304, 307, 313, 328, 419, 443–447, 454–455, 458, 461
Hopfer, Daniel 463–464, 499
horses 49, 114, 199, 317, 321–322, 326, 334, 345, 353, 357, 393, 447, 505
Höschel, David 478–479
households 9–10, 25–26, 28–29, 73, 80, 82, 89, 113, 116, 209, 257–258, 264, 271–274, 276, 283–284, 286, 295–299, 303–305, 307, 309, 318, 375, 423, 440, 442, 446, 450–451, 454, 461, 495, 507; see also children, families
Huber, Johann Josef Anton 38
humanism, humanists 4, 7–8, 10–11, 32–33, 59–60, 71, 77, 89–90, 132–133, 202, 222–224, 243, 310, 323, 377, 417–418, 422, 474–483, 499, 503, 505, 526, 533–534, 536–537, 539–541, 554–555, 562
Hungary 105, 107–109, 114, 230, 405, 442, 481, 520
Hurlacher, Jakob 554
Hut, Hans 233
Hutten, Ulrich von 56–57, 477

illegitimacy 301–303, 419
illumination 88, 417, 496
Ilsung family 158, 530
Imhof family 112, 231
Imhof, Hieronymus 231
Imperial Aulic Court 207
Imperial Chamber Court 152, 207
imperial diets 4, 21, 136–137, 146–147, 149, 208, 221, 224, 233–234, 240, 242, 249, 251–252, 289, 344, 348, 372, 378, 408, 443, 447, 477, 482, 505, 508, 512, 545, 553, 556
imperial police ordinance 253, 419
India 110–111, 290, 476, 500
indirect lordship 129–130, 141–142
inequality 28, 64, 271–276
infanticide 189, 302
inflation 115, 154, 261, 285, 349, 372, 564
Ingolstadt 226, 430–431, 473–474, 477–478, 483
inheritance law 197, 199–201, 203–204
innkeepers, tavernkeepers 164, 274–275, 298, 317, 331, 333–335; see also taverns
Innsbruck 431, 566
instruments (musical) 495, 556, 558–563, 565, 567; (scientific) 11, 482, 512–513, 515–517; (of torture) 178, 181
Interim, see Augsburg Interim
Isaac, Heinrich 555
Israel 344, 348, 351–352, 360, 367
Italy 12, 24, 77, 80, 102, 110, 112, 115–117, 173, 199, 201–202, 205, 209, 222, 284, 328, 353, 373, 392–395, 398–400, 405, 428–429, 432–433, 442, 445–446, 460, 466, 473–476, 478–479, 481–482, 500, 503, 507, 508–509, 512–513, 518, 520, 522, 526, 534–537, 553, 558–559, 561, 563–565

Jäger, Clemens 83, 87–88
Jahn, Joachim 26
Jardine, Lisa 442–443
Jerusalem 344, 352–353, 360, 516
Jesuits 151, 153, 241, 255–257, 322–323, 421, 427, 431–432, 479–480, 483, 485–486, 488, 511–512, 545, 559, 563, 565–567
Jews 162, 367–386, 418, 444, 450–451; see also anti-Judaism; court Jews
Johann of Saxony, Elector 235
Johann Frederick of Saxony, Elector 240
joiners 113, 128, 282, 287
Joseph I, Emperor 566, 569
Joseph I Ignaz Philipp Landgraf von Hessen-Darmstadt, Bishop 566
journeymen 9, 31, 114, 183, 271, 276–278, 280–283, 286–289, 296, 300–301, 303–305, 331, 420, 423, 444, 454, 496–497

jousting 320–321, 328, 334
Jubal 503
Jung family 60

Kager, Matthias 511
Kant, Immanuel 488
Karg, Johannes 241
Kaufbeuren 30, 102, 141, 281
Kaula Bank 383
Kellenbenz, Hermann 6
Keller, Hans 459
Keller, Michael 141, 229, 231, 236, 239
Kempten 234, 281
Kepler, Johannes 483
Kerle, Jacobus de 557–558
Kern, Blasius 226
keyboards 559, 561–562, 565, 567, 569
Kiesow, Johann Georg 63
Kießling, Rolf 7, 25, 129, 277, 290
Kilian, Lucas 35
Kilian, Wolfgang 36, 540
kinship 9, 81–83, 112, 153, 274, 401; see also families
Kitzinger family 380
Klausen (South Tyrol) 117
Klingenstein family 559, 564
Klingenstein, Bernhard 559
Knoder family 496
Knopf, Hans Jakob 452
Knöringen, Heinrich von, Bishop 154, 350, 559
Kölderer, Georg 11, 78, 153, 402
Köpplin, Jakob 508, 560
Koppmayer, Jakob 406–407, 423, 567
Köthen 116
Kötzler, Franz 207
Kraffter family 111
Krakow 102, 105, 516
Krämer, Gode 512
Krauss family 36, 487
Krauss, Johann Thomas 36
Kriegsdorfer, Tobias 566
Kriegshaber 373–374, 380–384
Kriesstein, Melchior 557
Kron family 496
Küchlin family 76, 86, 89
Kugelmann, Anna 451
Kugelmann, Johann 557

Kulmbach 376
Künast, Hans-Jörg 310
Künle, Martin 260
Kusser, Johann Sigismund 569

Lake Como 117
Lake Constance 24, 102, 406
Landau family 380
Lang, Matthäus 556
Langenbucher, Achilles 562
Langenmantel family 79, 158, 233–234, 289
Langenmantel, Christoph 223–224
Langenmantel, David 79
Langenmantel, Joseph Anton Leopold Wolfgang 158
Langenmantel, Ulrich 133
language learning 4, 11, 296, 311, 417, 472–473, 477, 480
Large Council 125–127, 148, 156; see also city council
Lasso, Orlando di 560–561
Latin 32, 55, 75–76, 138, 209, 310, 323, 351, 415, 421–422, 424–428, 430, 432–433, 477, 479–480, 499, 503, 517, 540, 555, 557, 559–561
Lauginger family 273
Lauingen 102, 149, 431
law 46, 48, 156–157, 171–178, 181–182, 185, 188, 190–191, 196–211, 222, 228, 231, 236, 255, 275, 294, 297–298, 301, 305–306, 309, 312, 317–318, 368–369, 372, 374, 377, 385, 401, 419, 421, 471–473, 475; see also bankruptcy law; canon law; commercial law; common law; contract law; corporate law; family law; inheritance law; matrimonial law; Roman law; statutory law
Lech 20–21, 23–25, 27–28, 31, 35, 102, 114, 161–162, 164, 281, 374
Lech Quarter 21, 27–28, 330
Lechhausen 25, 282
legal history 171–191, 196–211
Leipzig 115, 287, 407, 418, 420, 429–431, 443, 566
legislation 156, 176, 203–204, 206, 443, 446, 454; see also decrees, laws, legal history, ordinances
Leibniz, Gottfried Wilhelm 485

INDEX

Leichnam, Michael 265
Leipzig 287, 407, 418, 420, 429–431, 443, 566
leisure 316–336; see also entertainment, games, music, sociability, sports
Leo X, Pope 224
Leopold I, Emperor 407
Lestainnier, Jean 557
Leupold, Hans 233
libraries 4, 8, 10, 13, 78, 117, 201, 329, 404, 421, 471, 476, 478–479, 481, 484, 539–540, 541–542, 554, 560, 562
Licinio, Bernardino 512
Lieb, Norbert 7, 535
Liebert (von Liebenhofen), Johann Adam 116, 380, 522
Liechtenstein, Ursula von 256
Linay, Josef 335
Lindau 116, 234, 372
Lippi, Filippino 503
Lipsius, Justus 481
Lisbon 108, 110, 443, 505, 516
literacy 12, 70, 73, 310, 343, 422, 430, 470, 473, 480
liturgy 222, 238–239, 241, 256, 417; liturgical drama 554; liturgical music 222, 553–555, 559
livery 444, 446–447
locksmiths 282, 288, 547
Lombardo, Pietro 503
London 183, 516
Lords' drinking hall 36, 87, 157–160, 274, 444
Lotter, Johann Jakob 569
Lotter, Tobias Conrad 37
lotteries 326–327, 409
Low Countries 430, 450, 553; see also Netherlands
Loyola, Ignatius of 241
Ludwig of Bavaria-Landshut, Duke 103
Lully, Jean-Baptiste 567, 569
Lur, Heinrich 474
lutes 332, 554, 561–562, 567
Luther, Martin 133–134, 223–226, 229, 231, 237–238, 250, 309, 376, 425–426, 432, 478, 505, 556
Lutheranism, Lutherans 30–31, 59, 133, 147, 151, 154, 183, 221, 226, 229, 231–232, 234–236, 238, 240–242, 247–248, 252, 255, 257–258, 260, 262, 264–267, 276, 343–344, 348–354, 360, 423, 445, 486, 505, 540, 557; see also Protestantism
luxury trades 101, 105, 225, 279, 322, 379, 429, 442, 445–446, 467, 495, 499, 513, 518, 572
Luython, Carl 562
Lyons 108, 112, 115, 296, 392, 442, 452

Mader, Johann 477
Mader, Valentin 37
Maestrazgos 107
Mainz 32, 289, 373
Mair, Alexander 36
Mair, Paul Hektor 83–85, 87, 447–448, 461–462
Mair, Paulus 508
Mändle family 379–380
Mang, Christoph 423
Manger, Michael 406, 418, 423
Manlich family 109
Manlich, Melchior 111
Manlich-Katzbeck Company 109
Mansfeld 108–109, 116
Manutius, Aldus 499
maps 28, 32, 35–37, 418, 476, 487, 500, 516
Maria Stern, convent 222
Marie Antoinette, princess (later Queen of France) 38
markets 5, 13, 20, 28, 35, 47–49, 57, 59–61, 64–65, 83, 87–88, 101–102, 104–105, 107–109, 111–112, 114–116, 118, 132, 150, 157, 164, 177, 197, 204, 208, 271, 277, 283, 288, 303, 318, 320, 322, 324, 328, 334–335, 374–377, 381–382, 385, 391, 395, 398, 401, 408–409, 422, 424–425, 428–429, 432, 443, 459, 472, 484, 507, 511–512, 518, 520, 531, 535, 539, 545–546, 563
marriage 10, 26, 30–31, 59–60, 81, 87–88, 132, 134, 140, 156, 158–159, 200, 205–206, 225–226, 234, 239, 241, 251, 253–254, 256–257, 265, 274, 276–277, 282, 288, 294–296, 298–310, 333, 398, 423, 446, 456, 475–476, 496; see also families, weddings
Marseilles 111
Maschenbauer family 408–409
Maschenbauer, Andreas 408, 567

Maschenbauer, Johann Andreas Erdmann   408–409
masons   547
material culture   11, 440–467, 512–520
mathematics   377, 482–484, 486, 512, 515
matrimonial law, marriage Law   199–200, 206
Mauermüller family   496
Maximilian I, Emperor   4, 33, 77, 86, 105, 107, 109, 130–132, 209, 224, 466, 475–476, 478, 499–500, 533, 553, 555–556, 562
Maximilian I of Bavaria, Elector   349
Maximilian II Emanuel of Bavaria, Elector   355
Maximilian IV of Bavaria, Elector   358
mayors   3, 12, 23, 31, 38, 76, 79, 87–88, 111, 125–129, 133, 137, 139–141, 148–149, 151, 155, 157, 182, 226, 236–237 239–240, 295, 346, 418–419, 474, 479, 537, 545, 562
Mayr, Georg   353
Mayr, Johann Georg   569
Mayr, Leonhard Christian   548
Meadow, Mark   512
Meckhart, Johannes   253
media   37, 69–70, 74–75, 89–90, 261, 349–350, 357, 385, 391, 406–410, 415, 499; see also news, printing
medical marketplace   47–48, 57, 59–61, 64–65
Medici, Francesco I de', Grand Duke of Tuscany   466
medicine   11, 46–65, 164, 189, 306–307, 320, 344, 425, 432, 473, 482, 484, 486; see also health care institutions
Mediterranean   101, 111, 117
Mehrer, Hans   403
Meisterlin, Sigismund   32–33, 76–77, 86, 89, 471, 475
Meistersinger   323–324, 554, 569
Melanchthon, Philipp   234, 238, 252
Melhorn, Georg   253
Melk   470
Meltzer, Adam   563
Memmingen   102, 234, 265, 281
Memory memory   3, 53, 69–72, 80–81, 83, 89–90, 255, 284, 450, 511; see also commemoration

merchants   3–5, 7, 9, 11, 36, 49, 58, 72–73, 77–78, 83, 89, 101–105, 107, 109–112, 114–118, 125, 130, 132–133, 147–149, 153, 156–157, 159, 161–164, 186, 199, 201, 204–205, 224–225, 228, 242, 249, 273–276, 279, 287, 295–296, 307–308, 310, 317, 346, 349, 359–360, 369, 376, 379–380, 383–384, 391–395, 397–398, 400, 402–403, 426, 429–430, 443–445, 467, 472–473, 475–476, 479, 503, 507, 510, 512, 515, 518, 520, 537, 544, 562
Merchants' drinking hall   36, 159, 274–275, 444
Merck, Johann   560
mercury trade   108–109, 116
Merian, Matthäus   36
Meuting family   82, 104, 111, 308, 392
Mexico   108
microscopes   484
Middle Ages   7, 10, 20, 24–26, 28, 48, 75–76, 90, 101–102, 161, 172–174, 196–201, 203–204, 208–209, 211, 222–223, 239, 272, 284, 300, 311, 325, 348, 367, 373, 376, 385, 391, 421, 470, 527–528, 532
midwives   58, 60, 302, 306–307, 311
migrations   26, 30–31, 112, 140, 248, 256, 264, 271, 280–283, 343, 346, 373, 385, 406, 424, 486
Milan   108, 475, 563
Miller, Jacob   300
Miller, Matthäus (Matheus)   11
Mindelheim   280
mining   104–105, 107–109, 112, 114, 130, 273, 392, 431, 518, 520
Mittenwald   24
Moehner, Reginbald   353
monks   32, 73, 76–77, 86, 89, 128, 227, 237, 241, 309, 471, 477, 517, 557; see also convents
Montaigne, Michel de   254, 299, 539
Monte, Philippe de   562
Montesquieu, Charles-Louis de Secondat, Baron de   46–47
More, Thomas   477
Moritz of Saxony, Elector   240, 242
motets   555, 557–559, 561, 566
Moy, Josef Anton   408

INDEX

Mozart, Leopold   565, 567, 569
Mozart, Wolfgang Amadeus   565, 567, 569
Muffat, Georg   566–567
Mühlberg, Battle of   240, 508, 512
Müller (Mylius), Georg   152, 255
Mülich family   32–33, 38, 77, 82, 89
Münster, Sebastian   36
mumming   318, 322
Münch, Christian von   116
Munich   5, 24, 58, 69, 82, 116, 329, 383, 428, 479, 507, 539, 544–545, 557
Musculus, Wolfgang   236, 239, 241
music   317–318, 322–323, 326–328, 332, 334–335, 353, 357, 418, 503, 512, 515, 553–569; see also singing, songs; instruments (musical)
music printing   555–556, 562–563, 567
Mylius, Georg, see Müller

Nachtigall, Ottmar   225, 230–231
Naples   104
Napoleonic Wars   27, 345, 358–359
Negker, Jobst de   500
Neidhardt, Wolfgang   510
Netherlands   112, 117, 146, 230, 284, 392–393, 400–401; see also Low Countries
Neuburger family   380
Neuhofer family   117, 280
Neuhofer, Georg   117
Neusidler, Melchior   561
Neusohl   105, 109
news, newspapers, newsprints, newsletters   78, 261, 332, 391–410, 418, 426–427, 433, 472, 480
Nicolai, Friedrich   428
Nidermair, Anna   52, 54, 57
Niger, Theobald   236
Nijmwegen   407
Nördlingen   102, 104, 372–373
nuns   25, 128, 222, 237, 241, 248–249, 252, 308–309, 311, 330–331, 458, 497; see also convents
Nuremberg   21, 76, 82, 101, 104, 109, 116, 133, 137–138, 149, 176, 186, 201, 203–205, 223, 229, 235, 282, 300, 310, 355, 372–373, 392, 394–395, 413, 428, 430, 446, 474, 479, 486, 513, 520, 549, 555, 562

Oberhausen   23, 25, 282, 373–374
Obermayer-Kaula, Jakob   383
Obwexer family   117–118, 159
Obwexer, Johann   117
Obwexer, Joseph Anton   118
Obwexer, Peter Paul   118
Occo family   60
Ödenhofer, Thomas   474
Öfelin family   530
Öglin, Erhard   395, 555
Öhringen   430
opera   324, 335, 566, 569
Oppenheimer family   380
optics   484, 517, 533
Ott, David   508
Ottoman Empire   107, 111, 116, 406, 476–477, 480–481
ordinances   59, 104, 112, 133, 138–140, 150, 155, 175–176, 179, 200, 205–211, 230, 238–239, 253, 275, 278, 284–285, 289, 295, 299, 302, 305, 316, 318, 327, 329, 349, 357, 419–420, 443, 445, 454, 456, 547, 558; see also decrees, imperial police ordinances, wedding ordinances
Ordinari-Post-Zeitung   407–409
organs (human)   56–57; (musical)   126, 503, 518, 554–556, 558–562, 564–567
orphans, orphanages   10, 115, 200, 285–286, 302, 452
Österreicher, Georg   149
Otmar, Silvan   378
Our Lady's Suburb (*Frauenvorstadt*)   21, 27–29, 368, 527
overseas trade   3, 7, 53, 101, 105, 110–111, 118, 221, 443

Padua   474–475
painting, painters   33, 35, 37–38, 76, 78, 87, 329, 333, 443, 463, 495–497, 499–500, 505, 507–508, 511–512, 515, 522, 536, 539, 546, 556, 558
Paler, Wolfgang   103
Paler-Weiß Company   11
Palmer Wandel, Lee   442
pamphlets   5, 63, 74, 78, 90, 225, 232, 248, 257, 349, 351, 395, 397, 406, 420, 423, 425–427, 488
Panvinio, Onophrio   479

Panzau, Octavian 565
Paracelsus 59, 484
Paris 63, 258, 407–408, 479, 497, 515, 520
parity 3, 29, 46, 154–156, 207, 248–249, 264–265, 323, 354, 371, 420, 564
Passau 242, 252, 566
patricians, patriciate 3, 11–12, 23, 31, 36, 48, 50, 59–60, 78–79, 82–83, 87–89, 102, 125–126, 128, 133, 139–140, 142, 146–150, 153–159, 161–162, 165, 174, 208, 224, 231, 235, 240, 251, 273–275, 278, 289, 310, 320–321, 325, 328–329, 346, 348, 351, 354, 359–360, 381, 400, 403, 444–445, 452, 458, 461, 463, 471–476, 482, 488, 507, 509, 518, 530, 536, 539, 542–543, 553–554, 562
patronage 7, 13, 61, 71, 74, 78, 86, 128, 495, 499, 503, 505, 507–508, 513, 520, 523, 526–527, 529, 534–536, 548, 562
Paul IV, Pope 376
Paumann, Jakob 558
Pavia 474
pawnbroking, pawning 113, 369, 374–375, 380–381, 442, 450–451
Payen, Nicolas 557
Peace of Westphalia 10, 29, 46, 115, 154–155, 249, 264–266, 354, 424, 481, 564, 566
peasants 258, 310, 353, 381, 454, 459
Peasants' War 135–136, 228–229, 344, 426
peddlers 317, 327, 431
Pedroni Company 117
Pembold, Maria 451
pepper 110–111
Perlach Tower, Perlach Square 20–21, 33, 185, 530, 543, 546
Peru 108
Petel, Georg 518
Peutinger, Claudius Pius 147, 237
Peutinger, Conrad 7, 44, 77, 89, 132–133, 135, 202, 223, 230, 310, 422, 475–477, 499–500, 536–537, 555
Pfalz-Neuburg, principality 149, 398
Pfersee 23, 373–374, 380–384
Philidor, François-André Danican 569
Philip II of Spain, King 88, 107, 461, 466
Philip of Hesse, Landgrave 235, 239–240, 345
philosophy 46, 433, 487–488

physics 486
physicians 46–47, 51–65, 153, 239, 275, 306–307, 346, 350, 474, 479–480, 482, 484, 486
Piccinni, Niccolò 569
Pilgrim House 49, 51–52, 285
Pinicianus, Johannes 477
Pirckheimer, Willibald 477
plague, plague houses 50, 53–57, 60–61, 115, 261, 318, 322, 349, 353
Plummer, Marjorie E. 309
Poland 373, 405, 430, 520
politics 3, 5–7, 9–10, 26, 30, 33, 46, 48, 58–60, 62, 64, 70–73, 76–79, 86, 88–89, 101–103, 105, 107, 111, 123–143, 146–165, 171–172, 190, 221, 236, 241, 243, 247, 249–250, 253, 257–258, 261–262, 266, 273, 295, 303, 311–312, 316–318, 324, 332, 336, 342, 344, 346–347, 349, 351–352, 355, 357, 359–360, 372, 376–377, 379, 382, 385, 391–392, 395, 397, 401, 405, 407, 415, 421, 426, 432, 444, 447, 470, 472, 474–476, 481, 488, 496, 509–510, 526, 529–530, 532, 534–535, 539, 543–545, 553, 557
Pölnitz, Götz von 6
Pomerania 279, 513, 562
Pontanus, Jakob 479
poor relief 49–51, 118, 133, 150, 154, 163–164, 239, 276, 283–286, 301, 306, 318, 324, 335, 350, 535; see also Alms Office, Fuggerei, poverty
population 9, 25–32, 49–50, 53, 73, 88, 115, 127, 140, 148, 172, 186–187, 206, 222, 226, 243, 248, 251–252, 256, 266, 271, 275, 276, 283, 285, 301–302, 310, 318, 320, 343, 351, 354, 359, 371, 373, 378, 380, 381, 397, 481, 546
Portugal 6, 110–111, 115, 392, 399
postal routes, postal system 114, 393, 399–400, 402; see also courier service
Potsdam 116
poverty 8, 28, 31, 49, 51, 63–65, 101–103, 113, 115, 119, 125, 133–134, 141, 147, 158, 163–164, 176, 183, 223–225, 228, 271, 274–276, 283–286, 336, 349–350, 359, 445, 450, 535; see also Alms Office, Fuggerei, poor relief, workhouses

INDEX

Prague 102, 459, 511
Preiss, Sabina 312
privileges 3, 23, 110, 130, 146, 150, 153, 206, 206, 208, 210, 223, 228, 241, 272, 368, 372, 374–375, 377, 379, 383–384, 407, 421, 423–424, 444, 548, 554, 569
printing, printers 4, 11, 56, 74, 77, 79, 83, 86–87, 90, 114, 117–118, 134, 163, 223, 225, 256–257, 261–262, 276, 280, 282–283, 290, 308, 310, 345, 391, 394–395, 397, 401–403, 405–409, 415–433, 450, 470–471, 473, 475, 479–480, 482–487, 499–500, 512, 518, 520, 522, 533, 547–548, 555–557, 560–563, 567, 569; see also book production; broadsheets; music printing; news
propaganda 78, 86, 261, 397, 401, 427, 499–500
prostitution 298, 300–301, 329, 370, 444, 458
Protestantism, Protestants 3, 10, 27, 29–31, 47, 50–51, 54–55, 57, 111, 116–117, 138, 143, 146–149, 151–155, 157–158, 221, 226, 229–243, 247–267, 281–283, 295, 297, 308, 310, 323, 330, 348, 350–354, 357, 359–360, 376–377, 407, 420–421, 423–424, 426–428, 431, 447, 478–479, 481, 484–488, 508–509, 520, 543, 553, 556–557, 560, 563–564, 566, 569; see also Anabaptism, Lutheranism, Reformation, Zwinglianism
providence 343
psalters 557
psychology 181, 350, 355, 445
public houses, see innkeepers, taverns
publishing 10–11, 37, 83, 117, 284, 415–418, 421–424, 426–428, 431–433, 479, 483, 486–487, 500, 518, 547, 556, 569
punishment 54, 62, 146, 152, 171–172, 175–176, 178–179, 181–190, 255, 260–261, 263, 294, 297, 301, 318, 326, 344, 349, 357, 454
Purst, Peter 323
Pythagoras 503

quartering 115, 164, 242, 263, 343, 358
Quesnay, François 487

rabbis 368, 374
races 317, 322, 326
Rad-Hößlin Company 116
Rader, Matthäus 479, 511, 559
rape 172, 179, 299, 307
Ratdolt, Erhard 416, 499–500, 555
Rauner Company 116
Rauwolff, Leonhard 153, 480
Rauwolff, Sixt 562
Ravensburg 102, 154
Reformation 4–6, 9–11, 25, 35, 50, 55, 74, 78, 82, 88–89, 107, 123, 125, 128, 131, 133–142, 175–176, 184, 190, 201, 204, 221–243, 247, 250, 266, 284–285, 294–295, 297, 300–301, 303, 308–312, 316, 332, 336, 343–344, 349, 359, 376, 397, 415, 417, 419, 421–422, 425–427, 432, 444, 458, 477–478, 484, 505, 509, 540, 556, 559
Regensburg 149, 272, 403, 408
Regnart, Jakob 562
Rehlinger family 87, 139–140, 148, 151, 226, 230–231, 240, 273, 419
Rehlinger, Anton Christoph 151
Rehlinger, Bernhard 419
Rehlinger, Heinrich 148
Rehlinger, Konrad 231
Rehlinger, Ulrich 223, 231
Rehlinger, Wolfgang 139, 231
Reichle, Hans 511
Reiffenstein, Albrecht 399
Reinhard, Wolfgang 9
Reinhold, Johann 517
Reininghaus, Wilfried 287
Reith, Reinhold 9
Rem, Lucas 4, 82, 392
Renaissance 4–5, 7, 11–12, 33, 86, 88, 104, 222, 236, 325, 328, 442–444, 446, 503, 505, 508–509, 511, 526, 534–537
Rener, Adam 555
religious coexistence 10, 32, 50, 136, 140, 155, 242–243, 247–267, 348; see also bi-confessionalism, confessions, parity
religious conflict 78, 177, 249, 257–264, 266, 344, 357, 377, 401, 423, 476, 496; see also calendar; Schmalkaldic War
Religious Peace of Augsburg 151, 221, 243, 253, 344, 348, 391, 418, 481, 508, 518, 553, 557, 563

Remshart, Karl   37, 546
Reuchlin, Johannes   377, 477
Rhegius, Urbanus   226, 228, 231, 236, 478
Reith, Reinhold   9
Richenthal, Ulrich   74
Richter, Tobias   566
Riedenburger, Anton   260
Rieger, Matthias   431–432
riots, revolts   87, 102–103, 134–135, 140, 142, 146, 148–149, 152–153, 156, 158–159, 252, 290, 228, 252, 257–259, 264, 271, 286–287, 289–290, 294, 311, 348, 350, 359, 426, 488, 507; see also calendar; Peasants' War
Rococo   520, 522
Roeck, Bernd   9–10, 26, 28, 274, 353
Rogel, Hans   36–37
Rogendorf, Wilhelm Freiherr zu   463–464
Roll, Georg   517
Roman law   172–174, 199, 201, 204, 377, 475
Roman origins of Augsburg   3, 8, 20, 24, 32–35, 76–77, 89, 476, 479, 499, 509–10, 528, 534, 536–537, 540, 543–545
Rome   76, 105, 107, 159, 251, 344, 399, 404, 442, 475, 479, 483, 497, 503, 540, 541, 545, 563–564
Roper, Lyndal   276, 295, 304, 309
Rosenau   325, 334–335
Rosheim, Josel von   377
Rosselli Family   503
Roth, Friedrich   5–6
Rothenburg ob der Tauber   373
Rublack, Ulinka   442, 447, 458
Rudolf I, Emperor   4, 172, 192, 197
Rudolf II, Emperor   374
rumors   255, 257–258, 261
Ryff, Walter   544
Rynmann, Johannes   417, 430–431

Sachs, Hans   324
Safley, Thomas M.   10, 452
Sailer, Bartholomäus   374
Sailer, Gereon   239, 346
Sailer, Hieronymus   110
Sales, Pietro Pompeo   566
Salminger, Sigmund   557, 561
Salomon, Andreas   451
Salzburg   24, 30, 109, 431, 486

Sandrart, Joachim von   164, 522
Sansovino, Jacobo   541
Sauer, Manfred   417
Saxony   86, 104, 109, 111, 118, 149, 238, 242, 281–282, 290, 394, 406, 482
Schaezler Palace   522
Scharnitz   24
Schaumberg, Peter von, Bishop   33, 470–471, 474, 554
Schedel, Hartmann   479
Schedel, Hermann   474, 479
Scheiffelhut, Jakob   567
Scheiner, Christoph   483
Scheppelin, Johann   265
Schertlin von Burtenbach, Sebastian   239–240, 326, 346–347
Scheurl, Christoph   223
Schieler, Thomas   262
Schiffle, Jeremias   399
Schilling, Johann   87, 134–137, 226–228
Schilling, Michael   405
Schirle, Anton Maria   517
Schissler, Christoph   36, 483, 515–516
Schmalkaldic League   138–139, 141, 146, 238–240, 345, 420, 450, 508
Schmalkaldic War   141–142, 146–147, 241, 251, 308, 345–348, 426, 432, 557
Schmid, Joseph   60
Schnurbein, Markus von   116, 380
Schongau   559
Schönig family   418, 567
Schönig, Johann Jakob   567
Schönig, Johann Ulrich   563
schools   150, 164, 209, 237, 239, 251, 253, 256, 263, 266, 310, 322–324, 327–329, 344, 347, 349, 355, 368, 421–422, 427, 473, 477, 479, 517, 540, 541, 544, 554, 556, 559–570, 569
Schroeck, Lucas   486
Schüle, Johann Heinrich (von)   38, 117–118, 280, 547–548
Schultes, Hans   423–424, 427, 563
Schwartzkopf, Michael   186
Schwarz, Chajim   378
Schwarz, Hans   507
Schwarz, Matthäus   12, 83, 106, 447, 459–461
Schwarz, Veit Konrad   440, 459
Schwarz, Ulrich   77, 83, 89, 128–129

Schweingen family   530
Schwenckfeld, Kaspar   260, 431
Schwenckfelders   247, 253–254, 259–260, 312
science   5, 11, 58, 69, 223–224, 243, 256, 342–343, 409, 433, 481–487, 515–516, 547; see also physics, chemistry
sculpture, sculptors   34, 463, 495–497, 503, 505, 507–511, 515, 518, 522, 528, 539, 541–542, 545
Secret Council   139–141, 148, 155–156, 359, 545
Seehausen   431
Seida, Joseph Jakob Adam von   158
Seida und Landensberg, Franz Eugen von   4, 48, 158
Seitz family   83
Seitz, Mang   231, 236–237
Seld, Georg Sigmund   147
Seld, Jörg   35–36, 74
Sender, Clemens   77, 86, 443
Senfl, Ludwig   555
sermons   5, 33, 134, 140, 222, 226–227, 231–232, 236, 241, 266, 319, 349, 351–352, 372, 428, 431, 470
Seutter family   37, 487
Seutter, Matthäus   37
Seven Years' War   290, 358
sexuality   279, 294–304, 332–33, 453, 456, 458
shoemakers   104, 113–114, 227, 282, 289
shooting grounds, shooting matches   317, 320, 325–328, 334–335, 381, 451
Siber, Georg   451
Siedeler, Georg (Jörg)   78, 82
Sigismund, King/Emperor   23, 103, 371, 554
Sigismund of Tyrol, Archduke   104–105
Sieh-Burens, Katarina   10, 140, 149
Silbermann, Johann Andreas   567
Silesia   103, 118, 282
silk   112, 442, 445–446, 451–452, 459, 461
silversmiths   114, 117, 279, 283, 415, 454, 518, 520
silver trade   24, 101, 104–105, 108–109, 114, 116–117, 380–381, 442, 520, 522
singing, songs   69, 90, 149, 257, 261–262, 312, 318, 324, 329, 332, 336, 345, 347–348, 351–352, 395, 427, 554–555, 558–559, 563, 565, 567; see als Meistersinger
Singold   300, 329, 509
Sirturus, Hieronymus   481
Sixtus V, Pope   541
skinners   265, 279
slaves, slave trade   110, 184
sleigh-riding   318, 320–322, 353
Small Council   126–129, 134, 137, 140, 147–148, 150–151, 155–156, 174–175, 179–182, 185, 264, 531
Smith, Adam   487
sociability   9–10, 277, 316–317, 319, 322, 324, 327, 329–334
social discipline   117, 139–140, 150, 171, 175, 179, 183, 238–239, 247, 295, 316–318, 332, 536
social hierarchy   271–276, 295, 303, 317, 518
soldiers   27–28, 51, 107, 147, 152, 228, 232, 238–239, 252, 256–258, 263–264, 266, 288, 290, 311, 326, 330, 342, 345–346, 350–354, 357–358, 360, 374, 382, 403, 447, 451; see also troops
Sorg, Anton   74
Spain   6, 88, 107, 115, 146, 230, 355, 392, 395, 399–400, 428, 445, 459, 461, 466
Span, Anton   558
Späths, Franz Joseph   567
Speiser, Johann   226, 228
Speyer   136, 152, 234, 377
spices   24, 61, 101, 105, 110–111, 442
sports   317, 324–329, 455
Spreng, Johann   209
Springer, Balthasar   500
Stadion, Christoph von, Bishop   223, 225–226, 229, 234, 477
Stadtbuch of Augsburg   172, 176, 186, 197–202, 204
Stadtpfeifer (city piper corps)   332, 554, 562
Stadtpyr   445–446, 463, 511
St. Afra   38, 532
St. Anna   7, 151, 209, 222–223, 226, 231, 236–237, 241, 251, 255–256, 258, 323, 329, 354–355, 421–422, 477–478, 482–483, 503, 505, 517–518, 535, 540–542, 556, 560, 564, 566
St. Clara   222
St. Georg   222, 500, 505

St. Jacob   21, 528
St. Jacob's Suburb (*Jakobervorstadt*)   21, 27–29, 49, 152, 164, 264, 284, 330, 535–536
St. Katharina   222, 237, 497
St. Margaret   222
St. Martin   222
St. Moritz   222, 226, 230–231, 236
St. Nicholas   222
St. Peter   20, 546
St. Salvator   256, 323, 421, 479, 486, 488, 559, 567
St. Sebastian   49
St. Servatius   49
St. Stephan   222, 262
Sts. Ulrich and Afra   23, 33, 76, 222, 237, 252, 323, 416, 470–471, 474, 477, 496, 505, 508, 511, 526, 534, 536, 554, 559–561
St. Ursula   222, 237, 256, 330
St. Wolfgang   49
statutory law   171, 202–203, 206
Stein, Johann Andreas   567–568
Steiner, Heinrich   419, 427
Steppach   373–374, 380, 382, 384
stereotypes   375–378, 381, 383, 385, 401
Stetten family   83, 158
Stetten, Paul von, the Elder   3, 164, 354
Stetten, Paul von, the Younger   3–4, 12, 38, 79, 83, 164, 358, 495, 522
Steuer, Peter   10
stigmatization   370, 375
Stöcklein, Joseph   486
Stöer, Lorenz   513
Strasbourg   74, 86, 137, 139, 229, 234–236, 238, 407, 425, 430, 561
Strassburger Bank   383
Strada, Jacopo   479
Streber, Abraham   25
Strieder, Jakob   5–6
strikes   271, 286–289, 321
Stuart, Kathy   62, 287–288, 445, 447
Sturm, August   407–408, 423
Sturm, Paul   562
Stuttgart   289
suburbs, see Lech Quarter; Our Lady's Suburb; St. Jacob's Suburb
sugar   101, 110
Sulzer family   31, 82–83

Sulzer, Wolfgang Jakob   31
sumptuary legislation   150, 357, 443, 445–446, 454; see also wedding ordinances
Sustris, Friedrich   512, 539
Sustris, Lambert   512
Swabia   4, 6–7, 21, 86, 101–103, 108–110, 113, 117, 123, 131–132, 137–138, 160, 222–223, 233, 280–282, 373–374, 377, 430, 522, 549
Swabian League   131–132, 137–138, 233
Sweden   27, 115, 154, 263, 328, 351–354, 421, 427, 459, 515, 517, 564
swimming   318, 329–330; see also bathing
Switzerland   24, 107, 132, 141, 229, 281, 295, 382, 463, 520
sword-fighting   317, 326–328, 451
symphonies   558, 560, 565, 569
synagogues   368, 371, 379–380
Szczecin   105

Tagwercker, Martin   451
tailors   113, 282, 288, 394, 440, 450, 452, 459
tanners   459
tavernkeepers, see innkeepers
taverns   38, 164, 177, 247, 274, 266, 298, 304, 317–319, 323, 331–335, 378, 382, 384, 444; see also innkeepers
taxes   5, 8, 25–29, 102–103, 107, 113–114, 126, 146, 150, 153, 156, 158, 162, 164, 176, 197, 199, 222, 225, 228, 237, 240, 264, 271–276, 286, 305, 308, 311, 318, 355, 358, 368–369, 371–372, 379–380, 384, 398, 416, 496, 530; see also excise tax
Taxis (Tassis) family   114, 393
Tegernsee   470
Telemann, Georg Philipp   566
telescopes   483–484, 517
textile production   3, 13, 31, 38, 101–104, 113, 116–117, 161, 274–275, 277, 280–282, 287–288, 290, 381, 415, 442, 547–548, 553; see also weavers, weaving
theater   70, 164, 318, 323–324, 329, 335, 473–474, 480, 569
Thenn family   83
Thirty Years' War   4, 7, 9, 26, 28, 37, 50, 78, 101, 113, 115, 117, 154, 161, 187, 207, 248–249, 260–261, 266, 271, 275–276,

279, 285, 324, 326, 344–345, 348–349,
    357, 360, 378–379, 406, 421, 423–424,
    427, 432, 479, 481, 484, 513, 518, 545, 553,
    555, 563
Three Cities' League   137–139
Thuringia   105, 109, 116, 282, 355
Thurzo, Johann   105
Titian   512
Tlusty, B. Ann   454
toleration   3, 29, 221, 233, 243, 249, 252, 373;
    see also religious co-existance
topography   20–27, 34, 36, 271, 274, 391, 476,
    481, 483, 485, 528, 534–535
Torelli, Giuseppe   567
torture   110, 173, 180–182, 299, 312
tournaments   83, 320–322, 325, 461, 466; see
    also jousting
town hall, see city hall
trade   3, 5–7, 10, 23–24, 29, 31, 60–62,
    101–105, 109–118, 125, 156, 161, 197, 199,
    201–203, 208, 221, 225, 228, 235, 265,
    272, 275–280, 282, 288–289, 294, 296,
    303, 305–306, 310, 334, 368–369,
    374–376, 379–386, 391–392, 406, 415,
    417–421, 423–424, 427–433, 442–444,
    450–451, 466, 495–496, 500, 513, 515,
    518, 520, 522, 547, 553–554; see also
    commerce
trade bans   103, 280, 381
transportation   24, 112, 114, 391, 393, 487
Tremezzo   117
troops   27, 38, 107, 115–116, 142, 146, 164, 235,
    240–242, 251, 257, 263, 345–346, 349,
    351, 353–355, 358, 379–380, 383, 479,
    564; see also soldiers
Tübingen   152, 430–431
Tucher, Lienhart   394
Turks, see Ottoman Empire
Twinger, Jakob   74, 86
Tyrol   104, 107–109, 114, 117, 159, 282, 393, 431,
    442, 499

Ulhart, Philipp   395, 417, 427, 557, 563
Ullmann, Sabine   450
Ulm   21, 102, 131, 133, 137–139, 229, 235, 281,
    347, 355, 372–373, 409, 503
Ulman family   380
Ulman, Hendle Ephraim   383

Ulman, Löw Simon   280
Ulman, Samuel   380
universities   5, 8–9, 55, 59, 152, 156–157, 199,
    222, 226, 306, 400, 421–422, 430–431,
    433, 473–474, 477, 479, 483, 486, 526,
    563
Unterburger, Klaus   471
Urlsperger, Samuel   486

Veils   147, 277, 306, 456
Veith family   428
Veith, Franz Anton   79
velvet   112, 442, 445–446, 451, 461
Venezuela   110
Venice   101–105, 108, 111–112, 114–115, 117, 184,
    280, 296, 354, 392, 399, 404, 416, 425,
    430, 442, 459, 473, 478, 499–500, 503,
    505, 507–508, 512, 541, 559–561, 563
Verhelst, Egid   518, 522
Via Claudia Augusta   20, 24, 528
Vienna   102, 114–116, 155, 159–160, 162, 165,
    207, 380, 399–400, 407, 424, 431, 463,
    515, 548, 566
Villach   105
violence   62, 135, 179, 182, 184, 188, 226,
    228–229, 248, 254, 257, 259, 266, 296,
    298–299, 342, 350, 354, 367, 379, 451,
    455, 500, 563–564
violins   332, 554, 565, 567, 569
Virdung, Sebastian   555
Vitruvius   544
Vives, Juan Luis   477
Voch, Lucas   47, 51, 53
Vogel, Agnes   232, 312
Vogtherr, Heinrich   83
Vries, Adriaen de   509–511
Vries, Jan de   301

Wachsmuth, Jeremias   522
Wagner, Bernhart   300
Wagner, Jakob   78, 82, 349, 353
Wagner, Johann Christoph   486, 567
Wagner, Johann Michael   408
Wagner, Leonhard   554
Wahraus, Erhart   76
Waldburg, Otto Truchsess von, Bishop   88,
    146, 241, 251, 255, 346, 557–558
Waldkirch, Bernhard von   474

Walter, Caspar   21, 24
Walther, Marx   78, 83
Ward, Mary   310
War of the Austrian Succession   379
War of the Spanish Succession   27, 37, 161, 355–357, 360
warfare   4, 7, 9, 26–29, 37, 50–51, 78, 101, 103, 111–113, 115–118, 132, 135–136, 141–142, 146–147, 154, 161–162, 164–165, 187, 191, 207, 228–229, 234, 239–241, 243, 248–249, 251, 260–264, 266, 271, 275–276, 278–279, 285, 290, 308, 317–318, 322, 324–326, 328, 342–346, 348–351, 353–355, 357–360, 371, 378–380, 382–383, 386, 397, 400–401, 403, 406–408, 421, 423–424, 426–427, 432, 466, 479, 481, 484, 511, 518, 545, 553, 557, 561, 563, 565, 567; see also Napoleonic Wars; Peasants' War; Schmalkaldic War; Seven Years' War; Thirty Years' War
watchmakers   113, 445
water supply   24, 37, 114, 161, 353, 511, 541–543, 547
weapons   123, 152, 200, 239, 256, 258, 261, 263–264, 319, 325–326, 328, 355, 375, 442, 453–454, 456, 461; see also shooting matches, sword-fighting
weavers   8, 29, 35, 38, 87, 101–103, 113–115, 117–118, 125, 156, 158–159, 163, 228, 236, 260, 262, 271, 274–277, 280–283, 286–290, 305–306, 359, 442, 446, 451
weaving   101–104, 113, 118, 277, 281–282, 305–306, 311
Weber, Franz   38
Weber, Joseph von   488
Weber, Thomas   38
wedding ordinances   200, 456
weddings   30, 150, 158, 200, 258, 266, 317–318, 320–322, 332–333, 451, 456–458; see also marriage; matrimonial law
Weiditz, Christoph   83, 443, 447, 449–450, 454
Weil, Jakob b. Juda   368
Weilbächin, Anna   299
Weissenhorn, Alexander   417
Weiß family   11, 308, 402
Weißenau   373

Weißenburg   280
Welser family   11, 33, 64, 77, 82, 87, 89, 101, 104, 110–111, 132, 148–149, 230–231, 237, 240, 273, 308, 310, 346, 379, 394, 418, 422, 458, 475–476, 479–481, 483–485, 500, 503, 509, 537, 539
Welser, Anton   394
Welser, Bartholomäus   111, 148
Welser, Hans   231, 237
Welser, Lucas   104, 231
Welser, Margarete   310, 379, 475
Welser, Marcus (Marx)   33, 77, 89, 418, 422, 479–481, 483, 485, 537
Welser, Matthäus   111
Welser, Philippine   308
Welser-Vöhlin Company   110
Wenger, Gregor Ferdinand   567
Werkstetter, Christine   9, 305
Wertach   20, 23–25, 29, 509
Westheimer Bank   383
Weyden, Rogier van der   497
Weyer Company   111
Weyermann, Jacob Christian   37
Widemann, Karl   484
Widmann, Johann Georg   569
Wiesel, Johann   484
Wiesner-Hanks, Merry   304–306, 311
Wild, Sebastian   324
Wilhelm IV of Bavaria, Duke   347, 507
Wilhelm V of Bavaria, Duke   400, 539
Willer, Elias   426, 431
Willer, Georg   426, 430–431, 563
Wirsung, Marcus   555
witchcraft   179, 182, 186, 189–190, 261, 488
Wittenberg   223, 234, 238, 252–253, 255, 426, 556
Wittwer, Wilhelm   471
Wolf, Hieronymus   89, 422, 478–479, 517, 541
Wolf, Joseph   428
Wolfart, Bonifatius   236, 378
Wolff, Christian   488
Wolter, Anton von   63
women   9, 25, 31, 51, 80, 147, 156, 182, 186, 222, 248, 252, 264, 274, 277, 279, 283, 288, 294–313, 324, 326–327, 329, 331, 333, 336, 360, 445–446, 451, 456, 458, 461, 507; see also nuns

INDEX

women's work   9, 80, 277, 283, 288, 303–308, 311–313, 333
workhouses   163, 183–184, 289
Worms   134, 201, 419
writing   3, 12, 55, 69–78, 80–82, 86–90, 153, 156, 164, 208, 225, 260, 262, 336, 343, 394–395, 398–399, 417, 422, 425–426, 471, 477, 480, 515, 520
Wrocław   102, 116
Wunder, Heide   295
Württemberg   248, 281, 372, 380, 431
Würzburg   289, 373

Zainer, Günther   415–416, 422, 424, 499, 555
Zan family   496
Zangmeister Company   111

Zapf, Georg Wilhelm   79, 416
Zelinsky Hanson, Michele   253, 312
Zimmermann, Hans   395
Zimmermann, Wilhelm Peter   320
Zindelin, Philipp   558, 562
Zink, Burkhard   78, 82, 295
Zobel, Martin   374
Zorn, Wolfgang   7
Zöschinger, Ludwig   565
Zurich   133, 141, 229, 346
Zwickau   104
Zwingli, Ulrich   133, 147, 229, 231–232, 234, 236, 238, 250
Zwinglianism, Zwinglians   133, 141, 221, 230–233, 236–238, 242–243, 247, 250, 318, 346
Zwitzel, Bernhard   540

Printed in the United States
By Bookmasters